SCHOOLS OF THE AIR

SCHOOLS OF THE AIR

A History of
Instructional Programs on
Radio in the United States

William Bianchi

McFarland & Company, Inc., Publishers
Jefferson, North Carolina, and London

LIBRARY OF CONGRESS CATALOGUING-IN-PUBLICATION DATA

Bianchi, William, 1943–
Schools of the air : a history of instructional programs
on radio in the United States / William Bianchi.
p.   cm.
Includes bibliographical references and index.

ISBN: 978-0-7864-3058-1
softcover : 50# alkaline paper ∞

1. Radio in education — United States — History.
2. Distance education — United States — History.
I. Title.   II. Title: Instructional programs on
radio in the Unites States.
LB1044.5.B45   2008   371.33'310973 — dc22   2007052542

British Library cataloguing data are available

On the cover: *With Radio the Unprivileged School Becomes the Privileged One,*
Levenson, 1945 (Courtesy of University of Kentucky); background ©2008 Photodisc

Manufactured in the United States of America

McFarland & Company, Inc., Publishers
Box 611, Jefferson, North Carolina 28640
www.mcfarlandpub.com

To Judy, with love and gratitude

Contents

List of Tables

Abbreviations Used

ABESA   Akron Board of Education School of the Air

ABC   American Broadcasting Company

ACSA   Alameda City School of the Air

ASA   American School of the Air

AT&T   American Telephone and Telegraph

BBC   British Broadcasting Corporation

CBS   Columbia Broadcasting System

CPS   Chicago Public Schools

CPSA   Chicago Public School of the Air

CSA   Cleveland School of the Air

ECB   Educational Communications Board

ESB   Evaluation of School Broadcasts

ESR   Evaluation of School Radio (project)

ESSA   Empire State FM School of the Air

ETV   Educational Television

FCC   Federal Communications Commission

FRC   Federal Radio Commission

GE   General Electric

IQ   Intelligence Quotient

MAH   Music Appreciation Hour

MBS   Mutual Broadcasting System

MSA   Minnesota School of the Air

NACRE   National Advisory Council on Radio Education

NAEB   National Association of Educational Broadcasters

NBC   National Broadcasting Company

NCER	National Committee on Education by Radio
NCLB	No Child Left Behind
NEA	National Education Association
NPR	National Public Radio
NSD	No Significant Differences
NSoA	National School of the Air
NYA	National Youth Administration
NYC	New York City
OPB	Oregon Public Broadcasting
ORSA	Oregon School of the Air
OSA	Ohio School of the Air
OSAC	Oregon State Agricultural College
OSU	Ohio State University
PA	Public Address
PE	Physical Education
PSA	Portland School of the Air
PTA	Parent Teacher Association
RCA	Radio Corporation of America
RRN	Rural Radio Network
RSA	Rochester School of the Air
SOA	School of the Air
TEA	Texas Education Agency
TSA	Texas School of the Air
UIB	United Independent Broadcasters
UM	University of Minnesota
UMR	University Media Resources
UW	University of Wisconsin
WHA	Call letters for UW's educational radio station
WSA	Wisconsin School of the Air

Preface

In their heyday, radio schools of the air broadcast daily instructional programs during school hours to millions of American schoolchildren. They offered a broad curriculum of educational programs for the classrooms including art appreciation, drawing, music, science, history, literature, current events, citizenship, and rhythmic movement. Schools of the air (SOAs) were operated by the commercial broadcast networks, state universities, state departments of education, and local school boards. Pioneering SOAs started in the late 1920s and early 1930s. The most successful continued broadcasting up through the late 1970s and one until 1995. SOAs involved tens of thousands of teachers and children in the act of radio broadcasting and generated reams of scholarly studies by universities, government agencies, and foundations.

As the name implies, schools of the air were more than just another form of educational technology, such as film or records. They were, in fact, very much like schools. Their organizational structures resembled those of regular schools with administrators, teachers, educational consultants, and curriculum developers. They operated as schools did, offering semester-long schedules of graded programs presented by radio teachers. They issued teacher manuals and student learning materials, conducted extracurricular activities, and presented awards but did not take attendance or give grades. Most attempted to evaluate their programs or at least collect feedback from school administrators, classroom teachers, and parents.

Scholars writing during the mid–1940s identified dozens of radio efforts intended for classroom use in the United States, but only 18 were deemed to have reached a level of success worthy of being called a school of the air. They operated at three levels—national, state, and local. Of those, adequate documentation exists for 14, and they are the subject of this work. Their treatment varies according to the availability of documentation.[1]

Schools of the air delivered enormous educational resources to millions of students in rural and urban schools who otherwise would have gone without. Students sitting in one room, rural schools and big city classrooms alike heard the voices of leaders from government and business as well as the great literary artists of the day. They received instruction of a quality and kind usually available only in privileged schools—art appreciation taught by curators from leading museums, music appreciation by the conductor of the nation's most prominent symphony orchestra, and science, literature and history taught by master teachers. Most important, however, radio was flexible. It allowed educators to customize instruction in a timely manner to meet the

---

[1]Three limited-documentation curiosities are also presented: Prairie Farmer's *School of the Air, The Alameda City, California School of the Air,* and Akron, Ohio's *School of the Air.*

1

needs of local and state curricula and culture. That flexibility proved radio's most enduring quality. We can't quantify the value of radio's contribution to education, but we can document what schools of the air did and the appreciation of those who listened.

Schools of the air represented the largest application of technology to U.S. classrooms up to that time and also opened up the dark possibility, thankfully unrealized, of teachers being displaced by machines. They soon became a politicized issue at the center of a battle for the control of media in this country. The outcome of that battle still affects what we hear on radio today. Not surprisingly, radio in the classroom paved the way for subsequent waves of innovations in educational technology, namely: educational television, computers, and today's mania for online education.

When I began my studies in educational technology, I had expected to do research on the latest technology, namely online education. Perhaps because I am a child of the radio age, during a graduate course covering the history of educational technology, I was drawn instead to educational radio. I was amazed and pleased to learn that, at one time, schools of the air flourished in Wisconsin, Ohio, Texas, Minnesota, Chicago and Portland, Oregon, among other places; that for 18 years the Columbia Broadcasting System, a private commercial network, produced and broadcast a school of the air to the entire nation; and that even individual, privately owned stations broadcast programs for the classroom. Furthermore, boards of education in many cites and counties experimented with education by radio (Atkinson, 1942a). Of all this, I had been completely ignorant, despite my experience in the field of educational technology. It was like discovering remnants of a long-forgotten civilization in one's backyard.

I wondered about the schools of the air. What motivated their founders and what kind of programming did they offer? What educational philosophies shaped the curricula, and what instructional methods did they use? Why and how did the classroom teachers use SOAs, and how many tuned in regularly? Moreover, how did such an extensive application of educational technology affect the educational mainstream, and do SOAs have any relevance for today? I realized that these questions could be answered only through historical research.

During the research, I found many striking parallels between the widely enthusiastic predictions of ground-shaking, life-altering effects made on behalf of the Internet throughout the 1990s and the similarly exuberant claims made in the early days of radio. According to excitable proponents in the early 1920s, radio would foster world peace, bring about informed democratic government, and end poverty. But its greatest value, they asserted, would be as a tool for education. It would draw the people of the world together into one giant educational village, create an international People's University, and ultimately, some hoped, usher in a "new enlightenment" (Barnouw, 1966; Carpini, 1995, p. 21; Darrow, 1932). Perhaps their expectations were too high. Yet to understand the role technology has played in American education and is likely to play in the future, we must become familiar with the story of the radio schools of the air. Without that, our high expectations for the next innovation in educational media will be similarly dashed.

I started by reviewing the works of scholars from the 1930s and 1940s who had documented the operations of then existing SOAs. In particular, Carroll Atkinson dedicated nearly a decade of his professional work to creating a near-encyclopedic source of basic facts about SOAs that operated up to 1942. Unfortunately, his work ended too early to reflect the vigorous growth of schools of the air that took place at the state and local levels starting in the mid–1940s after the Federal Communications Commission had set aside a portion of the then new FM bandwidth for educational broadcasting. In addition to Atkinson's work, primary source materials are scattered in archives and many university and public libraries. These materials include program schedules and descriptions, teacher guides, promotional materials, and journal articles, all of which provide little windows on SOA operations.

Writings of SOA founders such as Ben Darrow, the founder of the Ohio School of the Air,

Walter Damrosch, founder of NBC's *Music Appreciation Hour*, and William S. Paley, president of Columbia Broadcasting System (CBS), provide rich sources of factual data and humanizing insight into their personalities and motives. Research studies conducted in the early 1940s by the federally funded Evaluation of School Broadcasts, headed by I. Keith Tyler and Seerley Reid at The Ohio State University, made available reliable data on SOA audiences, classroom teacher usage, and educational effectiveness.

Around 1980, after a 30-year hiatus, scholars began to take another look at educational radio. George Martin's (1983) fine biography of Walter Damrosch provides the story of one man's passion to develop appreciation for European classical music among average Americans. Two contemporary scholars of educational technology, Paul Saettler (1990) and Larry Cuban (1986), provide excellent overviews of SOA activity as well as some of the motivation for undertaking this work, though Cuban tends to be dismissive of radio in education. Another contemporary, Mary Kelly (1990) wrote an excellent, detailed study of *Let's Draw,* a nationally popular series from the Wisconsin School of the Air that taught drawing by radio! Media scholar Paul McChesney (1993) provided crucial background and analysis on the fight between educators and the networks for control of radio broadcasting. Finally, everyone who has written about the history of radio is indebted to Erik Barnouw's landmark work on the history of broadcasting in the U.S.

In addition to the many useful sources in university and public libraries, archive collections hold much in-depth information on the most successful SOAs. Those collections include internal memos, budgets, correspondence, internal evaluations, audience survey reports, and plans for expansion or reversing decline. In other words, archives contain the stuff that makes history come alive. The archives I found most useful included those at the University of Wisconsin, the State Historical Society of Wisconsin, the University of Minnesota, the Ohio State University, Oregon State University Archive, and the National Public Radio Archive at the University of Maryland. Without these sources and the help of staff, this work would not have been completed.

Finally, this work has been guided by the words of this country's preeminent historian of educational technology, Paul Saettler (1990), who observed, "The most frequent failing of educational reformers and futurists is to predict the future with little or no reference to the past" (p. 538). This book tells the story of this country's school of the air movement with the hope that future historians and scholars will make use of it.

Introduction

Interest in the history of radio extends mostly to its influence on popular entertainment, marketing, and American popular culture. The popular stories are important and worthy of our attention, but they tend to crowd out the other substantial influences that radio worked in society, particularly on education, the use of educational technology in the schools, and media use in general. To fully appreciate how schools of the air arose and evolved, it is important to become familiar with broadcast radio's dramatic rise following World War I. In many ways the wonder of radio exceeded that of the internet 70 years later.

Section I of this work traces the meteoric rise of broadcast radio from 1920 to 1929. During that period, as radio permeated much of American life, colleges, universities, and local school boards experimented with educational broadcasting. Unfortunately, as the number of radio stations multiplied, chaos spread across the airwaves. The federal government brought order through regulation, but in the process, crippled many fledgling educational radio stations. Not surprisingly a movement emerged among social progressives and college-based radio educators to establish a federally supported national school of the air. Soon battle lines were drawn between those who wanted the federal government to set aside part of the radio airwaves for exclusive educational use and corporate and private broadcasters who claimed that the American system of private ownership of radio offered the best educational potential. The outcome of that battle dug the contours of broadcasting in the U.S. for generations to come. It also laid the groundwork for the development of multiple schools of the air.

The bulk of this work tells the individual stories of schools of the air that flourished in the United States at three levels. Section II covers the schools of the air developed by the two national broadcast networks, NBC and CBS. They supported national SOAs in order to show that the dazzling new communication medium was in the hands of responsible business people who understood their civic duty and could be trusted to make education available to the public. In fact both networks used their formidable resources to create what turned out to be a unique and productive marriage between corporate and educational goals, a marriage that is unlikely to ever occur again in this country.

Section III documents state-level schools of the air. In Ohio, Wisconsin, Minnesota, Oregon, and Texas, universities and state boards of education saw in radio the potential to deliver rich educational resources to rural students at relatively low cost, a goal not driven solely by altruism. In fact, in many states, farmers collectively represented substantial political power in the legislatures that set university budgets. Meanwhile in up state New York, dozens of local school boards and operators of FM stations developed a unique grassroots radio service for the schools that required no help from state legislatures or universities. Section IV covers the schools of the air developed by local school boards. As you might expect, many big city schools adapted radio to enhance their already rich educational resources. Surprisingly, several successful schools of the air were developed in relatively small cities with limited budgets. One of the most positive outcomes was that nearly all the publicly owned state and local FM stations that carried school of the air broadcasts became the foundation of today's National Public Radio network.

It is unlikely that any one reader will want to read about all of the schools of the air included in this work. A suggested approach would be to read Section I for context, at least one school from Sections II, III and IV, and any specific stories of personal interest.

SECTION I

Radio Becomes an Educational Medium

It set off a mania for radio. When the Westinghouse radio station KDKA broadcast the first live report of a U.S. presidential election, in November 1920, news that Warren G. Harding had won reached only a few thousand listeners in the Pittsburgh area. Nevertheless, that event marks the beginning of broadcasting in the United States (Barnouw, 1966). Before then, radio had been used for point-to-point communication, as in ship-to-shore communication and for amateurs fascinated by the challenge of picking a distant signal from the air. The broadcast of a presidential election demonstrated the real value of radio—live communication to the masses. Twenty-eight stations went on the air in 1921 nationally, and by the end of the next year, nearly 700 licensed stations were broadcasting, many on the same wavelength[1] (Barnouw, 1966). Stations were started by a bedazzling array of would-be broadcasters, including furniture stores, hotels, newspapers, churches, city governments,[2] police and fire departments, and YMCAs—and those were the typical ones. Some of the more inexplicable station owners included a piano company in Youngstown, Ohio, a chiropractic school in Iowa, a gravestone distributor in Colorado, a roller skating rink in Chicago, and perhaps the strangest, the Nushawg Poultry Farm of New Lebanon, Ohio (Douglas, 1987). The radio boom expanded rapidly, catching most Americans by surprise. Then Secretary of Commerce Herbert Hoover, who held radio station licensing authority, described the radio phenomenon as "one of the most astounding things that come under my observation of American life" (Douglas, 1999, p. 65).

The meteoric rise of broadcast radio was slowed briefly by the lack of ready-made receiving sets. Government regulations had stifled the development of commercial radio during World War I. Fearing radio-equipped spies, the government had banished amateur radio operators from the air, sealed their equipment, and given control of the airwaves to the Navy (Witherspoon & Kovitz, 1989). While the Navy introduced many innovations in the technology for radio transmission, they ignored receiving sets for the home listener. Consequently, two years after the government had lifted wartime regulations, amateurs still found it necessary to assemble radio

---

[1]The chaos of multiple stations on the same wavelength was partly addressed by Secretary of Commerce Hoover in 1923. He assigned a range of wavelengths to high-powered stations but left all low-powered stations at one dial position, 360 meters. To limit interference, many low-power stations were restricted to daytime broadcasts so as not to interfere with the more powerful commercial stations that were free to broadcast during evening hours (Barnouw, 1966, p. 122).

[2]In 1921, WRR, the first municipally owned station, went on the air in Dallas. It continues broadcasting today.

equipment using component parts. Following the presidential election broadcast, however, demand for ready-made radio sets surged in Pittsburgh and across the nation. In Chicago, the demand for radio receiving equipment grew tremendously following the decision by a radio station to broadcast the Chicago Opera Company's entire season's performance, afternoons and evenings, six days a week — and nothing else (Barnouw, 1966). At the beginning of the 1921 opera season, perhaps 1,300 receivers existed in the Chicago area, mostly in the hands of technologically inclined young men (radio geeks). During the winter, however, listening in on the opera became "the most fashionable and popular of winter sports. Home, it seemed could not be home without a radio set" (Stone, 1922, p. 503). However, no sets were available in the stores. The problem was solved by bootleg manufacturers who ignored patent restrictions and built sets often using pilfered parts. By the end of the opera season, Chicago could boast of 20,000 receiving sets tuned to opera (Barnouw, 1966), a testament to either American ingenuity or our love for the art. Across the nation, broadcasts of baseball and boxing further fueled the growing radio fever.

Entrepreneurial minds quickly grasped that a huge market potential was opening in radio receivers. General Electric, the electric industry giant that had supplied the Navy with radio equipment during the war, along with partners Westinghouse, American Telephone & Telegraph (AT&T), and United Fruit,[3] formed the Radio Corporation of America (RCA). By mid–1921, RCA started producing complete radio receiving sets for the consumer market. Soon dozens of other manufacturers entered the market, and at the end of 1922 the number of radio receivers nationwide had mushroomed to almost 2 million.[4] According to Barnouw (1966), by the end of 1924, the public investment in radio equipment reached more than $300 million, an incredible sum in those days, and by 1928, the number of radio receivers had soared past 12 million, a 600 percent increase in six years. Indeed, within a decade of that KDKA broadcast, nearly two-thirds of American homes were supplied with radios, and by the early 1930s, the "astounding" new medium had become "an established feature of everyday life in the United States" (Douglas, 1999, p. 128).

Early Years: Idealism and Commerce

Visions of a People's University

During those incubator years, there arose utopian visions of radio as a vast and powerful medium for public service, education, cultural uplift, and the unification of contentious populations. In many ways these visions of radio were similar to those that arose during the incubator years of the Internet. Nikola Tesla, developer of alternating electric current, predicted that international peace could be realized only by annihilating distance through the use of radio (Taylor, 1974, p. 35). In 1922, editors of the new trade publication *Radio Broadcast* heralded radio as the "people's university."[5] The editors confidently predicted that radio would become a public resource that would make government "a living thing to its citizens" (*Broadcast*, 1922). Foreshadowing the many predictions about Web-based communication, a writer in 1927 asserted that radio "will bring about changes in every way comparable to those following the invention of printing in the fifteenth century" (Bliven, 1927). Media historian Eric Barnouw (1968) stated that to the radio innovators the new medium symbolized a unifying social force that could link rich and

---

[3]The United Fruit Company held important patents on key radio equipment.

[4]The Federal Bureau of Education's Biennial Survey of Education compiled in 1922 reported between 1 and 1.5 million receivers in the United States and from 3 to 4 million listeners (Perry, 1929, p. 41).

[5]The term "people's university" was appropriated by radio enthusiasts from public library advocates who were the first to use it.

poor, young and old, and end the isolation of rural life (Carpini, 1995). In their enthusiasm for the new medium, some clearly got carried away. For example, the former secretary of the Navy at the dedication of a new radio station in 1922 asserted, "Nobody now fears that a Japanese fleet could deal an unexpected blow on our Pacific possessions.... Radio makes surprises impossible" (Barnouw, 1966, p. 103).

Radio attracted the attention of government, business, universities, colleges, and local boards of education as a radical new way to communicate, sell products, and educate the public (Douglas, 1987). In 1923, educators viewed radio as a leading-edge technology that belonged in the academic sphere. They speculated wildly about its potential as a teaching device. As with the Internet today, it seemed that through the connectivity of radio, a single dazzling teacher could inspire thousands of bored students to learn and become educated (Douglas, 1987).

For a few years following the broadcast of the 1920 presidential election, radio in the U.S. came remarkably close to becoming a people's university, much as *Radio Broadcast* editors had predicted. Of the hundreds of stations that went on the air from 1920 to 1925, by far most were run by public, civic, religious, and educational institutions. In 1922 alone, 70 college and university stations went on the air (Carpini, 1995). Within a few years, 128 college stations broadcast programs that ran the "gamut from culture (drama and classical music) to politics, but the ideas of mass and continuing college education broadcasts became paramount" (Carpini, 1995, pp. 21–22).[6] "For a while it almost seemed that no educational institution worthy of the name could be without a radio station of its own" (Douglas, 1987, p. 142). During the utopian period, college-based educational broadcasters filled the airwaves with college lectures, vocational training, information talks, and a growing segment of home-study for-credit college extension courses (Barnouw, 1966).

Educational programming, however, was not the exclusive terrain of college stations. Many commercially owned stations offered programming with a hefty mix of education, informative

talks, self-improvement, and cultural programs. At Chicago's WMAQ, station manager Judith Waller's[7] program schedule for 1924 featured evening lectures from the faculty at the University of Chicago and Northwestern University on topics ranging from political science, sociology, and biology to crime prevention and the value of higher education. The station also featured informative and self-improvement programming, covering such diverse topics

Herbert C. Hoover Secretary of Commerce and Radio (circa 1922) (Underwood &Underwood).

---

[6]Improving public relations represented a common purpose for many college-operated stations (Saettler, 1990).

[7]The story of WMAQ's early years illustrates the innovative "seat of the pants" operation typical of the new broadcast industry. WMAQ was started in 1922 by the Chicago Daily News. WMAQ's business manager, Walter Strong, offered the job of station manager to a family friend, Judith Waller. According to her biography, Waller confessed that she knew nothing about radio. Strong responded that neither did he nor anyone else. "Radio was a new and untested medium and Waller had the freedom to learn by doing." With technical assistance from an engineer, Waller ran the station, wrote the shows, recruited talent, announced the news, and occasionally played drums when scheduled musicians failed to show up.

as child psychology, lawn care, and Midwestern art. In fact, 15 percent of the programs heard on WMAQ during 1924–25 were educational or informative (Caton, 1951; Linton, 1953).

Waller's programming choices in part reflected the values of WMAQ's owners, who believed that radio should be used for public service first and commercial ends second. They consciously used the station to elevate listeners' tastes (Caton, 1951). Because other Chicago stations played mostly popular music and jazz, Waller decided to feature classical music, the opera in particular.[8] An early radio trade magazine described Waller as an educator whose aim was to "elevate the standard of broadcasted programs." The publication quotes Waller: "Now, we could let the fad [radio] go on being a fad and only hear the inferior programs by amateurs, the jazz bands, the cheaper ballads ... if we preferred to do so.... We want to keep it an educational opportunity, a means of giving people better things" (Waller, 1923, in Caton, 1951, p. 97).

The statement showed that Waller shared a utopian vision of radio's vast educational potential but from the perspective of high culture versus low culture. Like many other upper-middle-class radio pioneers, Waller believed radio could uplift the low cultural standard of average people by exposing them to "high culture"—which I define as the European classical traditions in music, fine arts, and literature—and recognized experts in various fields. It seems to have worked. All the musical arts flourished during the early days of broadcasting,[9] but classical music and opera received a special windfall (Douglas, 1987). In 1920, the great majority of Americans had never attended an opera or a symphony, but thanks to radio, by the end of the decade, "a cultural miracle had occurred. Classical music,[10] which had never played a significant role in American life, became a widespread form of entertainment"[11] (Douglas, 1987, p. 153). Radio seemed to be fulfilling the utopian vision that saw common people, sitting in their living rooms, being uplifted to higher levels of culture and learning through the miracle of broadcast radio. Others believed it would become a money maker.

Commercial Considerations

During the incubator years, both for-profit and nonprofit stations struggled to find firm financial footing.[12] While manufacturers of radio equipment made substantial profits, broadcasters had little idea of how to make money from radio programming itself. Many business owners saw radio not as a profit-making vehicle but as a means of gaining the public's goodwill for their real businesses, such as hotels, newspapers, furniture stores, real estate firms, and the like (Barnouw, 1968; Carpini, 1995). Spot ads became common, but station owners had no idea that commercial advertising would eventually create huge revenue streams.

As with Internet providers in the late 1990s, radio broadcasters gradually discovered how to make money in radio through trial and error. Unlike today, in the late 1920s "there was widespread antipathy" to commercializing the new medium (McChesney, 1993, pp. 15–16). AT&T experimented with a novel commercial concept, the toll station. After opening in 1922 the most advanced radio transmission studio in the country—New York's WEFE[13]—AT&T offered airtime to all for a flat fee. Under this concept, private citizens, churches, store owners, politicians,

---

[8]Douglas (1999) suggests that frequent opera broadcasts caused the popularity of that art form to soar.

[9]Throughout the 1920s, broadcasters struggled to find enough programs to fill available airtime. Music was the perfect time filler, cheap and entertaining.

[10]During the decade from 1928 through 1939, the number of major symphony orchestras in the United States increased from 10 to 17 (Douglas, 1987).

[11]Radio was one of many forces that helped develop Americans' appetite for European music traditions, but radio was clearly a very important element in the mix.

[12]Barnouw (1966) asserts that stable financing for educational stations came only from state governments, particularly state universities, a claim born out by the WSA experience.

[13]WEFE was the precursor to New York's WNBC.

schools, businesses, or anyone who paid the toll could broadcast their message. Many who did were business advertisers, and even though they were limited to brief mentions of their company and product, the reaction was uniformly negative (McChesney, 1993). That same year, Secretary of Commerce Hoover alerted the nation to the as-yet hidden danger of allowing commercial advertising to gain a stranglehold on the new medium: "It is impossible that we should allow so great a possibility for service ... to be drowned in advertising chatter" (Carpini, 1995, p. 22). Hoover's words carried weight because, as secretary of commerce, he held sole authority to license stations and assign frequencies and hours of operation. Aversion to commercial broadcasting continued to the end of the decade. As late as 1929, the National Association of Broadcasters, while advocating unrestricted advertising during daytime hours, freely acknowledged that "When evening comes, the average [radio] fan ... is grateful to the sponsor who does not din his wares throughout the program" (Caton, 1951, p. 328).

Doubts about the financial viability of broadcasting and commercialism remained. In 1924, AT&T asked station WEAF in New York to solicit donations from listeners. A contest conducted by trade publication *Radio Broadcast* in 1925 asked readers to determine how best to support broadcasting. First prize was awarded to the suggestion that the government administer a fund collected from an annual radio set fee, a system used in Britain by the British Broadcasting Corporation (BBC).[14] The publication backed government financing, an approach that later would be called socialistic and un–American by network executives (Barnouw, 1966, p. 155). The state of radio broadcast financing at the beginning of 1926 remained quite unsettled (McChesney, 1993). Few stations were making money. "It's striking how infrequently direct advertising is mentioned as an acceptable source for revenues" (McChesney, 1993, p. 15).

The environment changed quickly. Confidence in the new medium's ability to attract dollars rose dramatically after a New York real estate developer reported increased sales of $127,000 as the result of a 10-minute, $50 broadcast on WEFE (Carpini, 1995, p. 22). As station owners became more aware of how to make radio broadcasting pay, they quickly adapted the practice of offering programming that attracted sponsorship. That shift was demonstrated by WMAQ's changing policy toward public service broadcasting. During the first half of the 1920s, the station boasted that its mission was one of public service, which it fulfilled by broadcasting educational, informative, and cultural programs. In the second half of the decade, management's attitudes toward commercialism shifted. While it continued to broadcast educational and cultural programs, WMAQ gradually accommodated the demands of commercialism by adding light entertainment to its schedule. "As radio became a big business, the profits to be made by amusing the largest possible audience multiplied and soared" (Caton, 1951, p. 398). Faced with a conflict between educational and cultural responsibilities and the commercial potential, WMAQ and other broadcasters who ascribed to the public service philosophy found the attraction of commercialism irresistible.

Despite the growth in advertising, most commercial stations continued to provide free airtime for cultural and educational programming, and some broadcasters actively sought opportunities to broadcast to the schools. Their motives varied, but just as with computer software manufacturers in the mid 1990s, they probably saw broadcasting for the schools as a marketing activity as well as a public service. Also, few stations were able to sell all their available airtime to sponsors; nevertheless, stations had to fill up hours of operation with some kind of programming. To fill the program void, they created the category of "sustaining" programs, usually public service shows of a cultural, educational, or religious nature that the station or the network broadcast without sponsorship. Several schools of the air started as sustaining programs on commercial stations (Atkinson, 1942c, 1942d; Smith, 1990).

---

[14]In England, the government took control of radio in the early 1920s and vested that authority in the newly formed BBC, which was supported by an annual fee on receivers. Through the 1920s and 1930s, America's commercial broadcasters fought any attempts to impose that system here.

Broadcast Networks

From the early 1920s, AT&T managers had experimented with network broadcasting. This made good business and technological sense to them because the company already owned a network of long-distance telephone lines capable of carrying radio signals. By 1924, AT&T managers operated several small regional radio networks, but they had a bigger vision. In early 1926, they proposed connecting the nations' largest stations to form a national network. Through such a network, programming from one hub station could reach national audiences, and such large audiences would appeal to national advertisers. However, executives at RCA and General Electric did not want to share control with a phone company. Only after AT&T agreed to bow out of an ownership position did the major corporate players in radio— RCA,[15] Westinghouse, and GE —form the National Broadcasting Company (NBC),[16] one of several media giants to emerge from radio (Douglas, 1987). AT&T executives rightly understood that the company would reap fortunes leasing the telephone lines needed to create the new network (McChesney, 1993).

The specter of network control of radio by the RCA group raised fears across the land of ruthless monopoly powers, excess commercialization, and inappropriate programming. To fend off the threat of government regulation, NBC managers launched a huge public relations campaign portraying the new network with an air of distinction and vision and as a guardian of the public trust (Smith, 1990). The new network would "speak at once to east and west, city and country, rich and poor" (Barnouw, 1966, p. 189). The network campaign helped assure the public and the government that radio broadcasting was now in the "best possible hands" and would remain responsive to public demands. To this end, it created an advisory council of "outstanding citizens" who, the publicity said, could overrule the network's operating executives, an extraordinary step in business-oriented America (Barnouw, 1966, p. 204). For seven years, the council of 16 men and one woman, most likely Judith Waller of WMAQ, suggested cultural, educational, and public service programming to be aired on the network. The schedule included lessons in music appreciation, concerts, Shakespearian productions, political debates, religious sermons, and lectures on the workings of government. Broadcast reformers dismissed the advisory council, saying that it worked under network control and served as little more than a smokescreen to protect the industry from criticism (McChesney, 1993, p. 119). Ploy or not, the public bought in as millions of listeners tuned in, advertisers eagerly signed up, and in 1928 NBC made its first profit (Smith, 1990).

Less than a year after the formation of NBC, William S. Paley, impressed with how radio advertising had boosted sales of his father's La Palina cigars, bought control of a struggling network of 17 stations and renamed it the Columbia Broadcasting System (CBS). To meet the challenge from the stronger NBC, Paley also pursued the path of highbrow programming with heavy emphasis on classical music. "That approach won public favor and that attracted advertisers" (Smith, 1990, p. 72).

To demonstrate their commitment to responsible broadcasting, both NBC and CBS competed in the arena of educational and cultural programming. By 1930, the two networks had formed departments of education responsible for conceiving and producing a wide range of cultural and educational programs including panel and forum discussions; drama; classical music and opera; programs devoted to specific subjects such as science, health, or politics; children's

---

[15]The ownership of radio broadcasting was clearly incestuous because the original investors in RCA itself were GE, Westinghouse, AT&T, and United Fruit.

[16]NBC actually formed two networks, the Red, using WEFE as the nucleus, and the Blue, using WJZ also in New York as its hub. Blue became the prestige network while Red made all the money. In the early 1940s, the Federal Communications Commission forced NBC to sell one of the networks. That became a new network, the American Broadcasting Company (ABC) (Atkinson, 1942c).

programming; and schools of the air (Atkinson, 1942c). Even more surprising, the networks appointed directors of education recruited from the ranks of distinguished faculty and administrators from big-name universities. Dr. James Roland Angell, president emeritus of Yale University, served for several years as NBC's education director. At CBS, education directors included Dr. Lyman Bryson from Columbia University and, for a short period, Edward R. Murrow. It can be argued that during radio's first two decades competition for advertisers and the need to allay public concerns drove both networks to broadcast high-quality educational and cultural programming that set a standard unmatched since.

AMOS AND ANDY

No historical account of radio's early days is complete without mentioning the spectacular success of the *Amos and Andy* radio show, which got its start in Chicago. Signed by WMAQ's Judith Waller in the mid–1920s, it hit gold almost immediately and soon moved to NBC where it achieved spectacular national success. More than 40 million Americans religiously followed the comic exploits of the African-American characters. Evening meetings of lodges, churches, and volunteer groups of all kinds had to be rescheduled in order to avoid conflicting with the program, else face meager attendance. When the show was on the air, President Coolidge instructed his staff that he did not want to be disturbed (Barnouw, 1966). Jim Morris, long-time director of Oregon's educational station KOAC, recalled that his station actually signed off the air and some movie theatres interrupted films during the broadcasts. "...downtown at the theater — I've been there when they turned off the movie that was on the screen, wherever it was, and rolled a console radio out onto the stage so people sitting there could listen to *Amos and Andy*. When it was over, the lights went on for a moment and then the movie started again. Right where it left off" (Harrison, 1978).

The success of *Amos and Andy* profoundly affected the direction of broadcasting in this country. First, it demonstrated the appeal of a continuing story that unfolds over weeks and attracts greater and greater numbers to the ranks of committed listeners. In presenting the ongoing series, it pioneered the serial format that within five years came to dominate daytime radio (Barnouw, 1966). More important, the show demonstrated once and for all the tremendous money-making power of popular entertainment. A huge hit at NBC, *Amos and Andy* inspired CBS's chief, William S. Paley, even more. "While NBC opened the door to light entertainment by signing *Amos and Andy* in 1929, it was Paley who flooded his network with escapist fare and strident commercials. NBC had little choice but to follow" (Smith, 1990, p. 132). Smith asserts that from that point on, educational and cultural programs, though substantial and impressive, served as window dressing for increasingly lowbrow commercial programming that soon dominated at both networks. Such a charge would be difficult to prove, but regardless of their motives during the 1930s and early 1940s, NBC and CBS broadcast impressive educational programming for adults and children.

Education and Regulation

Since probably the 1970s, the concept of educational broadcasting has largely been superseded by the notion of public broadcasting. As Saettler (1990) points out, the two terms carry distinctly different educational implications. Public broadcasting is defined as "all that is of human interest and importance which is not supported by advertising and is not arranged for formal instruction" (Saettler, 1990, p. 359), while educational broadcasting today implies programs that aim to instruct listeners on some topic. Saettler summarizes the dominant characteristics of educational programs as being (1) arranged in a series to assist cumulative learning, (2) explicitly planned in consultation with educational advisors, (3) usually accompanied by supplemental learning material such as texts or illustrations, and (4) usually subject to some form of evaluation.

In the early days, the concept of educational radio combined both notions, public and educational broadcasting, and all types of stations aired educational programs. Some commercial stations reflected Waller's public service view by broadcasting everything from college lectures, inspirational talks, and how-to programs to roundtable discussions conducted by experts and high-culture programs featuring operatic and classical music. Educational stations licensed to colleges and universities focused more on purely instructional programs such as for-credit adult home-study and certification programs. They also did some of what we today recognize as public broadcasting as defined by Saettler. That included general education and information, public service such as weather, and how-to programs. Much of the college broadcasting aimed at rural listeners.

As the networks came to dominate radio, they continued to define educational broadcasting in the broadest terms. In the mid–1930s Judith Waller, then educational director for NBC's central division, defined educational radio in the broadest possible sense as "any material ... which adds to the knowledge and culture of mankind and which ... helps us think and understand" (Waller, 1937 in Bird, 1939, p. 15). This broad view encompassed educational efforts aimed at adults such as NBC's *America's Town Meeting*, a panel discussion of current events, and programming aimed directly at schoolchildren such as CBS's *American School of the Air*. Meanwhile, educators working at college stations and local school boards struggled to establish viable educational efforts.

College Stations

During radio's booming first decade, 1921 to 1931, educational institutions started more than 200 radio stations (Barnouw, 1966). Among the early pioneers in this group were WCM, University of Texas; WRM, University of Illinois; WLB, University of Minnesota; and WHA, University of Wisconsin.[17] Like colleges in the early 1990s that experimented with online education, the pioneers of educational radio struggled to discover how to use a powerful new communication medium. Some saw radio merely as a promotional tool for attracting more students, while for others radio technology became a hot topic in the curriculum. Many colleges, however, were attracted by radio's immense instructional possibilities (Douglas, 1987). A number of colleges such as the University of Kansas and Connecticut State Teachers College invested heavily in developing and broadcasting for-credit home-study courses. By the end of the 1920s, a handful experimented with broadcasting instruction intended for elementary and high school classrooms, some of which became the SOAs that are covered in this study.

However, the boom in college or educational stations quickly ran out of gas. Many — too small and under funded to justify continued operation — gave up their licenses or had them taken away relatively soon (Douglas, 1987), but even those that enjoyed adequate support from state universities struggled to stay on the air. By the end of 1928, 31 educational stations quit broadcasting, and 13 more ceased operation the following year (Barnouw, 1966). By 1937, the count of educational stations had dwindled to just 38. What accounted for this dramatic drop? Most scholars of the day, writing in the 1940s and later, tick off a list of the usual suspects. Schools that used radio as a publicity tool found that it did not pay off in increased enrollment. Educators were apathetic and dismissive to the new medium, and those who tried it were unimaginative and dull in their presentation (Saettler, 1990; White, 1947). Little research exists to support these allegations. Furthermore, how can we today judge the appeal of a presentation made

---

[17]Private universities also showed interest. By 1922, Tulane in New Orleans and Washington University in St. Louis had inaugurated radio stations.

generations ago to listeners from a culture vastly different from our own? More significant, the Great Depression of the early 1930s undoubtedly forced many institutions into a cash crunch; selling the station offered a ready source of money (Witherspoon & Kovitz, 1989).

Several scholars present well-documented arguments blaming the actions of the Federal Radio Commission (FRC) for driving educators away from educational radio. Saettler (1990) asserts that the FRC "ostracized educational stations" and thereby enabled the increase in the number, power, and operating hours of commercial stations. White (1947) believes that the owners of commercial stations intent on taking scarce frequencies for themselves used their lobbying influence at the FRC to drive many educational stations from the airwaves.[18] Barnouw (1966) documents the woeful tales of several educational stations that were forced off the air. The University of Arkansas's KFMQ, for example, was forced to share time with a commercial station. KFMQ received one-quarter of the daytime hours and no nighttime hours at all and felt as a result, "its arms, its legs and its head had been cut off," so it quit educational broadcasting (Barnouw, 1966, p. 218). The Connecticut State College station had been a pioneer in adult for-credit educational broadcasting. Licensed at 500 watts in 1923 for full-time operation, two years later the FRC ordered it to another frequency where it shared time with a commercial station. Then, over the next six years, it was shifted eight times more, forced to reduce hours of operation, and reduced to 250 watts of power. By 1931, the college recognized that it had little chance of developing a significant state educational project under such conditions. Finally, the school gave up on educational radio. These stories paint a sad but clear picture of why many educational stations declined and how the actions of the FRC helped drive proponents of educational radio to seek political solutions to their dilemma (Barnouw, 1968; Saettler, 1990). Their efforts are discussed later in this chapter.

Chaos in the Ether

Throughout 1925 and 1926, radio reception became increasingly problematic. "All the virtues and defects of unfettered enterprise were exemplified in the mad rush to develop the new market — rapid expansion, ingenious improvisation, reckless and often unscrupulous competition..." (Witherspoon & Kovitz, 1989, pp. 8–9). Broadcasting faced a growing crisis. New stations arose like mushrooms, and since they all clustered on one of two available wavelengths, 360 meters (833 kilocycles) or 400 meters (750 kilocycles) (Douglas, 1987), they increasingly drowned out each other. The distinct voices and clear music of a few years earlier, by mid-decade had blurred into a cacophony of voices, music bursts, static, and weird noises. Seeking to restore order, Secretary of Commerce Hoover issued a flurry of orders for innumerable shifts in wavelength, changes in broadcasting power, and restrictions on broadcast hours (Barnouw, 1966). His actions had little impact on the handful of high-powered commercial stations, but they presented small and midsized stations with a dilemma — either accept the restricted broadcast hours and frequency changes issued by the secretary of commerce, or ignore them and hope for the best. Either way, conflicting broadcasts continued to garble radio messages.

Then things got worse. Litigation brought by station owners undermined the government's ability to assign and control radio channels, ushering in a complete breakdown of control in 1926. Soon the airwaves became a spectrum free-for-all. "Within six months more than 200 new broadcasters began to operate ... many did not respect the frequencies being used by others." The ether had become chaotic (McChesney, 1993, p. 17).

Chaos and the government's multiple frequency reassignments put great stress on educational broadcasters, particularly those who had developed substantial educational programs. The

---

[18]The University of Wisconsin fought off a determined effort by several Wisconsin newspapers intent on taking control of the school's educational station, WHA.

University of Kansas, for example, had jumped into the educational broadcasting arena early on and at first was licensed without time restrictions. It organized an extensive program of home-study courses for credit. According to Barnouw (1966), faculty from all departments rushed to offer courses by radio, but by 1925, 26 other stations had crowded onto their channel. The government imposed time-sharing but with limited success. "Enrolled home study students said they could not hear the broadcasts. Faculty members became disillusioned and withdrew. The home study courses were abandoned" (Barnouw, 1966, p. 173).[19] Barnouw implies that the Kansas experience was common. If so, it would explain, in part, the so-called indifference of educators to education by radio, to which Saettler (1990) also refers. Rather than being indifferent to radio education, it appears that educators became disillusioned with broadcast restrictions that prevented them from reaching their students.

Regulation and Ruin

A growing chorus of voices from broadcasters across the country called on the government to calm the airwaves through stricter regulation. In response, Congress provided new rules of operation designed to end broadcast chaos. The Radio Act of 1927 gave the U.S. government licensing control, but not ownership, over all channels. The most startling provision stated that in 60 days all existing licenses would be void; nearly 700 former licensees would have to reapply. In granting new licenses to stations, the "guiding standard was to be *public interest, convenience, or necessity*," [italics added] but in a telling omission, the act makes no mention of education (Barnouw, 1966, pp. 195–201).

In March of 1927, responsibility for administering the Radio Act was given to the Federal Radio Commission (FRC). Out of the broadcast chaos of the mid–1920s, the FRC brought order, but not necessarily fairness. In place of the obviously misguided practice of having all stations operate at just two wavelengths, 360 meters (833 kilocycles) and 400 meters (750 kilocycles), the commission expanded the radio band to dozens of frequencies on which local stations could operate without conflicting with other nearby stations. Moreover, the FRC created a number of clear channel frequencies, on which only one station could operate. Stations blessed with a clear channel were also free to broadcast at up to 50,000 watts of power, enough to project their signal clearly for hundreds of miles. In effect, a clear channel station operated as a regional broadcast monopoly. Of the 24 clear channel frequencies awarded by the FRC, all went to commercial operators and 21 of them went to network owned or affiliated stations (Douglas, 1987).

The order imposed by the FRC crippled educational radio in several ways. In the allocation of channels and airtime, FRC regulators favored commercial stations over public nonprofit stations. Using odd logic, they claimed that nonprofits were less public than the toll stations that were theoretically available to anyone who was willing and able to pay for airtime (McChesney, 1993). As a result, large commercial stations received clear channel licenses and precious evening hours while educational stations received local frequencies with significant restrictions on transmitting power and broadcast hours. The Commission's actions "impeded [educational stations] in their development by placing severe restrictions on them" (Douglas, 1987). Virtually all college and university stations were banned from broadcasting during the choice evening hours when most adults could listen. College based broadcasters focused on adult education, but after being restricted to daytime operation, they found the potential audience for adult home-study and for-credit extension courses greatly diminished (Barnouw, 1966). Saddled with daytime-only operation, some university- and college-based educational stations turned to broadcasting for the schools.

---

[19]After abandoning the for-credit home-study courses, the University of Kansas station continued broadcasting noncredit educational and informative programs for many years.

Three Experiments

During radio's early growth period, educators and radio innovators began experimenting with broadcasting educational programs intended for the classroom. Three of these efforts are worth looking at. In the spring of 1924, Chicago based Sears, Roebuck and Company through its Agricultural Foundation[20] funded the first true SOA, giving it the charming name *Little Red Schoolhouse of the Air*. Remarkably, Sears provided free airtime on its fledgling but powerful Chicago-based radio station, WLS,[21] and a small salary for the schoolmaster, "Uncle Ben" Darrow, who later would play a major role in the SOA movement (Lawson, 1942; Leach, 1983; Taylor 1974). Under Darrow's direction, the school launched an innovative and diverse program that quickly appealed to city and rural students in elementary and high school grades. The school broadcast programs in art, music appreciation, geography, science, and farming. Surprisingly, though Darrow aimed the effort primarily at rural kids, he soon learned that city children were also curious about cows and tractors. Most remarkable was Darrow's resourcefulness. Because the only funds available were those for broadcasting and paying his salary, Darrow had to figure out how to produce programs that were educationally effective and acceptable to his audience, with no money. His solution was simple: let the children and teachers do it. "Several days prior to the broadcast the pupils and teachers were called into the studio for one rehearsal and to learn microphone techniques. They were then encouraged to continue rehearsing in their own classrooms until the date of the program. Darrow discovered that even young children were able to present satisfactory programs and that the children in the listening audience preferred them to adult presenters" (Lawson, 1942, pp. 5–6).

Within a year, the school's claimed an audience of 23,000[22] schoolchildren plus an unknown number of listeners at home across northeastern Illinois, northwestern Indiana, and even into Michigan (Lawson, 1942). School superintendents from Illinois and Michigan showed their approval by appearing on the programs as special guests. Edward Tobin, superintendent of Cook County (Illinois) public schools, was an especially enthusiastic supporter. He predicted that radio would become a potent educational medium and foresaw the need to distribute program schedules and brochures prior to broadcasts so that teachers could prepare their classes for the broadcasts. He also noted that only commercial stations were available at that time and recommended constructing public stations to be used for educational purposes.[23]

The *Little Red Schoolhouse* broadcast for little more than a year. The exact cause of its demise is unclear, but there is some evidence that Darrow decided to develop the TABL-TUB, his own invention that combined a kitchen table with a bathtub (Saettler, 1990). At any rate, it seems that the managers of WLS did not wish to continue funding a staff dedicated to the school of the air. Consequently, no one at WLS wanted to assume the responsibility of the series in addition to regular responsibilities (Lawson, 1942, p. 7). Lack of funding would be a common complaint throughout the history of the SOA movement. Darrow, however, did continue working with SOAs for the next 16 years, and throughout that period he continued to build on the knowledge and skill that he gained directing the *Little Red Schoolhouse*.

Another early SOA experiment also took place in Chicago. Judith Waller, manager of station WMAQ and one of the pioneers of educational broadcasting, became interested in broadcasting to the classroom in 1925, but she was confronted with a dilemma. After Darrow had left

[20]Sears mail order operations served a mostly rural market.

[21]The call letters, WLS, stood for, "World's Largest Store."

[22]Lawson (1942) got the audience estimate from Darrow himself, but Darrow did not explain how he derived the number.

[23]This was not a revolutionary idea; several cities at that time owned and operated radio stations, such as New York City and Dallas.

town, educational broadcasting for the classroom ceased in Chicago. Consequently, the school officials believed that with no scheduled educational broadcasts, purchasing radios was useless. On the other hand, station owners asserted that without receivers in the classrooms, broadcasting programs to the classroom was a waste of time. Waller approached the Chicago Board of Education but failed to convince board members to take the first step. One might also surmise that Waller could not persuade the owners of her station to take action. Then, in the fall of 1926, Fanny Smith, the principal of Goudy Elementary,[24] asked Waller if WMAQ would broadcast programs especially for her school. The Goudy Parent-Teacher Association had presented the school a new radio receiver with the expectation that it would be used for educational purposes. Waller obliged (Atkinson, 1942c; Lawson, 1942).

To get programs on the air, Waller, like Darrow before her, improvised. She worked with Goudy's principal and faculty to plan and develop a weekly schedule of three programs: music appreciation, art appreciation, and presentations of general interest by prominent scientists and businesspeople. According to Waller, all the work was contributed: "Back in those early days, there was no such thing as a script nor a Radio School Committee. The programs were written and put on by the individual who did the broadcasting" (Lawson, 1942, p. 10).

These early broadcasts to schools used primitive pedagogy. Children sat for 30 minutes in an assembly hall listening to tinny voices on a loudspeaker[25] talk about music, art, or current events. Following the broadcasts, the children "wrote ten minute themes describing what they heard" (Caton, 1951, p. 226). Atkinson (1942c) describes these initial educational efforts as "very poor at the start" (p. 37). Nevertheless, by the end of the first year the single school of listeners had grown to 11 schools, and at the end of the second year, 1928, the program schedule expanded to daily broadcasts (Lawson, 1942, p. 7). For the 1929–30 year, WMAQ's school curriculum grew into a full schedule of 10 programs, 2 each school day, including music and art appreciation, a book club, current events, geography, history, math, household science, character training, nature study, poetry, a primary story hour, and social studies. The station printed and distributed to all teachers who requested it a monthly bulletin that listed and described the lessons to be presented, enabling teachers to prepare for the broadcasts. All of this activity suggests a flourishing demand for educational radio programs.

At this point, Waller recognized that conducting 10 school broadcasts each week was too much for her to handle. She appealed to the Chicago Public Schools (CPS) board to support the program (Lawson, 1942). Fortunately, the board agreed. They assumed responsibility for developing the programs, and WMAQ continued to broadcast them at no charge. The board appointed a radio committee responsible for planning, writing, and producing the broadcasts (Lawson, 1942), and initially they continued with Waller's schedule of 20-minute programs in the early morning. But the board also sought input from teachers and pupils. The committee soon discovered that 20-minute periods were too long and mornings not the most receptive time. They eventually settled on a schedule of 10 lessons per week, two 15-minute lessons daily, broadcast between 1:30 and 2:00 P.M. Following is the program listing for the 1932–33 school year. The list shows more than 10 programs because some first-semester programs were replaced during the second semester.

Music	Health	Poetry
Social Studies	Prominent Citizen's Series	Art
Geography	The Century of Progress	Guidance
History	Exposition	Character Inspiration
Household Science	Natural Science	Book Club
Current Events	Stories in Mathematics	Primary Story Hour

[Lawson, 1942, p. 51]

---

[24]Located in Chicago's Uptown, at that time, an affluent neighborhood.

[25]Probably the school owned only one radio receiver.

Most programs were adapted for specific grade ranges. Broadcast instructors included teachers, principals, supervisors, and specialists in a variety of educational fields. It is not known whether the pedagogy improved or whether all the programs continued to be piped into a packed auditorium. However, no budget was available to compensate those involved. All services were donated[26] (Atkinson, 1942b, p. 38).

Perhaps it was the financial strain of the Depression or just fatigue, but by the 1933–34 school year, CPS officials expressed a concern that continuing such an extensive program, without reimbursement, was too taxing on those involved and perhaps caused them to ignore their regular duties. Therefore, school officials requested a reduction in the broadcast schedule from 30 to 15 minutes daily and from five to four days per week. The board filled the broadcasting slot on the fifth day with NBC's popular *Music Appreciation Hour*, presented by Walter Damrosch, director of the New York Philharmonic, whose story is told in the next section. The following broadcast schedule for the school year 1933–34 shows how the board's decision restricted education by radio (Atkinson, 1942b; Lawson, 1942).

Monday	Civics and Social Studies
Tuesday	Nature Study and Health
Wednesday	Book Club and Literature Reading
Thursday	Mathematics
Friday	Damrosch's *Music Appreciation Hour*

(Where two subjects are listed, each was aimed at a different grade level and broadcast on alternate weeks.)

At the end of that year, the school board decided to end its SOA activity. Atkinson (1942c) says the board's action was forced by the lack of funds due to the Depression. Indeed, in 1934 there was talk of shutting down the entire school system.

Waller remained active in educational broadcasting well after the school board had taken over her SOA project at the Goudy school. From 1932 to 1934, she produced and broadcast over WMAQ a *Summer School of the Air*, an ambitious set of programs complete with supplemental workbooks covering eight weeks and featuring classes broadcast from the Hall of the Social Sciences at Chicago's Century of Progress Exposition. Students in the classroom joined those on the air in laboratory work (Atkinson, 1942b; Lawson, 1942).

Waller's summer school effort brings up a sensitive political issue that confronted all those involved in the SOA movement. Was radio an enrichment to classroom education or an alternative? Almost all schools in the SOA movement would claim that they were enriching classroom instruction, yet most offered some programs that clearly went beyond enrichment. Waller's summer school seemed to do just that. It is unlikely that during the Depression years, the Chicago Public Schools was able to offer summer school. Apparently, Waller developed and broadcast the summer programs and distributed accompanying workbooks with little involvement from school board personnel.[27] Clearly, Waller's summer school programs were not designed as enrichment to regular classroom instruction but represented a separate or alternative channel of instruction.

The year 1934 marked the end of all the WMAQ[28]–CPS cooperation on school of the air programming. While the CPS did return to education by radio years later, WMAQ never again broadcast juvenile educational programs originating from its studio (Lawson, 1942). However, Waller's initial effort, started at a single school, had lasted six years and grew to a huge project

[26]While I found no evidence for this point, it seems likely that Waller also received no extra compensation from WMAQ for her involvement in the SOA effort.

[27]Neither Atkinson (1942b) nor Lawson (1942) mentions school board involvement in the summer school broadcasts. I conclude that there was none.

[28]WMAQ was purchased by the National Broadcasting Company in 1931.

RCA Radiola 62 ... Combines the sensitive RCA Super-Heterodyne circuit and the famous RCA Dynamic Loudspeaker built in a walnut cabinet. *For use in school auditoriums $375* (courtesy of Wisconsin Historical Society Whi 44043).

serving the entire Chicago area. Throughout her career as an executive in commercial radio and television broadcasting, Judith Waller continued promoting educational programming. Atkinson, who chronicled education by radio in a multibook series published in 1942, praises Waller's work in education: "Probably no other American has contributed so much to the early pioneer work of making radio a tool of education" (1942b, p. 17).

Another radio education pioneer, Alice Keith, organized radio courses in music appreciation. Working in the Cleveland Public Schools in 1926, Keith arranged for special broadcasts of the Cleveland Symphony Orchestra aimed at upper-elementary grades and high schools. She developed other music programs for primary and intermediate grades (Atkinson, 1942b). "Records show a 100 percent increase in attendance at children's concerts of the Cleveland Sympathy" during the following year (Levenson, 1945, p. 32). Keith also introduced the first education by radio textbook, *Listening in on the Masters*, which she wrote for the music course. Her music series ran from 1926 to 1928 and ended when Keith left to become director of education for RCA, one of the owners of the newly formed NBC network. It is not surprising that in her new position Keith would help organize and promote NBC's acclaimed *Music Appreciation Hour* featuring Walter Damrosch, who had pioneered music education for children well before the advent of radio. As a result of Keith's efforts, the Cleveland School Board was sold on educational radio and decided to continue and expand her initiative. In 1929, they developed what was then the most advanced radio education project in the country (Atkinson, 1942b). The Cleveland SOA continued until the mid–1970s (John Basala, personal communication).

The early experimenters, Darrow, Waller, and Keith, were indeed trailblazers—dynamic, resourceful leaders who could play all positions. They built their SOAs without the benefit of budgets or trained staff. Like the Internet pioneers, Darrow, Waller, and Keith relied on the excitement and curiosity surrounding the new medium to attract the people and resources they needed. All three efforts relied on commercial stations to donate broadcast facilities, technical expertise, and production assistance. All three came to different ends. When Darrow left WLS, the *Little Red Schoolhouse* vanished without a trace, though his career in educational radio was just starting. As the WMAQ station manager, Waller was able to build and carry her SOA effort for several years until she convinced the Chicago Board of Education to take it over. Keith's initial effort died with her exit, but her legacy inspired the Cleveland School Board to launch an ambitious SOA that lasted for many years. Keith went on to play a leadership role in the country's two network-sponsored national schools of the air, whose stories are told in later chapters.

These early experiments led by Darrow, Waller, and Keith served as unofficial pilot programs for the school of the air movement. Using little or no money, these initial SOAs achieved limited successes that built basic repositories of knowledge about the skills, practices, and talents required to make an SOA successful. Out of these efforts emerged leaders who would play key roles in the SOA movement for years to come.

A National School of the Air?

Early experiments with radio as an educational medium soon inspired efforts to establish a national school of the air (NSoA). These efforts, in turn, sparked a political battle for control of the airwaves, a battle whose outcome affected not only broadcasting ever since but also how educators view education technology.

One of the first to understand that the new technology of broadcast radio had created the possibility of a "global village" was Ben Darrow, schoolmaster of the *Little Red Schoolhouse*. He stood in awe of radio's fantastic possibilities. "Who can vision the significance of the fact that distance for the ear has been annihilated: that by voice the world becomes one neighborhood." He envisioned that radio would "blow the roof off the classroom and expand the walls to the circumference of the globe" (Darrow, 1932, p. 79). Darrow said that he wanted to create an NSoA, an endeavor that he described in a letter to the networks in 1927 as potentially, "the biggest feature in all broadcasting," reaching the largest audience in the radio world (Taylor, 1974, pp. 57–58). Clearly, Darrow had a salesperson's gift for gab, and for the next two years he used that gift to promote the NSoA idea. The challenge he undertook was not easy.

After leaving the *Little Red Schoolhouse* in 1925, Darrow had returned to his Ohio farm where he spent two lean years struggling to support his family. A self-reliant, resourceful entrepreneur in the 19th-century tradition, Darrow dabbled in an astonishing variety of career and business activities. He sold rugs door-to-door, marketed his own invention the TABL-TUB, wrote a mystery story, and invented a youth card game. Though he succeeded in selling a few freelance articles to the *New York Times* and the *Christian Science Monitor*, all the other endeavors failed. Darrow was reduced to working as a farm laborer, cutting corn (Taylor, 1974).

Despite his humble circumstances, Darrow's work in educational radio had earned him respect, and by 1927 he was in contact with several influential people who shared his interest in establishing an NSoA. He joined with Gifford Pinchot, educator and former governor of Pennsylvania, and Admiral W. G. H. Bullard, member of the Federal Radio Commission, to form an informal committee dedicated to promoting the NSoA idea (Taylor, 1974). Probably on behalf of that group, Darrow pitched the NSoA concept to the Crosley Manufacturing Company of Cincinnati, one of the country's largest producers of radio receivers and owner of the country's most powerful radio station, WLW. Using an unabashed sales approach, Darrow proposed naming the new school "The Crosley School of the Air." Excerpts from a letter to Crosley management demonstrate that Darrow knew how to appeal to bottom-line-oriented businesspeople. He said: "It [NSoA] will reach the largest regular audience in the world. 32,000,000 children — 800,000 teachers—countless others. IMMEDIATE SALES Children are the best advertisers in the world. TWO LEGGED CROSLEY ADS will go home to 20,000,000 radio-less homes coaxing dad to buy a Crosley" (Taylor, 1974, p. 63). Educational objectives or benefits were not mentioned, a lack that probably resulted from Darrow's desire to tailor his message to the buyer (Taylor, 1974).

Later that year, Darrow and his group presented to the newly formed broadcast networks[29] an extensive school plan that included an ambitious full-day schedule of radio programs for high school and elementary grades. While Darrow made no direct reference to educational philosophy or pedagogy, his presentation demonstrates how he envisioned radio: "Only recognized leaders in each subject will be considered for the faculty of the School of the Air; the music instruction will be by a nationally famous teacher of school music; Nature Studies will be given by leading Naturalists. Health talks will be given by nationally known physicians and surgeons" (Taylor, 1974, p. 59). Darrow appreciated educational radio because it could expose the average student to the influence of master teachers and authorities from many fields. In that same appeal, Darrow emphasized that great prestige would accrue to the network that agreed to carry the school of the air.

While the networks expressed interest, negotiations bogged down over two issues. With NBC, the issue was increasing the number of receivers in the schools. The network would support the NSoA when the schools committed to equipping classrooms with receivers. This position is not surprising considering that the network's owners included two major radio equipment manufacturers, RCA and GE. At the CBS precursor network, the issue was scheduling. Management could not force its affiliates to surrender large blocks of time to the NSoA effort (Taylor, 1974).

Armstrong Perry and the Payne Fund

Just when Darrow's effort to establish an NSoA seems to have reached a dead end, he received a message from an acquaintance stating that the Payne Fund was very interested in his plans. Armstrong Perry, a freelance journalist specializing in broadcasting, had demonstrated an interest in radio early on when, as an executive of the Boy Scouts, he testified before the First National Radio Conference in 1922, calling for government-run public stations (McChesney, 1993, p. 40). He was later hired by the Payne Fund to promote the NSoA concept. Contact between Darrow and the Payne Fund revitalized the drive for an NSoA and had long-term consequences for the entire SOA movement. The Payne Fund, founded by Mrs. Frances Payne Bolton,[30] wife of an Ohio Congressman and one of the heirs to Standard Oil money, had demonstrated a concern with educational media by funding major studies of the educational use of movies and juvenile reading habits. As early as 1921, the fund had expressed an interest in educational radio, but to no effect. That interest was reinvigorated in 1926 when its president, H. M. Clymer, inspected the British Broadcasting Corporation's (BBC) educational programs. Impressed with what he saw, Clymer expressed his intention to launch a national school of the air in the United States. As a result, the Payne Fund staff including Darrow and Perry formulated a four-part plan for developing radio service to the nation's schools:

---

[29]NBC began operations in the fall of 1926. The precursor to CBS started in 1927. CBS, as we know it today, came under the control of William S. Paley in the summer of 1928.

[30]Frances Payne, an heir to portions of the Standard Oil of Indiana fortune, married staunch Republican congressman James Bolton. Upon his death, she succeeded him and served 29 years in Congress.

1. Complete a national survey of schools to determine the need for school broadcasting and whether schools were equipped with receivers.
2. Form a Preliminary Committee on Educational Broadcasting whose objective would be to gain the approval of the Executive Committee of the National Education Association (NEA) to provide educational leadership and to "oversee the establishment of a NSoA to be broadcast on commercial stations" (McChesney, 1993, p. 39).
3. Secure a grant from the Commonwealth Fund for operating the NSoA.
4. Establish a school of the air demonstration project [McChesney, 1993; Taylor, 1974].

Perry designed and conducted the survey, which was widely praised for its precision and usefulness (McChesney, 1993). He said that the national study was conducted specifically to determine whether schools would be willing to equip their classes with radios and, if so, what subjects they wanted to hear on the air (Perry, 1929, pp. 11–12). The survey questionnaire was mailed to 3,000 county superintendents, principals, and classroom teachers of public schools. Of 475 returns, 441 expressed positive attitudes toward educational radio for the classroom (Darrow, 1977; Quinton, 1977; Stead, 1937, p. 12). Meanwhile, Darrow worked with the preliminary committee to lobby the NEA.

However much involved the Payne Fund seemed to be, it would not commit to any major funding to launch an NSoA on its own. Instead it sought operational funding from another foundation, the Commonwealth Fund. After almost a year of efforts, everything seemed to hang on gaining approval from the NEA. Several times during 1928, the group's approval seemed assured, but in the end, the NEA executive committee referred the Payne proposal to a committee for further study,[31] effectively killing hopes for endorsement of the NSoA plan. Almost immediately, the Commonwealth Fund denied the Payne Fund's grant request (Taylor, 1974). Once again the effort to establish an NSoA had hit a wall.

At this point, Darrow abandoned the NSoA quest and returned to Ohio to try to stimulate interest in a state-wide effort. Perry, however, continued to fight for an NSoA. Immediately following the NEA's negative decision, Perry redirected the Payne strategy for establishing an NSoA along two different but parallel tracks. First, he asked the two broadcast networks to donate the airtime needed for the NSoA broadcasts, a request that both networks quickly agreed to in writing. However, Perry believed strongly that the effort must be supervised and largely operated by the NEA or some other national educational organization. After attempting to "rouse enthusiasm among educators," he soon realized that such a commitment would not be possible unless he could find funding to operate the school (McChesney, 1993, p. 40). Without operating funds, the network offers of free airtime would be wasted. Perry became pessimistic. In early 1929, CBS, now under the control of William S. Paley, informed Perry that to produce the school on their network required half a million dollars. If the money could not be found, CBS was prepared to launch its own scaled-down educational program. Despite months of solicitation, Perry was unable to raise the money from foundations or private donors (McChesney, 1993).

Meanwhile, Ben Darrow used his personal connections to entice educational leaders in his home state of Ohio to launch a radio education demonstration project. He succeeded. The plan was approved in the fall of 1928. With generous help from the Payne Fund, the first semester of classes began in January 1929 (Perry, 1929). The full story of the Ohio School of the Air is presented in Section III. Darrow's success affected Perry's work substantially.

The effort to establish an NSoA presented Perry with a new and more complex challenge. He opposed the idea of a commercial entity, such as CBS, conducting a large-scale educational activity, yet no other group seemed to have the resources to launch the effort — no other group,

---

[31]The NEA Committee on "Lay Relations" did study the issue and found: "the problem of educational broadcasting is too indefinite and involves too many unknown factors ... to admit our present acceptance" (Perry, 1929, p. 12).

that is, except the federal government. Perry initiated an effort to get the federal government involved. First he asked the NEA to pass a resolution calling for the secretary of the interior,[32] Ray Wilbur, to convene a commission to study the "crisis afflicting education radio broadcasting in the U.S." (McChesney, 1993, p. 40). With Darrow's Ohio School of the Air providing an example of successful operation, the NEA group readily agreed. Then Perry got the Payne Fund to put up $5,000 to cover the committee's expenses. With urging from a nationally recognized educational body and outside funding, the government could not refuse (McChesney, 1993).

In May of 1929, Secretary Wilbur convened the Radio Education Conference. Participants included representatives from the networks, independent stations, and the Rockefeller and Carnegie Foundations, both of which, according to Leach (1983), were partial toward commercial interests. Perry was the only participant who advocated unequivocally for a federally supported NSoA. Curiously, no one was invited from the Ohio School of the Air, which had just completed successfully its first semester of operation. Perry was highly capable, but the omission of Darrow, the man most experienced in developing schools of the air, seemed glaring (Taylor, 1974).

The conference's work spanned several months during 1929 and entailed a great deal of research on the state of educational radio. Perry conducted part of the research, and during this phase his thinking evolved. First, he became increasingly skeptical of the networks' offer to provide free airtime. Any resource offered by the commercial interest, he believed, would be bound to commercial considerations. Eventually, all the available airtime might be sold to advertisers. The meaning was clear: education would not survive long in a totally commercial environment. Perry also found among college and university broadcasters a group who understood the potential of educational radio and were willing to advocate for involvement by the federal government. By the end of 1929, Perry had shifted his focus from trying to establish an NSoA to agitating for the political changes necessary to make an NSoA possible. He urged the Payne Fund to cease working with commercial broadcasters and to focus instead on preserving and developing state and college broadcasting stations for educational purposes (McChesney, 1993).

The results of the Wilbur Conference disappointed Perry and the other NSoA advocates. In his report, Perry emphasized that the most important issue for the committee to address was control of radio channels; specifically, quick action was needed to protect the remaining college-based educational stations. Network representatives quickly dismissed his concerns, saying that "broadcast companies are willing to give ample time for educational programs and would exercise no censorship whatsoever" (McChesney, 1993, p. 43). The final report accepted the commercial broadcasters' promise, though it recommended a permanent radio section be established within the Office of Education, which was then part of the Department of Interior. The radio section's role according to McChesney was confined to coordinating the use of commercial facilities by educational interests. The report failed to mention the need to reserve channels for educational uses. Perhaps the only consolation Perry received is that he was appointed the first radio education specialist in the new radio section office within the Office of Education. From that position, he continued to advocate for government intervention and setting aside channels for education. He urged educators to quickly develop a consensus of opinion and submit a unified plan for developing educational radio that included the assistance of the federal government, or, he warned, "The broadcasting facilities of the country [will] come so firmly under the control of commercial groups that education by radio would be directed by business men instead of professional educators" (Hill, 1942, p. 10).

While Perry succeeded in persuading the federal government to take an interest in education by radio, he did not solve the more immediate problem of how to support the NSoA. Following the Wilbur Conference reports, released in early 1930, leaders of college-based educational

[32]The Office of Education was then part of the Department of the Interior.

radio stations and proponents of a national school of the air turned increasingly to the federal government to achieve their aims. They lobbied and petitioned to have the government set aside 15 percent of the radio channels for educational purposes, thus creating the technical facilities needed to support a national school of the air (Leach, 1983; McChesney, 1993; Saettler, 1990). Suffice to say that the effort reached a dead end in 1934 when the newly created Federal Communications Commission (FCC) ignored the channel set-aside issue and instead endorsed the "Cooperation Policy." In this policy, commercial broadcasters agreed to provide resources for educational broadcasting, including free access to airwaves and research and support for program development. However, the agreement was purely voluntary. Private owners of radio stations were in no way obligated to support educational radio[33] (Leach, 1983).

Out of the political battles two opposing associations formed, each supported by different foundations: the National Advisory Council on Radio Education (NACRE) backed by the Carnegie Foundation versus the National Committee on Education by Radio (NCER) backed by the Payne Fund. Supported by the commercial broadcasters, NACRE developed its Cooperation Policy stating that the "needs of education would be best served by not disturbing the status quo" (Saettler, 1990, p. 207). The status quo at that time meant commercial control of the new medium with no exceptions. Leach (1983) is more explicit, describing NACRE's goal as "to buffer educators' distrust of the [radio] industry and induce them to cooperate" (p. 20). Leach's skeptical view should not cloud the good work NACRE did in prodding the networks to produce high-quality cultural and educational programming and in producing educational programming for the networks.

NCER backers, on the other hand, believed that educational radio could gain neither stability nor a long-term future within a commercial system. During the first half of the 1930s, they mounted a spirited campaign on behalf of the channel set-aside issue, and even though they lost the war, they did win some battles. For instance, commercial forces felt compelled by the Cooperation Policy to demonstrate their commitment to quality educational and cultural programs, and as a result the networks produced a "great flowering of cultural and public affairs programs that has never been equaled" (Smith, 1990, pp. 140–141). Some credit for that "great flowering" should go to NCER and other like-minded groups.

Perhaps the leaders of the NSoA movement were fighting for an impossible dream. In his book, Armstrong Perry (1929) provides insight. In 1921, at the very dawn of the broadcast era, the Radio Council of what would later become the Payne Fund recommended that the U.S. Office of Education in the Department of Interior propose national radio education programs for the public schools. Fund representatives provided statistics on the rapidly growing number of radio receivers and broadcasting stations. After some internal consultation, Commissioner J. J. Tigert responded, saying that while he favored providing some educational programming by radio, "the feeling against Federal control of education was strong and growing stronger, and that the Bureau did not operate anywhere without the consent of state and local authorities." In fact, the bureau had responsibility for the education of Native Americans and the children of Alaska only (Perry, 1929, p. 41). This story shows that there existed at the federal level in this country no public organization, no legal structure, and no funding sources capable of launching and conducting a national educational radio effort. Furthermore, many were biased against federal involvement in education. Finally, broadcast facilities needed for national programming were available only at the discretion of private owners who might withdraw their cooperation any time. These barriers to a federally supported NSoA proved insurmountable but did leave

---

[33] According to Barnouw (1966), commercial spokesmen had a big advantage over educators because they could speak of program examples that were familiar to most listeners such as *Music Appreciation Hour, American School of the Air,* and broadcasts of major symphonies. Educators could invoke no such examples known to a national audience. Therefore, protesting educators were talking about abstractions while commercial broadcasters could talk about a reality that was part of the nation's daily life (p. 278).

the door open for the networks. The development of two commercially directed SOAs is described in the following sections.

Ideals of the Movement

Ironically, most of the philosophical rationale for developing a publicly run NSoA seems to have been articulated only after any realistic possibility for creating such an entity had diminished. Two respected spokespersons for educational radio stated their views in the early 1940s. Seerley Reid served as lead researcher for the federally funded Evaluation of School Broadcasts Project conducted at The Ohio State University's Bureau of Educational Research. Reid stated the following ideas about the value of national radio education broadcasts to the schools:

> Imaginatively and carefully planned, dramatically written and produced, school broadcasts can provide worth-while educational experiences not otherwise available in thousands of classrooms. Planned and produced in New York, network school broadcasts can make use of expert curricular advice, skillful writers and dramatists, excellent production facilities and resources. Broadcast over a nation-wide radio hook-up, the radio programs heard in classrooms from New York to San Francisco can be an integrative factor in an educational program to achieve national unity around the ideals, the achievements, and the potentialities of American democracy [Reid, 1941a, p.1].

I. Keith Tyler, director of the project, added:

> Through school broadcasts, centrally produced and widely distributed by affiliated stations throughout the country, it is possible for schools of varied types located in all parts of America to utilize common curriculum elements. All American children rural and city, southern and northern, Negro and white, poor and wealthy, have a similar heritage, face common problems and need a better understanding of each other. It is clear that programs dealing with these common elements can enrich, enliven, stimulate, and unify the education of boys and girls of America [Reid, 1941a, Introduction].

Later, Woelfel and Tyler (1945) published the major findings of the evaluation project in a very readable book entitled *Radio and the School*. In it, Seerley spells out several distinct benefits offered by national school broadcasting. Foremost is the ability to emphasize in a coordinated fashion to all listeners the major purposes and values of American democracy. Second, radio can address what he identified as the great problem facing American education, namely, anarchy. By that he meant education in the United States was fragmented among thousands of small school districts. Even though Americans by the early 1940s had become a highly mobile population in which social and economic barriers were diminishing, "American education holds to a nineteenth-century belief in small and autonomous school districts" that spawned a bewildering variety of curricula (Woelfel & Tyler, 1945, pp. 49–50). As a result, he said, the American people remained apprehensive and confused. According to Reid, an NSoA offered the potential of a common core of intellectual and emotional experience throughout the schools of America. Anarchy also characterized the philosophy and methodology that operated within many schools. Teachers and whole departments worked behind enclosures of classroom and subject matter. A unified national school broadcast, Reid asserted, could break down the barriers that existed between classroom teachers and fields of study.

Finally, while acknowledging that a local or regional approach to radio education offered effective programs, Reid believed that radio's educational potential could be achieved only through a unified national effort. NSoAs, he argued, could provide rich resources for planning and production that local groups could not match. "Even the most ardent believer in local broadcasting has to admit that the networks have advantages in resources and personnel" (Woelfel & Tyler,

1945, p. 52). Given Reid's assessment that the problem was fragmentation or "anarchy," his solution of a unified national approach made sense.

However, support of such a national effort seems to have waned considerably by the time Reid wrote. Woelfel, who along with Tyler edited the evaluation report, expressed his doubts as early as 1941: "If educators think about nation-wide school broadcasts at all, it is to regard them either as one more applicant for time in an already crowded course of study, or as something for a department of audio-instruction to plan for. The rich educational potentialities of a nation-wide school broadcast seem to have been completely overlooked both by educators and civic leaders" (Waller, 1946, p. 410). Thus, by the early 1940s, the movement to create a federally-backed national school of the air was dead.

The Great FM Set-Aside

During the first half of the 1940s, the struggle for educational set-asides began to bear fruit, though it took a while for that fruit to ripen. In May of 1940, the Federal Communications Commission (FCC) affirmed the right of educational agencies to the exclusive use of radio channels, but as it turned on, they would be on the new FM band. The war seems to have slowed down consideration of educational set-asides, but during the next five years, FM operating licenses were granted to six educational entities: the boards of education in New York City, Chicago, San Francisco, and Cleveland. The other two were granted to the Universities of Illinois and Kentucky. Finally on January 15, 1945, the Federal Communications Commission (FCC) announced that twenty channels, each 200 kilocycles wide, from 84 to 88 megacycles, would be allocated for educational stations. These 20 channels used throughout the country would enable thousands of FM educational stations. By the end of 1945, 37 educational institutions across the country had submitted applications to construct FM stations. The applicants included state boards of higher education, individual universities and colleges, local school boards, and the Sewanhaka High School in Floral Park, N. Y. The following year, the University of Wisconsin submitted its application to build a network of 8 FM stations (Woelfel and Tyler, 1945).

However, educators did not rush to own and operate educational channels. In fact by 1948 FCC Chairman Wayne Coy expressed disappointment that more school districts and colleges had not applied. He issued a warning: "I must point out that radio channels are too valuable to be left in idleness. If educators fail to utilize them, they will have lost their second and perhaps last chance to own and operate radio stations" (Coy in Field, 1991, p. 128).

Despite Coy's concern, by 1948 19 FM stations were in operation, 51 new construction permits had been issued and 8 applications for new stations were pending (Dunham, 1948). At a time when commercial stations began to curtail their involvement in educational radio, due the pressure of increased profits, the availability of FM stations fostered the continued development of existing SOAs and the development of new ones. We should all be aware that the stations developed from the set-aside form the core of today's NPR network.

Schools of the Air Emerge

The struggle to create a federally supported national school of the air, though unsuccessful, helped to create conditions that favored the development of SOAs at different levels throughout the country. Instead of the single coordinated national effort that Reid and others had hoped for, many independent schools of the air were conceived, developed and operated by three types of entities: commercial broadcast networks, state legislatures and universities, and local school districts. During the decade of the 1940s, perhaps half the elementary and high school teachers in the United States could have tuned in at least one SOA program every day of the week, and many teachers would have had a choice of several on the same day. Not surprisingly, with so many independent entities operated by different institutions and organizations, there developed distinct goals, philosophies, methods, audiences, and results.

So what exactly was a School of the Air? In this work, schools of the air are defined as radio programs intended for in-school use that:

1. Presented courses of study (series) in a subject that paralleled or was integrated with either a specific or typical school curricula.
2. Arranged programs in a series to assist in cumulative learning.
3. Designed individual program series for specific grade levels.
4. Developed broadcast schedules that coincided with the school year.
5. Designed series for students between kindergarten and grade 12.

Entities that broadcast individual radio programs for occasional in-school use are not considered schools of the air.

Following is a summary of the SOAs that are covered in this work.

Section II, National Broadcast Networks:
• NBC's *Music Appreciation Hour.*
• CBS's American School of the Air (ASA).

Section III, State-Level SOAs:
• By the middle of radio's golden age, the early 1940s, 38 state colleges and universities and 13 state or territorial boards of education offered or had offered at least one educational broadcast intended for classroom use. However, according to Atkinson (1942c), some were classroom instruction only by virtue of being named so. Five at the state level are identified as having had successful runs lasting at least a decade or more, and developed impressive followings among the schools of their respective states. They include: Ohio, Wisconsin, Texas, Minnesota, and Oregon Schools of the Air (Woelfel and Tyler, 1945). In the late 1940s the Empire State FM School of the Air was formed in New York State.

Section IV, Local School Boards:
• Thirty-one local school districts offered some kind of radio programming intended for the classroom, but radio scholars of the day deemed that only nine could be called schools of the air (Atkinson, 1942b; Saettler, 1990, p. 197; Woelfel & Tyler, 1945, p. 89). However, lack of documentation limits coverage in this work to seven including Cleveland; Chicago; Rochester, New York; Portland, Oregon; Detroit; Alameda, California; and Akron, Ohio.

Benefits of Education by Radio

While each SOA operated independently, proponents of education by radio agreed that all SOAs provided their listeners with a common core of benefits. Here is Darrow's list of the benefits of education by radio:

• Enables master teachers to share their expertise with a great number of pupils
• Exposes students to world figures
• Stimulates student imagination through the use of drama, music, and sound
• Puts students in contact with events as they happened
• Reunites the home and school in the educational process[34]
• Deemphasizes drill and practice

---

[34]Darrow asserted that because parents listened to the instructional broadcasts at home or work, families were stimulated to continue discussion in the evenings when children were home.

Ben Darrow saw radio as an "Electric Chautauqua." He believed that hearing world leaders on radio inspired students and stimulated clear thinking (Darrow, 1940).

William Levenson, supervisor of Cleveland's Radio Board of Education, suggested the following ways that radio helped achieve educational goals:

- It creates a sense of timeliness because it presents and interprets the event while it is still current and before it becomes history.
- It creates a sense of participation and opens the classroom doors to the outside world.
- It creates emotional impact using drama and music. Emotions have a powerful influence over learning and attitude development.
- It integrates knowledge from different subject areas into a more comprehensive learning experience.
- It services "homebound students" (Levenson, 1945, pp. 6–14).

Levenson (1945) names ten common ways to structure instruction on radio. They are: straight talk (lecture), interview, panel or round table, actuality (live pick-ups), quiz bee, classroom "pickup" (entire class brought to studio), forum or debate, dramatization, music, and demonstration (p. 48). These can be thought of as the basic pedagogy of educational radio.

Finally several local and state-based SOAs, Cleveland and Rochester to name the most prominent, used radio as the primary tool for delivering instruction. The Wisconsin School of the Air offered several of the series designed to fill voids in the curricula of the many small and one-room schools it served.

Mastering the Technology

Advocates of education by radio soon learned that piping broadcasts into school auditoriums packed with students was a bad idea. As early as 1929, radio educators were urging principals and teachers to put radios in the classroom rather than in large, open spaces such as auditoriums — or worse, lunch rooms. For one thing, large spaces such as school auditoriums required powerful speakers and amplifiers, far beyond what was available from most radios of the day, not to mention sound-deadening surfaces to reduce echo, all of which entailed additional expense and expertise that few schools were prepared to take on. Even if they were, the experts discouraged them; the educational environment of large spaces, they said, was inferior to that of classrooms (Darrow, 1940; Harrison, 1937; Stead, 1937). Probably most teachers then and today would agree.

Classroom broadcasting was achieved with either a centralized system or portable sets in the classroom. In the first case, large schools found it more economical to hardwire many classroom speakers to a central receiver and tuner located in or near the principal's office. According to Reid (1942), by 1941, 11 percent of all Ohio schools, including one-third of its high schools, were equipped with central radio sound systems. A central system probably provided the most reliable reception and could easily be adapted to give the principal a central address system. Also, a phonograph player could be added to the system. With a central system, however, teachers had no control over program selection.

For small schools, portable receivers in the classroom made sense economically, but while the individual sets gave the classroom teacher more control, they were more prone to reception problems. Harrison (1937) described portables as a set in which the speaker is separate from the receiver. If both were attached in the same wood cabinet, then the set would be too heavy to move easily from room to room. Medium-sized schools could compromise by stringing a few speakers to one set and then placing the speakers in several classrooms. However, the number of speakers that one set could support was limited (Harrison, 1937). Just as today, 2005, school administrators strive to get computers into the classroom; then, they sought creative ways to

With Radio the Unprivileged School Becomes the Privileged One (©University of Kentucky, all rights reserved, Louis Edward Nollan F Series Photographic Print Collection, circa 1885–1966, Special Collections and Digital Programs, University of Kentucky Libraries).

make radio available to the classrooms. Harrison reports that some schools put a home-style receiver on wheels so it could be quickly wheeled from classroom to classroom, and others, probably wealthier schools, wired classrooms with an outlet, aerial, and ground so that the portable sets could provide good, reliable reception. Harrison provides no data to back up these claims, though they seem credible.

From our perspective, one of the advantages of radio over computers would seem to be ease of operation. What could be easier to operate than a radio? Perhaps we should not take that ease for granted. In her text, Harrison (1937) found it necessary to remind teachers of this fact: "Teachers must not forget that only one program may be tuned in at one time for each radio set ... no matter how many loudspeakers are available" (p. 145). Harrison also provided detailed guidance on highly technical topics such as tuning a radio set and adjusting the volume (p. 147). She warns teachers to *never* slightly "tune out" the station as a means of reducing the volume. For that task, she recommends using the set's volume-control knob.

Radio: A New Form of Educational Technology

By the mid–1930s, many schools made regular use of film, records, and slides to supplement instruction, but in limited ways. For example a specific concept or process might be best presented or demonstrated with a slide, film or recording better than a competent teacher could do. But this technology was seldom used to supplement curricula to any degree or to achieve learning objectives.

Compared to film or records, radio SOAs offered a more flexible and powerful educational medium. Though radio was frequently used to enrich or to supplement curriculum in limited ways, it offered the opportunity to design instruction to meet specific educational goals for specific subjects and grade levels. In this sense radio could deliver instruction with effectiveness equal to or surpassing in some cases live instruction. This was true, particularly in rural schools where

First-grade classroom equipped with a radio speaker wired to a central receiver (circa 1930) (courtesy of the Ohio State University Archive).

teachers with limited training might be responsible for covering multiple subjects and grade levels. In those situations, classroom teachers could use radio lessons to deliver specialized topics such as science, music, art, and literature prepared by specialists and delivered by master teachers. Radio broadcasters commonly used direct instruction to which students responded during the broadcasts with any number of learning activities such as drawing, rhythmic movement, verbal responses, and even performing simple science experiments. Radio instruction often generated a surprising amount of interactivity between classroom and broadcast teacher.

Radio was adaptable. State and local SOAs could synchronize radio instruction with school curricula. Programs that highlighted state and local

Centralized Radio Receiver ... *provides for reception, control and distribution of radio programs from a single point in a place convenient for supervision by the proper authorities* (courtesy of Wisconsin Historical Society Whi 44046).

topics and historical personalities could be developed fairly cheaply. Programming could be updated fairly rapidly to reflect current events and seasonal topics. Moreover, radio offered creative potential. Tens of thousands of students and teachers participated in the creative and technical work of writing, producing, and broadcasting instructional and informational programs. Nothing similar was possible with the traditional forms of educational technology.

The stories of individual schools of the air that follow tell how some mined radio's rich creative and educational potential while others saw it as just another instructional aid, a classification that relegated radio to the realm of the static educational technologies. Some understood that radio was a new form of educational media enabling users and learners to design and create original instructional materials, mold them to fit various curricula, and alter them rapidly to suit local needs.

Evaluating SOAs

By the mid–1940s, schools of the air had reached a zenith of sorts, with CBS and NBC broadcasting programs to the nation's schools; state-funded SOAs operating in Ohio, Texas, Minnesota, Oregon, and Wisconsin; and many county and urban school districts broadcasting locally. For most schools of the air, evaluation consisted mainly of getting feedback from teachers and school administrators on what they thought of the programs. More rigorous evaluations of the learning that resulted from education by radio also took place, but it was conducted primarily by university based researchers

Thanks to Darrow's efforts, Ohio had become the center of educational radio, so it is not surprising that The Ohio State University sponsored the nation's premier research center for educational radio. Funded chiefly by the Federal Radio Education Committee of the FCC, the Evaluation of School Broadcasts (ESB) project was dedicated to researching and analyzing the educational value of radio in schools and classrooms. By the end of 1942, the project, under the direction of I. Keith Tyler and Norman Woelfel, had published 39 reports dealing with education by radio. Several of them will be covered later in this study. Chief researcher Seerley Reid oversaw much of the research and implemented rigorous standards. Two questions attracted the most attention of researchers: who listened, and what difference did it make? As it turned out, both questions proved difficult to answer (Reid, 1941a).

Directors of the ESB project, based on their findings on usage of radio in the schools, concluded that as of 1943 radio "has not been accepted as a full-fledged member of the educational family." Rather, it remained a "stepchild of education" (Woelfel & Tyler, 1945, p. 2). Cuban (1986) cites Woelfel and Tyler to support his assertion that teachers never truly accepted educational technology as part of their teaching practice. However, the evidence developed in this work leads us to conclude that in several state and local school systems, teachers did eagerly integrate radio into their classroom curricula. Further, the stories of the SOAs documented here illuminate the complex set of reasons why teachers embraced or avoided radio in their classrooms. It suggests that in evaluating SOAs, researchers placed too much emphasis on audience size and overlooked the fact that SOAs were launched with a variety of goals in mind, education being just one. In evaluating the success of an SOA, the goals of the founders should be taken into consideration.

Concern about the educational value of radio grew along with the use of radio in the classrooms. By 1940, several million schoolchildren were exposed regularly to radio lessons of one kind or another, and research efforts grew accordingly. In their extensive report on radio in the school, Woelfel and Tyler (1945) reviewed research and evaluation studies of radio up to that point. They identified three types of radio studies:

• Media comparison studies in which radio instruction is compared to traditional classroom instruction

• Media attribute studies aimed at identifying and analyzing radio's unique contribution to content instruction and methods
• Survey studies of teachers' opinions concerning the use of radio in the classroom

Most of the comparison studies investigated the difference between learning with and without radio; these studies found no significant difference. Such results provoked skepticism in Woelfel and Tyler, who asserted that radio educators should never have expected a difference between listening to a lecture on radio and listening to it in person. Subsequent researchers have thoroughly documented the common weakness found in media comparison studies, namely the confounding of variables[35] (Seels, Berry, Fullerton, & Horn, 1996).

In what later came to be called media attribute studies, Lazarsfeld (1940) found that radio appealed more to people from lower cultural and educational levels and less to those at higher cultural and educational levels. The latter preferred reading, in part, Lazarsfeld said, because they are more skilled at reading than those in the lower levels. Radio's unique educational attribute might be that it can appeal to those who are less skilled at reading, but it is not that simple. Other factors such as interest and subject play a role in determining whether one prefers to learn by reading or by listening. Lazarsfeld found that avid baseball fans would rather listen to a game on the radio, while people interested in current events prefer reading about them in a newspaper. Lazarsfeld concluded that learning outcomes are not determined by the means of perception. Crucial factors are situation, habits of the learner, and the nature of the subject. Given various arrangements of these variables, radio could be either superior or inferior to rival instructional media or live presentations (Lazarfield, 1940).

Woelfel and Tyler (1945) reviewed the extensive history of research that used teacher surveys to identify and establish the educational values of radio in school. They concluded, "Subject to the usual qualifications concerning questionnaire data, the findings indicate quite clearly that teachers who have used radio believe in the educational values of radio in school" (Woelfel & Tyler, 1945, p. 38). Overall, then, it appears that up to 1945, research into radio produced results quite similar to research performed since then with other media.

Another form of evaluation can be found in the opinions and comments made by knowledgeable observers and participants of the day. These include classroom teachers, school principals, scholars, and social critics. To the extent that their observations and opinions are available, we have a window in time that lets us understand what SOAs meant to educators of the day. Given that so much of educational research produces inconclusive or unreliable results, I believe the thoughts of proficient observers contemporary with events provide insight into historical phenomena that might otherwise be unavailable to today's readers.

Audience

Exactly who was receiving the benefits of education by radio? In his 1940 *Annual Report of the Columbia Broadcasting System*, Chairman William S. Paley claimed that Columbia's American School of the Air reached 8 million pupils in more than 200,000 classrooms (Atkinson, 1942b, p. 27). Atkinson quoted the source material without comment, but other scholars have disputed such claims. Cuban (1986) and Woelfel and Reid (1945) call Paley's claims absurd. If true, ASA's audience would have equaled well over 30 percent of all the public school children in America at that time. Citing a survey of ASA classroom audiences conducted in Ohio in 1940–41, Cuban projected the Ohio results nationally and shrank Paley's numbers down to fewer than one million listeners (Cuban, 1986, p. 23). However, the whole idea of basing national audience estimates on Ohio's atypical experience may have been faulty. Another study estimated the ASA audience to approximately 1.5 million listeners (Reid 1941a).

---

[35]As examples of studies that provide a more valid view of how and when radio can best be used for education, the authors point to Paul Lazarsfeld's (1940) research at Columbia's Office of Radio Research.

Developing accurate estimates of SOA audience size is a complicated and imprecise business in which both proponents and skeptics could easily err. For example, estimates for NBC's *Music Appreciation Hour* ran a wide range from half a million to as many as 7 million listeners at its peak of appeal in the late 1930s (Taylor, 1974). Some SOAs such as WSA made earnest efforts to determine audience size, but most did not. Few scholars tried to estimate the national audience because most likely it changed from year to year, and besides no national entity supported such research.

Despite these ambiguities, it *is* important to develop reasonable, accurate estimates of audience size in order to gauge the likelihood that SOAs affected educational achievement or practice. Based on a conservative reading and analysis of available data, at its height the entire SOA movement attracted roughly 3 million regular classroom listeners, approximately 10 percent of America's schoolchildren, plus an unknown number of at-home listeners. Because SOAs were not uniformly available to all the nation's school classrooms, in those areas where they were heard, audience size may have represented substantially more than 10 percent of the student population. The key point is that radio schools of the air regularly reached a substantial number of students, but the audience in certain states was much greater than in others. In Wisconsin, for example, during the period 1945 to 1965, listeners to the Wisconsin School of the Air (WSA) ranged between 25 percent and 50 percent of the state's elementary school population. This degree of penetration demonstrated that schools of the air had the potential to impact education in America. The study identifies factors that resulted in differences in audience size among the SOAs studied.

Finally, any discussion of audience size should also consider several related questions such as, what is the significance of audience size. What size audience would confirm success? In making judgments about success and failure, should we apply the same standard to SOAs that was applied to commercial broadcasting? What other standards of success, if any, should we use to evaluate SOA accomplishments or, for that matter, any educational experiment?

Summary

The dramatic emergence of broadcast radio stimulated a period of wild experimentation in programming, commerce, and education. Individuals, schools, organizations, and business corporations found it easy to get into radio, but at first few were sure what to do with it. Visionaries saw radio as a vehicle for world peace, universal education, religious conversion, enlightenment, cultural uplift, improved citizenship, and, of course, profit. At the same time, manufacturers of radio hardware played a major role in the development of the new medium and related technology. However, programming remained an open question for nearly the entire first decade. In that experimental period, colleges and universities, state and local educators, and social activists developed dozens of worthwhile educational endeavors, but the chaotic, open-market state of broadcasting discouraged these early efforts. Many educational stations were crippled by federal regulations that strongly favored the commercial broadcasters. A movement to establish a national SOA was hampered by the fragmented nature of American education and by political opposition from radio's commercial interests. Nevertheless, in radio's second decade, schools of the air took root and flourished at three different levels: (1) national commercial networks, (2) state legislatures and universities, and (3) local school boards. The next section investigates the network SOAs starting with the remarkable, though limited, *Music Appreciation Hour*; the educational benefits and innovations they delivered; and the reasons behind their demise.

Network Schools of the Air

While the government, private foundations, and even educational organizations avoided making a commitment to a national radio school of the air, the new commercial networks saw benefit in such programming. For a complex of business, political, and social reasons both NBC and CBS launched schools of the air and carried the cost of these non-profit entities for many years. Undoubtedly, the network efforts contributed to the educational resources available to U. S. students, but it's also true that the schools of the air contributed to network objectives. Fortunately, rich documentation exists for both.

NBC's Music Appreciation Hour

In October 1928, the National Broadcasting Company (NBC) launched the first national educational radio program designed for use in the schools. It has been acclaimed the most successful application of technology to education. Under the direction of Walter Damrosch, long-time conductor of the New York Symphony Orchestra and self-proclaimed missionary of European classical music to the American hinterland, the *Music Appreciation Hour* (MAH) soon became "the most popular school radio program throughout the country" (Woelfel & Reid, 1945).

Broadcast for 14 years by NBC, the MAH offered quality instruction on European classical music that probably has had no peer in broadcast media since. Through its network of affiliated stations, NBC delivered the MAH to schools in almost all sections of this country. By the late 1930s, at least 600,000 students nationally tuned in regularly to Damrosch's challenging classical music series (Reid, 1941a). Atkinson (1942a) called MAH "undoubtedly, the best known and most widely used [radio program] in classrooms of the U.S." (Atkinson, 1942a, p. 78); "unquestionably, [MAH] was responsible, more than any other program, for the introduction of radios into the American classroom" (Atkinson, 1942b, p. 42). Other SOAs often filled their Friday offerings with the MAH, providing additional evidence that Damrosch's approach to music appreciation was widely regarded as excellent and hard to top.[1]

---

[1]To today's no-nonsense educators and the politicians who control education, presenting courses in art and music appreciation to elementary students would probably seem frivolous. Yet SOAs at all levels presented such courses, reflecting the contemporary view of that time about what constituted an appropriate curriculum for elementary or high school students. That view has certainly changed over the intervening years. Today, learning about the fine arts seems to be outside of the purview of the schools.

We might question whether a single series dedicated to music education truly constituted a school of the air. Scholars since the 1940s have hailed the MAH for its accomplishments and popularity. In addition, as the first national program dedicated to classroom instruction, it provided a model that generated interest and goodwill for the schools of the air that followed.

Damrosch's Dream

For almost two decades prior to his radio work, Walter Damrosch had developed a reputation for his educational symphony concerts and in particular his Saturday morning Symphony Concerts for Children at Carnegie Hall. A gifted and energetic teacher, Damrosch was drawn to radio's educational potential shortly after the birth of broadcast radio. In 1923, Damrosch made his radio debut conducting the New York Symphony Orchestra in a short series of lecture recitals and concerts. The series prompted many letters from an appreciative audience, including a heart-warming one from Helen Keller, who described her joy at "listening" to Beethoven by touching the diaphragm speaker in the radio receiver. Though deaf and blind, she said she could actually distinguish different instruments and the human voice (Martin, 1983, 361). Three years later, in 1926, Damrosch conducted the New York Symphony in a regular series of Saturday evening radio programs (for adults) that featured lectures and impromptu comments. Sponsored by the maker of Balkite radios and carrying the inglorious name of the *Balkite Hour*, the series consisted of 22 weekly programs with alternating lecture-recitals and concerts, and it was presented over the newly formed NBC network. Damrosch claimed he had reached millions of listeners and received more than 30,000 letters, many complimenting him on his fine voice and diction. The following year Damrosch continued his educational concerts under the sponsorship of another radio manufacturer, RCA. The program was renamed the *RCA Hour*, and then when sponsorship changed, it was renamed again to the *General Electric Hour*.[2] This last name continued for several years more. The success of these broadcasts elevated Damrosch to the status of national figure.[3]

Damrosch quickly fell in love with the new medium and began to see the exciting possibility of "audiences of millions at one concert instead of three thousand in a concert hall" (Damrosch, 1930, p. 369). Moreover, as a teacher, he saw that through radio, young people all over the country could be exposed to the cultural influences of what he considered the world's finest music. He soon began promoting his idea of educational broadcasts to the schools. In the spring of 1927, with approval of NBC's president, Merlin Aylesworth, he revealed plans for a school of the air consisting of 24 radio concerts with explanations and demonstrations[4] (Martin, 1983). The series would be designed for different grade levels— elementary, high school, and college — and the format would be patterned after his children's and young peoples' concerts. Damrosch stressed that the series would be a collaboration between himself and the classroom teachers who would play a vital role in preparing students for the broadcasts (Martin, 1983; Sanders, 1990).

Before the advent of broadcast radio, Walter Damrosch had played a major role in the development of America's cultural life. In the early 1880s, his father, Leopold, had managed the newly formed Metropolitan Opera, and upon Leopold's death in 1885, young Walter took over as assistant manager. He also succeeded his father as conductor of the Oratorio Society and the New York Symphony Orchestra (Atkinson, 1942b). Soon Damrosch began touring around the country introduc-

[2]RCA was one of the major corporate owners of NBC, and GE was a major shareholder of RCA and through that, NBC.

[3]NBC appointed Damrosch to its prestigious National Advisory Council (see Section I), which probably had little power but gave him access to top executives such as GE's Owen Young (Martin, 1983).

[4]It's not known if Damrosch had been aware of early attempts at broadcasting to schools that were described earlier in this work. If not, it means he conceived of the school of the air concept completely on his own.

Walter Damrosch receiving flowers after the broadcast of his first Educational concert for school children on 28 NBC stations (February 10, 1928) (courtesy of State Historical Society of Wisconsin).

ing European symphonic music to wealthy and appreciative townsfolk throughout the Midwest and South, but he had more to do. Tireless and optimistic, he also founded his own opera company, the Damrosch Grand Opera Company. Dedicated to German opera, Damrosch toured relentlessly about the country bringing lengthy Wagnerian operas to curious folks in Boston, Chicago, Cincinnati, St. Louis, and more. As a result, by the end of the 19th century, Walter Damrosch was probably the best-known classical musician and orchestra director in the country (Martin, 1983).

In his biography, Damrosch credits his years of tireless missionary work in the name of classical music and opera with awakening cultural interest throughout the hinterlands of America. He also credits himself with inspiring and hastening the founding of symphony orchestras and opera companies in dozens of American cities including Philadelphia, Rochester, Detroit, St. Louis, and Los Angeles. By 1925, he said that he believed his work to be nearly complete, and at age 60 he found himself unexcited by public applause. Then, "out of the blue, came radio ... [it] beckoned to me with such allure of new possibilities and attachments to fellow citizens. I found myself with an intense and happy conviction that there was still work for me to do" (Damrosch, 1930, p. 368). Damrosch soon gave up almost all of his other work to devote himself to educational broadcasting.

While Damrosch's motivation for getting involved in educational radio was clear, NBC's motivations were more complex. Though clearly impressed with Damrosch's approach and public reception, network executives were concerned about getting sponsorship for his proposed school broadcasts and the estimated cost of roughly $100,000[5] annually (Martin, 1983). During the summer of 1927, when sponsors failed to sign up, NBC dropped the idea (Sanders, 1990). Undeterred, Damrosch proposed a short series of test broadcasts aimed at educators. He played to the interests of NBC executives by saying that his radio program would introduce the RCA line of radio receivers[6] for the classroom to educators. Apparently, that argument worked and the test was approved because RCA, one of NBC's owners,[7] agreed to sponsor the series.

In January of 1928, NBC broadcast several Damrosch music educational programs intended for the schools to an in-studio audience of 300 members of the School Masters Association of New York. The broadcasts were carried nationally on the NBC blue network. After the broadcasts, Damrosch discussed with the educators possibilities for coordinating the broadcasts with music education curricula in the schools. In February, additional test programs were aired primarily for the benefit of classroom teachers and students. These tests produced successful results; Damrosch was hopeful.

However, network executives remained skeptical about the appeal of classical music to the average American student. Atkinson (1942b) relates a story about a dinner meeting in spring of 1928, between Damrosch and Albert Lasker, head of NBC's advertising firm and a powerful molder of American public opinion. When asked by Lasker what he planned to play on the programs, Damrosch responded, "I will play the classics." "What is a classic?" Lasker demanded. "If a picture hangs in the Louvre for thirty years it becomes a classic," Damrosch responded. "Well then,

Top: RCA Radiola 16 with RCA Loudspeaker 100-A ... *a six-tube battery receiver that is ideally suited for use in rural schools $82.75* (courtesy of Wisconsin Historical Society Whi 44040). *Bottom:* RCA Radiola 18 with Loudspeaker 100-A ... *requires no batteries ... operates directly from the light socket $95* (courtesy of Wisconsin Historical Society Whi 44040).

---

[5]$100,000 in 1928 dollars would be worth approximately, $1,136,363 in 2005 dollars (Sahr, 2005).

[6]RCA marketed a line of radio receivers especially designed for classroom use (Keith, 1928).

[7]As mentioned earlier, NBC was owned by an investor group composed of the Radio Corporation of America (RCA) (50 percent), General Electric (30 percent), and Westinghouse (20 percent), all of whom had manufactured radio equipment at one time or another (Martin, 1983).

[Lasker said,] you'll play 'Carry Me Back to Old Virginia,' 'After the Ball Is Over,' and 'My Old Kentucky Home,' I presume." Damrosch thought for a moment, realizing the delicate situation the proposed program was in. "Yes, I will play them" (Atkinson, 1942b, pp. 43–44).

The series began broadcasting in the fall of 1928 as the *RCA Music Appreciation Hour*, and Damrosch played none of Lasker's suggestions (Atkinson, 1942b). Twenty-nine NBC network stations made it possible for most schools east of the Rocky Mountains to receive the broadcast. Damrosch's early success and untiring promotion of the series put to rest network apprehension about classical music.

NBC's decision to broadcast for the schools was probably only partly motivated by the desire to sell RCA radio receivers. In fact, RCA's sponsorship of the *Music Appreciation Hour* lasted but one year. After that, NBC offered the series as a sustaining program over its Blue network for the next 13 years. A deeper motive for broadcasting to the schools lay in the concern shared by NBC executives about how the American public would react to the newly formed broadcast networks. The public feared monopoly control of a powerful medium and, unlike today, was intolerant of excessive advertising. Many people believed radio should be used not just for commerce but for public service as well. To overcome possible public and thus governmental opposition to network control of the airwaves, in 1926 and 1927, NBC had launched a multifaceted public relations campaign to assure the public that the airwaves were in good hands (Barnouw, 1966). Clearly, that effort could be advanced by Damrosch and his prestigious reputation as a man devoted to education at the highest standards. Moreover, the network continued to use Damrosch's reputation and the school broadcasts as tools for marketing and political influence.

Administration, Organization, and Staff

After gaining approval, Damrosch began to recruit the orchestra for the programs. The network's house orchestra was deemed too small for symphonic works and too inexperienced for a demanding perfectionist such as Damrosch. Instead, he proposed that NBC form a whole new top-quality orchestra that he said would greatly enhance the network's reputation. Network executives agreed wholeheartedly that an NBC symphony orchestra devoted to radio with Damrosch as conductor would be "monumental" (Martin, 1983, p. 368). Eventually, this idea evolved into NBC's world-famous 95-member orchestra under the baton of Arturo Toscanini. However, that did not occur until 1937. In 1928, Damrosch settled for a smaller National Orchestra that, although it never developed an international reputation, served the MAH series well.

The MAH evolved and revolved around Damrosch, but at the beginning, he tapped the talents of two music educators and administrators to help launch the series successfully. To assist in developing the program and the educational support materials, Damrosch selected Ernest La Prade. A violinist and program annotator for the New York Symphony, La Prade received most attention for writing the teacher and student manuals that supplemented the broadcasts. The manuals are discussed later. However, after a disagreement, Damrosch dismissed La Prade.

More notable was Alice Keith, who had gained fame for initiating educational broadcasts of the Cleveland Symphony to the Cleveland public schools (see Section I), probably the first such use of radio by a local school board in the nation. A former consultant for RCA Victor,[8] in 1928 Keith was asked to become education director for RCA (Atkinson, 1942c). Her responsibilities included creating liaisons for the MAH with teacher and parent groups across the country. During her one-year tenure in the position, Keith quickly established contact with superintendents of schools in almost every state, in many cities and counties, and with the state presidents of the Federated Music Clubs. She placed advertisements in all of the state journals

---

[8]Keith's previous employer, Victor Talking Machine Co., had merged with RCA to form RCA Victor. That name in turn was shortened to RCA (Teaching Appreciation, 1925).

of education and music education to keep educators and scholars informed of MAH developments, including the dates and hours of the broadcasts (Martin, 1983). In addition, she worked with authorized RCA dealers to help advertise the program (Goodell, 1973). Among the pieces distributed to the schools was a list of do's and don'ts for radio listening, as shown in Table 1.

TABLE 1. TEACHER DO'S AND DON'TS FOR LISTENING TO MAH

Do's

1. Do get the best receiving equipment possible.
2. Do listen under ordinary classroom conditions.
3. Do appoint teachers to take charge of the listening audience.
4. Do use visual aids.
5. Do prepare by reading program notes and listening to recorded music.

Don'ts

1. Don't crowd children into a large auditorium.
2. Don't upset the entire school.
3. Don't mix younger and older students in the same audience. Musical concerts are graded for different age groups*   (Goodell, 1973, p. 326).

*This point suggests that Keith wasn't thinking about one-room schools.

Keith's efforts, including her numerous articles and appearances at teacher conventions and on radio, successfully promoted the series into a nationally recognized education event.

Keith organized MAH's Advisory Council and Committee. The Council, given the ostensible role of assisting Damrosch in preparing his radio concerts, included ten administrators and music educators. They met with Damrosch shortly before the first broadcast. The Committee consisted of 38 people, most with educational credentials, and included state and local directors of music education programs as well as professors of music education. In the second year of broadcasts, both groups were consolidated into one advisory board (Sanders, 1990). However, Sanders doubts that the board exercised much influence on Damrosch, particularly after the first few years. The purpose of the large board appears to have been to add prestige and to serve as contacts with and barometers of public opinion in the various cities that they represented (Sanders, 1990).

Keith's association with the MAH ended after the first year, when RCA stopped sponsoring the broadcasts. She went on to play a central role in the development of CBS's American School of the Air.

Philosophy

While Walter Damrosch did not express an educational philosophy as such, his writings and biography are filled with statements that point to deeply felt beliefs about education and culture. Not surprisingly, Damrosch greatly admired European culture, particularly its classical music tradition. His father, a noted musician in Germany,[9] had started a concert series there that became famous and attracted illustrious musicians and composers of the day such as Franz Liszt, Richard Wagner, Clara Schumann, and Arthur Rubinstein, many of whom dined and lodged at the Damrosch home (Damrosch, 1930).

With such childhood memories, it is understandable that Damrosch viewed European classical music as the pinnacle of human culture. He also believed that American culture had developed in an atmosphere that was artistically sterile, overly devoted to business, and devoid of

[9]Born in Germany in 1868, Damrosch moved to the United States at the age of eight when his father received an offer to head the New York Choral Society, a group made up of German immigrants.

deep musical traditions. American men, he argued, had been retarded in their artistic development by a Puritan heritage that frowned on the joys of life. As a result, men focused exclusively on work and business and considered the arts, including music, effeminate (Damrosch, 1930). He argued that the growth of America's musical life had been fostered almost exclusively by women. To overcome a heritage that dismissed the arts, well-to-do and educated women in the towns and villages of 19th-century America had formed music societies. These groups hosted musical performances and developed musical skills locally, particularly in the schools. "I don't think there has ever been a country whose musical development has been fostered so almost exclusively by women as America" (Damrosch, 1930, p. 323).

Early in his career, Damrosch became determined to bring Europe's musical heritage to the new world. During his 40-year reign as conductor of the New York Symphony, Damrosch toured the country every spring delivering educational concerts and giving audiences in the South, Midwest, and West their first taste of Wagner, Brahms, Beethoven, and Tchaikovsky. Apparently, his efforts were well received by the natives. By the early 1920s, Damrosch believed that, due to the efforts of women and his own missionary work, the country was freeing itself from those Puritanical limitations, and a European music culture was taking root (Damrosch, 1930).

For Damrosch, then, teaching and education in general were similar to missionary work, bringing the true faith to heathens in the new world. Radio did not change that fundamental concept; it merely gave him a bigger platform and a larger audience. He felt that radio offered the opportunity to "inaugurate a gigantic and new system of music education" (p. 371) that could address the challenges facing music educators of the day.[10]

The educational challenge, he believed, lay in the fact that few young people in America at that time had had an opportunity to hear an orchestral concert. Consequently, few realized that music was a universal and highly developed language, a vehicle for human emotions and aesthetic perceptions. While many schools conducted at least rudimentary music education, there existed a great need to stimulate awareness of the "higher possibilities of music and to develop a joy in hearing and cultivating it themselves" (Damrosch, 1930, p. 372). Furthermore, children in all areas of the country were being exposed to jazz, which, he said, "excites the nerves without feeding either the heart or head" (p. 372). "Something had to be done and done quickly in order to balance the marvelous material development of our people and to teach the younger generation that all this prosperity was useless unless it not only permitted but encouraged beauty and its cultivation through art to permeate our lives" (Damrosch, 1930, p. 372).

The solution of course was radio because it had proved itself, Damrosch said, as the great democratic leveler and uplifter.

He described his hope that radio broadcasts to the schools would lead to the growth of music not only in the schools but throughout the towns and villages. Town bands composed of former high school students—who had listened to his programs—would meet weekly for rehearsals and on holidays and ceremonial occasions would give performances to the delight of all in the community. "This means an America in which music will be cultivated not only by a small, over-fed ... community [those who attended his live concerts], but by millions of farmers, carpenters, plumbers and factory employees all over the country, to whom the names of Mozart, Beethoven, and Wagner will be household words, and all this, thanks to the greatest invention of our age—the radio" (Damrosch, 1930, p. 378).

I find in Damrosch's words a narrative that is simultaneously culturally elitist and naively democratic. Clearly, Damrosch felt he was delivering the truth to deprived students, that European musical traditions were superior to other forms. However, he also believed that through

---

[10]The task of cultivating a taste in American students for "good" music has perplexed music educators since the days of Lowell Mason, the father of public school music, who in 1838 introduced singing into Boston schools (Wiebe & O'Steen, 1942).

radio less privileged students could receive the same quality education as the rich and powerful and would accept it eagerly, recognizing its great worth. In that sense radio was a tool for social and cultural uplift. Similar ideas were expressed by many of the pioneers of educational radio.

Damrosch also stressed that the concerts were not to be a substitute for local instruction but were primarily to simulate the love of and interest in music. He warned schools against giving up their local teaching. Though his lectures and teachers manuals provided good instruction, he said that they would not fulfill their proper mission unless supported by the classroom teachers' instruction and encouragement (Damrosch, 1930).

Educational Programs and Methods

In developing the series, Damrosch faced the problem of how to present a complex subject for different age groups. To answer this problem, Damrosch created a four-level instructional design, which is shown in Table 2.

TABLE 2. MAH SERIES ORGANIZATION
(Damrosch, 1930, p. 373)

Series	Grades	Subject
A	4–6	Orchestral instruments
B	7–9	Music as expressive media
C	10–12	Musical structure and form
D	Colleges and adult clubs	Specific composers

Later, however, Series A, B, and C were adjusted downward to target younger children. At any rate, the grade levels were only suggestions. Classroom teachers were encouraged from the start to have their students listen to whatever series seemed most suitable for their experience, regardless of grade or age. In later years, the series were designated first, second, third, and fourth year of a progressive course (Atkinson, 1942b).

Each series was 30 minutes long, and two were coupled to fill the one-hour MAH broadcast that took place every Friday. After the first year, the combinations were Series A and B one week and C and D the next. This allowed schools that wished to give a class a full hour of music to combine series that were close to the same level of experience. Because of this structure, few large works could be used. For the most part, the selections consisted of movements, shorter works, or songs.

Each series had a specific educational focus. Series A highlighted the orchestral instruments, which Damrosch described as members of his musical family (Martin, 1983; Sanders, 1990). He described them with colorful, imaginative language and illustrated their special qualities with short piano pieces. Series B was devoted to music as an expressive and emotional medium. The programs dealt with subjects such as "Nature in Music," "Fairy Tales in Music," "The Dance," and "The March." Series C explored musical structure and form, such as the round, the canon, and the symphony. Series D studied specific composers from early polyphonic composers to late–19th-century ones such as Brahms and Wagner (Wiebe & O'Steen, 1942, p. 2). The final program of each series, the *Students' Achievement Program,* served as a review and test (Martin, 1983). Of course, only the classroom teacher could grade the results.

The musical content remained much the same over MAH's entire history. Damrosch favored the German composers— Bach, Haydn, Mozart, Beethoven, and Wagner — and he gave privileged position to the 19th-century composers. At the request of some educators, he occasionally included vocal and chamber music, but orchestral works remained the mainstay (Sanders, 1990). The composer most frequently studied was Beethoven, and the piece most frequently performed was Saint-Saens' *Carnival of the Animals,* because it best illustrated in solo most instruments of the orchestra.

Damrosch disapproved publicly of using contemporary music for instruction. He considered inappropriate for young children any composer still living or not working in the symphonic tradition.[11] When in 1932 the Philadelphia orchestra proposed to broadcast an educational musical program of Stravinsky, Schoenberg, and Berg, Damrosch hastily criticized the effort saying, "Children should not be confused by experiments ... which have not and never will be proven. Only that which has been proven worthy should be used to build the foundation of their knowledge" (Martin, 1983, p. 369).

Despite his strong opinions, Damrosch was not completely inflexible. He occasionally included 20th-century works such as Stravinsky's Firebird Suite and even George Gershwin's "I Got Rhythm," probably because those pieces illustrated well a point that he wished to make (Sanders, 1990). Also, he acknowledged that the "best of jazz had made its mark and would leave some impression on the real music ... in our country" (Martin, 1983, p. 370).

METHODS

By the time he started the MAH, Damrosch had honed his instructional technique to a fine point in his live symphony concerts for young people and children. He brought the technique to radio. It consisted of a five-step process: greeting, recall, preview, demonstration, and presentation. He started with a warm greeting that avoided condescension. For the younger students it was, "Good morning, dear children," for the older students, "Good afternoon, young friends" (Sanders, 1990, p. 98). Next, the orchestra played a review number from the previous lesson, which Damrosch asked his listeners to identify. He gave the answer at beginning of the following broadcast. This served as a stimulus to recall and helped tie the programs together. Next, he gave a lesson preview in which for each topic he stated relevant information, related a story that illustrated the point, and played themes on the piano to demonstrate the point. Then the orchestra or specific instrument played the main selection(s) for the program. Damrosch worked without a script (Sanders, 1990). He believed that his impromptu remarks made him more convincing and helped to relax the students by taking some of the formality away from the topic (Goodell, 1973).

Damrosch faced criticism from some music educators and critics for his subjective descriptions and interpretations and for embellishing his descriptions and instruction with highly visual and narrative language. He asserted that the final movement of Beethoven's Fifth Symphony expressed, "triumphant joy at victory over the adverse forces of Destiny" (Martin, 1983). (Beethoven, of course, never made such claims.) He said that Mozart's Symphony no. 40 expressed the sadder and more serious side of life. In another lesson, he described the role of the double bass as the foundation of a house. He described the elfin characters in *A Midsummer Night's Dream*: "I've seen them often dancing in the moonlight in the woods ... they are no taller than your thumb" (Sanders, 1990, p. 100). He even wrote words to accompany short motifs in the music of Beethoven and others.

This approach irritated some music professionals; one claimed that potential music lovers could be "maimed by this idiotic approach" (Martin, 1983, p. 371). However, Martin asserts that Damrosch's subjective approach did no harm. Rather, it helped young people appreciate the music. Martin concedes that Damrosch could be at times too cute, too pictorial, but stresses that these very qualities made the music more accessible and enjoyable to the many who were new to classical music. Had Damrosch employed the typical music school instructional approach, which focused on analysis of movements, harmony, and motives, the MAH would have been much less effective, Martin suggests. Sanders (1990) supports that position, explaining that Damrosch used the imaginative language mostly in programs aimed at younger children to make the music

---

[11]Perhaps Damrosch feared that modern composers threatened to replace those early Germanic composers that he had grown to love in his youth.

more meaningful to them, but much less with older students who, it was assumed, were able to appreciate the music with less imaginative stimulation.

A similar point was made by Damrosch in his autobiography. Comparing several pages of questions and answers from the teachers manual of 1930, Damrosch points out that the questions for the lower grades stress feelings and emotional words, while the questions for the older students stress cognitive ideas such as musical forms and development of concepts (Damrosch, 1930, pp. 374–378). This point is supported by comments in the first teachers manual in which the editor states that Damrosch used pictorial interpretations of certain works to stimulate the pupils' imagination — not to impose his own interpretation on the pupil (RCA, 1928).

Undoubtedly, Damrosch's success can be attributed in part to his charisma, which was transmitted through the airwaves by his deep mellifluous voice to the ears of his listeners. Damrosch himself modestly remarked on the number of letters he received from listeners complimenting him for having a voice that was "particularly adapted to radio transmission" (Damrosch, 1930, p. 369). Martin (1983) asserts that Damrosch possessed an appealing avuncular manner that captivated young children and put them at ease. Such testimonials raise our awareness that teaching — then, as now — is as much art as science.

TEACHERS MANUALS AND STUDENT GUIDES

From the first, Damrosch and his assistants made extensive teacher manuals available to classroom teachers. The first year's manual, issued in 1928 under the title *RCA Educational Hour*, offered 65 pages of information mostly organized by the four series. For each series, A through D, the manual provided a listing of the recordings available for all the selections to be covered in the series and between eight and twelve questions and answers to be used by the teacher following the broadcasts. The manual also presented names of members of the MAH advisory council and committee, one page of suggestions on how to use the manual, the broadcast schedule, and names and locations of stations that would carry the broadcasts. At the back were attached three pages of advertisements for RCA classroom radios (RCA, 1928).

For the 1931–32 school year, the program and manual title had been changed to *NBC Music Appreciation Hour*, and that change was emphasized by printing the names of the NBC board of directors. Content had also changed. The "Suggestions to Teachers" section was expanded from one to five pages with the material organized by series and broken down into general and specific preparations. The questions were moved from the teachers manual to a student notebook, described later. In place of the questions, the editors wrote detailed notes about each music selection featured in the lesson (Goodell, 1973). A diagram of the orchestra illustrated the positioning of the various types of instruments in the orchestra (NBC, 1931).

Starting in 1931–32, manual editor Ernst La Prade in the "Suggestions for Teachers" provided extensive guidance for the classroom teacher on how to use the broadcasts appropriately. In a sense, the suggestions were an extension of Damrosch's teaching methods. The key points made were preparation, repetition, and concentration on affective rather than cognitive learning. Teachers were advised to acquire phonograph records of the selections before the broadcasts. A list of the upcoming selections was provided in the manual. La Prade advised teachers to avoid asking students to analyze or react after just one hearing. He stressed the need for repeated listening to the records in order to let the children become familiar with the music. Throughout, La Prade encouraged teachers to take a facilitative approach to instruction in order to encourage and nurture budding student budding interest, rather than a directive approach which would tend to squash student confidence. "Do not ask pupils to analyze or react to the music in any detail after just one hearing. Be prepared to answer (though not stimulate) questions that may arise because of a spontaneous interest and curiosity" (NBC, 1931, Suggestions to Teachers).

La Prade assured teachers that as students grew more familiar with the music, their observations would improve and that would stimulate discussion about the cognitive aspects of the music, such as title, composer, and the qualities of specific passages (NBC, 1931). I found this approach surprising in its similarity to constructivist educators of the late 1990s who gave class-room teachers similar advice, namely to avoid being the "sage on the stage," and instead act like a "guide on the side" (King, 1993, p. 32).

In 1930–31, Ernst La Prade prepared the first student notebooks. They sold for 10 cents. Each notebook covered all four series, A through D, and typically included several pages for each lesson. The lessons supplied musical notation for the themes to be covered as well as blank spaces for pasting pictures of composers or drawings of instruments. For each broadcast, five to eight questions were printed. At the end of each lesson there was a blank page where the learner could note key points and comments. The final lesson usually included blank pages on which a student could write the answers to the review quizzes. On the final page, students found a brief biography of Damrosch (Sanders, 1990).

The teacher manuals, distributed freely during the first four years of the MAH broadcasts, reached approximately 56,000 teachers for the year 1930–31. The distribution of student note-books, however, was based on orders from the schools. Data from the same year show that 120,000 student notebooks were shipped.[12] Since each notebook covered all four series, up to four students could use one notebook. We can assume then that in 1930–31 up to 500,000 students might have listened to Damrosch's broadcasts.

Broadcasting System

In the first broadcast year, the MAH was carried by 27 NBC stations across the country. Four years later, that number had expanded to more than 60, including a number of clear chan-nel stations, such as WGN in Chicago, whose signal could be heard hundreds of miles in all direc-tions. One issue that Damrosch had been concerned with in 1928 seems to have resolved itself, namely the quality of sound reproduction. By the early 1930s, he no longer refers to the issue, perhaps because by then quality had improved.

Depression Years

While the Depression years took a toll on many educational programs, the national financial contraction seems to have left MAH relatively unaffected. NBC executives had always hoped to find a sponsor for the MAH, and when by 1932 they had not, they sounded alarm bells saying the series might have to be discontinued. Probably they were looking for some relief from Damrosch's enormous salary of $42,000[13] per year, a huge compensation for the day, equivalent to roughly $592,000 in 2005 dollars (Sahr, 2005). The maestro offered to take a 25 percent pay cut, and with the blessing of NBC's president, he set about to raise half a million dollars to ensure the program's survival for at least three years. Damrosch probably would have succeeded — he had many wealthy and influential friends and contacts — but just as the effort got under way, NBC announced that it would continue to sustain the program. Apparently, NBC executives felt that abandoning the series would result in negative public relations (Martin, 1983) just at a time when the future of the radio channel set-aside issue[14] was being considered by Congress. After NBC's generous offer, the pro-gram sailed along on Damrosch's popularity and skill and with the approval of most educators.

---

[12]Goodell, S. M. E. (1973). Walter Damrosch and his contributions to music education. Catholic University of Amer-ica, Washington, D. C.

[13]The salary covered all of Damrosch's activities for NBC, but his principle activity was that of director of the MAH (Martin, 1983).

[14]During the early 1930s, the NCER with support from the Payne Fund agitated for a total reallocation of radio chan-nels and a 15 percent set-aside for nonprofits and educational institutions. The proposal found a Congressional voice in the Fess Bill of 1931, which caused determined opposition among commercial broadcasters (Barnouw, 1968).

Audience

While it appears that nearly everyone who heard Walter Damrosch loved him, it is unclear how many students listened regularly. Given that the MAH attracted a broad national audience that involved thousands of schools, it is a daunting task to determine with precision how many listeners tuned in regularly[15] nearly 70 years ago. During the 1930s, NBC executives admitted that determining accurately the number of individuals listening to the MAH was "difficult, if not impossible" (Goodell, 1973, p. 391). Despite that admission, NBC regularly produced MAH audience estimates, all showing that Damrosch attracted millions of listeners. However, one outside researcher found the MAH audience to be much smaller than that claimed by NBC. I present both sets of estimates and the methods used to make them and offer an explanation for the discrepancy between the two.

During the second year of MAH broadcasts, NBC estimated that regular student listeners numbered between 4 million and 5 million, and for 1933–34, the number had grown to about 6 million student listeners. In addition, the receipt of thousands of letters annually[16] made the MAH administrators aware of a sizable number of adults who listened at home. In fact, Goodell (1973) asserts that one-third of the MAH mail came from adults. In 1938 NBC issued a brochure that cited an independent survey of the series' audience. It reported that 70,000 schools included the broadcasts in their curriculums and as a result the MAH listening audience totaled 7 million students and between 3 and 4 million adults—an audience that exceeded those of many popular daytime soap operas (Martin, 1983). If these figures were accurate, the MAH audience would have equaled approximately 25 percent of the nation's schoolchildren, kindergarten through 12th grade. These astounding figures were generally accepted then and now. In his autobiography, Damrosch (1930) mentioned the fact that up to 5 million children heard his broadcasts in 1930, and Martin (1983) in his excellent biography of Damrosch reports the NBC figures cited here without a trace of skepticism.

A quick look at the methods NBC used to develop the estimates reveals that they were faulty and designed to produce large numbers. According to Goodell (1973), "The approximate size of the total school audience was estimated by determining the ratio between the number of listeners in the New York City schools and the number of teacher's manuals mailed to those schools and then by projecting that ratio to the country as a whole" (p. 391).

The number of listeners in New York City schools was in turn determined from a 1929 survey conducted by NBC. It found that for each teachers manual used in the schools, 129 students listened to the program (Goodell, 1973). The author does not disclose how this high ratio was computed. However, Goodell does mention that until 1933, NBC distributed teachers manuals free of charge to "practically every school in the country"[17] (p. 338). We can see then the NBC estimates depended on several unsupported assumptions: (1) that every unsolicited teachers manual mailed represented a school that wanted to listen to MAH, (2) that every manual mailed represented 129 listening students, and (3) that the listening habits of New Yorkers were comparable to those found in the rest of the country.

To check the accuracy of their assumptions, NBC did conduct at least one small nationwide survey. Goodell (1973) reports that a 1933 mail survey to 24 states produced 67 replies and a ratio of 77 listeners to each teacher manual distributed. That finding reduced the estimate of the national audience to roughly 3.5 million, still a sizable group. Furthermore, Armstrong Perry, then working in the U.S. Office of Education, gave tepid support to NBC's estimates saying they were, "somewhat high ... but not unlikely" (Goodell, 1973, p. 392). Neither the results of the study nor Perry's support is sufficient to erase doubts about the network's huge audience estimates.

[15]Researcher Seerley Reid defined regular listeners as those who listened to 10 or more programs per semester (Reid, 1941a).

[16]Goodell (1973) reports that from 1931 through 1934 MAH received between 12,000 and 15,000 listener letters annually (p. 394).

[17]Starting in the fall of 1933, MAH charged 25 cents for each teachers manual (Goodell, 1973).

SERIES A   *For Grades 3 & 4 (or Grades 4, 5, & 6*

1st Concert, October 26, 1928, at 11:00 A. M.

MUSICAL FAMILY

Scherzo from symphony No 5 (Dance of the Raindrops) ...*Glazounow.*
Whispering of the Flowers...*Von Blon*
March from the "Lenore" Symphony...........................*Raff*

1.   Q. *What does Mr. Damrosch call his orchestra?*

    A.   His musical family.

2.   Q. *Mention some of the instruments of an orchestra.*

    A.   Violins, violas, violoncellos, double basses; flutes, piccolo, oboes, English horn, clarinets, bass clarinet, bassoons, double bassoon horns, trumpets, trombones, bass tuba; kettledrums, bass .drum, military drum, cymbals, triangle, bells, xylophone, celesta, harp.   (*The pupil is not expected to give the entire list of instruments. Four or more correctly names will be satisfactory).*

3.   Q. *What kind of language is music?*

    A. A language of our feelings.

4.   Q. *How does the language of music differ from other languages?*
    A. It can be understood and enjoyed even when the whole orchestral family speaks at the same time.

5.   Q.   *What feelings can music express?*

    A. Joy, sorrow, hope, despair, love, anger. courage, fear, peace, excitement, reverence for God, etc. * *

6.   Q.   *What words did the "Scherzo" by Glazounow suggest to Mr. Damrosch?*

    A.   Happy excitement.

7.   Q. *What feeling does the "Scherzo" by Glazounow express?*

    A.   "Rain is falling, dancing up and down
    Drenching all the children in the town."

8.   Q. *What can music do besides express feelings?*

    A. It can describe scenes.

9.   Q. *What scene does the March from the "Lenore" Symphony describe?*

    A. The passing of soldiers as they march away to war.

10. Q. *How does it describe this scene?*

    A. By beginning softly, as if the soldiers came from afar; then growing louder, as the soldiers pass by, an dying away, as the soldiers disappear in the distance.

Test Questions from the Music Appreciation Hour Student's Notebook (1930–1931).

It is odd that Goodell (1973) did not mention that instead of basing audience estimates on the teachers manuals, the estimates might also have been more reliably tied to the number of student notebooks distributed. Her study documents data on the number of student handbooks that NBC distributed from 1930 through 1934. Had that data been used, audience estimates would have been substantially lower. However, even that approach is based on a somewhat shaky assumption that teachers ordered one handbook for each student. Given those were Depression years, teachers might well have had students double up, ordering only one handbook for two or even three students to use at one time.

Academic Research

By the late 1930s, network broadcasting to the schools had attracted the attention of the educational researchers at The Ohio State University's Evaluation of School Broadcasts project that is described in Chapter 2. Funded by a New Deal agency and dedicated to studying the reach and effect of radio education, the project, directed by I. Keith Tyler, conducted several studies of NBC's MAH programs. One in particular, *The Classroom Audience of Network School Broadcasts: Bulletin 34* (Reid, 1941a), addressed the key question of who listened. In the introduction to this study, Seerley Reid, the chief researcher, derided the huge audience estimates issued occasionally by network executives or compliant journalists as being "grossly inflated" (p.1). Reid also went to great lengths to assure the reader that his research had been conducted with the utmost rigor.

The researchers mailed their questionnaire to roughly 2,500 members of the Department of Elementary and Secondary School Principals of the National Education Association (NEA). Questions included these: (1) Did the school use radio in the classroom? (2) How many teachers use radio regularly, e.g., 10 times per semester or more? (3) What grade levels participated? The first mailing was followed up with a second to the non-responders. Analysis of return rates from both mailings found no significant variance between the two waves. Based on these methods, the researchers felt confident that their data would accurately represent the entire sample (Reid, 1941a).

Because the sample was drawn from elementary and secondary school principals and teachers who were members of the NEA, the researchers readily conceded that the responses did not truly represent the nation's public school educators. To overcome that bias, they built in a fix to their data analysis: they reduced the actual response rates by 50 percent and used the reduced figures to make their estimates. The researchers explained that they had started with an assumption that NEA members were twice as likely as nonmembers to use radio. A 50 percent reduction of response rates, according to the researchers, represented an accurate estimate of radio usage in all of the nation's schools (Reid, 1941a). This sounds plausible, but the researchers give no data or solid reasons why they think their sample represented schools that were much more likely to listen to classical music instruction than others.

After analyzing the data, Reid concluded that the likely school-based audience for Damrosch's MAH was approximately 600,000, or about 2.2 percent of the nation's schoolchildren. When the primary grades were eliminated from the sample (because the program was intended for 4th through 12th grades), then the percentage rose to approximately 3 percent of the possible audience — either way, a far cry from the 20 to 25 percent touted by NBC (Reid, 1941a).

The available data present widely varying audience estimates, ranging between 500,000 and 6 million student listeners. It's clear that NBC's results were based on doubtful assumptions designed to produce exaggerated numbers. Researchers at The Ohio State University produced results from more reliable methods, but they were not definitive either. They also made assumptions about their sample — that it was more likely to listen to classical music instruction — assumptions that also were unsupported by the research and that reduced the estimated audience size. Given the available evidence, however, it does seem that audience estimates at the lower end of the range were more accurate. All in all, the evidence seems most supportive of

RCA Radiola 60 with RCA Loudspeaker 103 ... *provides a powerful combination that is capable of filling the largest class rooms with full, clear tones. $175.00* (courtesy of Wisconsin Historical Society Whi 44043).

the observation by NBC executives that accurately estimating audience size was a nearly impossible task.

More important, how should we view the fact that the MAH's audience probably fell far short of millions of schoolchildren touted by network executives? Should we be disappointed or impressed that Damrosch used technology to attract probably the largest classroom in the world? Should we acknowledge that the NBC executives had been correct when they cautioned that Americans would never tune in en masse to classical music? Or should we see the MAH as a brilliant fulfillment of radio's potential to provide educational enrichment to tens of thousands of classrooms, exposing hundreds of thousands of American students to a music tradition that they might otherwise never have heard? Answers to these questions will probably vary according to the readers' tastes and values. However, audience size was just one focus of researchers who studied the MAH.

Evaluation and Impact

The Ohio State University–based Evaluation of School Broadcasts project also studied the educational effectiveness of radio broadcasts directed at the classroom. Study number 39, "A Study of Series A: Damrosch *Music Appreciation Hour*," focused on determining the educational effectiveness of the MAH programs aimed at the youngest or least experienced listeners. According to the researchers, the general purpose of Series A was to acquaint students with the instruments of the orchestra. An examination of the instructor manual and student notebook revealed several specific learning objectives. Students should be able to do the following:

• Recognize the instruments of the orchestra by sight and sound.
• Classify instruments correctly as woodwind, brass, string, or percussion.
• Recognize the tonal characteristics of the instruments.
• Demonstrate knowledge of a vocabulary with which to discuss the characteristics listed.

Damrosch envisioned that both the classroom teacher and the students must participate actively in the instructional process. After ensuring that the students listened carefully to MAH Series A broadcasts, the classroom teacher led a discussion of the music and then guided students to read and do the activities suggested in the student notebook (Wiebe & O'Steen, 1942, p. 2).

Researchers conducted a two-tracked study. The first was aimed at gathering data on the students' general opinion of the broadcasts. In his autobiography, Damrosch claims that the real goal of the series was to increase the students' love for and understanding of great music (Damrosch, 1930). Results of the study suggest that Damrosch's goal was largely realized. Three-fourths of the students consistently asserted that they enjoyed the programs, wished all students could hear them, liked Mr. Damrosch, and wanted to know more about the symphony orchestra and its music (Wiebe & O'Steen, 1942).

The second research track focused on determining how well students who heard the broadcasts achieved the learning objectives set out in the printed manuals. To answer this question, researchers designed a standard comparison study composed of a treatment group that heard the broadcasts regularly, called the radio group (n = 169), and a control group (n = 120) who did not hear the programs.

The authors identified five related research questions. In comparison to the control group, how well did the radio group learn to: (1) recognize instruments by sound, (2) classify instruments in their proper orchestral family (winds, strings, etc.), (3) recognize instruments from photographs, (4) recognize instruments by their tonal characteristics, and (5) demonstrate an enlarged musical vocabulary. In four of the five tests, the radio group outperformed the control group, but the differences were *not* statistically significant (Wiebe & O'Steen, 1942).

The authors concluded that as a result of the broadcasts, students reported enjoyment and learning readiness. However, in terms of the stated objectives of the series, learning was small and about equal for those who did and did not hear the broadcasts. According to the authors, the series' major contribution appeared to lay in "certain long term values such as dispelling the concept of a symphony orchestra as [being] a formidable institution, [that] students find certain classical selections to be enjoyable, [and] looking forward to hear Dr. Damrosch's upbeat voice" (Wiebe & O'Steen, 1942, p. 9). These latter findings seem in line with Damrosch's larger goals. The editors of the teachers manuals consistently placed more importance on getting students to become familiar with the music than on mastering learning objectives. For example, in the 1937 teachers manual, in the "Suggestions" section for Series C, the editors stated, "Approach gradually anything like 'lessons' on the pieces. It is more important that the music make itself heard and known than that you talk about it — that is, until after it has ... become fairly familiar" (NBC, 1937, p. 13). The editors go on to advise that familiarity breeds appreciation, which was the overall goal as stated in the series' title, *Music Appreciation Hour*. This suggests that Damrosch and the editors were more concerned with bringing about affective learning rather than cognitive learning.

Any possible limitations of Reid's study are not known. For example, the author gave no information about the selection of the control and experimental groups. Did they truly represent MAH's listening universe? How did the groups compare with each other in terms of prior musical knowledge? Did the control group receive any kind of musical instruction, and if so, what kind? Also, did the dissimilar group sizes (169 versus 120) affect the results? Without answers to any of these questions, it's difficult to ascertain the reliability or usefulness of Reid's study.

I found no other rigorous research evaluations of the MAH's educational effectiveness. However, many observers with and without musical background commented on the worthiness of Damrosch's work; most were highly favorable. Atkinson (1942b) described the series as "the best known and most widely used in classrooms ... radio education program" (p. 42). Music biographer George Martin (1983) characterized the MAH in this way: "In the opinion of many persons, looking back on fifty years of radio and television in the United States, it is still the best use made of either medium for an educational purpose" (Martin, 1983, pp. 372). Martin fails to document that claim, but he asserts that the supporters based their belief on several factors: "[Damrosch supporters are] apt to stress the program's long life which gave teachers time to learn how to use it; the quality of the material presented, the quality of the man presenting; the skill of the pedagogy ... and the work constantly required of students and teachers, which kept the program for both an active experience" (Martin, 1983, p. 373).

As mentioned earlier, Martin (1983) asserts that the MAH had a powerful impact on adult listeners, particularly music teachers who themselves received "the equivalent of a college course in music appreciation" (p. 373). The teachers in turn exerted incalculable influence on their students. According to Martin, traces of Damrosch's methods remained visible (at the time of Martin's writing) in books and classrooms.

Another method for evaluating the MAH's impact and effectiveness can be found in the thousands of letters that NBC received every year from listeners. Goodell (1973) asserts the comments in letters, reports, and newspapers provide insight into the "striking impact that the MAH had in the field of music education throughout the nation." From her survey of letters received by the MAH, Goodell cites numerous expressions of appreciation and effectiveness from individual teachers, school principals and superintendents, and boards of education including those in St. Louis and Kansas City. A survey by the Chicago Board of Education found that the student audience for the MAH numbered more than 20,000. Many newspaper articles from around the country attested to Damrosch's popularity. The general tone of these testimonials is that the MAH brought something of value to the children and that they were as a result much more receptive to music education (Goodell, 1973). Finally, Goodell concludes that the major impact of the MAH was that it served as a model for music teachers at the local level to improve their music teaching or to initiate music education via radio at the local level (Goodell, 1973).

Another form of data from which we can make inferences about the MAH's educational effectiveness exists in the comments of knowledgeable observers and testimonials of music teachers and educational administrators. Data in this form provide insight into what contemporaries believed about the MAH's educational impact. The overall impression one gets from this data is that while a few knowledgeable musical critics disapproved of Damrosch's approach, the vast majority praised his series primarily for effectively introducing European classical music to millions of American students and adults. They also lauded his pedagogy, boundless enthusiasm, and effective use of a new communication technology (Atkinson, 1942a; Goodell, 1973; Martin, 1983).

Demise

By 1940, the commercial environment in which radio networks operated had changed substantially from the previous decade. Radio had grown into an enormously powerful and popular medium, and the networks no longer struggled to sell airtime to advertisers. The commercial value of Damrosch's one-hour program grew more tempting, but NBC never suggested a change. Instead, the federal government intervened and inadvertently presented the opportunity to get rid of a costly educational endeavor. As part of a long-term antitrust action, the FCC required NBC to divest itself of one of its two networks, the Red or the Blue. Because the Red was substantially more profitable, NBC chose to sell the Blue network, which reputedly carried more quality programs including the MAH (Martin, 1983). For a year, Blue operated independently but then was transformed into the new American Broadcasting Company (ABC). Blue network executives took a more businesslike approach to broadcasting. For the 1942 broadcast season they offered Damrosch only half an hour of airtime, even though the season's broadcasts were already planned and prepared. Unwilling to compromise, the 80-year-old Damrosch resigned. Neither ABC nor NBC wanted to re-launch the series with a new personality. After a 14-year run, the first and some say best educational program on radio ended abruptly.

Summary

As the first national school of the air, NBC's MAH set a high standard for educational broadcasting that inspired many others to consider the possibilities of broadcasting to the schools. Its director and only teacher, Walter Damrosch, quickly saw the potential of radio broadcasting, and drawing on his long experience with live educational concerts for children, he developed content and teaching techniques that soon captured the admiration of music educators and the affection of students across the country. Damrosch's programming demonstrated an educational philosophy that combined respect for democratic goals with culture elitism. He believed radio would enable working people in America's villages and towns to appreciate and participate in the glories of the European classical music tradition.

The network's decision to air and support instructional programs aimed at the schools grew out of a complex stew of motives, starting with a desire to sell radio receivers. A bigger concern was the need to mollify the public's distrust of chain broadcasting and their fear that crass advertising would completely dominate the airwaves. Some scholars assert that the main impetus was to fend off the growing movement among educators to have the federal government reorganize radio station ownership and set aside 15 percent of all channels for public service and education. They argue that the network used Damrosch's dedication to the highest standards of music education as a shield against government interference in their dominance of the radio dial (Barnouw, 1966; McChesney, 1993).

Despite the fact that he became a nationally recognized personality, Damrosch's audience probably never grew larger than 2.2 percent of the nation's school population, but the question remains, was his audience a disappointment? If so, what figure would be satisfactory? Ten percent? Twenty-five percent? No standards have been set.

Skimpy data make a definitive evaluation of the MAH's educational effectiveness unsure, but we do know that music educators across the country embraced Damrosch's use of radio. Probably, his 14 years of programs spread awareness of and respect for classical music throughout the country, but his dream of making Bach, Beethoven, and Mozart household names to average Americans most likely went unrealized.

Despite its many successes and wide recognition, NBC's MAH suffered from a curriculum limited to one subject and a once-a-week broadcast. A rival network, CBS, was eager to outdo NBC in any way possible. One of its competitive efforts resulted in the formation of the American School of the Air.

CBS and The American School of the Air

The narrative of the American School of the Air (ASA) represents one of the more remarkable and ironic stories in the history of educational technology. It is a typically American narrative of conflict between profit and social obligation, between private media and public education. Broadcast for 18 years by the Columbia Broadcasting System (CBS), the ASA offered a schedule of curriculum-enrichment programs sometimes characterized by imaginative subject matter and innovative methods. Through a network of more than 100 CBS-affiliated stations, the ASA reached schools in all sections of this country, attracting one and a half million regular classroom listeners as well as the attention of many educational researchers. Though supported by a purely commercial entity, the ASA became this country's only truly national school of the air, thereby confounding many who had strongly supported schools of the air but had scorned the idea of commercially supported educational radio.

Paley the Educator

The origins of the ASA were intimately intertwined with the birth and early growth of the Columbia Broadcasting System and the vision and ambition of its young president, William S. Paley. As a youth, Paley had become intrigued by the sound of a singing voice picked from the air by a friend's crystal set. His interest in radio's commercial potential was spurred by his small but successful experiment in on-air advertising. While Paley's father and uncle were traveling in Europe, they left young William in charge of the family's thriving cigar manufacturing company. On impulse, Paley bought an hour program on a local radio station to advertise his company's La Palina cigars. The cost was $50 per program. The results were impressive, but when his dad and uncle returned, they immediately uncovered the new expenditure and ordered the "foolishness" canceled (Paley, 1979). The elder Paley soon changed his tune. A few weeks later, he told his son, "Hundreds of thousands of dollars we've been spending on newspaper and magazine ads, and no one has ever said anything to me about those ads, but now people are asking me, 'What happened to the La Palina Hour?'" (Paley, 1979, p. 33).

That experience may have been the key to Paley becoming a broadcasting mogul. In the late 1920s, concert manager Arthur Judson, in partnership with the Columbia Phonograph Company, had formed United Independent Broadcasters (UIB) as a vehicle for putting classical musicians on the air. Incorporated January 27, 1927, the company struggled, unable to debut until September of that year. Soon facing bankruptcy, the UIB group sold out to wealthy investor Jerome Louchheim. Columbia Phonograph also withdrew, accepting payment in the form of free advertising and granting the new owners use of its name. After 10 months of rough sledding,

Louchheim offered the stumbling operation to Paley's father, Sam, who promptly declined, only to hear his 26-year-old son, William, express interest in using part of his own money[18] to buy control of the fledgling network (Paley, 1979). William Paley closed the deal on September 9, 1928, had himself elected chairman of the board the next day, and named the new network the Columbia Broadcasting System (CBS).

Paley immediately set out to build CBS into the country's premier network, but he realized that his was a small operation compared to NBC and its mighty corporate backers. He believed that the key to growing bigger and faster than his competitor was to develop top programming that would attract advertisers. One key to achieving this goal would be educational programming (Paley, 1979).

In his definitive history of radio broadcasting in the United States, Erik Barnouw (1968) says that the ASA was launched in response to the agitation over the 1931 Fess congressional legislation that called for the reallocation of radio channels to benefit educational radio.[19] No doubt all commercial broadcasters at that time felt pressured to provide at least the appearance of public service and educational programming, and later on, during his battle to prevent educators from playing any controlling role in broadcasting, Paley certainly highlighted ASA. However, in 1929, several years before the Fess Bill became an issue, Paley had expressed interest in broadcasting to schools (McChesney, 1993). ASA's birth and early development probably owed more to Paley's competitive aspirations than it did to his fear of government intervention.

Foremost among CBS's advertisers in early 1929 was the Grigsby-Grunow Company, manufacturers of Majestic radios, the most popular sets in the country at that time.[20] According to Paley (1979), "they [Grigsby-Grunow] loved CBS because they hated RCA [NBC's parent]," their chief competitor with whom they were locked in endless court battles over patent rights (p. 65). Like computer manufacturers of the 1990s, who offer computer software to schools as a means of selling their products to schools and home users, Grigsby-Grunow probably viewed the SOA concept as a vehicle for marketing their Majestic radio receivers.[21] In fact, NBC had already begun broadcasting to the classroom, partly as a promotion for their RCA line of classroom radios. In late 1928, NBC launched Walter Damrosch's *Music Appreciation Hour*, specifically directed to schools.[22] In that competitive climate, it is highly likely that both Grigsby-Grunow and Paley saw mutual benefit in broadcasting to the schools (Atkinson, 1942b).

Paley countered the rival network's entry into school broadcasting by hiring away from NBC the marketing and promotions director for the *Music Appreciation Hour*. By 1929, Alice Keith had established herself as one of the country's leading experts in music education by radio.[23] After

[18]When Sam Paley took his cigar company public, he placed a block of stock in his son's name.

[19]During 1930, the National Committee for Educational Radio (NCER) with support from the Payne Fund agitated for a total reallocation of radio channels and a 15 percent set-aside for nonprofits and educational institutions. The proposal found a congressional voice in the Fess Bill of 1931, which aroused determined opposition among commercial broadcasters (Barnouw, 1968).

[20]According to Paley (1979), in 1929, Majestic sold one million radio receivers, a figure representing 25percent of the U.S. market.

[21]Ben Darrow had pitched a similar idea to the Crosley Radio company. He presented Crosley executives with the following enticement to back a proposed NSOA:

IMMEDIATE SALES Children are the best advertisers in the world. TWO LEGGED CROSLEY ADS will go home to 20,000,000 radio-less homes coaxing dad to buy a Crosley. (Taylor, 1974, p. 63)

[22]Atkinson (1942c) asserts that the *Music Appreciation Hour* did more than any other program to introduce radios into the American classroom.

[23]Following World War I, Keith joined the educational staff of the Victor Talking Machine Company, lecturing before civic clubs and educational group across the country and writing articles for the *Cleveland Plain Dealer* on the potential of educational radio. That activity led to a position developing radio music lessons for the Cleveland Board of Education.

having gained fame for initiating educational broadcasts of the Cleveland Symphony to the Cleveland public schools, Keith received an offer from her previous employer, RCA,[24] to promote education by radio in the schools (Ray, 1928). For RCA, she promoted the music series featuring Walter Damrosch, former conductor of the New York Symphony Orchestra. The series, mentioned previously, was broadcast over the entire NBC network. Barely a year after that effort aired, CBS and sponsor Grigsby-Grunow enticed Keith to become the director of their proposed classroom-oriented educational series (Lincoln, 1938) by offering her a compensation package of nearly $8,000 per year (Ensign, 1930), a sum equal to approximately $110,000 in the year 2005 (Sahr, 2005).

While there existed some confusion at first over exactly who Keith worked for, CBS or the Grigsby-Grunow company, it is clear that Keith developed all the programming because CBS specifically gave her reproduction rights to all materials barring only rebroadcast over another network. Keith set to work building a school of impeccable credentials, if scant programming. She recruited 20 people with prestigious titles in education, educational administration, broadcasting, and the social services to serve on the school's advisory faculty. Headed by Dr. William C. Bagley, noted professor of education from Columbia University's Teacher College, the advisory faculty included other prominent individuals such as the director of Yale's School of Drama; sculptor Lorado Taft, then director of the Chicago Art Institute; the national commissioner of the Boy Scouts; and the assistant secretary of commerce. The advisory faculty members were organized into eight areas of curricula: music, literature, drama, art, nature study, the social sciences, health, and library. Their role was to suggest the main thrust of the semester's programs as well as the individual lesson topics. In addition to the faculty advisory group, Keith also recruited an advisory committee of 32 prominent persons from around the country including the U.S. Secretary of the Interior and the Commissioner of Education, who were highlighted as honorary members (ASA, 1930). It was an impressive list, but because the available data gives no indication of the committee's function, one wonders what contributions the nearly three dozen busy professionals and administrators could have made to the initial offering of exactly two programs.

CBS first aired the ASA on February 4, 1930, as a sponsored experiment in educational broadcasting. The experiment included two 30-minute programs each week throughout the spring of 1930. At the end of the semester, though the experiment was said to have received encouraging responses from teachers, Grigsby-Grunow bowed out as the sponsor (Atkinson, 1942c; School and Society 1930b). Undeterred by the loss of a sponsor, and apparently satisfied with the results of the radio experiment, Paley forged ahead with the ASA. Continuing under Keith's direction, ASA increased the broadcast schedule for the 1930–31 school year from two, 30 minute programs to five per week. CBS offered the entire package, 2.5 hours of weekly broadcasts to the classroom for 23 weeks, October to May, to its affiliated stations as a sustaining program; in other words, CBS paid the affiliates to air the broadcasts.

Paley described himself as a manager who believed in hiring the best talent and letting them work, but given his driving ambition, it seems likely that he, not Keith, set the school's purpose and direction (Paley, 1979). His vision for the school in the early years is perhaps best expressed in one word: *prestige*. The ASA would lend prestige to CBS, and that in turn would serve as a key tool for overcoming the challenges facing his network. Prestige would help convince advertisers that compared to NBC, CBS represented a more responsible,[25] or at least equally responsible, investment. It would attract big-name talent and also serve as a powerful weapon in the battle against the educators who wanted to reserve a portion of the radio spectrum for education and public service. To build the ASA's prestige, Paley consistently recruited prominent edu-

[24]Keith's previous employer, Victor Recording, had merged with RCA to form RCA Victor.

[25]As mentioned earlier, at that time, the public held a negative view of on-air advertising (Barnouw, 1966).

cators and talented writers. As a result, the ASA served as an entry point for a number of talented people who went on to fame and fortune, including Edward R. Murrow, William Shire, and Orson Welles.

Administration, Organization, and Staff

Both NBC and CBS competed for prestige in the educational arena by establishing departments of education and appointing full-time administrators who oversaw all the network educational programming including broadcasting for the schools.[26] Between 1930 and 1942, CBS appointed four network directors of education: Frederic Willis, 1930–35; Edward R. Murrow,[27] 1935–37; Sterling Fisher, 1938–41; and Lyman Bryson, 1942–48 (Atkinson, 1942b). Neither Willis nor Murrow had educational credentials, which suggests that at first CBS executives saw the director of education as an administrative position responsible for policy, personnel, and budget but not for the content and delivery of educational programs.

Serving with the title of director of broadcasting, American School of the Air, Keith directed the school's operations assisted by a staff of six: Dean Bagley's son, William Bagley Jr., educational research; Helen Johnson, Alice Keith's secretary, who would eventually replace Keith; a production manager for history and literature; a director of music for history and literature dramas; a dramatic director for history and literature dramas; and a conductor of the musical programs (ASA, 1930). In addition to the full-time staff, the ASA employed part-time writing and on-air talent, many of them borrowed from other CBS programs.

During the first year of full operation, 1930–31, either Keith or Willis determined that the school required an even larger group of advisors. The advisory faculty was expanded from 20 to 32 members and the advisory committee from 32 to 44 members. All had impressive titles; the group included, for example, several university presidents, but what was their purpose? Atkinson (1942c) guesses their role was not to guide programming but to establish connections for ASA with influential people across the nation.

The working relationship between the ASA staff and the advisory faculty is not spelled out in the documentation, but personal communications between Keith, Willis, and several faculty advisors give strong hints about how the relationship worked. It appears that Keith frequently generated ideas for program topics and approaches and submitted them to the faculty advisors for their opinion and approval. The advisory faculty member for history and civics was Carl R. Fish, professor of American history at the University of Wisconsin. In a letter to Fish, Keith asks the professor for his suggestions for the coming year, but then goes on to state her own ideas.

> Suppose we select events to dramatize, rather than personalities...? Do you think we could arrange thirteen programs devoted entirely to the history of inventions and their effect on the economic and social life of the country? Both transportation and communication could play an important part in these programs.
> What in your opinion, would be an interesting central thought for the European history program? [Keith, 1932a].

Although she was trained in music, Keith's letter to Fish shows that she was knowledgeable enough to suggest topic and development ideas for the history series, seeking only validation and approval from the eminent faculty advisor. Other correspondence reveals that after the staff developed the program scripts and musical accompaniment, they submitted them to the appro-

---

[26]In addition to broadcasting for the schools, CBS and NBC offered a number of educational and public service programs aimed at adults during evening and weekend hours (Bird, 1939)

[27]Little documentation exists showing that Murrow devoted much time to the School of the Air.

priate advisors who checked for accuracy and appropriateness for the intended grade (Willis, 1932). The data seem to indicate that advisory faculty played no direct role in developing scripts. Because the school was housed in CBS offices, technical support for conducting the broadcasts was readily available. The organizational structure described here remained consistent through 1938, though significant staff changes took place, including Keith's dismissal and changes in the position of network educational director.

Philosophy and Purpose

While neither CBS nor the ASA advocated a specific educational philosophy as such, William Bagley, the dean of the advisory faculty, was a prominent educational thinker and one of the founders of the educational movement known as Essentialism (Null, 2003). Like John Dewey, Bagley also sought to extend the opportunities of democratic living to all students. However, in contrast to Dewey's child-centered progressivism, Essentialists placed little value on learner initiative in the educational process. Bagley asserted that adult (teacher) responsibility for guidance, control, and direction of the immature (students) is inherent in human nature (Bagley, 1940b). He believed firmly that democracy in the classroom resulted from powerful teaching that could be realized only through the "placement of knowledgeable, cultured, academically prepared, technically competent and professionally educated, caring teachers" (Null, 2003, p. 240). With regard to curriculum, Dewey emphasized subject matter that was grounded in the child's world, while Bagley "stressed the centrality of the academic discipline" (Null, 2003, p. 241). Essentialists insisted on the value of knowledge for its own sake, not merely as an instrument. Bagley often criticized his colleagues for their failure to emphasize systematic study of academic subjects (Null, 2003).

Bagley's essentialism shared values with Judith Waller and other pioneers of educational radio who saw their role as bringing high culture to the masses, what I earlier called the "great mind" approach to educational radio (Darrow, 1932; Waller, 1923). To Bagley, democratic education consisted of sharing the highest academic and cultural resources with less-privileged students who typically might not be exposed to quality teaching and prep school curriculum. Radio provided an excellent vehicle for implementing Bagley's ideas, and undoubtedly he influenced the ASA program topics and development.

Some notion of William S. Paley's educational ideas can be inferred from his introductory statements written for the teacher guides that CBS distributed to schools. Paley's ideas seem to fit comfortably with Bagley's essentialism. In his foreword to the 1930–31 teachers manual, Paley states that the purpose of the ASA broadcasts is to bring to the classroom "the foremost authorities of our day, the best in art, music, and literature" (ASA, 1930, p. 1). This statement echoes Bagley, Judith Waller, and many other SOA proponents and demonstrates Paley's belief that radio should be used to expose the average student to high culture and to the thoughts and works of the great minds, an approach that complemented Paley's goal of gaining prestige for his network.

Paley and others at CBS apparently appreciated the key role that teachers played in deciding whether or not to tune in. They wanted to avoid conveying any hint that the ASA might compete with the classroom teacher. From its beginning, the ASA administrators described the school as an enrichment to classroom teaching. They gave assurances that the broadcasts were never intended to compete with or replace traditional classroom instruction (ASA, 1938; Atkinson, 1942a; School and Society, 1930a). In testimony before the Federal Communications Commission in 1934, Paley expanded on the theme. "In my judgment, educational radio must be regarded as supplemental[28] to formal educational agencies and methods. It cannot be a substitute for them. It cannot take the place of the classroom and lecture platform" (Paley, 1934, pp. 14–15). He

---

[28]Paley's use of the word "supplemental" is confusing. He actually means what I defined earlier as "enrichment."

asserted that the ASA programs supplemented school resources and helped the teacher achieve the larger aims of education (Paley, 1934). Many of the ASA teachers manuals and program guides distributed by CBS spelled out the school's goals, namely to enrich and vitalize classroom learning by extending horizons, arousing and stimulating interest, and bringing new ideas in a vivid and impressive form (ASA, 1938).

In his address, 10/17/1934, to the Federal Communications Commission in its inquiry into proposals to allot fixed percentages of the nation's broadcasting channels to special non-profit, mainly educational groups, Paley laid out his ideal about how best to use radio in the classroom.

> To radio's democratic audience, history must be made to seem not a recitation of facts and dates, but rather a spy-glass into the past where characters live again. Science must be discussed not as a series of abstract phenomena, but as an answer to the daily needs of man in his struggle with his environment. Classic literature must become a living expression of today's thought in yesterday's imagery. Geography can be no mere description, but rather an actual experience of the world. Every listener in short, must be made so aware of the direct application of this material to his own life that he listens as avidly as to sheer entertainment. We consider the criterion of success in such educational programs a presentation so dramatic that the listener could distinguish it from pure entertainment only with difficulty [Paley, 1934, pp. 14–15].

While Paley asserted the benefit of dramatic presentation over lecture, he also seems to have advocated a learner centered approach to instruction, one that privileges the students' perceptions and experience over the demands of subject matter. This was a pioneering idea for radio in 1934, but one that seems to conflict with Bagley's Essentialist approach. In addition, the idea that through radio, education could be made as appealing as "sheer entertainment" was a goal that many SOAs aspired to, but seldom achieved. In my opinion it is an inappropriate goal for any form of education.

Educational Programs

After the small pilot effort was deemed a great success, CBS expanded the ASA to 30-minute broadcasts, five days a week. By the following year, the ASA had settled into a somewhat complicated schedule that included alternating weekly programs as shown in Table 3.

TABLE 3. ASA PROGRAM SCHEDULE, 1931–32
(ASA, 1931)

Day	Time	Course	Grades
Monday	2:30–3:00	*History Dramas*	Upper grades and high school
Tuesday	2:30–3:00	*Geography and Music*	Upper grades and high school
Wednesday	2:30–2:45	*Art Appreciation*	Upper grades and high school
	2:45–3:00	*Literature*	
Thursday	2:30–2:45	*Radio Picture Book series* alternating every other week with *Children's Plays*	Primary
Thursday	2:45–3:00	*Radio Journeys to Music Land* alternating every other week with *Elementary Science*	Intermediate
Friday	2:30–2:45	*Current Events*	High school
	2:45–3:00	*Vocational Guidance*	

From the beginning, CBS annually prepared and distributed a substantial publication that served as the teachers guide, program schedule, and promotion vehicle. In a formal — almost pompous—passive voice, the guides provided descriptions of the school's education programs, suggestions for pre- and post-broadcast activities, related readings, follow-up-learning activities, and assurances that the school grew increasingly popular among teachers and students of America (ASA, 1931). The descriptions given below are taken from the *American School of the Air Teachers Manual and Classroom Guide* issued for 1931–32. They provide insight into program content, instructional methods and the educational views of Keith, Bagley, and, to a certain extent, Paley himself.

PROGRAM DESCRIPTIONS, 1931–32

History. The guide describes this series of historical dramas as being influenced by the disarmament conference taking place in Geneva, Switzerland, and being unified by the thought of "world brotherhood" (ASA, 1932, p. 13). It's unclear what impact this description would have on a classroom teacher. No information is provided on instructional methods used by the radio teachers.

Geography and Music. This series also was guided by the theme of world brotherhood. Famous "travelers and geographers of note will discuss each country and race.... The geography programs may be correlated with history and literature without any difficulty" (ASA, 1931, p. 25). The persons of note are identified as Madame D. Pirie-Beyea, "Lecturer and World Citizen"; the president of the World Federation of Education Associations; and a professor of economic geography from Columbia University (p. 25). Because the guide mentions discussion, it seems likely that the instructional methods included narration and dialogue among the famous personages.

Art Appreciation. The stated objectives for this series were:

• To stimulate an interest in art in general
• To awaken a particular interest in American art
• To inspire a desire to create pictures and other forms of original artwork

To motivate students in the last objective, prizes were offered for the best pictures and best examples of clay modeling; prizes of artwork reproductions were awarded to schools that submitted the most winning entries. In addition, winning entries were displayed in a gallery in New York City.

Literature. The literature selections for this series, according to the guide, were drawn from 10 countries and were of such universal interest that the programs would appeal to "students from 5th grade through high school" (p. 39). The series consisted of dramatizations of literature segments and commentary by literary figures, apparently well known in their day.

Radio Picture Book series, primary grades. Consisting of music programs designed for primary grades one through three, the series alternated weekly with music programs for the intermediate grades four through six. The broadcasts employed a variety of instructional methods including dramas played by children, direct instruction involving rhythmic activities, recognition activities in which children in the classroom were asked to identify instruments, and quiet listening. Teachers were strongly urged to have the children follow the broadcast using the radio picture books made available to students at a cost of 25 cents each.

Radio Journeys to Music Land. The radio teacher for this series led children in intermediate grades in the singing of folk songs from Europe and the Americas. The classroom teacher was encouraged to make sure that each student had a copy of the text for this program (25 cents). Also, students were encouraged to submit original tunes with the promise that those with merit would be played on air. This series alternated weekly with the primary series, *Radio Picture Book*.

Elementary Science. The purpose of this series, according to the guide, was to make students familiar with the world around them, to supplement classroom instruction, and to help the teacher make science a real experience for the pupils. Each program stressed observations of some aspect of the visible world. Methods appear to be limited to narration and discussion. No radio teacher is identified. For each program, the guide provides suggestions for pre- and post broadcast activities.

Vocational Guidance. This series featured conversational interviews with successful men and women. Nine speakers are pictured and identified as likely participants. They include many from federal government such as the Secretary of Agriculture, an assistant secretary of the Navy, an assistant secretary of commerce, and the Commissioner of the Civil Service.

Current Events. This series is the second one of only two that identified the on-air personality. Dr. Charles Fleischer is identified as an eminent lecturer and teacher. He interprets the daily news and introduces guest speakers who are prominent news makers.

These program descriptions raise several issues about the effectiveness or appropriateness of various ASA offerings. (1) Radio teachers are identified for only a few of the programs, and those fall into the category of renowned experts with impressive titles. This raises the question of whether renowned experts are appropriate teachers and speakers on a regular basis. Renowned expertise might soon lose its appeal. The programs seem to lack involvement from actual teachers experienced in elementary or high school education. (2) Most ASA programs were aimed at the upper grades and high school; only Wednesday's programming was intended for primary grade students. This focus was inappropriate because radio was better suited for elementary schools because teachers there were less hampered by rigid class schedules. (3) The curriculum and school administration do not seem guided by clear educational objectives. Rather, one might conjecture that the driving force behind ASA programs in the early years was Paley's desire to generate prestige for the network, not the need to attain any specific educational objectives.

Depression Years and Keith's Departure

The Great Depression disrupted activities and plans of most public and private educational organizations across the United States, and the ASA was no exception. Early in 1932, the worsening financial situation and loss of some advertisers prompted CBS to fire nearly 100 employees and cut salaries for the remaining ones by 15 percent. Keith wrote that "due to the panic of fear" she was asked to take a summer's vacation without pay (Keith, 1932a). Director of Education Frederic Willis told Keith that he and Keith's former secretary Helen Johnson could carry on during the summer of that year and that if the ASA continued, she, Keith, would be called back (Keith, 1932a). Keith had met Helen Johnson in Cleveland while developing the music radio programs for the school board there. She then invited Johnson to become her secretary at the Victor Recording Company where Keith was employed as the director of educational programs. Keith said, "I trusted her more than anyone" (Keith, 1932b).

As it turned out, despite the Depression, the advertisers returned to CBS. The company, like most of the radio industry, prospered, the former secretary continued to direct the ASA, but Alice Keith never again worked with the school. To protest her dismissal, Keith sent off a flurry of letters to members of the advisory faculty and other influential people including Eleanor Roosevelt, complaining that CBS was very "short sighted" in placing the planning of the school programs into the hands of a person "who has never taught school nor attended college" (Keith, 1932b). She stressed the possible negative consequences of having a mere secretary (Johnson) run a complex educational endeavor.

In protest of Keith's dismissal, several of the advisory faculty, including Professor Fish, threatened to resign. They voiced concern about whether a former secretary possessed the skills and prestige needed to maintain the school's standards, not to mention the respect of the educational community. Willis assured the advisors that the high standards of the ASA would be upheld under the new leadership of Johnson, who, he corrected, had served as Alice Keith's assistant, not her secretary. He explained that her responsibilities would be mostly administrative and that the role of the advisory faculty would become even more important. Moreover, CBS would continue to contribute its "vast resources of experience, time, and money" that had helped to make the ASA a recognized success as the only nationwide educational curriculum for the schools[29] (Willis, 1932). The faculty advisors apparently became reconciled to the new leadership, and the tempest soon passed.

Keith's relationship with the ASA might have ended there had not Paley decided in 1935 to recognize William Bagley, the dean of the ASA advisory faculty, as the originator of the school. Stung by this obvious and deliberate neglect of her role, Keith sued CBS to force its executives to recognize her as the founder and director of the ASA during the first three years of its operation. She wrote to anyone she felt could validate her role at the ASA, including Ben Darrow and Armstrong Perry. In a scathing letter to Bagley, she asked him pointedly, "Is it your belief that the idea [of ASA] originated with you?" She detailed her involvement as the founder and director from the beginning, pointing out that others on the advisory faculty did as much or more to launch the school than he had. "I cannot understand how you are willing to accept credit for having started the American School of the Air any more than Will Earhart, Chairman of the Damrosch Committee (which I organized) can claim to have started the Damrosch hour." She goes on to say that repeated statements about the founding of the ASA that left her out of the picture injured her professional reputation (Keith, 1936). Probably most hurtful to Keith was a letter of reference sent to a prospective employer by Frederic Willis, the former director of education, who in 1936 was serving as Paley's assistant. In cool, terse terms he acknowledged, "Miss Keith's statement that she took an active and principal part in the early organization of the American School of the Air is quite correct" (Willis, 1936). He also states quite inaccurately that she served as ASA's director only from the summer of 1929 to the autumn of 1930, a span two years less than her actual tenure.[30] The outcome of her suit is unknown. Keith went on to found the National Academy of Broadcasting, a private school dedicated to teaching broadcast-related skills. In 1934, Keith wrote a scathing and comprehensive attack on the state of educational radio in the United States compared to that in Europe. She characterized educational radio here as being in a state of chaos and laid the blame on commercial control of radio. She did not, however, mention CBS or the ASA (Keith, 1934). Over the next three years, 1932 to 1935, Helen Johnson and Willis made only minor changes to the curriculum established by Keith.

PALEY'S TESTIMONY

The six-year-long battle to have the federal government set aside 15 percent of the radio channels for education finally came to a vote in 1934 before the Roosevelt administration's newly formed Federal Communications Commission (FCC).[31] The forces in favor included Armstrong Perry, the Payne Fund, administrators of the many college educational stations, and members of National Committee on Education by Radio (NCER). Against them were aligned the full power of commercial broadcasting including the heads of both networks (Barnouw, 1968; McChesney, 1993). In his testimony of October 17, 1934, William Paley told the FCC that educational broadcasting appealed to elite tastes and that the call to set aside 15 percent of the radio channels for public service and education would reduce the service the commercial broadcasters provided for free "To destroy what has been built, or seriously to limit its usefulness— to weaken radio's economic structure — to attempt to widen the service the public is receiving by subtracting from that

---

[29]I found no data suggesting that the advisory faculty received any financial compensation, but such compensations would have been customary.

[30] It is curious that Keith acquired and retained this letter sent by Willis to a prospective employer. It's even more curious that Keith attached a newspaper clipping to it dated 12/28/38. The clipping announced the suicide of Willis' ex-wife who died penniless in a modest Manhattan apartment not far from Willis' office at the CBS headquarters building that came to be called "Black Rock" (Willis, 1936).

[31]The proposal would have meant a large-scale reassignment of most radio channels.

service or to lessen radio facilities so as to make unavailable to any portion of our population the broadcast they now receive — would seem to us a cause for real regret" (Paley, 1934, p. 29).

The FCC voted against the set-aside and instead urged the commercial broadcasters to fulfill their promise to bring quality broadcasting to the American public.

Welles and Murrow

Though Paley considered himself a hands-off manager, his guidance was felt at the school in the quality of people who started their radio careers at the ASA. In 1934, 19-year-old Orson Welles first entered radio through the ASA. Even as a youth, Welles' organ-toned voice suited broadcasting perfectly. To supplement his earnings from his work in live theater, Welles performed in a variety of ASA literature and history programs serving as narrator, reading poetry, and acting in various character roles, often augmented with his superb accents. Paley (1979) says that Welles' work in the live theater captivated CBS executives and prompted them to ask Welles to form his own radio theater group, the Mercury Theater of the Air. In that CBS group, Welles performed famous stories such as *Dracula, Treasure Island, A Tale of Two Cities, Julius Caesar,* and then, of course, H. G. Wells' *The War of the Worlds* (Barnouw, 1968).

In 1935, CBS hired Edward R. Murrow, then in his mid–20s, to serve as the "Director of Talks," a position he gained based on his previous work as president of the National Student Federation. In this new position, Murrow scheduled prominent speakers and panelists to participate in the network's various educational programs, including panel shows, talk programs, and the ASA (Atkinson, 1942a). In 1936, Murrow replaced Willis as the CBS director of education and served in that role until sometime in 1938.[32] Under Murrow's tenure, the ASA's educational purpose took a new turn. Previously, ASA lessons were designed to complement and supplement specific school subjects. To enhance their value, Murrow announced that the programs would become more interdisciplinary with the purpose of interrelating standard classroom subjects. As an example, he offered a new music series that traced the development of great historical figures such as Jean-Jacques Rousseau and Friedrich Nietzsche by focusing on the music they wrote in their spare time (School and Society, 1937). Another innovation under Murrow was a series of folk music broadcasts from foreign countries. These were two intriguing ideas to be sure; how well they appealed to the typical American high school student is unknown.

During his tenure as education director Murrow traveled extensively in Europe, ostensibly to arrange broadcasts of folk music via shortwave relay for use in ASA music and history programs. However, Paley probably had other duties in mind for Murrow. As signs in Europe pointed more and more to war, CBS appointed Murrow its European bureau director. Over the next year, he and another soon-to-be-famous CBS journalist and author, William L. Shirer,[33] were frequently dispatched to Europe, both men apparently serving dual roles as reporters and ASA musicologists (Barnouw, 1968). At first, the ASA assignments took up much of their time. In fact, on March 10, 1938, the day before Hitler's Nazi army marched unopposed into Austria, Murrow and Shirer were nearby — Murrow in Poland, Shirer in Yugoslavia — still collecting folk songs. Shirer rushed to Vienna in time to witness Hitler's troops entering the city, an event that signaled the beginning of World War II. Within two days, Murrow made the first of what became his famous wartime broadcasts to the United States (Paley, 1979). Needless to say, both men dropped their ASA duties and initiated what soon became CBS' European news operation, where both men — along with others such as Walter Cronkite — built international reputations as radio journalists.

---

[32]It is unclear whether the position of director of talks was abolished or whether it was combined with that of director of education. This may indicate that the latter position was not clearly defined.

[33]Shirer authored the monumental work *The Rise and Fall of the Third Reich.*

1936–37 Programs

Table 4 shows the schedule for the ASA programs offered under Murrow's tenure as educational director. *Art Appreciation* and the *Radio Picture Book* series have been dropped, replaced by a greater emphasis on science, music, European folk roots, and geography. The schedule also reflects an apparent shift away from programs for upper grades (five through eight) to more programs for high school students. The rationale for this move is unknown.

TABLE 4. ASA Program Schedule, 1936–37
(ASA, 1936)

Day	Time	Course	Grades
Monday	2:15–2:45	*History Dramas*	High school
Tuesday	2:15–2:45	*Music* alternating weekly with *Literature*	High school
Wednesday	2:15–2:45	*Geography*	Intermediate
Thursday	2:15–2:30	*Dramatized Folk Tales* alternating weekly with *Science Club of the Air*	Intermediate
Thursday	2:30–2:45	*Music*	Primary
Friday	2:15–2:30	*Current Events*	High school
	2:30–2:45	*Vocational G uidance*	High school

Here are some program highlights for the 1936–37 year taken from the teachers guide for that year:

Literature. The series broadcast two types of literature: poetry appreciation alternating with excerpts from Shakespearian plays. The poetry programs featured readings by well-known poets of the day, which demonstrated a unique capability of radio, namely exposing students directly to the voice of famous artists. The Shakespearian programs consisted of excerpts that were chosen in part because they conformed to an examination of college entrance board and other similar requirements. Overall, the mix of narration, reading, and dramatization demonstrated good use of radio's capabilities, but the alternating schedule—the literature series alternated weekly with the music series—required classroom teachers to do a lot of advanced planning.

Science Club of the Air. The series presented simple science experiments dealing with things such as carbon dioxide, air pressure, and magnetism performed before the microphone by an in-studio class of intermediate grade students. Dubbed the *Science Club of the Air*, the in-studio students worked under the direction of an actual science teacher who directed them and conducted a follow-up discussion of results and applications. During the broadcast, the radio audience just listened, but the intent was to have them repeat the simple experiments following the broadcasts.

Dramatized Folk Tales. This series introduced students in intermediate grades to "humanity's oldest form of literature." The tales included several from non–Western cultures, reflecting perhaps Murrow's international outlook:

• The earliest experience of peoples: *The Origins of Fire*
• Greek mythology: *Jason and the Golden Fleece*
• Early Western European: *Beowulf* and *The Song of Roland*
• Middle Eastern culture: *Sohrab and Rustam*
• Chinese literature: *Lo-sun the Blind Boy*
• Christian legend: *The Christmas Nightingale and The Other Cross*
• American: *Johnny Appleseed*   (ASA, 1936)

A lengthy description of the series is signed by the script author, Courtenay Savage (p. 17), but there is no indication of involvement by an educator or anyone else for that matter.

Music. This series demonstrated Murrow's interdisciplinary approach to curriculum. Intended for the upper-elementary grades through high school, it presented music composed by famous historical characters whom the world does not know as musicians, such as Henry VIII, Frederick the Great of Prussia, Jean-Jacques Rousseau, and Friedrich Nietzsche, among others. The rationale given was that the series provided insight into historical characters through music. It also contributed to an appreciation of music as a form of creative expression within everyone's reach, "no matter how busy, rich or humble" (ASA, 1937a, p. 18). The writers of the series made an assumption that students in grades 6 through 12 were familiar with such historical figures as Frederick the Great and Nietzsche.

Music for the Primary Grades. Traditional goals of music instruction for young children drove this series, namely to develop a sense of rhythm through listening and responding to rhythmic activities, to encourage individual singing, and to build the child's song repertoire. The song list was selected to coordinate with poems, stories, and topics familiar to children. Dorothy Gordon, a well-known music teacher of the day, utilized a variety of instructional techniques to get children involved in rhythmic movement and singing in the classroom.

Geography. Developed in cooperation with the National Council of Geography Teachers, the series presented the dramatized travels of the Hamilton family—a father, his two sons, and occasionally several cousins. Covering all regions of the world, the dramas revealed facts about the location as well as the characters' impressions and feelings about the enjoyment and difficulties of foreign travel. Humor and conflict between characters added human interest; music and sound effects enhanced the dramatic effects. The geography series demonstrated high production values and the fact that CBS invested substantial amounts to make the series appealing to listeners (ASA, 1937).

However, the geography series was criticized for overindulging in dramatization of "inherently expository material." As a result, many programs in the series "lacked reality" (Bird, 1939, p. 48). By this statement, Bird meant that the programs often sacrificed educational rigor for entertainment value.

The teachers guide for 1936–37 also provided insights about the administration and vision that controlled the ASA at that time. William Bagley's role as the school's dean continued to be highlighted along with other members of the advisory faculty and cooperating committee. The scriptwriters were identified, but, oddly, the school's director, editor of the teachers guide, and the other administrators remained anonymous. No indication is given of Helen Johnson's role or that of the then unknown Murrow. Perhaps their names were omitted because they lacked academic titles or experience, so they contributed little to the ASA's prestige.

Overall, the 1936–37 schedule continued to reflect Dean Bagley's traditional curriculum, modified by Murrow's interdisciplinary approach. Absent, however, were influences of the progressive educational movement or the enormous social changes brought about by the Depression and Roosevelt's New Deal policies.

Methods

Despite the fact that radio appealed to only one sense, the ASA—like most schools of the air—quickly adopted a repertoire of instructional methods that worked well for on-air instruction. These methods included (1) exposition using narration, dialogue, or simulation and (2) imaginative presentations using storytelling or dramatizations (Darrow, 1940). Direct teaching, which meant that the classroom students responded directly to the radio teacher's instructions during the broadcast, was not frequently used in ASA programs. The appropriate instructional method was determined in part by the program's subject matter. Literature and history programs cried out for storytelling and dramatization, while science and art appreciation programs demanded more dialogue and exposition (Bird, 1939). However, creative scriptwriters could and did apply different instructional methods to any type of subject matter, and in fact, most programs combined methods, though typically one dominated. Table 5 shows the ASA program offerings for 1936–37 and the principal instructional methods used for each.

TABLE 5. ASA INSTRUCTIONAL METHODS, 1936–37
(ASA, 1936)

Day	Subject	Method
Monday	*History*	Dramatization
Tuesday	*Music* alternating with	Demonstration
	Literature	Dramatization and exposition
Wednesday	*Geography*	Dramatization and narration
Thursday	*Dramatized Folk Tales* alternating	Dramatization
	with *Science Club of the Air*	Exposition and simulation
Thursday	*Music*	Audio demonstration and exposition
Friday	*Current Events*	Exposition
	Vocational Guidance	Exposition and dramatization

Compared to that of 1931–32, the 1936–37 schedule showed changing methods: an increased use of dramatization, a decrease in narration, and the apparent elimination of direct instruction. It appears that the ASA staff relied less on innovative methodology and experts and more on its ability to hire or borrow from CBS's stable of talented writers to create dramatizations. For example, it is known that Orson Welles wrote some ASA scripts in the early 1930s, but it is not known which ones (Barnouw, 1968). More important, the best-known and most admired radio writer of the day, Norman Corwin, also wrote scripts for ASA (Bannerman, 1986); which ones, however, are unknown. It certainly made sense that a company whose business consisted heavily of soap opera drama would bring the same approach to its educational broadcasts.

A New Direction

According to Atkinson (1942b), by late 1937 the ASA had become an "orphan child" (p. 13). CBS executives were losing interest and had seriously considered dropping the project because of its big expense. Atkinson provides no evidence to support his claim, but we might infer top management's waning interest in the school from the fact that during the preceding years, the network's director of education, Murrow, was running around Europe collecting folk songs, acting more as staff than as management. Also, his responsibilities seemed to have been divided among several areas, including education, talks, and news. Possibly, by the late 1930s, as networks found it easier to sell daytime hours to advertisers, the need to build prestige on the domestic front had diminished. It might also have been that Paley saw news as a better weapon than education for conducting the competitive battle with rival NBC.

At any rate, in the following year, 1938, the orphan became the prodigal son. CBS named a new school director, defined a new emphasis and purpose, created new programs, and increased funding substantially. Atkinson (1942b) credits the change to the appointment in 1938 of a new director of education, Sterling Fisher, a man with academic credentials and a vision for the ASA's future. Fisher sold CBS executives on the idea that refurbishing the ASA as an international educational service would earn CBS substantial benefits in goodwill and public relations. Most likely Fisher's argument appealed to Paley and other top CBS executives as a brilliant competitive move to counter NBC, which was then experimenting with shortwave broadcasts into Latin America. In the late 1930s, the entire radio industry had become aware of the commercial potential of shortwave as a means of rebroadcasting programs including commercials to foreign countries. When in June of 1939 the FCC authorized the sale of commercial time over shortwave, a struggle ensued between CBS and NBC to get their programming in place (Barnouw, 1968). Once again, the ASA would become a chess piece in Paley's competitive game with NBC, but the outcome benefited the ASA and its audience.

Fisher articulated two strategic goals that would guide the ASA's future operation: (1) obtain official recognition for the nation's educational leadership, and (2) decentralize ASA activities in order to develop close relationships with local superintendents, principals, teachers, and pupils (Atkinson, 1942b).

To implement his vision, Fisher substantially reorganized the school's academic governance by disbanding the ASA's faculty advisors and the cooperating committee[34] and developing a close working relationship with the National Education Association (NEA), a significant feat as the NEA leaders had never been enthusiastic about educational radio. The NEA in turn nominated a national board of consultants that served as the ASA steering committee and that also set up local boards of consultants in roughly 80 cities across the country. In addition, CBS-affiliated stations were asked to appoint educational directors or at least to name a staff person responsible for educational broadcasts. Approximately 100 stations did so. Furthermore, the CBS director of education established, across the nation, six regional directors of education whose jobs were to promote wider and effective use of ASA broadcasts and seek means to relate both network and station presentations to community needs (Atkinson, 1942b).

By 1940, Fisher had largely achieved his two goals. He had gained recognition from national educators— the NEA adopted the ASA as its official radio project, the National Catholic Education Association endorsed it for use in parochial elementary and secondary schools, and the boards of education in 11 states gave the ASA their recognition and endorsement (ASA, 1939; Atkinson, 1942a). In addition, thanks to the NEA, ASA had direct connections to educators in local communities.

The new organization and direction in ASA's program development were reflected in the 1938–39 teachers manual and classroom guide. The front cover prominently mentions the new director of education, Sterling Fisher. Gone are the long lists of high-powered advisors, consultants, and cooperators. In their place, the guide names educators with backgrounds in kindergarten through 12th-grade schooling as the actual planners and writers of specific courses, along with collaborating organizations. For example, the program *Frontiers of Democracy* was planned by Dr. Alice V. Keliher, chairperson of the Commission on Human Relations of the Progressive Education Association (ASA, 1938).

Fisher revamped the program offering substantially by adding snappy titles, as shown in the schedule for 1938–39 in Table 6.

TABLE 6. ASA PROGRAM SCHEDULE, 1938–39
(ASA, 1938)

Day	Time	Course	Grades
Monday	2:30–3:00	*Frontiers of Democracy*	Upper grades, junior and senior high schools
Tuesday	2:30–3:00	*Music of America*	Senior high
Wednesday	2:30–3:00	*This Living World*	Upper grades, high schools, colleges, and adult clubs
Thursday	2:30–3:00	*New Horizons*	Elementary grades
		Lives Between the Lines	Junior and senior high school
Friday	2:30–3:00	(replaced in 1939–40 with) *Tales from Far and Near*	Upper grades, junior and senior high schools

[34]Dean Bagley retained an affiliation with CBS as a figurehead for the educational programs.

Following are descriptions of the five new programs identified in Table 6 that Fisher launched for the 1938–39 year.

Frontiers of Democracy. This program covered contemporary issues and problems in national life. The semester-long series was organized into five "frontier" topic areas: frontiers of science, health, work, community planning, and education. Each program presented the historical background and scope of the problem and posed the question, "What could we do about it through joint democratic action?" (ASA, 1938, p. 10). In addition, the guide provided suggestions for student engagement through reading, research, information dissemination, and action programs. Especially imaginative, the guide suggested that students conduct a survey around a problem or issue of interest to local residents and prepare a report of their findings. The guide assured teachers that local radio stations would broadcast well-prepared student reports (ASA, 1938). All in all, the series demonstrated a startlingly contemporary approach to learning.

Music of America. Designed to celebrate American music and its roots in Euro-American, Indian, and European folk traditions, this series surveyed practically all aspects of American music from colonial days to folk music and modern jazz from all eras and sections of the country. Program titles included *American Indians, Colonial New England, The Southern Colonies, Music of the Negro, American Symphonic Music, American Light and Grand Opera,* as well as music composed by high school students. ASA program developers were able to draw from CBS's rich musical resources.

This Living World. This series provided scenes and commentary from significant events in the world's news in order to integrate current events, social studies, and civics through a problem-based approach (ASA, 1938). The authors of the guide envisioned interest extending to adult listeners outside the classroom including clubs, parent-teacher associations, community organizations, and veterans groups. A variety of instructional methods were employed, including dramatization, question and answer sessions, panel and classroom discussion, and debates.

Lives Between the Lines/Tales from Far and Near. The description of the *Lives ...* series in the guide evokes a college-level course: "American literature in terms of the human implications of the literary work" (ASA, 1938, p. 63). The following year, 1939–40, the *Lives* series was replaced with *Tales from Far and Near,* which presented radio adaptations of modern children's stories of the Americas. The *Tales* series had two educational goals: (1) stimulate interest in reading books, and (2) develop an understanding and sympathetic appreciation of the lives and customs of people throughout the Americas (Reid, 1941c). This latter goal complemented the network's business goal of competing with NBC for market share in Latin America. The series became the most popular ASA offering, attracting approximately 400,000 regular listeners across the country (Reid, 1941a). It also became a subject of extensive research conducted by Seerley Reid and the Evaluation of School Broadcasts group at The Ohio State University (Reid, 1941c), Reid's findings are presented later in this chapter.

New Horizons. According to the 1938–39 Teachers Manual, this natural history series would open up new horizons in natural history for students in grades four through eight and supplement the study of elementary science and geography. The series focused on scientific concepts relevant to children rather than traditional content, a more contemporary learner-centered approach. From the halls of the American Museum of Natural History in Washington, D.C., museum director Dr. Roy Chapman Andres, "noted explorer and scientist," served as the radio teacher (ASA, 1938, p. 35). Combining narration and stories, Andres related adventures associated with scientific discovery. Brief dramatizations served to demonstrate and elaborate his points (ASA, 1938).

ALAN LOMAX'S FOLK MUSIC SERIES

With solid financial backing, Fisher was able to develop some truly innovative programming that built on radio's unique attributes. In 1937, he invited Alan Lomax, who had recently taken charge of the folk music archives of the Library of Congress, to produce a folk song series for the ASA. Lomax wrote and directed *American Folk Songs*, a 26-week music survey for 1939–40 featuring artists such as Woody Guthrie, Leadbelly, the Golden Gate Quartet, Burl Ives, Aunt Molly Jackson, and field pickups of square dancing and French-Canadian and lumberjack songs (Barnouw, 1968; Rounder, 2004). Lomax served as the radio teacher, singing on many programs while accompanying himself on the guitar. His goal for the programs was "to bring the listeners as close as possible to authentic folk songs and show how it is really sung and how it functions in the American community" (Sanders, 1990). The following year, the ASA revised the series as the *Wellsprings of Music*, a "more refined version" of *Folk Music of America*, which combined the music of professional composers with the folk repertoire. The *Wellsprings* series continued the trend toward increased integration of music with other subjects. The ASA guide for 1941 describes *Wellsprings* as a combination of music and social studies based on the concept that good music is "never a thing apart but a result of man's experience and a common function of daily living" (Sanders, 1990).

Overall, Fisher's program offerings for the years 1938 through 1941 reflected a fresh and imaginative approach. In essence, the new ASA curriculum represented a departure from Bagley's strict emphasis on traditional and classical subject matter and toward a more contemporary, problem-based, learner-centered, interdisciplinary curriculum that Fisher hoped would appeal to students in North and South America. The new curriculum also seemed more cognizant than in previous years of the social and political changes occurring across the country as a result of the nation's response to the Depression. However, most of the programs still catered to junior and senior high school students. Though the guide describes that several programs were intended for "upper grades through high school," the span was too great. Teachers complained that the vocabulary and subjects were too difficult for younger students. The programs better suited junior and senior high school students, and that focus was problematic. Rigid class schedules followed in high schools and some junior high schools often did not coincide with radio broadcast schedules. This issue will be discussed later in more detail.

Paley backed up Fisher's new schedule with money and resources. According to CBS, the annual investment in the ASA during the early 1940s—counting production, music, scriptwriting, and salaries—reached $250,000, excluding the value of donated airtime[35] (Atkinson, 1942b). This amount was huge in comparison to what state and local SOAs spent on their programs.

SCHOOL OF THE AIR OF THE AMERICAS

As part of Paley's grander plan to challenge NBC's Latin American thrust, in early 1940, CBS renamed the ASA the School of the Air of the Americas and began multilingual broadcasting in English, Spanish, and Portuguese. The stated purpose was to provide the people of the Western Hemisphere with a better understanding of each other's cultures, but this purpose also paralleled the network's expansion southward. During 1940, CBS affiliated with 64 Latin-American stations creating, in effect, a Pan American CBS and helping to make the School of the Air of the Americas the world's largest educational organization (School and Society, 1941).

Programming for the new international school of the air was intended to reflect the cultures and histories of all the Americas. To achieve that end, Fisher invited the ministers of education from Latin American countries to send CBS material on their countries' literature, history, economy, and culture suitable for inclusion in School of the Air of the Americas radio programs. CBS would then translate the material, create scripts in Spanish or Portuguese, and furnish the scripts to the various countries for broadcast over their public or private stations using the stations' production and acting staff. In addition to the scripts, CBS also provided translated copies of the teach-

---

[35]If the value of airtime is included, then CBS asserted that its investment in ASA was approximately $1,000,000 annually.

ers manuals. Both scripts and guides were offered free of charge (Atkinson, 1942b). President Roosevelt's secretary of state praised the new broadcast concept as a form of international cooperation that would deepen and broaden understanding among peoples (Bagley, 1940a, p. 40).

To promote the new school's international focus, Fisher had CBS sponsor, in cooperation with the NEA, the First International Conference of the School of the Air of the Americas. This event was held in conjunction with the 1940 annual meeting of the Pan-American Union. At the conference, Fisher showcased several ASA programs, including a story of the Yucatan, "Dark Star of Itza," from the *Tales from Far and Near* series. Also featured was a program from the *New Horizons* series at a conference session held at the American Museum of Natural History (School and Society, 1941).

To accommodate the international character of the broadcasts, the School of the Air of the Americas adopted a more flexible broadcast schedule for the 1941–42 school year:

• Eastern time zone: 9:15–9:45 A.M.
• Central time zone: 2:30–2:55 P.M.
• Mountain time zone: 9:30–10:00 A.M.
• Pacific time zone: 1:30–2:00 P.M.   (ASA, 1941, p. 11)

All in all, it appeared that under Fisher's direction and CBS's generous support, the School of the Air of the Americas was off to a roaring start, but the growing European war brought changes to the school.

During the war, the school played an important role nationally. The U.S. government announced that it was the official channel through which the Office of War Information would "convey news, information, and instruction for civilian activities to children, teachers, and parents of America" (ASA, 1943). Selection of the School of the Air of the Americas for this task was not surprising considering that early in the war Paley had served as a civilian consultant to the Office of War Information. Then, in 1942, he took a leave of absence from CBS and joined the army. After meeting with General Dwight Eisenhower, he was named chief of radio broadcasting within the Psychological Warfare Division of Eisenhower's command (Paley, 1979).

AUDIENCE AND EVALUATION

Throughout nearly two decades of operation, the ASA issued no credible reports on the size and demographics of its audience. That omission is ironic given that CBS was renowned as an innovator in the field of audience survey and measurement[36] (Smith, 1990). In 1938, CBS's research department did conduct a comprehensive nationwide survey on the use of CBS and NBC school broadcasts in classrooms, but the results were never released (Reid, 1941a). That refusal suggests the results of the study had fallen far short of the inflated claims often made by network executives.

By the late 1930s, the ASA had attracted the attention of educational researchers associated with the Evaluation of School Broadcasts (ESB) project[37] at The Ohio State University and funded by the federal government. Dedicated to studying the reach and effect of radio education, the project, directed by I. Keith Tyler, conducted dozens of research studies, many of which focused on the ASA programs including the key question of who listened. As mentioned earlier, chief researcher Seerley Reid derided the audience estimates issued by CBS as being "grossly inflated" (p. 1). Chairman Paley, in his 1940 annual report to CBS shareholders, had claimed that the ASA reached 8,000,000 pupils in more than 200,000 classrooms (Atkinson 1942d, p. 27). Those claims were repeated in a

---

[36]In 1935, CBS hired Frank Stanton, a young psychologist from OSU, to head up the network's research department. Stanton's statistical research intrigued network executives because it showed that information is absorbed better through the ear than the eye. Stanton went on to become president of CBS (Paley, 1979).

[37]The Evaluation of School Broadcasts project is described in Chapter 1.

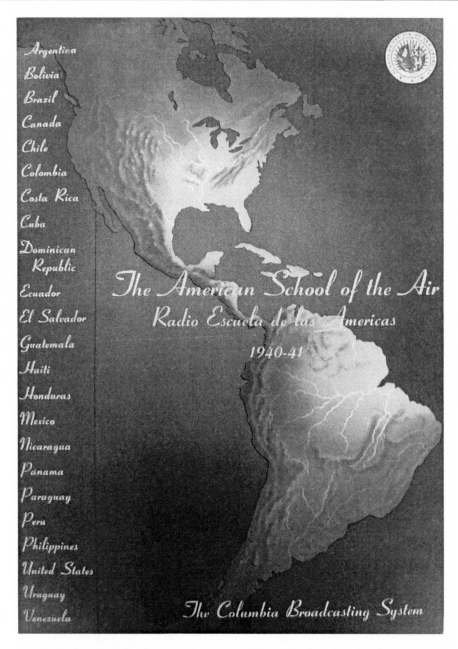

Argentina
Bolivia
Brazil
Canada
Chile
Colombia
Costa Rica
Cuba
Dominican Republic
Ecuador
El Salvador
Guatemala
Haiti
Honduras
Mexico
Nicaragua
Panama
Paraguay
Peru
Philippines
United States
Uruguay
Venezuela

The American School of the Air
Radio Escuela de las Americas
1940-41

The Columbia Broadcasting System

Radio Escuela de las Americas (courtesy, of Columbia Broadcasting System).

CBS print ad that appeared in a national magazine, and an even higher estimate of nearly 10,000,000 listeners appeared in the *New York Times*. Those numbers, Reid asserted, were ridiculous (Reid, 1941a, 1941c). CBS's estimates and the public debunking are discussed extensively by Cuban (1986), who used them to support his claims that teachers never accepted radio in the classroom.

Based on the results of their mail survey study, I. Keith Tyler estimated the combined audience of regular listeners for CBS and NBC network SOA broadcasts at a little more than 2 million, and even that number might have included some duplication of students who listened to two or more series (Reid, 1941a). Of those 2 million listeners, approximately 600,000 listened to

NBC's Damrosch *Music Appreciation Hour*, and the remaining 1.46 million to various ASA programs. The audience estimates for the five ASA programs are shown in Table 7.

TABLE 7. ESTIMATES OF THE CLASSROOM AUDIENCE FOR ASA BROADCASTS, 1940
(Reid, 1941a)

Course	Audience
Frontiers of Democracy	210,000
Folk Music of America	330,000
New Horizons	330,000
Tales from Far and Near	400,000
This Living World	195,000

According to the data, in 1940 1,465,000 students listened regularly to at least one ASA program, and that number represented between 5 percent and 6 percent of the nation's schoolchildren, kindergarten through 12th grade. Tyler states that although the ASA's actual audience size was substantially smaller than the boasts of network executives, it still represented a sizable portion of America's schoolchildren and clearly constituted the country's largest single educational institution (Reid, 1941a).

Another ESB project study conducted by Reid appraised the educational value of the ASA's most popular program, *Tales from Far and Near.* With an eye to building its new image as the *School of the Air of the Americas*, CBS described the series as radio adaptations of modern children's stories of the Americas. The broad target audience included students in the fourth through the ninth grades (Reid, 1941c). The study's goal, according to Reid, was to provide CBS executives and interested educators with timely information on teacher reactions to the broadcasts in three criteria: (1) educational value, (2) clarity and comprehensibility, and (3) audience appeal. The study consisted of recruiting a panel of cooperating teachers; collecting, interpreting, and summarizing their judgments and opinions regarding the full semester of 25 broadcasts; and distributing the results to the interested parties. Study results were presented in each of the three criteria areas.

Criterion number one: educational value. Researchers provided the panel with four questions for evaluating the broadcasts' educational value:

1. Did the broadcasts contribute to increased appreciation of radio drama as a unique form of literature?
2. Did the broadcasts contribute to educational experiences that you could not provide in the classroom?
3. Did the broadcasts avoid undesirable social concepts, race stereotypes, and human prejudice?
4. Did the broadcasts stimulate listeners to desirable educational activities? (Reid, 1941c)

According to Reid's summary, the panel gave qualified approval to the series overall but complained that individual programs fluctuated widely in educational value. Some of the programs were judged to be too mature for younger students in the stated target audience.[38] According to the panel, fourth, fifth, and sixth graders struggled to understand the vocabulary and the story line.

Criterion number two: clarity and comprehensibility. Again the panel gave only qualified support to the series, for the same reason as cited in criterion number one. The maturity level of some programs was felt to be too high for lower grades. Other programs were judged unsatisfactory because they consisted of too many short episodes and failed to develop sufficient interest in character or plot. Reid concluded that this problem resulted from the radio writer's desire to cram long stories into half-hour formats (Reid, 1941c).

---

[38]Part of the problem derived from ASA's assertion that the series was suitable for a very broad range of students from 4th through 12th grades. Apparently, it was more suitable for older students.

Criterion number three: audience appeal. Seventeen of the twenty-five broadcasts were enjoyed by the students, and eight were not. Reid noted a clear positive relationship between high ratings for educational value and student enjoyment. Generally, teachers stressed that compared to narration, dramatization had a strong appeal and offered higher educational values.

Despite these specific criticisms, which made the series "less valuable and enjoyable than they otherwise might have been" (Reid, 1941c, p. 35), Reid acknowledged that a substantial majority of the participating teachers attested to the educational value of using *Tales from Near and Far* in their classrooms as an enrichment and supplement to reading (Reid, 1941c). Reid, however, provides 20 recommendations for improving the series. The most significant urged ASA administrators to first set clear educational objectives and then select only programs that met those objectives. Others urged careful matching of broadcasts to the audience maturity levels, use of drama over narration, and logical sequencing of presentations. Unfortunately, Reid provides no information about how CBS and ASA executives responded to the reports of teachers' evaluations or researchers' recommendations.

Another college-based researcher studied the educational broadcasts of both NBC and CBS, including the ASA. Winfred Bird, a speech instructor at the University of Washington, established a set of 14 criteria for evaluating SOA programs. These are listed in Table 8.

TABLE 8. CRITERIA FOR JUDGING EDUCATIONAL MERIT OF PROGRAMS

1. Has educationally significant subject matter
2. Captures the immediate interest of the listener
3. Has a unified theme
4. Is consistent with the established political and social order
5. Provides strong motivation to the listener
6. Is available at a suitable hour for classroom use
7. Does not take the place of the teacher
8. Has clearly defined educational areas
9. Provides for student participation or appreciation
10. Is authoritative
11. Does a unique educational job
12. Is related to the school curriculum
13. Has no advertising
14. Has educationally measurable results (Bird, 1939)

While Bird's list represents an admirable collection of qualitative criteria, it also demonstrates the complexity associated with evaluating any broad educational effort. Some of the criteria — 1, 3, 10, and 11, for example — seem highly subjective. Other criteria such as numbers 2, 6, and 9 do seem objectively observable. Bird gives no information as to how the criteria were applied and interpreted or who did so. Presumably, he did it all.

Based on his analysis and criteria, Bird's (1939) overall conclusions about several programs sound reasonable. He found ASA programs in current events, literature, and music to be highly successful educationally. He praised their content selection and blending of narrative and dramatic techniques. In his analysis of the geography and the elementary science series, Bird offered one of the few critiques of instructional methods found in the radio literature. He said that due to over reliance on dramatization of inherently expository material, many programs in the series "lacked reality" (p. 48). By that he meant that the programs often sacrificed educational rigor for entertainment value. At the bottom of his effectiveness list, Bird placed the series on vocational guidance. The problem, he felt, was that the subject is inherently personal and requires customization to individual needs, and that could not be done on air (Bird, 1939).

Overall, the evaluations performed by Reid and Bird seem to support the CBS contention that the ASA contributed substantially to American education for those who tuned in by supplementing and enriching classroom instruction. In another study covering network school broadcasts, Reid characterized ASA programs as, "excellent, educationally worth while, clearly understandable, and highly enjoyable" (Reid, 1941b, p. 1). Even though the number of regular student listeners fell short of their claims, still CBS executives could have boasted that ASA broadcasts were heard by the largest schoolroom ever assembled in America.

Demise

The year 1942 was a turning point for network-sponsored SOAs. In the year that Walter Damrosch retired, effectively ending broadcasts of his popular MAH series, an ominous event signaled change for the ASA also. Director Fisher "transferred his allegiance [from CBS] to NBC," where he took on the responsibility of organizing NBC's Inter-American University of the Air (Atkinson, 1942b, p. 14). Atkinson comments on the possible reason behind this move: "In those playful little interchanges of executives among networks, NBC undoubtedly acquired from its rival the man [Fisher] most capable of approaching Latin America with an educational service that eventually would lead to sizeable commercial profits" (Atkinson, 1942b, p. 17).

Fisher's replacement at CBS was Lyman Bryson, a man whom Atkinson (1942a) believed to be more interested in using radio for adult education than for classroom education. The change was discouraging. In 1938, Fisher had infused new life into the ASA with the idea of making it an international educational broadcaster to the schools, but by 1942, he was replaced with someone whose interests lay elsewhere. Bryson was described as being "so adult-educational conscious that he may neglect the broadcasting to classrooms" (Atkinson, 1942b, p. 14). The change of director may explain what happened next. Starting in 1945, CBS decided to offer the ASA only as an after-school program, broadcasting from 5:00 to 5:30 P.M. eastern standard time (Summers, 1958). This time slot effectively ended ASA's service to the schools.[39]

During the next three years, CBS continued broadcasting ASA programs five days a week at the new time. In 1945, the network issued a 200-page manual that served as program schedule and teacher guide. In it, CBS interim President Paul Kesten[40] maintained an upbeat tone, expressing the hope that the late-afternoon broadcasts would enable parents and children in many parts of the country to "listen and learn together," and that the programs might become a regular part of family listening. He further asserted that listening to broadcasts that educate and entertain was becoming a national cultural pattern (ASA, 1945, p. 4). Lyman Bryson, CBS' director of education, also attempted to explain and rationalize the ominous time change. He candidly cited three motives: the impossibility of broadcasting ASA programs at a time that fits all school schedules, the obsolescence of classroom radio equipment, and the rapid growth of FM stations. (FM was being used increasingly by local school boards to broadcast SOAs that could be adapted to the local curriculum.)[41] He ends on an upbeat but unconvincing note saying that at the new time, the ASA could reach more schoolchildren out of their classrooms than in them (ASA, 1945). William C. Bagley, the original dean of the school, now sporting the title of chairman, CBS National Board of Consultants, provides still another rationale that combines a note of concern with false hope: "In the judgment of the present writer, who has had the good fortune to be associated with the ASA since the preparation of its first programs, the new hour, while representing a now-necessary change in the purpose as originally

[39]Broadcasting at 5:00 pm Eastern time, ASA programs reached only schools in the Pacific time zone during school hours.

[40]During the war years, in Paley's absence, Kesten served as president of CBS.

[41]In 1940, the FCC announced that educational stations would be given exclusive rights to develop part of the new FM band that was authorized to begin operations in 1941 (McChesney, 1993).

conceived, will in no way diminish the significance of the School of the Air; rather by broadening its scope, it may well enhance its influence for good" (Bagley in ASA, 1945, p. 1).

Twenty years earlier, Armstrong Perry had expressed concern about the wisdom of developing SOAs dependent on commercial broadcasters. The resources offered by commercial broadcasters, he believed, would be bound to commercial considerations, and eventually, all the available airtime would be sold to advertisers (McChesney, 1993). While his concerns seemed well founded, the ASA did broadcast successfully for 15 years as America's only national school of the air. In its time, many ASA programs were heralded as educational gems.

Why did CBS change the broadcast time and then terminate the ASA? Perhaps NBC's decision to abandon school broadcasts in 1942 was a causal factor. Because competition with NBC had always been a chief motive for starting and continuing the ASA, the end of that competition might well have reduced the importance of the ASA in the eyes of CBS executives. Another reason might have been that the public's expectations for radio had changed. Compared to the late 1920s, postwar America was a much different society, and those differences were reflected in the public attitude toward radio. In the late 1920s, as Keith noted, idealism about the new medium's potential had burned brightly. "When broadcasting first made its appearance, ... it was looked upon by socially minded people as the greatest emancipator of the intellect since the invention of printing" (Keith, 1934, p. 9). People then expected the new medium to become a force for uplifting culture, extending education, and stimulating involvement in civic life (Carpini, 1995). Clearly, by the late 1940s, the flame of idealism was nearly extinguished. In the postwar era, entertainment was accepted as the norm and major purpose of broadcasting. Not surprisingly, commercialism had triumphed over idealism.

Nothing demonstrates that triumph better than Paley's own thoughts on the period following the war when he returned to the network's helm. In his reflection on CBS's situation and prospects, Paley (1979) complained that despite its accolades and financial strength, compared to NBC, his network remained "a poor second" in ratings and advertising revenue (p. 173). His goal of overcoming NBC and making CBS the country's premier network had remained unfulfilled. Shortly after V-E day, 1945, CBS Vice President Paul Kesten outlined a strategy for the future of CBS. Paley recalls:

In essence he [Kesten] proposed turning CBS from a mass medium into an elite network, beamed at ten or perhaps 15 million homes rather than 30 million. He wanted CBS to become "the one network that never offends with over-commercialism, in content, in quantity or in tone, that presents superb and sparkling entertainment ... [and] an important forum for great public figures and great public issues, for education, for thoughtful and challenging presentation of the news and issues growing out of it.

"Bill, [said Kesten] I've merely expressed briefly the things we've told ourselves we've been — or wanted to be — these many years" [Paley, 1979, p. 173].

Paley castigated Kesten's ideas for "giving up the fight against NBC" and for advocating a small, specialized network of dubious potential. "His was not the answer I sought" (Paley, 1979, p. 173). Paley goes on to say that he had always seen radio as a mass medium, and that meant fulfilling the majority's taste for popular entertainment. Given Paley's vision, and a market environment where all daytime could be sold to advertisers, it is hard to see where the ASA could fit in. The ASA programs were aired for the final time in May of 1948 (Summers, 1958).

A more cynical rendition of why CBS cancelled what was hailed to the end as the best example of commercial radio operating in the public interest can be found in Robert Metz's book, *CBS: Reflections in a Blood Shot Eye.* Metz says that near the end of the war, CBS executives were looking for ways to pump up advertising revenue required to develop television. A little known disc-jockey from Washington D.C. asked the network for the time period with the lowest rating so he could prove that he was a personality that could bring in advertising dollars. CBS agreed. They cancelled the award winning American School of the Air which of course brought in no advertising dollars and replaced it with a man named Arthur Godfrey, whose show soon became a CBS power house drawing many big named advertisers and many new station affiliates to the network (Metz, 1975).

ASA Summary

Given that its origin was driven chiefly by the objectives of commerce, public relations, and Paley's ambitions, it is surprising that the ASA endured for 18 years and achieved notable results. From 1930 to 1948, the ASA served as a unique national educational resource regularly reaching students in nearly 50,000 American classrooms.[42] It received official recognition from 11 state school boards, the NEA, and the nation's Catholic school system. At the beginning, Director Alice Keith and Dean William Bagley established a traditional subject-oriented curriculum that featured literature, geography, history, music, and art appreciation, all of which apparently appealed to many teachers and principals. Meanwhile, Paley used the school as a tool for competing with rival NBC and as a means of foiling the movement that advocated a government set-aside of radio channels for education (Paley, 1934). Following Keith's forced departure in 1932, caretaker directors changed little over the next four years, offering only a few new programs, in science and folk music. During the mid–1930s, under Edward R. Murrow's tenure as the CBS director of education, the school seemed to lose direction, perhaps because Murrow's time was divided among several responsibilities and CBS executives were focused on the brewing conflict (World War II) in Europe.

However, in the late 1930s, the ASA received a shot in arm when CBS retooled the ASA as a competitive weapon in the network's battle to counter NBC's Latin-American initiative. The new director, Sterling Fisher, revamped the curriculum. Moving away from Bagley's traditional subject matter, Fisher developed an interdisciplinary, problem-based, learner-centered curriculum with a contemporary appeal, stressing issues of democracy, the living roots of folk music, popular science, and literature with a contemporary appeal. As a result of Fisher's work and the influx of resources and attention from CBS executives, the ASA thrived, receiving official recognition from many educational organizations.

World War II, however, brought yet another puzzling change in focus. Despite Fisher's accomplishments, he abruptly departed the ASA. Then, as the war neared its end, the ASA ceased broadcasting to the classroom.

Among those associated with the ASA and involved in serious evaluation of its programs, there exists a sense of genuine satisfaction tempered with disappointment. Satisfaction came from the realization that the ASA was truly a national school of the air that counted one and half million regular listeners among America's schoolchildren. But disappointment arose because the programs reached only about 5.5 percent of the potential national audience. There was pride in the production and airing of quality programs, but disappointment in the realization that intended benefits were not being appreciated by all of the listening audience. The causes of these disappointments are suggested in the conclusions stated in Bird's and Reid's research, which point to several fundamental problems with the ASA:

1) Overemphasis on content and traditional subjects saddled the ASA with a prep school curriculum that may have been inappropriate for the broader American student body. As a result, the ASA curriculum tilted extremely toward junior and high school grades, neglecting elementary students. By 1940, it was clear that educational radio appealed more to elementary students and their teachers than to high school students.
2) The school's advisory faculty was overloaded with university academics, while the school's staff of writers and producers lacked teaching experience. As a consequence, the school suffered from the absence of people experienced in primary and secondary pedagogy.

---

[42]One and a half million students divided by an average of 30 students per classroom (Reid, 1941a).

3) ASA administrators failed to articulate appropriate educational objectives and grade levels for specific programs. They billed programs as being appropriate for wide grade ranges—for 9-year-old fourth graders to 18-year-old twelfth graders. As a result, many teachers judged even the best ASA programs as inappropriate for their younger students.

When CBS pulled the plug on the ASA, it ended a unique or at least unusual marriage between commercial interests and public need. Its achievements were significant and should be neither ignored nor underrated. No other commercial broadcast organization in the United States ever again attempted such an ambitious educational effort.

But, those very commercial roots—CBS's not-so-hidden agenda to use the ASA as a weapon in its competitive battle with NBC—may in fact be the deeper reason why the ASA failed to reach its potential. Could it be that if an educational institution backed by adequate resources had developed the ASA, as Armstrong Perry and others in the NSoA movement had hoped, then perhaps the ASA would have evolved in a way that classroom teachers would have found not just nice, but necessary? This question informs the next section of this study, which presents the history of the state-sanctioned radio schools of the air, starting with the Ohio School of the Air.

Summary: Network Schools of the Air

As the movement to establish a publicly supported radio school of the air grew, managers of the newly established private radio networks, NBC and CBS, saw benefit in broadcasting to the schools. NBC executives were persuaded by the ebullient Damrosch to launch the *Music Appreciation Hour* (MAH) while CBS's Paley drove the development of the *American School of the Air* (ASA). The national scope of each network and their focused marketing campaigns enabled them to quickly gain the attention and approval of educators across the nation. Yet both developed in markedly different ways. Table 9 summarizes the operations of the network SOAs. Following that are brief discussions of the highlights.

TABLE 9. SUMMARY OF FINDINGS: NETWORK SCHOOLS OF THE AIR

FINDINGS	MAH	ASA
Longevity (Approx)	14 years 1928–1942	15 years 1930–1945 (1945–1948 as an after school program)
Major Personalities	Walter Damrosch, founder and director 1928–1942	William Paley, president CBS Directors: Alice Keith, Helen Johnson, Edward R. Murrow, Sterling Fisher, and Lyman Bryson Dean of Faculty Advisors, William C. Bagley
Supporting Institutions	National Broadcasting Company (NBC)	Columbia Broadcasting System (CBS)
Broadcast Facility	NBC's national network of over 100 stations NBC provides studio orchestra	CBS's national network CBS provides administrative staff, script writers and educational consultants
Educational Philosophy	Affective learning before cognitive learning Classroom teacher plays crucial role Subject matter is paramount	First decade, Bagley's Essentialism guided the ASA: education resulted from powerful teaching and stress on the academic discipline Last five years, programming become more learner centered with focus on arts, culture and current affairs

	NBC:	CBS:
School Goals	Maintain network's positive public image Demonstrate network's intention to provide quality educational service Market the use of radio **Damrosch:** Develop appreciation and involvement in classical music throughout U.S.	Maintain network's positive public image Demonstrate network's ability to provide quality educational service Prestige for network Gain competitive advantage over NBC **ASA:** Enrich school curricula with quality programs in a variety of subject areas
Instruction Methods	5 step instructional process: greetings, recall, preview, demonstration, presentation	No specific pedagogy Drama, discussion, dialogue
Support Materials	Teacher manuals and student guides for all programs	Annual catalog and schedule of program series which included mini-teacher guides Student guides for a few programs
Audience — % of Potential Universe	600,000 regular listeners approximately 2.15% of the nation's school population, K–12, 1950 Audience data developed by Reid and Tyler based at The OSU's Evaluation of School Broadcasts project	1.5 million regular listeners, approximately 5.5% of the nation's school population, K–12 Audience data developed by Reid and Tyler based at The OSU's Evaluation of School Broadcasts project
Evaluations and Surveys Conducted	Major study conducted by Reid at OSU's Evaluation of School Broadcast project Findings: MAH lessons increased student appreciation of music and learning readiness, but compared to non-radio instruction produced no significant improvement in learning program objectives	Several major studies of ASA programs conducted by Reid at OSU's Evaluation of School Broadcast project Findings: *Tales from Far and Near* was found to provide "qualified" educational value by: (1) increasing appreciation of radio drama, (2) contributing to an educational experience, (3) avoiding undesirable social and racial stereotypes, (4) stimulating desirable educational activities
Impact	Increased awareness of and appreciation for European classical music Served as a model for teaching music and for using radio to teach music	Seems to have left little documented evidence of its impact on education at the national level

Demise	Immediate reason: NBC forced to sell the Blue network. New owners were unwilling to donate a full hour to the program Deeper reasons: (1) the public no longer demanded that networks provide educational programming; (2) daytime became more valuable	Public no longer demanded that networks provide educational programming Set aside of FM channels for education undercut the need for network SOAs Need to maximize profits in order to fund the networks' move to television

Within just a few years of starting operations, the major broadcast networks launched radio schools of the air; both operated continually for approximately 15 years. The networks acted out of similar motivations, which included a mix of public relations, product marketing, and political maneuvering. Despite their mostly commercial motivation, the networks applied radio to education successfully and captured the attention of educators nation-wide, drawing mostly praise and admiration. Even though Woelfel and Tyler (1945) described their efforts as modest endeavors, NBC and CBS succeeded in doing what Darrow, Perry, the Payne Fund and many others educators could not, namely they built national schools of the air (Woelfel and Tyler 1945).

Each network developed a different approach to the use of radio in education. NBC's *Music Appreciation Hour* (MAH) relied on the gifted master teacher, Walter Damrosch, who selected and organized the lessons and presented them using his proven instructional approach. Damrosch's charisma and passion accounted for the series' popularity. The ASA on the other hand never highlighted radio teachers; consequently no radio "stars" emerged. For the first decade, the ASA followed a staid instructional approach guided chiefly by Bagley's Essentialism and perhaps resulting from the dismissal of Alice Keith as school director. During its early years, Keith had been the only full-time staff person who could boast a background in education and radio instruction. Not until the late 1930s did another educator, Sterling Fisher, assume control of the school. Fisher transformed the ASA pedagogy from Bagley's Essentialism to a more contemporary, learner centered approach that highlighted the contributions of global culture and American folklore, music and history to contemporary life.

Both CBS and NBC claimed many millions of regular listeners, gross exaggerations that frequently went unquestioned by the media and even by scholars who followed educational radio. However, reliable research carried out by university-based scholars determined that the two SOAs reached a regular audience of two million, approximately 7 percent of the nation's school children. The discrepancy between network claims and research findings was often cited as indirect evidence that the SOA movement failed or was irrelevant to American education. However Woelfel and Tyler (1945) expressed ambivalence over the results of these audience studies—should they be disappointed that more students did not tune in or pleased that several millions of students did?

University based researchers also studied the educational effectiveness of several network instruction series compared to traditional classroom instruction unsupported by radio. These studies usually uncovered no significant differences (NSD), a finding replicated many times in subsequent media comparison studies.

Gauging the impact of the ASA on education and culture proved difficult as few scholars or writers have commented. The situation is quite different for the MAH; its impact on music education and the use of technology in education continued to be discussed at least until the early

1980s. The consensus is that Damrosch's 15 years of music appreciation broadcasts had at least three major impacts, (1) it served as a teacher training series for thousands of music teachers, (2) it set the standard for music appreciation and theory instruction by radio, and (3) it stimulated interest in European classical music for at least a generation.

The demise of both network SOAs by the mid 1940s proved the validity of Armstrong Perry's prescient prediction made in 1929 that when commercial broadcasters could sell their day time to advertisers, they would cease supporting their schools of the air. However, the networks made American educators aware of radio educational potential and stimulated SOA development at the state and local levels.

SECTION III

State-Based Schools of the Air

While the networks operated national schools of the air (SOAs), educators at the state level forged ahead with the development of SOAs that could offer programming more in tune with the educational needs and preferences of their students. According to the top scholars of educational radio[1] at that time, successful state-based schools of the air (SOAs) arose in Ohio, Wisconsin, Texas, Oregon, and Minnesota (Woelfel and Tyler, 1945). A sixth, New York's Empire State FM School of the Air, began operation in 1948. All the state-based SOAs operated for periods much longer than did the networks. At least one powerfully affected education in its state, others paved the way for educational television, and all helped build acceptance of educational technology of any form in the classroom. While none of the state-based schools could offer the rich production values of the networks, most offered their listeners valuable educational resources, and one far exceeded the network efforts. State-based SOAs shared common characteristics, namely, they received support primarily from state universities, they broadcast over state owned radio facilities, and all but one chiefly served the needs of rural students. What's surprising is how different their stories are.

Broadcasting for the schools had received a shot in the arm when the Federal Communications Commission (FCC) allocated part of the FM radio band for educational use. Several states such as Indiana, Minnesota, Texas, Wisconsin and New York set up comprehensive state FM radio networks (Saettler, 1990). Wisconsin and Minnesota used their FM systems to build popular schools of the air.

The existing documentation allow us to tell the rich and complex stories of the Wisconsin and Ohio SOAs and moderately full stories with some gaps for Minnesota, New York, Texas and Oregon. Missing from the stories of Texas, New York, Oregon and Minnesota are the personal stories of leaders, radio teachers, and organizations. Nevertheless, enough data exist to confirm that they all made important contributions to education by radio and the educational culture of their states. Finally in this section you find a brief treatment of WLS's School Time, a curiosity, the only commercially run regional SOA.

This section focuses on uncovering the origins of the state-based SOAs and their operations and struggles particularly after 1950 when instructional television appeared on the scene and government agencies and foundations lost interest in funding research in educational radio. Though incomplete, the data show that after 1950, instead of withering, SOAs at the state level experienced some of their most remarkable growth.

---

[1]Norman Woelfel and I. Keith Tyler ran the federally funded Evaluation of Educational Broadcast Project located at The Ohio State University.

Ohio School of the Air

It is not surprising that the Ohio School of the Air (OSA) quickly became the nation's show-case for educational broadcasting to the schools, K through 12. The states, not the federal government, were the logical home base for new educational endeavors. As proponents of a national school of the air (NSoA) had discovered, the U.S. federal government played no significant role in education (Perry, 1929, p. 41). Unlike governments in Europe that exercised near proprietary control over the new medium, the U.S. government had rejected any ownership position in radio, and though it regulated broadcasting, as of 1930, the government put no pressure on radio station owners to provide educational programming. The states, on the other hand, bore primary legal responsibility for funding and controlling American education. Furthermore, because many state universities had jumped into radio early on, a number of them operated radio stations that could provide fledgling SOAs with a nurturing home.

In 1929, several months after the OSA went on the air, it received support from the Ohio state legislature and educational bureaucracy. Within a year, approximately 100,000 students in Ohio and nearby states were listening regularly to the OSA programs. "That success and resulting national publicity crystallized radio's possibilities in education" throughout the nation (Taylor, 1974, p. 96). Under Ben Darrow's direction, the OSA initiated and refined instructional methods for education by radio and set the pattern that would be duplicated and refined by SOAs at all levels. The OSA also became a prime example of the perils that threaten attempts at experimentation in America's fragmented and politically charged educational system.

Darrow's Experiment

Early in 1928, as hope for a national school of the air (NSoA) faded, Ben Darrow told Armstrong Perry that he was interested in creating an experimental effort in Ohio, a plan that fit well with the Payne Fund's goal of starting SOA demonstration projects (McChesney, 1993; Taylor, 1974). Earlier, the Payne Fund had sponsored a national study among educators to determine their level of interest in education by radio. The study discovered that educators at the local level were eager to equip their classes with radios as soon as appropriate programming became available. Overall, the results pointed to substantial support for educational radio (Perry, 1929, pp. 11–12.). With these facts in hand, Darrow introduced his idea for an Ohio-based experimental radio school of the air to Dr. John Clifton, director of the Ohio Department of Education.

An early backer of the NSoA effort,[2] Clifton expressed support for the Ohio experiment but cautioned that he could offer neither radio facilities nor funds for staff. Darrow relates this event in his typical folksy way: "It was a repetition of that old saw 'If I had some ham, I'd have ham and eggs, if I had some eggs'" (Darrow, 1940, p. 11). Obviously, Darrow had some eggs up his sleeve. He soon returned to Clifton with a promise from the Payne Fund to provide money for his (Darrow's) salary and administrative expenses until such time as the Ohio state legislature either provided or refused funds.[3] In return, Payne asked the state to provide offices and administrative staff and take responsibility for (1) determining the course of study, (2) gaining acceptance from Ohio's schools, and (3) enlisting the talent for planning and presenting the broadcasts.

To show his enthusiasm, Clifton named Darrow the Director of Radio for the State of Ohio, probably the first such title in the United States (Taylor, 1974). Clifton then used his influence to gain commitments from other Ohio educators including Dr. Randall Condon, superintendent

---

[2]Secretary of the Interior Ray Lyman appointed Clifton to the committee that would advise the new Federal Radio in Education section of the Department of Education.

[3]According to Darrow, Mrs. Bolton, whose fortune financed the Payne Fund, told Darrow directly, "Go to Dr. Clifton and tell him your salary is paid for this test period" (Darrow, 1940, p. 12).

of schools in Cincinnati; D. E. Lewis, head of the Department of School Administration at The Ohio State University (The OSU); and Dr. W. Charters, head of the Bureau of Educational Research of The OSU. All proved helpful to the effort (Perry, 1929).

Broadcast Facility

At that point Darrow's plan was coming together nicely, but it still lacked one crucial element, a broadcast facility. Apparently, Darrow planned early on to originate programming from The OSU's college station, WEAO[4] in Columbus, and transmit the signal by long-distance lines to a commercial station in either Cleveland or Cincinnati. This arrangement was necessary because at only 5,000 watts, the college station's signal had limited range, and Darrow wanted to reach students in all of Ohio (Taylor, 1974). His optimistic plan also called for the long-distance lines and broadcast facilities to be donated. Fortunately, a small commercial station in Columbus, WAIU, agreed to carry the broadcasts gratis, if the FCC would permit the station to increase its transmitting power 10-fold in order to reach schools throughout Ohio. The offer heartened Darrow; his goal was in sight. But barely a month later the picture clouded. WAIU pulled out of the deal because the FCC refused to grant the station permission to increase its transmitting power (Darrow, 1940). With only two months to go, Darrow had no way to make his school heard statewide.

Dr. Condon saved the day. He approached Powell Crosley Jr., owner of WLW in Cincinnati, the most powerful station in the nation. When Crosley welcomed the school of the air,[5] Darrow rejoiced. WLW's half million watts of power[6] meant that the OSA broadcasts could be heard during daytime hours not only throughout Ohio but in parts of nine other states as well (Perry, 1929, p. 12; Taylor, 1974, p. 82).

Darrow reflected on how frequently and unpredictably the scope of his program changed. First he had envisioned a nation wide educational effort. That vision was trimmed down to a state-wide program, and then reduced further to only central Ohio. When WLW came on board, the scope expanded again to all the central states. "Such are the vicissitudes of promoting" (Darrow, 1940, pp. 13–14).

Now the OSA programs could originate in The OSU's Columbus studio or from WLW's Cincinnati studio, but that raised another problem. AT&T refused to donate the long-distance lines. That meant that Darrow needed several thousand dollars annually to pay the long-distance charges required to connect The OSU station in Columbus with WLW in Cincinnati. He succeeded quickly in his classic way by what he called "panhandling." He personally appealed for donations from dozens of groups and individuals sympathetic to educational radio. By early December of 1928, all the building blocks were in place (Taylor, 1974).

Darrow had never specified whether the OSA programs should be focused on city or rural students, but he anticipated that 1,000 of Ohio's 9,000 schools were radio equipped. From that number, he calculated that the OSA's first broadcasts could be heard by as many as 200,000 students, or roughly 20 percent of Ohio's schoolchildren, easily the largest classroom ever assembled in America up to that time (Taylor, 1974). That estimate is unsupported because Darrow gives no indication of the size of the radio-equipped schools. Obviously, school enrollments varied from a few dozen students in one-room rural schools to several thousand in large urban

---

[4]Later, in the 1940s, the call letters became WOSU.

[5]At this point in radio's development, manufacturers of receiver sets saw educational radio as a marketing tool for promoting the sale of hardware, just as manufacturers of computers do today.

[6]By a fluke and with clever lobbying, Crosley's WLW was allowed to broadcast at 500,000 watts, 10 times the power of the other clear channel stations. The extra power enabled WLW to charge advertisers substantially more than competing stations did. Crosley's extraordinary exception was terminated by the FCC in 1939 (Barnouw, 1968).

schools. At any rate, Darrow had little time to worry about the audience. The first broadcast was scheduled for January 7, 1929. Time was short, and, unfortunately, Darrow had done little to develop the educational programs or select teachers (Taylor, 1974). Would he be ready in time?

Teacher Selection

The Payne survey results had already identified the kinds of programs that school leaders wanted, but to develop effective educational programs required good radio teachers who could develop and deliver instruction. Not surprisingly, Darrow selected the broadcast teachers himself. Though he said that he had sought the advice of "many leading educators," he named none. As one of the few in the country with a background in educational radio, Darrow undoubtedly knew a good radio teacher when he heard one. He interviewed all candidates and made his selections based on "personality and voice" (Darrow, 1940, p. 18), but he did not explain what qualities of personality and voice he sought; nor did he make any reference to the candidates' ideas about or experience in education. Instead, he said that radio teachers should project a sense of spontaneity and immediacy (Darrow, 1940). As it turned out, all the selected radio teachers were either experienced teachers from urban Ohio schools or professors affiliated with The OSU.

Darrow (1940) did explain his training methods. He said that he asked one teacher who seemed overly self-conscious to "forget everybody but the listening child, to speak directly to him with all of the little railleries and good humor that would be used with a single group of children in a classroom" (p. 44). To help achieve this state of direct talk, Darrow encouraged his radio teachers to shut their eyes and imagine a classroom of children (Darrow, 1940).

When the big day arrived, excitement filled the radio studio at The Ohio State University. Darrow describes what must have been a fulfilling moment for him. At exactly 1:30 P.M. the organist at WLW began playing "America the Beautiful" and a chorus of tens of thousands of children across Ohio sang along (Darrow, 1940). Next, Darrow introduced Dr. Clifton, who welcomed the radio audience to what was then a momentous experiment in education. After Clifton, Dr. Condon, superintendent of Cincinnati schools, explained that now great minds of the period would speak directly to students in the classroom. He also reassured teachers that radio would supplement, not supplant, their work (Taylor, 1974). Then the first lesson was broadcast. A decade later, Darrow proudly asserted that on that day an audience of 50,000 students listened in (Darrow, 1940, p.19).

A Good Start

The OSA was off to a good start, broadcasting a full hour of programs daily to at least 50,000 student listeners. The effort stimulated thousands of encouraging letters from every state in the union and from many foreign lands (Darrow, 1940). Darrow summed up his thoughts about the first month of operations: "The first period had proved that a School of the Air was feasible — that schools, colleges, libraries, magazines, schools of drama theatres and radio stations could furnish broadcasting teachers of worth — that schools could and would equip to hear the broadcasts — that teachers and pupils received added benefits from the introduction of radio. The big unanswered question was 'Will the State of Ohio provide funds?'" (Darrow, 1940, p 30).

The answer came quickly. In April of the demonstration semester, the Ohio legislature appropriated $40,000 to cover two years of operation for the OSA, or $20,000 per year.[7] Of this amount, $7,800 went for salaries, $5,000 for telephone lines to connect the OSU broadcasting studio with transmitting stations, and $7,200 for speakers and musicians. Smaller administrative costs such as postage were covered by the OSU department of education. Darrow valued the

---

[7]$20,000 in 1929 dollars was equivalent to approximately $225,000 in 2005 dollars (Sahr, 2005).

WLW donated airtime at $60,000 annually and estimated that another $10,000 would have been necessary to pay the teachers if they had not donated their time (Perry, 1929). All in all, SOA's total annual budget including state funds, the estimated value of donated airtime, and teachers' time came to $90,000. Darrow and the Payne Fund were pleased. A radio school of the air with public financial support was a reality.

THE *COURIER*

Darrow admitted one significant mistake during the first semester of operation. His failure to distribute what he called "lesson leaflets" beforehand made it impossible for teachers to prepare for the lessons adequately, and that undercut educational effectiveness. Most likely, during that first semester, many teachers had no idea what programs were to be broadcast or when. Darrow claimed that the oversight was compensated for to some degree by the widespread publicity that the school received in the daily press and periodicals. Also, the backing of the Ohio Department of Education encouraged school teachers and administrators to take the broadcasts seriously (Darrow, 1940).

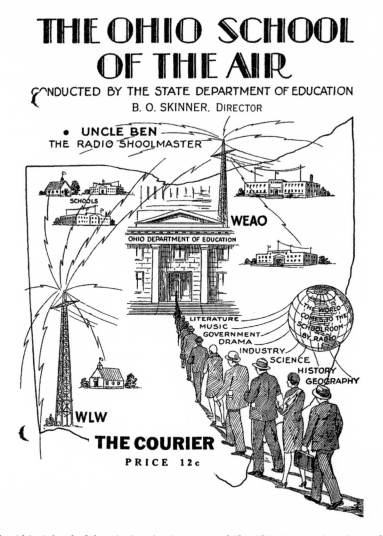

The Ohio School of the Air Courier (courtesy of The Ohio State University Archive).

Darrow made up for his mistake in September of 1929 by issuing an impressive monthly program guide called the *Ohio School of the Air Courier*. The *Courier* was intended as a combined teachers manual, program announcement, and newsletter, and editor Cline Koon packed the publication with program schedules and descriptions, teacher profiles, follow-up study questions, illustrations, references, suggested readings, numerous ideas for pre- and post broadcast activities, news about the school, and hints for how to get the best radio reception in the classroom. The publication was distributed monthly, free to all principals and teachers who showed interest in the radio lessons, though Darrow provided no detail on how these recipients were identified. Significantly, the *Courier* was clearly identified as a publication of the (Ohio) State Department of Education.

Educational Programs

In their curriculum, Darrow and his staff attempted to tailor the programs to the needs of children in different grades from kindergarten through 12th. The schedule for fall 1929 included the foundation offerings that were continued for years as shown in Table 10.

TABLE 10. OSA PROGRAM SCHEDULE, FALL 1929
(Darrow, 1940; Taylor, 1974)

Day	Time	Course	Grades*
Monday	2:00–2:20	*Current Events* by Harrison Sayre	6–8, high school
	2:20–2:40	*Out to Old Aunt Mary's*	K–6
	2:40–3:00	*Story Plays and Rhythmics*	K–3
Tuesday	2:00–2:20	*Chemistry* and *French*, alternating	High school
	2:20–2:40	*History Dramalog* by the OSA Players	6–8, high school
	2:40–3:00	*The Constitution of the United States or Citizenship*	6–8 and high school
Wednesday	2:00–2:40	*Literature by Living Writers*	6–8, high school
	2:40–3:00	*Health* by Anna Drake	3–8
Thursday	2:00–2:20	*Stories for the Primary Grades*	K–3
	2:20–2:40	*Geography of Our Country* by Dr. McConnell	
	2:40–3:00	*Geography of Foreign Lands* by Dr. McConnell	4–8
Friday	2:00–2:30	*Little Red Schoolhouse Course in Music*	K–8
	2:30–3:00	*Drama* by the Stuart-Walker Theatres and the Schuster-Martin School of Drama	6–8, high school

*Grade levels shown in the right column were inferred from course descriptions provided in the *Courier*.

Following are summary descriptions for the OSA programs offered during spring and fall of 1929. They are taken from the *Couriers* (1929 through 1931) and from Taylor, 1974.

Current Events. Teacher Harrison Sayre, managing editor of the publication *Current Events*, described the program not as facts to be learned, but rather "as experiences to be visualized" (*Courier*, 1929, p. A-1). He said that classroom teachers of current events could unify the curriculum by referencing information from many subject areas. He also encouraged teachers to make available a world map for reference during the broadcast (*Courier*, 1929).

Out to Old Aunt Mary's — Nature Study. Designed to help children become better acquainted with country life and the common things typically found in a rural environment, this series introduced the teacher as the Pied Piper and invited the children to be his or her helpers. Helpers were asked to bring to class items to be covered in the next broadcast such as cornstalks, old bees' nests, leaves, and weeds from cultivated fields. The children would hold up these items as they were mentioned in the broadcast (*Courier*, 1929, pp. B1–B3).

Story Plays and Rhythmics. A kind of aerobics for children in kindergarten through third grade, the radio teacher was an enthusiastic physical education teacher from the Dayton public school, Alma Ruhmschussel. She used what Darrow called "direct teaching"[8] to get children doing rhythmic exercises and acting out story plays using simple movements during the broadcast. Darrow (1940) noted with pleasure that the children were able to follow and enjoy the radio teacher's directions with little input from the classroom teacher. He asserts that this program was among the most popular and waxes so euphorically in praise of the teacher that one can appreciate Darrow's skill as a spin doctor as well as the teacher's skill: "Mrs. Ruhmschussel ... succeeded in sending such a pleasing personality through the microphone and into the hearts of the boys and girls that teachers reported the children as looking forward to her visits almost as if she were coming 'in person' ... [her] secret was that her smile was not only on her face, but also in her voice and the listening children felt it" (Darrow, 1940, p. 19).

Chemistry and French, alternating. Darrow describes the chemistry course as a series of talks on specific topics, but he acknowledges that they may have been pitched at too high a level even for Ohio's high school students. The French teacher describes his series as an "experiment to awake and maintain an interest in French languages, but not intended to form a complete course of instruction or to supplement classroom work in competent hands" (*Courier*, 1929, p. D-1). From this vague description it seems that the real intent of the radio French program may have been to stimulate the creation of French programs in schools where none existed.

History Dramalog. This series demonstrated how schools of the air quickly adapted the new medium to education. Dispensing entirely with lecture, these history programs dramatized historical events using student actors from The OSU's drama and speech departments. Scripts were prepared in part by the OSU's English department. Darrow described this method saying that the series infused a "spirit of actuality to history" by having the audience hear voices reenact some of the crucial periods of the nation's history (Darrow, 1940, p. 21). By "actuality," Darrow seems to mean learning that is more closely connected with real life as compared to the artificiality of traditional classroom instruction. The series included titles such as The Hamilton-Burr Duel, the Inauguration of President Hoover, the Boston Tea Party, and the Underground Railroad.

Literature by Living Writers. In this series, Darrow introduced, or perhaps borrowed, an innovation that seemed perfect for radio. Instead of having a learned teacher talk about the literature of the dead masters, he engaged living authors of some reputation to read and speak about their own works. This approach also fit in with Darrow's ideas about using radio to expose students to great minds and master teachers. As news of OSA's accomplishments spread across the nation, Darrow was able to attract prominent literary figures to his microphones, including Carl Sandburg and Hamlin Garland.

Health. Primarily lecture, this series aimed at keeping home, school, and neighborhood as healthful as possible. The *Courier* description also stresses goals such as keeping a healthy mind and preventing accidents.

Stories for the Primary Grades. For the youngest schoolchildren, the series told of playthings, pets, flowers, birds, and birdcalls. Darrow (1940) says that the storyteller, Cincinnati teacher Bessie Gabbard, gained instant favor as the "Story Lady" (p. 24). This series also continued through most of the OSA's rocky history. Storytelling became one of the enduring strengths of

---

[8]According to Darrow, "direct teaching" meant that listening students responded to the radio teacher's instructions during the broadcast instead of just passively listening (Darrow, 1932).

educational radio used by all SOAs in this study for primary and intermediate grades, though seldom for high school.

Geography of Our Country and of Foreign Lands. Consisting of two separate programs aired alternately, the series employed a straight lecture format to take students on tours. The original plan had been to teach geography through travelogues, a form that in addition to geographic facts, included dramatizations and realistic sounds that convey the traveler's sensual impressions. These ideas remained undeveloped due to a lack of funds. Surprisingly, the lecture-only series proved popular with students and teachers alike. Darrow, who always discouraged on-air lectures, attributed the series' popularity to the fact that Dr. McConnell "was an unusually interesting lecturer" (Darrow, 1940, p. 28).

Little Red Schoolhouse Course in Music. This series offered another example of direct instruction. The teacher, "Song Lady" Donezella Boyle, described herself as a "visiting teacher" who presented and demonstrated musical ideas that were to be sung aloud by the students during the broadcast. Boyle encouraged classroom teachers to continue the singing after the broadcast. While the series is described as a supplement to the school's regular musical curriculum, it is also described as being designed for schools that had "the least musical leadership," meaning the thousands of country schools that had little or no music curriculum (*Courier*, 1929, p. H-1).

Drama by the Stuart-Walker Theatres and the Schuster-Martin School of Drama. Aimed at high school students and performed by students of Cincinnati's Schuster-Martin School of Drama, this series provided a high-quality dramatic experience that was greatly appreciated, according to the many letters received by the OSA from pupils, classroom teachers, and "the great audience of home listeners" (Darrow, 1940, p. 27). The series' purpose was to help "establish regional and local theatre and to bring the playhouse close to the real life of America" (*Courier*, 1929, p. I-1). It presented a good example of radio's ability to provide a unique educational resource to classrooms at no cost to the school.

Administration and Staff

After obtaining state funding, the OSA became part of Ohio's educational bureaucracy as a division of the Ohio State Department of Education. Darrow received the title of State Director of Radio and a salary, the first since his days as schoolmaster of the Little Red Schoolhouse in Chicago (Taylor, 1974). Darrow set up the following staff:

• Director: Darrow served as the school's director and backup announcer.
• Assistant director: Cline Koon, a doctoral student in educational radio at The OSU, edited the *Courier*, developed curriculum, and conducted research. Koon set up the first research study on the classroom use of the school of the air and went on to serve with Armstrong Perry in the federal Office of Education's Radio Division.
• Drama coach: Gwendolyn Jenkins wrote or adapted program scripts and rehearsed the players who read the historical dramalogs.
• Secretary: Ruth Carter served as Darrow's secretary and oversaw audience contact (Darrow, 1940, p. 34).

This staff structure continued during the first two years of funding provided by the Ohio legislature. Significantly, Darrow does not mention any type of curriculum or administrative board to advise him, a lack that suggests how much the whole operation centered on Darrow.

Accomplishments

By the fall of 1929, Darrow could boast of an impressive list of accomplishments. He had established a functioning SOA that broadcast 13 programs weekly throughout the school year.

He had recruited a professional teaching staff made up of OSU faculty members and full-time teachers, all of whom either received small honorariums or donated their time. The OSA had received substantial backing from the most powerful commercial radio station in the nation, and it distributed a combined teacher guide and program bulletin to thousands of schools. Most important, Darrow had secured legislative funding for the OSA and official status as a part of the state's educational bureaucracy. Not surprisingly, recognition of his accomplishments spread rapidly in educational circles, and in November of 1929, the OSA became the subject of the first statewide educational conference devoted to educational broadcasts intended for the classroom (Darrow, 1940).

Darrow sought to extend the OSA's influence further. To engage a wider audience of parents and teachers in classroom broadcasting, he arranged to broadcast in cooperation with the Ohio Parent-Teacher Association, a monthly evening forum dealing with the OSA and radio education in general. He also initiated the highly successful monthly "Teacher Radio Forum" aimed at teacher-training institutions within the listening area (Darrow, 1940; Taylor, 1974). By 1930, Darrow and the OSA were on the cutting edge of educational technology.[9]

Program Changes. Despite the attention and successes, Darrow remained attentive to his audience. To solicit classroom teachers' opinions about the OSA programs, the staff devised, during the first year, the Daily Report Blank, which was sent to all listening teachers. Darrow says that hundreds responded regularly, though he offers no supporting data (Darrow, 1940). Nevertheless, the completed Daily Report forms provided a steady stream of suggestions for programming improvements. In response to these, the OSA modified the schedule for the spring 1930 semester (Darrow, 1940; Taylor, 1974). The changes are shown in Table 11.

TABLE 11. OSA PROGRAM SCHEDULE CHANGES, SPRING 1930
(Darrow, 1940; Taylor, 1974)

Day	Time	Course
Tuesday	2:00–2:20	*Mound Builders* by Dr. Shetrone
	2:40–3:00	*Every Pupil Test* by members of the state board of education
Wednesday	2:00–2:20	*Literature by Living Writers* alternating with *History Dramalogs*
	2:40–3:00	*Health* by Anna Drake alternating with *Physics*
Friday	2:00–2:30	*Art Appreciation* by William Vogel

Mound Builders. Presented by the director of the Ohio State Archeology Museum, this series uncovered the culture and mysteries of Ohio's early Native American inhabitants. The radio teacher asserted that knowing the past promoted better understanding of the future (*Courier*, 1929). Methods included lecture and dialogue.

Every Pupil Test. A special lesson series developed by the state education department to assist Ohio high school students to improve their scores on statewide tests, the Every Pupil Test represented a unique application of educational radio (*Courier*, 1929, p. 24). Unfortunately, Darrow offers no information on the instructional methods used, and based on the responses in the Daily Reports, the series never became popular.

Art Appreciation. Schools that participated in this series had to acquire prints of the works to be discussed prior to the broadcasts. It's unclear whether classroom teachers had to gather the prints or the OSA supplied them. During the broadcast, as the listeners looked at the prints, the radio teacher, Dr. Henry Bailey of the Cleveland Art Museum, explained and interpreted the

[9]Internationally, the OSA's achievements were probably less noteworthy. By 1930, the BBC had been broadcasting educational programs to classrooms throughout England for six years (BBC, 1945).

works and told intimate stories of the artist's life. This series represented the widespread belief that radio education could serve as a vehicle of cultural uplift through exposure to great works (*Courier*, 1929).

During the summer of 1930, Darrow continued to revise the schedule based on teacher responses to the Daily Reports. Table 12 shows the revised schedule that remained relatively unchanged for several years.

TABLE 12. OSA PROGRAM SCHEDULE, 1931–32
(*Courier*, 1931)

Day	Time	Course
Monday	2:00–2:30	*Literature by Living Writers*
	2:30–3:00	*Our Government* by various Ohio state officials
Tuesday	2:00–2:20	*Current Events* by Harrison M. Sayre
	2:20–2:40	*Citizenship* by John W. Pontius
	2:40–3:00	*Nature Study* by Harry E. Eswine
Wednesday	2:00–2:20	*Botany* and *Physics*, alternating
	2:20–2:40	*History Dramalogs* by the Crosley Players
	2:40–3:00	*Art Appreciation* by William H. Vogel
Thursday	2:00–2:20	*Geography of Our Country* by Dr. McConnell
	2:20–2:40	*Geography of Foreign Lands* by Dr. McConnell
	2:40–3:00	*Stories for the Primary Grades* by Bessie Gabbard
Friday	2:00–2:20	*General Science* by Hanor A. Webb
	2:20–2:40	*Health* by Anna M. Drake
	2:40–3:00	*Story Plays and Rhythmics* by Alma Ruhmschussel

Several new classes were added and are described here:

Our Government. The concept behind this program was, "government by those who governed." It grew directly out of Darrow's desire to expose the average student to society's movers and shakers. Prominent Ohio politicians, including the governor and state bureaucrats, took turns at the microphone to explain their roles in government and the functions of their offices (Darrow, 1940). This series had the quality of what Darrow called, "immediacy," that is, radio students get a sense of being in the presence of those who actually make history rather than those who merely write or talk about it. Darrow believed immediacy to be a powerful motivator (Darrow, 1932).

Two years of adequate funding and staffing, 1929–31, enabled Darrow to demonstrate his vision of educational radio, namely to open the classroom to the contemporary world by exposing students to the great minds, leaders, and illustrious personalities of the day. He achieved the zenith of this vision by moving two of the most innovative programs from Ohio to Washington, D.C., where more illustrious persons lived and worked. In 1931, he oversaw broadcasts of *Literature by Living Writers* from NEA's radio studios in Washington, D.C. The program introduced many of the famous literary names of the day, people that Darrow felt were sure to excite students. A few of those literary lights may still be remembered and studied in 2005, such as poets Vachel Lindsay and Carl Sandburg, novelist Hamlin Garland, and humorist Wallace Irwin (Darrow, 1940; Taylor, 1974). Remarkably, Darrow did not bother to describe what the literary figures said or did during the broadcasts. To Darrow, merely having them on the air was fulfilling.

What better place to originate a series on government than the nation's capital? The format of *Our Government* had been popular in Ohio, so Darrow used it to launch a similar series on the national government. Members of President Herbert Hoover's cabinet presented 20-minute reports describing the workings of their offices. The vice president, several senators, and an Ohio congressional representative also contributed. Secretary of the Interior[10] Ray Lyman Wilbur introduced the series, and, following the reports, he quizzed each participant for 10 minutes. According to Darrow, the series generated enormous publicity. For some reason, people were skeptical about whether cabinet members could communicate with schoolchildren. Newspaper people in particular were intrigued and perhaps apprehensive at the idea of cabinet members teaching an enormous class of young people on air.[11] Darrow asserts that these concerns were unfounded because the politicians and government people proved to be good teachers (Darrow, 1940). He described the broadcasts as "splendid bits of teaching..., fresh, vital, interesting to school and home" (p. 49). The Washington broadcasts also served as an excellent example of Darrow's belief that the greatest educational strength of radio lay in its ability to bring society's leaders and great minds into the classroom and make the average student feel part of great social and national processes.

Philosophy and Methods

Darrow was unlikely to have developed a broad philosophical outlook on education. He had not majored in education during his college years, and in his writings, he showed little interest in the topic (Taylor 1974). Above all, Darrow was a doer, not a thinker. However, we can glean some idea of his thoughts about radio as an educational medium through his writings and actions. From them emerges a belief in a "great mind" philosophy of education mixed with echoes of John Dewey's progressive ideas about actualizing classroom experiences. The three media attributes of education by radio according to Darrow were these:

• It enables master teachers to share their expertise with a great number of pupils.
• It stimulates student imagination through the use of drama, music, and sound effects.
• It puts students in contact with events as they happen, i.e., immediacy (Darrow, 1940).

Like many others in the early days of radio, such as Judith Waller, Darrow was genuinely excited by the new technology's potential to expand students' horizons, to open up the classroom to the world and bring students in auditory contact with great minds, artists, authoritative voices, and heroes. During the initial OSA broadcast, Dr. Condon, the Cincinnati school superintendent, asserted that through radio the great minds of the day could reach students in the classroom. Later, in the first issue of the OSA *Courier*, September 1929, Darrow expanded on Condon's thoughts. He said, "Radio permits the living voice of the specialist, the great educator, the statesman, or captain of industry to give first hand accounts and the last word on the subject and thereby increase the impression of actuality" (*Courier*, 1929, p. 3).

That approach was best exemplified by two OSA programs that Darrow was most proud of: *Our Government* and *Literature by Living Writers*. Both programs brought students into direct audio contact with national leaders and famous writers.

Though Darrow never mentioned John Dewey in the writings, his writings echo ideas and values that we associate with Dewey and the progressive movement, namely that education must be an active endeavor that connects classroom students to the "real" world (Quinton, 1977). Darrow's frequent use of the words *actuality* and *immediacy* suggests Dewey's persistent urging to make education a real, rather than an abstract, event. Darrow consistently voiced enthusiasm for radio's unique attribute, namely live communication. To Darrow, hearing the live voices of leaders, artists, and great minds made learning real for students, especially when compared to the abstract reality found in books.

Darrow described other benefits of educational radio; it added variety to the school day and

---

[10]At that time, the U.S. Bureau of Education was under the Department of Interior.

[11]By 1930, radio competed with newspapers for advertising revenue (Barnouw, 1966).

enabled pupils to assemble information quickly with ease and sureness that could not be accomplished with books (*Courier*, 1929). Darrow offered no support for such claims—possibly because he was too busy to engage in research, but more likely because he believed detailed investigation detracted from the magic of radio (Taylor, 1974). Solid research on learning by radio was at least a decade off.

Dewey's ideas also echo in Darrow's assertion that learning by radio helped to reunite the home and school in the educational process. Darrow reasoned that because parents could listen to the instructional broadcasts at home or work, families were stimulated to continue discussion and dialog at home. For example in his description of the program, *Current Events*, he says: "[Current Events programs] were unquestionably the basis of thousands of supper-table talks. The mother, especially, welcomed this contact with the school and her own child, for it gave her an opportunity to discuss with her family the mutually interesting topics upon which she might not otherwise have been informed" (Darrow, 1940, pp. 20–21).

It was an intriguing idea, but Darrow offered no substantiating data (Darrow, 1940).

INNOVATIONS IN LEARNING

From its beginning the OSA set the pedagogical pattern for educational radio. Earlier attempts at educational radio, particularly those originating from colleges, were criticized for their verbosity. Some scholars named the academic lecture hall approach as one of the major culprits behind the fall of educational radio (Saettler, 1990; White, 1947). While that conclusion is debatable,[12] it is likely that Darrow learned from his experience with the Little Red Schoolhouse in Chicago that lecture was the least appropriate instructional method for the radio classroom. In place of lectures, the OSA demonstrated three successful pedagogical approaches (Tyler, 1939):

1) Talk and dialogue. On the surface, radio talking was not much different from the lecture hall, but Darrow refined the technique by simplifying the language and having radio teachers imagine that they were talking directly to individual students or engaging with them in small group discussion. Introducing other characters with whom the radio teacher could converse added the dimension of question and answer—the listener is subtly invited to identify with the questioner, and thus is more receptive to the radio teacher's answer—a technique used widely in radio ever since.
2) Storytelling and drama. Radio had the power to touch the emotions and stir the imagination in ways that reading could not; at least that was a commonly held belief of the day. Consequently, storytelling proved to be effective for getting younger children interested in literature. In this instructional approach, the speaker's voice could convey passion, irony, and humor, all important in attracting and holding listener attention. Also music and sound effects increased the illusion of reality (Darrow, 1940; Tyler, 1939).
To avoid the demotivating sound of lecture, OSA radio educators dramatized history, literature, social science, and even geography. From the very first semester of its operation, the OSA used a troupe of semiprofessional actors to present literary dramas and The OSU college players to dramatize the history series. Music and sound effects intensified the emotional impact (Tyler, 1939; Woelfel & Reid, 1945). Quality dramatic broadcasts provided classroom teachers with an effective instructional resource not available by other means.
3) Direct instruction. Darrow was lucky to engage Ms. Ruhmschussel, a dynamic physical education teacher from Dayton, to present story plays and rhythmics for the primary grades. From the microphone in Cincinnati, she took control of young student listeners throughout Ohio's classrooms, giving them direct instruction for physical activity, which they carried out during the broadcast. Her program became one of the OSA's most popular and set a pattern that was repeated for similar programs by other SOAs.

[12]As presented in Section I, the key factor in the demise of college-based educational radio stations was governmental regulation that favored commercial as opposed to nonprofit development.

For the classroom teacher, Darrow recommended a simple three-step approach to make the most of educational broadcasting: (1) preparation, (2) purposeful listening, (3) follow-up (Atkinson, 1942b, p. 118). Editors of the *Courier* and teachers manuals issued later in the mid–1940s encouraged classroom teachers to get students actively engaged in learning during the broadcasts. Purposeful or attentive listening was important, but the OSA staff recognized that listening, no matter how attentive, was too passive; other activities were required. Consequently, they encouraged teachers to get students involved by using the same learning techniques that teachers used in their classrooms such as note taking, watching visuals that supported the broadcast lesson, drawing, and even verbal response. For example, the art appreciation series supplemented the broadcasts with prints of the artworks to be discussed. During the broadcast, students were expected to study the features described by the radio teacher, and then following the broadcast they were asked to write or discuss their reactions to the works (*Courier*, 1931; Darrow, 1932).

The Depression and the Struggle for Survival

While the Depression of the early 1930s forced many state-funded educational bodies to struggle for survival, the OSA remained relatively unaffected by the great national dilemma, at least for a while. The two-year state funding appropriation, augmented by gifts from the Payne Fund, extended to January 1, 1931. But storm clouds were forming, and everyone plainly saw trouble ahead. As in most states, the Ohio educational system was supported by property tax levies. By 1931, much of Ohio's realty was revalued downward, and the tax base on which education depended shrank. As a consequence, the state's annual education budget fell from $85 million to less than $60 million and then to $44 million the following year[13] (Darrow, 1940; Stead, 1937; Taylor, 1974).

With the state budget slashed by nearly one-third in 1931, the outlook for the OSA's budget for the next school year was ominous. Darrow rose to the challenge. The first big problem he faced was simple; the state legislature had cut the OSA from the 1931 budget. No money was available for continued operations. Through a frantic public relations effort, Darrow got supporters to flood the legislature with protests and requests to continue the OSA funding. His efforts paid off, but not immediately. The politicians restored some funding, but it would not be available until January 1, 1932. Darrow faced the prospect of no state funds during all of 1931. Fortunately, he had anticipated trouble and had banked enough money to carry on operations through June of that year. However, for the second half, July through December, he would have to beg. And beg he did. Darrow asked for money from almost every person or organization that had shown a past interest in educational radio: NCER, NEA, the Payne Fund, the PTA, the Women's Club, plus many individuals. Almost all donated (Darrow, 1940), and the OSA made it through 1931 with flying colors. The future, however, was uncertain. From a lean but adequate annual budget of $20,000, the OSA was forced to operate over the next four year on substantially less money, as shown in Table 13.

Table 13. OSA Annual State Funding, 1932–35
(Darrow, 1940, pp. 69, 85)

Year	Funding Amount	% budget reduction compared to 1930
1932	$11,000	45% less
1933	$9,349	53% less
1934	$13,320	33% less
1935	$11,660	42% less

[13]All the dollar amounts come from Darrow (1940). In comparison, Massachusetts, with a smaller population, had educational expenditures for the year 1929 of $69 million (Society, 1930a).

The reduced budgets of the Depression years shook the OSA staff and seriously affected their educational offerings, yet Darrow's determination never flagged. He attacked problems with his usual energy and flexibility, cutting costs and reengineering the OSA operations. He made the formerly free *Courier* available for a subscription fee; organized the OSA radio scripts into a library, lending them to other stations for a rental fee; and eliminated long-distance transmission costs by originating all programs from Crosley's WLW studios in Cincinnati. That last arrangement was short-lived, because WLW engineers soon discovered that they could pick the WOSU broadcast out of the air and rebroadcast it from WLW. As a result, programming returned to Columbus. Crosley also increased its in-kind aid to the OSA by writing some of the broadcast scripts. In this manner, Darrow continued his radio education innovation, bowed and partially crippled, but still on the air.

During the period of reduced budgets, from the beginning of 1932 to the end of 1936, Darrow continued to produce a full schedule of educational programming. The schedule for 1933–34 shown in Table 14 reflected expansion and refinements to meet demand. Several new programs on the 1933–34 schedule reflected a shift in emphasis for Darrow and the OSA. Perhaps influenced by the Depression and the government's reaction to it, in place of bringing great leaders and artists into the classroom, the new programs introduced students to social reality and critical thinking. Also, all programs were reduced to 15 minutes, a change that allowed OSA to broadcast more programs in the allotted hour.

TABLE 14. OSA PROGRAM SCHEDULE, 1933–34
(Darrow, 1932; Taylor, 1974)

Day	Time	Course	Grades*
Monday	2:00–2:15	*Modern Problems*	10–12
	2:15–2:30	*Learn to Sing*	1–4
	2:30–2:45	*Inventors and Inventions*	5–8
	2:45–3:00	*Little Visits to Great Industries*	7–8
Tuesday	2:00–2:15	*Civil Government*	7–8
	2:15–2:30	*Stories*	1–8
	2:30–2:45	*Nature*	4–8
	2:45–3:00	*Mound Builders*	5–8
Wednesday	2:00–2:15	*History Dramalogs*	7–8
	2:15–2:30	*Story Drama*	2–4
	2:30–2:45	*Touring America by Plane*	4–5
	2:45–3:00	*Know Ohio*	5–8
Thursday	2:00–2:15	*Botany*	8–12
	2:15–2:30	*Stories*	3–4
	2:30–3:00	*Geography of Our Country/of Foreign Lands*	7–8
Friday	2:00–2:30	*Literature*	7–12
	2:30–2:45	*Story Plays and Rhythmics*	1–4
	2:45–3:00	*Art Appreciation*	6–8

Modern Problems. Aimed at high school students, this series provided insight into the Depression-era economy, the causes of the downturn and unemployment, and the government's reaction. Darrow (1940) described the series as "the most provocative ever aired by the OSA" because the teacher took "a stand well to the left and fearlessly discussed issues of Capitalism,

Fascism, and Communism, calling on students to evaluate the claims of each" (p. 76). Clearly, Darrow was proud of this one. However, Barnouw, (1968) says that management at Crosley's WLW station occasionally censored scripts and on one occasion took the instructor off the air.[14]

Little Visits to Great Industries. Led by renowned professor and pioneer in the field of educational technology, Edgar Dale of The OSU, the series introduced various industries to students as a backdrop for a deeper exploration of how industrialization had affected American life. Dale led the seventh and eighth graders on radio tours of the coal, steel, railroad, oil, and motion picture industries, among others.

Uncle Sam at Work. Offered in 1934–35, this series modified the *Our Government* program by focusing on the new government agencies that had been created in response to the Depression (Darrow, 1940; Taylor, 1974).

With no money for honorariums, the OSA curtailed the *Literature by Living Writers* series and replaced it with the *Contemporary Writers* series that dealt with all categories of modern literature, humor, biography, and novels. This marked a difficult change for Darrow, because students now heard the voice of an academic talking about writers, rather than the writers themselves, which had been the case earlier.

Demise and Arise

By 1935, the Depression was abating, but the OSA's problems were increasing. Ohio voters had elected a new governor, Democrat Martin Davey, who promised to cut fat from the state's budget. From the very beginning of his term in 1935, Davey targeted the OSA for trimming, and Darrow soon felt the effects. Davey's proposed budget for 1936 slashed the school's appropriation to less than $9,000, an all-time low that would seriously strain the school's operations. The governor followed that up with a request that the state's Department of Education survey Ohio schools to gauge interest in educational radio. Darrow felt confident that he would receive support from the state's educators, but Davey had one more shock in store. He had the new director of education request that the OSA suspend all preparations for the 1936 fall semester, pending the results of the survey. This meant the *Courier* might not be issued until after the new semester began. When it became obvious that the OSA enjoyed wide support throughout Ohio, the governor removed restrictions on the school's operation, but the damage had been done. The staff quickly printed and distributed the *Courier*, but its late arrival prompted some schools to strike the OSA from their fall curriculum (Taylor, 1974).

The reduced budget forced other unwanted changes. Working with a reduced staff, Darrow found it necessary to cut four popular programs because they were the most costly or required teacher honorariums. *Story Plays and Rhythmics,* the two geography series, and *When They Were Young* were replaced with less expensive programs. By fall of 1936, Darrow was compelled to use donated talent for all operations (Atkinson, 1942d; Darrow, 1940).

Darrow refused to remain passive in the face of what seemed to him a personal assault. He solicited donations from past supporters—individuals and organizations—and enough money flowed in to keep the OSA operating. One group even donated the printing of the *Courier,* enabling the OSA for one year to once again distribute it for free. Darrow also fought the cuts with information that highlighted what a terrific bargain the OSA was for the people of Ohio. A handbill that he distributed throughout the state compared the value of all the donated services with the actual allocation from the state legislature, as shown in Table 15.

---

[14]Crosley Management was fiercely anti-labor. During the mid–1930s, it imposed a blackout on labor news stories. When Norman Corwin, then a WLW writer, argued for running labor stories because newspapers were doing so, he was immediately fired (Bannerman, 1986).

TABLE 15. WHO PAYS FOR THE OHIO SCHOOL OF THE AIR?

Free Services from Individuals	$6,000
Other Radio Workshops	$9,600
State of Ohio	$12,000
Radio Workshops Federal Government	$21,500
Other Radio Stations	$30,000[15]
Crosley Radio Stations (WLW)	$26,000
Total:	$105,100

In April of 1936, Davey continued his crippling tactics by requesting another survey, this time of the home audience. With no advanced warning, the director of education, who often introduced the broadcasts, suddenly asked the listening audience their opinion of the value of the OSA to Ohio. Despite the surprise, Darrow says he was gratified when "over 75,000 people demanded that the School of the Air be not only continued but strengthened" (Darrow, 1940, p. 96). This claim raises many problematic questions. Who received those 75,000 demands, the state legislature or the OSA? If they were directed to the OSA, how were Darrow and his small staff able to process that great volume of letters or phone calls? Darrow provided no answers.

By late fall of 1936, Darrow must have realized that the school's survival was in doubt. At that point it is likely that he was already looking for another job, because in late 1936, Davey released his proposed budget for the coming biennium. It contained no money for the OSA. Darrow responded bitterly, characterizing Davey as a powerful demagogue intent on destroying the OSA. Despite a chorus of protests, appeals from the state director of education, and last-minute political lobbying and maneuvering on behalf of the school, the new budget passed with no appropriation for the OSA (Stead, 1937, p. 25). As of June 30, 1937, Darrow's role in a great experiment in educational technology was finished.

The OSA's demise apparently had little to do with issues of education; rather, it seems to have fallen victim to rough-and-tumble statehouse politics and a personal clash between Darrow and the governor. Several observers attributed the governor's actions to anger over Darrow's refusal to allow a few on-air announcements supporting Davey's election or over Darrow's refusal to contribute part of his salary to the governor's campaign or simply to the fact that Darrow had quietly backed Davey's opponent (Taylor, 1974).

THE OSA RE-EMERGES

Saettler (1990) says that after Darrow's departure in 1938, the OSA was disbanded (p. 198). Despite that scholar's usual thoroughness, he apparently overlooked the fact that the OSA was soon resurrected and continued operating until the mid–1960s, though the road was ragged with many stops and starts. For several years following Darrow's departure, the OSA seemed an orphan. When state support ended, temporarily as it turned out, the whole OSA organization became a feature of Crosley's WLW in Cincinnati. Retitled the National School of the Air, the OSA programs became available nationally through WLW's affiliation with the Mutual Broadcasting System (MBS), a cooperative network that included Chicago's WLS.[16] Because Mutual stations were not bound to carry network programs, it is impossible to know which stations actually broadcast the OSA programs. At any rate, this arrangement lasted only a short while. In 1938, after joining the NBC network, which enforced a strong policy against broadcasting to the

---

[15]By the mid–1930s, daytime radio soap operas were popular, attracting lucrative ad revenues. Quite possibly Crosley could have sold the airtime that it donated to the OSA.

[16]WLS was Darrow's old employer when he was Uncle Ben, headmaster of the Little Red Schoolhouse.

schools, WLW stopped airing the National School of the Air. Consequently, all other MBS stations lost their access to the OSA programs.

Meanwhile, with Darrow out of the picture, the Ohio legislature transferred control of the OSA from the state Department of Education to The Ohio State University. Funds were appropriated, and the OSA returned to the air in the fall of 1938 via WOSU, the college station. With 5,000 watts of power, it could be heard clearly by about one-third of the state;[17] that arrangement soon faltered. Due to an apparent dispute between station WOSU and the university, neither party submitted a funding request to the legislature for the upcoming year. Consequently, no funds were appropriated for the 1939–41 biennium, and the OSA again ceased to exist. A few programs continued to be heard thanks to WOSU volunteer efforts, but with no director or special staff, the output was meager. Four series were broadcast for the 1939–40 school year — down from 17 in 1934 — and five in 1940–41, but it appears that no program bulletins were distributed either year (Tyler, 1946–1953). In 1941, the legislature restored funding and, a few years later, transferred administrative control from WOSU to the Bureau of Educational Research and Services of The OSU's College of Education, a more secure location, but one that guaranteed reduced visibility.

Perhaps what Saettler (1990) meant when he said that the OSA had been disbanded was that the revived OSA no longer resembled the school that Darrow had started a decade earlier (Atkinson, 1942a). During World War II and for a few years following, the OSA operated only half an hour per day, and its identity began to fade. Nevertheless, the program schedule gradually expanded — five programs in 1940–41, eight in 1941–42. By the end of the decade, when Margaret Tyler became director, the OSA offered a schedule similar to what Darrow had offered in that exciting first year of 1929. Tyler restored a formal school structure and budget and progressively built up program offerings until the OSA regained a full hour of daily operation (Taylor, 1974). Table 16 shows the OSA broadcasts in Tyler's first year.

TABLE 16. OSA PROGRAMS, 1948–49
(Tyler, 1946–1953)

Grades	Course
Primary	*Music Time*
	Story Time
	Play Time
Intermediate	*Boys and Girls of Bookland*
	Science Club of the Air
	Once Upon a Time in Ohio
	Time for Music
	News of the Week
Junior and high school	*The Economic Detective*
	The Columbus Philharmonic Orchestra

Tyler's schedule retained some but not all of Darrow's vision. It retained science and art appreciation. Missing, however, was the exposure to great minds, artists, and political leaders that had characterized early OSA programs. The programs continued to employ a variety of teaching methods: dramatized presentations were used in four programs including *The Economic Detective*, which purported to dramatize economic principles; storytelling was used in two programs for the primary grades; and direct teaching was used in *Play Time* and *Science Club of the Air* (Tyler, 1946–1953).

---

[17]During the 1938–39 school year, classroom teachers could choose to hear the OSA programs on several stations: WOSU, WLW, or perhaps another MBS station (Barnouw, 1968; Taylor, 1974).

Audience Size

Darrow and his staff conducted no definitive research on audience size, and, with one exception, neither did any outside researchers. Despite his boundless enthusiasm and salesman's tendency toward hyperbole, Darrow made only a few statements about the size and nature of OSA's listening audience. However, throughout its long history, OSA administrators conducted several surveys of teacher and audience opinions regarding the school. From these we can get some reliable ideas about the audience for the OSA.

Proponents of the schools of the air have often been prone to exaggerate audience size. Taylor (1974) states with little support that by the beginning of the 1930–31 school year, the OSA was reaching nearly half a million pupils;[18] the head of CBS radio network claimed in a speech that 8 million students listened to the ASA every day (Paley, 1940, in Atkinson, 1942d). Neither one backed up his claim with hard data.

Surprisingly, Darrow avoided making any inflated claims about the size of the OSA radio audience. Reactions to the initial broadcast in 1929 prompted him to estimate the first day's audience at approximately 50,000 students, and by the end of the first year, Darrow felt confident that his school broadcasts reached between 50,000 and 100,000 students. If he felt disappointment that regular listeners made up only 5 percent to 10 percent of the state's approximately 1.1 million public school students,[19] he never expressed it. Instead, he asserted the existence of a huge listening audience at home, curious listeners enjoying the programs and discussing them later with family members. Darrow conjured up pictures of a "vast audience" of at-home listeners (p. 65) that included sick children, "shut-ins," mothers wanting to escape domestic boredom or to stay abreast of their children's studies, adults trying to overcome an inadequate education, and — during the Depression — unemployed people hoping to improve their employment prospects. This audience profile was supported anecdotally by hundreds of letters sent to the school (Darrow, 1940).

However, the OSA did conduct several annual listener surveys, during and after Darrow's tenure. All suffer from methodological weaknesses, particularly in failing to make clear how the survey sample related to the universe of listeners. Nevertheless, the results of these surveys enable the reader in 2005 to make inferences and educated guesses about how many students listened regularly to the OSA. The most complete survey conducted during Darrow's years was the *Annual Report of the Ohio School of the Air, 1933–34* (Reichelderfer, 1934), published by the Ohio State Department of Education. The survey consisted of a two-part questionnaire sent to *Courier* subscribers, part one for school principals and part two for teachers.[20] The key question, addressed to principals, asked how many pupils in each grade listened to the OSA. The results are shown in Table 17.

TABLE 17. SELECTED RESULTS FROM *ANNUAL REPORT OF THE OHIO SCHOOL OF THE AIR, 1933–34* (REICHELDERFER, 1934)

Surveys Sent	476
Not Returned	182 (43%)
Returned:	270 (57%)
- Listened to the OSA	182
- Number of Pupils Listening	50,181
- Did Not Listen to the OSA	88

[18]It is doubtful that in 1930, 500,000 Ohio students, K through 12, attended radio-equipped classrooms. In 1929, Darrow had estimated that only 1,000 of Ohio's 9,000 schools were radio equipped (Darrow, 1940). Perhaps Taylor was thinking that the 500,000 figure was possible because WLW's signal reached such a large area.

[19]According to Reid (1942), the census of Ohio's public schools in 1941 was around 1.2 million. I assume the count was smaller in 1934.

[20]Reichelderfer's report seems to contradict Cuban's (1986) charge that surveys conducted by the radio schools of the air were faulty because they never involved teachers, only the school superintendents or principals.

The data in Table 17 show 50,000-plus listeners, a credible number, but these results require more analysis. First, it is unclear whether the 476 surveys mailed represent the whole universe of schools that received the *Courier* or just a representative sample of those recipients. If the latter is true, then the results should be projected to all *Courier* recipients, a projection that likely would yield a listening audience much larger than 50,000. Also, we can assume that the "not returned" category contained some additional listeners. While the report leaves key questions unanswered, it does point to the possibility that the OSA's regular audience was substantially greater than the 50,000 mentioned in the survey.

In the early 1950s, I. Keith Tyler, professor of educational radio at The OSU and longtime OSA associate, estimated the OSA's listening audience at approximately 190,000 or roughly 15 percent of Ohio's school population, kindergarten through twelfth grade. Although Tyler drew his figures from what he termed a careful study, he presented no supporting data (Tyler, 1946–1953). In 1959, the number of regular OSA listeners was estimated at more than 100,000 (Carle, 1959). That number may also be suspect, however, because the OSA researcher made a doubtful assumption that teachers who did *not* respond to a survey used the OSA programs as frequently as teachers who did respond. Given that dubious assumption, it is probably safer to say that the OSA audience in 1959 ranged between 50,000 and 100,000 regular listeners. Ironically, that is about the same range that Darrow had estimated 35 years earlier (Darrow, 1940).

After having reviewed all the various estimates and the studies on which they were based, I infer that the OSA's regular listener base fluctuated between 75,000 to 150,000 pupils, a range that represented between 10 percent and 15 percent of Ohio's elementary school population. In addition, the audience included an unknown number of at-home listeners.

Why did not more teachers use the OSA programs? The OSA Annual Reports ignore the question, but I. Keith Tyler, writing in the early 1950s, briefly mentions two issues that might have curtailed usage. One is that any regularly scheduled broadcast probably conflicted with the lockstep schedules found in most high schools. Indeed, by the early 1950s, the OSA programs were designed to serve chiefly elementary students. The other issue was that in the post–Darrow era, university station WOSU's primary and secondary coverage areas included only about half of Ohio, and that area did not include the large cities of Cleveland, Toledo, and Cincinnati (Tyler, 1946–1953). Consequently, many of Ohio's schools could not receive the OSA broadcasts.

Analysis of the data points to several other factors that may have affected usage, at least during Darrow's reign. One was the lack of radios in the schools. Using data from the study *Radio in the Schools of Ohio*[21] (Reid, 1942), we can safely estimate the percentage of radio-equipped schools in Ohio by 1935 at between 30 and 40 percent. That range most likely understates the numbers of students in radio-equipped classrooms.[22] Nevertheless, during Darrow's era, a significant portion — perhaps half — of all Ohio schools were without radios, and that lack clearly limited the OSA audience. Cuban (1986) asserts that any teacher who believed in educational radio could probably get one for the classroom. His point might have been true during the 1940s,

[21] The Reid (1942) study represents one of the few solid studies devoted to radio usage in Ohio schools. It documents usage of all SOA programs available to Ohio schools including offerings by CBS and NBC, four local school boards, and the OSA. Unfortunately, the work was conducted in spring of 1941, near the absolute low point of the OSA's existence, as mentioned earlier. Given the OSA's erratic operation during the period from 1938 through 1942, it is likely that many Ohio teachers and administrators lost interest in the school, if not in radio education altogether. For that reason, Reid's excellent research is not helpful in determining the size of the listening audience during Darrow's time at the OSA.

[22] Reid found that 80 percent of Ohio's urban schools but only 46 percent of its rural schools were radio equipped (Reid, 1942). Because the urban schools had substantially greater enrollments than rural schools, the percentage of students with access to radio in the classroom must have been substantially greater than the percent of schools with radios.

but in the midst of the Depression, when many teachers were being paid in script, acquiring a radio adequate for classroom listening might have been problematic.

Meanwhile, competition from other SOAs undoubtedly drew listeners away from the OSA. By the mid–1930s, Ohio teachers could have listened to several SOAs including the OSA, the American School of the Air (ASA) and the Cleveland Board of Education's long-running and successful SOA (Atkinson, 1942b). ASA was available throughout Ohio, while the Cleveland broadcasts could be heard only in a small part of the state, one that contained a large proportion of the state's pupils.

Most significant, Darrow never focused the OSA on meeting the educational needs of rural communities. Reid's study, *Radio in the Schools of Ohio* (1942) found that although rural one-room schools made up 23 percent of Ohio's schools, only 23 schools (2.1 percent) reported listening to OSA programs. Farm families and the isolated one and two room schools that served most of them were the natural constituency of state-based SOAs. This assertion is supported by the experience of SOAs in Wisconsin, Minnesota, Oregon and Texas, all of which will be covered later in this section.

Evaluation

From the very beginning of the OSA, the Payne Fund had wanted to assess the effectiveness of the school's radio broadcasts on student learning. To conduct a quality study, the fund appointed Dr. W. Charters, head of Ohio State's Bureau of Educational Research. Charters found a resistant Darrow, who said that researchers might handicap his efforts. According to Taylor (1974), Darrow, ever the practical man of action, had little appreciation for the time-consuming detail work required by empirical research. However, in order to improve programming, Darrow did need information on how the broadcasts were being received. To fill that need, in the second school year Darrow devised and distributed a Daily Report form to all listening teachers. He stated that he received hundreds of completed replies full of teacher input on topics such as preparation, reception, suitability of subject matter, the speakers' presentation qualities and vocabulary, pupil reaction, and more (Darrow, 1940). Darrow credited the responses from the teachers with helping the school improve programming, but his methods for conducting surveys would probably be considered unscientific today. He offered no supporting information about how the listening teachers were identified or how the report data were analyzed. In fact, Taylor (1974) asserts that Darrow relied on a cadre of schools that sent in their reports regularly, ignoring those that responded sporadically.

The OSA conducted year-end listener surveys that unfortunately told little about the learning that took place as a result of the broadcasts. They did, however, provide insight into how teachers incorporated the OSA programs into their instructional effort and what teachers thought of the programs. The *Annual Report of the Ohio School of the Air 1933–34* (Reichelderfer, 1934) describes three aspects of teacher program usage: pre-broadcast preparation, during-broadcast activity, and post broadcast review. In general, the primary teachers prepared for the broadcasts by summarizing the stories prior to the broadcast. Teachers in the intermediate grades and high school used questions provided in the *Courier* as the basis for pre-broadcast discussion. For example, to prepare for broadcasts on current events and geography, students studied maps. Students in art appreciation looked over the artwork.

During broadcasts, students engaged in a variety of learning behaviors, according to the teacher reports that are summarized in Table 18.

TABLE 18. TEACHER RESPONSES TO THE QUESTION,
"WHAT DID THE PUPILS DO DURING THE BROADCAST?"

Activities	Responses
Studied Maps	105
Took Notes	124
Followed Radio Directions	97
Read Book	44
Studied Pictures	41
Wrote Difficult Words on Board	12
Just Listened Attentively	84

(Reichelderfer, 1934)

OHIO SCHOOL OF THE AIR
STATE DEPARTMENT OF EDUCATION
COLUMBUS, OHIO

A RATING SCALE FOR RADIO LESSONS
Being a Confidential Report by Cooperating Teachers

Date of Broadcast..

....Lesson Topic...
Radio Teacher's Name

Reported by..Address...............................

Grade.........
or
School...No. Pupils in Listening Class............. Grades........

Please rate the radio lesson on each of the six main items listed below by placing an X in the proper column at the right of the page. In the column headings, E means excellent, G—good, F—fair, and P—poor. Underline thus_____ any sub-item on which you judge the radio lesson to be especially good, and enclose in parentheses thus (   ) any sub-item on which you consider the radio lesson was especially poor.

Use a separate rating scale for each lesson and mail as early as practical after the presentation of the radio lesson to C. M. KOON, State Department of Education, Columbus, Ohio.

ITEMS	E	G	F	P
1. **Pupil Attitude During the Broadcast**......... Attentive, thoughtful, responsive, continued actively interested throughout the broadcast.				
2. **Subject-Matter of the Radio Lesson**......... Closely related to the curriculum, suitable, valuable, proper amount presented, well organized.				
3. **The Radio Teacher's Method of Presenting the Lesson**......... Should be a skillful instructional performance before the microphone. Style clear, sufficient repetition and proper emphasis. Vocabulary suitable, common, vivid words. Called for sufficient active pupil participation. Lesson plan and objectives clear to the classroom teacher.				
4. **Personality of the Radio Teacher**......... Manner attractive, forceful, vital, stimulating, likable. Voice pleasing, magnetic, clear, expressive, natural, distinct enunciation, intonation varied and stimulating.				
5. **Results of the Radio Lesson**......... Attitudes of the pupils: stimulated the imagination, aroused curiosity, awakened interest, provoked thinking, stirred ambition. Achievements of the pupils: The pupils should have a reasonable grasp of the subject matter, as determined by discussion, reports, oral and written tests, etc. (Copies of any written tests given, together with results should be attached.)				
6. **General Estimate of the Value of the Radio Lesson**.........				

How many lessons in this series have your pupils heard?..

How many rating scales would you like for us to send you?..

Suggestions for improving the radio lesson:..

The Ohio School of the Air Daily Report Form (courtesy of The Ohio State University Archive).

The numbers in Table 18 are not statistically meaningful because many teachers reported several activities. However, the tallies do show that rather than remaining passive, most OSA students engaged actively during the radio lesson. Not all SOAs encouraged active learning during radio lessons. For example the director of the Alameda City SOA said that he did everything he could to discourage teachers from requiring any pupil activity.

The follow-up behaviors described in the 1933–34 report included typical instructional activities such as recall of radio-received facts, tests, discussions, and writing summaries.

The *Annual Report of the Ohio School of the Air 1933–34* (Reichelderfer, 1934) also presents the teachers' views of the chief benefits derived from the OSA programs. Teachers in the primary grades reported that the programs brought relaxation, enjoyment, expression, and appreciation for good music. Some teachers also mentioned improved concentration. Teachers in the intermediate grades identified benefits such as a wider knowledge of the world, appreciation for fine pictures and music, and increased vocabulary. It is worth noting that the first benefit reflects Darrow's belief about radio education, while the second mirrors the idea of cultural uplift. Pupils also improved their abilities at note taking, attentive listening, and summarizing. High school teachers reported that the programs *Current Events* and *Modern Problems* had increased interest in current affairs, news, and politics. All in all, the report lists an impressive range of educational benefits in which any teacher or administrator could take pride. However, almost all the data are descriptive and anecdotal (Tyler, 1946–1953).

The 1959 *Evaluation of the Ohio School of the Air* uncovered an interesting correlation between years of teaching experience and the use of the OSA programs. Teachers with the least teaching experience were more than twice as likely to use the OSA programs than teachers with six or more years of experience (Carle, 1959). From that data, I infer that younger teachers were far more open to radio than older teachers. I suspect that similar correlations exist today with regard to teacher adoption of the latest technology into their practice.

Awards and Recognition

In November of 1929, as the OSA was completing its first full year of operation, Dr. John Clifton, director of the Ohio Department of Education, called a conference to discuss the work of the OSA. Forty Ohio educators attended. After a round of speeches and presentations, the participants split into three committees that studied and reported on various radio education topics: present uses and effectiveness of broadcasts, difficulties encountered in using radio lessons, and future plans and policies. Later, Darrow proudly termed that meeting, "the first of its kind in educational history" (Taylor, 1974, p. 108). However, the committees put forth several tough recommendations to Darrow. They called on Darrow to survey all users about the effectiveness of the educational broadcasts. They also asked him to formulate an unambiguous statement of purpose for the OSA. Another committee, chaired by Dr. Edgar Dale of The Ohio State University, recommended launching a research study that would gather the opinions of participating teachers and principals concerning any difficulties and possible solutions uncovered in their use of educational radio. A third group suggested conducting surveys to make certain that the broadcasts covered the subject matter of greatest interest to teachers (Taylor, 1974, pp. 108–110). Taylor concludes that the conference was a fitting tribute to Darrow's hard work and dedication to radio education.

The OSA also received a vote of approval from the people of Ohio. The state had been hardhit by the national economic troubles, and education was severely stricken. The legislature, forced to make drastic cuts in many established programs, was poised to slash all OSA funds and redirect them to struggling schools. After all, the OSA was the youngest of all departments in the state educational system and therefore a likely target for cutting. Instead, citizens inundated the legislators with messages of support and persuaded them to continue funding the OSA, albeit at a lower level. Nevertheless, it was enough to continue operating. The school had built a good reputation throughout Ohio (Taylor, 1974).

Darrow became a celebrity in educational circles and is one of the few directly involved with educational radio who are mentioned by contemporary scholars such as Cuban (1986) and Saettler (1990).

The OSA in the Television Era

What purpose could educational radio serve in the television era? That is one of the questions the OSA administrators addressed in their 1959 evaluation of the OSA nearly a decade after the introduction of TV. The response, drawn from a panel of 11 educational experts, gave radio a surprising, if somewhat wishful, endorsement. A majority of the experts said that (educational) radio would continue to grow and that in fact, use of radio in the schools had actually increased since the advent of TV. They stated emphatically that radio and TV did not compete with each other. Then, in a somewhat competitive vein, the experts listed ways in which radio education was superior to televised education, particularly in the area of broadcasting drama, music, news, and "imaginative" programs. Furthermore, they said that in subjects such as science and drawing, radio allowed students to be active learners, listening *and* doing, while television restricted students to passive viewing (Carle, 1959, pp. 58–61). Unfortunately, the experts' positive outlook does not seem to be reflected in the OSA's program offering for that year. The 1959 report names only eight programs, as shown in Table 19.

TABLE 19. OSA PROGRAMS, 1959–60
(Carle, 1959, p. 3)

Grade Group	Program	Local Production	Purchased Programs
Primary	*Play Time*	X	
	Story Time	X	
	Fun to Sing		X
Intermediate	*Boys and Girls of Bookland*	X	
	Once Upon a Time in Ohio*	X	
	Newspaper of the Air	X	
	Uncle Dan at Froggy Hollow (nature study)	X	
	Chevron School Broadcasts (music)	X	

During the late 1940s, *Once Upon a Time in Ohio* was the most popular OSA program, probably because the legislature had mandated that state history be taught in the schools. Radio proved to be an effective, convenient, and inexpensive way to cover the required material (Tyler, 1946–1953).

Thirty years after the first broadcasts, the OSA schedule showed a marked shift away from Darrow's grand vision of educational radio toward a more limited role. Gone from the 1959 schedule were programs that attempted to link classroom students to society's leaders, artists, and great minds. Missing also were programs aimed at cultural uplift in art, music, and drama, the latter once considered one of radio's strong points. Absent also were the challenging subjects in the sciences or languages. In part, the limited schedule recognized that the OSA never was that successful with high school students, mainly because inflexible broadcast schedules did not mesh well with the rigid time frames that regulate learning in secondary schools. The schedule seems to confirm that 30 years after Darrow's triumph, radio had become just another teaching aid. In fact, one of the questions in the 1959 evaluation asks teachers "to compare the OSA with other teaching aids" (Carle, 1959 p. 38). That is a question Darrow would have rejected because for him radio was so much more than merely a teaching aid. In fact his most revealing comment about the value of educational radio was stated in response to a teacher who said she thought that educational radio had proved itself a successful experiment. Darrow responded: "Frankly, I have never considered radio education as being on trial ... it was not the radio on trial. It is you and I who are on trial to determine whether or not we have the vision and the genius to make this wonderful discovery serve the classroom" (Darrow, 1940, pp. 67–68).

Summary

After Darrow realized that the effort to create an NSoA was floundering and likely to fail, he focused on developing a pilot project in his home state of Ohio. Drawing on the contacts and spadework of the previous four years, Darrow soon gathered all the pieces necessary for launching the nation's first state-supported school of the air. In January of 1929, the OSA, broadcasting from the most powerful radio station in the nation, aired an innovative program of 13 to 15 radio programs each school semester for the following eight years. Under Darrow's direction, the OSA quickly established a pattern for educational broadcasting to the schools that would be taken up by a dozen other SOAs in the years that followed. The OSA introduced and adapted instructional methods suitable for radio, such as historical dramalog, direct instruction, and storytelling. It broke new ground in subject matter by introducing into the kindergarten through 12th-grade classrooms the voices of the political leaders, noted writers, and experts from many fields and provided schoolchildren throughout the state with exposure to the classics in art and literature. More important, educational radio broke down the isolation of the classroom by bringing in authentic voices from the real world.

The Depression of the 1930s restricted the OSA's growth possibilities. Following that, a political vendetta perpetrated by Ohio's governor eventually forced Darrow out as the OSA's director, but the OSA continued for at least another 25 years operating from The OSU educational station in Columbus. It is doubtful, however, that it ever conveyed the sense of relevance and energy that it had under "Uncle Ben's" direction.

What finally happened to the OSA? That part of the story remains unclear. It appears that The OSA apparently never died officially. "It simply faded slowly away" (Taylor, 1974, p. 163).

Wisconsin School of the Air

The few contemporary education scholars who mention radio schools of the air dismiss them as another failed experiment in educational technology. Cuban (1986) argues essentially that teachers never accepted radio in the classroom and that only a small fraction of them used radio regularly. Others asserted that radio never really was accepted as a "full-fledged member of America's education family" (Woelfel and Reid, 1945, p. 2). Saettler (1990), while more supportive, implies that educational radio declined rapidly after World War II and was pretty much finished by 1950.

But these scholars rushed to judgment. They over-emphasized audience studies and audience size. Their misplaced focus masked many significant accomplishments of the SOAs. More important these scholars overlooked the Wisconsin School of the Air (WSA). A rousing success that became an integral part of Wisconsin's educational system, the WSA represented one of the most successful applications of communication technology to education.

For nearly a half century, the WSA broadcast a curriculum of music, art, science, literature, current events, social studies, government, and conservation to hundreds of thousands of elementary students in Wisconsin and neighboring states. Its success was confirmed by high enrollment, longevity, numerous awards, and personal testimonials, some of which are included in this work. The WSA succeeded because it: (1) used a new communication technology appropriately to meet specific educational needs, (2) built communities of learners, (3) focused on supporting classroom teachers, (4) encouraged feeling, creativity, and values, and (5) became part of a powerful statewide broadcasting network dedicated to education. Also, it pioneered the development of award-winning pedagogy such as the early use of active and collaborative learning and creative expression via radio.

Saettler (1990) says that too often in the history of the field, there has been a "one sided emphasis on media ... an excessive concentration on hardware, at the expense of process, feeling, motivation, art, and values" (p. 538). The WSA largely avoided many of these mistakes, primarily because it was focused on meeting educational needs through the use of technology rather than seeking to find applications for technology in education.

The Wisconsin Idea

The WSA was created at the University of Wisconsin at Madison (UW) and represented a logical outgrowth of the school's guiding philosophy known as the "Wisconsin Idea." The term carried several meanings, but the one that inspired the WSA is captured in a slogan: "The boundaries of the campus are the boundaries of the state" (Apps, 1996, p. 97). This meant that the UW was dedicated to serving the educational needs of all the people of the state no matter what their occupation or economic status. To help fulfill that mission, UW faculty and administrators realized early on that radio would be an excellent tool. The UW became a pioneer in educational radio through what it claimed was the "oldest station in the nation," WHA AM, which began broadcasting in 1917[23] (WHA, 1969b, front page). During the early 1920s, as broadcast radio was just getting off the ground, WHA offered a variety of educational programs such as a homemaker show, market news, and agricultural programs (Apps, 1996, p. 90). A few years later, WHA became the home base for the WSA.

Origins

In 1929, the Payne Fund, which had been instrumental in launching Ben Darrow's Ohio experiment, agreed to fund an experiment in broadcasting to the schools of Wisconsin. By the spring of 1930, the UW's Radio Research Committee, long concerned with improving education for Wisconsin's rural school population, designed an experiment to measure the effectiveness of radio for teaching current events and music to sixth-, seventh-, and eighth-grade students in rural schools. Researchers believed that in those areas of curriculum, the rural schools were unable to provide appropriate educational offerings. Their two-part study included an experimental group and a control group, each comprised of 25 rural schools. The radio lessons were broadcast over WHA for 10 weeks, and the results were encouraging. The experimental group, those who received lessons via radio, outperformed the control group. The researchers concluded that radio could be used to teach subjects when no qualified teachers were available (Barr, Ewbank, & McCormick, 1942; Schneiker, 1949). However, researchers emphasized that radio's greatest potential lay in supplementing, not replacing, the teacher (Schneiker, 1949). This approach, advocated by all other SOAs, remained WSA's stated policy throughout its history.

In contrast to the clear organizational structure that marked the beginnings of the Ohio and

---

[23]*WHA, the University of Wisconsin.* 9XM-WHA achieved its first successful transmission of voice and music in 1917 from the University of Wisconsin campus in Madison. Pioneers in the establishment of the station were Malcolm Hansen and Professor Earle Terry (Radio, Roots of Broadcasting).

American schools of the air, the WSA's origins seemed informal, lacking a clearly defined admin-istration. This informality grew out of the fact that the school was started and always remained a function of radio station WHA, which itself was not set up as a separate agency but instead was fostered early on by a joint effort of the UW's education and speech departments and the Radio Research Committee[24] (Lowe, 1972; Schneiker, 1949).

Following the successful experiment, the Radio Research Committee planned to broadcast to the schools. The person most responsible for carrying out those plans and starting the WSA was Harold B. McCarty, whose introduction to educational radio occurred by accident. A grad-uate student in speech and theater with experience in vaudeville, McCarty said "yes" when asked by the head of the UW speech department, in the fall of 1929, to do some announcing for the campus radio station. Later he said that he, "instantly fell in love with WHA and the idea of using radio to extend the UW [to all of Wisconsin]" (Lowe, 1972, p. 1).

In February of 1931, McCarty became the program director for WHA, making him the sta-tion's top administrator and soon after the de facto director of the WSA as well. During that summer, McCarty planned WSA programs using volunteer help from UW faculty and Madison teachers. Prominent among the volunteers was H. A. Engel, a former teacher and UW graduate student who would continue to serve as the WHA assistant director for many years. Several of the original volunteers would also continue to serve as broadcaster "radio teachers" for decades.

"On October 5, 1931, with no public fanfare, a student announcer stepped up to the big box-like microphone [and said], 'Station WHA presents the first broadcast of the Wisconsin School of the Air!' So began a[n instructional] service that spanned a period of more than forty years" (McCarty, nd). From the very first day, WSA offered a full schedule of ten 15- to 20-minute pro-gram series, one in the morning and one in the afternoon five days a week, as shown in Table 20.

TABLE 20. WSA PROGRAM SCHEDULE, 1931–32
(Schneiker, 1949)

Day	Time	Program	Grades
Monday	9:35 A.M.	You and Your Government	7–9
	2:10 P.M.	Counseling and Guidance	9–12
Tuesday	9:35 A.M.	Dramatization and Stories for Children	1–4
	2:10 P.M.	Wisconsin History	7–8
Wednesday	9:35 A.M.	Let's Sing	4–8
	2:10 P.M.	Art Appreciation	5–9
Thursday	9:35 A.M.	Birds in Autumn and Winter	3–6
	2:10 P.M.	What Makes a House a Home	7–9
Friday	9:35 A.M.	Health and Safety	1–4
	2:10 P.M.	Poetry Club	7–9

WSA's first-year programs are unremarkable for their subject matter or methods. True, *You and Your Government* included an initial broadcast by Wisconsin governor Philip La Follette, but similar titles had been offered by the ASA and OSA for nearly two years. What was different, however, was broadcasting programs in the mornings and afternoons. This flexibility probably enabled the WSA to attract more students in its listening area than the other SOAs. Despite its

---

[24]The Radio Research Committee was in turn established by the Committee on Radio Broadcasting, which had been appointed in 1928 by UW President Glenn Frank (Lowe, 1972).

limited budget, WSA offered more programs per week than did the well-funded ASA. Also, the schedule shows that WSA focused on programming for elementary grades. With the exception of Counseling, programs for high school students did not appeared on the schedule until 1935. This focus on elementary rather than high school students served the WSA well, because as mentioned, radio instruction served the schedule of elementary and junior high school teachers better than it did high school teachers.[25]

One major failing, however, was the lack of any printed teacher guides. During the first two years, mimeographed program schedules were mailed out sporadically, but not until 1933 did McCarty schedule the full semester in advance. In 1938, the WSA finally distributed teacher guides that included pedagogical tips, resources, and instructional aids, the kind of things ASA had done from the very first.

WSA's Mission

One of the key factors in WSA's long-term success was its dedication to serving the educational needs of rural Wisconsin. That dedication was highlighted in a statement by E. B. Gordon, UW music professor and one of the original and most popular WSA teachers. Speaking before the WSA went on the air, Gordon highlighted the WSA mission: "Do you know there are still more than 4,000 one-room rural and small state-graded schools in this state? Just think of those poor gals out there, trying to teach all subjects and all grade levels. Most of them have had no training in music or art and the creative activities that children need. Let's see how we can help them by radio" (McCarty, nd, quote from speech).

While the OSA saw its mission as bringing the voice of great thinkers, artists, and leaders into all the classrooms of Ohio, and the ASA was preoccupied with building prestige for the CBS network, WSA's directors saw their mission differently. They wanted to serve the unmet educational needs of the majority of the state's elementary population, namely rural students who attended one-room, state graded, or county elementary schools,[26] a mission that paralleled the mission of station WHA and indeed the University of Wisconsin.

Limited Reach

Although the WSA got off to a successful start in 1931, its programs reached only a portion of the state's schools. WHA, like most educational stations, had been limited by the Federal Radio Commission (FRC) to operating as a regional daytime station (Lowe, 1972). Furthermore, WHA's legally mandated weak signal of 1,000 watts reached only 75 miles at best (McCarty, 1967). Only a fraction of Wisconsin residents could receive WHA's programs. To overcome that limitation, in 1931, McCarty and Engel proposed merging WHA with WLBL, a 2,500-watt station operated by the Wisconsin Department of Agriculture from broadcast facilities located about 100 miles north of Madison in Stevens Point, Wisconsin. The merger was denied by the FRC, but the two stations joined forces informally by having WLBL rebroadcast WHA programs via a rented long-distance phone line (WHA, 1969b). By this arrangement, WSA programs could be carried to more Wisconsin schoolchildren in the northern part of the state, though many more lay beyond the signal of either station. The relationship with WLBL proved valuable to WHA and the WSA for another reason as well. During the dark days of the Depression, the Department of Agriculture rescued the WSA and WHA from near extinction.

[25]The problem of using radio in high school was mentioned in a letter from the Newark school board: "Because of conflicting bell schedules and lack of uniformity in the high school class period ... it is almost impossible to cultivate and sustain a steady high school listening audience" (WSA, various dates).

[26]According to WSA archival data, for the year 1945–46, the State Department of Public Instruction reported that pupils in one-room rural, state graded, and county elementary schools constituted 52 percent of Wisconsin's elementary school population, kindergarten through eighth grade.

THREATS

During the first five years, the WSA faced two threats to its existence. One was the financial strain caused by the Great Depression, and the other was the attempt by commercial interests to strip the UW of its radio station and turn WHA into a commercial outlet. Both hit simultaneously. Many commercial stations and networks fiercely fought for control of all radio outlets including those owned by education stations. They argued, often persuasively, that commercial stations would provide educational programs; consequently, there was no need for the state to fund public education by radio. McCarty recalls that just such a threat hit WHA in the early 1930s when all state institutions were scrambling to justify their share of scarce state dollars. He said:

> During the week when our bill for appropriation of funds [for WHA] was to come before the [Wisconsin] legislature, there appeared in the headlines of the two local newspapers an announcement of the plan for two commercial stations to take over the educational work of the state station. [Their proposal to] launch a program of public service without cost to the taxpayers, served to block the introduction of our bill for appropriations from the legislature of Wisconsin. The result was that we got no appropriation from the legislature. We had to go before the emergency board of the state, and for seven weeks we were entirely without funds. This is the kind of thing that puts educators on the defensive [McCarty, 1935, p. 38].

While McCarty, Engel, and WHA survived the threat from commercial stations, they were also involved in fighting off the effects of the Great Depression. From 1932 to 1936, the UW excluded WHA operating funds from its appropriation request.[27] UW President Glenn Frank conceded that broadcasting was a worthy activity — but believed that classroom operation must take precedence. During those years, however, the station (and WSA indirectly) was funded with small grants from the Wisconsin State Emergency Board. For the year 1934–35, WHA received $15,723 for operations out of which WSA represented only one of the station's activities. In 1935, McCarty submitted a request to the legislature for $42,000 for two years of WHA operations. The legislature denied his request, but subsequently WHA's friends in agricultural broadcasting came to the rescue. From 1936 to 1941, operating funds for WHA were appropriated through the State Department of Agriculture and Markets, which administered radio station WLBL. However, control and supervision of WHA and the WSA remained with the UW[28] (Lowe, 1972, p. 19–20).

Administration, Organization, and Staff

Because station WHA was wholly owned by the University of Wisconsin, the WSA was a part of the UW, a relationship that proved beneficial to both parties. It enabled McCarty to recruit technical and educational volunteers from various UW departments to run the station and to help plan and implement the school's educational programs. In return, the WSA helped the UW carry out its mission of serving the educational needs of all the state's citizens. McCarty said that the WSA programs built a reservoir of support for WHA not just from professional educators but also from parents whose children listened to the WSA at school.

Such interconnected relationships make it difficult for us today to identify the school's staff and budget. In the 1935–1936 WSA schedule McCarty is identified as "Program Director, WHA," but because his picture and greeting are featured on the inside cover, it appears that he is the

---

[27]Despite the lack of operating funds, the university and the legislature, curiously, continued to demonstrate a commitment to public radio by funding the construction of new offices and a transmitter for WHA completed in 1935. Engel described the new facility as the most modern and spacious, consisting of three studios surrounding a central control room, appointed with furniture designed by the university's art department, and featuring a large pipe organ to provide musical accompaniment. The new facility was augmented with a new transmitter (Engel, 1935a).

[28]It is unclear whether the funds came out of the Agriculture and Marketing Department's budget or the department merely served as conduit for the funds.

WSA's director also. Each radio teacher is featured with picture and name next to the appropriate program description and schedule. No others are identified in the schedule, even though there must have been scriptwriters and production people who worked on the WSA programs. The schedule also prominently states that the WHA programs were approved for classroom use by both the State Department of Public Instruction and the Wisconsin Teachers Association (WSA, 1935). Other records from 1935 show annual salary and wages of approximately $14,500 for WHA's full- and part-time staff, including McCarty and radio announcer Verner Hansen, both of whom probably devoted substantial time to the WSA (Engel, 1935b).

Curriculum and program planning were carried out as a cooperative effort by classroom teachers and administrators from the Madison schools, the staff of the State Department of Public Instruction, and faculty from the University of Wisconsin. These groups analyzed the state curriculum to discover the opportunities for radio to contribute to educational objectives (Barr et al., 1942). McCarty recalls that some from this diverse group not only helped with planning but also produced and broadcast the programs. "We were fortunate in having a number of inspiring teachers, such as Professor Edgar B. Gordon, Wakelin McNeel, Mrs. Fannie Steve, James Schwalbach, and others whose names became bywords throughout the state" (Lowe, 1972, p. 16). Gordon was a UW professor of Music, McNeel worked out of the Department of Agriculture, Steve was a Madison school teacher and Schwalbach's salary was paid in part by the UW Extension and part by WHA.

The link between the WSA and the UW was the Committee on Radio Broadcasting, which by the mid–1930s consisted of just three faculty, representing speech, agricultural journalism, and electrical engineering. Surprisingly, it involved no one from education. According to McCarty, the committee set policy for the station and served as liaison with the UW faculty. They also advocated that UW's administration support WHA radio largely on the basis that the station in turn supported the school of the air[29] (McCarty, 1941). In addition, the WSA received a boost in prestige when the state's Department of Public Instruction and the Wisconsin Teachers Association approved the programs for classroom use. This enabled WHA to advertise the programs as, "State Approved Broadcasts" (WSA, 1935).

Educational Programs

Despite difficult financial times and the circuitous founding route, the WSA gradually improved the quality and quantity of its instructional offerings. As shown in Table 21, by the 1935–36 school year, WSA broadcast 13 programs per week.

TABLE 21. WSA PROGRAM SCHEDULE, 1935–36
(WSA, 1935)

Day	Time	Program	Grades
Monday	9:35–9:50 A.M.	*Afield with Ranger Mac*	4–8
	1:30–1:50 P.M.	*History Dramas*	9–12
	2:05–2:20 P.M.	*Little Stories of Great Lives*	4–7
Tuesday	9:35–9:50 A.M.	*Story Time for Little Foxes*	K–3
	2:05–2:20 P.M.	*Dramatic Moments in History*	6–9

[29]In a report on the WSA's first 10 years, an anonymous author emphasizes the key role played by the University of Wisconsin in WSA success. The writer says UW, "which is essentially an institution for higher education, is assisting in the teaching of huge classes of elementary school children.... No other agency in the state has had the facilities or the inclination to render the service." Not only did the university provide the radio station WHA, it also provided most of the management, many of the teachers, and the goodwill of its name among the residents of Wisconsin. In addition, the UW Department of Education encouraged the UW teacher preparation program to participate and cooperate with the WSA program.

Wednesday	9:35–9:50 A.M.	*Nature Tales*	K–3
	1:30–1:50 P.M.	*Gems of Literature*	9–12
	2:05–2:25 P.M.	*Journeys in Music Land (Let's Sing)*	4–8
Thursday	9:35–9:50 A.M.	*Creative Art*	6–9
	2:05–2:20 P.M.	*Exploring Distant Lands*	5–8
Friday	9:35–9:50 A.M.	*Rhythm and Games*	K–3
	1:30–1:50 P.M.	*American Problems*	9–12
	2:05–2:20 P.M.	*Dial News*	6–9

The schedule in Table 21 shows the addition of three programs for high school grades, an experiment that lasted only a few years. Most significantly, the schedule for 1935 includes several of the beloved radio teachers (Pop Gordon, Wakelin McNeel, Mrs. Fannie Steve, and James Schwalbach) who became well-known personalities and who played a significant role in the education of tens of thousands of students across the state, both in and out of school (Apps, 1996, p. 92). The program titles and descriptions given here are taken from the teachers guide for 1935–36. The descriptions are limited to programs that demonstrate an emphasis on active engagement of listeners, an educational approach that contrasts with those of the ASA and OSA.

PROGRAM DESCRIPTIONS, 1935–1936

Afield with Ranger Mac. The ranger, Wakelin McNeel, an official in the state's 4-H movement, broadcast talks on nature and conservation that remained popular with young students of Wisconsin for more than 21 years. Apps (1996) tells a story that seems to have attained the status of rural legend in Wisconsin but testifies to *Ranger Mac's* popularity with rural classroom teachers. It is about a country teacher in a school so poor it could not afford a radio. The teacher found a way to overcome this obstacle because he was dedicated to *Ranger Mac*. When it was time to listen to the program, he took his class outside, gathered around his Ford, and listened on the car radio. "Got a little cold sometimes," the teacher recalled, "but we never missed a program" (p. 91).

McNeel wrote his own scripts, which were straight talks that required little editing (Barr et al., 1942). The talks helped students understand and appreciate the importance of soil conservation, the majesty of trees, and the need to observe nature carefully to learn her secrets. *Ranger Mac* is credited with inspiring thousands of children to participate in Wisconsin's successful school-based reforestation program, in which Wisconsin schoolchildren planted more than 7 million trees in 214 school forest plots throughout the state.

At the urging of Ranger Mac, hundreds of schools also developed and maintained classroom nature exhibits and recorded their observations in nature logs (Apps, 1996). Literally hundreds of these exhibits, dubbed "Conservation Corners," served as living demonstrations of the topics, plants, and animals covered in Ranger Mac's broadcasts. Classmates worked together to develop their exhibits, and many sought special recognition for their efforts. Somehow, McNeel arranged to have state agriculture extension employees tour local schools to evaluate the Conservation Corners. Selected exhibits were rewarded with equipment for building better exhibits (Schneiker, 1949; WSA, 1935). *Afield with Ranger Mac* motivated literally hundreds of thousands of children to observe nature, take notes, read, reflect, create exhibits, and plant trees throughout Wisconsin.

Journeys in Music Land (Let's Sing). When the WSA took to the air in the fall of 1931, listeners heard Professor E. B. Gordon's *Journeys in Music Land*[30] for the first time. They continued listening to him for 24 years, until the mid–1950s. No scripts were prepared for the program; Professor

---

[30]After Gordon retired in 1955, the series continued under the title of *Let's Sing*. Warren Wooldridge served as instructor, but the format remained exactly as developed by Gordon (Sanders, 1990).

Gordon,[31] who soon earned the affectionate title "Pop," spoke extemporaneously from a simple outline (Barr et al., 1942). Retitled *Let's Sing* in the mid–1950s, the series emphasized singing and note reading and became one of many WSA programs that engaged children in active learning. Because all of the students in *Journeys/Let's Sing* had their own songbooks (WSA, 1948), it is not surprising that they were actively involved in making music. A vivid description of student involvement is presented by the testimonial of Bonnie Trudell, a student at the Squaw Lake School in the late 1940s and early 1950s. She said: "We'd tune in the radio, all sitting at our desks with our song books, and there would be talk about where these songs came from and a demonstration of the song. Then we'd all sing along. I remember the theme song, Sing, sing the whole day through. The best of things will come to you. A song will always see you through, so sing, just sing'" (Apps, 1996, p. 94).

Gordon, a UW music professor, conveyed his enthusiasm for music to tens of thousands of Wisconsin schoolchildren. During the long tenure of *Journey's/Let's Sing* on the WSA, it is estimated that as many as 70,000 students sang along at one time (Schneiker, 1949).

Rhythm and Games. Probably the longest-running WSA program, *Rhythm and Games* was essentially a radio-based physical education (PE) class for five- to seven-year-olds. The radio teacher, Fannie Steve, started the series on the first day that WSA hit the air in 1931 and continued her broadcasts until 1965. According to the description in the 1948 WSA program brochure, Mrs. Steve uses "original and adapted music to help teach games, dances, rhythmics, and pantomimes which are more than just fun. They developed coordination, poise, and rhythmic sense" (WSA, 1948, p. 22). During the entire broadcast, tens of thousands of students across the state were on their feet, engaged in rhythmic action, games, and pantomime. Children discovered that taking turns and following directions were part of the game and improved the fun. According to observers, "this program was literally non-stop student participation and activity, though, at times, chaotic.... Mrs. Steve can give lessons to anyone on anticipating children's responses ... she's practically infallible" (Barts, 1945, p. 2).

Nature Tales. One series that lasted only a brief time was presented by the "Bird Girl, [who] whistled her way straight into the hearts of the youngsters" (WSA, 1935). Using birdcalls to announce the program, the "Bird Girl" spun adventure stories involving feathery and furry creatures that the writers believed appealed irresistibly to "tiny tots." We're assured that each week children looked forward eagerly to the Bird Girl's merry whistle. Despite its irresistible appeal, the series was discontinued after a year.

PROGRAM HIGHLIGHTS, 1938–1949

By the 1938 school year, the broadcast schedule included the big four programs that would achieve surprising popularity and make their teachers household names throughout Wisconsin. Previously mentioned were *Afield with Ranger Mac, Let's Sing,* and *Rhythm and Games.* The fourth program, *Let's Draw,* was initiated in the 1938–39 school year. Table 22 shows the schedule for 1938–39.

TABLE 22. WSA PROGRAMS, 1938–39
(Barr et al., 1942)

Program	Grades	Subject
Afield with Ranger Mac	4–8	Conservation and natural science
Journeys in Music Land/		
Let's Sing	4–8	Music, singing, and note reading
Rhythm and Games	K–3	Rhythmic movement, games, cooperation

[31]A pioneer in music education by radio, Gordon did his first music broadcast in 1921 over WHA. According to Sanders (1990), the instructional techniques he developed were imitated in a number of subsequent educational music programs.

Let's Draw	4–8	Drawing
Radio Reading Club	6–9	Literature and storytelling
Peggy and Paul	3–6	Primary social studies
Neighbors 'Round the World	??	Geography, world studies
Pictures Studies	??	Art appreciation
Music Enjoyment for Children	1–4	Music appreciation
Nature Tales	K–3	Nature study for primary grades
Community Living	5–9	Social skills

Let's Draw. This long-running series of 35 years was designed and developed by radio teacher Jim Schwalbach, who also served as an extension specialist in art and design for the UW College of Agriculture. Schwalbach delivered art education and drawing instruction to tens of thousands of students in rural and small-town classrooms. At first, the idea of teaching drawing by radio seems curious, but in fact the program was very effective. Schwalbach usually started by introducing the theme for the day's art activity and using several minutes of storytelling and music to stimulate young imaginations. Then, while the music continued, students were invited to draw. Most students could not finish their drawings in the remaining broadcast time; consequently, they had to continue working after the broadcast (Kelly, 1990). The teachers manual for *Let's Draw* asked teachers to facilitate follow-up work by encouraging students to finish, giving praise when appropriate, and withholding criticism.

It's easy to imagine, then, that a typical *Let's Draw* lesson might have required 45 to 60 minutes of class time per week, a fact that contradicts Cuban's (1986) criticism that radio instruction lasted for only 15 to 20 minutes per week and therefore was inconsequential. When they

A 6th Grade Art Class Listening and Drawing — *Let's Draw* (courtesy of Wisconsin Historical Society Whi 23503).

finished the drawings, students were asked to select up to five of the best to represent the class.[32] These were to be sent to Madison for "criticism and honor role evaluation" (Schwalbach, 1948–1949). Schwalbach reviewed every piece of student art sent to him and featured the best work in the teachers manuals. Schwalbach's program set a high standard for radio instruction, received awards and national recognition, and, according to one scholar, affected how art was taught in Wisconsin schools for decades (Kelly, 1990).

Other notable programs offered in the 1938–39 year included these:

Pictures Studies. This series offered art appreciation for elementary grades and should be clearly distinguished from *Let's Draw,* which offered creative arts for grades four through eight.

Music Enjoyment for Children. Based on the assumption that if children became familiar with great (classical) music at an early age, they would adopt it as their own, this series used riddles and games to enhance the listening pleasure for grades one through four. The series proved popular for more than a decade.

The WSA also offered a radio program for teachers, *Problems in Classroom Instruction.* Presented by the UW School of Education and aired in the late afternoon, the series provided round-table discussions of typical problems in classroom instruction and new developments in the field of education.

It's instructive to compare the schedule from 1938 with that of a decade later. By the end of the war, WSA had rooted itself in the educational environment of rural and small-town Wisconsin. Its program offerings built on a bedrock of five well-accepted and highly regarded programs plus several new programs that achieved notable results. Table 23 shows the program schedule for 1948–49.

TABLE 23. WSA PROGRAM SCHEDULE, 1948–49
(WSA, 1948)

Program	Time	Grade	Subject
Monday			
Afield with Ranger Mac	9:30	5–8	Conservation and natural science
Democracy in Action	1:30	5–8	Social studies
Tuesday			
Let's Find Out	9:30	2–4	Natural science
Let's Draw	1:30	4–8	Drawing and art skills
Wednesday			
Exploring Science	9:30	5–8	Experiments in physical science
Journeys in Music Land	1:30	4–8	Music, singing, and note reading
Thursday			
Music Enjoyment for Children	9:30	1–4	Music appreciation for youngsters
News of the Week	1:30	5–8	News and background
Friday			
Rhythm and Games	9:30	K–3	Games and rhythmic movement
Book Trails	1:30	3–8	Dramatic reading of children's literature

The schedule shows a reduction in the number of programs from 13 in 1938 to 10 in 1948 and that 5 programs were continued from the earlier decade. They constituted the foundation of the WSA's offerings: *Afield with Ranger Mac, Let's Draw, Journeys in Music Land/Let's Sing, News of the Week,* and *Rhythm and Games.* These programs all continued to be popular for

---

[32]In the Let's Draw teacher manual for 1952–1953, Schwalbach insisted that students, not teachers, select drawings for submission for Honor Role evaluation. Teacher's evaluation would be too adult, he said.

another decade (or two in some cases). Several of the newer programs also attained long tenures. They included these:

Book Trails. The series provided dramatic narrations taken from one of 28 featured books selected by the radio teacher. Dramatic reading was widely used by all SOAs and proved effective for almost all elementary grades. In order to synchronize the broadcast with classroom readings, the WSA's assistant director, Arlene McKellar, mailed out in the spring the list of books to be used in *Book Trails* the following year. Usually the selections were made around a unifying theme such as growth of a child as an individual and in the community. The list enabled rural schools to order the books to be read ahead of time from their county libraries. In this way, the WSA informally established the reading curricula followed by several thousand Wisconsin schools. The program remained a WSA mainstay from the early 1940s to the mid–1960s.

Let's Find Out. This series presented children in grades two through four with natural science and social studies stories. The radio characters, all children similar in age to the listeners, provided answers to questions about the natural and social world.

Democracy in Action. This social science series for the upper grades documented how everyday people use the services of state government.

Exploring Science and Young Experimenters. It seems remarkable that elementary students could perform science experiments in their classrooms under the direction of a distant radio teacher, but for nearly 30 years that is exactly what tens of thousands of students did in schoolrooms across Wisconsin. The broadcasts, known as *Exploring Science* in the 1940s and 1950s and *Young Experimenters* in the late 1950s and 1960s, were geared to fifth through eighth graders. Design and instruction of the series were the responsibility of Lloyd and Sylvia Liedtke. They shaped the series on the premise that listeners should participate actively in the learning process. A class that subscribed to the series organized itself into several experiment committees. Each week, one committee performed the experiment for that week while other class members observed and took notes. The following week another committee did the work, and so on until all the committees had performed an experiment. Preparation was the key. The teachers manual directed each class to set up a science shelf at the beginning of the semester. Students stocked the shelf with all the materials they would need to perform the experiments for the entire semester. The manual also instructed the committees to read through their experiment prior to the broadcast and to have the necessary materials on hand. Preparation, it stressed, was the responsibility of students, not teachers (WSA, 1947–1948).

The teachers manuals were addressed more to the students than to the classroom teachers. For example, the teachers manual for 1946–47 said: "Hello, Young Experimenters, this is your science program. You can do a great deal to make it more interesting for yourself by accepting the responsibility for gathering the necessary materials each week and conducting the experiments" (WSA, 1946–1947, 1947–1948).

For more than 30 years, during a period when few elementary schools could boast of having a science lab or even a science teacher, *Exploring Science* and *Young Experimenters* brought activity-based instruction on science to as many as 20,000 Wisconsin students per year.

MANUALS AND SCHEDULES

Starting in the mid–1930s, WSA began distributing, each semester, a brochure with program schedules and descriptions. One page was devoted to each program. By providing an overview of the semester's offering, the brochures made advance planning possible. These were distributed free of charge to teachers in the WHA listening area (WSA, 1935). In the late 1930s, some WSA teachers took the brochure idea a step further. At their own expense, they began developing teacher manuals for their programs. In addition to the semester schedule, the manuals described topics, suggested preparation and follow-up activities, gave advice on instruction, and explained any reward or recognition programs that might be part of the series. They

Using the [Radio] Science Lesson (courtesy of U.S. Office of Education).

frequently included study support meant to be used by the students. Most likely, this latter material was packaged with the teachers manual to avoid asking schools or students to pay for individual manuals, a requirement that might have limited participation. Only one program, *Let's Sing,* issued a student manual that students had to pay for.

Teacher manuals proved very popular, and by 1940 they were produced and distributed for all programs. However, they were not distributed freely. Teachers or schools had to order and pay for them. In the late 1940s, fees for the manuals ran from 20 cents to a high of 50 cents for the *Let's Draw* manual. In comparison, the student manual required to participate in *Let's Sing* cost 15 cents (WSA, 1948). If we assume prices in 2005 to be at least 10 times those of the 1940s, the cost for teacher manuals in today's dollars would be $2 to $5. This was not an insurmountable amount, but it was enough to discourage the merely curious from enrolling. Charging for the manuals not only provided a source of income, it enabled the WSA to gather enrollment data that proved more reliable than the mail surveys that were used by other SOAs. The topic of how the WSA gathered enrollment data is discussed later in this chapter.

Broadcasting System

By 1938, WHA was on fairly solid footing financially and boasted fine new facilities. In addition, nearly 25 percent of Wisconsin elementary schoolchildren were tuned in to at least one WSA program (Barr et al., 1942, p. 8). Even with that apparent popularity, a substantial portion of the state's rural and small-town residents lived beyond the reach of WHA or WLBL signals. To solve this problem, McCarty and Engel, perhaps emboldened by their relative success, concocted an audacious scheme. They decided to take advantage of a little-known and seldom-enforced FCC regulation and have WHA designated as a clear channel station. As a clear channel,

WHA could have broadcast at 50,000 watts, prevent any other stations from using its frequency, and be easily heard throughout Wisconsin, thereby fulfilling the Wisconsin Idea.[33] However, the plan meant putting a major commercial station out of business. Engel recounts the background to their plan: "The [FCC] rules said that the clear channels were to be distributed equitably among the states.... Chicago has five clear channels and Wisconsin nary a one. It looked like a very good case" (Lowe, 1972, p. 7).

As such, Engel and McCarty boldly applied to take over the frequency of Chicago's WMAQ, a station wholly owned by the mighty NBC. "We knew that we were fighting a lot of money with NBC, but we decided we might as well get ... the best [frequency available]. And that really did stir up a storm" (Lowe, 1972, p. 7). The proposal sparked furious outrage from editors of the *Chicago Tribune*, who were appalled at the audacity of educational radio attempting to take over a commercial channel (*Tribune*, 1938). In articles and editorials spanning a six-month period, *Tribune* editors attacked educational radio for what they called a blatant attempt to conquer the commercial broadcast establishment, and they attacked WHA in particular for doing the bidding of the LaFollette political machine (*Tribune*, 1939). McCarty and Engel were soon summoned to a meeting in the governor's office to explain their request. Engel recounts that contentious meeting:

When we arrived at Governor Heil's office he was behind his big mahogany desk, with a few other representatives of the state; McCarty and I sat in. [University of Wisconsin] Professor Edward Bennett was there with a model and graphic depiction of the [clear] channels and how they were distributed [across the United States]. Across the table from the governor sat a vice-president from NBC, a man named Bill Hedges, and on either side of him sat an attorney. They had an array of legal talent there and were ready to do battle. They listened very intently and quietly until we had presented the case. Then this vice-president of the network stood up and leaned across the table and shook a finger under the governor's nose and said, "Governor, we don't like this and we're going to lick you. We've got three million dollars to spend on this and we're going lick you."

Governor Heil said, "Now, hold on, I don't like the way you said that." Well nobody liked the way he said it or what he said, but there was nothing we could do but withdraw our application, because we could not get the necessary money to fight a corporation like that (Lowe, 1972, pp. 7–8).

Once again McCarty was frustrated in his dream of bringing public radio and WSA programs to all Wisconsin citizens.

Philosophy and Methods

Perhaps one of the reasons WSA gained popularity with Wisconsin teachers was its unacknowledged adherence to Dewey's progressive philosophy and the application of his ideas to radio education. Like the other SOAs of the day, WSA administrators and teachers did not formally advocate a philosophical approach as such, but clearly the environment of state educational bureaucracy and the UW favored those ideas. By 1935, the Wisconsin State Department of Public Instruction had approved WSA broadcasts for classroom use (WSA, 1935). A year later, prominent educators within that office began advocating a progressive philosophy, based on John Dewey's teachings (Kelly, 1990). One major instructional approach associated with John Dewey and progressivism was activity-based learning. Methods included cooperative exploration, project-based learning, problem solving, and experiments using the scientific method (Kelly, 1990, pp. 15–17). These ideas were supported by the state educational administrators. In official reports,

[33]As mentioned earlier, the Wisconsin Idea was that UW was dedicated to serving the educational needs of all the people of the state no matter what their occupation or economic status.

they advanced the idea of replacing "older methods such as passive memory work" with the progressive idea of "learning by doing." Experience was seen as the best teacher, and even at this early date, radio was recommended as an instructional tool that lent itself to active learning (Kelly, 1990, p. 95). Kelly also asserts that WSA's mother institution, the UW Madison, had long been considered a prime example of progressivism in higher education (Kelly, 1990, p. 15).

Despite the rich context of progressivism that surrounded them, WSA administrators and teachers avoided making any official pronouncements about their educational philosophy. Perhaps they felt that stating an educational philosophy would raise opposition to their efforts. However, some insight into the educational philosophy that guided the radio teachers can be obtained from the WSA teachers manuals. The manuals enabled radio teachers to communicate directly to classroom teachers about issues such as teaching methods to be used with their programs. For the most part, these expressions reflected the strong influence of Dewey's progressive thought, which focused on activity-based learning.

For example, Jim Schwalbach states that "Actual experience is the best teacher. By looking at a cow, a child learns to draw a cow" (Schwalbach, 1952). Another radio teacher echoed similar ideas about methods. In his teachers manual for 1952–53, under the title, "Listening Only is Not Enough," Wakelin McNeel (Ranger Mac) laid out his basic idea that activity is the key to learning. "With children ... the secret of ... keeping interest is to have something to do" (WSA, 1953b). He urged teachers to encourage students to create and maintain a Conservation Corner in their classes and also to keep a logbook of all their observations of nature. He described the purpose behind the Conservation Corners and logbooks as, "a way to strengthen the teachings of the broadcasts by activity. They are the means of arousing interest in the surroundings and of fixing in memory the lessons presented." McNeel also said that when learning activities are closely related to life, they "integrate naturally with spelling, composition, art and social studies" (WSA, 1953b). The idea that learning is best achieved through activity based in the real world is fundamental to progressive thought (Null, 2003).[34] To encourage students to develop their logs, McNeel developed an annual state conservation contest with more than 100 awards of prizes and cash (Schneiker, 1949).

Other progressive values that influenced WSA programming were democracy and child-centered curriculum. Radio art education creators William Claxton and Jim Schwalbach shared a philosophy that art should be a daily source of enjoyment for all and not just a privilege of a talented few. They shaped the *Let's Draw* radio series to foster the development of self-confidence, self-expression, and self-evaluation within an environment of social cooperation. These ideas parallel Dewey's ideas about child-centered learning and teaching for life in a democracy (Kelly, 1990, p. 14). In his teachers manuals, Schwalbach articulated his philosophy that art education should be about individual expression, not about learning a set of predetermined skills. Young students should follow their inner ear rather than the outside authority. He tells the teachers: "There's no compulsion about 'Let's Draw.'" Some children may not find the subject suggested by the broadcast appealing and prefer to draw boats or fashion models. Let them express themselves as they choose. To force them to conform ... might remove all inclination to express themselves creatively (WSA, 1948–1949, p. 8).

While Schwalbach's desire to stimulate spontaneous creative expression blended well with Dewey's focus on the individual learner, his teachers manual also shows a desire to get students

---

[35]Probably the strongest advocate of activity-based curriculum was Dewey's disciple at Columbia, William Kilpatrick, best known for his advocacy of project learning. However, the two actually disagreed on the role of activity in learning. Kilpatrick believed that activity had value in itself and that mastery of subject matter was relatively unimportant. Dewey, while he wanted to make thinking and learning "active business," opposed reducing education to undisciplined activities meant to keep children interested. He supported project learning "only so long as the teacher had a clear end in view" (Null, 2003, p. 166).

working together cooperatively instead of competitively. He asks teachers to encourage the children not only to work together but also to evaluate each other's work in a cooperative spirit (Kelly, 1990, p. 95).

In her 1963–64 manual for *Let's Write*, radio teacher Maureen Applegate offered a just-in-time self-directed approach to learning that seems to have a lot in common with more recent ideas about "authentic learning." For example, she advises teachers: "The mechanics of English are easy if children learn them when they need them. Direct conversation, for instance, needs quotation marks to fence it in. Send your pupils to their language books [during the writing task] to find how to punctuate and to paragraph direct quotations.... Urge children to develop the habit of using their books for self help (WSA, 1967–1968, p. 6).

The radio teachers' instructions sound similar to discussions of authentic learning advocated by some current constructivist educational scholars, such as Brown, Collins, and Duguid (1989). They propose that learning rules and cognitive tools, such as punctuation, be presented in a situated context such as a writing assignment rather than in the abstract, separated from the cognitive task. They recommended teaching rules and the use of cognitive tools "in the framework of the context that produced them ... in real time," just as the radio teacher suggested (Brown, et al., 1989, pp. 32–42). Applegate's instructions seem to have captured the essence of authentic learning at least as described by these scholars.

The manuals for *Exploring Science/Young Experimenters* exemplify a total dedication to the activist, problem-solving approach to learning. In fact, radio teachers Lloyd and Sylvia Liedtke condensed their educational philosophy into one word: *busy*. The heading on page one of the teachers manual for 1962–63 states, "Young Experimenters Are Busy Doing Things" (WSA, 1962–1963). According to the manual, students are busy planning, preparing, performing experiments (under the direction of the radio teacher), thinking, discussing, and cleaning up. In an earlier manual, Lloyd Liedtke sums up his approach to science education with the word *exploring*, by which he means identifying and solving problems (WSA, 1962–1963). I reviewed program scripts and teachers manuals for this science education program, and they contain no instance of lecture or narrative text; they are all problem-based learning.

The following report of an *Exploring Science* classroom experiment portrays the active learning approach suggested by Lloyd Liedtke in his manual:

> The [radio] program began with a dramatization, by radio actors, of the moment when Daguerre in France stumbled on a method of capturing a portrait on paper. Then, with guidance directions from the radio teacher, the experiment committee and their watching classmates relived this moment of discovery by performing their own experiment. The radio teacher then discussed some of the effects on science, art, and industry of this discovery and its later development, a discussion that was continued by classroom teacher and pupils after the program was over [Milbauer, 1949, p. 1].

As Milbauer points out, the lesson used dramatization to create context for the ideas demonstrated in the experiment and then carried out by the students. Milbauer goes on to say that the program was not simply a classroom activity for the children. The lesson and experiment had "assumed for the children a real meaning in the world about them" (Milbauer, 1949, p. 3). The report probably reflects a somewhat idealized version of what the reporter saw. Nevertheless, it explains how the radio teacher created a learning event characterized by active involvement and richly supplemented with contextual information. This approach to instruction would have been supported by the progressives of the day.[35]

---

[35]Most likely, today's constructivist theorists would also approve of the instructional approach used in *Exploring Science*.

Table 24 summarizes the instructional approaches used in WSA programs.

TABLE 24. WSA INSTRUCTIONAL METHODS, 1948–49
(WSA, 1948b)

Program	Method
Afield with Ranger Mac	Imaginative narration, extracurricular learning activities
Democracy in Action	Dramatization, narration
Let's Find Out	Dramatization, narration
Let's Draw	Direct teaching, active involvement, extracurricular learning activities
Exploring Science	Direct teaching, active involvement, observation, narration
Journeys in Music Land (Let's Sing)	Direct teaching, active involvement
Music Enjoyment for Children	Listening
News of the Week	Narration, reading
Rhythm and Games	Direct teaching, active involvement
Book Trails	Dramatic reading

While similar methods were attempted by the other SOAs covered in this study, the WSA far exceeded them in implementing innovative methods successfully.

A COMMUNITY OF LISTENERS AND LEARNERS

Many educators and instructional designers involved with online (Web-based) instruction are concerned with creating a sense of community among online learners.[36] These scholars and practitioners assert that community-building can generate student satisfaction with online learning and improve learning performance. The high dropout rates and dissatisfaction in many online courses are attributed in part to a lack of community among online learners (Hill & Raven, 2002). A half century before the internet, the WSA was fostering a strong sense of community among its listeners. Apps (1996) comments on the community-building aspect of the WSA broadcasts: "There was also a kind of camaraderie that developed among the school children who participated in the radio programs. They knew that they were listening with thousands of other young people each week, and now, at least for a few minutes, they were not a little crossroads school, but part of a huge congregation of students all gathered by their radios at the same time (Apps, 1996, p. 97).

I infer that this general sense of community contributed to WSA's acceptance throughout thousands of Wisconsin's schoolrooms. Moreover, many WSA programs included activities that fostered the development of learning communities and task groups among students. Table 25 summarizes WSA programs that included notable learning-community-building activities based on their source material.

TABLE 25. WSA GROUP AND COMMUNITY-BUILDING PROGRAMS

WSA Program	Group/Community-Building Activity
Let's Sing	Regional and statewide music festivals
Let's Draw	Round-robin and regional art shows, honor rolls (students selected artwork for submission)
Ranger Mac	Conservation Corners, reforestation projects

[36]Online education and education by radio can be considered different facets of distance education. Saettler (1990) treats them as branches of educational technology.

| *Let's Write* | Radio teacher solicits children's best writing to be read on-air |
| *Exploring Science*
  (later *Young Experimenters*) | Students work in groups to prepare for and conduct experiments |

Let's Sing. In 1949, up to 12,000[37] students, teachers, and parents got a chance to meet each other and Professor Gordon annually at the many regional and statewide music gatherings that were part of the *Let's Sing* experience (Schneiker, 1949, p. 27). Those large group events served as outside-the-classroom extensions of the music instruction offered by the radio series *Let's Sing* and *Journeys to Music Land.* If educators of that day had wanted to evaluate the educational effectiveness of *Let's Sing,* somehow they would have had to find a way to measure the effects of participating in the various regional and statewide events that were so much a part of the program. These events helped transform isolated, scattered student groups into a huge community that sang and learned together. One such gathering of the *Let's Sing* clan is recalled by Linda Clauder, whose teacher took the pupils in her one-room school near Prairie du Chien, Wisconsin, on a field trip to Madison in the early 1950s. Clauder recalls: "I still have a memory of Professor Gordon [the *Let's Sing* radio teacher] ... in the [UW] stock pavilion[38] filled with children and he'd say, 'Now boys and girls we're going to sing' ... and of course we knew the songs by heart. And so the whole stock pavilion was filled with these children singing songs. It was just beautiful (Clauder, Personal Communication, Nov. 7, 2003).

Let's Draw. As community outreach during the late 1930s and early 1940s, Jim Schwalbach established Round Robin Art Exhibits. A group of local schools with students enrolled in Schwalbach's drawing program would join together to exhibit the artwork of their student listeners (Kelly, 1990). It must have been an interesting day when students and teachers from a group of nearby schools gathered, perhaps at one school, in a church basement, or even in a barn, to appreciate each other's creative work. By the mid–1940s, however, Schwalbach redesigned the Round Robin idea. Schools, groups of schools, or county superintendents who wanted to participate received a traveling exhibit of the best student artwork selected mostly by Schwalbach himself. Usually the exhibits were held as part of a local meeting or event such as a graduation, holiday celebration, etc. Following the exhibit, Schwalbach sent out an evaluation form that asked the local contact person to report the number of participating schools and students. The form also served as a reminder to return the exhibit.

Schwalbach also organized, in cooperation with the county agricultural extension office, regional art shows. The 1952–53 *Let's Draw* teachers manual announced 12 "One-Day Art School," events scattered throughout the state. Schwalbach sent works to exhibit and invited the local children to exhibit their own work. In addition, he presented statewide *Let's Draw* exhibits annually at the UW Madison during the summer, creating another opportunity to build community among *Let's Draw* students. The regional art shows helped embed the WSA into the state's education and culture. Such a high level of community outreach was made possible because Schwalbach, in addition to teaching for the WSA, also served as an extension specialist for the UW's College of Agriculture. This connection enabled him to draw on the resources and contacts of agriculture extension agents throughout the state (Schwalbach, 1952).

The Honor Role of Student Talent represented another form of post-broadcast student engagement. Schwalbach invited classroom teachers to send in good student work for comment. As many as 500 classes per year sent in multiple samples of student work, and Schwalbach

---

[37]By the mid–1950s, over 25,000 Wisconsin students participated in *Let's Sing* festivals (Sanders, 1990).

[38]The WSA meetings at the University of Wisconsin's Stock Pavilion typically attracted between 4,000 and 5,000 students (Apps, 1996).

Let's Draw Honor Roll Artwork (University of Wisconsin–Madison Archives).

returned a card to each one with suggestions for improvement (Milbauer, 1949). He also selected examples of excellent work for inclusion in the Honor Role. The work of Honor Role artists was featured in the teacher manual for the following semester's program. Most significant, Schwalbach directed the classroom teachers to allow their students to take part in classroom discussions to identify those art pieces that were to be sent to the radio station for feedback or Honor Roll consideration (Kelly, 1990, p. 113).

We can infer that a classroom where students discuss the relative merits of their artwork and select work for submission qualifies as a good example of a learning community. No doubt, participating in the Honor Role, Round Robin exhibits, regional art shows, and local art exhibits helped reduce the physical and psychological isolation that separated country students and teachers from each other and contributed to a sense of inclusion among the program's listeners.

Ranger Mac. The Ranger, Wakelin McNeel, encouraged his listeners to develop classroom nature exhibits. Literally hundreds of these exhibits, dubbed Conservation Corners, served as living demonstrations of the nature topics, plants, and animals covered in the Ranger's broadcasts. Somehow, McNeel arranged to have State Conservation Department employees tour local schools to evaluate the Conservation Corners. Selected exhibits were rewarded with equipment for building better exhibits, certificates of recognition, and, most important, special mention on the Ranger's radio program (WSA, 1953b). As mentioned earlier, listeners to *Ranger Mac* participated in the school-based reforestation efforts that McNeel promoted on his program.

Exploring Science/Young Experimenters. Students were organized into the experiment committees that took turns performing the experiment during the broadcast and prepared for the experiment by ensuring that all materials were available. Performing real-world tasks together to achieve a common learning goal suggests that students were engaged in a classroom-based learning community (Badger, 1953; Milbauer, 1949).

The WSA exceeded all other SOAs in building learning communities. It would be interesting to compare its achievements in this area with those of online learning communities.

Building a Statewide Network

Though frustrated twice in 10 years, McCarty and Engel did not abandon their quest to make WHA a statewide radio service. They saw the opportunity present itself again with the rise of FM radio. In 1940, the FCC announced that educational stations would be given exclusive rights to develop a part of the new FM band, authorized to begin operations in 1941 (McChesney, 1993). Within a few years, 20 channels on the FM band were designated for educational use only (WHA, 1969a). Finally, after more than a decade, radio channels were set aside for education, and this time the federal government acted in the public interest before commercial broadcasters could dominate the new technology.[39] As noted in previous chapters, both NBC and CBS were battling in a misguided effort to dominate shortwave technology rather than FM.

By the early 1940s, McCarty and Engel saw the promise of FM — static-free, clear, high-fidelity reception — and soon became determined to establish a network of FM stations throughout the state. It was a long-term proposition. In 1943 and 1944, they made the plan that started the ball rolling. The following year, 1945, a State Radio Council was set up to oversee the network's development, and by 1947, Wisconsin constructed the first of what would become an eight-station network (WHA, 1969a). McCarty recalls, "[19]45 was the key year. We created the council, filed the application [with the FCC] and got funding approval from the state legislature which not only established the Radio Council but made the initial appropriation for two stations" (WHA, 1969a, p. 10). The first station went on the air in March of 1947, "and thereafter each legislature provided us funds for the establishment of two additional FM stations. So they

[39]In the early 1940s FM radios were a novelty; few receivers existed.

were built over a period of years, roughly one a year" (p. 10). According to McCarty and Engel, Wisconsin's FM network was a unique accomplishment in many ways: "The eight stations were interconnected through their own signals, not by land lines, a unique feature not only in the U.S., but in the world. According to C. M. Jansky ... a top consulting communications engineer, 'this Wisconsin State Radio Network is truly a unique application of FM and its capabilities.'" (WHA, 1969a, p. 9).

Another unique feature of the network, according to Engel, was that it was completely planned before a single station was built, the only example of this kind in the country.[40] "Professor Koehler and Professor Bennett laid out a map of the state and located FM stations where they thought they should be to give complete statewide coverage" (WHA, 1969a, p. 9). Their plan was sent to the FCC engineers, and to the surprise of McCarty and Engel it was approved exactly as requested. Engel said, "This is very significant as it probably never happened anywhere else throughout the country" (p. 9).

At any rate, the network carried the WHA signal to the far corners of the state, and as each new station went on the air, more and more schools were able to tune in to WSA programs. Potentially that meant a big expansion of the audience for WSA programs, but there was no guarantee that teachers and supervisors in the newly covered school districts would want to participate in educational radio. WSA programs had to be sold to teachers and school administrators.

During construction of the FM network, the WSA administrators and staff mounted an aggressive marketing effort. They conducted a series of teacher workshop presentations designed to promote educational radio and educate teachers and supervisors on how to use radio effectively. One of the workshop presenters, E. B. Gordon, said of his 1949 presentation to teachers at the Eagle River Public School in far northern Vilas County, "There were few [WSA] listeners in this area; hence we were doing pioneering" (WSA, 1944). His presentation covered the basics that teachers needed to know to get the most out of the radio broadcasts including preparation, follow-up, and the use of FM radio. Gordon said that he received a very positive reception at the Indian schools in Oneida County and those near Lac du Flambeau, but at other schools "it was important to sell them on the idea." During his presentation to teachers in Minocqua, Gordon was confronted with a tough technical question: "How many radios can work off one antenna?" "That stumped me," Gordon says. He promised to check with WHA engineers and get right back to the questioner (WSA, 1949). During November and December of 1949, the WSA team conducted four workshops reaching an audience of 352 teachers, supervisors, and even some school board members. Gordon concluded: "These gatherings are golden opportunities for public relations for the School of the Air. They all liked the 'honor' of having people from the station [visit]. That in itself makes them accept suggestions and makes them willing to see radio as a tool" (WSA, 1949).

These promotional efforts demonstrate the WSA's proactive attitude toward building and retaining its audience.

In addition to promoting the WSA, McCarty also found it necessary to explain FM radio. During the 1940s, when FM channels were set aside for education, probably few if any schools were equipped with FM receivers. While Wisconsin busily erected its FM network, McCarty and others at the WSA realized they needed to inform Wisconsin educators and parents about the benefits of switching to FM radio, otherwise the network would be worthless. During the early and mid–1950s, the WSA regularly mailed school districts, schools, teachers, and community organizations information describing the benefits of FM radio over AM. It also distributed information about good-quality radios and FM antennas to assure good reception. Almost all WSA printed materials identified the network's eight repeater FM stations as well as their call letters

---

[40]It seems odd that Engel considered advanced planning for such a large endeavor to be a unique occurrence. One would expect planning to be the norm.

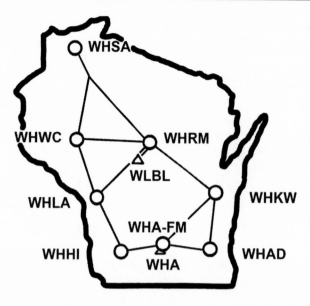

The Wisconsin Radio Network (University of Wisconsin–Madison Archives).

and numbers and location (McCarty, 1956). Clearly, WSA administrators understood the need to educate Wisconsin educators about radio instruction and to familiarize them with the new technology of FM radio. Consequently, while SOAs in the rest of the country were barely holding their own or fading, the WSA was growing in audience and prestige.

Audience

Cuban (1986) hypothesizes that SOA administrators often overstated their enrollment figures. They typically based their audience estimates on the results of mail survey studies, which, Cuban says, were frequently completed by school administrators, not teachers. When one or two teachers in a school used radio, the administrators falsely indicated that all teachers did, thereby inflating audience numbers. In previous chapters it was reported that NBC and CBS executives exaggerated audience figures for the MAH and the ASA and that OSA administrators reported little about enrollment data. The WSA, however, was different.

Cuban's argument does *not* apply to the WSA. McCarty and his associates continually gathered and analyzed enrollment data, and, more important, they did not rely on surveys to count ears. Instead they used more reliable methods and reported their findings annually. They also compared their audience to the total school population in the listening area, something no other SOA did or at least reported doing. Their findings consistently show that a substantial portion of the state's elementary students listened regularly to the WSA programs.

The key to the WSA's audience data collection was an enrollment form and a fee charged for the teachers manuals. From 1938 on, all schools in the WSA listening area received a program schedule for the upcoming semester that included the combination enrollment and order form. For each program selected, the administrator or teacher was asked to order the accompanying teachers manual. Requiring payment helped assure that the teacher in fact did plan to have her class listen to the program. This practice contrasted with most other SOAs that distributed teachers manuals for free, often without a request, and thereby undercut their own ability to gather accurate enrollment data. Support for the WSA method of calculating enrollment is provided in the "Wisconsin Research Project in School Broadcasting" (to be described later). In this study, UW researchers emphasized that the number of teachers manuals sold provided a reliable indicator of genuine teacher interest in WSA programs (Barr et al., 1942).

The enrollment form asked for a substantial amount of data, including:

• School: name, location, county, and type (one room, state graded, city elementary, parochial, or high school)
• Teacher's name
• Programs of interest (including a request to order teachers manuals)
• Number of pupils enrolling in each program
• Payment information

The returned forms provided a wealth of raw audience data from which WSA enrollments were projected annually from the late 1930s to 1970. A summary of enrollment data is provided in Table 26.

TABLE 26. WSA ENROLLMENTS AND ANALYSIS, 1938–69
(WSA, 1932–1971)

Year	Total WSA Course Registrations	Total Students Enrolled in WSA*	Total State Enrollment, K–8**	Percent WSA of Total State
1938–1939	285,172†	95,013	381,973	25%
1948–1949	394,911†	121,570	339,352	36%
1950–1951	457,478†	124,782	355,668	35%
1953–1954	639,864†	213,288	389,602	54%
1959–1960	704,614§	281,845	504,688	56%
1968–1969	770,326§	308,130	657,409	47%
1970–1971	603,695	241,478	679,887	36%

*Based on data gathered from the registration forms.

†Based on the assumption that each pupil is enrolled in three WSA classes.

§Based on the assumption that each pupil is enrolled in 2.5 WSA classes. Historical enrollment data for Wisconsin schools can be found on the Wisconsin Department of Public Instruction Web site.

**Does not include parochial schools.

Data in Table 26 were derived from the returned enrollment/order forms using the following somewhat complex process. First, the number of schools purchasing manuals was calculated. Then, using enrollment data provided, the "Total Students Enrolled in WSA" was determined. However, the raw data were always incomplete because some schools failed to provide enrollment figures. For example, data for 1953–54 show that of 4,578 schools ordering manuals, 4,015 indicated student enrollment numbers, but 563 schools did not. To arrive at the 213,288 figure shown in the "Total Students Enrolled" column, WSA administrators simply extended the average of 46.6 pupil-listeners per school to those schools that failed to provide enrollment data. However, other data suggest that in some cases the "Total Students Enrolled" figures were calculated by simply multiplying the number of teachers manuals ordered for each program by 25, the assumed number of students in each class. This calculation was unnecessary for *Let's Sing* because the number of student books ordered reflected the actual enrollment.

Data shown in the "Total WSA Course Registrations" column were calculated by multiplying the number of individual students enrolled by 3, and later, after 1955, by 2.5. These numbers reflect an assumption that the average student was registered in 3 programs and then apparently only 2.5 programs per year. The course registrations are *not* used to calculate the percentages shown in the last column. Finally, the column "Percent WSA of Total State" shows WSA individual student enrollment as a percentage of total state public school enrollments, kindergarten through eighth-grade (WSA, 1932–1971).

ENROLLMENT DATA ANALYSIS

While conceding that the WSA statistics are far superior to any available from other SOAs, a healthy skepticism should be applied to the data. For some years, the figures in the "Total Students Enrolled" column seem to be based on the questionable assumption that each teachers manual order represented 25 students. That seems high. Data from the 1943–1944 year give an average class size of 18.5, a figure 25 percent lower than the number used in later years. Moreover, the assumptions about class size do not apply to one-room schools where the student body ranged

File No. _____

ENROLLMENT and ORDER FORM

Separate enrollment is required from each teacher even when manuals are ordered in lots by school board, principal or superintendent.

PLEASE GIVE **ALL** REQUESTED INFORMATION

Failure to do so will mean delay in shipment of your order.

TYPE OF SCHOOL

	Check
One-room rural	
1st class state graded	
2nd class state graded	
Elem. under county supervision	
Elem. under city supervision	
Teacher training	
Handicapped children	
Parochial	
Private	

CITY and STATE _____
(P. O. Address of School)

STREET or R. R. _____

COUNTY _____

SCHOOL _____

TEACHER _____
Which
Grade(s)
Enrolling _____

No. of
Pupils
Enrolling _____

COURSE	Enrollment		Order		
	Which Grades Listening	No. of Pupils Listening	Price of Manual	Number Wanted	Cost
AFIELD WITH RANGER MAC			20c		
EXPLORING SCIENCE (1st Sem.)			20c		
ON WISCONSIN (2nd Sem.)			20c		
LET'S FIND OUT			20c		
LET'S DRAW			50c		
NEWS OF THE WEEK			20c		
JOURNEYS IN MUSIC LAND, Song Book			15c		
Piano Accompaniment Book	X	X	30c		
MUSIC ENJOYMENT			20c		
Music Instrument Chart	X	X	10c		
ADVENTURES IN OUR TOWN			20c		
RHYTHM AND GAMES			50c		
BOOK TRAILS			20c		
			TOTAL		

NOTE: Payment must accompany all orders of less than $1.00. Larger orders may be charged to the school board, but not to the individual. No C.O.D. shipments. Currency sent at own risk. No stamps except on orders of less than 50¢, please.

PAYMENT ENCLOSED _____ or CHARGE MY SCHOOL BOARD _____

STOP!. HAVE YOU GIVEN COMPLETE ENROLLMENT INFORMATION FOR ALL COURSES? Save possible delay of days in shipment of your order by a two-minute check for thoroughness now!

_____
(Clerk)

_____
(Address)

OFFICE RECORD (*Do not write below this line*)

Order Rec'd _____

Shipped _____

Correspondence

_____
_____
_____
_____

Mail to

WISCONSIN SCHOOL OF THE AIR—Station WHA—Madison 6

WSA Course Enrollment and Order Form (University of Wisconsin–Madison Archives).

from first through eighth graders. When a teacher bought the manual for *Rhythm and Games*, a program intended for grades one through four, it is unlikely the older kids would have participated (though there was nothing to stop them from doing so).[41]

Table 26 shows the WSA listening audience as a percentage of the state's kindergarten through eighth-grade population to be sizable indeed. Starting in 1938, when more than 25 percent of the state's public elementary students tuned in, the WSA audience grew steadily through the 1940s to 35 percent, in the 1960s peaked at more than 50 percent, and by 1970 fell back into the 35 percent range.

However, these percentages may be somewhat misleading; the state enrollment figures do not include parochial school students, but the WSA enrollment figures may have. Data from 1948–1949 show that parochial school students made up approximately 13 percent of WSA listeners that year (WSA, 1932–1971). No other data on parochial students are available. Based on that one year, it could be argued that the percentages shown in Table 26 should be adjusted to reflect parochial students, which would reduce the WSA percentages by that 13 percent.

Ultimately, without access to the raw data, reliability can not be assured. No doubt, WSA administrators had a strong interest in reporting increased enrollment to the UW and the legislature. The available data, though copious, are not definitive, and analysis was sometimes inconsistent. Nevertheless, even if we adjust the WSA data to reflect smaller class size assumptions and to account for parochial school students, WSA enrollments as a percentage of state elementary population for the years shown in Table 26 would change little. The range would drop from 56 percent down to 48 percent. Even these lower numbers seem a laudable achievement, particularly if we compare them to the anemic audience penetration achieved by the national and other state SOAs, which could not count even 10 percent of their potential audience as regular listeners.

What accounted for this astounding penetration? In one sense, that question is the subject of this entire work. In addition to the focus of the programs and appeal of the instructors, several outside factors also may have contributed. First, by the late 1940s, no competing SOAs reached Wisconsin; the WSA was the only game in town. More important, the gradual completion of the FM network, from 1947 through 1953, enabled many more teachers to tune in to WSA programs (WHA, 1969a). In those areas of the state where FM service was being inaugurated, WSA staff and administration actively promoted the WSA. They personally addressed school boards and visited schools in those new areas to explain and demonstrate the radio programs. Additionally, the visits were announced and supported by WHA's on-air promotional efforts. Perhaps most important, WHA and WSA were part of the state's educational apparatus. Educators in each newly served community most likely felt they had a right to receive all the educational benefits provided by the state. One such benefit was the WSA.

The WSA's audience data seem relatively reliable because their results were based on good-faith assumptions and clear procedures designed to gather accurate information: (1) Instead of relying on mail surveys, the WSA linked enrollment data collection with the process for ordering manuals. (2) They required payment for teachers manuals. This improved the reliability of enrollment data because it discouraged orders from those who were not serious about listening to the programs.[42] (3) They collected enrollment data each semester and reported findings annually, which enabled year-to-year comparison with state enrollment figures. (4) They collected data about pupils, class size, school type, and programs. This information provided a clearer picture of the audience, which helped the WSA to stay focused.

---

[41]In 1949, one-room schools accounted for 36 percent of the WSA enrollments. State-graded and city elementary schools accounted for 30 percent and 33 percent, respectively (WSA, 1932-1971).

[42]It is still possible that someone other than a teacher provided enrollment data.

Evaluation, Feedback, and Field Visits

During its first years of operation, WSA administrators attempted to evaluate their performance using the same tactics as other SOAs, namely mail surveys to schools. In June of 1937, for example, WSA sent out 2,000 surveys to classroom teachers and received 430 replies, about a 22 percent return. The survey sought to collect data on the size of the radio audience, program popularity, and reception conditions and to gather suggestions for improvement. On almost all counts, the report authors admit the results were unhelpful. Audience size could not be determined because too many teachers failed to indicate the number of students in their classes. Reports of program popularity included contradictory responses, and the reports on radio reception only confirmed what was already known, that many schools in the WSA listening area were receiving either a weak signal or in some cases none at all and that was definitely holding down enrollment (Schneiker, 1949).

Early on in the WSA's history, the state's General Education Board received a $41,000 grant from the Rockefeller Foundation to conduct an extensive evaluation of the educational effectiveness of radio (Barr et al., 1942). Known as the "Wisconsin Research Project in School Broadcasting," the study ran for two years, from 1938 to 1940, and the results were published in 1942. The overall goal was to "measure the educational effectiveness of each series of school broadcasts" (Barr et al., 1942, p. 7). Cuban (1986) refers to this study.

The study yielded three kinds of data. First, researchers conducted a comparison study that matched listening classes against non-listening classes in six subject areas:

Subject Area	Radio Program
Music:	*Journeys in Music Land*
Nature study:	*Afield with Ranger Mac*
Geography:	*Neighbors 'Round the World*
Social studies:	*Community Living*
English:	*English As You Like It* and *Good Books*
Speech:	*Good Speech*

Second, researchers administered a survey to gather "subjective findings," e.g., teachers' opinions concerning the value of the radio programs they used. Third, to follow up on the expressions of interest, researchers analyzed enrollment data for the following semesters to see if teachers continued to use the radio programs in their classrooms. The control group was supplied with the same materials as the experimental group (Barr et al., 1942).

The comparison study reached a predictable finding of no significant differences between control and experimental groups. Since that time, decades of comparative media studies have yielded similar disappointing results due mainly to the fact that comparative media studies suffer from confounded variables (Seels, Berry, Fullerton, & Horn, 1996). However, the Wisconsin researchers speculated that the results of their study were affected by the fact that the control group teachers received the same outlines and materials that the radio teachers used. Those materials and the fact of participating in the experiment might have prompted special effort by the classroom teachers in the control group. Had the control group teachers not received the materials, the experimenters speculated, the results might have better reflected the difference that radio makes in the classroom (Barr et al., 1942).

The data collected from the questionnaires and interviews uniformly favored the radio lessons. The teachers all agreed that WSA programs made "valuable contributions to the curricula of individual schools" (Barr et al., 1942, p. 195). Most teachers also reported using the teachers manuals and found them helpful. The analysis of enrollment data strongly supported the conclusion that teachers continued to be interested in WSA programs in the years following the study.

Data for the first semester following the study, 1940–41, show that enrollments rose about 4 percent over the previous year.

Overall, then, the results of the only major summative evaluation conducted by outsider researchers did not confirm the instructional superiority of the WSA programs versus traditional classroom instruction. Significantly for this study, the results from the Wisconsin study do support the assertion that Wisconsin teachers and administrators perceived the WSA programs to be valuable educationally, primarily because they filled their schools' critical educational needs.

FIELD VISITS

The WSA did conduct substantial efforts at formative evaluation. From 1944 to the early 1950s, administrators, radio teachers, staff, and volunteer professionals gathered user feedback and observed firsthand how WSA programs were received and used in the schools. The data from these efforts provided anecdotal evidence of how classroom teachers used WSA and also of what WSA educators and other staff thought of their own work. Furthermore, we can see how feedback from users prompted the WSA management to make better educational judgments.

At the beginning of the 1944–45 year, 16 WSA staff members visited eight listening schools in the Madison area to observe educational radio in action. The observers included, among others, Mac McCarty, the WSA director; Professor E. B. Gordon from *Let's Sing*; Wakelin McNeel from *Afield with Ranger Mac*; Fannie Steve of *Rhythm and Games*; and Roy Vogleman from *Exploring the News*. They made a total of 13 visits and listened to nine programs, four of them twice. During the visits, they recorded their observations and impressions on preprinted WSA School Visit Report forms. The forms were organized into three sections—before, during, and after the broadcast—and they also provided ample room for additional comments and general conclusions. Overall, it seems the observers completed about 25 reports (WSA, 1949).

The reports provide detailed observations about such things as broadcast quality, narrator attributes, level of student attentiveness, and participation in learning activities. They also provided detailed comments and information on the classroom teachers' broadcast preparation, facilitation, and follow-up. In some cases, the observers gave their overall sense of how well a specific program contributed to learning.

The data do not tell exactly how the observations were used, but based on review of the available reports as well as a report summary, it seems that WSA management intended to use them as the basis for refining individual programs in order to improve overall effectiveness, not to mention popularity (WSA, 1944). Regardless of how they were ultimately used, the completed reports provide a wonderful "fly on the wall" view of radio use in the classroom as well as the comments and critique by people who were deeply involved in the process. No program failed to receive some critical marks. The following sampling gives an idea of what the reports said.

Let's Draw. Two observers complained of too much warm-up time. They said that the introduction and musical warm-up ran to 17 minutes, and that the students were ready to start drawing well before the radio teacher instructed them to do so. One observer noted, "the children were fully stimulated long before they were unleashed" (WSA, 1944). However, another observed that the program offered good opportunity for cooperation among students and the teacher, and that the students were happy during the program.

Exploring the News. Observers recommended more variety in tone and style of narrator's presentation. They also called for a reduction in the number of topics covered in a broadcast. On the positive side, one observer noted that the classroom teacher had prepared by discussing the broadcast topic beforehand and had appropriate maps and pictures available for reference during the broadcast. As a result, student interest was high.

Rhythm and Games. The observers said that the children got so worked up, they drowned out the radio and that it was hard to work with large groups. But special praise went to Mrs. Steve, the radio teacher: "Mrs. Steve can give lessons to anyone who wants to listen, she's prac-

#19a

Report made by. Rome X.
Date of visit Jan. 30, 1945

WISCONSIN SCHOOL OF THE AIR - REPORT OF SCHOOL VISIT

Series and program heard __Let's Find Out - "Milly Finds a Lake "__

School _Lowell_   Teacher _Mrs. Stoddard_   Grade(s) _3_

Type of school _City elementary_   No. of pupils listening __44 (2 cl__

General impression of classroom Excellent. Alert teacher. Comfortable seats,
                                        good lighting, much available material
Quality and placement of receiver Fine. Front of room, just above heads of ch

BEFORE THE BROADCAST

Any special provisions for radio listening? _Yes/_ Other room came in, to sha
            radio.
Preparation (length, nature, use of manual, exhibit of materials, questions
    on blackboard, etc.) We arrived at 9:15. Preparation had been in progres
    and was continued while we were there. Must have been begun several days
    before, for there were maps, made by the youngsters, posters of early Wis.c
    and so on posted. Students were discussing Belmont, mining, the reason Wis
    is called Badger State, prncipal cities and rivers when we arrived. Used m
    of the activities listed for after the broadcast , before the broadcast.

DURING THE BROADCAST

Was program heard from beginning to end, including announcements? Missed first
                                                of Bill's opening sentence.
Could children hear the broadcast easily and distinctly? Yes   Comment on the
    broadcaster's voice and projection Too soft, generally. Not enough life
        except toward end. Children reacted visibly when broadcaster "perked"
        up, and exaggerated.

What reception difficulties were encountered? Some interference at first...soun
                    remarkably like a railroad train. Faded out after teacher adjusted
What was teacher's attitude and actions during broadcast? Sat at desk , taking
            notes and smiling when children reacted. Second teacher sat at si
How long before children's interest was caught and held? Immediate. Had been w
            built up by teacher who set the scene for the story before program
If interest and attention lagged, indicate at which points It's hard to tell w
    is lagging interest and what simply unconcsious movement. There was no time
    interest seemed to lag, when attention was not on radio, but there were tim
    when interest was higher ....see second page of report.
If participation was invited, did the children respond? Raised hands when aske
    "How many of you heard what I said?"
Did the children seem to comprehend all the ideas in the program as they were
    presented? Yes   What parts, if any, were too difficult for the children?
    None.   ad been well prepared by teacher for all ideas presented.

    What parts too simple? None.

List words that might have been too difficult Teacher asked after the broadca
    wanted to be sure understood word "explore." All did, but apparently she
    how many children
Was pacing of program satisfactory? __A little slow at first.__

Did production techniques (sound, music, drama, etc.) contribute to or detract
    from comprehension? Be specific. __A narration technique.....exaggerated__
    voice for speaking character's line....and exaggerated build up helped.

Above and opposite: WSA Report of School Visit (University of Wisconsin–Madison Archives).

AFTER THE BROADCAST

Observation

Immediate follow-up: extent, nature (spontaneous, eager? perfunctory? uninspired?) character They get milk at 10, and program, with better listening section, lasted 18 minutes. Follow-up was therefor shorter than it might have been. Program should be 15 minutes only, and thi could have been speeded up without loss of clarity at the beginning. Teacher had used follow-up material before hand, and questioned chil on story itself after broadcast, Apparently she has plan of radio us Was effect of teacher's manual felt in the follow-up? Yes.

Judging from the reactions and discussion, what in the broadcast seemed most to have impressed the children? Milly leaving the bread; the Indian; finding a lake for her moth er. Trees of Wisconsin. Pet who come here from other lands. (Many in class had parents from Switz Norway, and Germany)

Questions

What part did the children like best? The Indian

What part did they like least? I'd judge page 2 and 3.

What do they think of the series as a whole? Like it very much, accord
                                        to teacher
How did this broadcast compare in their estimation with others in the series? Average

Additional comments

This was an exceptional school. The youngsters could have taken

much more information, but I think the imaginative appeal of the

story heightened their interest in the subject, and that the school

is not typical. The teacher had so well prepared and interested the

that the broadcast was frosting on a cake full of plums. They knew

the background of the story , so that it was full of meaning for then

This teacher could use a lot more pre-broadcast material (as see
above, she used follow-up for pre-broadcast)

General conclusions

It all mde me feel real good. Radio is a stimulus ...in this case
the radio program tied together and clarified information the
youngsters had been absorbing. Without the radio program, I think
their study of Wisconsin would have been purely factucal. Through
the story they got a sense of people having lived in the days and
the land they had mapped and charted.

tically infallible. If the *Young Experimenters* broadcaster could have that same feeling in relation to upper grades, I feel the experiments would go much better" (WSA, 1944).

Young Experimenters. Observers reported that the classroom teacher remained passive during the broadcast and used questions in the teachers manual to conduct the follow-up discussion. One observer told of a problem that arose during the program because the preparatory instructions had been unclear. As part of an experiment on pendulums, the manual had asked the children to bring string and a nut. The meaning apparently was a metal nut for a metal bolt, but most of the children brought walnuts. They struggled to tie string around the nuts.

Fannie Steve, the radio teacher for *Rhythm and Games*, paid nine impromptu visits to WSA schools around Madison. Based on those observations, she concluded that the classroom teacher played a crucial role in the success or failure of WSA programs. When the classroom teacher actively facilitated learning,[43] students were attentive and involved and participated in the follow-up. When teachers remained passive or, worse, used the broadcast time to do other work, students tended to be inattentive and less involved and avoided participation in the follow-up activities (WSA, 1944).

Clearly, WSA observers do not qualify as disinterested. However, the visits demonstrated management's commitment to improve their offerings using the time-tested field observation technique. It is easy to believe that the longevity of many WSA programs is due in part to the frequent on-site observations conducted by many of the radio teachers.

CONTEMPORARY EVALUATION

While acknowledging the value of radio in furthering science education, King (2001) asserts that in the popular WSA program *Afield with Ranger Mac,* instructor Wakelin McNeel imposed on mid–20th-century students a vision of elementary science curriculum that was a generation out of date. He says the program, like similar nature study programs on other SOAs, was informed by the nature study movement of the late 19th and early 20th centuries, a movement that promoted observing nature and developing empathy for the agricultural life. King highlights the irony of McNeel using the most up-to-date technology (radio) to communicate out-of-date ideas. He says that a more appropriate approach for science education by radio should have involved activity-driven experiences similar to those proposed by progressive educators and widely adapted by public schools of the period. In an activity-driven curriculum students should interact with materials, something not attempted by McNeel (King, 2001, pp. 11–13).

Unfortunately, King does not comment on the WSA series *Exploring Science* and *Young Experimenters.*[44] As described earlier, both employed an action-oriented experimental approach to science education. In fact, the description of *Young Experimenters* in the 1949–1950 teachers manual has the heading, "Learn by Doing."

Kelly's (1990) historical study of *Let's Draw* found that "radio [effectively] disseminated creative art education instruction for students and in-service training teachers throughout Wisconsin before districts hired elementary art specialists" (p. v). She found that teachers in small rural schools "needed and welcomed help with classroom art instruction" and that radio as a mass-communication medium was effective in providing an interesting variety of creative art activities for students. She also concluded that the formation of the Wisconsin Art Education Association in 1950 was linked to the activities of the *Let's Draw* advisory committee (Kelly, 1990).

Sanders' (1990) study uncovered descriptions of the *Let's Sing* regional and state music fests that can be interpreted in an evaluative mode. Stressing that Professor Gordon placed a priority on learning at these events, Sanders says: "In 1956, about 27,300 children were participating in the regional festivals [throughout Wisconsin].... Even with audiences of some 3400 children, there was absolute quiet between songs. When [Pop] Gordon addressed the children, or asked them a question, they responded in unison, and their singing was remarkably together, in light of the number ... present" (Sanders, 1990, p. 176).

These comments support the finding that Gordon's radio lessons succeeded in teaching thousands of young students how to sing in unison and on key.

---

[43]The word facilitated is mine, not Steve's. I use the word to capture the classroom teacher activities that Steve praised, namely preparing the students prior to the broadcast, showing interest and participating during the broadcast, and following up with the students after the broadcast.

[44]Both series represent the same approach and philosophy and were taught by the same teacher.

Oral Testimonials

Fortunately, a number of people who had direct experience with the WSA were willing to share their memories. Life history data, even if only in brief excerpts, provide details, perceptions, and interpretations that illuminate historical events. Following are comments and quotes selected from longer interviews. The participants include three former WSA students and a rural teacher who used WSA programs in her classrooms Some interviews were conducted in person and others by phone. Questionnaires were used to guide the interviews but were not followed rigidly.

1. Mary Michie Udall attended Maple Lawn School, a one-room school in Green Lake County, Wisconsin. She recalls a WSA program from the very earliest days, 1932 to 1935, when she attended fifth through eighth grades:

Q. *What WSA radio program(s) did you hear?*
A. The music one. Don't know what it was called. It had male voices including Professor Gordon. Like music appreciation. (We listened weekly.)
Q. *What do you remember about that program?*
A. Well, I just remember the general feeling; it was always good fun, but it was serious. It was educational, not meant to be entertaining. Kind of a nice pleasant teacher kind of educational [program], nothing stern, very friendly. Like Mr. Rodgers, [*sic*] only on an older child's level.... The whole school listened for that fifteen minutes in one room.... It was sort of a very special diversion of the week.... We thought it was special for rural school children, and we enjoyed it for that reason. And it was coming from Madison and from the University. That meant something.
Q. *What do you remember about the radio?*
A. I think the radio probably belonged to the teacher and she just brought it with her.... It was battery because we didn't have electricity in the school.
Q. *Did you participate in any extracurricular activities related to the WSA programs that brought you in contact with WSA students from other schools?*
A. We took one big trip to Marchisand. Our parents volunteered to drive us because we didn't have a school bus ... to meet the voices of the WSA at the Marchisand High School, and they put on a special program. It was sort of like a super duper music time and Pop Gordon was there ... and four or five of the narrators of these programs. I think it was one day and we took our lunches. We sat and listened to these people who explained and gave samples of the programs. Other students were there.
Q. *What did the other kids think of the radio programs?*
A. Well some of the farm boys weren't particularly interested in music. But they all liked it because of the diversion. I think that was the biggest draw.
Q. *For the teachers too?*
A. Yes, they [teachers] didn't have any other teaching aides or ... TV. We didn't have mimeograph machines or much of anything. So anything a little out of the ordinary was welcome.
Q. *What did you think about those programs then? What value did it have for you?*
A. It was our connection to the world outside of our little corner of Wisconsin. And it gave us a feeling of being connected to all the other schools, and in a way of being up to date with the schools in town. We weren't just a hick school; after all, we had a radio that worked! (M. Michie Udall, personal communication, December 29, 2003)

2. Linda Clauder attended first through fifth grades in a one-room rural school near Prairie du Chien, Wisconsin, roughly from the late 1940s through the early 1950s. At that time, the WSA was well established throughout the state. She recalls that there were approximately 25 students, grades one through eight, and the teacher was Bridget Murphy.

Q. *What WSA radio program(s) did you hear?*

A. *Let's Draw* and *Let's Sing* regularly and *Ranger Mac* occasionally.

Q. *What do you remember about the radio?*

A. There was this glorious radio, very special radio that sat near the teacher's desk. The dial was set on one station; that was the big thing and at the right volume. It was only turned on and off, and that was it. It was not used for anything else.

Q. *How did your teacher prepare you for the program(s)?*

A. Students were given pictures of art work to refer to during the *Let's Draw* programs.... They had their singing books ready for *Let's Sing* and kids were asked to bring items to class to coincide with *Ranger Mac* programs.

Q. *Did you participate in any extracurricular activities related to the WSA programs that brought you in contact with WSA students from other schools?*

A. The class would go on "field" trips to collect nature items for the *Ranger Mac* class and *Let's Sing*. [The class went on a field trip to Madison to participate in *Let's Sing* singing festival held in the University of Wisconsin Stock Pavilion.] I still have a memory of Professor Gordon. In the stock pavilion filled with children and he'd say, 'Now boys and girls we're going to sing' ... and of course we knew the songs by heart. And so the whole stock pavilion was these children singing songs. It was just magnificent."[45]

Q. *Looking back, what do you think about the WSA programs now? What value did they have for you?*

A. They provided a great enrichment for a small school. It's a cliché, but it was our window on the world (L. Clauder, personal communication, November 7, 2003).

3. Julienne Reimann attended first through eighth grades in a one-room rural school in Whittlesey, Wisconsin, roughly from the late 1940s through the mid–1950s. She recalls that during those years, the student population varied from 30 to 40 students, ranging in grades from first through eighth. During her school years, four different teachers served, teaching all subjects.

Q. *What WSA radio program(s) did you hear?*

A. *Let's Draw, Rhythm and Games, Let's Sing, Ranger Mac.* Schwalbach (*Let's Draw*) would teach us how to use different media, chalk, color. He gave instruction, but it was up to us how we wanted to create. Everyone painted the same subject. We could send in our drawing. I got more than one honorable mention. We got them back. He would write things on them, I'm pretty sure. I remember one of my classmates created a watercolor and I thought, "oh man that was great." Everyone in the room followed *Let's Draw*.

Q. *Describe the WSA radio teacher(s), if possible.*

A. All [radio] teachers were very enthusiastic about what they [were] teaching, they loved their subjects, consequently made us love them too.

Q. *What do you remember most about the programs you heard?*

A. *Let's Sing*, I loved it. We had a book, and we would follow along in the book. He taught us something about keys too. It opened ears to classical music. They played themes from various well known works of classics that they put words to, and we learned them by singing them. [*She sings.*] It's from Brahms. They made up the words. Dvorak. There were other things too, American folk songs and spirituals. He would teach us the song, they had singers, the Minnesingers. Every morning we started class with a song we learned in *Let's Sing*.

Q. *Looking back, what do you think about them now? What value did they have for you?*

A. They taught me an appreciation of art and music (J. Reimann, personal communication, November 6, 2003).

---

[45]It is estimated that the Stock Pavilion held approximately 4,000 people.

4. Lola Mader taught at Welsh Prairie, a one-room school near Cambria, Wisconsin, from 1953 to 1955. She used WSA programs.

Q. *Tell me about the school.*

A. [Welsh Prairie] was a one room school. There was a little well outside and we had to carry our water in. We had an oil burner, and we had to get our fire going. Turned up in the morning and down at night. There were two outhouses, one for the boys and one for the girls. A regular one room school! We did have electricity. They did have a film strip projector. No copy machine of any sort and no telephone!

[The area was] all farmers. Children were highly motivated and so were the parents. The children were well behaved. The school had a small enrollment, it was winding down, less than 20 students. The school was still the social center of the community. Parents showed up for the children's performances. The school was consolidated in 1960.

Q. *How many students were in the school/class you taught?*

A. [Twenty], all grades, one year I recall, I had one eighth grader, two first graders and in between. I taught all subjects.

Q. *How did you learn about WSA?*

A. The county supervisor visited regularly and was in touch with the State Department of Public Instruction. Her name was Dorothy Balliet, very well known in Columbia county. She set the curriculum and selected the texts. We wrote our own lesson plans, but she checked everything and told us what was available on the radio. She told me what radio programs she thought would be useful depending on the grade.

Q. *What WSA radio program(s) did you use?*

A. *Let's Draw, Let's Sing, Rhythm and Games,* and *Book Trails.* Some in the morning and some in the afternoon.

Q. *Describe the WSA program(s) and the radio teacher(s), if possible.*

A. I thought they were very good. I was 20 years old. I didn't have a lot of knowledge in the variety of subjects. For instance, drawing or singing. So it was wonderful to be able to pull that stuff in with some people who knew what they were doing. And then we followed through on that afterwards.

The *Book Trails*, of course in a country school you don't have a library, but we did have several [book] shelves. Periodically we received a shipment of books from our county for our reading and we kept those for a month and that would be picked up. And we could request certain books that we wanted that had come to our attention through *Book Trails*. That was another resource.

Q. *How did the program go, starting with* Let's Draw, *and what were the kids doing?*

A. *Let's Draw.* The instructor would tell a story to get the children started on a subject. Children were given materials, pencils, paper, or chalk and paper. We had the manual, and we knew what was going to happen. It might have been drawing animals, we had the manual and there were some ideas for how the children should get started. We decorated the room [with the artwork children produced during the program] and made up booklets that they took home. *Let's Sing*: Again we had the manual so we knew what was going to happen. Every child had the song pages. [She remembered Professor Gordon.] So there was a piano accompaniment and we sang along with that.

Book Trails. Again we would know what books would be talked about. So we tried to prepare. We would read the book chapter by chapter. Normally I would read.

Normally when the program was over, they [the students] would finish their activity. Sometimes another day when we had time, we would go back and use the art lesson to review.

Q. *What programs made the biggest impression on you, on the kids?*

A. *Book Trails* was reinforcing the whole thing we were trying to do. The children liked to read or be read to. They didn't have a library.

Q. *What do you remember about the classroom radio?*
A. We would listen to weather reports. We had no telephone. So the radio was our source of information for weather and news. It worked well.
Q. *Sounds like you thought highly of those programs.*
A. The children learned to follow directions and listen closely. They all had radio at home. I tried to write it up on the blackboard if we had a radio program that day.
Q. *Did you participate in any extracurricular activities related to the WSA programs?*
A. No.
Q. *Looking back, what do you think about them now? What were the strengths and weakness?*
A. Weaknesses: a few students in each grade. No reinforcement, no feedback.
   Strengths: The variety of instructors [enabled us] to listen to another voice. Most children didn't receive much outside stimulation. They saw few movies. I recall it as a very good experience. You know I didn't see or talk to any other adults. It had to be a broadening experience for me (L. Mader, personal communication, November 19, 2003).

The student excerpts speak of three main benefits derived from the WSA. Namely, it (1) fulfilled their need for instruction in music, art, literature, and nature study; (2) developed a sense of belonging or camaraderie with other WSA students; and (3) helped to draw back the curtain of rural isolation and inferiority. For the classroom teacher, the WSA broadcasts provided valuable curriculum resources that helped her give more to students. It also helped expand her horizons. It's remarkable how well these echo the goals and vision expressed by some of the founders of radio education. One of the WSA founders, E. B. Gordon, had expressed the desire early on that radio could help the thousands of teachers in rural schools who lacked the skills to give children the creative education they craved (Gordon, 1930, quoted in McCarty, nd). His words are echoed faithfully by Lola Mader. Several students express the idea that radio brought them in part a sense of greater connection to the outside world, a result predicted by the OSA's Ben Darrow in his hyperbolic expression about how radio instruction would, "blow the roof off the classroom and expand the walls to the circumference of the globe" (Darrow, 1932, p. 79).

While anecdotal data should never be used as a basis for generalizing to larger populations, it does provide insight into how an educational service can powerfully influence participants of that service.

In the Age of Television

By the late 1950s and early 1960s, the WSA stood out as a remarkable example of educational radio, listened to regularly by roughly half of the state's elementary students. Its success and accomplishment were recognized by the federal government. In 1961, on the occasion of the WSA's 30th anniversary, the Department of Health, Education, and Welfare officially congratulated the WSA on having served longer than any other similar SOA in the country, on serving schools in every county of Wisconsin, and on demonstrating the most effective utilization of technology in education. Moreover, the agency lauded the WSA for ably demonstrating to "citizens in all the States how non-commercial, educational broadcasting can well serve the public interest" (Lloyd, 1960 in Kentzler correspondence, 1970–76). In some ways, the last line partially fulfills the vision promoted by the early proponents of a national school of the air.

Amazingly, the WSA program schedule for the late 1950s resembled that of a decade earlier. The popular programs of the late 1940s held their audiences throughout the 1950s, and two radio teachers from the mid–1930s were still broadcasting in 1958, Fannie Steve and Jim Schwalbach. Tables 27 and 28 display WSA schedules for 1948–1949 and 1958–1959.

TABLE 27. WSA PROGRAM SCHEDULE, 1948–49
(WSA, 1948)

Program	Time	Grade	Subject
Monday			
Afield with Ranger Mac	9:30	5–8	Conservation and natural science
Democracy in Action	1:30	5–8	Social studies
Tuesday			
Let's Find Out	9:30	2–4	Natural science
Let's Draw	1:30	4–8	Drawing and art skills
Wednesday			
Exploring Science (Young Experimenters)	9:30	5–8	Experiments in physical science
Journeys in Music Land (Let's Sing)	1:30	4–8	Music, singing, and note reading
Thursday			
Music Enjoyment for Children	9:30	1–4	Music appreciation for youngsters
News of the Week	1:30	5–8	News and background
Friday			
Rhythm and Games	9:30	K–3	Games and rhythmic movement
Book Trails	1:30	3–8	Dramatic reading and short stories

✦ ✦ ✦

TABLE 28. WSA PROGRAM SCHEDULE, 1958–59
(WSA, 1958)

Program	Time	Grade	Subject
Monday			
Wonderful World of Nature	9:30	5–8	Conservation and natural science
Footsteps of the Free	1:30	4–8	American history and citizenship
Tuesday			
Young Experimenters (Exploring Science)	9:30	5–8	Experiments in science
Let's Draw	1:30	4–8	Drawing and art skills
Let's Find Out	2.45	1–3	Basic science, answers, and activities
Wednesday			
Let's Write	9:30	5–8	Writing skills and expression
Let's Sing (Journeys in Music Land)	1:30	4–8	Music, singing, and note reading
Early Wisconsin II	2:45	4–8	State history
Thursday			
Exploring the News	9:30	5–9	The story behind the news
Music Time	9:45	1–4	Music appreciation for youngsters
When Men Are Free	1:30	4–8	American democratic values
Friday			
Rhythm and Games	9:30	K–3	Games and rhythmic movement
Book Trails	1:30	3–8	Dramatic reading and short stories

Of the 10 weekly programs listed in the 1948–49 schedule, five titles appear a decade later in the 1958–59 schedule; *Let's Sing, Let's Find Out, Exploring Science/Young Experimenters, Rhythm and Games,* and *Book Trails.* Three other programs from 1948,

Afield with Ranger Mac, Music Enjoyment for Children, and *News of the Week* are also continued in 1958 as are the *Wonderful World of Nature, Music Time,* and *Exploring the News.* The titles and teachers were different, but the programs' content and format remained the same. This continuity represents a testament to how well WSA served the needs of its target audience.

Another sign of the WSA's vitality is that the 1958 schedule offers 13 programs, 3 more than a decade earlier. The four new programs on the 1958–59 schedule are described briefly here. Three of them focused on the need to make America's democracy available to all members of society.

When Men Are Free. This award-winning series used narrative and dramatizations to introduce a "fresh and clear view of the foundations of American democracy" (WSA, 1958, p. 10). Individual programs highlighted the legal basis of specific American freedoms such as representative government, freedom of the press, rules regarding search and seizure, equal protection, etc.

Footsteps of the Free. A sequel and companion to *When Men Are Free,* this series sought to enrich the study of American history and citizenship. Using drama and documentary form, individual programs highlighted the words and activities of the great American leaders who helped establish human rights and democratic freedoms.

Early Wisconsin II. This series provided dramatized overviews of Wisconsin's early history from the territorial days through the years of early statehood and of the people who helped shape the state's history. Also, the program fulfilled the state requirement for a course in Wisconsin history. This program alone may have boosted the WSA audience.

Let's Write. This series encouraged and instructed listeners in self-expression through the written word. Its teacher, Maureen Applegate, designed each program around a specific topic and filled the broadcast with examples and ideas that helped recall experiences that could nourish creative thought and feeling (WSA, 1958).

Overall, the 1958 schedule reflected the best that WSA had offered in the past with the addition of new programs that appear designed to address social and political changes beginning to take place in American society such as the growing movement for civil rights.

COPING WITH CHANGE

Despite having reached a lofty pinnacle of success, by the early 1960s, the WSA faced a new and potentially threatening environment. In 1964, in a letter to the WSA family, Associate Director Arlene McKellar addressed the serious issues that the school had to face. First, how should the WSA serve the newly reorganized schools of Wisconsin? In the 1940s the state had begun to reorganize Wisconsin school districts mainly by consolidating the many small schools into fewer large ones. The process accelerated during the 1950s, and by 1965, many of the consolidated districts had hired (teacher) specialists[46] and expanded their curricula. Should the WSA continue to offer courses with specific curriculum orientation as it had been doing, or should it focus more on enrichment for broad subject areas? And what role should radio play in the era of many competing instructional media, such as television, films, filmstrips, and tape recorders (McKellar, 1964)? These questions highlighted the fundamental problem that WSA faced. The world which the WSA had been developed to serve — the rural world of one- and two-room schools, rural isolation, and one teacher having to teach all subjects and grades — was disappearing. Consequently, the challenge facing the WSA was nothing less than to reinvent itself.

---

[46]In 1955, 25 percent of Wisconsin's school districts employed art teachers; by 1965, 75 percent had hired one or more visual arts specialists (Kelly, 1990).

McKellar asserted that WSA must, at the very least, project a more contemporary sound and image. Based on feedback from a telephone survey of Wisconsin teachers, McKellar advised bluntly that the radio teachers talk to students more as young adults and less as children. "No more, 'Hello boys and girls! Are you sitting up nice and tall? I'd like to tell you a story.'" She admonished, "We can be friendly without being sappy" (McKellar, 1964). Other needs she highlighted were for more substance, less entertainment, and more involvement — a tall order for radio, but one that the WSA had delivered in the past.

Disengagement

In 1967, Director Harold McCarty resigned. After 36 years, the man who planned and administrated the WSA and oversaw the development of Wisconsin's unique public radio network stepped down. Taking his place was then Associate Director Claire Kentzler. While the WSA continued operation for at least seven years more under Kentzler, the data suggest that with McCarty's departure, the University of Wisconsin began a long, slow, painful process of disengaging from the WSA, an event that threatened the school of the air's existence.

The slippery slope on which WSA was lodged became clear during the budget crisis of 1969, a crisis that apparently affected the entire UW and resulted in a proposal to severely cut the budget for the WSA.[47] Kentzler objected strenuously. In a lengthy memo to her boss, the director of WHA, she provided much useful data about the challenges facing the WSA at the end of the 1960s. She described her perception, derived from reading the budget and accompanying explanations for that year, that "somehow the WSA is not a proper activity for the UW," that the UW ought not to be in the business of in-school broadcasting (Kentzler, 1969). She argued that the WSA advanced many of the UW's important responsibilities. It helped teachers on the job and should be seen as a continuation of the UW's key service of teacher preparation and support. She pointed out that the WSA also furthered the UW's general educational mission by allowing the UW to make "good music" available to citizens via the state-owned radio network; the WSA educated Wisconsin students in music appreciation and music skills. Kentzler said that not only had the WSA received national recognition from broadcasters for its program excellence, but also, many educational stations throughout the nation broadcast WSA programs on tape, a testament to the WSA's ability to identify teacher needs.

Kentzler's memo discussed issues of funding and governance. She said that responsibility for funding and directing the WSA had recently been passed to the UW Extension, a move with which she agreed, because the extension service was designed to make the resources of the UW usable to the public, and the WSA was the "most usable version of the University of Wisconsin." She also anticipated the likelihood that responsibility for funding and management might be moved again to other agencies within state government. She expressed no disagreement with those moves; her main concern was to maintain the relationship between the UW and the WSA. She stressed that the WSA's excellence was the result of the relationship with two entities, WHA and the UW. Both had provided the volunteer talent and creativity that made the WSA's success possible.

Kentzler addressed the proposed cuts to the WSA budget by saying that the UW, WHA, and the extension service could not afford to *not* fund the WSA: "You know the stories as well as I. How, when the FM network was threatened, or budget cuts [to WHA] were suggested, the mere mention of our in-school broadcasts saved the entire operation" (Kentzler, 1969).

She asserted that one reason for the decline in sales of manuals and enrollment over the previous few years was that due to lack of funds, the WSA had "rebroadcast the same old pro-

[47]Most likely the Legislature cut the University budget as a form of retaliation for campus anti-war protests. (Bates, Tom, 1992 Rads, New York: Harper Collins).

grams for several years..., not the same old series..., but actually the same programs." Usage was bound to fall, she explained, because the children had heard the programs in previous years. She appealed for funds to underwrite the development of new programs. Finally, Kentzler complained about the proposal to give the Television School of the Air[48] more money than radio. She pointed out that unlike television, radio operation originated most of its own series and reached a statewide audience (Kentzler, 1969).

Programs in the 1970s

Kentzler's forceful defense of the WSA may have had the intended effect because the next year the school celebrated its 40th anniversary of broadcasting and issued a stylish glossy black-and-white booklet announcing the WSA programs for 1970–1971, as shown in Table 29.

TABLE 29. WSA PROGRAM SCHEDULE, 1970–71
(WSA, 1970)

Program	Time	Grade	Subject
Monday			
Wonderful World of Nature	9:30	5–6	Ecology and environmental programs
The Darker Brother	1:30	5–6	Builds white people's awareness of black people
A World of Music	2:00	4–7	Supplements and enriches music and social science
Tuesday			
Reckoning with Boris	9:30	3	Promotes the understanding and enjoyment of mathematics
Let's Ask Dr. Tenny	1:30	4–6	The human body
Let's Find Out	2:00	2–3	Science for the lower grades
Wednesday			
Old Stories and New Ideas	9:30	4–6	Stories appropriate for many subjects
Let's Sing	1:30	4–8	Music, singing, and note reading
Exploring Science	2:00	3–4	Science for the lower grades
Thursday			
Exploring the News	9:30	1–4	Examines important news stories in depth
Music Time	1:30	1–3	Introduces a wide variety of music — classic, folk, and jazz
Worlds of Art	2:00	4–8	Problems and aesthetics
Friday			
The Author Is You	9:30	4–6	Creative writing
Book Trails	1:30	N/A	Literature study
It Happened When	2:00	K–3	Readings for children

Despite its declining audience, surprisingly the 1970 schedule included 15 weekly programs, more than ever before. The list included several old favorites, *Let's Find Out, Let's Sing,* and *Book*

---

[48]Though started in the mid–1950s, WHA's television signals reached only a fraction of the state's residents well into the 1970s.

Trails, presented on tape because many teachers asked for them in that format[49] (Kentzler, 1972b). The other 12 programs were presented live. A quick scan of the subject descriptions reveals that Kentzler's question about how the WSA should serve schools—with curriculum courses or enrichment courses—had been answered in favor of enrichment. Here are descriptions of many of the school's innovative enrichment offerings.

Reckoning with Boris. This series, designed to "correlate well with most [math] textbooks now in use," (WSA, 1970) included two types of programs, one to promote the understanding of math and the other to stimulate enjoyment of mathematics. Dramatizations featuring Boris, a dedicated math hater, used humorous, often silly but familiar situations to introduce the idea that math is a human invention, useful in everyday life.

The Darker Brother. An early example of diversity education, this innovative series introduced Joe, an African-American boy, and invited Wisconsin's white children to understand what it feels like to be Joe. The emphasis was on empathy and feelings instead of sympathy and intellect. The teacher manual describes one program in the series that captures the essence and power of the series: "In a program entitled, 'I, Too, Am American,' Joe keeps insisting, 'They can't see me.' Of course he's right. Like any radio character he is invisible to the audience; but the invisibility carried another meaning. Joe's identity as a Negro emerged only gradually in the course of the program. More importantly, it symbolized the theme that is primary in this program and implicit in most others—the general failure of white Americans, in the present as in the past, to perceive the black American as an individual human being" (WSA 1969–1971).

Based on these descriptions, the program seemed like a good example of broadcasting harnessed to the purpose of introducing racial awareness and understanding.

A World of Music. Representing a departure from the music appreciation courses presented in past years, this series supplemented and enriched the music and social studies curricula. Programs covered a variety of music traditions: ancient, Western classical, folk, and regional music. No attempt was made to teach music; rather, the series developed awareness that music is a normal human activity. The manual encouraged teachers to use music to build awareness of customs and traditions from other areas. It also encouraged project work.

Let's Ask Dr. Tenny. To stimulate interest in, understanding of, and appreciation for the amazing human body, Dr. Tenny responded to questions with enthusiastic presentations that provided knowledge and motivated students to practice good health habits and strive for physical fitness. Each program in the series stimulated classroom discussion and provided opportunities for extended study.

Worlds of Art. Probably unique among SOA programs, this series claimed to teach elementary school children aesthetics. The description in the schedule said the series was about "dresses, automobiles, chairs, houses, cans..., [and] also about politics, ecology, ethics, pollution and change" (WSA, 1970). The aim was to stimulate the use of aesthetics as a consideration in judging the quality of our lives and environment. The series could be used to supplement art, social science, language, and science classes. All of these ambitious goals had to be accomplished with no visual component (WSA, 1970).

Overall the schedule for 1970–1971 demonstrated how the WSA changed its approach from curricular to enrichment programming. Few of the 1970 series offered the subject matter programs that had been the staple of the WSA in its early years. Implicit in this difference was the recognition that the educational needs of Wisconsin schools had changed. By 1970, Wisconsin schools were providing their students with a full range of subjects taught by specialists in many cases. What the schools seemed to need, at least from the WSA perspective, was integration of subjects, subtlety, diverse perspectives, and, in particular, a more complex approach to learning that involved problem solving, project work, and open-minded exploration. The 1970 series

[49]By the early 1970s the WSA provided teachers with many programs on tape.

titles demonstrate this approach. The word *world* appears in three titles, suggesting a desire to widen student awareness to global perspectives.[50] *Darker Brother* suggests issues of racial diversity. Seven titles include action verbs: *reckoning, ask, find, sing, exploring* (twice), and *happened*, emphasizing the aim of engaging students in active learning. Perhaps it was the WSA's ability to adapt to a new social environment and new educational needs that enabled it to continue operation well into the 1970s[51] (WSA, 1970).

TAPING

By the early 1970s, taped programs became an important part of the WSA offering The WSA had developed a library of program tapes and distributed them on request to schools. Also, by 1970, most schools had capability to tape programs directly off the air, so teachers could choose between taping programs themselves or buying taped programs from the WSA. The latter option offered better audio quality. For the WSA, the option to broadcast live and sell taped copies, what Kentzler called dual service, provided flexibility. New programs could be developed, tested for a year or two, and then retired to the tape library freeing a time slot for new programs. Other programs deemed more popular would continue through rebroadcast so that classroom teachers could tape them off the air. This arrangement enabled the WSA to design programs for just one grade level, something that in the past was considered an uneconomical use of staff and airtime (WSA, Various dates). Taped copies of popular old favorites could also be broadcast, as was done in 1970–71 with *Let's Find Out, Let's Sing,* and *Book Trails.*

Demise

Despite the apparently successful transition to a curriculum of enrichment programming and the added flexibility of taping, the WSA increasingly faced not a hostile environment but a less accommodating one within the UW community and state government. In the spring of 1972, Kentzler realized that the state's Educational Communications Board (ECB) would assume responsibility and budget for all educational broadcasting in Wisconsin including the WSA. She looked on the change hopefully. She believed this move might result in more money for the WSA, and she assumed that the ECB would want the WSA to define a new role for instructional radio, one of experimentation and innovation rather than "serving the schools." Kentzler accepted that charge eagerly, saying that the WSA was already the most innovative thing on educational radio. However, another directive from the ECB asked not for innovative programming but that the WSA remain in "stand-still mode" during the coming school year. Kentzler's response was to proceed at full speed with the planning and writing of several new projects, without incurring extra expenses. "It is not possible for instructional radio to innovate on short notice" (Kentzler, 1972a). Her concern was that when ECB removed the stand-still request, the WSA would need another year to plan and produce innovative programming. In that time, who knows what could happen? Kentzler wanted to be ready to go as soon as possible. By November of 1972, she reported that the WSA had prepared about the same number of new programs as in the previous year (Kentzler, 1972b).

[50]This echoes Darrow's claim that radio would move the schoolroom walls out to the circumference of the globe (Darrow, 1932).

[51]A testament to the changing social values that the WSA faced can be found in a listener's letter, dated October 1975. The writer, a grandmother, expressed her disappointment with the sexist tone expressed in an episode of Reckoning with Boris. "I was appalled by the appearance of a gaggle of giggling girls. At first I thought, Oh good, at last girls are going to have a part in this clever presentation, and they will show that girls may be just as interested in and proficient with mathematics as boys. But alas the use of girls was only to distract, annoy, and at last be submissive.... This is a tragedy, in this age of struggle for women's rights.... Indeed in this International Women's Year, 1975, it is careless ... to permit discrimination in thought, word, or deed (G. Plumb, letter October 22, 1975, in Kentzler, 1969).

By early 1973, new evidence emerged that the support of institutions that had contributed to the WSA's success was eroding. A memo from WHA to the UW chancellor stated that the station would cease contributing its 14 percent of Jim Schwalbach's salary[52] (Johnson, 1972). The administration responded by asking the station to please reconsider because Schwalbach was just one year away from retirement, but station management replied that it had no choice; the station had ceased to carry Schwalbach's *Let's Draw* program (Long, 1973). Both promised the other that they would look for a way to maintain Schwalbach's salary. They failed to find one, and thus ended a relationship of nearly 40 years.

The trend continued slowly. By 1975, the UW had ceased printing or mailing the WSA manual; that responsibility had been turned over to the ECB, which had responsibility for the WSA budget as well. A memo from the ECB, dated March of 1975 and entitled "Production of ECB Instructional Radio Programming 1975–76," makes no mention of the WSA (Bauer, 1975). In the memo, the ECB director stated that station WHA-AM would stop contributing to personnel and production services for instructional radio programs carried on WERN, Madison[53] (Bauer, 1975). This decision seems to signal the end of WHA's role as the producer of the WSA programs and its withdrawal from broadcasting to the schools.[54] By 1975, the two pillars supporting the WSA had disengaged from it.

From the ECB perspective, the WHA decision simply meant that less money was available for instructional radio, but from Kentzler's perspective, WHA's withdrawal probably had more serious consequences. In a letter from June of 1975 addressed to the director of WHA, she expressed a desire to be relieved of her WSA responsibilities. She also discussed a likely successor for whom she suggested the title of coordinator of instructional production services. She made no mention of the WSA; nor is it mentioned on the letterhead where Kentzler is identified with the peculiar title of "associate director of radio station manager: WHA" (Kentzler, 1975). This letter is the last data item available at the UW archive from people directly involved with the Wisconsin School of the Air.

And so, the Wisconsin School of the Air, like the OSA, slowly faded away. In the early days of radio its origins resembled an idea that, seed like, fell into the fertile soil of the University of Wisconsin, and nearly 45 years later its days ended in a similarly bionic fashion. It seems to have biodegraded into various broadcasting and state entities that no longer would support something called the WSA but nevertheless continued broadcasting educational and instructional programs of one kind or another to the schools. This suggests that the demand for broadcasting to the schools remained.

Even though the WSA had all but disappeared, its reputation lived on. In 1974 and 1975, educational stations and state agencies from around the country continued to request taped versions of WSA programs. Newark, New Jersey's board of education station, WBGO, requested permission to use taped programs to augment high school curricula. The inquiry was prompted by many requests from Newark high school teachers for several WSA programs. Milwaukee's public schools notified Claire Kentzler that they wanted to simulcast 11 WSA programs during the 1975–1976 school year (Milwaukee, 1975). The Nebraska State Educational Television Commission expressed a desire to inaugurate a public radio system similar to Wisconsin's. To convince the "powers that be" — the state legislature and governor — the commission administrators needed to demonstrate how radio could be used in the schools. For that reason, they requested

---

[52]For many years the bulk of Schwalbach's salary was paid by University Extension, which employed him. When he started the *Let's Draw* series, he was an extension specialist in art and design for the UW College of Agriculture (Kelly, 1990).

[53]WERN-FM, Madison, was the hub of the Wisconsin FM network.

[54]By the late 1960s, the Public Broadcasting Network had been established. Many educational radio stations transformed their operations from instructional to public broadcasting (Saettler, 1990).

tape copies of several WSA programs to use as examples of radio instruction for the schools (Nebraska, 1975). In an internal memo to Claire Kentzler, Ron Borstein, director of WHA, explained that the Nebraska Commission had great plans and good dedication to public radio, but had "... encountered considerable adverse pressure from the many 'mom and pop' commercial radio owners in Nebraska who believe that Public Radio is both an unnecessary competitor and luxury for the people of their own state (Borstein, 1975).

The quote highlights how wise Engel and McCarty had been in the mid–1940s to fight for Wisconsin's FM system, before commercial stations were established. Thirty years later, small commercial FM stations were strong enough to block public radio in Nebraska, a state that no doubt had a substantial portion of its children attending small isolated rural schools where one teacher had to teach multiple grades.

The University of Wisconsin Archive contains no WSA data dated later than 1975. Therefore, we must conclude that the radio school disappeared as an entity in that year. WHA no longer broadcasts in-school programs; however, as of 1990 the FM network continued to make taped programs available to schools through a service known as the Wisconsin School Radio Service (Sanders, 1990).

Impact

Tracing the actual impact of any educational experience on generations of students or a state's bureaucracy is difficult, to say the least. The WSA, like most SOAs, conducted no summary evaluations. However, the extensive Wisconsin Research Project in School Broadcasting conducted in the late 1930s by outside researchers produced three types of findings. One part of the study compared music instruction delivered by radio versus a traditional classroom. The findings, predictably, showed no significant differences in learning outcomes. An accompanying survey of teacher opinions, however, showed that most teachers and administrators believed the educational value of the WSA broadcasts to be high. Follow-up interviews with teachers who had participated in the study revealed that one year later, the participating teachers continued to incorporate WSA programs into their curriculum (Barr et al., 1942). Unfortunately, this research, though well funded and rigorous, was conducted years before the WSA hit its stride.

Some contemporary scholars have studied the impact of specific WSA programs. Kelly's (1990) historical study of *Let's Draw* found that "radio was an effective means of disseminating creative art education instruction for students and in-service training teachers throughout Wisconsin before districts hired elementary art specialists" (p. v). She found that teachers in small rural schools "needed and welcomed help with classroom art instruction" and that radio as a mass-communication medium was effective in providing an interesting variety of creative art activities for students. She also concluded that the formation of the Wisconsin Art Education Association in 1950 was linked to the activities of the *Let's Draw* Advisory Committee (Kelly, 1990).

As mentioned earlier, King (2001), in his study of technology and science education, asserts that in the popular WSA program *Afield with Ranger Mac,* Wakelin McNeel imposed on mid–20th-century students a vision of elementary science curriculum that was a generation out of date.

On the other hand, Apps (1996) credits *Afield with Ranger Mac* for getting Wisconsin school-children involved in statewide conservation efforts. Specifically, he suggests that Ranger Mac inspired thousands of children to participate in a successful school-based reforestation program, in which Wisconsin school kids planted millions of trees in school forest plots throughout the state.

Sanders' (1990) study uncovered descriptions of the *Let's Sing* regional and state music fests that can be interpreted in an evaluative mode. Stressing that Professor Gordon placed the priority on learning at these events, she says: "In 1956, about 27,300 children were participating in the regional festivals ... even with audiences of some 3400 children, there was absolute quiet between songs. When Gordon addressed the children, or asked them a question, they responded in unison, and their singing was remarkably together, in light of the number ... present" (Sanders, 1990, p. 176).

These comments imply that Gordon's radio instruction was successful in preparing children to sing in unison and on key. Overall then, spotty evidence does exist to suggest that the WSA had a broad positive educational impact on Wisconsin schoolchildren.

Summary

The long history of the nation's foremost SOA offers many indicators of its success. They include longevity, audience size, and national recognition, far exceeding those of other state and national SOAs. That success was driven by several factors. From the beginning the WSA was dedicated to supporting the UW's mission to serve all the people of Wisconsin. The WSA implemented that ideal by using radio to help teachers in rural and small-town schools. They provided the curriculum support those teachers needed most; such a focus resulted in programs that had a particularly Wisconsin appeal and also provided means by which the customs and values of older Wisconsin residents could be transmitted to young people. Programs in science, history, conservation, and literature all included themes, characters, and activities familiar to older generations of Wisconsin residents.

Moreover, a half-dozen of the WSA's most popular programs cultivated communities of learners. These programs brought students together, engaging them in cooperative learning activities that built connection and loyalty to the WSA. Another aspect was the encouragement of feeling, creativity, and values. While other SOAs often tried to awe students (and parents) by bringing the voices of society's prestigious leaders, artists, and thinkers into the classroom, the WSA developed a more child-centered approach. WSA programs aimed at helping individual students become engaged with learning about their own world and their individual talents.

Probably the single most important factor in the WSA's success was its connection with the state university and its powerful statewide broadcasting network. That university radio connection enabled the WSA's director, scriptwriters, and radio teachers to focus on their core activity, education by radio. Atkinson (1938) made a similar observation. He described the WSA as a "cooperative adventure among state university, state department of education, state teachers association, Madison public schools and other groups" (Atkinson, 1938, p. 105). This involvement stands in contrast to what seemed a one-man show conducted by Ben Darrow at the Ohio School of the Air (OSA). This connectedness with many groups explains in part how the WSA remained plugged into the needs of Wisconsin's teachers, and became part of the Wisconsin educational family.

Minnesota School of the Air

The Minnesota School of the Air (MSA) vied with the Wisconsin School of the Air (WSA) for the title of the longest running state-based school of the air (SOA). Beginning operation in 1938 as an arm of the University of Minnesota's (UM) educational station, WLB, the MSA operated continually for at least 41 years and perhaps longer. Early in its history the first director, E. W. Ziebarth, envisioned a grand plan. The MSA would become the school of the air for the entire Upper Midwestern United States— Minnesota, Wisconsin, North and South Dakota and Iowa — this despite the Wisconsin School of the Air that operated next door.[55] While the grand plan failed, the MSA

---

[55]By 1940, the WSA programs reached only a portion of Wisconsin's schools and probably none along the Minnesota border.

did succeed in providing well-received curriculum supplement programs to public and parochial schools throughout southern Minnesota, serving at one time up to 140,000 school children.

The MSA faced many of the same challenges as the WSA, threats from commercial stations, the competition from instructional television, and in the later years, growing indifference from its university-based supporters. Moreover, it lacked some of Wisconsin's support systems, such as a statewide FM network, strong legislative support, and adequate budget and staff. Nevertheless, the MSA broadcast a full range of quality programs for in-school use; its programs received 25 awards for programming excellence from various national groups; and it continued developing original programming even in the late 1970s. Much credit for MSA's survival and achievements belonged to its long time director, Betty Thomas Girling, a writer and educator, who fought tenaciously for the MSA's survival while continuing to oversee the development and production of effective instructional programs. The end was contentious, but the MSA faced its demise with what may have been its most ambitious and interesting program schedule.

Origins

On January 13, 1922, the University of Minnesota (UM) received a license to operate station WLB, allowing the university to claim the distinction of being the second oldest continually operating educational station in the nation. Wisconsin's WHA was the first. In 1931, WLB presented its first course intended for classroom room use, *A Radio Course in Music Appreciation*. Developed by Burton Paulu, the course introduced basic principles and facts needed to appreciate fine music[56] and composition. Course bulletins were distributed annually to participating schools. Although intended for high school students, the course quickly drew adult listeners and that fact influenced program development. (Atkinson, 1942d). In a sense, the music appreciation course introduced hundreds of teachers throughout Minnesota to the idea of using radio in the classroom, thus paving the way for easy acceptance of a formal school of the air. The course would later become a regular feature of the MSA. In the mean time, Paulu was appointed manager of station WLB, a position he held for several decades.

The idea of a school of the air as such percolated for a few years and got its official start in the fall of 1938, under the direction E. W. Ziebarth (Atkinson, 1942d). Ziebarth stated early-on that the radio courses should be developed as supplements to the state's school curricula and as motivational learning aids. To this end, all the programs were one semester long and paralleled, to some degree, the subjects being taught in Minnesota schools. Table 29 shows the MSA programs for the 1938–1939 school year.

TABLE 30. MSA PROGRAM SCHEDULE, 1938–1939

Day	Time	Course	Grades
Monday	11:05–11:20 A.M.	*Old Tales and New*	K–3
	2:05–2:20 P.M.	*Countries and Cities Around the World*	7–12
Tuesday	2:05–2:20 P.M.	*German and French*	HS and college
Wednesday	11:05–11:20 A.M.	*Current Events*	6–8
	2:05–2:20 P.M.	*Representative Authors*	9–12
Thursday	11:00–11:30 A.M.	*Music Appreciation*	7–12, adults
	2:05–2:20 P.M.	*Representative Authors*	7–12
Friday	11:05–11:20 A.M.	*Guidance for the Future Worker*	9–12
	2:05–2:20 P.M.	*Episodes in American History*	Not Specified

[56]The course covered music in the European classical tradition.

The schedule in Table 30 demonstrates the typical program offerings for the state-based SOAs of the day: stories for the primary grades, geography, literature, music appreciation, current events, career guidance, and American History. Each series was one semester long, and all programs ran for 15 minutes except for *Music Appreciation* which was 30 minutes long. Ziebarth repeated the error of many other SOAs; he emphasized programming for high schools and all but ignored the elementary grades, which were the more fertile ground for instructional radio. Nevertheless, a few of the early programs endured many decades and became hallmarks of the MSA effort, for example, *Old Tales and New.* The longest running MSA series, *Old Tales and New* continued on air even in the school's last year, 1979. Its basic story telling remained popular with primary teachers throughout the listening areas. The key was a warm voice that could put drama into a story. Starting in 1940, many of the scripts were selected, written, and narrated by children's author Betty Girling, who would go on to serve for many years as the MSA director.

Basic German and French. Designed to supplement high school and college class work, this series presented readings, songs, and plays in the two languages. Printed texts were provided to support the broadcasts. The MSA was one of the few SOAs to continue language instruction by radio well into the 1960s.

Music Appreciation. The series started by Burton Paulu in 1931 continued to focus on European classical music until the mid–1940s. Paulu believed that many adults listened in.

Representative Authors. Titles for this literature series came from the State Course of Study reading lists, and were selected by a committee of English teachers from Minnesota schools. As such it represents a program that closely supported the actual subject curricula in use at many Minnesota junior and senior high schools.

The state's Department of Education and many other state-based organizations participated to some extent in reviewing and approving program content. But development depended mostly on Mr. Ziebarth. He explained:

> The administrative set-up of the Minnesota School of the Air is a relatively simple one in which I take the responsibility for planning programs with the schools, for the determination of objectives ... [and] content-areas which the programs are designed to supplement.... In making plans for the programs, we of course consult committees drawn from the public schools in this area, as well as committees made up of members of the University faculty.
> We are helped by an NYA [National Youth Administration] script writing project which does research and some writing for the series. We use many student actors for the dramatic broadcasts [Atkinson, 1942d, p. 63].

Ziebarth's statement makes clear that in the area of program planning and development, he worked with the local schools and university faculty to set program objectives and content and to coordinate broadcasting. Ziebarth overcame the barrier of having no paid staff to write scripts by acquiring script writing help from the NYA (National Youth Administration).[57] He also took responsibility for developing educational programs for the general public that were broadcast either after school hours or on the week end. These included programs in child development, music appreciation, American government, and the WLB Playhouse.

PROGRAM SCHEDULE 1943

Five years after its launch, the MSA offered a mix of continuing and new programs; several of the latter reflected the on-going great war and its consequences as shown in Table 31.

---

[57]The NYA was a New Deal agency spearheaded by Eleanor Roosevelt to provide vocational and education support to youth during the Depression. Apparently, one NYA project focused on writing scripts for radio.

TABLE 31. MSA PROGRAM SCHEDULE, 1943–1944
(WOELFEL AND TYLER, 1945)

Day	Time	Course	Grades
Monday	11:00 A.M.	*Old Tales and New*	K-3
	2:00 P.M.	*Your Job and the War*	7–12
Tuesday	2:00 P.M.	*We, the United Nations*	7–12
Wednesday	11:00 A.M.	*Your Health and You*	6–9
	2:00 P.M.	*Current Events*	6–9
Thursday	11:00 A.M.	*Music Appreciation*	7–12
	2:00 P.M.	*Representative Authors*	7–12
Friday	11:00 A.M.	*Current Events*	6–9
	2:00 P.M.	*Land Alive*	4–8

By the mid–1940s, surveys of school listeners had repeatedly indicated that the bulk of schoolroom listeners are in elementary schools (Woelfel and Tyler 1945, p. 83). The schedule for 1943–1944 does shows a gradual shift toward more programming for elementary grades. Program highlights are given below.

Your Job and the War. A vocational series designed to help high school students make good career choices.

We, the United Nations. Aimed at junior and senior high school students, this series was designed to build respect for the USA's wartime allies.

You and Your Health. Presented by Dr. William O'Brian, whom the schedule described as "One of the best known radio personalities in the entire Northwest." The series description conveys the sense of war-time patriotism, "Wartime regulations in civilian goods necessitate not only changes in diet, but also special precautions in regard to other aspects of the health of school children" (MSA Bulletin, 1943, p. 6).

Current Events. Because the war heightened interest in events taking place in the world, *Current Events* was presented twice a week. It provided what the writers called an objective analysis of significant news over the week, edited and presented for young people, grades six through junior high.

Music Appreciation. The original WLB program started by station manager Burton Paulu in 1931 (before the MSA was initiated) and billed as the oldest music appreciation program in the nation.[58] The programs were intended for listeners in junior and senior high schools and at-home.

Land Alive. Intended for a mix of conservation and social studies classes, the series consisted of taped radio dramas that told the story of a wounded war veteran and his family who recuperates in Northern Minnesota. Many aspects of life in the north woods highlighted the importance of conservation during the war. Scripts were developed by the State Department of Conservation.

Broadcast

As a University owned station, WLB broadcast, by the late 1930s, a nearly full day from 10:30 a. m. to sunset.[59] One and half hours of that time was devoted to the MSA programs. Even though the MSA program Bulletin assured listeners that WLB's 5,000 watt station could be heard in most of Minnesota, it's unlikely that reception was reliable much beyond 100 miles

---

[58]Though Walter Damrosch's *Music Appreciation Hour* went on the air in 1929, it was terminated in 1942.

[59]FCC required WLB to share its evening hours with another station.

from Minneapolis. With this limitation in mind, Director Ziebarth advanced a vision to expand the reach of station WLB using the MSA as a chief attraction. By affiliating WLB with the 10 station North Central radio network, the MSA programs became available to students throughout the upper Midwest: "Last year [1939] the startling concept of the state as a classroom was developed in connection with the Minnesota School of the Air. Today we should like to bring to your attention an even more startling concept — that of the entire Northwest as a classroom. Cooperation between the North Central Broadcasting System and WLB has made possible an extension of school services equaled in importance only by the major [commercial] networks" (Atkinson, 1942d, p. 63).

Had Ziebarth's vision of creating one big radio classroom in the North Central United States come to pass, MSA programs would have served schools in Wisconsin, North and South Dakota, Iowa and Minnesota. Audience research, conducted by the MSA in 1947, showed that the MSA programs reached few schools outside Minnesota.

In 1945, station WLB was renamed KUOM. Its 5,000 watt signal reached most of southern Minnesota, but even there AM reception could be unreliable. As a consequence, reception of the MSA programs occurred mainly in the southern part of Minnesota and near-by portions of bordering states. It is unclear what portion of the state's schools could actually tune into the MSA programs. Oddly, neither University administrators nor station director Paulu seems to have been enticed by the Wisconsin model of developing a state-wide educational radio network, or by the idea of switching from AM to FM broadcasting. The reasons why are not documented Fortunately, by the mid–1950s station KROC in Rochester, Minnesota began carrying select MSA programs, improving coverage in southern Minnesota.

Administration and the Girling Years

The MSA existed as an activity of radio station WLB, which in turn was under the administrative control of the UM's Extension Division. While the Dean of the Division held ultimate authority over the station and consequently the school, there is little evidence that he interfered much in MSA management — even in the mid–1940s, radio was still considered a new and somewhat mysterious medium. The Dean did however appoint many members of the MSA Advisory Committee. The Committee made policy recommendations, met twice during the school year to examine new trends or ideas, and recommended changes in program emphasis. One of the few SOA policy committees to include representatives from Parochial school systems, The Advisory Committee members included a representative from the State Superintendent of Education, two members of the UM College of Education, one each from the Minneapolis and St. Paul Boards of Education, the Arch-diocesan Catholic schools and the Missouri Synod Lutheran Schools.

The Advisory Committee structure enabled the MSA to serve more of the state's students, but it also created barriers in terms of communicating with classroom teachers. Because teacher use of MSA programs was voluntary, communication with large numbers of teachers was important. However, direct contact was not possible. Each administrative body represented on the Advisory Council had it own supervisor of radio activities; it was only through the radio supervisors that MSA could contact large numbers of teachers (MSA Bulletin, 1950).

While the Advisory committee could make recommendations, the MSA director was not bound to follow them (MSA, Annual Report, 1948). Consequently, the director answered only to the KUOM station manager. In 1946, manager Burton Paulu appointed Betty Girling director of the MSA; she would shape and defend radio instruction for the schools in Minnesota for over thirty years. Girling had been hired by the station in 1940 primarily as a scriptwriter (Girling, 1978). Over her long tenure she wrote literally hundreds of scripts and some for television as well. On becoming director, her title changed and her responsibilities expanded, but writing remained a large part of what she did even to the very end of her career at the MSA.

Probably Girling's first and most significant action was to undertake a comprehensive study of the MSA programs and audience, the findings of which are reported later in this section. Out of that 1947 study came a key finding concerning the popularity of individual programs, as shown in Table 32.

TABLE 32. MSA PROGRAM SCHEDULE BY POPULARITY,
1946–1947 (GIRLING, 1947)

Course	Popularity	Course	Popularity
Books Bring Adventure	1	*Your Health and You*	10
Old Tales and New	2	*Our America*	11
Adventures in Music	3	*Art and Artists*	12
Young People's Concert	4	*News X-Ray*	13
Penny and Paul	5	*United Neighbors*	14
Let Science Tell Us	6	*Representative Authors*	15
Journeys in Art	7	*Your Job — Your Future*	16
Current Events	8	*High School Workshop*	17
Music Appreciation	9		

Girling attributed low popularity ratings of the four least popular programs to the fact that they were intended for high school use, where rigid schedules inhibited teachers from using the programs. Also affecting popularity, some MSA programs were designed specifically for rural teachers while others were intended for urban school children. Based on these findings, Girling changed the schedule to eliminate high school programming, and to focus instead on the grades known to be most receptive to radio instruction, K through 8. Girling's changes are demonstrated in Table 33.

TABLE 33. MSA PROGRAM SCHEDULE, 1949–1950 (MSA, BULLETIN, 1950)

Day	Time	Course	Grades
Monday	11:00 A.M.	*Old Tales and New*	K–3
	2:15 P.M.	*Let Science Tell Us*	4–8
Tuesday	11:00 A.M.	*Look What We Found*	4–8
Wednesday	11:00 A.M.	*Penny and Paul*	4–8
	11:15 P.M.	*Your Health and You*	5–9
	2:15 P.M.	*Journeys in Art*	4–6
Thursday	10:30 A.M.	*Let's Sing*	K–3
	2:15 P.M.	*Old Tales and New*	K–3
Friday	11:00 A.M.	*Current Events*	4–9
	2:15 P.M.	*Following Conservation Trails*	4–8

Girling also added *Following Conservation Trails,* which was developed by the state's Department of Conservation. The program become very popular, but more important it gained for the MSA a powerful ally within state government. Descriptions of programs not described previously are given below.

Books Bring Adventures. Intended to be of high value to rural teachers who had a limited supply of children's books, the program was indeed popular with the state-graded elementary school teachers, but it attracted the largest audience from urban schools. This fact underscores one of instructional radio's greatest strengths — story telling for young children.

Art and Artists. The series presented new methods and materials for art expression. It was designed especially for rural teachers whose background in art and access to art supplies were limited.

Journeys in Art. Aimed specifically at students in the Minneapolis/St. Paul Metropolitan Area, this series was planned, developed, and presented cooperatively by the Minneapolis Schools and the staff of the Minneapolis Institute of Art. Its relatively high popularity reflects the fact that Minneapolis and St. Paul made up a high proportion of the MSA listening audience.

Following Conservation Trails. The MSA's popular conservation series highlighted the Minnesota environment. It was presented by Nat Johnson, educational adviser for the State Department of Conservation, who asserted that the programs were the only conservation broadcast series in the United States. Topics covered included historic Minnesota sites, hunting and winter recreation in Minnesota, birds, game fishing, boating and camp grounds. The Bulletin for 1952–53 reflected the growing Cold War tensions of the time by dramatically stressing how progress strained the nation's natural resources, and consequently made conservation education "more vital to the defense of the free world and the ultimate existence of Democracy" (MSA Bulletin, 1952).

Support Materials

For the very first semester of broadcasting, the MSA distributed print materials for use by classroom teachers. The *Bulletin of the Minnesota School of the Air* provided classroom teachers with a weekly schedule of the upcoming programs for an entire semester. The Bulletins included a description for each series, the intended grade level, the broadcast date and time for each program in a series, individual program titles, and basic information about authors and composers, where appropriate. They also provided suggestions on how to prepare for the broadcasts and for follow-up discussion and activities. The bulletins enabled classroom teachers to incorporate the radio programs into their semester lesson plans. The MSA continued issuing the professional looking program schedules annually for over forty years. The last available sample is dated 1979.

Girling's writing background is evident in the program Bulletin for 1949; it identifies the writer and producer for every program. In that year, Girling wrote most of the scripts for the MSA's popular primary series, *Old Tales and New.*

In addition to the schedule, at some point in the late 1940s or early 1950s, the school issued teacher manuals for individual programs or at least groups of programs. Bulletins contained forms for ordering the manual, usually with a separate envelope. By 1960, the order form was printed in the Bulletin. At that time, two Teacher Manuals were offered, one for the primary grade programs and one for the intermediate grade programs. The fee was $.75 and $1.25, respectively. Curiously, by the late 1960s and early 1970s, when most SOAs were winding down, the MSA had expanded its offerings by preparing a separate manual for every two courses and then in the late 1970s, a separate manual for each course. The available documentation suggests that the MSA did not make extensive use of visual aids.

Philosophy, Methods, and Challenges

Statements from the MSA Bulletin for the fall semester of 1941–42 reveal that Director Ziebarth held strong views about how students learned best from radio in the classroom. He recommended a strictly passive listening approach. Teachers were urged to create a listening environment free of any possible distractions. Note taking was discouraged. Visual aids such as maps and pictures were to be kept out of sight until after the broadcast. Apparently, Ziebarth was in no way influenced by Dewey's thought about active learning, which was widely popular at that time. To Ziebarth, students learned best by listening attentively, and nothing else. Visual aids or note taking merely distracted students from the message being delivered by the radio voice (Atkinson, 1942d). This view is in opposition to ideas suggested by educators associated with the Wisconsin and Texas schools of the air who often encouraged teachers during the broadcasts to make visuals available and get children engaged in activities such as note taking, drawing, singing and doing experiments. The dichotomy over methods could be found among many SOAs at the state and local levels.

With a change in director came a change in philosophy. In the 1949–1950 program Bulletin, director Betty Girling said that the MSA programs did not aim primarily to give facts. Rather they presented hard to measure learning areas such as expanding horizons, enriched experience, understanding of human relationships, and attitude development. For example, in the science program, *Let Science Tell Us,* developing enthusiasm for science took precedent over teaching science facts. Girling offered eight recommendations for getting the most out of radio, the key points being to precede each broadcast with a short warm-up introduction and to follow-up by integrating facts with ideas and discussing concepts and perception (MSA Bulletin, 1950, p. 3). She said little about what students should or should not do during the broadcasts.

Girling also said little about whether radio should be used as lesson enrichment or curricular supplement. However, in her Annual Report of 1949, she laid out the difficulty she faced in trying to develop programs that would meet the curricular needs of four different educational districts. To accommodate the curricula of the State Department of Education, the Metropolitan County Schools, city and parochial schools— each with different curriculum syllabi and all using MSA programs— Girling believed that the MSA had to address broad subject areas rather that specific ones (MSA Bulletin, 1950).

Tapes for Teaching

In 1948, aided by the University's Foundation Funds, the MSA helped establish the *Tapes for Teaching Project,* which made audio tapes of many MSA programs available to the schools. The project solved the problem faced by teachers who could not fit their class schedules to the broadcast times of the MSA programs. Order forms were enclosed with the program bulletins. To receive a taped program, the teacher or school was asked to send a blank tape and pay postage. The *Tapes for Teaching Project* copied the desired programs onto the blank tape and returned it to the school or teacher who requested it. The tapes program grew steadily; in 1970, Girling reported filling over 1,700 tape requests, and we can assume that teachers used each tape at least once per semester. Unfortunately, no data exist on how many students listened to the taped versions of the programs.

The project also made tapes available nationwide through such organizations as the National Association of Educational Broadcasters (NAEB) and the National Education Association (NEA). Girling reports that requests for tapes from out-of-state SOAs and schools had reached over 100 per year. The tape program demonstrates that despite the availability of instructional television, demand for the MSA's radio offerings, though not huge, remained strong well into the 1970s.

MSA and the Minnesota Centennial Celebration

A decade after Girling became the MSA director, the broadcast schedule remained very similar to that of the late 1940s except for the big role that MSA played in celebrating Minnesota's Centennial. During the three years prior to the 1958 grand event, the MSA developed programs to support and celebrate the state's 100th anniversary. Four new series were developed as described below:

Minnesota Honor Role. The series provided biographical sketches of famous Minnesotans who had achieved world-wide recognition such as Charles Lindbergh and novelists Ole Rolvag and F. Scott Fitzgerald.

Minnesota Events that Changed the World. A series of seven programs highlighting events that had significant effect not only on the people of the State, but on the nation and the globe.

Crystal Gazing: A series that invited students to imagine the future in their state.

Adventuring with a Road Map. The series explored Minnesota by radio.

In addition to the special series many programs with Centennial themes were developed for the regular series such as *Conservation Trails, Adventures in Music,* and *Your Health and You.* In all, 132 Centennial theme programs were aired as part of the MSA's three year celebration (MSA, Teacher Manual, 1958).

After a decade in the role of director, Girling grew more adventurous. During the late 1950s she gradually initiated programming changes that gained for the MSA national recognition as an innovator in radio programming. In her annual report for 1956–1957, she described two special series that featured reports from around the world and harkened back to Ben Darrow's ideas about bringing the world to the classroom. One was a short series by Dr. Laurence Gould, President of Minnesota's Carlton College, who broadcast from Operation Deep Freeze II in connection with a 15 year study of the Antarctic. Short wave connections brought live interviews with the explorers and scientists at the bottom of the world into classrooms of southern Minnesota. Another special program was arranged by MSA staffer, Lotte Seidler, who recorded a series of special interviews with children in Europe for a five week unit of programs called *Meet Your Neighbors.*

The innovations continued in 1957–58 with the introduction of instruction in German and Spanish, an effort that ran counter to what almost every other SOA in the country was doing, namely moving away from rigorous instruction in language and science. *Espanol Si Si* and *Gesundheit* were intended to spark interest in language study and supplement the study of foreign countries and cultures. In 1960, the German language programs *Gesundheit* and *Die Flotte Liesselotte* were approved by the Modern Language Association for distribution to language teachers across the country (MSA, Annual Report, 1960). The program schedule for 1959–1960 shown in Table 34 reflects Girling's changes.

TABLE 34. MSA PROGRAM SCHEDULE, 1959–1960 (MSA, BULLETIN, 1960)

Day	Time	Course	Grades
Monday	11:00 — 11:15	*Old Tales and New*	K–3
	2:15–2:30	*Let's Sing*	K–3
Tuesday	11:00–11:15	*Carnival of Books**	5–9
	2:15–2:30	*Exploring Nature with Mr. B.*	K–3
Wednesday	11:00–11:15	*Espanol Si Si* (1st Semester)	4–6
		Gesundheit (2nd Semester)	4–6
	11:15 — 11:30	*Your Health and You*	Not specified
	2:15–2:30	*Adventures in Music*	4–8
Thursday	10:30 — 10:45	*Let's Sing*	K–3
	11:00 — 11:15	*People Like You and Me* and	4–8
		A Day to Remember§	4–9
	2:15–2:30	*Old Tales and New*	K–3
Friday	10:30 — 10:45	*Young People's University Theatre*	4–8
	11:00–11:15	*Current Events*	5–8
	2:15–2:30	*Following Conservation Trails*	5–8

* Programs acquired from New York radio station, WNYE

§ Created by the National Broadcasting Company (NBC) and distributed by NAEB

The schedule in Table 34 also shows two programs acquired from sources outside of the MSA, *Carnival of Books* and *A Day to Remember*. Program tapes were acquired from the National Association of Educational Broadcasters (NAEB)[60] which had created a library of tapes produced by its member stations. Two other noteworthy new programs are described below:

People Like You and Me: In observance of the International Refugee Year, 1959, the MSA offered stories of five refugee children. Written by Lotte Seidler, the school's Administration Fellow in Radio, the short series introduced Minnesota children to the plight of refugee children and encouraged them to help rescue the refugees.

A Day to Remember. Developed by New York City's educational station, WNYE, this prize winning series chronicled the events and celebrations that occur during the year. Each program developed the idea that behind every date is a man or woman who is making history.

Another first from the early 1960s was *A Sense of the World*. The idea, according to Girling, was to arouse the students' sensory perception and then present "artistic manifestations of their aroused perceptions and urge them to express themselves in a variety of artistic formats, painting, stories, music, poetry, creative drama, gallery visits, etc. (MSA Annual Report, 1960). The NAEB chose *A Sense of the World* for distribution to all its member stations.

Girling engaged the services of young music composer Lynn Olson to develop a music series for the primary grades that would feature Olson's original compositions. In 1963, Olson's *It's Time for Music* received a First Educational Broadcasters award at the Ohio State University. Later, Olsen went on to write music for the children's television series *Captain Kangaroo* (MSA Annual Report, 1960).

The Sixties Bring a New Look

The 1960s brought change to the MSA. Instructional television became well established, radio became old news, and the space program stimulated the imagination of young people across the country. Girling seems to have absorbed these changes because by 1966, she extensively revised the MSA program schedule compared with just six years earlier, as shown in Table 35.

TABLE 35. MSA PROGRAM SCHEDULE, 1965–1966 (MSA, BULLETIN, 1966)

Day	Time	Course	Grades
Monday	10:30 — 10:45	Old Tales and New	K–3
	2:15–2:30	Let's Write*	4–6
Tuesday	10:30 — 10:45	Make Mine Music*	4–6
	11:00–11:15	The Book Detective	4–8
	2:15–2:30	They Stride the Land* (1st semester)	5–9
		Aero-Space Age* (2nd semester)	5–9
Wednesday	10:30 — 10:45	Your Health and You	4–6
	2:15–2:30	The Golden Shoes (1st semester)	4–6
		The Earth's Circle (2nd semester)	4–6
Thursday	10:30–10:45	It's Time for Music!	K–3
	11:00 — 11:15	Pioneers of Science	5–9
	2:15–2:30	Old Tales and New	K–3
Friday	10:30–10:45	Young People's Play (Once each semester)	4–8
10:30–10:45	Current Events	5–9	
2:15–2:30	Following Conservation Trails		5–8

* Programs acquired from outside sources.

[60]NAEB tapes became a mixed blessing in my opinion. On the one hand, they made available an extensive collection of quality radio series enabling all to expand their program offerings. On the other hand, they also encouraged SOAs to cut back on producing their own programs.

Only four of 14 programs from the 1959–1960 schedule survived in 1965–66. They were *Old Tales and New, Current Events, Your Health and You,* and *Following Conservation Trails.* Several of the 11 new programs demonstrated the country's deep interest in the space program and science in general. Three of the new programs were acquired from other schools of the air. Below are descriptions of the new programs.

Let's Write. The series was borrowed from the Wisconsin School of the Air. Girling admired radio teacher Maureen Applegate's unique creative writing series and acknowledged Applegate's warmth and effective pedagogy, which stressed teaching skills as-needed by student writers. Applegate stated that her goal was to aid students in expressing themselves clearly and imaginatively. The acquisition was supported with help from the Minneapolis Public schools.

Make Mine Music. An upgraded music appreciation series that was designed to lead "intermediate students to the romance of musical discovery." Using casual dramatic vignettes and accessible musical selections, the programs introduced young people to the various modes of musical expression used in serious, i.e., classical music (MSA Bulletin, 1966, p 10).

Book Detective. A literature series comprised of informal but informative book reviews. For each semester, the Minneapolis and St. Paul library staffs selected 30 or so books that covered a wide range of ages and interests. The book detective briefly discussed each book and read selections to demonstrate the book's style. Story synopses and notes were included in the Teachers Manual. Child author Richard Stevens served as the first on-air book detective and he continued in the role for many years.

They Stride the Land. Thirteen programs that dramatized giants of American legend and song. Primarily designed to supplement English classes, the programs could be used to enrich lessons in music, art, geography and history. The series was produced by the Newark, New Jersey school board's educational station, WBGO, and distributed by the National Association of Educational Broadcasters.

The Aero-Space Age. This series brought the space-age to the classroom. Made available by New York City's WNYE, the programs helped classroom teachers relate various school subjects with the space age. Interest in space must have declined soon, because within a few years this series had been dropped.

Golden Shoes. The series used drama to make students in grades 4–6 familiar with European myths and legends from Greece, Rome, France, and Scandinavia. Girling asserted that the radio dramas brought to life gods, heroes, monsters and amazing deeds "which cannot be convincingly represented visually," emphasizing radio's power to stimulate the imagination (MSA Teacher Manuals, 1979, *Golden Shoes,* p. 1). She recommended that teachers use the series as a supplement to the study of literature, social studies, history, even art. A teacher manual provided background information and suggestions for follow-up discussion and learning activities.

The Earth's Circle. A companion to *Golden Shoes,* the series presented a collection of folk tales from around the world. Billed as a supplement for the language arts, each program included a narrator who played the guitar and read stories typical of a specific country.

It's Time for Music. A popular series designed to supplement the core music curriculum in the primary grades, K–3. Girling said the programs had become a well used teaching aid in school systems across Minnesota and in several other states. The key character, a musical elf, Chipper, received huge amounts of fan mail while the program's originator, composer, and radio teacher, Lynn Freeman Olson, became familiar to thousands of school children, in part due to frequent school visits. The series represented one of the MSA's most creative efforts.

Pioneers of Science. Produced by WNYE, the series presented dramatized biographies of scientists whose basic research and discoveries have added to our understanding and knowledge of the natural world. Similar series were presented by most SOAs with the idea of simulating student interest in learning about science. While the productions were usually good, they probably represented a way for schools to avoid the difficult job of actually teaching science.

Teacher manuals were available for all programs, most at the cost of $1.25 each. The schedule for 1965–1966 shows the MSA shifting gears and making adjustments to a new era, though curiously, unlike in previous years, Girling's name appears nowhere in the schedule (Girling, 1978).

Evaluation

It appears that the MSA's two directors, Zeibarth and Girling, did little in the way of summary evaluation, or at least documented little of it. Lotte Seidler, the MSA administrative fellow, during the late 1950s organized regular school visits to observe classrooms during the in-school broadcasts. She recruited a group of university graduate students and teaching assistants and together visited 62 classrooms in the Twin Cities area. During their visits they completed an evaluation of broadcast and student and teacher reactions. Girling said the visits helped revise programs and also promoted the MSA to many teachers. Unfortunately, she gave little information about what the visitors actually saw or heard.

Audience

Almost immediately after the start of the MSA broadcasts in 1938, then director Ziebarth conducted surveys to determine who was listening. In the fall of 1938, just a few weeks after the initial broadcasts, survey results indicated approximately 17,000 classroom listeners. Results of a spring 1939 survey showed 32,000 listeners and by 1941–1942, the number of listeners topped 95,000 (Atkinson, 1942d). No data is available on how the survey sample was selected, the questions, or how results were tabulated or analyzed. Ziebarth continued his surveys annually until 1942.

In 1947, shortly after being named MSA director, Betty Girling authored a report on the most extensive survey of the MSA listening audience conducted to that date. In it, she asserted that the results presented a more accurate picture of the MSA listening audience than did the results from earlier surveys, which were projected from smaller bases of returns. Results from the 1947 survey were based on actual counts of responses.

To conduct the survey, Girling sent a two-part postcard mailer to 1,442 schools in the KUOM listening area. A listing of the types of school surveyed included the following categories:

- Minnesota Public Graded Schools (Outside the metropolitan area)   647
- Minneapolis and St. Paul public schools   176
- Hennepin and Ramsey County public schools (part of the Minneapolis
  and St. Paul metropolitan areas)   95
- All Catholic Schools in Minnesota   287
- Schools in the neighboring areas of Wisconsin and Iowa   229
- Private schools in Minnesota   8

                                                                  (Girling, 1947)

The list included all the schools in the Minneapolis/St. Paul metropolitan areas and all of the state's Catholic schools, some of the state graded schools, which represented small towns and rural areas, and some schools in nearby areas of Wisconsin and Iowa.[61] Apparently, not included were one-room schools, a glaring omission. Even in the late 1940s, one-room rural schools served a significant portion of the state's school children. In Wisconsin, teachers in one-room schools proved to be the most enthusiastic users of radio instruction.

The mailer collected a great deal of information, including how many students listened to

---

[61] As it turned out, no schools in Iowa reported listening regularly to the MSA programs, and the main reason given was poor reception (Girling, 1947).

each program and whether they listened regularly or irregularly. Regular listeners were defined as those who listened ten or more times to programs in one series per semester, while the irregular listeners were those who listened fewer than ten times. Girling (1947) received replies from over half the schools that were mailed, a very impressive return rate. A simple tally of the replies revealed that in the 745 schools that replied, 95,562 students listened regularly to at least one series. Irregular listeners totaled 4,909. Girling said she made no attempt to estimate listeners in schools that did not reply. If she had, the projected total of listeners might easily have exceeded 150,000, a not unreasonable projection. Nevertheless, the results confirmed that the MSA programs were used regularly in a substantial number of Minnesota's schools though she does not compare her estimates to the total number of potential listeners.

Girling's (1947) survey did suffer from the weakness described by Cuban (1986) and discussed earlier in this study. The individual postcard surveys went to schools, not teachers. Who completed the survey forms? Was it the school principal, a superintendent, or one of the classroom teachers who actually used radio programs? We don't know, but Cuban asserted that when principals and superintendents completed surveys on radio usage, they often exaggerated the number of students who listened.

By 1957, however, Girling's estimates grew to perhaps inflated levels. In her bi-annual report of 1956–1957, she alluded to a 1957 survey that found 220,000 MSA listeners in Minnesota elementary schools. Beyond that, she speculated that even more listeners were tuning in from Western Wisconsin, at home, and in Minnesota's high schools. Girling's estimates seem fanciful, given the realities of a radio station that reached only a portion of the state, that the MSA offered no programs for high school students, and that by the mid–1950s, Wisconsin's powerful FM network reached all of that state's schools and probably more in Minnesota. No doubt Girling, like all directors of many SOAs, faced pressure to justify the expense of the MSA, as small as it was.

In 1965, in response to a request from KUOM station director Burton Paulu, the acting director of the MSA, Nancy Eubank,[62] developed estimates of the MSA audience. Eubanks used a simple method for making her estimate. She merely counted the number of manuals sold to teachers and multiplied by 30. Her assumptions were that teachers who bought the manuals used at least one program and that each teacher who ordered a manual represented 30 student listeners. Using that method, she came up with 45,150 weekly student listeners for the 1964–1965 school year. That number sounded rather small compared to the hundreds of thousands listeners estimated by Girling earlier. Several factors might have limited the MSA audience. (1) Programs were intended for the grade ranges, K–3, 4–6, and 4–8, so the total possible audience for each program was relatively small. (2) MSA broadcasts reached only part of the state; students in northern and western Minnesota did not receive the broadcasts. (3) Because manuals for twelve intermediate series were bound into one book, the purchaser of one book could represent multiple users. Also, by duplicating a manual at the schools, teachers who had not ordered could use the programs. At any rate the Dean of the Extension Division which controlled the station seemed more than satisfied with Eubank's numbers. In fact, he wrote to Paulu and said: "I agree with you that it (the MSA) does represent one of our best electronic education bargains...." (MSA, Thompson, 1965).

Five years later, more than half of Betty Girling's 1971 annual report dealt with audience estimates, perhaps underscoring a perceived attack on the MSA from University administrators who were starting to question the relevance of radio education in the television age. Girling, assuming one manual equaled 30 students, came up with 36,259 regular listeners in the 42 counties of southern Minnesota that were served by KUOM and KROC in Rochester. Girling tried

[62]During the mid–1960s, Betty Girling apparently took a leave of absence from her position as director. But she returned and remained in that position until at least the late 1970s.

to put a positive spin on her estimate by asserting that 36,000 equaled 3/4s of the University of Minnesota's population.

Girling argued convincingly that the 36,000 number did not accurately reflect the full MSA audience because at many schools manuals were duplicated. In those schools each purchased manual could represent substantially more than 30 student listeners. As evidence, she claimed that on many teacher manual order forms teachers had indicated that substantially more than 30 students listened to the programs. In addition to listeners to the live program, Girling asserted that many more listened to taped versions of the programs. In the 1970—1971 year, the Department of Audio Visual Extension distributed 1,766 MSA tapes to the schools. Since teachers or schools ordered the tapes and paid postage, it could be assumed that each tape was used for at least one classroom, but probably more used them. Added to that were tape requests from out of state SOAs. According to Girling, the Portland Public Schools rebroadcast 90 MSA programs during 1970–1971, and 25 programs were distributed through the National Tape Library. It's clear that the MSA never reached the penetration levels recorded by Wisconsin School of the Air, but then neither did Minnesota make the investment in education by radio that Wisconsin did.

FIGHTING TO STAY ON THE AIR

Throughout Girling's short 1970–71 annual report there lurks a sense of her fighting to preserve not just her job, but the MSA itself, something Girling had contributed most of her working life to and had done so much to shape. Girling argued that if the audience numbers were not what they should be, it was the fault of stringent budgets. With a trace of bitterness in her words, she compared the MSA situation with other SOAs that received much greater resources:

> The University's investment in an operation of this considerable size, is regrettably minimal. Two and one-half staff people, plus one secretary; a miscellaneous payroll budget for talent of $2,260; a printing budget for Bulletins and Manuals for $4,000. The New York City Schools have 38 full-time people in radio, The Wisconsin School of the Air with 300,000 children, is budgeted directly by the State Legislature at $125,000 per year. Their 15 programs on Black Americans cost $30,000; our 15 programs on American Indians cost about $1,000. I strongly suggest that a value assessment of the Minnesota School of the Air is long overdue [MSA Annual Report, 1971].

During the 1970s Girling often seemed to be defending the MSA from possible attackers who included the University's President and Vice President. In 1975, Girling became aware of a move by those administrators to transfer the KUOM radio license for the sum of $1.00 to station KSJN — part of the newly formed Minnesota Public Radio network, a private (non-profit) corporation. Apparently, the University administration thought that by merging KUOM with the Minnesota Public Radio network, the University could withdraw from educational broadcasting to the schools. In a scathing and detailed letter to the University Faculty Senate, Girling pointed out that the move would have meant transferring KUOM's equipment and staff, who included civil service employees, to a private corporation. Furthermore, she, an employee of 33 years, was never consulted. Girling dismissed the reason given for the transfer, namely that KUOM's programming duplicated that of KSJN. Girling stated: "The charge of duplication is patently unsupportable.... The University Station (KUOM) is the oldest licensed station in the state, dating back to 1922 — and KSJN's license was born in the late 1960s— it is difficult to understand the logic of *our* fault in duplicating *their* barely dry program service" (Girling, 1975).

She praised the accomplishments of KUOM and the numerous awards won by the MSA programs and asserted that the charge of duplication was made only to stir up legislators and KSJN supporters in order to pressure the University administration for action against KUOM. She called on the University Faculty Senate to review the "mechanics of this so-called merger, along with its effect on the University" (Girling, 1975).

Apparently, Girling's letter had some effect, because no other references to the proposed transfer exist in the archives, and station KUOM remained independent of the Minnesota Public Radio network. Nevertheless during the period 1976 through 1978, support for the MSA among its university supporters continued to slip. In 1978, with the retirement of long time radio administrator, Barton Paulu, the question of whether to continue the MSA arose publicly. Girling maintained a witty defiance, but it was apparent that her days and probably those of the MSA were numbered.

The Final Schedule

Despite the storm clouds that blew over Girling's office during spring of 1978, the MSA showed little signs of diminishment. In the fall of the year, the MSA issued a broadcast schedule that included some truly innovative programs as well as refurbished versions of the older favorites that many Minnesota teachers had come to rely on. In fact, during the years 1977 through 1979, while almost every other SOA had died or was gasping, the MSA programs demonstrated creative vitality, as evidenced by the Teacher Manuals for those years. A list of the series scheduled for 1976 through 1979 is reproduced in Table 36.

TABLE 36. MSA PROGRAM SCHEDULE, 1976–1979
(MSA, TEACHER MANUALS, 1979)

Day	Program Series and Description	Grades
Monday	*Old Tales and New*	K–3
	Whatcha See is Whatcha Get (1st semester)	7–8
	Book Detective (2nd semester)	4–6
Tuesday	*Getting to Know Yourself*	5–9
	Meet Me in the Closet	K–3
Wednesday	*It's Time for Music*	K–3
	Sound Ideas (1st semester)	4–8
	Poem Maker (2nd semester)	4–8
Thursday	*Make Mine Music*	K–3
	People Worth Hearing About	4–9
Friday	*Newscast and Current Events*	4–8
	Golden Shoes	4–6

Below are descriptions of some of the programs shown in Table 36.

Old Tales and New. A favorite of primary teachers since the MSA's first year of operation, 1938, the series presented stories for young students, K–3. Girling herself wrote many program scripts. In the 1978 Teachers Manual, she stated that the underlying idea for all the stories was human dignity and that the people, animals and things in the stories treat one another with respect and humor. Of all the series broadcast by all the SOAs covered in this work, *Old Tales and New* probably had the longest run.

Whatcha See is Whatcha Get. A consumer education series for 7th and 8th graders developed with the goal of creating wise consumer awareness. With humor and clever techniques, students were alerted to the tricks of the marketplace and encouraged to apply their own values to the claims of advertising. Portland Schools station KBPS wrote and produced the scripts and teacher manuals.

Getting to Know Yourself. Started in 1972, the series addressed children's mental and emotional health by helping children understand their feelings and why emotions sometimes grow at a different pace than their bodies or minds. Students heard how to deal with everyday emotions such as fear, joy, shame, and anger. Dr. George Williams, psychiatrist and Associate Dean of the UM School of Medicine, brought credentials and superior skills for reaching children. Girling described Dr. Williams as having magnetic warmth and a superb ability to communicate with children. In 1975, his program was awarded 1st prize for excellence from the Institute for Education by Radio.

Meet Me in the Closet. A provocative title for a new series designed to help teachers and students use creative dramatics to learn together about themselves and each other. Possibly one of the most ambitious programs attempted on radio. Girling believed in the power of creative dramatics and worked the idea into several other series. The goal was to promote emotional growth and learning through improvisational performance. Exactly what happened during the broadcasts is not clear (at least to the author), and Girling herself admitted that she could not describe precisely "what it is, nor do I advocate a method of working," but she assured teachers that the children will understand what to do. Girling promised teachers that "through patience and selection, trial and problem solving, you and your students will grow closer and closer together as you both become more and more vulnerable" (MSA, Teacher Manuals, 1979, *Meet Me in the Closet,* p. 1). She urged teachers to avoid judging student performances, to have patience and let the children get comfortable with the exercises.

People Worth Hearing About. Started in 1968, this engaging series featured biographical vignettes of outstanding Americans. At first the series highlighted minority men and women, but by the mid 1970s it focused on women of achievement in many fields. Women of achievement, Girling stated, were themselves a minority. "Increasingly, as education is equalized for minorities, it will be equalized for girls " (MSA, Teacher Manuals, 1979, *People Worth Hearing About,* p. 1). Girling hoped that the stories of female achievers in various fields would inspire young girls to set their sights on careers of achievement.

Make Mine Music. An upgraded music appreciation series. These programs led "intermediate students to the romance of musical discovery." Using casual dramatic vignettes and accessible musical selections, the programs provided introductions to various music forms that acquaint young people with specific modes of musical expression in serious music (MSA, Teacher Manuals, 1979).

Sound Ideas. An unusual series that attempted to teach and encourage children of any age, grades 2–12, to use inexpensive tape recorders to turn their own ideas into sound productions. "... [T]he spoken voice, music, and sound effects on tape make powerful tools of communication" (MSA, Teacher Manuals, 1979, *Sound Ideas,* p. 1). Through the activity of recording, children would learn how the recorded messages that they heard on radio and TV were used to manipulate people's thinking and action. The teacher manual provided suggestions for acquiring and using tape recording equipment. Girling expressed her belief that the series gave children the opportunity to explore their own neighborhood or city and in that way create their own field trips. The MSA ran a contest for the best audio recording projects.

Poem Maker. Designed to help students express the poetry within them, each lesson built on a theme, gave poetic illustrations—some written by MSA students—and ended with an exercise in poetry writing. The Manual provided many examples of poetry to share with the students. The series developer Vicki Gaylord suggested that following the broadcast, teachers provide time for poetry writing as well as give students the freedom to write on any topic of interest.

Demise

As with many other SOAs, the end point for the MSA cannot be clearly defined. The schedule for the 1978–1979 school year appeared enticing and innovative, giving little hint of an organization in decline. However, the exchange of memos and letters[63] between Girling, Paulu, Harold Miller, Dean of Continuing Education and Extension, and two other administrators from that office, Marion Watson and Donald Woods, contained much discussion about the MSA's possible demise. The correspondence also reflected the tensions and harsh feelings that arose over that issue but gave no definitive statement about the outcome. The discussion started with Paulu's summary of the May 17th meeting in which Paulu, Girling, Miller, Watson and Woods agreed that Paulu's successor — Paulu was retiring that year as the Director of the University Media Resources after more than 40 years with the University's radio operation — would make a survey and appraisal of the entire KUOM mission and all aspects of the MSA, including its continuation. But the status of the MSA during that appraisal period remained unclear.

Within a few days, Girling responded with two memos; one delivered a five page explanation as to why she had not been in the office for several months. A skin infection had forced her to stay home, but during that time at home, she said, she continued writing scripts, something she had done for nearly forty years. In her second memo, Girling replied to Paulu's agreement memo with a two-column response. On one side were key phrases from Paulu's memo, on the other side Girling restated his phrases more to her liking. The memo fairly crackled with sarcasm and wit. It appears, however, that Paulu took no offense and in a follow-up memo agreed to Girling's terms, namely that the MSA would continue in its present form until Paulu's replacement had made a decision (MSA, Paulu, 1978; Girling, 1978).

The most definitive statements of regret about the MSA's possible demise came from two executives of the EMC Corporation, which produced taped copies of the MSA programs. The executives clearly had a financial interest in seeing the MSA continued. Richard Stevens from EMC wrote the following to Girling on May 19th just two days after Paulu's meeting: "I was shocked and distressed by your telling me of KUOM's contemplated decision to dismantle the Minnesota School of the Air after its nearly 40 years of continuous in-school program to classrooms throughout Minnesota — and the nation. I can only hope that this ill-conceived notion is abandoned as a capricious impulse not justified by the facts...." (Girling, 1978). Stevens goes on to say that despite occasional variations in quality [due to limited resources] KUOM was a leader among public radio stations — with in-school radio programs on many subjects such as Health Care, Conservation and Ecology, Communications, science that pre-dated commercially-produced multimedia materials which today have come to the fore.

In a letter dated July 19th 1978, Dean Miller expressed the hope that the new director of the University Media Resources (UMR) will be "sensitized to the historical differences" that had developed over the years between Girling and the former UMR director [Paulu]. He also affirmed that the new director's review would determine whether or not the MSA should be continued. In her response, Girling said that past issues should not be a factor in future decisions. She thanked the Dean for replying, but she recognized that most likely her participation in the MSA would "die on September first ... unless someone else brings the matter [her future] to light" (Girling, 1978b). These words seem to imply that either the MSA's 1978–1979 schedule was not broadcast, or that it was without Girling as director. There is no evidence of MSA broadcasts after 1979.

However, CDs of old MSA programs are still available online. The collection includes many popular programs such as *Old Tales and New*. The online address is: http://live-artist.com/fairytales/minnesota.html, as of the printing of this book.

As for station KUOM, it continues to broadcast under the direction of the College of Continuing Education at the University of Minnesota's Twin City Campus. It receives donations from the public. During the 1980s, KUOM carried a variety of educational programs, but not as the MSA. Early in the 1990s, the university re-examined the idea of merging KUOM with another station. As the educational function of radio came into question, the University reviewed more

---

[63]The collection of letters and memos was left by Betty Girling to the University of Minnesota's archive.

critically KUOM's funding, and it came up with a surprisingly progressive solution. In 1991, amid controversy, the College of Continuing Education which owned the license decided to turn the station over to the University students, and also to fund a small full-time professional staff. On October 1 of 1993, KUOM was merged with station WMMR and "Radio K" was born. The small full-time staff oversees operations and provides continuity, while students provide much of the on-air talent. Radio K broadcasts as an AM station during the day and as an FM station at night. Eighty-four years after its first broadcast, KUOM continues to serve Minnesota students, but in a different capacity.

Summary

The MSA was created in 1938 as part of the educational service of the University of Minnesota's radio station KUOM, which still exists today. In 1931, KUOM, then operating as WLB, had broadcast its first educational program for in-school use, Burton Paulu's *Music Appreciation*. By the early 1940s, the MSA was broadcasting at least two in-school series a day and reaching nearly 100,000 students in southern Minnesota, but its 5,000 watt station could not bring MSA programs to the entire state. MSA director E. W. Ziebarth developed a plan to link up with the North Central radio network, which he thought would make MSA programs accessible throughout the upper Midwest. That dream failed to materialize.

With Betty Girling's appointment as director in 1946, the MSA focused exclusively on elementary grades and gradually became a standard fixture in the public and parochial schools of southern Minnesota. Her biggest challenge was finding the right mix of programming to suit the different school groups— urban, rural, public and parochial — that listened to the MSA. From the 1950s through the early 1970s, Girling balanced competing demands with a mix of new and old programs. New programs such as *People Worth Knowing* and *Let's Write* stayed abreast of current events and needs, while old favorites such as *Following Conservation Trails* and *Old Tales and New* provided teachers with programs that they had come to rely on. In the final years, Girling added a burst of complex and innovative programs such as *Meet Me in the Closet* and *Sound Ideas*. Unfortunately, before these programs could make their marks, the MSA was discontinued. Girling expressed few ideas about educational philosophy, but she offered many ideas on methods, mostly suggesting ideas recognized as fundamental to good teaching, namely that teachers show enjoyment, give positive reinforcement, and encourage student expression.

Audience estimates suggested that in the late 1930s the MSA started with roughly 35,000 regular listeners. That number quickly grew to between 100,000 and 150,000 and remained there until the late 1960s when it gradually fell into the range of 40,000. Evaluating the MSA audience is difficult because we don't know the total size of the student body that existed within the range of KUOM and the few commercial stations that carried MSA programs. Nor do we know how many student listeners were represented by each teachers manual sold.

MSA broadcast for over forty years on a shoestring budget and staff. Unlike the other state SOAs, the MSA never received direct funding from the state legislature, and that limited its development. Nor did it enjoy the benefit of a state-wide FM network. While several sound reasons for its low funding might be offered, one could argue that the MSA received limited funds because its director was female. In the days before woman's liberation in this country, a female director had to struggle. Possibly, males in charge of Minnesota purse strings might have consciously or unconsciously given less resources to a woman than they would have to a man.

Nevertheless, the MSA shared with the WSA honors for broadcasting high quality programs for in-school use, forty-plus years, well into the television age. Like Wisconsin, the state of Minnesota effectively used technology to deliver educational resources to the schools at a relatively low cost, which is what technology is supposed to do.

Texas School of the Air[64]

Not surprisingly a Texas educator, A. L Chapman,[65] proclaimed that in the six year period from 1941 to 1947, the Texas School of the Air (TSA) had grown from this nation's smallest to the largest state supported school of the air (SOA).[66] Such oversized claims might be expected out of Texas, even though the documentation supporting such claims is slim and unreliable. What is clear, however, is that the TSA grew rapidly during the mid 1940s. Although hobbled by a lack of funds and a small staff, the TSA broadcast programs in natural science, literature, music, citizenship, history and vocational guidance five days a week for 20 years, contributing valuable educational resources to several hundred thousand Texas school children across an area larger than France.

In a region of the U.S. not noted for educational innovation, a complicated web of institutions and organizations formed a uniquely cooperative approach that brought broadcast technology into the service of public education. Organized by the State Department of Education, the TSA was a broad-based cooperative effort that included four Texas universities, a network of commercial radio stations, the Texas Congress of Parents and Teachers, the state teachers association, and literally dozens of volunteer and civic groups. The universities planned and developed the courses and provided talent and technical support. The State Department of Education provided administration, coordination, and later funding. The numerous civic and educational improvement organizations contributed moral and financial support and helped gain acceptance throughout the state. After two years of precarious operation, TSA proponents persuaded Texas legislators to provide funds for a small but effective staff that continued educational broadcasts for nearly two decades (Hill 1997, pp. 137–38).

Origins

The birth and development of the TSA was carefully cultivated by the same school of the air (SOA) proponents who played key roles in initiating the Ohio and Wisconsin SOAs. Those proponents included the Payne Fund, Ben Darrow, and the National Committee for Education by Radio (NCER). In 1937, NCER chairman Dr. A. Crane helped form the Texas Radio Council to study the broadcasting facilities and resources available in the state. With Crane's help, the Council received a Payne Fund grant to bring Ben Darrow, founder of the OSA,[67] to serve as an instructor and lecturer on education by radio at Southern Methodist University and the University of Texas. Both institutions offered courses in radio workshop and broadcasting. Darrow helped write a preliminary draft plan outlining a cooperative public radio effort in Texas. Out of that work grew a detailed plan for initiating the publicly supported Texas School of the Air (Hill, 1997). Hill asserts that without Darrow's guidance, the TSA might never have gotten off the ground.

Unlike other state-based SOAs which operated from a central hub, the TSA plan dispersed activities among four universities and colleges, a network of CBS affiliated radio stations, and the State Department of Education. A summary of the organizational web that administered and operated the TSA is provided in the pages of a teacher's manual and classroom guide distributed in the late 1940s. It says that the TSA "... is a division of the State Department of Educa-

---

[64]The section on the Texas School of the Air draws heavily from Angela Hill's 1997 fine dissertation, *The Texas School of the Air: An educational endeavor.*

[65]Chapman was the Director of the Bureau of Research in Education by Radio at the University of Texas.

[66]Chapman, A. L., 1947 in Hill, Angela, N. C., 1997, *Texas School of the Air: an educational radio endeavor. Austin,* University of Texas, p. 6).

[67]Due to a political dispute with Ohio's governor, Darrow had recently been dismissed as director of the Ohio School of the Air. See Section II.

tion, organized in cooperation with University of Texas, North Texas State Teachers College, Texas State College for Women, Texas Congress of Parents and Teachers, and other recognized educational institutions and organizations" (TSA, n/d, p. 1).

Each university took responsibility for developing at least one program while the State Department of Education provided resources for script writing, administrative services, and coordination with the CBS stations that aired the programs. The Department also helped ensure that the school administrators across the vast state were aware of the TSA and that the program content supported the state's core curriculum. Table 37 below shows how program responsibilities were assigned for the 1940–1941 school year.

TABLE 37. TSA PROGRAM SCHEDULE AND COOPERATING INSTITUTIONS, 1940–41 (ATKINSON, 1942D; HILL, 1997)

Program	Institution(s) and Responsibility	Cooperating Entity
Nature science: *Open your eyes* 3rd — 8th grades	N. Texas Teachers Col Texas State College for Woman - Script Writing, production, direction and sound engineering	State Dept. of Education - Paid for script writers and line chargers - Administration, coordination with radio network
Language arts: *Reading is Adventure* Grades: 7–12	University Of Texas - Script writing, production, direction and sound engineering	State Dept. of Education - Paid for script writers and line chargers - Administration, coordination with radio network
Music: *Music is Yours:* *Vocal, Instrumental* *and Folk* Upper elementary and junior high	University of Texas - Script writing, production, direction and sound engineering	State Dept. of Education - Paid for script writers and line chargers - Administration, coordination with radio network
Vocation information: *Jobs Ahead* High school	Texas A & M - Script writing - Production, direction and engineering provided by the college radio station	State Dept. of Education - Paid for script writers and line chargers
Social Relations: *Living With Others*	Dallas Radio Workshop	State Dept. of Education

Broadcast times— between 11:15 and 12 noon — were selected because research conducted at the Bureau of Research in Education by Radio at the University of Texas revealed that the fewest class changes occurred during that period in departmentalized junior and senior highs (Hill, 1997).

Additional support for the TSA in the form of advice, promotion, and networking came from over a dozen volunteer organizations including the Texas Congress of Parents and Teachers, Texas Teachers Association, and the Junior League. Policy and overall direction for the TSA were provided by a board made up of university presidents, state and local educators and representatives from NCER.

An arrangement so diffuse, composed of so many different participants, universities, state bureaucrats, private radio stations, private donors, and inputs from literally dozens of civic and volunteer organizations, seemed destined to soon fail. Nevertheless the enterprise took off in February 1940 and continued operating for 20 years. According to Hill (1997) the TSA's lack of centralized structure and cooperative nature was actually a sign of strength. She characterized the school's cooperative planning and operation as "one of the most unique educational experiments in the development of radio in education" (p. 62). Hill goes on to cite the State Superintendent of Public Instruction who asserted that the TSA cooperative planning structure demonstrated the principles of democracy applied to an educational program. While such comments are unlikely to be proven, it does appear that the decentralized Texas approach worked well in that environment. Perhaps it was the only approach that would have succeeded there.

Broadcast Facilities

Unlike most other state-based SOAs covered in this work, the TSA never associated with a publicly owned radio station. Instead TSA programs were broadcast through a network of commercially owned CBS affiliated stations known as the Texas Broadcast Network and later as the Texas Quality Network. Four stations carried the TSA programs regularly: WBAP in Fort Worth, WFAA in Dallas, WOAI in San Antonio, and KPRC in Houston. All broadcast at high power, 50,000 watts, with the exception of the Houston's station which operated on 5,000 watts of power. In addition two other stations supplemented the network. They were located in Amarillo and Weslaco Texas (Woelfel & Tyler, 1945). While the publicly owned Wisconsin FM network certainly contributed to the success of the WSA, the Texas Quality Network seems to have provided good service to the TSA and at no cost. All TSA programs were sustaining and thus represented donated air time.

FUNDING

For its first two years, 1940 and 1941, the TSA operated without state funds. During that period, operations were supported mostly by contribution of services from the cooperating institutions and participating radio stations. Expenses that could not be handled through in-kind services were provided by a public spirited donor, Karl Hoblitzelle, President of the Dallas based Interstate Theatres and member of the TSA Advisory Committee. "A firm believer in the importance of educated citizenry, Hoblitzelle recognized that the TSA furthered this goal. Hoblitzelle's gifts enabled the TSA to provide rural schools more of the things that constituted a balanced education"[68] (TSA, 1941). In that sense, the TSA achieved a unique status as probably the only SOA to be substantially supported by private donations. In 1941, however, state officials and legislators acknowledged that the TSA had made substantial contributions to the Texas school children. Central to building this awareness was the work of the TSA Advisory Committee. Composed of nearly 50 leaders in Texas education, labor, business, publishing, and law, the members worked to build support for the TSA throughout Texas. They succeeded. The legislature appropriated funds for the 1941 and 1942 school year and continued funding the TSA until 1960. State funding enabled the state's education bureaucracy to establish a Department of Radio Education, which served as the TSA administrative center, vital to such a decentralized entity.

GOALS AND PURPOSE

TSA's goals and purpose were printed in every teacher manual in rather vague language. The radio broadcasts were intended to:

• Increase knowledge
• Cultivate discernment, appreciation, and taste

---

[68]Hoblitzelle's contributions were acknowledged at the beginning of all TSA teacher manuals and program guides.

• Enrich character by inspiring social ideals that may result in constructive citizenship (TSA Manual, n/d).

The manuals also included a more pointed educational objective, to supplement, enrich, and vitalize regular classroom teaching. This statement echoed that of other SOAs that had articulated similar objectives, namely to add to classroom curricula elements that might be missing in terms of content, embellishments, or excitement. Hill (1997) also adds that the TSA aimed to avoid duplicating programming or program topics offered by the national networks. It is unclear how such duplication could be avoided, given that all SOAs offered programs in the natural sciences and music appreciation.

Under the heading, "Suggestions to Teachers," TSA directors assured classroom teachers that they had no intention through the broadcasts or the supplemental manuals to "build a curriculum" (TSA, n/d, p. 6). They urged teachers to use the programs however they wanted. Teachers might wish to read the manual thoroughly and prepare a longer unit of study built around a radio series or use individual programs to initiate or to sum up a unit. In any case the choices of instructional method, sequence and emphasis were all up the classroom teacher. This tone contrasts with that found in the manuals for the OSA and WSA where classroom teachers were encouraged to follow the approach recommended by the radio teachers.

Programs, 1943—1944

Table 38 shows the core schedule of TSA series that ran from 1943 to 1944.

TABLE 38. TSA PROGRAM SCHEDULE, 1943–1944 (HILL, 1997)

Day	Time	Course	Grades
Monday	11:15 A.M.	*Stories Plus* (Earlier) *Your Story Parade*	K–3
Tuesday	11:15 A.M.	*Open Your Eyes*	4–7
Wednesday	11:15 A.M.	*Reading Is Adventure*	J & S. H S
Thursday	11:15 A.M.	*Jobs Ahead*	H. S. & Adult
Friday	11:15 A.M.	*Music Is Yours/Music for the Schools*	El. & H. S.

The five programs paralleled five core curricular areas advocated in the Texas public school curriculum: language arts, science, social studies, vocations, and music. Descriptions are provided below. Unless otherwise noted, they are taken from Hill (1997).

Stories Plus (earlier *Your Story Parade*). Intended for elementary students, this social relations series was designed to be instructive and entertaining. The programs consisted of children's stories that portrayed social themes relevant to successful living in a democracy. To build student understanding, the teacher manual and guide included specific questions related to the themes.

Open Your Eyes. Developed by the North Texas State Teachers College and the Texas State College for Women, the series dramatized natural science subjects in the social context for grades 4 to 8. The educational goal was simple, to demonstrate how by "opening your eyes" students will experience the beauty and excitement of every day living. Using recurring Texas based characters, the Potter family, the series incorporated many dramatic techniques found in commercial radio in order to hold listener interest. In the early 1940s, the series served as promotion for Texas' economy and hospitality. By 1944, due to the influence of the war, the series took a more worldly tact and explored life in many sections of the globe. The Teachers Manual described the series as emphasizing "parents participation in learning ... and the active learning-by-doing process that goes on in the schoolroom" (TSA, 1941, p. 55). Each program strove to involve listeners by asking students to help answer a question related to the main idea presented in the program (Hill, 1997, p. 83).

Music Is Yours. The Teacher's Guide described the series as taking a functional approach to music education in which children learn how to use various products of music and make them their own. Programs presented a variety of music types with the intention that children would choose the part music could play in their lives (TSA, 1941).

Reading Is Adventure. This language series from the University of Texas presented dramatized segments drawn from books selected on the basis of research into the reading preferences of junior and senior high school students. A typical program dramatized an episode from a selected story and stopped at a point of high suspense or tension. To find out what happened, students had to finish reading the story on their own (TSA, 1941, p. 55). Themes covered in the series included patriotism, the meaning of freedom, and the meaning of greatness.

The series encouraged a love for reading, more selective reading, and improved reading habits and ability. It showed students that they can broaden their experiences and discover new worlds simply by reading a book (Hill, 1997). To help achieve these goals, the manual asked teachers to avoid "spoiling" the lesson with formalized activities such as memory work, written book reports, assigned reading, and detailed analysis of the recommended books (TSA, 1941). The pedagogical approach suggested in this series represented, in this writer's view, an extreme example of the child centered progressive approach advocated by some in the progressive education movement.

Jobs Ahead. Presented by Texas A & M and Sam Houston State Teacher's College, the broadcasts presented discussions and dramatic situations treating the requirements for success in major vocations. Though aimed at seniors, the series producers also believed the programs could help students in junior high and even elementary grades. The writers took a practical "utilitarian" approach and made clear two points. (1) "There are all kinds of people, and (2) the world has a specific use for each kind" (TSA, 1941, p. 90). To address both points, the series was divided into two sections, "Mostly about People" and "Mostly about Jobs." The first looked at specialized abilities that everyone possesses, while the second part looked at the requirements of various types of job. The series concentrated on jobs available in Texas.

The teacher manual for *Open Your Eyes* said that each series was "planned by a committee

Texas School of the Air presents, "Music Is Yours" (courtesy of Texas School of the Air).

of selected teachers and authorities in the subject matter areas covered by the broadcasts" (TSA, 1943, p. 7). According to Hill (1997), limited resources and staff restricted TSA program development and innovation. Volunteers at each cooperating institution took responsibility for designing and producing programs while the State Office worked to coordinate the individual program efforts. As a result, Hill says, programs tended toward the formulaic. "Once an individual devised a format that worked, the pattern was used as template for every program. Only the content varied" (p. 5). Comparing that limited scenario to the national SOAs that could call on the vast network resources or even with the WSA where a large creative staff, paid and volunteer, worked under the direction of a fulltime director, the TSA accomplishments are impressive.

SUPPORT MATERIALS

For each of the broadcast series, the TSA provided teachers with a combined teachers manual and classroom guide at no cost. These comprehensive manuals presented the general purposes and function of radio education and discussed the potential benefits of classroom listening. The introduction of each manual presented the purpose of the TSA, described how the programs were produced, and listed the participating broadcast stations. The introduction also described the function of the listening committees (covered later in this section) and how visual aids should be used. The Suggestions to the Teacher section stressed an attentive but casual listening atmosphere and discouraged note-taking. It also presented a checklist of things to do and avoid before, during, and following the broadcasts. The remainder of each manual described the series and each program thoroughly and also included a summary of the subject, discussion questions, suggestions for classroom activities, and references for further reading (Woelfel and Tyler, 1945; TSA, 1944–1945). During the years 1946 through 1948, 35,000 *Teacher's Manuals and Classroom Guides* were mailed out each year.

Philosophy and Methods

While TSA probably did not introduce any innovations in radio instruction, it did refine a few practices in interesting ways. For example, the serial drama approach in which the same characters were depicted in new learning situations was used successfully in many SOAs programs, including in the TSA's elementary science series, *Open Your Eyes*. In the TSA series, however, the continuing character drama developed an interactive style that treated the listeners as the ones with the knowledge and the radio characters as learners.

In *Reading Is Adventure,* drama and narrative were used to entice students to finish the stories that were started on air. Nothing is new in that, but this series included one small innovation the stories to be included were selected through surveys of junior and senior high school students. Using this selection method, series planners could be fairly confident that students would enjoy the readings.

Jobs Ahead. By focusing on jobs available in Texas and stressing the relationship between the individual and the job, this series overcame some of the resistance that developed against putting general vocational education on the radio.

In *Music Is Yours* students were charged with the responsibility of figuring out how music can fit into their lives. This approach seems unique to the TSA.

Overall then the instructional methods and the suggestions offered in various TSA teacher manuals provides evidence that the TSA educators leaned philosophically toward a progressive, learner centered approach to instruction. For example the 1944–1945 teacher manual for *Reading is Adventure* stated specifically that the program's goal was to nurture a love of reading and enjoyment of good literature, not to build knowledge or analytical skills. To this end teachers were encouraged to "avoid ... assigning book reports or detailed analyses of the books.... Some teachers have found students read more ... if no outside reading requirements are imposed" (TSA

Manual, 1944, p. 12). These suggestions certainly conflicted with those presented by the Essentialist, William Bagley, dean of the American School of the Air, who admonished progressive educators and followers of John Dewey to emphasize subject knowledge acquisition above student preferences and affinities (Null, 2003).

The teachers manual and classroom guides did present specific pedagogical guidelines that paralleled those advocated by other SOAs, the key concept being that listening constituted only part of the learning experience. To gain full advantage of the learning opportunity presented in radio lessons, teachers must conduct pre-broadcast preparation and post-broadcast discussions. The latter was imperative to a complete learning experience (Hill, 1997; TSA, 1944).

Audience

A. L. Chapman asserted that by 1947 the TSA had grown into the largest state sponsored school of the air in the nation (Hill, 1997, p. 6). He backed up that assertion with the results of several survey studies conducted during the early and mid–1940s. Results from these studies, he said, proved that more schools reported listening to the TSA than another other SOA in the country. The surveys also found that, of the state's approximately 1.5 million school children, 260,000 (17 percent) listened regularly to TSA programs. If true, the Texas listenership would be well above that achieved by the OSA and close to that of the WSA.

Table 39 shows the results of several surveys conducted to determine usage of TSA among the state's public schools and students (Hill 1997).

TABLE 39. SURVEY RESULTS, TSA USAGE (HILL, 1997)

Survey	Audience	Response rate	Results
Composite 1943–1944 A. L. Chapman	4,500 Texas public schools	3,396 schools responded	Schools using TSA 2,591 (76.2% of responding schools)
1943–1944 Dept of Radio and Visual Education	4,500 Texas public schools	Unreported	Many schools outside coverage area of TSA stations
1945–1946 Superintendent of State Department of Education	1,300 Texas school superintendents	Responding: 714 (55%) (Represented 3,812 schools)	- 40% of responding schools reported no radios - Student listeners: 260,301 (Approx. 17%) of Texas school enrollment
1942 Deputy State Superintendents of A-V Education	All state public schools	3,616 schools responded	3,073 schools with radios 2,765 schools reported using TSA: - Teachers using TSA: 20,000 (approx.) Student listeners: 500,000 (approx.)
1946 State Depart. of Ed	4,500 public schools	3,830 schools responding	3,812 schools report using TSA

Hill (1997) reports these results in detail and seems to accept them with little question. However, Cuban (1986) raised strong objection to most survey research performed to measure usage of radio in the schools. In his seminal work, *Teachers and Machines* (1986), he asserts that the survey results were unreliable because "it was common practice for superintendents or their designees to answer the questionnaires. Few surveys ever asked teachers what programs they used" (p. 22). If one classroom teacher used the radio, then a whole school was identified as using radio, and all the students in the school were counted as listening to school of the air programs, according to Cuban. This approach resulted in inflated claims about audience size.

The surveys conducted for the TSA, shown in Table 39, may have suffered from just the sort of methodological weakness described by Cuban because they were in fact completed by superintendents or principals, not teachers. As a result, the TSA can offer reliable data on the number of schools that used TSA programs, but not on the number of student listeners. Was data on the student listenership collected from the surveys *or* was it estimated from the number of participating schools? That remains unknown. The survey conducted in 1945–1946 did ask whether the school received the teacher manuals, but it did not state how the receipt of teacher manuals could be translated into accurate audience estimates. Whatever the case, Cuban's assertion — that estimates of the size of student audience based on the report of superintendents and principals are probably unreliable — cannot be dismissed without data. On the other hand, Cuban offers no solid evidence that such practices were wide spread. We should not rule out the possibility that a high proportion of students in participating schools listened regularly to TSA programs.

With those cautions in mind, the data do seem to support the conclusion that a large number of Texas school children listened to TSA programs. 260,000 students and 17 percent may represent the very high end of the likely range of audience size. Hill's data do support the contention that the TSA rapidly grew into a "huge educational organization" (p. 133), and that for many years it delivered needed educational resources to a very large number of Texas school children and, with only two full time staff, at an extremely low cost. Furthermore, the state legislature confirmed this observation by voting continuously for 18 years to support the TSA.

TAPES FOR TEACHING

By 1952 low cost recording technology enabled local schools and individual teachers to use taped programs at their convenience. To take advantage of that development the Texas Education Agency (TEA) in Austin introduced the *Tapes for Teaching* program. Teachers sent in a blank tape, and the TEA recorded the requested program and returned the tape free of charge. Using the service, schools established in-house libraries of TSA programs and programs from other sources as well. Two years after *Tapes for Teaching* started it had supplied 5,512 taped broadcasts for a total of 1,210 hours on air. As schools expanded their audio libraries, tape duplication activity grew year by year reaching as high as 7,000 tapes per month. Unfortunately, as the popularity of tapes grew, interest in hearing live broadcasts may have declined (Hill, 1997).

Evaluation and Benefits

The TSA became one of the first state-based SOAs to evaluate educational broadcasts with listening committees. For each series the TSA formed a listening committee composed of "educated listeners" such as teachers, librarians, and others concerned with radio in education. The members listened to their assigned programs regularly and provided feedback on content, vocabulary, instructional methods and the children's reactions. Their suggestions and criticism were reviewed by the TSA script writers and production staff to determine how the broadcasts could be improved (TSA, 1943).

Based on her review of many TSA program scripts, Hill (1997) identified specific benefits that Texas school children received from listening to the TSA broadcasts, including stimulated imagination, expanded awareness, racial tolerance and the advancement of women. Through the broadcasts, students, isolated in far flung corners of that immense territory, could take mental "field trips across Texas," to view its cities and industries, and meet its influential leaders. *Reading is Adventure* extended those mental field trips around the entire world giving students a chance to learn about areas they probably would never visit in their lives. *Open Your Eyes* dramatized instances of how science affected students in their daily lives, thus helping to dissolve the barrier between academic and actual experience. From the *Music is Yours* series, Hill said, students encountered a wide variety of musical forms including opera, the European classical tradition, and forgotten folk tales.

While such claims could be made for any type of school music program, through *Music is Yours*, Hill says, students heard conductors, composers, and performers talking about their music, an experience which again helped dissolve the barrier between academic presentation and the listener's experience. The concept of "mental field trips" echoes the often repeated idea that live radio stimulated the imagination, allowing listeners to create their own ideas of the place, thing, or person that was presented in a broadcast. In its ability to spur the imagination, radio is often said to be superior to any other form of educational technology.

Hill (1997) lauds the insights that many TSA scripts offered into different cultures and customs. Through TSA programs, rural Texas farm children got to hear the dialect of Yankee dock workers, and city dwellers could listen to Negro spirituals. Moreover, Hill concludes that the TSA was remarkable for offering a largely white society "still struggling with the evils of segregation" (p. 139) glimpses into diverse cultures. "Long before political correctness and multi-cultural literature became prevalent," according to Hill, "every (TSA) script showed respect and kindness toward individuals of every race and nationality." In addition, "the TSA took special effort to provide literature and radios to Negro schools" (p. 140).

Hill also asserts that the TSA pioneered in educating women. Early scripts urged self-improvement and encouraged women toward life-long learning. Through tales of Amelia Erhardt and Florence Nightingale, young girls were exposed to new role models and heard the benefits of higher education. Finally, the TSA promoted reading through dramatizations of literature in some cases selected by students. Hill asserts, "the (TSA) programs offered an array of possibilities that were never before available in Texas schools" (p. 139).

While Hill's summary of the beneficial effects of TSA broadcasts makes intuitive sense and provokes good feelings about the TSA, the author offers no data to support her assertions. The benefits summary reflects the intentions of TSA script writers and staff rather than an objective report of what students actually gained from the broadcasts. That said, we should be aware that similar statements can be made for many forms of education.

Demise

No documentation exists regarding the final years, but by 1960, the "Texas School of the Air quickly evaporated without benediction" (Hill, 1997, p. 65). Hill names three decisive factors related to the TSA demise: the lack of a champion in the Texas school bureaucracy, the increasing popularity of educational TV, and the growing availability of low-cost tape recording and playback technology. Certainly, by the 1950s the sparkling novelty of radio had dulled. Without a leader to promote the TSA and update its programs, the TSA became more and more outmoded. Indeed, Hill documents that the TSA's small staff was unable to develop new programs or update the format of existing ones. Instead the TSA tended to repeat the formats of previously successful programs year after year. In this environment, classroom teachers had less incentive to listen to the TSA.

Also, educational television was stimulating great interest among educators and students at all levels, and it may have prompted neglect of what probably seemed by the mid 1950s the old technology of radio. However, that is conjecture for which little supporting evidence exists. Hill

(1997) also argues persuasively that the advance of recording technology did contribute to the TSA's demise. As the *Tapes for Teaching* program made taped versions of the TSA programs available, in-school tape libraries grew, and in turn the need to listen to the broadcasts at specific times declined. Consequently, she asserts that teacher interest in the live TSA waned.

Mostly likely the three factors named by Hill (1997) did contribute, to some degree, to the demise of the TSA, but her assertions remain hypothetical given the absence of teacher survey results. By comparison, the growing availability of recorded programs and educational television seems to have had little effect on the popularity of the Wisconsin and Minnesota Schools of the Air, at least through the mid–1960s.

Throughout this work, I have argued that a strong contributing factor to the demise of the SOA movement was the loss of interest in educational radio by commercial broadcasters. The TSA depended on the CBS affiliated stations to donate air time and technical support. By the late 1940s, most SOAs that depended on commercial radio stations felt the chill wind of unfavorable market conditions,[69] which made the practice of offering free air time increasingly unpopular with the managers and owners of the nation's private and corporate broadcast media.

When commercial radio broadcasters lost interest in educational programming, the TSA had nowhere to turn.[70] As of 1960 Texas had not developed a publicly owned statewide radio station or network. Meanwhile, by the early 1950s, schools of the air in Oregon, Minnesota, and Wisconsin broadcast their programs over publicly owned stations. Consequently, they continued broadcasting educational programs for decades after the commercial station had dropped that activity. One further point, the TSA never developed a firm connection with any one state university. For most state-based SOAs, the university connection proved to be the key to long term survival.

Summary

Compared to the other state-based SOAs, the TSA story provides a unique perspective of how one state used new technology to serve the educational needs of a far flung population in an environment characterized by conservative attitudes and a strong bias toward local control. The TSA's most unique accomplishment may have been its organizational structure. Bringing together a diverse group of institutions, social organizations, and private media shows the strong desire among some Texas educators and citizen leaders to develop radio education in a manner that suited the state's conservative opinions.

At first TSA producers and script writers demonstrated creativity in designing programs that proved popular with teachers and students throughout the huge state. Programs such as *Open Your Eyes* and *Reading is Adventure* gained wide acceptance because they presented important subjects in a manner that incorporated local culture and perceptions. Further, despite the lack of a central director, TSA programs demonstrated a consistent approach to pedagogy, one which seemed influenced by Dewey's ideas about active learning and a desire to situate learning in environments that were familiar to the students.

Despite working on a shoestring budget, the TSA offered effective educational programming that reflected the state's sense of pride in Texas heritage, culture, and customs. This approach enabled the TSA to provide badly needed educational resources to a large number of widely-scattered students for two decades.

The TSA's demise stemmed from several causes, but the key one, according to Hill (1997)

---

[69]By the mid–1940s broadcasters were able to sell most of their daytime hours to advertisers. Donating air time to school broadcasting represented reduced profit opportunity, just as Armstrong Perry had predicted.

[70]It is unknown how many stations in the Texas Quality Network continued to broadcast TSA programs during the late 1950s.

was the lack of a champion in the Texas educational bureaucracy. Without someone to carry the school's mission to the decision makers, there was little hope of encouraging the state to increase support or to develop its own educational radio network, a key to sustaining SOAs in other states. Also, by the 1950s, commercial broadcasters were unwilling to contribute valuable air time, a familiar narrative. Without the support of private media, the Texas School of the Air lost the vital lifeline that allowed it to operate, and the state had lost an important educational resource.

New York: The Empire State FM School of the Air

Neither a state educational bureaucracy nor state university played a role in establishing the Empire State FM School of the Air (ESSA). Rather it grew from the grassroots, from the cooperative efforts of individual principals and superintendents in New York State school districts who saw that educational radio could offer valuable resources for their students and teachers. With no budget and few resources, Paul Reed, former director of the Rochester School of the Air, and other educators in central New York school districts joined together to form what would soon become a radio operation that served schools in many areas of the state. The pioneers adapted the name Empire State FM School of the Air to reflect their state-wide vision. Soon, they were delivering a broad curriculum of music, literature, science, health, current events and modern languages to tens of thousands of students across central New York state, a substantial accomplishment given ESSA's grassroots origins and limited budget (Truscott, 1958, p. 54). Gradually, both the New York State educational bureaucracy and University Regents became involved, but the primary input and funding came from local school districts that participated in the programs.

ESSA's development owes much to a relationship between the goals of private media and public education. Its broadcasts depended almost entirely on the contributed services of the newly formed commercial FM stations. Starting with three stations and soon growing to as many as 22–21 privately owned, ESSA broadcasters formed a cooperative network that reached rural and urban schools throughout much of Central and Southern New York (Truscott, 1958, p. 28). This unique support system stood out among state-based SOAs, and allowed ESSA to expand rapidly, but it also became a source of weakness when changing market conditions allowed the commercial FM stations to attract advertising dollars.

Documentation for the ESSA story draws from a dissertation written by Natalie Truscott in 1958 and from the Syracuse University Archive which maintains a collection on the ESSA.

Origins

The ESSA essentially grew out of a conflict that arose between the Rochester School of the Air[71] (RSA) and its long time broadcast outlet, WHAM. Started in 1932, the RSA had developed into one of the nation's premier local SOAs, and that status owed much to the generosity of the owners of station WHAM. For over 15 years, WHAM broadcast RSA programs over its clear channel 50,000 watt AM outlet. By 1947, the growing potential of lucrative daytime advertising enticed WHAM managers to discontinue offering free AM time to RSA, but they compensated by offering free service over their newly built FM station, WHFM. Because the new facility broadcast at much lower power than the AM station, 100 schools outside of Rochester that had listened regularly to RSA were now out of range. RSA administrators soon developed a solution, simply relay the WHFM signal to an FM repeater station near Syracuse. As a result, signals from the two stations reached all schools that had previously received the RSA programs. In addition to solving

---

[71]The Rochester School of the Air story is told in Section IV.

RSA's problem, the relay solution planted an interesting idea in the minds of Paul Reed and others at the RSA, an idea that led to the formation of the ESSA network.

Within a month of the first two-station broadcast, local educators and broadcasters met to investigate the possibility of enlisting more FM stations in order to extend the RSA broadcasts further. A third station, WSYM in Syracuse joined the network and promoted its effort by distributing 70 FM receivers to Syracuse schools (Truscott, 1958). The idea of a state-wide network started to take shape as other FM stations asked to join.

In December of 1947, 28 educators and representatives of FM stations met to discuss developing a statewide school of the air. Participants agreed that the radio stations would supply the broadcasting facilities and the necessary announcing and engineering personnel at no cost. The group also agreed that while RSA programs offered a good foundation on which to build the new educational effort, they would not dominate it. Each participating school board could develop new programs. Most important, the group formed a steering committee to direct the effort, and decided on a name, the Empire State FM School of the Air. By the end of the December meeting, the ESSA consisted of three school districts, Rochester, Syracuse, and Hornell, and three local commercial FM radio stations. Five other local FM broadcasters in nearby Utica, Cortland, Corning, Ithaca, and Binghamton expressed a desire to join, and even approached their local school boards, urging them to get involved (Truscott, 1958).

PROGRAMS 1947–1948

During the spring of 1948, most of the ESSA programs originated from the RSA. Other local school districts soon contributed programs, but relying heavily at first on RSA series enabled the group to offer the first year a full five-day broadcast schedule of eleven programs as shown in Table 40. All programs were aimed at grades K–8.

TABLE 40. ESSA PROGRAM SCHEDULE, 1947–48 (TRUSCOTT, 1958)

Day	Time	Course	Produced by
Monday	1:30–1:45	*Magic Book Shop*	RSA
	1:45–2:00	*Our Heritage in Freedom*	Syracuse, WSYR
Tuesday	1:30–1:45	*The Singing Lady*	RSA
	1:45–2:00	*Garden Time*	Hornell, WWHG
		Rochester Concerts (1948)	RSA
Wednesday	1:30–1:45	*Science Adventure*	RSA
	1:45–2:00	*We are World Citizens*	RSA
Thursday	1:30–1:45	*People in the News*	RSA
	1:45–2:00	*Pathways to Health*	Syracuse, WSYR
Friday	1:30–1:45	*News Today — History Tomorrow*	RSA
	1:45–2:00	*Tell Us a Story*	Utica, WIRK

This cooperative approach worked primarily because the RSA already had developed a core of successful programs which the other school systems could use as models.

ESSA Broadcast System

One of the driving forces behind ESSA's rapid growth was the network of newly formed, privately owned local FM stations. By spring of 1949, the 15 station network broadcast 2.5 hours of ESSA programs per week, free of charge (ESSA, Cosgrove, 1967). Over the next three years, the ESSA network had grown to 22 stations including those in Buffalo, Niagara Falls, Rochester, Syracuse, Utica, Troy, Ithaca, Binghamton, Albany, Corning, Poughkeepsie, White Plains, and on Long Island. The New York City school system's public station, WNYE,[72] also participated, and several of its high production value programs became mainstays of the ESSA repertoire.

Next the Rural Radio Network (RRN) joined the ESSA broadcast family. Designed to serve the state's farming communities, the RRN connected its six transmitters by FM relay instead of wires and promoted FM radio use by distributing FM receivers to farmers through local Grange Federation (Tracking the old RRN, 2002). The entire ESSA broadcast network brought ESSA programs to students throughout most of New York's long central valley, the Hudson Valley, and Long Island.

Why were those small FM stations so ready to donate their air time to a non-profit cause? No documentation exists to answer that question, but most likely owners of the new FM stations, like broadcasters in previous decades, realized that broadcasting to the schools offered an excellent marketing opportunity. In the mid 1940s the new FM stations faced a big barrier; few people or businesses owned FM receivers. By broadcasting to the schools, and distributing FM receivers, the start-up broadcasters hoped to prompt the public to tune in to FM radio. Unfortunately for the ESSA, when the public did start listening to FM radio, the FM station managers reevaluated their commitment to educational radio.

Administration and Staff

The ESSA experiment in 1947–1948 had been well received, but the job of producing and airing ten radio programs weekly made evident the need for administrative and production staffs. Broadcasts needed to be planned, produced, and coordinated; advance information on programs had to be delivered to the participating schools; teachers needed help in using programs; and the effort required evaluation and refinement. Yet, at the end of 1948, ESSA had no formal structure for delivering these services; everything functioned ad hoc. The Steering Committee, headed by Paul Reed, recognized a pressing need for a central office, an administrative director, and clerical support, but how would that be supported? Other state-based SOAs received funding from state legislatures or out of university budgets; the ESSA Steering Committee came up with a unique solution — the users would tax themselves. School superintendents from the districts that used the programs agreed to provide the funds to support an administrative office.

An Executive Secretary was appointed and given an administrative office at Syracuse University's Radio Center. The Secretary essentially served as the director coordinating ESSA activities and broadcasts, distributing program support material, promoting the programs to schools in the radio service area, and providing counsel and advice to school personnel about how to use ESSA programs. Also hired was a part-time secretary.

Next the Steering Committee decided to place program selection and evaluation into the hands of experts. It created the Program Policy Committee, made up of teachers and supervisors drawn from ESSA affiliated schools, to evaluate the needs of participating schools and determine the subjects for which radio programs would be most effective. The ten committee members did not get involved with developing or broadcasting programs. Rather they evaluated current programs, recommended which should be continued and suggested new programs. The Advisory Committee's recommendations were then implemented by the Steering Committee (Truscott, 1958).

In June of 1949, the Steering Committee sought state recognition. State recognition would widen participation and attract in-kind services from educators in New York's universities and colleges and the state's educational bureaucracy. The Steering Committee recommended incorporation as an entity under the Regents of the University of the State of New York. Apparently,

[72]WNYE made ESSA programs available to all city schools, but each school decided whether or not to use the programs.

the Steering Committee felt the Regents provided the most authoritative educational body in the state and that authority would rub off on the ESSA.

As part of incorporation, an ESSA Board of Trustees was formed with authority to direct ESSA policy and appoint Steering Committee members. However, the Trustees' most important responsibility turned out to be setting the ESSA budget and the tax rate for the participating districts and schools. Unlike any other SOA in the country, the ESSA funded itself by charging the schools that received its broadcasts. The six contributing school districts, Syracuse, Rochester, Utica, Ithaca, Hornell and Cortland, paid a tax according to the size of their educational budgets (Truscott, 1958).

MEMBERSHIP

The tax system highlighted ESSA's membership structure. The participants in the ESSA were organized into three groups: (1) broadcasting members, those FM stations or groups of stations that regularly aired ESSA programs, (2) contributing members, those school systems that were approved by the Board of Trustees, and (3) participating members, those individual schools or school districts not designated as contributing members. The broadcasting and contributing members had voting privileges at the annual meeting; participating members did not. In the early years, fees collected from the contributing members represented the bulk of the ESSA budget, but as the number of participating members grew, so did the amount they contributed. By the late 1950s, participating members contributed more than half of the ESSA budget (Financial Statement, in Truscott, 1958).

LEAN BUDGETS

Throughout its history, the ESSA operated on relatively small amounts of money. The annual budget for 1949–1950 was roughly $6,000. By the mid–1950s ESSA's annual budget approached $20,000,[73] and by the mid–1960s it reached $30,000. For comparison consider that Ben Darrow's Ohio School of the Air started in 1930 with an annual budget of over $20,000, during the 1950s the Wisconsin's radio station WHA which operated the Wisconsin School of the Air had an annual budget of over $250,000[74] and New York's WNYE which was totally dedicated to in-school broadcasting received over $150,000 annually (Truscott, 1958).

Truscott (1958) acknowledges that ESSA's budget was small and covered only administration, communication, and printing of bulletins. The budget dollars cited above did not include donated services such as program development by various member schools and universities and the broadcast services donated by the cooperating radio stations. Were those assigned a dollar value, Truscott estimates that the ESSA's annual budget would be closer to $100,000.

While the ESSA accomplished a lot with little, the lean budgets restricted its growth, limiting the staff to one full-time and several part-time positions. Part of the problem could be found in its method of funding; direct grants from local school boards were almost guaranteed to restrict funds as local boards are continually looking for ways to cut costs (ESSA, Annual Meetings, 1959; Truscott, 1958).

EDUCATIONAL PROGRAM HIGHLIGHTS

During the decade of operation covered here, ESSA schools had developed several dozen program series that supported the core curricula used in New York schools, including music, literature, science, health, current events and modern languages. Table 41 lists the most popular programs or ones that had the longest broadcast life.

---

[73]$20,000 in 1950 dollars equals approximately $160,000 in 2005 dollars (Sahr, 2005).

[74]However, the Wisconsin figure probably represented the amount budgeted for the entire statewide WHA radio system, not just the WSA. Betty Girling of the MSA said that the WSA received $125,000 annually from the Wisconsin legislature.

TABLE 41. ESSA PROGRAM HIGHLIGHTS, 1949–1952 (TRUSCOTT, 1958)

Years	Course	Developer and Grades
	Music	
1948–1957	*Rochester Concerts*	Rochester school system and the Rochester Civic Orchestra, 5–7
	Literature	
1950–1957	*Adventure Trails*	Rochester, 5–7
	Science	
1948–1957	*Science Adventure*	Rochester, 5–8
1952–1957	*Exploring Science*	Cortland Teachers College, 1–5
	Health and Safety	
1948–1950	*Pathways to Health*	Syracuse Public Schools, 1–3
	Current Events	
1948–1953	*News Today — History Tomorrow*	Rochester and station WHAM, 5–7

All programs were 15 minutes long except the concerts which were 30 minutes. Programs were broadcast between 1:30 and 2:00 P.M. daily. Below are program descriptions.

Rochester Concerts. Presented by the Rochester Civic Orchestra, the format included a study of individual instruments that make up the orchestra, performance of descriptive and story telling musical segments, and "music for fun and humor" (Truscott, 1958, p. 56). Prior to the broadcasts, a course notebook prepared by Howard Hinga, music consultant for the Rochester schools, was distributed to participating students. The longest running ESSA series, aimed at grades 4 — 8, the programs were aired 30 minutes.

Adventure Trails. One of the most popular ESSA offerings, the series dramatized contemporary children's literature for students in the upper elementary grades. The series also supplemented social studies and language arts. Its popularity may have been due to the fact that each program was evaluated by city and rural teachers in the Ithaca school district. Their comments were used to revise and refine the productions.

Science Adventure. Another popular and long running series, *Science Adventure* was written and produced by Grace Boulton, a science teacher in the Rochester Public Schools. The series offered dramatized science lessons featuring the adventures of the Allen Family: Tom, Jane, parents and the family dog, Mr. Waggs. An unusually curious family, the Allens made interesting discoveries at home and on their travels. The goal was to motivate students for in-class science lessons and to help students enjoy science.

Exploring Science. Developed for grades 1–5, this series presented science experiments and activities that used materials available in the classroom or at home. The programs got the children actively involved in learning by doing, seeing, feeling, and hearing.

Pathways to Health. Prepared for primary grade students by the Syracuse Public Schools, the series focused on four phases of health teaching: health habits, manners, play habits and pets in the home. Probably recognizing that talks about health, whether live or by media, generally failed to engage students, the ESSA program planners tried a dramatized approach. In a short lived series called *Peter Pan and Patti,* children heard the adventures of Peter Pan, Patti, and other boys and girls. Mixed into the stories were health messages. Judging from the fact that the series lasted only two years, we can assume that even dramatized health programs carried little appeal for students.

You and Your Friends. Designed to address the social and personal concerns of pre-teens in grades 5–8, the action centered on the Harris Family, Bussy, 12 and Linda, 10. In each program the children confronted a problem about getting along with others, mental health, bad habits, or leisure time. With the help of mom and dad, the children worked out a practical solution. The goal was to encourage school children to discuss their problems with their parents.

News Today — History Tomorrow. Presented by station WHAM in Rochester, the series featured news commentary by a well-known local broadcaster, Jack Ross. Designed for students in grades 5–8, the program presented unscripted commentary on the day's top stories (Truscott, 1958).

WEEKLY BULLETINS

The ESSA central office distributed a bi-weekly Pre-program Bulletin that listed all the radio programs to be aired during the coming weeks. In newspaper format, teachers received summary descriptions of the upcoming programs, suggestions for pre- and post-broadcast learning activities and resources for further study. The bulletins also offered a set of guidelines intended to help teachers make effective use of the programs. The guidelines included:

• Read advance material on the upcoming programs
• Prepare the class to listen effectively be providing background information, conducting discussion, and suggesting research projects
• Provide best possible listening conditions
• Conduct follow-up discussion
• Suggest follow-up learning activities such as readings, drawings, field trips, etc.

The bulletins encouraged teachers to evaluate a program's usefulness and suggest ideas for improvement (Truscott, 1958).

Teachers received the Pre-program Bulletins every two weeks prior to the broadcasts, though some complained about late arrival and the bulky newspaper format. In addition, by the mid–1950s, at the beginning of each semester, the ESSA central office distributed *The News Bulletin,* also in newspaper format, which presented an overview of the program series, schedules for the entire semester, and news of the ESSA programs, stations and personalities.

Philosophy and Methods

According to an ESSA weekly bulletin distributed to the schools in 1949, radio should be considered in the same light as textbooks, maps, film and other audio-visual instructional aids which are furnished to the teachers and students in the classroom. It should contribute to the curriculum "experiences ... beyond those which could be expected to originate with the average classroom teachers or from other accepted teacher aids" (Truscott, 1958, pp. 54–55). Such language may hint at the fine line radio educators often walked to assure that they were not infringing on the prerogatives of the classroom teachers or school administrators. However, taking it at face value, the description also suggested that the ESSA educators held a limited view of radio as being very like other audio-visual aids, only a little different. Unfortunately, that language masked the true uniqueness of radio, namely that it allows users to creatively shape the final programs to meet the needs of the schools or specific curricula, or at least to the vision of the script writers and subject matter experts. Maps, films, and even textbooks allow no such freedom.

Truscott (1958) also says that the ESSA used radio to bring to the classroom experiences that were "uniquely adaptable to radio; experts who could never visit in person could through radio enrich the curriculum by bringing up-to-date information on issues of democracy" (p. 55), a view widely held then by proponents of educational radio. Truscott also shared some visionary ideas about the role of radio in the classroom. Echoing the words of Darrow and other early SOA proponents she says, "[I]t was hoped that the walls of the classroom would be pushed back, educational horizons broadened and the world brought to the children" ... throughout the state of New York (p. 55). Not clear is whether Truscott is speaking for the ESSA administrators or herself.

Though documentation is limited, it appears that the ESSA administrators seldom intentionally used radio to fill gaps in school curricula. Programs could parallel curricula and enrich lessons, but radio was seldom used as primary means of instruction for any course. Its role was to enrich the classroom lessons at the teacher's discretion. Exceptions existed. For example, the series *Exploring Science* encouraged children to get actively engaged in learning. Apparently, ESSA administrators did not think too deeply about how to best use radio in the classroom. If they did, they didn't record their thoughts.

PROGRAMS 1957–1962

By the late 1950s, the ESSA had developed efficient procedures for identifying and developing program series that New York state teachers used. Table 42 shows a mix of programs developed locally and borrowed from other SOAs.

TABLE 42. ESSA PROGRAM HIGHLIGHTS, 1957–1962
(ESSA, News Bulletin X, 1959; ESSA, Annual
Meeting, 1960; ESSA Program Evaluation, 1962)

Day	Time	Course and Grade Level	Produced by
Monday	11:15–11:30	*Spanish Today (4–6)*	University of Rochester
	1:30–1:45	*Animal Worlds (K–3)*	Utica Public Schools
	1:45–2:00	*Voici Mimi (Here's Mimi) (4–6)*	Minnesota SOA
Tuesday	11:00–11:15	*Understanding the News (7–8)*	ESSA Staff
	1:30–1:45	*Science at Our Door (4–6)*	WNYE (New York, Public Schools)
	1:45–2:00	*Science Adventure (5–8)*	Rochester Public Schools
Wednesday	1:30–1:45	*Rochester Concerts (4–8)* alternating with	Rochester Symphony
		New York, the Empire State (5–8)	WNYE
	1:45–2:00	*Health and Safety (K–3)*	Buffalo Public Schools
Thursday	1:30–1:45	*Let's Sing*	Rochester Public Schools
	1:45–2:00	*Tales from the Four Winds*	WNYE
Friday	1:30–1:45	*Tree Time Travels (4–6)*	Syracuse University, Dept. of Forestry
	1:45–2:00	*We Know a Story (K–3)*	Utica Public Schools

In the 1960s, ESSA programming drew from the best of WNYE in New York City and from local universities, but also many program series were developed by member school districts such as Rochester, Utica, and Buffalo. Highlights of several new program series are given below.

Spanish Today. This series for intermediate level students used an oral approach to teach Spanish. The creators believed that the grammar would be learned inductively. Each lesson presented an aspect of life in a particular Spanish speaking country.

Spanish for Today. Designed to continue language study begun in *Spanish Today,* the series dramatized the experiences of an American of Hispanic descent as he traveled through Mexico. The course objectives included: (1) improve pronunciation and intonation through imitation of dialogue and songs, (2) present idiomatic Spanish, (3) describe customs and culture of Mexico. Both Spanish language programs demonstrated effective use of radio for actual language instruction, instead of using it to merely encourage language study. It was developed by the faculty at the University of Rochester.

Tales from the Four Winds. "One of the nation's best known and most highly regarded in-school radio programs" (Truscott, 1958, p. 61), the series dramatized stories for children in grades 1–5. Developed by WNYE, New York, with high production values, the performers were members of an all-city children's radio workshop. When WNYE joined ESSA, it offered the Steering Committee a choice of any program on the station's schedule. Their unanimous choice was *Tales from the Four Winds*.

Speak My Language. Though not long running, the series did demonstrate an ambitious effort on the part of high school students to tackle a topic that challenges many American students, namely foreign languages. Produced by high school students in Long Island, New York, the program series introduced Spanish and French using basic words, conversation, songs, games, and stories. The series also presented information about geography, history and culture of French and Spanish speaking countries. As with other radio-based language series, the larger goal was to not to build language proficiency but to stimulate interest in language study.

Understanding the News. Designed to develop interest among upper elementary students in the world that surrounded them, the series gave background on current developments and recommended sources for following-up on local, national, and world news events. Programs followed a pattern: overview of the week's news, a feature story, news quiz based on "clues in the news." The series was developed with a special grant from Newhouse, a local media corporation, and supported with funding from the Buffalo Evening News.

Tree Time Travels. Presented from the wildlife forests of the Adirondacks State Park, this series described "exciting" visits to the forests and to nearby pulp and paper mills. It was developed by the State College of Forestry.

Audience

Who listened to ESSA programs? Getting a handle on audience size posed a very problematic issue for all schools of the air, and ESSA was no exception. In his report to the Trustees at the end of the 1951–52 school year, the Executive Secretary, Eugene Foster, claimed approximately 6,000 teachers worked in member schools and according to his calculations, each of these teachers tuned into 2.28 ESSA programs weekly. Estimating 30 pupils per class, Foster estimated approximately 375,000 students listened regularly. However, that same year, in a report to participating broadcasters, Foster estimated that approximately 10,000 classrooms used the programs every week and that added up to "about 300,000 school children on the elementary level" (Truscott, 1958, p. 276).

Foster's numbers represent between 30 percent and 37 percent of the school population of New York State, outside of New York City. If accurate, that percentage would substantiate Foster's observation that the size of the ESSA's audience, "… compares quite favorably with any school of the air in the country and is certainly most praiseworthy for a cooperative organization of this type" (Foster, 1952 in Truscott, 1958, p. 276). But were his numbers accurate?

Most likely Foster was guilty of the fallacy that Cuban (1986) identified: Foster assumed that because one teacher in a school used the ESSA programs, they all did. Obviously, that was not the case, and it seems Foster became aware of the problem. Later in 1955, he reported distributing Pre–program Bulletins to 11,000 elementary school teachers or 40 percent of all New York elementary school teachers outside of New York City, but he made no estimate of the size of the student audience. He went on to assert that the main obstacles to greater use of the programs in the schools were lack of FM receivers and scheduling conflicts (Foster, 1952 in Truscott, 1958, p. 263). In the end though, the data are insufficient to either accept or challenge Foster's estimates of audience size. However, one could argue that teachers in the ESSA schools were more likely to use radio than those in other schools, because each member school or school district contributed directly to the ESSA budget and mostly likely superintendents and principals encouraged the use of radio.

From the late 1950s to mid 1960s, the ESSA annually included in the Pre-program Bulletin a questionnaire form to be completed by teachers who used ESSA programs. One of the questions asked teachers to report the number of students in their classes that listened. Bases on 887 returned questionnaires for the 1961–1962 school year, the Executive Secretary, James Fellows, reported that students listening to ESSA programs totaled about 21,000, a low and probably inaccurate number (ESSA Annual Meeting, 1964). Fellows mentioned that the number was based on only those teachers who responded to the questionnaire and that the actual number of listeners was likely to be much higher, but he made no attempt to project the results to the universe of potential ESSA users. Experienced survey researchers know that in voluntary surveys, the non-responders typically include many users. We can assume that the ESSA probably attracted substantially more than 21,000 listeners in that year, but the data are not sufficient enough to venture a guess.

Furthermore the ESSA continued to attract more and more member schools and districts, despite the fact that every year a few dropped out. The 1960 Annual Report to the Trustees reported that the number of member schools and school districts totaled 169. That number compared favorably with the 42 districts and schools that made up the ESSA membership in 1949, its first full year of operation. How many schools and potential listeners that represented is difficult to calculate because some rural districts included only one school, while some urban ones included a half dozen schools or more. In addition 51 schools or school districts participated on a trial basis for a total of 230 members. The number of broadcast members remained at 19. By the 1960s, then, the ESSA had reached a plateau in terms of budget, membership, listening audience, and cooperating radio stations. It would remain at the plateau a few years more.

Evaluation

ESSA's staff made regular attempts to solicit the opinions of the local school superintendents and teachers regarding the radio programs. Starting in 1948 the steering committee sent a survey questionnaire to principals of member schools dealing with program selection. The eight questions solicited reactions to the entire broadcast program rather than any specific issues. Several years later, the Program Policy Committee issued a survey designed to uncover reactions to specific programs. It asked principals and superintendents to rate each program offered on a five point scale ranging from "Highly Significant" to "No Value." It also asked recipients to rate the programs that their teachers used according to how well they held student interest and attention and on the amount of follow-up activity generated. The same survey also asked which programs were most and least listened to. While responses to such questionnaires yielded little information about the educational effectiveness of the programs, they did tell ESSA administrators which were most popular. Not surprisingly, *We Know a Story,* a program for primary students proved to be the most popular (Truscott, 1958, pp. 305–310).

To streamline the survey distribution process, in 1953 the central office began including a shorter questionnaire once a year in the Pre-program bulletin. Recipients were asked to identify their position (superintendent, principal, or teacher) and how many ESSA programs they used each week. They were then asked to rate the programs they used according to whether the programs should be continued or dropped (Truscott, 1958).

Overall, the ESSA's evaluation process was designed only to gather reactions to the program and perhaps as a public relations gesture. The data show no attempt to determine educational effectiveness. Granted measuring educational effectiveness was something few SOAs did after 1950. Perhaps the job was just too daunting. Or maybe it was felt that such an effort would be misinterpreted by school people who might see it as prying.

Programs and Operations 1966

During the early 1960s the ESSA administration and oversight changed substantially. Paul C. Reed, one of the founders of the ESSA, had died, and the position of Executive Secretary changed hands several times. Programming also changed. By 1966, the number of programs offered expanded from 12 in 1960 to 16, mainly through the addition of morning broadcasts. Also the programming focus expanded to include mathematics and programs with a multicultural focus. Table 43 shows the schedule for the 1966–1967 year.

TABLE 43. ESSA PROGRAM HIGHLIGHTS, 1966 (ESSA, NEWS BULLETIN, 1966)

Day	Time*	Course and Grade Level	Production Notes
Monday	10:00	*Using Keys to Mathematics* (7–8)	ESSA member
	10:15	*Community Helpers* (K–3)	ESSA member
	1:30	*Animal Worlds* (K–3)	
	1:45	*Tree Time* (7–8)	
Monday	1:30–2:00	*Special Broadcast, such as* "Indian Legacy"	The Special Broadcasts pre–empted regular programs at several times throughout the semester.
Tuesday	10:00	*Exploring Science* (4–6)	
	10:15	*We Know a Story* (K–3)	ESSA member
	1:30	*Tales from the Four Winds* (4–6)	WNYE
	1:45	*Let's Find Out* (K–3)	
Tuesday	1:30–2:00	*Rochester Orchestra, Youth Concerts* (5–8)	Broadcasts of the Rochester Orchestra ran 30 minutes and pre-empted regular programs
Wednesday	10:00–10:30	*Special Broadcast, such as* "Indian Legacy"	The Special Broadcasts pre-empted regular programs several times throughout the semester.
Wednesday	10:00	*Understanding the News* (7–8)	Buffalo Evening News
	10:15	*Tree Time* (4–8)	Syracuse U. Forestry
	1:30	*Let's Sing* (K–3)	ESSA members
	1:45	*Science Adventure* (7–8)	ESSA members
Thursday	10:00	*The World of Myths and Legends* (4–6)	WNYE
	10:15	*Keys to Mathematics* (7–8)	ESSA members
	1:30	*Using Keys to Mathematics* (7–8)	ESSA members
	1:45	*Community Helpers* (K–3)	
Friday	10:00	*Our Neighbors Around the World* (7–8)	WNYE
	10:15	*Tales from the Four Winds* (4–6)	WNYE
	1:30	*Exploring Science* (4–6)	
	1:45	*We Know a Story* (K–3)	ESSA member

* All programs were 15 minutes except for the Rochester Concerts which ran 30 minutes.

The schedule for 1966 reflects a mix of traditional favorites such as *We Know a Story* and *Tales from the Four Winds* and new programs such as *Special Broadcasts* and *Keys to Mathematics*. Below several new programs are described.

Keys to Mathematics. An ambitious series that presented key ideas in order to stimulate thinking about mathematics; the programs also covered mathematics vocabulary and offered suggestions for class discussion to follow the broadcasts. Instructional methods included lecture and discussion.

Using Keys to Mathematics. A companion to *Keys to Mathematics,* this series was billed as "fun with mathematics puzzles." It presented puzzles that could be solved without resorting to previously learned math manipulations. The puzzles required a number of skills such as a play on words, detection of number patterns, and logical thinking. The Rochester School System produced both *Keys to Mathematics* and *Using Keys to Mathematics.*

Community Helpers. An odd series that aimed at making primary students aware of how parks and playgrounds improve life in the community. Programs also covered the different kinds of maintenance required to keep those facilities in good condition.

The Effects of Educational Television

Until 1960, the ESSA served large areas of New York State with little competition from other forms of educational technology. However, by the mid 1960s educational television (ETV) had become well established in many of New York's school districts, and it competed with the ESSA not in the economic sense, but rather it competed for "something more valuable, teacher's time" (ESSA, ETV, nd). During the 1950s increasing demands, special classes, and departmentalization had already reduced the amount of time classroom teachers could devote to radio, and by 1960, that time was further reduced by ETV. Furthermore, ETV became well established in New York State's larger urban school systems, the same systems that the ESSA served. In 1966, the Board of Trustees decided to study the effects of ETV on ESSA usage. They chose Buffalo as a test case for two reasons: Buffalo had the longest running ETV stations outside of NYC, and Buffalo's schools were the largest contributor to the ESSA.

The Executive Secretary sent a questionnaire to Buffalo's public school teachers with the stated purpose of determining the effect on the usage of ESSA programs in areas where ETV was also available. 396 teachers responded, roughly 18 percent of the 2,250 questionnaires sent. The major findings were that overall 30 percent of the responding teachers said they had reduced their use of the ESSA since ETV became available, 50 percent said their usage of radio had remained the same, and 20 percent said they had increased use of ESSA programs. Those results point to a 10 percent decrease in the use of ESSA programs due to competition from ETV.

On average the teachers reported using the ESSA only 20 minutes per week and ETV, on average, 31 minutes a week. Further analysis of the data showed that kindergarten, first, and second grade teachers used ETV substantially more than they used radio. The reasons given were that the ESSA material presented for the primary grades was too advanced, the vocabulary too difficult, and the speed of presentation too rapid, problems that visuals could easily overcome. Those findings highlight the power of visuals over audio, particularly with young children. The study found that educational television in the early 1960s did reduce use of educational radio in Buffalo, but not enough to seriously impact the ESSA's viability. In response to the study, the Board of Trustees asked the executive secretary to investigate ways that ESSA could cooperate with educational television.

Demise

In the ESSA annual meeting of 1964, executive secretary James Cosgrove first presented the Board of Trustees some good news about audience and school participation; both had risen slightly. Then he presented news of the problem that would grow substantially within a few years and gravely threaten ESSA's future. Public use of FM radio was on the rise and as a result, FM stations that made up the ESSA network began to re-evaluate their commitment to educational radio. It started when station WRUN FM in Utica alerted the ESSA executive secretary that as its general audience grew, it could not justify the free air time that it donated. The problem was not the loss of advertising dollars from the donated air time, but rather the loss of listeners. The station manager said that during the ESSA broadcasts its non-school listeners tuned to other stations and did not return (ESSA, Annual Meeting, 1964 and 1965).

The implications for this turn of events were ominous. If WRUN FM ceased airing ESSA programs and no other local outlet could be found, then the Utica schools would stop participating, resulting in a loss of audience and revenues. Cosgrove only hinted that the Utica situation could represent a first domino in a row that might soon start toppling. A year later, however, the Executive Secretary reported that the station WFAS FM in White Plains New York had canceled its membership and as a result so did the Mount Vernon school district, a former contributing member (ESSA, Annual Meetings, 1964 and 1965).

In his special report on the future of the ESSA, the new executive secretary, Donald Smith, asserted that while educational radio remained viable in New York, the ESSA faced a serious problem; members of the radio network were dropping out at an accelerated rate. As of mid–1967, stations serving White Plains, Utica, and Schenectady had all "been forced to cancel from the network," which meant that the surrounding schools also cancelled. The loss of Schenectady hit hard because it represented $2,000 of annual revenue. Furthermore the co-founding school districts of Hornell and Rochester had alerted Smith of their intention to cancel after the current year, a move that would put the ESSA budget into deficit. Smith pointed out several problem areas that if attended to might reverse the ESSA's downward drift. They included expanding their meager facilities, increasing the limited staff, promoting the ESSA to the tens of thousands of New York teachers who were unaware of the ESSA's existence and more (ESSA, Smith, 1968). Smith did not say where the money could be found to pay for his suggested improvements.

In 1967, former Executive Secretary Cosgrove presented a detailed report outlining the causes of what he called a near fatal crisis and offering ideas for altering the ESSA's old structure and policies. He asserted that, given the boom in educational technology that was taking place in the schools at that time, the ESSA should be in the forefront of education; instead he said, it was a mere holding action. He identified several fundamental causes for current crisis:

• Overemphasis on the mechanism of instructional radio at the expense of instruction by radio. He called for greater emphasis on curriculum, instructional methods and greater cooperation with school systems.
• Limitation of broadcast air-time. One hour of broadcasting per day was insufficient to attract additional teachers; and that hour was likely to be reduced because increasingly the cooperating commercial stations wanted to maintain a constant audience during the day.
• The rise of ETV threatened the ESSA's base of support in urban areas by competing for teachers' time.

Cosgrove offered the following list of solutions:

• Launch a promotional effort to attract more parochial schools to the ESSA. Usage among parochial schools was low, but a recent effort aimed at the Diocese of Buffalo had succeeded in signing up 20 new schools.
• Appeal to publicly owned educational FM stations that did not carry ESSA programs to do so. Cosgrove acknowledged that continued reliance on commercial broadcasters would ultimately be a dead end. He identified seven locally owned educational FM stations in the ESSA service area, plus three FM stations operated by the State University of New York.
• Develop a cooperative relationship with operators of educational television stations that would allow the ESSA programs to piggy-back on the ETV broadcasts.

• Establish a tape service — similar to those operated by many state-based SOAs — that could overcome the problem of differing class schedules and curriculum.
• Seek grants from foundation.

(ESSA, Cosgrove, 1967)

Where would the money come from to implement these recommendations? Cosgrove offered a number of suggestions that included many of the usual suspects. Increasing the number of participating parochial schools would provide modest amounts of additional moneys, but not enough to make a difference. Seeking grants from private foundations such as Ford or Kettering offered possibilities, though even Cosgrove admitted that these organizations had recently shown much more interest in educational television than in radio. The most promising source of new money, he asserted, was the federal government. New legislation recently passed by then President Johnson — Titles II, III, and IV of the Education Act — made monies available to local school boards for a variety of purposes, but to qualify, ESSA would have to affiliate with a local school, a lengthy process. Finally the Public Broadcasting Act of 1967 which created the Corporation for Public Broadcasts represented another possible funding source (ESSA, Cosgrove, 1967).

Were the ESSA a new idea or a vigorous start-up that showed great promise, Cosgrove's ideas would have been worth pursuing, but how likely was it that any of these agencies he mentioned would agree to fund a failing entity built on what was then perceived to be old technology? No definitive answer exists, but six months later, in February of 1968, executive secretary Smith sent a memo to the Board of Trustees saying the Steering Committee had decided that the ESSA no longer played an effective role in New York State education. Several representatives from the State University of New York had expressed interest in taking over the ESSA operation, but if that initiative failed, the Steering Committee would recommend the ESSA be terminated. In May of that year, the Board agreed and voted to cease operations. Several Board members justified their action by saying that the radio operation could no longer compete with other teaching tools and besides the Board faced a $9,000 deficit. Thus the experiment in grassroots educational technology came to a close, a victim of technological change and over reliance on America's privately owned broadcast system.

Summary

The ESSA delivered a curriculum favored by most of the state-based schools of the air: literature, science, current events, health, and of course music. The programs, most developed by member schools or school districts, were designed primarily to enrich school curricula, but also to expand it in areas where local schools were deficient. In all that, the ESSA varied little from other state-based SOAs. What was different was its development from the grassroots up. Local superintendents and principals organized and developed a system that soon served several hundred thousand students. Starting with the Rochester school system, the ESSA spread from one school system to another until the participating schools encompassed a large part of Upstate New York. The ESSA grew because teachers found the programs to be valuable additions to their classroom instruction. Remarkably, the ESSA self funded through the participating school districts. Incorporation under the state university's Board of Regents stimulated cooperation and participation from University based educators. A key driving force came from owners of the new FM radio stations who recognized in the ESSA an opportunity to perform a public serve while also promoting their fledgling businesses. One wonders why such cooperation didn't occur in many other states.

Another remarkable feature of ESSA was the cooperative arrangement that developed between educators and commercial broadcasters. A 1949 letter from the ESSA Board of Trustees to the New York University Regents describes the ESSA as an educational experiment unique in the U.S. It represented, the writer said, a "one-of-kind pooling of effort from educators and commercial broadcasters for the benefit of the state's school children" (Foster, 1955 in Truscott, 1958 p. 282). Apparently, the writer had no knowledge of similar cooperative ventures between educators and commercial broadcasters that had taken place in Texas. The writer went on to praise the American radio system: "... never before has there been a public service by radio which has been of such immediate and significant value to the public schools of a large segment of our country. This is American Radio at its best" (Foster, 1955, in Truscott, 1958 p. 282).

The Board certainly did represent a unique cooperation between the newly established FM commercial stations and public education. Only the Texas School of the Air relied as heavily on commercial broadcasters. In both cases the environment that enabled that level of cooperation had been transitory. When new market conditions arose, both lost their connection to commercial radio and soon faded.

Oregon School of the Air[75]

The origin of the Oregon School of the Air owes more to the state's struggle to keep the license for state-owned station KOAC than to any overarching vision of radio's educational potential. Nevertheless, in-school broadcasting became deeply rooted in the state's rural areas as attested to by its long operating history, spanning roughly forty years from January of 1933 to the early 1970s. Starting with just one broadcast for in-school listening per week, KOAC soon expanded its offerings and dubbed the in-school effort the Oregon School of the Air (ORSA). Like many educational stations during the 1930s, KOAC faced challenges from the federal government and from local commercial broadcasters eager to take over the station's place on the AM dial. KOAC's major function as a service for Oregon's far flung agricultural communities built the political support needed in the state legislature to fend off any potential enemies and retain the station under state ownership. Broadcasting for the schools became one more tactic to cement its popular support. Though never as well funded or supported as the Wisconsin School of the Air, the ORSA thrived well enough as an entity of the state's higher education system — and specifically the General Extension Division — providing rural schools with valuable educational resources that might otherwise be unavailable.

Origins

One of the nation's original educational stations, KOAC was licensed in 1922 to the Oregon State Agricultural College (OSAC) in Corvallis, Oregon. For nearly ten years it operated, primarily as a technical learning tool for scientifically inclined agriculture students. In that service, for four to five hours a day, the station offered a variety of general education programs, intended chiefly for Oregon's rural population who lived close enough to pick up the low power transmission. That schedule fit comfortably with the school's resources (Atkinson, 1942d; Morris, 1972).

Broadcasting in-school educational programs began as the result of pressure from the Federal government. In 1931, the Federal Radio Commission (FRC) ruled that operators of full-time radio stations must broadcast for at least 12 hours per day. OSAC administrators recognized that they lacked the resources to conduct full-time operations, and appealed to the state educational officials for help. KOAC's situation presented state educators with a dilemma; either give up one

[75]Documentation for the Oregon School of the Air (ORSA) is limited, particularly for later years. Much of the information on the Oregon School of the Air comes from the recollections of James Morris, who served several year as the director of KOAC-School of the Air and several decades as the director of station KOAC.

of the few radio licenses remaining in the hands of an educational institution or expand the small radio operation into a state-wide institution. They chose the latter.

In 1932, station KOAC became a department of the General Extension Division of the state's higher education system. With this designation, KOAC could draw talent from Oregon's colleges and universities including Oregon State College, the University of Oregon, and the Oregon College of Education (Morris, 1972). In 1937 the state legislature expanded KOAC's mission to also serve other departments of state government. KOAC managers used this designation to promote the station as belonging to all the people of Oregon. The idea was expressed in the motto, *KOAC, Oregon's Own Station*.

Despite the connection to higher learning, the founders of the ORSA did not share the same sort of cosmic aspirations that propelled Ben Darrow's work in Ohio. Their vision was much closer to the ground, in fact rooted in the specific business needs and concerns of Oregon's farmers. Starting in 1933 with just one course, *Rural Electrification*, ORSA aimed to help prepare high school students in rural areas who were concerned with bringing electric service to the family farm. The positive response from rural schools and the need to fill up air time drove KOAC administrators to develop more programs for the school. By 1934–1935, KOAC aired eight in-school programs, four days a week.

The increased pace of activity called for a dedicated manager. In 1935, Alexander Blair Hull, an assistant professor of radio education at Corvallis, was appointed the full-time director of the ORSA. In addition to his managerial responsibilities, Hull also planned and wrote many new series. In his first year, Hull increased the number of weekly ORSA broadcasts to 14, and then in the following year to 20 programs—a full hour per day, five days a week. Divided into four 15 minute broadcast periods, each period consisted of 13 minutes of speaking and two minutes of music. It is unclear how Hull developed and produced such an ambitious schedule of live programs. Most likely he played many roles including that of announcer and radio teacher. Presumably, volunteer teachers and professors from the college assisted with planning and script writing services. Table 44 shows the ORSA program offerings for 1935–1936.

While impressive in its scope, the schedule suffered from an abundance of programs for junior and senior high students and few for elementary students. Hull apparently had not yet discovered that elementary teachers used radio much more frequently than did high school teachers. Also, the programs probably were not coordinated with the state curricula.

TABLE 44. ORSA PROGRAM SCHEDULE, 1935–1936 (ATKINSON, 1942D)

Course and Description	Weekly Frequency	Grades
Lessons in German	Four days per week	High school
History and Appreciation of Music, two series:	Four days	Intermediate High school
- Story of Music		
- Growth of Music		
National and International Problems	Two days	High school
History and Story of Oregon State history, geography, stories and legends	Four days	Intermediate and high school
High School Radio Guild Techniques of writing for radio	One day	High school
Drama Folk tales dramatized by the KOAC Drama Guild Players	One day	High school
Geography	One day	Not specified

Romance of Words	One day	Not specified
Talks on language, its origins and use		
Vocational Counsel	One day	High school seniors
Interviews and lectures in voc ed. from "authoritative sources"		
Out of the Zoo	One day	Not specified
Director Hull talks about wild life		
History in the Making	One day	Junior or senior high
Director Hull comments upon news events		
Facts and Affairs	Two days	Not specified
Series prepared by Director Hull on natural and social sciences		
Science in Everyday Living	Two days	High school
Occasional discussions on science as applied to everyday life		
Through the School Day	One day	Intermediate grade teachers
Broadcasts on the activities of grade school; aimed at teachers		

Hull continued to increase the number of offerings. By 1937–1938, the ORSA broadcast four series daily during the fall semester and three each day during the spring term, for a total of 35 offerings to the classroom during the time slot from 11:00 A.M. to 12:00 noon. In part, the large number of programs resulted from ORSA broadcasting on a quarterly, rather than a semester, schedule. No teacher support materials such as program schedules or teacher manuals were mentioned in the documentation. One wonders how teachers frequently integrated these broadcasts into their semester lesson plans.

One of the key staffers at this time was Helen Senn. By the late 1930s, radio educators recognized that the medium's greatest instructional strength lay with dramatic presentation. Unfortunately, the technically trained KOAC staff knew little about producing or performing on air drama. Long time KOAC program manager James Morris recalls his early years at the station, when he learned dramatic techniques from Senn:

> I'd never done dramatics; I was green in this area. But they assigned me to learn the job from Helen Senn; so I was present as a part of all her rehearsals, and her casting, auditions, etc. and I produced all the sound effects, all the musical background, and everything that she needed, and soaked up all the advice she gave college kids on how to interpret dramatic lines, etc. When Mrs. Senn left us after a year and a half, why then dramatics were my responsibility. So I took over the School of the Air, carrying on the production of the dramatic programs, etc. [Harrison, 1978, p. 13].

Morris' quote shows how SOAs in the early years found the talent needed for on air performance. While Senn was a paid staffer, volunteer college students performed all or nearly all of the character roles required in the ORSA dramatic scripts.

Apparently state legislatures were pleased with the radio service because in 1939, the state provided KOAC with additional funds to support increasing its broadcasting power to 5,000 watts, enough to cover a large part of the state's population.[76] That increase naturally benefited

---

[76]AM coverage was problematic. On a good day, a 5,000 watt signal might reach 75 miles in all directions, but on stormy days, atmospheric interference could hamper clear reception beyond 25 miles.

the ORSA, but it appears that little state money was devoted to the school of the air activities beyond Hull's salary as the full-time director. One exception is that the state's General Extension Division did "loan" Helen Senn to the station part-time at no cost. As mentioned above, she developed dramatic productions for KOAC including some for the school of the air programs. In addition, announcers for the school programs were drawn from the station's paid staff. All other KOAC SOA activities were supported by volunteers. Actors for the in-school dramatic programs formed the KOAC Radio Guild, which consisted of 75 students from Corvallis junior and senior high school as well as college students, all volunteers (Atkinson, 1942d; Morris, 1972). It's likely that the scripts were written either by Hull or college faculty members who volunteered their work. While this arrangement delivered some note worthy programming to the schools of Oregon, the demands of producing 14 weekly broadcasts apparently required more work and resources than the KOAC staff could offer. Within a few years, the schedule would be reduced substantially.

By 1941, the ORSA broadcast schedule was pared down to six programs per week. However, the reduced schedule also showed that ORSA had become better focused on serving teacher needs. Programs ran a full semester to better coordinate with actual schedules in the schools. Programming for high school students was discontinued, and all programs were aimed at the elementary and intermediate grades. Table 45 shows the reduced schedule for 1941—1942.

TABLE 45. ORSA PROGRAM SCHEDULE, 1941–42 (ATKINSON, 1942D)

Course and Description	Grades
This, Our Community	4–9
Designed to show how civic life relates to students. Children interview public official.	
Land of Empire Builders	5–9
Significant episodes in Oregon history	
Magic Casement	3–7
Classic tales and folk tales	
Safe and Healthy	Not specified
Informal talks and dramatizations on topics of safety and health	
Lest We Forget	5–9
The story of the American Constitution	
This Week's News	4–8
A review of the week's news in terms appropriate for elementary grade students	

The schedule shown in Table 45 demonstrates that the ORSA directors had developed a clearer understanding of the kinds of radio programs Oregon teachers wanted. The schedule highlights state history, news, civics, safety, and the students' responsibility to be good citizens, all aimed at the elementary and intermediate grades. In other words, radio delivered specialized subjects and difficult or unpopular topics such as safety and current events. One of the most popular and long lasting programs aired for years and is described below:

Land of the Empire Builders. Also know by the less dynamic title, *Significant Episodes in Oregon History,* the series was developed by a superintendent of a local school district who intended to vitalize the state history classes for elementary grades 4–6. The series covered topics from Oregon's pioneer history such as "The Journey of Lewis and Clark," The Discovery of the Columbia River," and "With a Bible and a Rifle." Each lesson included a brief narrative introduction followed by dramatization of the lesson topic. Historical characters were naturally highlighted over events or interpretation. The series served as good example of how radio was used by many SOAs to supplement and deliver curriculum — as opposed to mere enrichment — in those topics, such as local and state history, for which few texts or other resources were available.

The stress and strain of producing 14 weekly broadcasts with very limited staff may also have taken a toll on the ORSA directors. Alexander Hull served in that position for four years, but after he left, the directorship changed hands frequently. Between 1939 and 1945, five ORSA directors came and went, and each brought specific expertise and goals. Jerry Walker was good at writing news that children could understand. Since few daily newspapers were available in rural areas, radio served as the primary news source. After Walker, the next director, Betty Jo Bouska, built a network of "radio teachers" throughout the listening area. They served as in-school representative for ORSA and other KOAC programs. In 1946, James Morris took up duties as school director. His strengths, he said, were in news casting and drama production, skills he learned from Helen Senn.

POST WAR ADMINISTRATION AND GROWTH

Following the war, the ORSA developed more consistent leadership and entered a period of stable program development. Perhaps the key to that stability was put in place when James Morris became program director for station KOAC. Since the station was owned by the University's General Extension Division, its administrators were ultimately responsible for the station and the ORSA, but Morris also directed daily operations at the station. During the period from 1946 to 1950, Morris also seems to have taken on the many duties of the ORSA director even though another person filled that position. The documentation covering the ORSA's relationship with other SOAs during the period 1946 through 1949 shows correspondence conducted almost entirely by Morris with little from the ORSA director Lana Lu Hull, or her replacement in 1949, Elizabeth Dotson. During the late 1940s and early 1950s KOAC shared a great deal of ORSA's programming and some operations with Portland's school of the air (KBPS),[77] the educational station operated by the school board of Eugene, Oregon, and with several of Portland's commercial radio stations. Morris conducted nearly all of the correspondence concerning these relationships (Morris, 1946–1949).

In 1947, the ORSA aired 14 semester-long programs weekly. Proud of that accomplishment, Morris submitted the entire ORSA schedule in competition for the national Peabody Radio Awards. While ORSA did not win, the competition brought national attention to the Oregon's educational radio effort. In the application document, Morris described the role and purpose of KOAC programs within the state's schools: "Today [1947] the Oregon School of the Air features fourteen programs and endeavors to correlate planning and production of these broadcasts with curriculum of as many schools as possible in the state of Oregon. Radio supplements classroom work, stimulates student interest and offers a sound tool of instruction" (Morris, 1972, p. 78).

It's significant that Morris says the ORSA endeavored to correlate programming with Oregon school curricula, suggesting a desired goal that had not yet been reached. Morris also stated typical thinking about the role and value of in-school radio education, namely, that it motivated students through the emotional appeal of drama, sound effects, and stories and extended the teacher's instructional tool box. The quote also highlights Morris's role as the de facto director of the ORSA. Within the next few years, Morris trimmed the KOAC schedule to between 10 and 12 program series per semester.

Shared Broadcasts

Station KOAC-AM carried all ORSA programs, but its 5,000 watt AM signal could not reach all of Oregon's school children. Typically, the Corvallis, Oregon-based KOAC had a dependable

[77]The story of Portland's local school of the air and station KBPS is told in Section IV of this study.

broadcast range of roughly 75 miles with variations, more or less than that, depending on atmospheric conditions and geography. That meant that KOAC's reception was problematic in Portland, the state's main population center, approximately 85 miles distant. As part of the state's General Extension Division, KOAC was originally intended to serve the state's agricultural population, but clearly, Morris and others at the ORSA wanted to reach as many Oregon schools as possible, including its urban areas. Morris partially addressed the problem by offering KOAC programs to other Oregon educational and commercial stations that broadcast to the schools. Its primary broadcast partner, however, was the station owned by the Portland Board of Education, KBPS, which had developed its own school of the air.[78] KBPS made the ORSA programs available to teachers throughout the Portland area, and for many years, it carried the entire KOAC weekly schedule as shown in Table 46.

TABLE 46. ORSA PROGRAMS CARRIED BY PORTLAND'S KBPS IN 1948–49 (SWENSON, 1958)

Day	Course	Grade Level
Monday	*Especially for Women*	Parents
	Land of Make Believe	Primary
Tuesday	*The News Watch*	4–8
	Doctor Comes to School	N/A
Wednesday	*Stories that Live*	6–12
	What's that Word?	N/A
Thursday	*Let's Sing America*	1–8
	Lest We Forget	N/A
Friday	*Nature Trails*	2–4
	Tell a Story	Primary

KBPS carried all the ORSA programs because it needed to fill up a full day of programming, but it lacked the resources to produce many original programs. Fortunately, KOAC made its programs available at little or no cost. Only a few descriptions of the KOAC programs are available. They are given below.

Especially for Women. Intended for adults, not children, but nevertheless broadcast during morning hours, the series dealt chiefly with domestic issues, but also provided a forum for at-home women to hear discussion of issues related to education for adults and children.

Land of Make Believe. A combined art and literature program intended for the primary grades that included an imaginative method for engaging children in learning. Each program presented a story for children to enjoy and then asked to them draw an illustration suggested by the story's characters or events. Teachers submitted the best drawings to a contest run by the ORSA. Winning entries were announced during the series, and judging from several letters sent by classroom teachers, students were very excited if the announced winners included one of their works.

Nature Trails. A natural science series for the lower elementary grades, the series consisted mainly of mini-dramas featuring Jimmy and his dog, Rex, who have little adventures that result in learning about nature. In 1948, the ORSA director Lana Hull introduced a modest teacher's guide that listed and described each program in the series and offered a standard set of suggestions for conducting the broadcasts. These included pre-broadcast activities such as topic introductions and vocabulary word study. For post-broadcast, the manual offered review questions and additional readings. Teachers were asked to pay twenty-five cents for the guides.

[78]The KBPS story is told in the next section of this work.

The Doctor Comes to School. Developed by the State Medical Society in cooperation with the State Department of Education, the series presented round table discussion and question-and-answer on health matters for elementary grades. The topics were not new, but the process of student involvement was. Round table participants varied for each program but typically included a medical expert, two teachers and two students from various elementary schools. The appeal then, at least initially, was hearing young people ask questions on air (ORSA, Teacher Guides, 1963).

A difficult technical problem was raised by the round table discussion. In correspondence, KBPS's Patricia Green Swenson asks Morris how to best pick up the voices of multiple people participating in a discussion or talk program. Morris gave no easy answer, suggesting new equipment such as the "salt shaker" microphone which was specifically designed to pick up multiple voices. Apparently, Swenson believed no funds were available to buy new equipment (ORSA Correspondence, 1959).

Materials

Station KOAC and the ORSA's approach to the important task of creating and distributing program support materials was inconsistent at best. In the early 1940s, KOAC issued a fine looking weekly program schedule covering one semester. ORSA programs were listed in their time slots, but not described or highlighted in any way. It is unclear whether the station in later decades continued to distribute the schedule. Beginning also in the early 1940s, the ORSA prepared teacher manuals for many series. They were made available upon request for a small fee, but the whole effort appears to have been inconsistent. Not all series had a supporting teacher guide, and for those that did, the guides appeared irregularly. Furthermore, the greatest lack, at least judging from existing documentation, was that the ORSA failed to regularly issue an annual schedule of its broadcasts. Most other SOAs found it essential to publish a schedule that described the purpose of each series and listed each program in the series giving its title and broadcast time. Without an annual or semester schedule, how could Oregon's classroom teachers make lesson plans that included ORSA programs? ORSA schedules are available only for the years running from 1952 through 1958. None are available from the 1940s or the 1960s. The problem may be simply that the documentation no longer exists, but the lack fits in with the ORSA pattern of inconsistency in distributing basic support materials. The reason behind that inconsistency most likely was a shortage of funds.

Pedagogy

Neither Morris nor the ORSA directors expressed ideas about educational philosophy or about how teachers should use radio in the classroom. However, all ORSA teacher manuals included a page entitled *Some General Utilization Aids for In-School Listening.* This piece suggested how teachers could make the best use of the radio lessons. The key ideas were preparation, attentive listening, and student involvement. Prior to the broadcasts, teachers were urged to ask students to set standards for listening behavior and have paper and pencil available for note taking. The standards—to be achieved as a result of the broadcast—were to be set by the students themselves. The idea of elementary grade students setting learning goals reflected one of the dominant ideas associated with child centered learning. How frequently teachers actually carried out this recommendation is open to question (ORSA, Teacher Guides, 1963).

During the broadcasts, according to the suggestion sheet, teachers should avoid interruptions but be prepared to conduct any activities required during the broadcast. Following the broadcasts, teachers were to discuss questions raised during the broadcasts and to conduct discussions on the information, attitudes and skills that were gained and how well learning goals were achieved. All in all the list of suggestions include time-tested learning activities that good teachers everywhere would likely support whole-heartedly. They also reflect the subtle influence of progressivism and John Dewey's ideas about child centered learning.

PROGRAMMING IN THE 1950S AND 1960S

Program manager Morris avoided involvement in the day-to-day tasks associated with planning and developing ORSA programs. Presumably, that was the responsibility of the ORSA director and those who worked with her as writers or on-air talent. Concerning those tasks, little documentation exists. Consequently, while the ORSA continued to broadcast a full schedule during the 1950s, not much has been documented for that decade concerning the programming, the talent that produced it, or the educational vision that drove it. However, for the 1960s, many teacher manuals are available and from them we can gain a view of programming for the early 1960s.

Table 47 shows that by the early 1960s, the ORSA schedule was pared down and included a mix of home-grown programs and others acquired from outside sources.

TABLE 47. ORSA BROADCASTS, EARLY 1960S (ORSA, TEACHER GUIDES, 1963)

Course and Description	Grades
Adventure Time	2–6
A literature anthology series that featured narrative verse, ancient myths, legends and excerpts from novels.	
The series was an amalgam of several other series originally presented by KOAC and New York's WNYE.	
Living In Oregon:	3–6
Significant episodes in Oregon history, dramatized stories and museum visits to acquaint young people with life in early Oregon.	
Let's Find Out	1–2
Elementary science. Drama and narration acquainted primary school children with basic facts of the world around us and stimulated curiosity about science.	
Sense of the World	Not specified
Borrowed from the Minnesota School of the Air, this innovative series aroused the students' sensory perception and then presented "artistic manifestations of their aroused perceptions and urged them to express themselves in a variety of artistic formats, painting, stories, music, poetry, creative drama, gallery visits, etc. (MSA, Annual Report, 1960). The NAEB chose *A Sense of the World* for distribution to all its member stations.	
Conversational Spanish	Not specified
This foreign language series was presented through television and radio, though the radio role was supplementary. Lessons were presented on TV and practice and application lessons were broadcast only via radio.	

Two of the five programs are from other SOAs. By the early 1960s, the NAEB had made taped programs available throughout the nation.

Audience

Even though evidence points to fairly frequent audience survey activity, data regarding the results from those surveys is scarce. However, summary data and audience estimates for the years 1946 through 1949 do exist, but show some curious calculations.

Year	ORSA Estimated Audiences
1946–1947	113,085
1947–1948	138,635
1948–1949	212,283 (ORSA, Audience, 1962)

Given that Oregon's likely school population K–12 would have been roughly 270,000,[79] the estimate of 212,283 for 1948–1949, seems suspiciously high. Moreover, what caused the big jump in audience size from the previous year? Most important, how did ORSA administrators determine the number in the first place? We know that they sent mail surveys to a large number of schools asking for data on the number of teachers who used each ORSA program and the number of students who listened to each program. The data received was very useful, no doubt, but the survey required substantial effort from school personnel and consequently, response rates remained low, in the range of 13 percent to 17 percent. Apparently Jim Morris decided to project the results from the returned surveys to all schools that did not respond. His action was bound to produce inflated results because the non-responding schools undoubtedly included a higher percentage of non-users than did the responding schools.

A more realistic idea of audience size could have been obtained by taking the actual responses and adding a realistic factor, say 50 percent, to account for the users that existed among the non-responding schools. Had Morris or the ORSA used this method to estimate audience size, they would have obtained the following results:

Year	Unrealistic Audience Estimates	Realistic Audience Estimates Based on Actual Returns plus 50%
1946–1947	113,085	33,923: 12% of K–12 enrollment
1947–1948	138,635	41,591: 15% of K–12 enrollment
1948–1949	212,283	57,895: 21% of K–12 enrollment

The revised estimates, though substantially smaller, seem realistic, particularly when compared to Oregon's likely 1950 school population of 270,000.

Two factors that probably limited audience size should also be considered. The ORSA broadcast signal reached approximately 70 percent of Oregon's public schools and few ORSA programs were intended for high school students. When those factors are worked in, it seems safe to say that ORSA's audience of regular listeners probably included up to 30 percent of the potential universe of listeners. That was a significant accomplishment. Unfortunately, tallies of the responses to surveys conducted in later years are not available.

Estimates of audience size made in the late 1960s by staff of Oregon's Educational Coordinating Council seemed much more in tune with reality. That study found that the number of regular in-school listeners to ORSA programs totaled 43,880 out of a total elementary school population of 269,699. However, only 189,455 pupils attended schools that could actually receive ORSA broadcasts. Considering the latter figure, the ORSA listening audience represented approximately 23 percent of state's elementary students who could actually receive the broadcasts, a respectable number particularly considering the relatively small investment made by the state for in-school broadcasting (ORSA, Oregon, 1968).

In his memoir of his years spent at KOAC, *The Remembered Years,* James Morris (1972) reflected on the composition of the ORSA listening audience. Morris said that the rural schools made the greatest use of radio programs because "... these one and two-room buildings ... had few reference books, activities and resources as compared to the larger schools." He also offered

---

[79]School enrollments for K—12 were estimated by multiplying the state population by a factor of .18. Oregon's population in 1950 stood at 1,521,341 (Infoplease, 2006).

conjectures about what kinds of programs appealed most to individual teachers and students. "They [rural teachers] made extensive use of radio, especially those (programs) that developed student participation: art contests correlated with *Land of Make Believe* stories (and) club membership to go along with astronomy lectures" (Morris, 1972, p 84). Morris's observations were not surprising, given that until the 1960s, farming made up the preponderance of Oregon's economy and farm families most of its population. They suggest the correctness of the Wisconsin approach which focused from its beginning on the educational needs of teachers in rural schools.

Evaluation

The ORSA consistently mailed Teacher Evaluation forms to schools that ordered teacher manuals. The forms asked teachers to identify the specific programs they used, the grade level for which they were used, and number of pupils involved. It also asked teachers to give simple yes or no answers to 6 questions regarding the program. Probably the most important question asked teachers to indicate whether the program content fit into their basic curriculum or whether it was used as enrichment. Unfortunately, summaries of the responses to the evaluation questionnaires are not available.

However, in his memoir, Morris offers anecdotal evidence of the educational effectiveness of at least one program. Morris describes *Lets Sing, America* as the radio school's most popular program, attracting as many as 40,000 student listeners every week (Morris's estimate). With songs performed in studio by university music students, the radio teacher invited her tens of thousands of listeners to sing along. Echoing Wisconsin's *Let's Sing,* the Oregon version also held gatherings of thousands of pupils to sing together the songs they had learned separately in their small one and two room schools. "And everyone knew the songs in exactly the same way: same words, same tune, same tempo, same emphasis! The instruction was proven successful. It was a thrill to see these youngsters together each year" (Morris, 1972, p. 85).

Radio Sets the Table for ETV

One of the key contributions made by radio during this period was that it prepared educators and parents for the coming of educational television. Morris (1972) asserts that "teachers, administrators, parents, and politicians gathered in the forefront of the ETV [educational television] movement because [they saw] the contributions that radio had made to education in Oregon" (Morris, 1972, p. 84). When ETV was proposed for the state, parent-teacher associations and clubs quickly expressed interest. They provided a ready audience for educational television because, according to Morris, educational radio had raised their expectations.

Demise

The ORSA story followed a trajectory of strong growth in the post-war years followed by gradual decline in the late 1960s and early 1970s. In guarded language Morris (1972) attributes that decline to the school consolidation movement which combined many small separate schools into larger units that could provide more educational resources and specialized teachers. "Changes came to the School of the Air with the ground swell of school consolidation in Oregon. Those schools that made the greatest use of in-school radio now are gone and the youngsters are bused to larger schools. Today there are other media which share the teaching time in the classroom. Radio takes its place along with the other media and each assumes its own role" (Morris, 1972, p. 85).

This quote implies that by the date of publication, 1972, the ORSA was reduced to just another form of instructional aid. The available documentation for 1970 and later includes no teacher guides or program schedules. We can assume then that by 1972, KOAC continued to broadcast some programs for in-school education, but that for the most part they were taped programs obtained from outside sources or taped versions of older ORSA programs. No original programs were developed by KOAC.

In writing his memoir, *The Remembered Years,* (1972) Morris had the opportunity to give real insight into how a deep rooted educational institution got started, developed, and eventually expired. He could have provided the intimate and often fascinating details about the challenges he faced and the forces that aided and opposed the growth of educational radio in Oregon. Such a memoir would have been deeply rewarding to him and edifying to those who seek better understanding of the history of educational technology and media. Unfortunately, Morris chose to do little of that. Instead his memoir consists mainly of reminiscences about the nice people he worked with. He gives only vague hints about the struggles and passions that went into his work and made it so valuable.

In 1981, the State System of Higher Education divested itself of its radio and television stations, including both KOAC-AM and KOAC-TV. By the early 1990s these stations had became part of the public corporation, Oregon Public Broadcasting (OPB), and the administration, TV studio, and production functions were all moved to Portland. KOAC radio studios and transmitters, however, remained on the OSU campus and in the Corvallis area (KOAC Records, 1965).

Summary

Unlike schools of the air that flourished in Minnesota and Wisconsin, the ORSA never developed an identity separate from its broadcasting station, KOAC. In-school broadcasting was seen as another service provided by the station. In fact some sources referred to the ORSA as the *KOAC School of the Air.* Initially the station's mission was to serve the information needs of Oregon's agriculture communities. Weather, news, farm markets, and home making became staples of KOAC's broadcast day. Broadcasting for the schools began almost incidentally, but once KOAC station management realized that in-school educational programs fit the station's mission perfectly, they quickly established a dedicated school of the air.

From the late 1930s to the mid–1940s the ORSA had five directors; each brought special talents and new ideas. The first ORSA director, Andrew Hull, used his multiple talents to expand programming from a few per week to a dozen or more. Unfortunately, he tailored too many to the needs of high school teachers, rather than to the more receptive elementary teachers. Subsequent directors quickly shifted focus by filling the schedule with programs for the elementary grades. Another director, Betty Jo Bouska, built a network of teachers in the schools who supported and explained ORSA programs to their colleagues. That network helped overcome one of the ORSA's deficiencies, namely the lack of semester schedules dedicated to the in-school series. By the end of World War II, the ORSA offered fewer program series than it had before the war, but the post-war schedule was better focused on the needs of elementary school teachers. Following the War, James Morris served as ORSA director for several years and then as KOAC program manager until the early 1960s.

Possibly, the frequent management changes impeded important foundation building efforts. At any rate throughout its years, the ORSA remained under funded even by the lean standards of public broadcasting. In later years the ORSA seemed to rely more and more on taped programming from outside sources and less on developing original programs or live broadcasting.

Audience studies conducted during the 1940s and then again during the 1960s found that the school attracted perhaps 20 percent to 25 percent of the elementary school children who lived within the broadcast area. However, fully 30 percent of Oregon's school children lived beyond KOAC's broadcast range. The fact that the state never built broadcast facilities to service children in isolated areas— presumably the ones most in need of additional educational resources—

suggests a lack of commitment on the part of KOAC managers or the state's educational establishment.

KOAC became known as "Oregon's Own Station," but in-school instruction, though important, never was touted as the station's primary purpose. Owned by the state department of higher education, administered by the University Extension Division, KOAC served the needs of all of Oregon's public colleges and universities and other state entities as well. That arrangement enabled the station to call on resources of other state schools and agencies, but in trying to serve so many different constituencies, KOAC may also have diluted its limited resources. As a result, the ORSA never became as well entrenched in the state's educational culture as did some other state-based SOAs.

The *Prairie Farmer*, WLS's *School Time*

Spurred by the terrible polio epidemic that struck Chicago in 1937 and forced the schools to close, Burridge Butler, president of Chicago's WLS radio, placed the station at the service of Chicago's school officials (Atkinson, 1942b). (The story of how the polio epidemic rekindled the Chicago Public School Board's interest in education by radio is told in Section IV). Within a month, the epidemic was sufficiently under control and the schools reopened, but Butler saw such great value in education by radio that he decided to expand and continue his station's broadcasts to the school. The new service would be called *School Time*. Butler had in mind a radio education service not for the school children of Chicago but for children in the myriad small towns and rural areas where WLS had great appeal.

Originally owned by Sears, WLS had been purchased around 1930 by *Prairie Farmer* publications.[80] A clear channel station, WLS became known as The Voice of the Prairie serving the rural Midwest; its *National Barn Dance* had become one of the most popular programs in the WLS broadcast area. Providing educational service to rural children then was a natural outgrowth of the station's mission. Butler stated that *School Time* would provide rural schools with the educational resources and advantages that traditionally had been available only to schools in large cities (Atkinson, 1942b). The station's interest in educational broadcasting was not unprecedented. Back in 1924, WLS broadcast the first SOA in the nation, Ben Darrow's *The Little Red School House*. Fifteen years later, *School Time* represented a unique event in American broadcasting; it was the only school of the air operated entirely by an independent, privately owned radio station.

Butler launched *School Time* in February 1937 with John Baker as Director, but Butler soon realized that the position required someone with a background in education. In fall of 1938, he appointed Harriet Hester the new director of *School Time*. A graduate of Northern Illinois Teachers College and a graduate student at Northwestern University, Hester had made an intensive study of rural school music education. Her work led to an educational series broadcast by station WROK in Rockford, Illinois that attracted the attention of educators nationally. She had described the broadcasts as being designed to "enrich music lessons and to stimulate purposeful learning activity" (Atkinson, 1942b, p. 54).

Programs

By 1940, *School Time* provided one 15 minute program per day, five days a week, a schedule that continued at least until 1945. Table 48 shows some of the series presented in the years 1941 and 1942.

[80]*Prairie Farmer*, an agrarian bulletin, began as a newspaper in 1841. It was a popular agricultural magazine in the late 1920s when it bought its radio arm, WLS, which emphasized farm news, livestock reports, and country music from its inception. For the next quarter century, the editor of *Prairie Farmer* would also serve as the president of WLS.

TABLE 48. SCHOOL TIME BROADCASTS, 1941—1942 (LAWSON, 1942)

Course and Description	Day
Let's Sing	Monday

Let's Sing   **Monday**
  Harriet Hester led this music appreciation series in front of a live studio audience made up primarily of Chicago school children. She started each lesson with a fundamental point about music and then led the group in songs. She encouraged listening students to sing along at their desks.
  Copies of the songs, games and drills appeared a week in advance in the *Prairie Farmer*.

Our World Today   **Tuesday**
  Julian Bentley conducted current events discussions in studio with four eighth grade pupils.

Rainbow's End   **Wednesday**
  The subject for this ambitious series included fine arts, especially painting. Each program focused on a painting whose original hung in the Art Institute of Chicago. Postcard sized copies of all the paintings covered in the lessons were made available through *School Time* for $1.10. One wonders how many rural teachers ordered the postcards.

The Adventures of Polly and Pat   **Thursday**
  A story period for lower elementary grades. Stories dealt with nature study, citizenship, character training and neighborhood helpers. Hester read the stories, but also encouraged listening students to take part through singing, rhythm activities and games.

America's Friends   **Friday**
  A travel series that acquainted students with the cultures and economies of neighboring countries. John Strohm, Assistant Editor of *Prairie Farmer*, focused on South America where he had traveled extensively. Each program featured a dramatization of life in a South American country. Resource material selected by the Illinois State Library was made available to participating schools. The series alternative with *The Bookworm Club*.

The Bookworm Club   **Friday**
  Dramatized reviews of "good books," the series was intended for 5th through 8th graders. We can assume that classroom teachers were encouraged to have their children read the books, but what's not clear is whether WLS helped make the books available.

School Time topics covered basic music, current events, fine art, stories and participation, cultural geography, and literature.

WLS was a highly successful commercial station, and it made rich resources available for Hester's operation. Hester said that a staff of eight worked on *School Time* program development and production (Atkinson, 1942b). If true, it demonstrated a substantial investment in educational programming for the schools. The WLS Studio Orchestra participated in the musical features, and all the dramatized segments were produced using professional voices, a feature well beyond the budgets of state-owned SOAs. Hester claimed that among other benefits, *School Time* introduced other cultures to isolated rural students.

Supplemental Material

Teacher manuals for individual series were first issued in the spring of 1939; it's likely that that practice continued throughout the school's operations. As mentioned above, the station made some additional resource materials available such as the postcard pictures for the art appreciation series, *Rainbow's End*. It also cooperated with the Illinois State Library to make appropriate reading resources available. It is unclear whether *School Time* distributed a regular program schedule. Such schedules made it possible for classroom teachers to plan to use radio well in advance.

Audience

Atkinson (1942b) cites WLS figures that show that enrollment for *School Time* climbed from 412 schools in 1937 to 5,400 schools by 1940–41 in the WLS broadcast area, which included parts of Illinois, Wisconsin, Indiana, and Michigan. By 1942, the station claimed 870,000 listeners in 24,000 classrooms (Atkinson, 1942b). That estimate exceeded estimates from any other SOAs excepting the *American School of the Air*. However, neither WLS nor Atkinson offered any supporting data, nor did they describe the methods used to make the audience estimates. While it is unknown how the *School Time* attendance figures were developed, most likely they were inflated and the estimates unreliable. Probably WLS used the tabulation process that Cuban (1986) criticized, namely, if one teacher in a school used radio, then all teachers were counted as users and all pupils as listeners. Whatever the case was, the data required to make a sound evaluation of *School Time's* audience are unavailable. Perhaps rather than trying to determine the exact size of the *School Time* audience, it would be more fruitful to discover what impact the broadcasts had on the school children and teachers who did tune in.

Demise

Little documentation is available about *School Time's* operation after the early 1940s. It is known that by 1944, the director was Jerry Weller, and that the station rebroadcast some CBS educational programs for the school.

Summary

WLS managers devoted substantial resources to developing *School Time*. They hired a full-time director, Harriet Hester; donated between 15 and 30 minutes of air time per day, five days a week; provided creative and production services; and printed and distributed support materials. The only thing lacking was direct connection with educational administrators in the many rural schools that *School Time* was designed to serve. While our knowledge of WLS's unique *School Time* is limited, enough is known to conclude that the station's decision to operate a school of the air entirely on its own reflected a market environment that has long since passed, an era when an individual business owner could and did indulge a desire to mix business with social responsibility. Clearly, *School Time* helped WLS maintain its strong ties to listeners throughout the rural Midwest, but probably it went well beyond what was actually necessary for the station's financial health. By broadcasting an educational series intended for classroom use, station managers probably did succeed to some degree in providing rural students with some of the rich resources available to urban students. Feedback from the Wisconsin School of the Air and other state-based SOAs suggests that those rural students often were more appreciative of those resources than were their urban cousins.

Summary: State-Based Schools of the Air

While the effort to establish a publicly supported radio school of the air foundered at the national level, it flourished at least in six states where they operated separately, but in many ways similarly. All six SOAs developed semester long program series synchronized with the typical

TABLE 49. SUMMARY OF FINDINGS: STATE-BASED SCHOOLS OF THE AIR

FINDINGS	OSA	WSA	MSA	TSA	ORSA	ESSA
Longevity (Approx.)	28 years 1929–1937 and 1940–1960	44 years 1931–1976	41 years 1938–1979?	20 years 1940–1960	Approximately 40 years 1933–1970s	20 years 1948–1968
Major Personalities	Ben Darrow, founder and director 1929–1937 Margaret Tyler, director of revived OSA	- Director, Harold McCarty - Radio teachers: - Edgar Gordon - Fanny Steve -Jim Schwalbach -Maureen Applegate -Wakelin McNeel	- Barton Paulu, director of KUOM - E. W. Ziebarth, director of MSA 1938–1946 - Betty T. Girling, director of MSA, 1946 to 1978	Ben Darrow - created the development plan - Hill (1997) said that the TSA lacked a champion	- Alexander Hull, 1935—1939 - James Morris, KOAC station manager	Paul C. Reed, Steering Committee Chairman, 1948 to 1964 ESSA Executive Secretaries: - Eugene Foster, 1948–1956 - James Fellows, 1956–1962 - Coy Ludwig, 1962–1966
Supporting Institutions	- OSU and Ohio legislature - Crosley Broadcasting Co. - Approval from state educational agencies	UW - State Board of Education - Cooperation from various state agencies - Madison, WI public schools	- U of Minnesota - UM General Extension Division	- Origins: NCRE and Payne Fund - Administration: State Department of Education - Funding: Texas legislature - Operations: four Texas universities	Developed as a service of the General Extension Division of Oregon's higher education system.	Local school districts mostly in central New York state
Broadcast Facility	- WLW, owned by Crosley Broadcasting - The OSU station	- UW station WHA - Wisconsin's FM Network	UM radio station KUOM	Texas Quality Network (CBS affiliated stations)	KOAC, owned by the state and administrated by the General Extension Div.	Network of local privately owned FM radio stations

Educational Philosophy	- Master teachers and great minds deliver appropriate curricula and motivate students to learn - Education must be based on "actuality" rather than abstraction	- Radio serves the curricular needs of rural teachers - The "Wisconsin Idea" - Progressivism - Radio is integral part of Wisconsin educational service	- Ziebarth stressed passive listening, and no activity during broadcasts - Girling urged teachers to develop interest through pre- and post-broadcast discussion	- Learner-centered instruction situating in a Texas culture and economy - For literature programs, the goal was to nurture enjoyment of reading	- Students need to be engaged in setting standards for listening behavior and learning - Extensive interaction between students and teacher	- Curriculum enrichment and experiences that otherwise might not be available
School Goals	- Expose students to great minds - Expand student awareness - Demonstrate radio's educational power - Equity in education - De-emphasize drill and practice	- Develop student-centered curricula featuring active learning - Expand rural school curriculum - Overcome rural isolation - Make WSA an integral part of K–8 education in Wisconsin	- Provide classroom enrichment and supplement - Meet the curricula needs of different school districts: urban, suburban, rural, and parochial	- Supplement, enrich, vitalize classroom teaching - Increase knowledge - Cultivate appreciation and taste - Inspire social ideals that build constructive citizenship	Encourage student participation in learning	- Bring to the classroom experiences, experts, and up-to-date information on issues of democracy - Serve rural schools - Use local resources where possible to create programming
Instruction Methods	Pioneered radio instruction techniques: - Exposition: "plain talk" and dialogue - Imaginative presentations, storytelling and drama	- Extensive use of direct teaching, dramatization, and storytelling - Emphasis on active learning - Extensive extracurricular activities	- Drama and storytelling - Creative dramatics, Girling introduced technique of improvisation into elementary classrooms	- Utilized drama that featured local Texas characters in familiar surroundings - Invited listener to identify with main characters	Drama and story telling	No documentation

TABLE 49 (continued)

FINDINGS	OSA	WSA	MSA	TSA	ORSA	ESSA
	- Direct teaching - Music and sounds to stir the imagination	- Statewide programs and contests				- Weekly bulletins that listed and described programs - Semester schedules, problematic
Support Materials	- Combined teachers manual for all programs	- Semester program schedules - A teachers manual for each program - Student guides for a few programs	- Annual bulletins provided semester schedules - Teacher manuals for most programs - Student guides for a few programs	- Combined teachers manual and classroom guides provided for most programs	- Inconsistent approach - Semester schedule offered irregularly - Teacher guides available for some programs	
Estimated Audience —% of Potential Universe	- Btw 50,000 and 100,000, 1935 - 150,000, 1950 - Btw 8% and 10% of the state enrollment, K-12 - Weak supporting data	- Highpoint, 308,000, 1968 - 47% of state enrollment K-8 - Strong supporting data	- 95,000, 1942 - 150,000, 1952, approx 28% of state enrollment - 45,000, mid 1960s, (13%) - Strong supporting data	- 260,000, mid 1940s - Approx. 17% of state enrollment, K-12 - Weak supporting data	- 58,000, 1949–1950 - 43,880, 1967–68 - Claim 23% of elementary students in listening area	- 300,000 claimed early 1950s. Later surveys revealed around 50,000–75,000 - Enrollment data for service area not available - Weak supporting data
Evaluations and Surveys Conducted	- All evaluations and surveys were internal: - Daily Report forms from select group of teachers - Year-end listener surveys - Annual reports	- External and internal studies: - Wisconsin Research Project in School Broadcasting[81] - Frequent mail surveys to participating schools	- No documentation available on summary evaluations - Classroom visits conducted in the 1950s, but results not reported	- Listening committees critiqued programs - No documentation of formative evaluations or classroom visits	Teacher evaluation forms mailed regularly to schools that ordered teacher manuals. No reports on results	- Frequent surveys made to determine teacher and principal opinions about programs - Information on educational effectiveness was not gathered

[81]See (Barr et al., 1942)

	- Field visits to schools - Contemporary studies of specific programs					
Community-Based Learning	No documentation of OSA's community-based learning programs	Extensive: - Regional and statewide singing festivals and art exhibits - Statewide programs to encourage conservation - Statewide contests in writing and science	No documentation available on community-based learning programs	No documentation available on community-based learning programs	In his memoirs, Morris refers to singing festivals conducted for *Let's Sing* students	No documentation available on community-based learning programs
Impact	- Established first state-supported SOA - Introduced many methods of radio instruction - Set model for education by radio	- Supplemented school curricula throughout Wisconsin - Set reading curricula for some schools - Created communities of learners - Influenced art education in Wisconsin - Got students involved in conservation - Left a legacy of endearment	Established radio instruction as a regular part of rural elementary curricula - Helped infuse Minnesota geography, history and environment into state curricula - Encouraged widespread use of audio-taped programs in schools	- Developed a community of citizens, agencies and universities involved in education by radio - Established radio instruction as a regular part of rural elementary curricula - Encouraged widespread use of audio-taped programs in schools	- Established radio instruction as a regular part of rural elementary curricula - Delivered much of the curriculum for Oregon's pioneer history - Scant documentation	- Established radio instruction as a regular part of rural elementary curricula - Created a community of school districts managing the integration of technology into the schools - Scant documentation

TABLE 49 (*continued*)

FINDINGS	OSA	WSA	MSA	TSA	ORSA	ESSA
Demise	- Initial demise caused by political retaliation against Darrow - Final demise, unclear	- Left a legacy of endearment - School consolidation and decline of rural isolation - UW and station WHA slowly withdrew support for in-school broadcasting	- UM admin. may have wanted to withdraw from in-school broadcasting - Declining usage	- Lack of a champion to attract support - Lack of funds to update programs - Educational TV diverted interest away from radio - Lack of support from a university or state-owned radio station	Morris said that the school consolidation movement lessened demand for ORSA programs	- Members of the FM broadcast network discontinued contributing free air time - Rise of ETV

school calendar. They quickly adopted instructional methods that had proved most effective with radio, namely drama, dialog, and story telling, augmented by music and sound effects. Surprisingly, many of their radio lessons asked the listening students to perform learning activities during the broadcasts. All SOAs distributed program support materials throughout their listening areas including semester broadcast schedules, teacher guides for each series, and student guides for some programs. Five of the six were birthed by universities or a university extension division.[82] Universities provided lean but sufficient support, enabling the SOAs to establish roots to one degree or another in their state's educational communities. Even in the case of the ESSA which did not arise within the confines of a state supported university, approval from the state University system gave it credibility among New York teachers. WLS *School Time* obviously represents a unique experience.

Despite the similar background, the state-based SOAs' programming and educational philosophy varied substantially from one another. Furthermore, each SOA experienced varying degrees of success in terms of audience, longevity, innovative educational production and educational impact on the state's children. Table 49 summarizes SOA operations, characteristics, and accomplishments. Below is a brief discussion of similarities and differences and discussion of factors that may have accounted for differences.

The summary of findings shows that three state-based schools of the air broadcast instructional programs for at least 40 years. Such longevity attests to the fact that in those states education by radio enjoyed strong support from educators, universities, legislators and parents. But what accounted for the sharp differences in longevity demonstrated by the WSA, MSA and ORSA, which operated forty years or more and the TSA and ESSA, which had comparatively shorter life spans?[83] Two factors may explain the differences, university support and a close relationship with a university owned or state owned radio station. The university connection provided SOAs with a lean but secure foundation of funding, a broadcast facility, and access to low-cost or volunteer talent and expertise. The university budgets included salaries for a school director, full and or part-time creative staff, and a reliable broadcast facility. With the broadcast facility assured, SOA directors could concentrate on developing and broadcasting programs that best met the needs of teachers and communities in their broadcast areas.

Equally important, the university connections bestowed legitimacy on the SOAs as bona fide members of each state's educational community and therefore deserving of respect from teachers, administrators, and parents. Additionally, the WSA, MSA, and ORSA operated as divisions of a state or university owned radio station, which provided ample free air time and valuable technical support. The TSA, on the other hand, while it worked cooperatively with several universities, was forced to depend on commercial radio stations for its broadcasts. When those stations lost interest in educational radio, the TSA faded. The ESSA enjoyed neither a connection to a state university nor a close relationship with a state owned radio station, deficiencies that largely explain why the ESSA experienced a relatively short operating life.

In Wisconsin radio teachers emerged as popular figures in their own right. Wakelin McNeel (*Ranger Mac*), Jim Schwalbach (*Let's Draw*), Pop Gordon (*Let's Sing*), Maureen Applegate (*Book Trails*) and Fannie Steve (*Rhythm and Games*) all become well-known personalities among elementary teachers, school children, and their parents, particularly in rural Wisconsin.

Significant variation existed among SOAs in their education philosophy and their ideas about how to use radio for instruction. Those differences affected programming in several ways. The OSA emphasized radio's role in bringing the master teacher and the authoritative voice to

[82]While the Texas School of the Air was supported by the state legislature, volunteers from four Texas universities performed most of the curriculum planning, script writing, and program production.

[83]As documented earlier, OSA's longevity was affected by an atypical political conflict that arose between its director, Ben Darrow, and the then governor of Ohio.

the classroom. They valued radio's ability to expose students directly to prominent artists, experts, and political leaders. Consequently SOA programming highlighted a teacher-centered curriculum, content mastery, and the thoughts and experiences of prominent experts, leaders and artists.

On the other hand the WSA, MSA, and TSA viewed radio as a means to engage students by presenting familiar contexts and building on their interests. This view resulted in programming that was more student-centered — programs tended to feature characters with whom students could identify, characters who either possessed knowledge or were discovering it on their own. In particular, the WSA and TSA programs down-played experts and authority figures and focused instead on developing the student's talents and opinions. The WSA, MSA, and ORSA also emphasized student involvement in extra curricular learning.

ESSA programming, though hard to characterize, seemed to incorporate an eclectic approach that included many "home grown" productions such as *Animal Worlds* and *Science Adventure* with high quality production values from outside such as WNYE's *Tales from the Four Winds*.

Another important distinction among SOAs arose in regard to whether radio should be used for curricular enrichment or supplement. Should the radio lesson enhance the classroom lesson or deliver it? Few state-based SOAs took the latter position, but significant exceptions occurred. For example with the subject of state history, because adequate learning resources were unavailable, state educators often saw radio as the low-cost alternative for delivering content and structuring learning activities. All state-based SOAs offered program series on state history, and the ORSA and the MSA, in particular, made great use of radio to deliver curricula on state history, geography and economy. Early supporters of the WSA stated directly that radio should be used to fill in the gaps in rural curricula caused by the limitations of one teacher having to teach multiple grade levels. The local teachers focused on the three "Rs" but were less qualified to teach music, art, literature, or science. In these subjects, the WSA contributed most to the curricular resources available in rural areas.

State-based SOAs also differed in their use of direct instruction. In that method, students in the classroom responded directly in real time to broadcast instruction. Wisconsin led in the use of direct instruction, with programs such as *Let's Draw, Let's Sing, Young Experimenters,* and *Rhythm and Games.* Other state-based SOAs used direct instruction, but to a smaller extent.

State-based SOAs varied substantially in the size of their listening audiences as a percentage of their total potential audience, which is defined as all students who attended schools within each SOA's broadcast area. Table 50 compares the enrollment estimates and percent of potential audience at each SOA in its peak years.

TABLE 50. HIGH POINT AUDIENCE ESTIMATES FOR STATE-BASED SOAS

School of the Air	Enrollment estimates*	Year highest enrollment	% of potential audience§
Ohio School of the Air (SA)	100,000	1937, and the 1950s	8% — 10%
Wisconsin SA	308,000	1968–69	47%
Texas SA	260,000	1945–1946	17%
Empire State FM SA	300,000 claimed	1952	Insufficient documentation
Oregon SA	58,000	1949?	21%
Minnesota SA	95,000	1942	20%
TOTAL	1,121,000		22%

*Enrollment figures are based on credible estimates from the SOAs, the WSA being the most credible and ESSA's the least.

§Represents the enrollment estimates as a percentage of the state's school population.

Wisconsin's penetration of the student audience reached near 50 percent, a rousing success by any estimate. Three others hovered in the 20 percent area. The ESSA's numbers are doubtful. What accounted for Wisconsin's success? A number of likely factors have been documented but special credit should go to the state's FM network and to the fact that the WSA administrators focused relentlessly on weaving radio instruction into the fabric of Wisconsin's educational community.

Impact and Accomplishments

In their respective states, how did state-based SOAs affect education and the use of educational technology and media in the schools? This study doesn't definitively answer these questions, but it does shed some light on them.

State-based SOAs probably affected education in rural areas most. The point should not be over stated, many urban schools tuned in, but during the heyday of radio, in almost all the U S a substantial portion of school aged children attended one room and state-graded rural schools. Ben Darrow had predicted that radio would bring the world into the class room (Darrow, 1932). His prediction did come to pass, at least for children isolated in rural communities or in provincial urban enclaves. As one former student of a one-room rural Wisconsin school said of the WSA, "… it gave us a feeling of being connected to all the other schools, and in a way of being up to date with the schools in town" (M. Michie Udall, personal communication, December 29, 2003).

Not surprising then for rural schools in the six states covered in this work, radio became the most regular source of supplementary educational resources. The widespread use of audio tape in schools certainly got its original impetus from radio. It also paved the way for educational television and computers in the classrooms.

State-based SOAs customized their programs to reflect state history, culture, economy, and the state curricula, something the national SOAs were unable to do. Several SOAs, particularly the WSA and MSA, held large scale regional and state-based learning events for their music, art, and conservation students. Out of these events grew a sense of community among otherwise isolated school children and teachers, again an accomplishment beyond the reach of national SOAs.

In most areas shown in Table 50, the WSA stands out among the others particularly in terms of longevity, audience, building communities of learners, and educational impact. The most important factor in Wisconsin's success was it original vision of serving the curricular needs of rural teachers. From the very beginning, the WSA set as its goal to help rural teachers by providing the educational resources they lacked, by filling the gaps in local school curricula. This focus elevated radio in Wisconsin to that status of a vital component of local education, a status beyond the reach of those SOAs that saw radio only as a tool for curricular enrichment.

Another contributing factor to its success was the role the WSA played in fulfilling the "Wisconsin Idea," the University's vision of serving all the state's citizens. That vision seems to have prompted administrators to promote the WSA across the state. The best example of their inclusive effort was the role they played in establishing the state-wide FM network. As the network reached into new communities, WSA administrators and staff promoted the WSA to local school boards. By the mid–1950s, the WSA had become an integral part of Wisconsin's educational family. Of the six states that developed SOAs, only Wisconsin developed a state-wide radio network dedicated to education and in-school broadcasting. In many ways the WSA provided lessons and perhaps a model for technology integration into the schools.

SECTION IV

Local Schools of the Air

In addition to those at the national and state level, successful schools of the air (SOAs) were developed by nine local school boards (Atkinson, 1942c; Woelfel and Tyler, 1945). This section covers the local SOAs for which adequate documentation exists, including Cleveland; Chicago; Rochester; and Portland, Oregon, and four others for which sparse documentation allows only limited treatment, Alameda, California; Detroit; New York City; and Akron, Ohio.

While a few school systems developed effective SOAs using donated time from commercial AM stations, the dramatic growth of local SOAs occurred in the 1940s after the Federal Communications Commission (FCC) allocated part of the FM band for educational use. That action enabled school systems to own and operate radio stations. Starting in 1938 and finishing in 1945, the FCC set aside 20 FM channels between 88 and 92 megacycles (Field, 1991, p. 118; Saettler, 1990). Those 20 channels would have enabled approximately 800 educational stations to operate nationally (Field, 1991, p. 118), but far fewer than 800 state and local institutions took advantage of the opportunity. In fact, FCC Commissioner Wayne Coy complained in 1948 that educators had not rushed to take advantage of the opportunities created by the FM set aside. Nevertheless, by 1948, 19 new educational FM stations were operating, 24 more had received construction permits, and at that time another 9 applications were pending (Dunham, 1948, p. 2). One possibly negative consequence of the FM set aside for educational purposes emerged; it may have encouraged commercial AM stations to withdraw from in-school broadcasting. As day-time radio became more lucrative during the 1940s, the FM set-aside gave some commercial station managers an easy out. They could say their services were no longer needed.

FM radio offered educators a number of advantages over AM. With AM, atmospheric disturbances, electric storms, steel structures, and electric motors in buildings interfered with reception, causing distortion, static, and high-pitched whining. None of these problems occurred with FM broadcasting. Also from the lowest base to the highest treble, FM provided greater sound fidelity than AM signals, making FM better for music education. Another consideration, AM radios tended to disappear. Theft was a continuing problem with school based AM radios because they could be used at home. Since little consumer oriented broadcasting existed on the FM dial during the early years, FM radios were safe in the schools for a while. Finally, because FM was new, no big operation yet existed.

Substantial advantages accrued to schools from owning the radio station. Most important were stability and regularity. Time slots donated by commercial AM operators often changed abruptly due to the shifting desires of advertisers or to special events, such as baseball games. Commercial stations frequently offered schools different times on different days. For example a commercial station might make air time available at 10:00 A.M. on Monday, 2:00 P.M. on Tuesday, 11:00 A.M. on Wednesday, etc. Such irregularity discouraged teachers from becoming regular users of radio. By owning and operating its own FM radio station, a local school district gained the flexibility and control it needed to set a broadcast schedule based on teacher or school preferences and stick to it.

What ever the local SOAs may have lacked in resources, staff, and production values in comparison to the state and network SOAs, they made up for in their ability to synchronize radio instruction with the local school curricula. They could tailor a program series or individual lesson to specific courses and grades even to the topic being covered during a particular week. Cleveland and Rochester SOAs presented the best examples of radio instruction becoming a regular part of the school program, particularly in math and science. Also local SOAs frequently developed programs in cooperation with other community-based educational institutions such as museums and libraries.

Compared to other forms of educational technology available at that time, radio enabled educators to get large numbers of students active in applied learning, but only the local SOAs took advantage of that potential. At the local level, thousands of students participated regularly in the creative and technical aspects of radio broadcasting including production, performing, announcing, and, to a limited extent, script writing. Furthermore, local teachers and subject matter experts often planned, wrote and produced the local SOA radio programs.

Local school administrators all had to make one crucial decision early-on that affected the development of their SOAs for years after. That was whether radio should be used for lesson enrichment or to supplement various curricula. When they chose the enrichment options, then little curriculum changes were required, teachers could pick and choose from offerings as they saw fit. The more ambitious path of supplementing curricula required local radio educators to design and develop radio lessons that delivered a part of curricula. Often this required revising the school curricula (Tyler, 1967, pp. 25–30).

During the 1950s there began a movement toward the use of taped programs and fewer live broadcasts. A variety of motives drove this movement, one being tapes enabled local stations to repeat programs during the week so more teachers could take advantage. There were two tracks to the tape movement, one was where state or local educational agencies taped the state or local SOA programs and made them available to teachers who used those SOAs. The other was where the state or local SOAs borrowed taped programs from other stations through national agencies such as the National Association of Educational Broadcasters (NAEB), which had developed a cooperative tape library that made high quality productions available on tape to all member stations at low cost. The appeal of that is understandable. Small stations with limited budgets could acquire high quality programs from better funded stations such as New York City's WNYE. In the later years of the in-school broadcasting movement, tape programs from outside agencies provided clear benefits but also presented a problem for in-school broadcasting. They enabled local stations to broadcast a broad range of professional sounding programs, but they also encouraged local stations to stop developing original programs and in some ways led to a loss of their local connection.

Cleveland School of the Air

Building on the legacy of Alice Keith's experimental work with broadcasting music instruction for the schools,[1] the Cleveland school board developed a school of the air that became the bench mark example for the integration of educational technology into the curriculum and the model against which all other local schools of the air (SOAs) would be compared. Operated continuously from 1928 to 1978, its programs ranged from stories illustrated with "lantern slides"

---

[1]Alice Keith's work developing music instruction by radio for use in the Cleveland school system is described in Section II of this work.

to high school radio workshops in which hundreds of high school students annually participated in developing and presenting radio programs.

The Cleveland School of the Air (CSA)[2] introduced radio as a regular tool of classroom instruction, "similar to the textbook, and used for direct teaching" (Tyler, 1967, p. 31). While other SOAs often talked about radio being an "assistant teacher" or a supplement to the teacher, CSA educators spoke about radio being an integral part of the school curriculum, a vehicle for achieving learning objectives. Cleveland's radio educators also were dedicated to the ideal of using radio for teacher training. By introducing the master teacher into the classroom, radio would provide exemplary instruction that classroom teachers could emulate (Stewart, 1939; Atkinson, 1942c).

The CSA operated a two track system, one track for the elementary grades and the other for junior and senior high schools. The elementary track developed radio courses fully integrated into the curriculum while the latter offered supplementary and enrichment programs. Woelfel and Tyler (1945) described Cleveland's radio programs for the elementary grades as representing ..."the greatest use of radio as curricular content and teaching methodology made by any school system in the United States" (p. 91). Cleveland schools received praise for adjusting their curriculum, teaching processes and even administrative practices to take full advantage of radio as a learning aid (Levenson, 1945).

Finally, the CSA operated one of the few AM radio stations in the country to be licensed by the Federal Communications Commission (FCC) for educational non-commercial broadcasting and devoted to in-school broadcasting (Report of Activities, 1942). By operating its own station, the CSA was able to expand its schedule of instructional programming from less than an hour a day to eight hours a day.

Origins

Shortly after Keith left Cleveland to help promote Damrosch's Music Appreciation Hour, Dr. Ida Black started an experiment teaching arithmetic to second and third graders via radio. She initiated a formal and rigorous approach to radio program development that came to characterize all of the CSA's work. Planned and developed by a master teacher and subject matter expert, the arithmetic programs received a pilot test in a school especially equipped for radio experimentation (Atkinson, 1942c). The tests involved a matched group comparison study; one group listened to the radio instruction, the other did not, both groups received mimeographed worksheets covering the lessons. Positive test results encouraged school administrators to extend the radio experiment to other subject areas.

Within a few years, the CSA offered instruction to Cleveland elementary students in music, geography, elementary science, and English in a very focused and unique matter. Wishing to avoid overwhelming teachers and students with too many programs, the CSA offered one lesson per week, one grade per year. New series were introduced gradually and old ones after a while dropped. Table 51 shows the process of how new series were introduced and then retired over an eight year period.

TABLE 51. CSA RADIO CURRICULUM, 1929 TO 1938 (WOELFEL AND TYLER, 1945)

School Year	Courses	School Year	Courses
1929–30	2A Arithmetic 3B Arithmetic	1934–35	6B-A English 4B-A Geography

[2]From the time it began broadcasting from its station WBOE in 1938, the CSA announced itself "Your Pioneer School Station." I use the term Cleveland School of the Air (CSA) to remain consistent with other schools of air covered in this document.

	3B Arithmetic		4B-A Geography
			3B-A Music
			5b-A Elementary Science
			1B-A Music
1931–32	2A Arithmetic	1935–36	3B-A English
	3B-A Arithmetic		5B-A Geography
	4B Arithmetic		4B-A Music
	3B-A Music		6B-A Science
	7B-A Social Science		2B-A Music
1932–33	3A Arithmetic	1936–37	4B-A English
	4B Arithmetic		6B-A Geography
	4B-A Music		5B-A Music
	3B-A Social Science		3B-A Science
	5B Geography		1B-A Music
	1–6 Elementary Literature		
1933–34	5B-A Music	1937–38	5B-A English
	5A-6B Geography		6B-A Geography
	6B-A Elementary Science		3B-A Music
	6A English		4B-A Science
	7B Social Science		Upper Elementary Safety
	1–6 Elementary Literature		2B-A Music

Table 51 shows that the CSA developed radio instruction to support specific courses being offered in the schools, with each course designed for just one grade level. This approach differed markedly from the approach used by the network and most other state-based SOAs, which typically offered general programs spanning several grade levels. CSA administrators insisted that participation was voluntary. Elementary teachers could choose whether to teach a topic with or without radio, and participating teachers received no special recognition (Potter, 1942; Levenson, 1945).

By the late 1930s the procedures for developing new programs had evolved into a formal process. Unlike other big city SOAs, the CSA employed no specialists to write and produce scripts, but still conducted a rigorous development process. For the elementary division, the school board equipped its 12 curriculum centers or lab schools to function as laboratories for new radio lessons. There, school-based subject supervisors worked with master teachers to plan and write program scripts. The development personnel varied with the program schedule. For example, the development of a science series included a part-time subject matter supervisor, one full time science teacher, and two part-time science teachers. Teachers were selected for their teaching excellence and their flair for writing; some who possessed good speaking skills were asked to serve as the on-air radio teacher. Administrators freed selected teachers from classroom duties and hired substitute teachers to conduct their classes. In that sense the Cleveland schools paid for script development. After testing, the radio scripts were revised and finalized. Broadcast series for use in junior and senior high were developed later when the CSA operated from its own station, allowing it to overcome the barrier of rigid class schedules that didn't coincide with the broadcasts (Potter, 1942).

Support Materials

No other SOA made such extensive use of radio lesson support materials, and chief among them was the teacher guide. At the beginning of each semester, the CSA distributed a mimeographed teacher guide for every program to each participating school or classroom.[3] The guides ranged from a single page outline to a comprehensive booklet (Radio Activities, 1943). Like other SOA guides, the CSA guides gave the schedule of programs for the semester, listed materials needed to participate in the radio series, listed directions for using learning support materials such as slides, listed the classroom teacher's responsibilities, and suggested follow-up activities. Unlike other SOAs, the CSA guides for most elementary grade programs also included detailed information for conducting each lesson within the series. The guides specified lesson content and objectives, what to write on the blackboard, how to handle visual materials, and activities to be conducted during and after the broadcast. In many ways, the CSA guides served as a nearly complete lesson plan (Potter, 1942). The only missing part was the radio script.

CSA administrators recognized that the purely auditory approach had certain limitations so they designed many radio lessons as audio/visual education experiences. Participating teachers received an enormous amount of visual aids, carefully coordinated with each lesson. Chief among these were "glass lantern slides" and charts typically used in science and geography series, but in others as well. Prepared by the Board's "Education Museum," the slides and charts were assembled in box sets for the specific courses and grades, duplicated, and sent to all participating schools prior to the broadcasts. Often during the broadcasts, the classroom teacher or a trained student showed the lantern slides on directions from the radio teacher. Slide projectors were also made available to participating schools.

Preparation of the boxed sets of slides was an enormous undertaking. For the 1942–43 year, Education Museum workers copied and boxed over 1,700 different slides into 5,523 sets for a total of nearly 200,000 slides!

In addition to slides, visual support materials included pictures, plants, and posters of glossaries of words and phrases. All of these materials were used during and following the broadcasts (Stewart, 1939; Potter, 1942).

Broadcasting—WBOE

During the first six years of operation, CSA programs were broadcast by local commercial stations that donated air time on a sustaining basis. Beginning in the late fall of 1938, however, the CSA began operating its own station, WBOE, using the then new technology of short wave. After receiving a $42,000 grant from the Rockefeller Foundation, the Cleveland School Board built a short wave radio station including control room and studios, offices, transmitter, and antenna tower. The grant also supplied over 100 short wave receivers, enough to equip each school. Woelfel and Tyler (1945) explained the advantages for a local school of the air of owning its own station.

1. It made possible silent periods during the broadcast to give time for pupil activity, responses, or work. (Commercial stations prohibited silent periods.)
2. School administrators could select the best times to air programs.
3. The radio schedule could be adjusted to fit the school schedule.
4. The length of the radio lessons could be set to the needs and capacities of the learner (p. 94).

Furthermore, with its own station, the CSA could repeat programs either live or recorded at various times during the day. In this way, they overcame the barrier of fixed class schedule, which had made broadcasting to high schools and some junior highs impractical. Finally, using WBOE, the CSA expanded its broadcast day.

All of this activity required a substantial investment in studios and equipment well beyond what was purchased by the original Rockefeller grant. By the mid–1940s, WBOE operated out of

[3]It's unclear whether the teacher guides were sent to individual classroom teachers or to the school.

a ten-room studio space that included at least three broadcasting studios, one of which included a small auditorium for demonstrations, a control room, offices, reception area and workshop.

WBOE's staff included William Levenson, the school district's Supervisor of Radio, a studio engineer, a transmitting engineer, an announcer, and a clerk. Shortly after the CSA began operating its own radio facilities, director Levenson moved to expand broadcasting for the upper grades. Working with high school principals, the schools created a uniform city-wide bell schedule, which enabled the CSA to develop a broadcast schedules that best suited the largest number of students.

Because the Cleveland School Board was a strong advocate for educational radio and one of the first to own its own station, the CSA attracted many important visitors to tour the operation. Some, apparently inspired by what they saw, offered resources and money. One such offer came from Edwin Armstrong, inventor of the FM system. On a tour of the WBOE facility in 1942, Armstrong donated a complete FM transmission system. The CSA's FM license application had been approved the previous year. Within several years, CSA programs were broadcast mostly on WBOE-FM (Atkinson 1942c).

Programs 1939

Within a year of going on the air, WBOE broadcast eight hours per day, from 8:00 A.M. to 4:30 P.M. on school days.[4] Table 52 shows the extensive and ambitious WBOE program offerings for 1939–1940 for all grade levels.

Table 52. WBOE—Weekly Programs Offered, 1939–1940
(WBOE Teacher Guides, 1939–1942)

Programs for Elementary Grades		Programs for Junior High Grades	Programs for Senior High Grades
Arithmetic	Kindergarten	*Answer Me This	Art
Art	Stories	Art	Current Issues
French	Music for Young	Clevelanders at	French
Geography	Listeners	Work	German
Handicrafts	Rhythmic	Current Issues	Home Economics
Handwriting	Activities	French	*This Living World
Health	Rote Songs	German	* Gallant American
History	Safety	Great Moments	Women
*Tales from	Science	from JH literature	
Near and Far	Science Club	Pioneers of Health	
*Frontiers of	Song Study	Safety	
Democracy		*New Horizons	

Teachers	Parents	Public
Elem. Physical Education	Pre-School	*This Living World
Kindergarten Talks	Children	(CBS)
	Your Child and His	Your School
	School	

*After School Programs

Adventures in Science	Men Behind the Stars
Between the Bookends	Young People's Concert
Good Health and Training	Daily News and International Affairs
Intercollegiate Debates	Local Programs of Educational Interest

*Indicates broadcasts originating from other sources and rebroadcast by WBOE

[4]WBOE broadcasts were announced as "Your Pioneer School Station."

Comparing Tables 50 and 51 visually demonstrates how owning the broadcast facility enabled the CSA to substantially increase its annual program offerings. When the CSA relied on donated time from commercial stations, it aired only 5 to 6 series per week. With station WBOE up and running, the Cleveland School Board offered over 30 programs weekly for in-school use, grades K through 12, and in addition provided educational programs for the wider community.

PROGRAM DESCRIPTION HIGHLIGHTS

It's not possible in this space to describe all the programs shown in Table 52, but descriptions of the most appealing and significant that ran during the period from the late 1930s to the early 1940s are given below.

A Child's History of Numbers. Part of the curriculum for upper elementary grades, programs in this series presented the history of how humans developed numeric systems for measurement of weights, length, distance, and money. The series included slides to be shown during the broadcasts. The printed guide directed the teacher to select a child to run the lantern (slide projector) during the broadcast and another child to turn the lights on and off at the proper time (WBOE, 1942).

National Negro History Week. For high school classes, this innovative series gave an impressionistic account by voice and vocal music of the "age-old need of man to convert his fear of other men into free companionship" (Report of Activities, 1942). The Central High School radio workshop developed the script and the production. The program was aired several times on one day during Negro History Week (WBOE, 1942).

Radio History 5A. Intended for the fifth grade, this series covered American history from the Pilgrims to the Revolutionary War with a total of 17 lessons. It comprised a fifth grade history curriculum option that classroom teachers could choose to use. The Teacher's Guide provides specific directions for conducting the learning activities: "Have a clear space on the front blackboard. Stand in the front of the room and follow directions as given by the broadcaster as

Seeing and Hearing the Safety Lesson (CSA) (courtesy of Cleveland Board of Education).

exactly as possible. Call on children quickly so that they will have time for answering questions. Repeat the broadcaster's questions only when children have not heard them. Call on as many children as time allows" (WBOE, 1939).

The quote illustrates the direct instructional approach taken by the CSA, an approach duplicated by no other SOAs covered in this work.

Radio Art Appreciation. This sixth grade series and others like it for different grades provided an audio-visual experience intended to enrich the students' aesthetic and emotional experiences. The objectives for the course included such high-minded ideals as enabling the students to: (1) observe and interpret works of art, (2) recognize how closely art is related to life, and (3) develop judgment and discrimination. These ideals reflected the prevalent values among elementary educators of the period, values that seem to have largely disappeared from the schools of early 21st century America. The content of *Radio Art* covered a much wider range of art topics than did art appreciation series of most other SOAs, from the study of classical Renaissance masters, to art in nature, architecture, textiles, and woodcraft among others. Unlike the art appreciation series offered by the other SOAs, Cleveland's program required the classroom teacher to project "lantern" slides in the classroom during the broadcast as directed by the radio teacher (WBOE, 1939).

Elementary Radio Handicraft. Prepared by the Industrial Arts Department, this ambitious series was voted the most popular program by teachers and children in 1938. It taught sixth-grade children to follow directions for designing a simple toy and encouraged them to use their leisure time in making something with their hands. During the broadcast—following the radio teachers directions—students drew a pattern with which they were to make something following the broadcast or at home. Children chose the material to work in: wood, metal, clay, cloth, yarn, soap, cardboard, etc. (WBOE, 1938). No other SOA covered in this study attempted to teach handicrafts.

While the CSA's programs for elementary grades stressed the master teacher approach and close integration with the curricula for specific subjects and grades, the programs for the junior and senior highs took a different tack. Junior high script writers aimed at producing supplementary and enrichment programs. The purpose was not in-service teacher training, but "to bring to the schools in a pleasurable way, authentic and stimulating [learning] experiences" (Atkinson, 1942c, p. 34).

The high school programs were also developed in curriculum centers similar to those in the elementary schools. Written by teachers who were expert in the subject matter, the scripts were prepared for dramatic presentation, and produced by high school radio workshops. The script then became a school project, put on by the schools' radio directors and broadcast over the school's public address (PA) system[5]

Organization and Administration

The CSA operated as an integral part of the Cleveland's school bureaucracy, at least until the early 1950s. The Directing Supervisor of Radio for many years, William Levenson, reported directly to the Superintendent of Schools. Under Levenson, three program coordinators, one each for high school, junior high and elementary, along with a technical director supervised script writers, master teachers, and technicians at the school workshops and at the curriculum laboratory schools. Though the curricular lab schools pre-dated radio, by the late 1930s they had become centers for experimentation for testing and refining the unique Cleveland approach to radio pedagogy. For each subject and grade level, scripts and instructional approach were worked

[5]Atkinson (1942c) reported that almost all Cleveland high schools were equipped with public address systems and a radio workshop.

out by subject specialists and selected teachers. This same group then tested the radio scripts on small groups of students and made revisions as needed. The rigorous Cleveland approach reflected a high level of integration between radio and school curricula not achieved by any other SOA. After a while, a stable team for each subject area emerged and continued developing programs over the years. At one point there were two script writers for each subject area (Kline, personal communication). Overall, the CSA developed a remarkable mixture of paid staff, professional volunteers, and students to plan, write, produce and broadcast its many program series. Other local SOAs tried a similar approach, but few reached Cleveland's level of expertise and educational rigor.

Philosophy and Vision

The CSA's methodical and deliberate approach to radio instruction was rooted in the carefully thought-out vision that its founders had for radio education. While other SOAs articulated lofty but general goals such as enriching the curriculum or bringing high culture or the world into the classroom, CSA directors viewed radio as a medium for accomplishing two specific high level educational goals, at least at the elementary level. The first goal was to use radio as a direct teaching tool that carried specific curricular content. Each radio lesson addressed specific learning objectives for a specific grade level. The script development process, carried out at the curricular lab schools by subject specialists and master teachers, created complete lessons for direct instruction by radio, and they also carried the approval of school administrators. It was appropriate, therefore, for the radio teachers to direct the activities of the students and classroom teacher. Tyler (1967) praised the Cleveland approach saying it was the only one that used radio to its full educational potential.

The second major goal of radio instruction dealt with teacher training. Radio would bring the instructional skill and knowledge of master teachers into Cleveland's elementary classrooms. Master teachers would not only motivate student learning, they would also present for classroom teachers a model of the best instructional practices. Through radio that model would be transferred to inexperienced and ineffective teachers, helping them to improve their teaching performance. Clearly, in this vision lurked the unspoken assumption that even the average public school teacher was not quite up to the job. In effect, radio served as a powerful administrative tool for distributing expertise and curriculum control throughout the system.

To further illustrate how much CSA administrators believed that radio should be integrated with the classroom, the following note was included in the program bulletin for 1942–1943: "The synchronization of school clocks with those of the (radio) studio is essential. WBOE will announce the correct time several times daily. Schools are asked to check their time" (WBOE, 1942). In effect, radio set the school schedule.

An assistant superintendent of the Cleveland schools described two tiers of educational broadcasts; first were the broadcasts for the elementary grades, described above, where each radio lesson became a teaching and learning situation that as much as possible exemplified actual classroom experience. Radio delivered complete lesson plans integrated with subject curricula. Supporters of this approach argued that by freeing the teacher from the responsibility of making and conducting lesson plans, radio in fact freed teachers to devote more time to individual instruction (Potter, 1942). The second tier of broadcasts, aimed at junior and senior high school students, reflected the more widely used "general type" of radio instruction that included interesting information, dramatic presentation, entertainment, and material intended to enrich or supplement the regular classroom work (Potter, 1942).

According the CSA vision, broadcasts for both tiers should furnish information and inspiration, involve visual aides, include evaluations during the broadcasts, and provide worksheets for each listening student (Potter, 1942). For both tiers of broadcasts, CSA administrators viewed learning as an active process. During and after broadcasts students were expected to get involved in learning by viewing slides, taking notes, responding to questions and engaging in discussion. Other SOAs may have shared similar educational philosophy about radio, but none were documented and carried out with such a rigor and precision.

Instructional Methods

The CSA approach to instructional methods for radio featured specific instructions for each lesson. Literally, for many radio lessons, the radio teacher directed classroom activities, asking questions and pausing for student answers while the classroom teacher monitored responses. In many programs such as geography and science, teacher guides spelled out specific activities and guided the use of visual aids, giving page references to maps and pictures that were used during the broadcast. The radio teacher called for the slides by number. As the slides were shown in class, the radio teacher asked questions and then paused to allow responses or brief discussions between students and classroom teacher.[6]

During the broadcasts, students might engage in activities such as examining, experimenting, observing, responding to questions, and participating in brief discussions (Potter, 1942). In some cases, pauses to allow for student reactions accounted for 25 percent of the broadcast lesson. Depending on the content, instructional methods used before and after the broadcasts might include drama, map work, quiz bees, oral reports, and panel discussions (Potter, 1942). The Teachers Guide for a geography lesson broadcast on November 5, 1941, details the classroom teacher's duties:

Prior to the broadcast:
1. Read an overview of the lesson
2. Gather needed materials such as slides to be shown during the broadcast, text and any other visual aides
3. Insure that each student had the text marked at the proper pages
4. Write discussion questions on the board and review with class

During broadcast
1. Show slides or reference visual aids as directed by the radio teacher
2. Write words on board as directed
3. During pauses, call on children promptly to respond to the radio teacher's questions. Engage in discussion as required.

Follow-Up
1. Immediately following the broadcast: conduct discussion using questions given in the Guide for Discussion
2. During the week: Finish work on the unit and review lesson
3. Give the unit test (optional)
4. Keep detailed records of student strengths and weaknesses in responding to the broadcasts (Stewart, 1939; Atkinson, 1942c).

Other SOAs used the direct teaching methods shown above, but none as consistently as the CSA. One wonders how these rigorous instructions affected experienced classroom teachers.

While the CSA used direct teaching methods in the elementary grades, it followed more typical practices in the junior and senior high grades, namely dramatization and story telling. Master teachers and subject supervisors prepared dramatic scripts for use in Cleveland's high

---

[6]Pauses were only possible on programs originating from WBOE short wave or FM. Commercial stations frowned on having dead air time during broadcasts.

school programs, and high school radio workshops including students and teachers performed the scripts over school public address systems[7] (Atkinson, 1942c).

CSA script writers used the dramatic technique in imaginative ways that met the challenge of gaining and holding student interest. One such example was a 1946 program for senior high school English entitled *Trial by Reader*. Using the time-tested court room motif, the script writers presented discussion and critique of Mark Twain's novel *Huck Finn* to engage young listeners. With a judicious mix of live drama exposition and recorded excerpts the CSA created an amusing and educational listening experience. For example:

CLERK AND BAILIFF: Oyez! (THUMP) Oyez! (THUMP) Oyez! *Trial by Reader* is now in session. [Judge] Don Robertson of East High School presiding — with Lois Kozminski and Don Rank of Rhodes High School and Edith Katz of East as associates [judges].
JUDGE: The clerk will read the title on today's docket.
CLERK: Is *Huckleberry Finn* by Mark Twain still of real interest to modern readers?
JUDGE: What are the facts in the case of *Huckleberry Finn?*
CLERK: Your honor and readers, Mr. Bennet Cerf [New York publisher and editor] has several facts and opinions in respect to the book on trial.
JUDGE: Proceed with Mr. Cerf's testimony.
(A short except from Mr. Cerf's actual lecture on Mark Twain is then played).
JUDGE: Thank you Mr. Cerf. You may step down.
(The next piece of evidence is a recorded excerpt from *Huck Finn,* an original broadcast by NBC. Following that the Clerk adds more contextual information, after which the judge attempts to wrap up.)
JUDGE: Then this panel of readers will now consider the merits of the book in question — and its appeal to high school readers. (But one of the associated judges interrupts).
EDITH: Not quite yet, Don.... I question the right of this procedure ... the author himself forbids such an inquiry.
JUDGE: Oh, you mean his [Twain] "Notice to readers?"
The Clerk reads Twain's famous notices:
CLERK: "Notice, Persons attempting to find a motive in this narrative will be prosecuted, persons attempting to find a moral in it will be banished; persons attempting to find a plot in it will be shot."

The judge insists that Twain's book is too important to keep under wraps. He calls for a vote on whether the discussion of the book should continue, and the motion to continue wins. Then various participants discuss the nature of Twain's work, the various characters and events, and share some of their favorite passages. They conclude that *Huck Finn* is not a novel in the traditional sense because it has no central plot. Rather it is a series of episodes taking place along the Mississippi that portray life in America. After everyone has their say, the judge decides that *Huck Finn* should be read by all Americans. It's a classic.

Given the job of presenting in 15 minutes fairly complex literary ideas that could appeal to teenagers, the script writers succeeded admirably.

PROGRAMS AND OPERATIONS, MID 1940S

Through the 1940s the WBOE presented an amazing array of educational series for grades K–12 that included programs developed by the CSA and a few from network SOAs. Cooperation from local commercial stations using private lines made possible selective program service from all major networks. In addition tape recorded programs enabled repeat broadcasts of essential programs (Levenson, 1945). Table 52 demonstrates the station's impressive range of offerings for the year 1949–1950.

---

[7]Almost all of Cleveland's high schools were equipped with public address systems (Atkinson, 1942c).

TABLE 53. THE CSA, PROGRAM OFFERINGS, 1949–1950
(Levenson and Stasheff, 1952)

Divisions of Instruction	Elementary School Series	Junior and Senior High
Art	*Art Appreciation*, 6th grade	*7A, Artistic media used by artists* *8A, Creativity*
English and Language Arts	*The Storybook*, (6 and 7 year olds) *The Poetry Parade* *Story Lady* *The Treasure Chest of Poetry*	*Passing in Review* (JHS) *Weigh Your Word* (JHS) *The American Story* (HS) *Fun from the Dictionary* (HS)
Foreign Languages	*Elementary French* *Elementary Spanish*	*German and French* (JHS and HS)
Handicrafts	*The Village*	
Health	*Good Health*	
Home Economics		*Boy Dates Girl* (HS)
Industrial Arts		*The March of Production* (HS)
Kindergarten	*Once Upon a Time*	
Mathematics	*Primary Arithmetic* *4B Arithmetic*	*Get the Answer Right* (JHS)
Music	*Music for Young Listeners* *Rhythmic Activities* *Rote Songs* *Song Study*	*Musical Highways and Byways* (JHS)
Safety	*Safety-Sam, Detective*	
School Gardens	*The Garden Club*	
Science	*Fourth-Grade Science*	*Adventures in Research* (JHS) *Science for Better Living* (JHS) *Biology for Living Today* (HS) *Work Made Easier* (HS)
Social Studies	*Behind the Headlines* *Leaders of Colonial America*— 5A *The Story of Early Cleveland*	*The News: Places and People* (JHS) *The Ohio Story* (JHS) *Current Topics* (HS) *You Are There* (HS) *UN Story* (HS)

A quick review of the listings in Table 53 demonstrates the breadth of the CSA's offerings on WBOE. It also highlights the sharp difference between the offerings in the Elementary Division and those in the Junior and High School divisions. Elementary programs included specific lessons in arithmetic, music, science, social studies, physical education, health, foreign languages, and current events. Programs for the junior and high school division are mostly of the enrichment type. Many of the programs listed above were probably aired two or more times during the week.

Audience

The precise targeting of CSA programs at the elementary level affected audience size because the targeted classes represented a limited number of students. For that reason, CSA administrators seemed focused on the number of schools that used the radio programs rather than the number of students. Stewart (1939) reported that the number of participating schools[8] increased from 45 in 1933 to 105 by 1938, the year before WBOE went on the air. Irvin's numbers would have had more meaning if he had also cited the number of schools in the Cleveland system. Seerley Reid (1942), chief researcher at the Evaluation of School Broadcast project, reported that for the year 1940–1941, 65 percent of Cleveland's elementary and high schools used WBOE broadcasts (p. 20). However, citing only the number of schools left unanswered Cuban's (1986) suspicion that data on school listenership does not reflect the number of students who actually listened. Fortunately, Potter (1942) did cite pupil numbers. She said that in 1940–1941 the listening audience in Cleveland's elementary schools included 1,576 teachers and 65,370 pupils, roughly 60 percent of Cleveland's elementary population. The CSA programs were of course chiefly intended for use by students in the Cleveland public schools, but we can safely assume that some teachers and students in nearby communities also tuned in to the broadcasts.

How should we evaluate these numbers? Were CSA administrators happy or disappointed? Unfortunately, the two authors who reported the audience numbers given above did not explain how they acquired the data or whether the figures pleased or disappointed CSA administrators. Reid (1942) however lauds the level of participation reached by CSA saying: "In Cleveland approximately two-thirds of both elementary and secondary schools used the broadcasts of station WBOE, a tribute to the program of radio education in Cleveland and a fact of significance to those who maintain that school broadcasts cannot overcome the rigidity of secondary-school time schedules" (p. 20).

Reid's opinion should be taken seriously because his research was rigorous and comprehensive.

Evaluation

In a series of trial studies at the curricula laboratory schools, the CSA staff carried out systematic and rigorous formative and summary evaluations of radio programs for the elementary grades. In the formative evaluation the CSA administrators sought to test the effectiveness of new programs using two groups, differentiated by Intelligence Quotient (IQ) scores.[9] One group tested at the high end of the normal IQ range, 85 through 124, and the other at the lower end of that range. Both groups listened to a newly developed radio lesson and carried out learning activities as directed. Observers attending the trial lessons included principals, assistant principals, classroom teachers, and subject supervisors. They noted pupil reaction to the radio teacher's questions, directions, vocabulary, lesson content, the timing of pauses, as well as the level of pupil interest. Following the trial broadcasts, students were asked to do the follow-up work just as they would for a regular radio lesson. The student participants were also asked to give their opinions on how to improve the lesson. Cleveland's Supervisor of Social Studies said the he was constantly amazed at the "pertinence and number of suggestions" offered by the pupils when they were asked to evaluate a broadcast (Potter, 1942, p. 46).

Following the trial broadcasts, the CSA staff revised the program script based on observer comments and student suggestions and then submitted it to another trial broadcast similar to the first. The second revised script was then given to a curriculum supervisor for final approval. This process certainly ensured that the resulting program was completely synchronized with school curriculum, educational philosophy, and policy.

Summary evaluations were equally as rigorous. The process included three levels of testing and evaluation that sought to involve the classroom teachers. They were:

[8]A participating school is one in which one or more classes listened to one or more CSA programs (Stewart, 1939).

[9]Apparently researchers in the 1930s and 1940s commonly used IQ scores to define test groups. Seerley Reid did the same in his study of Chicago radio programs (Reid, 1939).

1. Asking a panel of teachers to fill out a rating scale for each broadcast series.
2. Using teacher-made tests for measuring student acquisition of information, attitudes and interests.
3. Using commercially available tests to measure subject matter learning in American history, literature, and critical thinking.

These evaluation activities continued over a number of years, though it is unclear when they ceased. The major findings associated with those evaluations were, according to the Cleveland Bureau of Educational Research, that children who participated in radio instruction regularly enjoyed increased proficiency in vocabulary, recognized a greater number of words, and demonstrated a better understanding of word meaning than did those who did not participate in radio instruction (Potter, 1942).

The reactions of classroom teachers became the standard for judging program effectiveness. A typical question to gain teacher reaction to the Handwriting class was, "Do the lessons help you in your teaching of Handwriting?" (WBOE, 1938, p. 97). The results were consistently and overwhelmingly positive.

One other type of evidence about the effectiveness of SOA programs can be found in the opinions and descriptions of contemporaries of the CSA. Many of the educators who observed CSA operations lauded the school for being an exceptional example of education by radio. They praised its dedication to using radio to bring the skills and knowledge of master teachers into the city's 100 plus schools.

Operations, 1950 to 1976

The CSA function as an important educational resource for the city's schools probably peaked during the late 1950s, but WBOE continued to broadcast instructional programming for school use until the mid–1970s. Documentation is lean, but station program logs reveal a good deal about WBOE's operations. For example, the program log dated May 18, 1970 shows that the station was on air from 7:55 A.M. to 4:25 P.M. and that all programs were taped. Most likely by 1970, live broadcasting had become far less common at all radio stations, commercial or public. Instructional programming still made up part of WBOE's daily offerings, but increasingly programs came from outside sources. The program log for one day in 1975 (Table 54) shows the instructional programs titles, the program originator, and program length.

TABLE 54. WBOE INSTRUCTIONAL BROADCASTS, SEPTEMBER 22, 1975

Program	Originator	Length
Who Are the Americans? (HS)	Network*	15 min
Yes, You Can Continue Your Education	Local	5 min
Elementary Math	Local	15 min
Elementary Music	Local	15 min
Elementary Art	Local	15 min
We're all Ears	Network*	15 min
World of Words	Network*	15 min

* Most likely the network originator was the National Public Radio (NPR).

Table 54 shows seven instructional programs all of which were rebroadcast during the day at least once and in the case of *Who Are the Americans?*, six times. All in all, instructional programs accounted for 15 of the 32 programs that WBOE broadcast during school hours, albeit many repeated programs.

During the 1970s the CSA continued developing some noteworthy new programs. In 1974, two new WBOE instructional programs received awards for excellence. *Billy Bumble and His Dragon*, a series for the elementary grades, received recognition for outstanding children's programming. *The Contribution of the Black Scientist* was recognized in the public service category.

Despite the awards, the station was short of funds and staff. To continue broadcasting as many hours as it did, the staff was forced to replay the old programs frequently, too frequently according to Jay Robert Kline, station director during the final years. Kline's career spanned over 40 years in the Cleveland schools as a teacher, assistant principal, principal and then in the 1970s as the last director of station WBOE. Appointed in 1973, Kline described his role, "I was like a receiver in bankruptcy ... I was responsible for keeping it [WBOE] alive" (Kline, personal communication). Kline recalled that in the years following World War II, for every subject area WBOE had two teacher script writers, who were relieved half-time from their classes to work on radio.[10] A large group of scriptwriters worked in virtually every school department. By the early 1970s, the staff had dwindled to a few. No one was fired, but during the 1960s and early 1970s reductions took place through attrition. Without program writers, Kline was forced to repeat old programs, which quickly lost favor among students.

Klein worked to keep teachers interested in radio. He visited faculty meetings at as many schools and attended new teacher orientations to talk about the radio station. It amazed him, "the large number of teachers who were totally unaware of the services offered by the radio station" (Kline, personal communication). By the mid–1970s, the Cleveland School Board faced many serious challenges, and apparently, it did not look to radio as a solution for any of them.

Demise

Undoubtedly, the rise of instructional television drained some interest and support from educational radio, but the most damaging forces came from outside the schools. Cleveland like many Northern industrial cities experienced a serious decline in population and the tax base. Between 1960 and 1980 the city's population fell from 876,000 to 574,000, a decline of nearly 35 percent. The school system in the 1940s and 1950s had served a population that was mostly middle class and solid working class. By the 1970s, as more and more industries closed or moved out of Cleveland, the schools served a poorer population who faced declining job prospects. In a school system increasingly strapped for funds, education by radio appeared more and more of a luxury.

In 1976, WBOE switched to the NPR format, which did include some general educational programs, but at that point the Cleveland School of the Air was effectively dead. In 1978, with the school population just half of what it was in 1950, the school board closed the station as part of a larger cost cutting move. Using an alternative sub carrier frequency, it continued to broadcast instructional programs for the visually impaired for several years. The station reopened in 1984 but no longer as the school's educational station. Instead it operated as Cleveland's NPR outlet, broadcasting a format of NPR news, jazz, and culture.

Summary

The notion that radio never became accepted into America's educational family did not apply to the Cleveland School of the Air, at least during the first two decades of its operation. No other SOA went as far as the CSA in integrating radio into the school curricula. Its curriculum centers, laboratories for developing superior teaching techniques, became the workshops for planning and writing CSA radio series that were fully integrated into the elementary curricula for specific subjects and grade levels. The CSA staff planned, wrote, and presented series for

---

[10]This represented a subsidy for the station, since the teacher's scriptwriting services were free to the station and their classes had to be filled by paid substitutes.

specific subjects and lessons designed to accomplish specific learning objectives. Further, the radio teacher not only presented information but directed classroom learning activities as well. In-service teacher education was also performed via radio. The radio master teacher modeled excellent pedagogy and desired subject content that classroom teachers were expected to follow. The CSA's achievements are summed up best by the dean of educational radio research, I. Keith Tyler. He said: "... in Cleveland radio was looked upon as a regular tool of instruction, similar to the text book, and used for direct teaching, with each program carefully planned and tried out in advance" (Tyler, 1967, p. 31).

It could also be said that since the radio lessons were seamlessly integrated with the schools' curricula, they served the aims of departments and supervisors more than teachers (Stewart, 1939).

The CSA backed up its radio effort with substantial amounts of visual support materials. Slides, charts, maps, even live specimens were delivered to the classroom "just in time" for the broadcast. During the lessons, the broadcasts directed teachers on how to incorporate the visuals. All of that was offered in addition to the customary support such as printed teacher guides, semester schedules and brochures, and weekly bulletins.

What's missing from the documentation is something that could give better understanding of the educational effectiveness and how teachers and principals accepted it. We do know that by the mid–1950s, confidence in radio education began to wane in Cleveland. Instructional television attracted foundation and government grant money, which in turn forced academics to shift their focus from the old but imaginative medium of radio to the didactic new medium of television. More significant, declining and changing student population strained the Cleveland School Board, forcing cut-backs at many levels. WBOE continued to broadcast instructional programs for classroom use, but found it difficult to develop new programs. The station filled more and more of its daily schedule by replaying tapes of the old popular programs, of which students and teachers soon tired. In end, as Kline attests, instructional radio became irrelevant.

Chicago Public School of the Air

Out of adversity came renewed enthusiasm for education by radio in Chicago. In late summer of 1937 a devastating epidemic washed through Chicago and its suburbs. Within weeks 250 children were stricken with polio. The image of hundreds, possibly thousands, of permanently crippled children wrenched Chicago residents. The board of health ordered the schools to remain closed until the epidemic abated. After the first week of extended vacation and with no idea when school could start again, the Chicago Public Schools (CPS) board decided to conduct school during the emergency for hundreds of thousands of home-bound students using radio.[11] It was a daring step.

The undertaking was daunting. Nevertheless, working with unaccustomed urgency, in a matter of weeks, the CPS prepared daily lessons in English, math, social studies, and science. Local radio stations broadcast the lessons in 15 minute slots while five Chicago newspapers published a daily digest of each lesson to be broadcast. These mini-textbooks included directions, questions, and assignments for the pupils. Aimed at 3rd through 8th grades, the programs started on September 13 and continued for only two weeks. When the students returned to school, follow-up evaluation showed that roughly 50 percent of the 317,000 students in the target audience had listened to the programs and that real learning had taken place particularly in social studies, though little in math (Lawson, 1942). The level of learning "was not particularly satisfactory" according to Harold Kent, who a few months later would be appointed director of the CPS

---

[11]Undoubtedly, some CPS board members remembered the Board's previous involvement with education by radio led by Judith Waller. See Chapter 1.

Radio Council (Atkinson, 1942c, p. 40). Nevertheless, the experiment set the stage for the development of one of the nation's largest and longest lasting radio schools of the air.[12]

Origins

The successful radio experiment had attracted national attention and stirred great interest among Chicago media and educators. The educational directors of Chicago's local radio stations and publishers of local newspapers eagerly embraced the spirit of pro-bono service and also saw an opportunity to enhance their public image. The experiment opened the eyes of school administrators to the power of education by radio. The Superintendent of Chicago Public Schools, Dr. Johnson, became sold on "the educational possibilities of using radio to supplement classroom education (Woelfel and Tyler, 1945, p. 98). Johnson remarked, "we have the opportunity to pioneer"[13] (Lawson, 1942, p. 33). Continuing the experiment seemed like the logical next step, but the venue for the pioneering work would have to shift from broadcasting for students at home to students sitting in classrooms, a much different situation.

After deliberation, the CPS administration and local radio station managers agreed to establish a joint organization that would plan and direct a program of educational broadcasts. Since the operation would rely entirely on donated air time and publicity, it seemed appropriate that the committee should include, in addition to CPS educators, representatives from radio stations that were to broadcast the educational programs and managers from cooperating newspapers (Atkinson, 1942c).

To head the operation, they selected Harold Kent, an elementary school principal who offered extensive experience in education by radio. Having worked on school radio programs with Judith Waller at WMAQ and with other local stations, Kent had experience with program development, script writing, and broadcast production. By October of 1937, the Chicago Radio Council was formally established with Kent as director and a staff of five teachers, all of whom had attended radio workshops. The Council's responsibilities included planning curricula, writing scripts, and promoting education by radio to Chicago's schools. In addition, they decided to adopt the name, the Chicago Public School of the Air (CPSA).[14]

One of the CPSA's first jobs was to determine how many Chicago schools were radio equipped. By the time of the epidemic, 1937, most homes had one or more radios, but what about the schools? How many had radios, and of those, how many were tuned to the existing network SOA programs? To get answers, the CPSA conducted a comprehensive survey of the schools. Not surprisingly, survey results revealed that few Chicago schools owned radios, and of those that did, fewer still used the educational programs broadcast by NBC or CBS. The survey also promoted the benefits of radio to thousands of CPS teachers and administrators. To begin the task of teacher education, the CPSA developed and distributed a radio bulletin that informed teachers about CPSA activities and plans for the coming semester. Much more would have to be done later.

During the fall semester of 1937 the CPSA produced no programs for in-school use, partly because it lacked a studio and partly because that first semester was a time of intense planning and preparation. However, CPSA members did cooperate with local commercial radio stations

---

[12]According to Woelful and Tyler (1945) the experiment raised concern among teachers about being replaced by the new "assistant teacher," radio. Though not well documented, such concerns played constantly in the background (Cuban, 1986).

[13]One reason for the Superintendent's keen interest in educational radio may have been that it offered an opportunity to enhance the reputation of a system that had been plagued with the reputation of political appointments (Atkinson, 1942).

[14]In most sources, authors continued to refer to the activities in Chicago as the Radio Council. For consistency in this work, I will use the title "Chicago Public School of the Air" (CPSA).

on developing out-of-school educational broadcasts. Members also worked with the Adult Education Bureau on the production of weekly citizenship broadcasts (Lawson, 1942).

Faced with the tasks of planning programs for the coming semester and the following year and with promoting radio to teachers, Kent decided that he needed more help. He invited principals and subject supervisors to form an advisory committee with the specific task of identifying topics and program approaches for the following school year. Meanwhile the CPSA focused on getting ready for the coming spring semester.

In February 1938, the CPSA presented its first schedule of broadcasts for in-school use, a modest offering of just one program, though two more would air later that semester. Perhaps it was the enigmatic title, *The Hour of Magic Boots*, that appealed to Chicago's primary teachers and their students for it soon became popular and proved long lasting. Primarily a literature storytime for grades K through 2, the series also included programs on social science, health and safety, and science. During its first semester, nearly 20,000 children listened in (Lawson, 1942). Proceeding cautiously, just two months after the program aired, the CPSA surveyed every elementary school principal in Chicago. The returns showed strong support for the new program and a big jump in the number of radio equipped schools.

PROGRAMS

By the end of the semester, the CPSA, working with a number of local radio stations, aired three in-school radio series. Table 55 lists the programs, subjects, intended grade level, and the broadcasting station.

TABLE 55. CPSA PROGRAMS, SPRING 1938 (LAWSON, 1942)

Date Initiated	Program and Subject	Grade	Station
February 1938	*The Hour of Magic Boots* Stories, also social science, health, and science	K–2	WAAF 1:30–1:45
March 1938	*Occupational Research* Survey of local industries and businesses and the kinds of jobs they offer.	8–12	WBBM Friday, 1:30
April	*Student Chorus* Music education	All elementary grades	WLS Thursdays, 11:00–11:15

To assist teachers in using the programs, the CPSA distributed a weekly radio bulletin that discussed the activities of the CPSA, described up coming broadcasts, and listed the in-school and out-of-school broadcasts by local stations including the network programs aired by NBC and CBS. The bulletin also served as an excellent vehicle for promoting the efforts of the Chicago CPSA. Kent sent it to educators across the country. He believed that it caught their attention (Lawson, 1942).

By the middle of spring 1938, the Chicago Public School of the Air had been successfully launched. Yet few classroom teachers were tuning in. Kent understood that to be successful, in-school radio would require more than just putting programs on the air. It also required continuous teacher education — pre-service and in-service demonstrations. Also required were effective promotion for each program and well thought out printed support materials. Every effort had to be made to get radio inside a school's curriculum (Woelfel and Tyler, 1945).

To sell teachers on the benefits of educational radio, Kent organized his staff into a sales team. Each week every staff member visited one classroom to listen along with the children to a CPSA program. A school visit had two purposes: (1) to record teacher and student responses to the broadcasts and (2) in those classes where radio was not used, to sell the concept of radio education to the teacher. In those cases where the classroom teacher knew little about CPSA programs and had no radio in class, the "sales" person brought a portable radio to demonstrate the programs and give tips on how to get the most out of them. Following the visit, the staff member wrote a report describing the highlights and reactions (Lawson, 1942, p. 48). In this way, radio was introduced in-person to hundreds of Chicago schools.

The first year of CPSA operation ended on a high note of optimism and anticipation. It had launched 3 in-school programs with an estimated audience of 33,000 students. It helped produce several out-of-school programs, wrote and distributed weekly program bulletins that received national recognition, and sponsored the successful Midwest School Board Conference, which evolved into a national conference (Lawson, 1942). Lawson asserted that these activities stirred interest in education by radio throughout Chicago schools. She reported that results from CPSA surveys showed that the listening audiences for the network SOA's and WLS's School Time broadcasts (see previous section) had increased dramatically during the past year. The number of classes listening to NBC's *Music Appreciation Hour* grew from 107 to 500, and the number listening to WLS's *School Time* ballooned from a miniscule 14 to almost 900. Lawson offers no documentation to back up her claims. She attributed the growth to the wide distribution of the program bulletin, the staff visits to school, and to publicity, all of which raised teacher awareness of radio programs for classroom use (Lawson, 1942, p. 52).

By the fall of 1938, the CPSA was rolling. It offered Chicago teachers seven weekly in-school radio series and helped develop six weekly out-of-school (free time) broadcasts. The in-school programs were aimed at grades K–8 while the out-of-school programs were designed for high school students. Another milestone occurred in the fall semester when construction started on a broadcast studio. When complete, the studio would enable the CPSA to produce its own programs, though they would continue to be transmitted by the commercial stations.

The following year, the CPSA scheduled ten in-school broadcasts weekly, two per day. That prompted two radio stations to donate a "strip across the board," jargon for the same time slot, five days a week, a feature that made it easier for teachers to plan their listening. Table 56 shows the broadcast schedule for the 1939–1940 school year.

TABLE 56. CPSA PROGRAMS, FALL 1939 (LAWSON, 1942)

Day	Program	Grade	Station
Monday	*The Hour of Magic Boots*	K–2	WAAF
	Your Science Reporter	7–8	WJJD
Tuesday	*That's News to Me*	8–12	WFFD
	Makers of Chicago	5	WAAF
Wednesday	*I Will / Let the Artist Speak*	8	WJJD
	Pieces of Eight	3–4	WAAF
Thursday	*Your Science Story Teller*	5–6	WAAF
	Let's Tell a Story	5–8	WJJD
Friday	*Student Chorus*	1–8	WJJD
	Open, Sesame!	5–6	WAAF

Program descriptions:

The Hour of Magic Boots. This popular series for the primary grades presented dramatized stories followed by discussion mostly on literature, but also on social studies, health and safety.

Your Science Reporter. Science information presented in a news format, the series supplemented the 7th and 8th grade science curriculum. As an additional feature, the series incorporated live lectures. Each weekly program bulletin included a page of tickets that would admit four students into science lectures offered by local museums or other science related organizations. Soon all the science programs featured tickets for live lectures.

That's News to Me. This series presented an interesting combination of reports on current events along with interviews with outstanding Chicago pupils. The strategy was that hearing Chicago students express their opinions would make current events more appealing to the average student.

Makers of Chicago. An early attempt at multicultural programming, the series described the nationalities who lived in Chicago. It featured folk songs and talks by people representing the different ethnic groups, for 5th grade.

I Will. Designed for 8th grade social studies, the programs brought to the microphone outstanding Chicagoans as guest speakers. Here was another example of schools hoping to motivate students with great personalities, but it was short lived.

Let the Artist Speak. One of its more ambitious efforts, CPSA developed this art appreciation series in cooperation with Chicago's Art Institute and Field Museum. These institutions, at the beginning of each semester, distributed prints and pictures to each school, enabling students to have a visual as well as audio learning experience. The institutions distributed tickets to free lectures. To support the program CPSA issued a teachers manual prepared by the CPS art department. This series replaced *I Will* in the spring of 1940 and continued for many years.

Pieces of Eight. Intended for third and fourth graders, the series featured mythical ship captain Lemuel Covington Ames, who told stories of treasure searches and sea adventures.

Your Science Story Teller. Intended to correlate and supplement the science curriculum for fifth and sixth grade students, the series listeners received free tickets to science lectures.

Let's Tell a Story and *Open, Sesame.* These series offered dramatization of books on the CPS library's approved list, for upper elementary grades.

Student Chorus. Rather than a typical music appreciation course, the series featured thematic programs built around holidays, seasons, and special events.

Battle of the Books. In December 1939, the CPSA started production of the program that became its best known and longest aired, lasting until at least the late 1950s. Using a quiz show format, teams from different schools were invited into the studio. There they competed in answering the questions, some of which were submitted by students in listening classes. The questions reflected the assigned readings selected from the school curricula, all of which represented a high degree of listener engagement in the action. Developed by Ruth Harshaw, the series became regular fare on several commercial radio stations. During the 1950s NBC's WMAQ ran the program with sponsorship from one of Chicago's leading department stores. Winning schools received a cash award for buying books.

Each program in the 1939 schedule supplemented a specific topic in the CPS curricula. Furthermore, the titles suggested that Kent and his staff took a learner-centered approach to program development; half the titles involve the personal pronouns I, Me, Your, and Us. Moreover, the focus was on the elementary grades, another good practice for education by radio.

SUPPORT MATERIALS

From the beginning Kent understood that in order to get teachers to use radio programs, they had to be informed and cajoled. For each series and each semester, the CPSA prepared a Broadcast Handbook that announced each series, identified the broadcasting station, and stated the learning objectives. It also provided program content summaries and suggested learning activities for pre-, during-, and post-broadcast learning. In addition to the Handbooks, the CPSA also issued a weekly four-page Program Bulletin that publicized important radio events of the week and listed by grades the broadcast schedule for the CPSA programs, the American School of the Air, the WLS School Time series, and later for the CPS's own station WBEZ (Woelfel and Tyler, 1945).

The wide distribution of the Handbook and Bulletin, Kent believed, prompted a substantial increase in in-school listening. In his dissertation on educational radio in Chicago, Jerry Field (1991) complains that he was unable to find any complete copies of the handbooks for CPSA programs. Nevertheless, he does report that for the 1948 spring semester, the CPSA distributed the radio Handbooks for Teachers to 15,000 teachers (p. 130). The following year it distributed 24,000, and the number would grow to over 75,000 by the early 1950s.

Special tours and lectures planned for young students represented another type of support available to teachers. Tickets of admission were printed in the Handbook or Bulletin so that listening classes could attend lectures at the Chicago Art Institute and the Field Museums of Natural History (Levenson, 1945).

Philosophy and Methods

Sparse existing documentation makes it difficult to get a picture of the educational philosophy that may have motivated CPSA leaders.[15] However, throughout his involvement with the CPSA, Harold Kent referred to the radio programs as a supplement to teacher activity in the classroom. Certainly, he chose this term carefully, being well aware of the suspicions that existed among some teachers that the new technology of radio might one day replace them in the classroom (Woelfel and Tyler, 1945). In his farewell address, Kent praised the CPSA for developing programs that covered "every supplemental area — news, English, science, history, music, art, vocations" (Field, 1991, p. 121). Apparently, he meant that the radio programs complemented the learning objectives and topics found in the CPS curricula. Kent characterized the teacher handbooks as being well coordinated with the CPS curriculum. Overall, he said that radio had been practically integrated with school procedures.

It appears that Kent thought radio had become part of the educational family in Chicago. Had it? Or was it, as Field (1991) suggests, merely an ornament on an otherwise complete curriculum? Did supplemental teaching aid mean the same as enrichment, something nice to do, but not necessary? From the distance of many decades the distinction is not clear. What we do know is that Kent never voiced the kind of idealistic vision of the role of radio in education that Ben Darrow, founder of the Ohio School of the Air, often articulated. Darrow had said that radio would blow the roof off the school and move the classroom walls back to the circumference of the globe. For the Chicago crew, the function of radio was to supplement the teacher's work, nothing more.

Kent's statements do give some indicators of what he thought the best way to utilize radio in the classroom. The following is Kent's advice to teachers:

> Methods in classroom utilization are largely an individual affair with the individual teacher. (but) ... the pre-broadcast period should concern itself chiefly with motivation ... (to) increase earnestness in listening. In after-broadcast activities, we are concerned with the entire potential situation. It may be to increase the amount of reading done, it may result in diaries and scrap books; it may result in creative dramatic and writing efforts; it may result in merely a pleased feeling. We are constantly improving our handbooks to the end that they may be practical servants of the teacher [Atkinson, 1942c, p. 43].

Kent advised teachers to motivate students prior to the broadcasts and to involve them in active learning afterward. He said nothing about what students do during the broadcasts.

---

[15]In interviews, CSPA script writer Herb Graham said he was not given any curricular guidelines and never questioned the educational philosophy behind the programs. Russell Reed, a performer for CSPA, said there was no formal philosophy or rationale behind the programs (Field, 1991, p. 170).

WBEZ-FM

It was certainly a milestone in April of 1943 when radio station WBEZ-FM went on the air as the "Radio Voice of the Chicago Public Schools." Unfortunately, in the following weeks, not many heard it. During the war, few FM receivers were produced, and in early 1943 only 25 of Chicago's 400+ public schools were equipped with FM receivers, though all had AM receivers.[16] As a result, for the next few years, most CPSA programs continued to be broadcast on commercial radio stations. Nevertheless, the wisdom of owning the station was confirmed a year later on baseball's Opening Day, April 10, 1944, when station WJJD abruptly announced that it was changing the broadcast time of the five CPSA program series it carried, from 2:15–2:30 P.M. to 9:45–10:00 A.M. As Kent explained later, "Cancellations of programs due to baseball broadcasts will be avoided" (Woelfel and Tyler, 1945, p. 101). With its own station and the Board's support, the CPSA anticipated that the number of FM equipped schools would grow quickly and planned accordingly. Within a year of WBEZ's first broadcasts, over 1,000 FM radios were available to Chicago's classroom teachers (Field, 1991).

In early 1941, John Kent joined the army, receiving rank of lieutenant colonel. His replacement, George Jennings, began utilizing the new FM outlet to expand the broadcast day. As of September 1943, from 10:30 A.M. to 1:30 P.M. daily WBEZ offered 15 broadcasts for the elementary grades and several more for the high schools. This latter step was significant; with its own station, the CPSA overcame a big barrier to high school use of in-school radio, namely their rigid classroom schedules. By recording and re-broadcasting programs at different times of the day, WBEZ made it possible for many more high school teachers to use radio in their classes.

CPSA programs moved from commercial broadcasting to WBEZ, but the pace of change was gradual. In December of 1947, a school board report showed that of a total of 176 hours programming during the year, 156 hours were aired over WBEZ and the rest on commercial stations. Finally, although the title Chicago Public School of the Air had been officially adopted several years earlier, it was seldom used. People referred to the radio effort as the Chicago Radio Council and after WBEZ was up and running as "WBEZ radio, the voice of the Chicago Public Schools." Identity focused on the station.

War-Time Programming

During the war the School Board directed that the radio programming reflect the war effort. As a result, WBEZ developed a schedule of programs that reflected the nation's new priorities as articulated by the superintendent. They were aviation, mathematics, languages, geography and social sciences. Table 57 shows the schedule for fall of 1943, the first semester of full-time broadcasting by WBEZ.

TABLE 57. WBEZ PROGRAM SCHEDULE, FALL 1943 (FIELD, 1991, P. 222)

Day	Program	Time
Monday	*Destination Unlimited	10:30 A.M.
	Before the Doctor Comes	10:45
	Lest We Forget	11:00
	*Languages in Action	11:30
Tuesday	The Mother Goose Lady	10:30 A.M.
	The Thousand Million	11:00
	*Numbers at Work	11:30

[16]The fact that all schools were equipped with AM radio receivers was a testament to the Board's determination and Kent's work in promoting radio to the schools. Recall that six years earlier, surveys showed few Chicago schools were radio equipped.

Wednesday	*New Worlds for Old	10:30 A.M.
	China and India Speak	10:45
	Pan-American News	11:00
	*Let's Tell a Story	11:30
Thursday	Life for Wildlife	10:30 A.M.
	China	11:00
	*By Freedom's Light	11:30
Friday	Contact	10:30

*Indicates repeat broadcast of programs heard on commercial stations WIND and WJJD.

No program descriptions are available, but it's obvious that the schedule is substantially different from that of 1939. The only program from that year still listed in 1943 was *Let's Tell a Story*. The titles show a strong emphasis on geography and social studies with programs such as *New Worlds for Old, China and India Speak, Destinations Unlimited* and *China*.

Audience

The CPSA learned who listened through mail surveys, classroom visits, and feedback from listening groups. A study conducted by the Council and submitted in August of 1944 claimed listeners to CPSA totaled 97,114. The study also reported on the listening audiences in Chicago schools for other SOAs. The figures are as follows:

CPSA programs:	97,114
American School of the Air	10,388
School Time, station WLS (Rebroadcasts of OSA programs)	14,964
Total SOA classroom listeners in the Chicago study:	*122,466*

(Woelfel and Tyler, 1945, pp. 101–102)[17]

The results show that approximately 20 percent of Chicago school children listened to in-school radio. Judith Waller (1946) said that the fact that more than 100,000 children in 362 schools in Chicago listened to the 25 weekly programs testified to how well-thought-out and integrated radio programs had met the needs of teachers and pupils alike.

Ten years later the data on audience size pointed to a much larger audience. A local newspaper reported that Chicago schools were equipped with between 2,500 and 3,000 radios, about 5 per school. During that same period, the WBEZ staff numbered 25, all involved in programming, and 75,000 program handbooks were distributed. Most significant, the station claimed to be reaching 400,000 pupils in Chicago and surrounding suburban schools (Field, 1991). It is likely that number reflects the total number of enrollments, not individual students. Many students listened to more than one program per week. If each student listened to an average 2 programs per week, that would mean that approximately 200,000 students were tuned-in to CPSA every week, nearly 40 percent of the total enrollment.

What did all the numbers mean? Probably, they meant that administrators who approved budgets wanted qualitative justification for funds. The existing documentation gives no clue about how the numbers were gathered, tallied, or analyzed. It seems likely, however, that the CPSA programs reached a substantial part of the students in Chicago public schools, and that many Chicago teachers believed in the educational value of radio.

[17]I respect Woelfel's numbers because he was so skeptical of ASA exaggerated claims about audience size.

Evaluation

For most schools of the air, evaluation consisted of gathering feedback from school administrators and teachers on what they thought of the programs. Kent believed strongly that the only evaluation that counted was what teachers who actually listened thought of the programs. To gather those valued opinions, he set up listening groups for each series. Composed of a number cooperating teachers, the groups enabled Kent and his staff to quickly gauge teacher opinion and to do so in depth. Four levels of feedback evaluation were employed:

1. Weekly check sheets. Sent to the listening groups, the sheets asked teachers to identify any production problems or writing that interfered with clarity, simplicity, and comprehension. The original checklist format was changed after a few years; instead of merely checking off an option, teachers were asked to express opinions, enabling script writers to respond quickly to problems identified.
2. End of semester report forms. These reports asked the teachers in each group to evaluate programs, offer new program ideas, comment on the usefulness of the broadcast handbook from the teacher's point of view, and describe how the follow-up activities suggested in the handbooks were utilized. The evaluation items included level of student interest in program content, what educational objectives were accomplished, and the teachers' overall evaluation of the use of radio in their classrooms. Unfortunately, no copies of the forms are available (Field, 1991).
3. School visits. Each week script writers visited classes that listened to their programs. They attended to how well students understood the language and how teachers used the programs in class. Based on what they saw and heard, the writers improved scripts and created more effective learning activities. After editing, the reports from the visits were published as "best practices" for integrating radio programs into their curricula and the most effective follow-up learning activities. The CPSA distributed the edited reports to the schools and to others interested in education by radio.
4. A summary report on school listening behavior. The report covered a variety of topics including radio equipment in the schools, effects of radio on school curricula, extent to which radio programs from other SOAs were used, summary of how teachers used the programs and student reactions. In addition, the summary also included data on quality of reception, reactions to the dramatizations, reactions to the number of facts presented, and program suitability to the intended grade level.

During the early years, the CPSA cooperated with outside researchers in evaluating the educational effectiveness of the radio programs. In 1939, Seerley Reid wrote his Master's thesis on the CPSA series *Let's Tell a Story,* and I. Keith Tyler served as Reid's thesis director. Both men went on to play prominent roles in The Evaluation of School Broadcasts (ESB) project based at The Ohio State University, funded in part by the Federal Radio Education Committee of the FCC — Reid as chief researcher and Tyler as director. Reid's work was characterized by rigor and a determination to cut through any spin put out by proponents of education by radio. He also developed a grand vision for the role that schools of the air should play in American education. That vision is described in Section I of this work.

Reid started his study by asking teachers and administrators to name the important learning goals for the *Let's Tell a Story* series. They responded with 3 outcomes that should be studied: (1) did the radio program broaden reading interests, (2) did it result in students reading more books of increasing variety and maturity, and (3) did listening students write more correctly and effectively? The research design compared the learning outcomes of two groups, a treatment and a control group. The treatment group consisted of 12 classes of 7th and 8th graders from 12 different Chicago schools who listened to the radio program. They were matched demographically by 12 classes that did not hear the radio programs. The period of investigation was short, only five weeks, and possibly that limited the value of the results (Reid, 1939).

The results were mostly positive. While there was no significant change in the number or type of reading interests in either group, pupils listening to the broadcasts reported reading more books during the test period than did pupils who did not listen. More significant, the listening students improved more than the non-listening pupils in writing ability. Given the shortness of the research period, these results seemed very encouraging. In another study dealing with the *Science Storytellers* series, similarly conducted with fifth and sixth grade students, the listening groups showed greater gains in information retention and positive attitudes toward science than did the non-listening groups (Woelfel and Tyler, 1945; Willey & Young, 1948). While neither study proved conclusively that classroom listening enhanced educational outcomes, they did point in that direction.

One of the more interesting points about the Reid study of *Let's Tell a Story* was what it revealed about the then current view of intelligence and how it might be rooted in class or ethnicity. In an attempt to balance the control and experimental groups in terms of intelligence, Reid described the participating groups variously as being "High, Average," or "Low" and "Low, Few Average" or "High, Few Low." He did something similar for ethnic and class background by matching the participating groups in terms of the following ethnicities: "Middle Class American; Residential Swedish; Good Home Scandinavian; 90 percent Italian; Poor Polish and Bohemian; Foreign Polish P.; Polish, Bohemian, Russian; Good"; and the enigmatic "Poor Pol. For Lan." How these group descriptions were worked into the statistical analysis is unclear.

Overall, it appears that the CPSA made good faith efforts to closely monitor the reactions of teachers and to adjust the programs accordingly. Also, recognized researchers found evidence that the radio programs enhanced learning.

Later Years

Claims by some scholars that educational radio had all but disappeared by 1950 seem exaggerated. In fact WBEZ-FM continued broadcasting a full schedule of programs for the school well into the 1970s. Even in the late 1970s when educational stations owned by universities and local school boards were transitioning away from instructional broadcasting to the National Public Radio (NPR) format familiar today,[18] WBEZ continued to offer a number of instructional series for in-school listening. Two types of data give insight into the station's in-school broadcasting operation during the period from the late 1950s to the mid–1970s. First, an interview with writer Jamie Gilson,[19] who got her start working at WBEZ from 1957 to 1960, reveals much about the operation of the CPSA during that time. Hired as a substitute teacher, Gilson became a certified teacher, but she never taught in the schools. Instead she wrote scripts for a number of radio series. As she explained, everyone at the station worked a number of jobs including on-air personality and occasionally sound engineer: "It was great fun. We were putting on shows in science, poetry, history and literature.... We all had our (subject) niches.... We were busy writing and producing things all the time. I don't know that we actually thought about an (education) philosophy.... We were told to augment the curriculum ... (and) told precisely what the need was" (Gilson, personal communication).

[18]In 1967 President Johnson signed the bill establishing the Corporation for Public Broadcasting which ushered in the era of National Public Radio (NPR). Over the next decade most educational stations adopted the NPR programming format which featured information, culture, and entertainment (Tenerelli, 1972).

[19]Gilson is an award winning author of children's literature. She has published nearly 20 books including her latest, *Stink Alley*, based on a child's life in 17 century Holland.

Gilson explained that since all the script writers were certified teachers, they were assumed to be qualified to write the programs. Gilson said she never talked to classroom teachers and regrets never having the opportunity to visit classrooms to see how students reacted to the programs she wrote.

Gilson said that they wrote programs for elementary and high school students, but "our sense was that no one in the high schools was listening." She wrote for several program series including *Safety Mates, This is Chicago,* a poetry series (Gilson doesn't remember the name), *Lady Bug,* and *Bag of Tales.* The latter was popular because teachers could just turn on the radio and hear a story.

Once a week, the CPSA invited fourth and fifth grade children from the schools to come in for radio workshops where they would learn how to do radio, acting, and even sound work. The children were used in the shows. "So when there was a [little] Betty or Bob in the script, the roles could be played by real children from the schools. And when we wrote, we had to write something that was comfortable for them to say" (Gilson, personal communication).

Following a terrible school fire in Chicago that killed nearly 100 children,[20] the Illinois Legislature mandated all state schools to conduct safety instruction for one half hour a week. The CPS responded by asking WBEZ to produce radio programs on safety. Gilson recalls:

> What do you do with that? Safety is fleeting and very difficult to write about. We developed a format of 15 minutes of radio dramatization to be followed by 15 minutes of discussion in the classroom. I came up with situation comedies in which children did something especially stupid, (such as) played with matches and suffered consequences. We developed a jingle. I wrote this program every week, and we got letters from children who said they listened. I was surprised, and we (created) a safety certificate with an owl and sent them out [Gilson, personal communication].

The most popular program by far was *Battle of the Books,* a series developed by Ruth Harshaw before WBEZ went on the air. It continued for nearly two decades. She brought small groups of children from various public schools into the studio where they formed school teams. Each team was asked questions about assigned books.

> It was always a heady time when the child came to the studio, they were excited, they were on the radio and this program, the *Battle of Books* was so much fun and generated so much excitement. It was a big thing. It spread across the nation, though not on radio. Just in the schools or in libraries, in Alaska, Michigan, Champaign-Urbana. In Evanston, Illinois for their year-end battle, they [the teams] had cheer leaders. That all came as a direct result of the early WBEZ programs. I don't know of any other program that had such a lasting effect [Gilson, personal communication].

NBC's Chicago outlet WMAQ aired Harshaw's program and the department store Carson Pierre Scott sponsored it.

WBEZ programs used lecture very sparingly. According to Gilson, almost all programs featured drama or interviews. Most programs were live radio, but some were taped. "I went to Goodman Theatre and taped T. S. Eliot reading his poetry and broadcast on the poetry series." As for feedback on the programs, Gilson knows that the CPS sent out surveys, but she (Gilson) never heard about the results. However, "we got letters from children and teachers saying they liked them, but never any critical letters." A final point made by Gilson, was that unlike at the WSA or OSA, at the CPSA radio teachers were not identified on air.

Gilson's recollections demonstrate that into the late 1950s the CPSA still developed programs that teachers used and children liked. But the operation seems to have lost close contact with

[20]The fire took place at Our Lady of Angels School in Chicago in December, 1958. It claimed the lives of 92 children and 3 nuns.

the schools. Writers such as Gilson did not visit classrooms, nor did she know how the programs she worked on fit into curricula.

WBEZ IN 1978

A "Radio Guide" issued by WBEZ in 1978, then under the direction of Carol Nolan, shows that the station offered a mix of programs, most for in-school use, but also some using the NPR format as shown in Table 58.

TABLE 58. WBEZ RADIO GUIDE, 1978 (WBEZ, 1978)

Day	Program	Time
Monday AM	*Morning News Service*	7:00 A.M.
	Man and Molecules (Interviews with scientists)	8:30
	Learning Exchange	8:45
	The Alphabet Show	9:00
	Pledge of Allegiance, Star Spangled Banner, and *Lift Every Voice and Sing*	9:10
	Let's Find Out	9:45
	+ 10 Vocabulary Booster	10:00
	Bag of Tales	10:30
Monday PM	*WBEZ Student Workshop on the Air*	1:45 P.M.
	Bag of Tales	2:00
	Let's Find Out	2:30
	Money Sense	4:15
	*All Things Considered	5:00
	Voices in the Wind, (a Portrait of the arts)	8:00
Tuesday	*Let's Pretend*	10:00 A.M.
	Science with the Count	10:45
	*The Sound of Illinois*11:00	
	The World of Myths and Legends	11:30
	*All Things Considered	5:00 P.M.

The schedules for Wednesday through Friday repeat.

The excerpts of the 1978 schedule show a few NPR programs such as *All Things Considered*, but most of the daytime schedule consisted of programs for in-school use. However, many program titles also appeared years earlier, a fact that offers support to Field's (1991) contention that in the later years the CPSA merely repeated the same programs without much updating. He says that as students were promoted, they often heard last year's program with new introductions aimed at the higher level (p. 195). Field does not specify which programs or which years, but his complaint is one repeated by researchers who studied other local SOAs. However, during Jamie Gilson's years, 1957 to 1960, it's clear that new program content was written regularly.

WBEZ TELEVISION

Paul Saettler (1990), the eminent historian of American educational technology, observed that all too often before educators properly learn to use one technology, their interest turns to a newer technology. Field (1991) makes a similar argument with the educational use of WBEZ-FM. Monthly reports for 1949 showed that administrators of the CPSA devoted more and more time and effort toward television; interest in radio would soon be overshadowed by television and tape recording. But Field's observations seem conflicted because he also reports that by 1950, television was starved for programming, while radio under George Jennings' leadership covered all aspects of the school curricula. Co-productions also flourished. CPSA developed programs in collaboration with the Western Arts Conference, the Mathematics Council, the Conference for Exceptional Children and the Principals' Workshop. If the CPSA radio effort was declining, it wasn't obvious from the number of teacher handbooks distributed. In 1951 over 50,000 were distributed and by the mid 1950s the number of handbooks distributed exceeded 75,000. It appears that Field's observations were appropriate for the years after 1965.

Demise

The date when WBEZ-FM broadcast its last radio program intended for classroom use is unknown (though it may yet be discovered), but we do know that the transition from instructional broadcasting to the NPR format occurred gradually during the late 1970s and early 1980s. Scholars such as Field (1991) assert several reasons for its demise. He argues that educational television appealed to CPS administrators and drew resources and budget away from instructional radio. That assertion can be refuted. Television certainly got more attention than radio, but during the 1950s at least, WBEZ-FM continued to develop and air a full schedule of programs intended for the classroom. Also, the lack of documentation today reflects as much on the thinking of WBEZ's management as it does on that of the CPS.

Teams from Two Chicago Schools Engage in "Battle of the Books" (CPSA) (courtesy of Chicago Radio Council).

More convincing is Field's assertion that the lack of CPSA records and documents proves that radio was not an integral part of the Chicago School curriculum. "It was treated like a stepchild" (p. 194). But it had not always been viewed that way. Under Kent and continuing to at least the early 1950s, the CPSA keep close contact with teachers and the schools. Staff including script writers visited schools to listen and learn. There was some sense that radio played a key role in the curricula and was a full-fledged member of the Chicago educational family (Woelfel and Tyler, 1945). Through the late 1950s, the CPS apparently provided adequate funds for a full staff. Perhaps the real cause of the demise of the CPSA was that it lost contact with the schools, that scriptwriters never visited schools or had any contact with classroom teachers, unless teachers visited the station. Nor was there any discussion at WBEZ of educational philosophy or how to use radio in the classroom. In that environment, radio seemed to be a nice but optional instructional aid that teachers might use now and then, not something integral to the city's educational family. Surprisingly, there is no evidence of teacher union hostility toward the CPSA, though it is likely that many teachers remained suspicious.

Summary

Kick-started by a devastating epidemic that engendered high public spirit among local broadcasters and publishers, educational radio was quickly adopted and supported by the Chicago Public Schools. Starting in 1938, under the direction of Harold Kent, radio instruction took root in the Chicago school system and developed quickly. With the establishment of WBEZ-FM, in 1943, the CPSA expanded program offerings, adapted to rigid high school schedules and got more students involved in the technical and creative processes of radio broadcasting. By the early 1950s, station WBEZ had assumed the identity of the "Voice of the Chicago Public Schools" and reached a plateau for its in-school operations.

From the beginning, the WBEZ/CPSA developed along the lines of a professional radio station with paid staff, but it also involved a number of students in the creative and technical activities associated with radio broadcasting. From the mid–1940s to at least 1960, local students performed on many programs.

Kent had envisioned radio instruction as enrichment to classroom instruction, not an integral part of curricula. That fundamental philosophy may have limited radio's development and kept it from becoming a part of Chicago's educational family. At any rate, by the mid- to late 1960s, the excitement had gone out of educational radio, at least in Chicago. Interest turned toward instructional television, and more and more the WBEZ FM broadcast schedule consisted of programs repeated from previous years. The operation lost close contact with the schools it was supposed to serve.

Rochester School of the Air

During its 15 years of operation, the Rochester School of the Air (RSA) became the largest and most effective school of the air launched by a mid-sized local school board. It gained national attention for fully integrating radio instruction with the school's science curricula and for incorporating the study of radio into the school curriculum and delivering that by radio. One of the earliest continually operating schools of the air, the RSA thrived despite a small budget, mainly through the generosity and enthusiastic support of a local philanthropist and a local commercial radio station. It accomplished one other unique feat; it transformed itself from a local school of the air to the state-based Empire State FM School of the Air. In that form it continued operating for at least another two decades.

Origins

Rochester, New York benefited from being home to one of this country's technology pioneers, George Eastman, the developer of Kodak film and cameras. A social progressive, Eastman in 1929 donated 36 auditorium sized radio receivers to the Rochester Board of Education with the purpose of bringing broadcasts of the Rochester Civic Orchestra into each of the city's schools.[21] The experimental radio concerts broadcast by station WHAM from various high school auditoriums became popular and laid the ground work for the RSA. The broadcasts demonstrated to the city's school teachers and administrators how well the new medium could serve as a tool of instruction.

While the music programs continued to be aired, the decision to develop a broader school of the air resulted largely from financial pressures. In 1932, a depression year budget forced the Rochester's school board to cancel summer school. In response, WHAM's manager, William Fay offered free use of the station's facilities and staff for an experimental "summer school by radio" (Crowley, 1971, p. 57). His offer was accepted by the Board's director of curriculum research, Laura McGregor. She organized three summer radio series, Algebra, Science, and English, and recruited volunteer teachers to help write and present the programs. After two successful experiences with education by radio, the Rochester Board of Education launched what became one of its most notable achievements, the long running series of science instruction programs developed by science supervisor, Harry Carpenter. The new radio effort however would be designed for classroom use.

The district had long placed high emphasis on teaching science beginning in the 7th grade, but a severe a lack of classroom space in junior high schools forced many 7th graders to continue attending the elementary schools. This situation presented the school board with a dilemma; the 7th graders in the elementary schools would receive science instruction from generalist teachers who had little training in science and no access to lab equipment. Not surprisingly, the solution the Board decided upon was radio. McGregor and WHAM's William Fey devised a plan to have a master teacher broadcast his lessons for use by 7th graders in the elementary schools. The master teacher chosen was Harry Carpenter (Crowley, 1971).

In February 1933, under Carpenter's direction the RSA broadcast two half-hour science programs per week aimed at the 7th grade. Carpenter's programs attracted national attention and became recognized as an outstanding example of science instruction (Atkinson, 1942c). Carpenter asserted that teaching science over radio offered several advantages as compared with the traditional method:

> First "lessons are developed with greater care than would be possible for an individual teacher who is meeting five classes daily.... Moreover, the lessons ... should serve as models of good teacher procedures. Second, the classroom teacher is relieved of routine lesson preparation, presentation, the writing and giving of tests, and is able to devote greater attention to individual pupils in her class. Third, parents listening in (at home) become familiar with the course of study ... and (are) able to discuss the work understandingly with the child. For the first time in the history of education, parents, teachers and pupils may effectively unite in a common purpose — the education of children [Carpenter, in Atkinson, 1942c, p. 63].

Based on Carpenter's work, science by radio became a prominent feature of the Rochester schools curriculum, though a voluntary option for teachers. In addition to science, in 1933–1934, the RSA also aired two 15 minute programs in social studies, a 15 minute geography talk by "world traveler" Mark Ewald, and a continuation of the Rochester Civic Orchestra concerts (Crowley, 1971; McKelvey, 1970).

[21]Eastman had a history of supporting music education. His multimillion dollar donation founded the Eastman School of Music at Rochester University (Crowley, 1971).

In 1937 the RSA implemented another notable curricular experiment—for high school students—by developing several courses that focused on the media, newspapers, radio and motion pictures. Part of that series, English 10A, recognized the fact that by 1937 radio had become an endemic part of American culture that powerfully influenced life, thought, and student language use. The course took full advantage of the language related educational opportunities offered by radio listening and production. In describing his vision for the series, the course writer said "since we live in a radio centered world ... education must provide a public trained to appreciate and demand the genuine and the artistic rather than the artificial and vulgar"[22] (Reid, 1941d, p. 1). Course objectives sought to develop student ability to listen critically to radio, improve speech by emulating the best examples on the air, and improve writing skills by creating original scripts. English 10A became a research subject for Seerley Reid (1941d) and the Evaluation of School Broadcasts project located at the Ohio State University.

Broadcast

Three commercial AM stations aired the RSA programs, WHEC (CBS), WSAY, and Rochester's most powerful, WHAM (NBC). Together the three stations provided the RSA with up to 3 and half hours weekly of free air time, though by the mid–1940s that amount had been scaled back. WHAM's clear channel, 50,000 watt signal made the RSA programs available to city and country schools in much of west-central New York State.

The WHAM story illustrates the nuanced relationships that developed between educational and commercial interests during the early days of radio. WHAM's origins stretch back to a collaboration in the early 1920s between Frank Gannett, founder of today's Gannett media conglomerate, and George Eastman. Eastman had invited Gannett to move his fledgling radio station into the newly built Eastman Theatre from which they would broadcast live performances such as those of the Rochester Philharmonic Orchestra. By 1927, both parties agreed that running a station out of the theatre was not working well. WHAM moved out to become an NBC affiliate, but continued its close cooperation with Eastman, and that made the development of the RSA fairly smooth (McKelvey, 1970). Eastman urged Rochester school administrators into action by donating radio receivers to the schools and arranging special broadcasts of the Rochester Civic Orchestra for in-school listening. WHAM provided the broadcast facilities and technical support.

By the mid–1930s, school administrators began investigating the possibility of establishing a public station to serve the city's educational needs. WHAM responded by offering more broadcasting services to the schools (McKelvey, 1970). For example, the station made possible remote broadcasts from high school auditoria from which performances of the Rochester Civic Orchestra—one of the RSA regular programs—could then be transmitted to the WHAM studios and on to many other NBC affiliates. As a result, Rochester's Orchestra and the RSA became widely known. WHAM engineers also installed portable short wave transmitters in classrooms, making it possible for students to interact with the radio teacher in the studio. Transmitters in one-room rural schools enabled those children to discuss topics with the city kids in the broadcast studio. These free services undoubtedly enhanced the RSA educational program, but they also cut off the effort to develop a publicly owned station dedicated to education (Stewart, 1939; Atkinson, 1942c). In addition, depending on commercial stations for access to the airwaves imposed some limitations. During the 1930s, most RSA broadcasts aired between 1:30 and 3:00 P.M., a timeframe not selected by the schools, but made available to the schools by the stations.

---

[22]Judith Waller made similar statements about the uses of radio instruction. See Chapter 1.

Administration and Staff

Depression era budgets made it nearly impossible for most local SOAs to hire full-time radio support staff, and the RSA was no exception. In 1935, when Paul Reed[23] assumed responsibility for directing the RSA, he faced the difficult job of developing programs without a paid staff. Nevertheless, in the tradition of the early innovators, Reed molded the RSA into one of the outstanding radio education operations in the country. He recruited volunteer teachers and subject supervisors to write and produce programs and in some cases to serve as on-air teachers. Radio stations donated technical support. The WHAM staff served as announcers and in one case as the on-air teacher.

Later on teachers were released from one fifth of their teaching load to work on a radio program. This concession did in fact represent a small subsidy for radio program production in that the board paid substitute teachers to fill in for those teachers who were released from classroom duties (Stewart, 1939). Part of the effort and expense of producing radio programs was borne by cooperating institutions such as the Rochester Public Library and the Rochester Civic Orchestra.

Programs, 1937–1938

The RSA broadcast schedule for 1937–1938 shown in Table 59 reflects the RSA dedication to science education, probably reinforced by the national attention garnered by Carpenter's work.

TABLE 59. PROGRAM SCHEDULE, ROCHESTER SCHOOL
OF THE AIR, 1937–1938 (STEWART, 1939)

Day	Time	Program and Grade	Producer/Writer
Monday	1:30–1:45	*Science*, 7th grade	Harry A. Carpenter
	2:00–2:15	*Books*, 5th and 6th grades	Public Library of Rochester
	3:00–3:15	*Let's Sing*	(WHEC)
Tuesday	1:45–2:00	*Science*, 6th grade	M. Elizabeth Tuttle
	1:45–2:15	*School Concerts of the*	Rochester Civic Orchestra
	2:30–3:00	Rochester Civic Orchestra,	
		Elementary Concerts of Orchestra	Civic Orchestra
Wednesday	1:30–1:45	*Science*, 7th grade	Harry A. Carpenter
	2:00–2:15	*Art Appreciations*, 5th and 6th grades	Elizabeth W. Cross
Thursday	1:45–2:00	*Science*, 6th grade	M. Elizabeth Tuttle
	2:15–2:30	*Science*, 5th grade	M. Elizabeth Tuttle
Friday	1:30–1:45	*News Today — History Tomorrow*, 7th and 8th grades	Paul C. Reed
	1:45–2:00	*Science*, 8th grade	M. Elizabeth Tuttle

Except for Monday's *Let's Sing* and the Tuesday *School Concerts*, all programs were broadcast by AM station WHAM. Of the eleven programs offered, six are science programs. Below are program descriptions.

Science. All the science series followed the Rochester school science curricula and met the

---

[23]Reed held the position of director until 1948 when the RSA merged with the Empire State FM School of the Air (ESSA). He continued his school of the air work by serving on the ESSA Steering Committee until 1964. The ESSA story is covered in Section III: State-based SOAs.

requirements of the New York State curriculum for seventh and eighth grade science. The series for fifth through eighth were arranged in grade sequence. In support of the science series the RSA mailed weekly bulletins to all participating teachers. The bulletins encouraged classroom teachers to organize their students for group study of science phenomena. Classroom teachers were asked to appoint students to various roles such as observer, recorder, and director in order to carry out simple experiments following the broadcasts. Carpenter's science series stood as one of the best examples of radio instruction being integrated with school curricula.

Books. This series demonstrated an unusual coordination between two community educational agencies, the public library and the schools. Staff from the Rochester Public Library planned, wrote, and broadcast the programs for fifth and sixth graders. Their objectives included developing desirable reading habits and making students aware of the resources of the public library. Instructional methods included a mix of talk, book reviews, and dramatization.

Music. This series represented another coordinated effort, this time between the music department of the Rochester schools and the Rochester Civic Orchestra. Howard Hinga, supervisor of music for Rochester's elementary and junior high grades, selected the music, prepared student notebooks, and commented on the selections played during the broadcasts. Performances for the high school classes were conducted from the assembly halls of selected school auditoria and broadcast by NBC's Blue network.

Let's Sing. The singing and rhythmic response of this series helped to fill the void in music instruction for primary children. Unfortunately, the musicians' union objected to having professional musicians perform without reimbursement, and the series was cancelled.

Art Appreciation. Like most other SOAs, the RSA offered a series in art appreciation. The quaint idea then was that an educated population should be familiar with society's arts, crafts, and artists. Surprisingly, radio, a non-visual medium, effectively introduced students to a visual art with the help of special drawings created by the radio teacher. The drawings were lithographed by students in a local technical high school and distributed to all student listeners prior to the broadcasts.

News Today, History Tomorrow. A summary of the day's news for seventh and eighth grades that proved popular. During the 1940s Paul Ross, news editor of station WHAM, planned and delivered the series, exemplifying the close cooperation that existed between the RSA and its commercial broadcast outlet (Willey and Young, 1948). The schedule shown above changed little until after the war.

Philosophy

Because Carpenter's science programs made up much of RSA's offerings, his outlook and methods dominated. In Carpenter's view radio instruction enabled a master teacher and subject specialist to organize and deliver a high quality of science instruction to the classroom. This capability was particularly important in those schools that had no specialized science teachers. In those cases deficiencies in subject expertise or in teaching skill could be overcome through radio. In addition he believed that radio relieved the classroom teacher of the work of preparing the science lesson plan, and freed her to work with individual students. "To some extent it (radio program) relieves the classroom teacher from the requirements of being a specialist in several fields of learning, and makes it possible for her to become more of a specialist in child training" (Carpenter in Atkinson, 1942c, p. 65). Carpenter thought of his lessons as the vehicle for the school's science curriculum and the classroom teacher as the facilitator of individual learning. Though he acknowledged that radio teaching could become a substitute for classroom teachers, it could, he asserted, make the work of the classroom teacher more productive. In Carpenter's view then, the radio instructor and classroom teacher formed a high-powered synergistic instructional team (Atkinson, 1942c).

Carpenter shared with the Cleveland school of the air the view that radio instruction also could serve as a form of in-service teacher education. In addition to the content provided, the radio instruction would serve as a model of science pedagogy that could be emulated by generalist and inexperienced teachers. Like Ben Darrow, Carpenter also asserted that many parents listened to the radio lessons and, "because parents are listening, they too understand better the objectives and methods of modern education and they are better able to supplement in the home the work of the school" (Carpenter, in Atkinson, 1942c, p. 65). Unfortunately, Carpenter offered no data on how many parents actually listened.

Materials

Support materials provided to teachers who used the radio programs were similar to those found in other local SOAs. Weekly bulletins informed all participating teachers about the topics and activities for the week's upcoming broadcasts. They also suggested pre-and post-learning activities as well as related reading materials. It's unclear whether the RSA distributed semester schedules, but without them, teacher planning would have been less effective. The RSA offered specialized materials in support of specialized topics. For example in art appreciation, the RSA distributed illustrations of the art to be discussed during the weekly broadcast. As mentioned earlier, in some cases the radio teacher created visual support materials (Atkinson, 1942c; Stewart, 1939).

After the war and nearly 15 years after its first broadcasts, the RSA seems to have scaled back its program offerings from two programs a day in 1937 to one per day in 1947. Table 59 shows the broadcast schedule for the 1946–1947 school year.

TABLE 60. RSA PROGRAM SCHEDULE, 1946–1947 (WILLEY AND YOUNG, 1948)

Day	Program and Description
Monday	*The Magic Book Shop* Dramatized selected books with the aim of motivating students to read good books
Tuesday	*The Rochester Civic Orchestra* Music selections keyed to the interests of young people (Alternating weekly with) *Science At Work* A series of interviews designed to give an understanding of how science affects our daily life
Wednesday	*Science Adventures* Dramas portraying the development of inventions and discoveries that have affected civilization greatly
Thursday	*People in the News* A popular series that brought interesting and important people to the microphone to talk about social and economic programs
Friday	*News Today — History Tomorrow* Long running series on current events prepared and broadcast by the news editor of station WHAM

Comparing this schedule for 1946–1947 (Table 60) with that for 1937–1938, (Table 59) we can see that the number of programs offered weekly had been reduced from 12 to 5. No data is available that might tell us why the schedule was reduced. Possibly radio station WHAM simply donated less time for RSA programs. We can also see that Carpenter's rigorous science instruction series are replaced with programs on science history and interviews with scientists. This change suggests that Carpenter's approach had been watered down to make science more appealing to a wider range of students.

Audience

Based on mailings of the weekly bulletin and surveys, RSA administrators claimed that more than 50,000 pupils enrolled in their programs. Atkinson (1942c) calls that estimate "fairly accurate" (p. 66), but he does not explain how the estimates were derived. Tabulations for the 1937–1938 school year showed that 171 schools participated in RSA programs with a total of 53,144 pupils, but that included schools in the entire WHAM listening area, not just Rochester. Nevertheless, if accurate, that estimate is quite impressive for a mid-sized city. When evaluating the credibility of estimates of listening audiences, we should keep in mind Cuban's (1986) warning that the results of school surveys of radio use tended to be exaggerated. Often, if even one class listened, all pupils in a school were counted as listeners. We do not know the procedure the RSA followed in tabulating their radio audience.

Evaluation

Information concerning the evaluations conducted on RSA programs includes brief accounts of two unusual efforts. In 1939, the RSA sent questionnaires to 168 teachers outside of Rochester who were known to be using the science radio lessons; 125 responded. The results showed that three quarters of the students expressed much greater interest in studying science than they had previous to the radio broadcasts. Increased interest in science was one of the original goals set for the RSA programs (Atkinson, 1942c).

The RSA science broadcasts became the subject of a national experiment designed to test whether the radio science approach would improve science education and student desire to study science. The researchers recorded forty of Carpenter's science broadcasts on phonographic records and distributed copies to 72 schools in New York State. They send additional copies to state departments of education in North and South Carolina, Texas, Minnesota, Nevada, and New Mexico. Each state selected a few schools to participate in the experiment. Overall, eleven thousand students and their teachers "completed a successful semester of science aided by recorded sound" (Willey and Young, 1948, p. 284). Teachers reported that the records promoted interest in science. At the end of the semester, participating students completed a science interest test. A summary of the results supported the conclusions that science records aided the teaching of science for several reasons. Listening to the science records increased knowledge of facts, improved scientific skills, improved understanding of the scientific method, and most important, increased interest in and appreciation of science related topics and ideas (Willey and Young, 1948, pp. 284–285).

Formative evaluations were conducted regularly for at least some RSA programs. For the series News Today, History Tomorrow, a listening committee composed of participating classroom teachers met periodically with the radio teacher. At these meetings the teachers shared their reactions and suggestions regarding such things as the type of subjects, number of topics covered in the broadcasts, vocabulary level and grammar. Presumably, the feedback helped RSA radio teachers to revise and improve the scripts and on-air presentations (Woelfel and Tyler, 1945).

Demise and Transition

In 1948, the RSA faced a crisis. Owners of its main broadcasting outlet WHAM decided to end their service to the schools or rather to shift it from their powerful 50,000 watt AM station to a much weaker 1,000 watt station, WHFM. Undoubtedly, WHAM's owners were motivated by financial considerations. By the late 1940s advertisers were paying high rates for daytime radio. The time slots that the station owners had donated to the RSA on a sustaining basis over the previous 15 years had become valuable commodities. Their generosity meant foregoing more and more profit. Besides, the school board had no basis for complaint since WHAM's owners offered free use of another outlet that would enable all schools in Rochester to receive the programs. The only problem was that nearly 100 schools outside of Rochester, which had participated in the radio lessons for many years, were now beyond of the range of the weaker sister FM station. Unwilling to cut off the outlying schools, RSA administrators devised a plan to make their radio programs available on a much wider basis. They asked a group of the new commercial FM stations to form a network that would make RSA programs available to schools in central New York State. The station managers liked the idea. Consequently, instead of fading away, the RSA transformed itself into the Empire State FM School of the Air (ESSA). That story is told in detail in Section III: State-based Schools of the Air.

Summary

Most SOAs needed a catalyst to transform general interest in education by radio into an active program. For the RSA, that catalyst was George Eastman. By funding the broadcasts of music concerts for the schools, Eastman demonstrated the potential value of radio instruction and that motivated school board and administrators to implement radio into the classrooms of Rochester. Once started, the radio effort was carried forward by Carpenter's dynamic science instruction, a radio series that gained national attention. Atkinson (1942b) praised the science series as "one of the major public [radio] developments in the United States" (p. 88). English 10A represented another innovation in radio instruction, a sophisticated program that studied radio language, aesthetics and writing, all taught by radio. Both the science series and English 10A represented an integration of radio instruction with school curricula that few other SOAs achieved. Following World War II, the RSA's creative edge seemed to dull. Its program schedule reflected more of what became the enrichment approach.

For a decade and a half, local commercial radio stations provided the RSA with excellent broadcast and technical services free of charge. But by the mid–1940s the RSA faced the dilemma predicted in 1928 by Armstrong Perry, namely that advertising would crowd educational programs off of day-time radio. Undaunted, the RSA administrators found a way to not only continue but expand their broadcasts, by joining with other school districts and the newly formed FM stations to create the Empire State FM School of the Air.

Portland, KBPS

Portland's school of the air (PSA) probably had the longest run of any SOA in the nation, over 60 years from 1933 to the mid 1990s. It distinguished itself in two ways. First, despite a very small professional staff, it continually broadcast a full day of in-school and after school programs; second, more than any other local SOA, the PSA got students and teachers directly involved with the full range of creative radio work-writing, producing, performing, announcing, and engineering. Several student written programs won national recognition and awards.

The PSA[24] is best understood through the story of its student-run radio station, KBPS. Started in March 1923 at Portland's Benson Polytechnic High School, KBPS still broadcast from the Benson facility as of March, 2006, making it undoubtedly the country's longest running and

[24]The term Portland School of the Air was used infrequently. Generally the sources refer to the Portland Program or just KBPS.

probably the only AM educational station. KBPS's story is unique for several reasons: (1) it was one of the few, if not the only, educational station effectively run by students, albeit under faculty direction; (2) it developed a long and mutually beneficial relationship with several Portland commercial stations which continued to write and produce programs that were aired on KBPS, even after those stations had stopped broadcasting educational programs; and (3) it rounded out its school-day broadcast schedule by re-broadcasting many programs from Oregon's station, KOAC. Moreover, KBPS directors decided early on that they wanted to serve the classroom, the student body, and the wider Portland community, and they succeeded in each area.

Throughout its history the "Benson boys" with faculty guidance operated KBPS, providing much of the station's technical and production staff (Swenson, 1958, p. 117). Today, 2006, the station serves as the focus of the Portland school system's curriculum in communications methods and technology. Remarkably, through the early 1990s, long after other educational stations had given up on in-school instruction and adopted the National Public Radio (NPR) format, KBPS continued to call itself the "Voice of the Portland Public Schools" and boasted a full schedule of programming for in-school use covering "nearly every subject area and at nearly every grade level-all planned in cooperation with the curriculum department of the Portland Public Schools" (KBPS, 1988).

Fortunately enough documentation is available to tell a fairly complete story of the Portland School of the Air (PSA)[25] stretching from the late 1930s to the mid 1990s. Much of the early period is documented in the thesis written by Patricia Green Swenson, who served as the chair of the Radio Programs sub-committee and, starting in 1947, as the KBPS station director.

Origins

In early 1923, students from Portland's Benson Polytechnic Institute's radio club talked Benson faculty members into purchasing used radio transmission equipment and applying for a commercial broadcast license. In March of that year, the school received a license to operate a small 100 watt AM station. At first the station was little more than a play thing for the technically inclined students, but soon administrators from the Portland Public Schools developed a greater vision. They decided to create a state of the art technical curriculum in radio. As with the internet pioneers of the early 1990s, the Benson program emphasized the how-to. School administrators hoped that a program covering the technical aspects of radio broadcasting would attract more students. They also hoped the excitement and glamour that then surrounded radio would help whitewash the school's image which had been tarnished somewhat by a "surge of juvenile delinquency" (Swenson, 1958, p. 5).

During the first ten years of operation, the station, guided by faculty and operated by the radio club, provided Benson students a laboratory for training in the technical skills needed to become station managers and broadcast engineers. Benson students built nearly all of the station's radio equipment. The station offered an eclectic palate of weekly programs developed by various Portland high schools consisting of music and "auditorium" programs, aired mostly at noon, when classes were not in session, or in the evening hours. The listening audience consisted largely of the students from the school that put on the program and, of course, their parents (Stewart, 1939). Clearly the focus was on radio's technical aspects.

In the early 1930s, after becoming interested in radio's educational potential, Portland's superintendent of schools encouraged the Benson radio club to experiment with day-time programs related to school curricula. He appointed a committee composed of faculty and principals to plan the development of radio programs for classroom use. The Principal's Radio

---

[25]The term Portland School of the Air was commonly used, but many sources referred to it as KBPS, Voice of the Portland Public Schools.

Committee would select topics and set policy, and the Benson Radio Club would write scripts, produce, broadcast, and announce the programs. In this round-about way, KBPS transformed itself into a school of the air. Two programs were soon developed, *Geography Travels* and *Music Appreciation.* The geography series dramatized the adventures of a character, "Mr. Travel," whose visits coincided exactly with the section of the globe being studied in Portland's geography classes (Stewart, 1939, p. 142). At roughly the same time, the local NBC stations, KEX/KGW, developed two programs for in-school use, *Nature Trails* and *Current Events,* using its in-house staff and resources. By the end of 1934 then, school station KPBS and commercial station KEX offered a total of four programs for Portland's elementary grades.

Benson's radio club soon discovered that they had taken on a daunting responsibility. Writing and producing two weekly 15 minute scripts required enormous amounts of time and more writing and broadcasting talent than was available at a boy's high school. Since depression era budgets prohibited hiring staff, KBPS could not continue the experiment with in-school programming. To the rescue came the management of NBC affiliates KEX/KGW.[26] They offered to assume complete responsibility for the in-school programs. Under this arrangement, the Principal's Radio Committee selected the topics for the in-school programs, but the KEX/KGW staff wrote, produced, and aired them with little input from the schools. KPBS was out of the in-school broadcast business, but the superintendent continued his strong support for educational radio. He directed all schools to set aside one period a day during which teachers could listen to the radio programs, if they desired to do so (Stewart, 1939).

In spring of 1937 a radio program evaluation survey, mailed to all school principals and teachers who used the broadcasts, uncovered a deep interest in using the radio lessons but also several pointed suggestions for improvement: (1) aim the programs at a single grade level, (2) provide more advance information about the programs so teachers can prepare adequately, (3) make sure language and topics are appropriate for the stated grade level, and (4) help with problems of poor radio reception. These responses prompted efforts to refine the in-school programs. The Principal's Radio Committee divided into five sub-committees each with responsibility to oversee one program. The subcommittees selected program topics that coincided better with topics being covered in the classroom and reviewed language to ensure comprehension by children in the intended grade level.[27] Actors were taught to improve diction, and the announcers gave highlights of upcoming programs so teachers could be prepared. Most important, KEX/KGW sent a technician to every school to evaluate the receiving sets and make recommendations for improving reception (Stewart, 1939; Atkinson, 1942c).

Broadcast

For the first decade of its existence, station KBPS was little more than an amateur operation broadcasting from the back of a boy's technical high school. Its 100 watt signal carried a few miles at best. Nevertheless, by the late 1940s, the little understaffed station had become a powerful source for in-school broadcasting. That transition occurred chiefly because Portland's school board and station management wisely cultivated beneficial relations with local commercial radio stations and with Oregon's state owned station, KOAC. Portland was blessed with several commercial stations whose managers strongly supported educational radio. Even before KBPS began its own in-school programs, NBC affiliates KEX/KGW planned an in-school effort, and for 10

[26]In many cities NBC affiliated with two stations, one for each of its two networks, the red and blue. KEX was red and KGW was blue. Since the documentation does not always distinguish between the two, they are identified as KEX/KGW. In 1943, the blue stations became part of the American Broadcasting Corporation (ABC).

[27]Despite efforts to make programs relevant to the subjects being taught in the schools, the radio programs at this point did not coincide with the actual lessons being conducted in the classrooms.

years from 1933 to 1943, KEX/KGW managers provided the Portland schools with a turn-key operation comprised of five in-school programs. The package included consultation with the schools on program topics, writing and production services from members of KEX/KGW's professional staff, and broadcasting over the stations' state of the art studios and transmitters.

KBPS's role in the broadcasting for the schools enlarged substantially in 1943 after the federal government's anti-trust suit forced NBC to sell off its blue network. As a result, KGW was sold, KEX remained with NBC, and both stations discontinued broadcasting the in-school programs from their facilities. However, KEX continued to write and produce the programs. They transmitted via phone line the finished broadcasts to KBPS, which in turn aired them. KEX continued that arrangement at least until the early 1950s (Stewart, 1939; Swenson, 1958).

Under the new arrangement KBPS not only took an active role broadcasting its own in-school programs, it also expanded its relationships with other commercial stations. For example it publicized and re-broadcast *Kid Critics,* a book review program for elementary students carried by station KOIN, the CBS affiliate. KOIN also provided KBPS with CBS's *American School of the Air* programs via a telephone line to the KBPS facility. Moreover for several years, KOIN, in co-operation with the Portland school board, sponsored a three-day radio institute for Portland teachers, which is described later in this section. KBPS also benefited from the state-based KOAC/Oregon School of the Air which provided the Portland schools with ten taped programs per week (Atkinson, 1942c; Swenson, 1958). As a result of all these relations with other stations, KBPS became one of the nation's premier local SOAs despite the fact it operated on a small budget and with only two paid staff.

Over the years, KBPS boosted its power in increments from 100 watts to 250 watts, then to 500 watts and by the 1960s, it broadcast at 1,000 watts of power, enough to reach a 30 mile radius. Its studio and broadcast facilities were also expanded. With the demise of Cleveland's WBOE-AM, Portland's School Board proudly proclaimed KBPS as the only AM station in the U.S. licensed and operated by a school board. Probably, it is the only AM station operated by high school students. In 1983 KBPS-FM debuted at 89.9 and five years later the two stations, KBPS AM and FM, broadcast 24 hours a day, 7 days a week.

From 1923 to 1939 Benson Polytechnic students and volunteer faculty members had completely staffed station KBPS. What's more, they financed it out of the Benson's school budget, but by 1939, the demands of running a radio station stretched the school's resources too far. Fortunately, the superintendent of Portland's schools enthusiastically backed the KBPS operation, and in 1939, the Portland school system assumed financial and administrative responsibility for the station, while the Benson students and faculty continued to run the station and build much of its equipment.

Lady in the Studio

As soon as the school board took responsibility for KBPS management, it hired a part-time station director, Hazel Kenyon. She was given the responsibility to shape a somewhat casual operation that was narrowly focused on technical training into a broader vision that would provide educational programs and services for the classroom, the school system, and to some extent the wider Portland community. Though well qualified for the job — a graduate of the University of Washington, she had done graduate work at Columbia University and La Sorbonne and taught speech and drama at a Portland high school — still Kenyon was at first not welcomed by Benson students: "The new lady program manager was received in September, 1939 with less than a cordial welcome to KBPS. Barricaded from the control room, considered as a definite interloper, feelings ran somewhat high at the beginning of her term of employment in a hitherto all-male sanctum" (Swenson, 1958, p. 42).

Kenyon soon overcame the Benson students' gender prejudice and began expanding the station's mission and scope of activities.[28] Her most important thrust was to gain the confidence and involvement of Portland's teachers and students. She started by inaugurating a daily all-city school news series, "What's Going On," making KPBS the first morning stop for many teachers and students. Then she invited high school drama clubs to broadcast their stage productions over the station and added ten student announcers, training each in radio speech. Kenyon reached out to Portland's high school teachers, asking them to develop program ideas and scripts in several subject areas and to furnish on-air talent. She visited the schools assisting teachers with the production of radio programs-to be broadcast on KBPS — and discussing ways to improve their classroom use of the in-school radio programs that were aired by the commercial stations (Swenson, 1958). Kenyon also furnished materials, conducted rehearsals and auditions, and scheduled broadcast time at the station, mostly after school hours (Swenson, 1958). Kenyon's approach made great sense given KBPS history and its lack of budget.

Kenyon had inherited a two-track system of programming at KBPS. One track consisted of in-school programs produced and aired by Portland's commercial stations and the other consisted of KBPS produced programs that were broadcast mostly at the noon-hour or after school (Atkinson, 1942c). Unhappy that KBPS programs lacked a clear connection to the classroom curricula, Kenyon asked the school administration to support better coordination of KBPS broadcasts with school curricula. At her suggestion, the school superintendent appointed subcommittees of subject area supervisors to advise the KBPS student staff and its faculty advisors on how to integrate classroom subjects into radio programs. However, Kenyon did not address the connection — or lack of — between school curricula and the programs produced by the commercial stations.

During her two years as program director, Kenyon laid the foundation of the KBPS approach to educational radio that gained national attention. It was remarkable because much of it was produced and broadcast by students. The Principal's Radio Committee set policy and identified topics, but local teachers, typically high school teachers, wrote scripts and the local school students performed the scripts at the KBPS studio. In some cases high school students shared writing credits (Swenson, 1958). Somehow Kenyon coordinated everyone's work. While the students probably produced a number of amateurish productions, they also produced programs that attracted national attention and garnered awards. During Kenyon's tenure, two student productions received national honors at the 12th Annual Institute for Education by Radio held at The Ohio State University. Recognized were the *Jeff Hi Latin Club* program produced by students from Jefferson High School and *Grant Dramateurs*, a production of the Grant High School Drama Club (Swenson, 1958, p. 51).

Gilmore Years

In 1941, Kenyon resigned her position with KBPS to become the educational director at Seattle's 50,000 watt CBS station. In her place the board appointed Mary Gilmore as the full-time program director and paid her the salary of a teacher with 5 years experience. Gilmore expanded the initiatives started by her predecessor, including the two-track broadcasting. Since the commercial stations carried most of the programming intended for classroom use, Gilmore spearheaded the effort to develop greater coordination between those programs and the specific subject areas covered in the school curricula. This meant getting the KEX staff to work closely with and accept direction from the schools, not an easy task. The Principal's Radio Committee

[28]Kenyon didn't completely overcome gender distinctions. It was noted that Miss Kenyon, "being a woman could not assume complete responsibility for station's engineering repairs." As a result, engineering was split from programming. Later, however, when another woman assumed the title of Assistant Supervisor of Radio, the school administration specifically stated that she was responsible for all station operations, programming and engineering (Swenson, 1958, p. 229).

developed a list of subjects to be presented during the 1942–43 school year and assigned five sub-committees composed of subject supervisors, teachers, and principals to guide the development of the five in-school programs that were written and produced by the commercial stations. The subcommittees prepared program titles, content outlines, and reference materials. They also reviewed scripts and prepared support materials for pre- and post-broadcast learning activities. Gilmore tried to ensure that each program was specifically planned to meet the needs of and supplement a specific grade level for an area of elementary school study (Swenson, 1958). Table 61 lists the in-school programs developed during the early 1940s through the cooperation between the school Radio Committee and the commercial stations.

TABLE 61. IN-SCHOOL BROADCASTS AIRED ON KEX/KGW
AND KBPS, 1943–1944 (Swenson, 1958, p. 60)

Day and Time	Program and Description	Grade
Monday — 11:15 A.M.	*Great Moments in Oregon History*	7–8
Tuesday — 11:15 A.M.	*They'll Always Be Heroes*	5–6
Wednesday — 11:15 A.M.	*What Am I?*	6–8
Thursday — 11:15 A.M.	*How Are You Feeling?*	4–8
Friday — 11:15 A.M.	*Current Events*	6–8

When possible, the programs were aired simultaneously over KBPS and the commercial stations. Principals were asked to arrange school schedules so that most teachers could use the programs.

Gilmore also oversaw a particularly productive period in which Portland high school teachers and students developed a large number of original series for in-school use that were broadcast exclusively over KBPS. Table 62 lists just five of the many in-school programs developed during that period, most for high school students.

TABLE 62. IN-SCHOOL PROGRAMS DEVELOPED BY PORTLAND
SCHOOLS FOR BROADCAST ON KBPS, 1943–1944
(Swenson, 1958, p. 61)

Program and Description

Oregon Authors
　　Interviews by members of high school journalism classes
　　with distinguished Oregon authors.

Pacific Northwest Tales
　　Legends of the Northwest region dramatized by high school drama clubs

Figure It Out
　　Planned and presented by the Supervisor of Mathematics, these programs featured
　　a student quiz, a number story and interview with people who use math in their jobs.

Great Composers
　　Featuring the lives and careers of six great composers, the series were dramatized by
　　three high school radio clubs.

Oregon Industries
　　A series of eight weekly programs dramatizing industries of Oregon, prepared
　　and produced by eighth grade students for use in social studies.

Though intended for in-school listening, these series were short term, 4 to 8 weeks; none spanned a full semester. Nevertheless, during this time, KBPS received an award from the Fifth School Broadcast Conference held in Chicago. Citations for excellence went to the Franklin High School

Radio Players for their original series, *Portrait of Empire Builders*, which was used in Oregon history classes.

In 1943, Gilmore faced a serious dilemma that had or would confront nearly every local school radio operation, namely the loss of their carefully nurture commercial broadcast outlets. In the aftermath of the break up of NBC's two networks, Portland stations KGW and KEX discontinued broadcasting the in-school educational programs that they had provided since 1934. While KEX managers did continue to write and produce the scripts, KBPS' small staff suddenly faced the big responsibility of becoming the city's major source for in-school educational broadcasts. The episode underscored the change that had taken place in market place dynamics; daytime radio had become too valuable to be donated freely.

Gilmore's most significant accomplishment turned out to be in organizational development rather than in programming. She believed making the most effective use of radio in the schools required an organizational framework that tied KBPS to each individual school. At her request, the school administration asked all school principals to appoint a teacher at their schools to serve as liaison between their school and the station. These teachers would be known as Radio Coordinators and would be responsible for successful utilization of the radio programs at each school. Their duties included routing broadcast support materials within the school, informing each teacher about the subject and grade level of the upcoming broadcasts, teaching classroom teachers how to make best use of the radio programs, and assisting teachers with the planning and development of original radio program scripts for production on KBPS. During the summer months, coordinators were urged to attend radio workshops—quite a lot for an unpaid effort.

The Radio Institute

In 1944, development of original radio scripts for broadcast over KBPS received a big boost when a local CBS affiliate station, KOIN, conducted Portland's first Radio Institute for Teachers. Jointly sponsored by KOIN and the school board, the three-week Institute attracted over 300 teachers from the greater Portland area, immersing them in topics such as writing radio drama, conducting radio forums, handling controversial issues, listening to news on radio, and, most popular, how best to utilize radio in the classroom. Teachers heard presentations by the authorities on educational radio such as I. Keith Tyler, Director of the Institute for Education by Radio, Dr. Lyman Bryson, Educational Director at CBS radio, and Norman Corwin, America's foremost radio dramatist. Teachers who attended received career advancement credit from the Portland Extension Division.

Gilmore credits the Institute with stimulating interest in radio throughout Portland's schools. In the year following the first KOIN Institute, three new in-school series were produced by teachers who had attended the Institute or by the classes of teachers who had attended. *The New China Program* presented a social studies series for seventh grade. *Fulton Park School Goes on the Air* was an all-school original radio production, and *Junior Town Meeting of the Air* featured social studies discussion by and for high school students. It was the only radio program in the country moderated by a student. The Institute was repeated the following year (Swenson, 1958).

In 1945, the Portland school board took two actions that communicated its support for radio education. First it promoted Gilmore from the position of teacher to that of Assistant Supervisor of Radio. The new position paid a higher salary and made Gilmore part of the school administration. That same year, the Portland school board rejected two offers from business groups to purchase KBPS. With the war's end in sight, many business people were excited by radio's expanding market potential. The Board's rejections signaled its belief that the station provided great educational value for the students of Portland (Swenson, 1958).

In same year, the American Council on Education invited the Portland school system to participate in the Council's national project on intercultural education. The school board took up the challenge immediately, in part because during and after World War II, Portland's African-American population had boomed from roughly 2,000 to more than 20,000. The board decided to use radio to promote intercultural projects throughout the city's schools; the responsibility fell naturally to KBPS and Gilmore. After researching the local stations for appropriate programming and finding none, Gilmore challenged classroom teachers and students to write scripts on the theme of intercultural understanding and promised air time for any worthy efforts. She urged high school radio workshops and clubs to produce scripts for national magazines that promoted the intercultural themes. One result from her efforts was a series on Intercultural Education that included both original scripts created by Portland high school teachers and programs from outside sources, including a series made available by the Urban League consisting of scripts treating prejudice called the *Loom of Life*.

In June of 1947, Director Gilmore submitted her resignation. Gilmore had requested promotion to the position of full supervisor, but the board refused saying that she lacked the Master Degree required of all supervisors. Gilmore argued that KBPS had earned a national reputation for its extensive educational and community programming, and as a result, she needed an assistant to maintain that high level of activity. The board refused saying that it lacked the money for an additional position.

In her six year tenure, Gilmore had established an impressive record of accomplishments. The station in cooperation with the commercial stations offered a broad range of programs for in-school and after school listening and also provided a publicity outlet for many community organizations. Most of all, KBPS continued to be a vehicle for student involvement in the technical aspects of broadcasting and in program production.

The Swenson Years

Gilmore's replacement was Patricia Green Swenson, who would serve as director of in-school programming and later as manager of KBPS until 1988. Swenson inherited a station that broadcast 12 hours a day from 10:00 A.M. to 10:00 P.M.[29] Its schedule during school hours included a fine mix of original instructional programs developed by Portland school teachers and students, in-school programs developed by Portland's commercial stations, taped contributions from the Oregon School of the Air and several network programs transmitted to KBPS from the commercial stations. The full week's program log for 1948–49 is too large to be reproduced here, but the excerpted part, shown in Table 63 gives an idea of the station's extensive offerings of programs intended for in-school use.

TABLE 63. EXCERPTS OF **KBPS** PROGRAM LOG, 1948–1949
(SWENSON, 1958, PP. 130–132)

Originating Station	In-school Programs	Time
	Monday	
KBPS	*The News*	10 A.M.
	Old Tales and New	11:00 A.M.
	Nuggets of Verse	11:30 A.M.
	Sons of Guns	11:45 A.M.
	Luncheon Concert	12:00 noon
	Bulletin Board	12:45 P.M.

[29]The KBPA broadcast day had been extended from 8 to 12 hours in order to fend off a challenge from a commercial station that wanted to use the frequency during the station's unused evening hours.

	French Folk Songs	1:30 P.M.
	Decision Now	2:00 P.M.
	A Look at Australia	2:15 P.M.
	Afternoon Varieties	2:30 P.M.
KGW (NBC)	*Great Moments in Oregon History*	11:15 A.M.
KOIN (CBS)	*Kid Critics*	2:45 P.M.
KOAC (Oregon School of the Air)	*Especially for Women*	10:15 A.M.
	Land of Make Believe	1:15 P.M.

Tuesday

KBPS	*Community Living*	10:15 A.M.
	Books Bring Adventure	11:00 A.M.
	Builders of Oregon	11:30 A.M.
	Music for All	1:00 P.M.
	Adventure in Research	1:30 P.M.
	Guest Star	1:45 P.M.
KGW (NBC)	*Our Magic World*	11:15 A.M.
	Chicago Round Table	2:00 P.M.
KOAC (Oregon School of the Air)	*The News Watch*	1:15 P.M.
	What's that Word?	2:30 P.M.

Wednesday

KBPS	*Junior Town Meeting*	10:15 A.M.
	Music for All	11:30 A.M.
	Journeys Behind the News	1:00 P.M.
	Rhythm and Reason	1:30 P.M.
	Safety Story Lady	1:45 P.M.
KGW (NBC)	*Science By-Ways*	11:15 A.M.
KOAC (Oregon School of the Air)	*Stories that Live*	2:00 P.M.
	What's that Word?	2:30 P.M.

Thursday

KBPS	*Storybook Land*	11:00 A.M.
	Music for All	11:30 A.M.
	Starry Skies	1:00 P.M.
	Homes on the Land	1:30 P.M.
	Jeff Latin Club	2:45 P.M.
KGW (NBC)	*Pan America*	11:15 A.M.
	Let's Be Healthy	2:30 P.M.
KOAC (Oregon School of the Air)	*Let's Sing America*	1:15 P.M.
	Lest We Forget	1:45 P.M.

Friday

KBPS	*Young Homemakers*	11:30 A.M.
	Five Centuries of French Music	1:30 P.M.
	Excursions in Science	1:45 P.M.
	Homes on the Land	2:30 P.M.
KGW	*Current Events*	11:15 A.M.
KOAC (Oregon School of the Air)	*Nature Trails*	11:00 A.M.
	Tell a Story	1:15 P.M.

Regardless of the originating station, KBPS also broadcast all programs shown in Table 63 except for KOIN's *Kid Critics*. Because many KBPS originated programs ran less than a full-semester — usually four to eight weeks in length — Swenson had to scramble to fill the 30 plus hours of in-school broadcasting each week with effective instructional programs, most of which ran only 15 minutes long. In addition to the daytime schedule, KBPS also broadcast programs after school and in the evening. All told, Swenson was responsible for broadcasting 135 programs a week. She did that with a staff of one and half positions, compared to other local educational stations that generally had 5 or 6 staff positions. How did they do it? They succeeded by coordinating a broad array of people and resources: (1) The "Benson boys" served as the station's production and technical staff. (2) New program series were developed by continually encouraging Portland high school teachers and students to plan and write them. That production was supported with teacher workshops and written guidelines on radio production and utilization. (3) Swenson and her staff worked hard at maintaining good relations with the commercial stations that contributed the semester long series. (4) She borrowed up to ten taped programs from the Oregon School of the Air (KOAC) each semester. Despite their successes, both Gilmore and Swenson had complained that inadequate staffing retarded the station's accomplishments. "Lack of staff constitutes the greatest difficulty in following through the KBPS program of educational radio" (Swenson, 1958, p. 124). The Portland school board continually refused requests to expand the KBPS staff.

Despite their consistently tight attitude toward adding staff, the school board did increase the KBPS operating budget steadily during the years 1943 to 1950, from $5,000 to nearly $22,000 annually. However, given an enrollment of 49,000 students, even in the latter years, the Portland school system spent less than fifty cents per pupil on educational radio.

One exception to the board's parsimonious attitude occurred in 1948 when it granted a half-day of release time to a teacher so she could write and present a music series called *Fun with Music*. Intended for primary grades, each 15 minute program presented music for rhythmic response, dramatic play and for quiet listening. It was the first time the board had agreed to hire a substitute in support of KBPS activities (Swenson, 1958).

Program Descriptions

During the 1948–1949 school year, in response to teacher requests, KBPS aired nine original programs to support curricula in art, literature and music. These programs demonstrated KBPS's ability to quickly respond to teacher needs, serve the needs of civic and cultural organizations, and get students involved at all levels. Several are described below:

Our Art Museum. This weekly series provided intermediate and upper grade students with informational reviews of current exhibitions at the Portland Art Museum. The goal was to stimulate young people to visit the exhibits in person.

Special Art Exhibition Interview Series. Planned by students with help from the Portland Public Schools Supervisor of Art, KBPS students interviewed, produced, and presented coverage of several exhibitions at the Portland Art Museum. The programs included live interviews from the galleries with artists and student visitors.

Theatre Lady. This series featured plays and characters from the Portland Junior Civic Theatre, a children's theatre that highlighted the KBPS policy of involving community groups in school education.

Nuggets of Verse. A response to teacher requests for help in developing poetry appreciation among children, the series was produced by the Radio Workshop classes of Jefferson and Franklin High Schools. It featured poetry selected by classes at several elementary schools.

Careers in Art. Designed to inform high school students about opportunities for careers in different fields of art, the monthly series was co-planned and moderated by Art Museum personnel.

"Kid Critics"— Budding Book Reviews on the Air (KBPS) (courtesy of Station KBPS, Portland, Oregon Public Schools).

KBPS's in-school programming was seriously threatened when KGW announced that as of January 1950 it would discontinue writing and producing the six in-school weekly radio series. That meant KBPS would lose the core of its in-school programming because the understaffed station lacked the resources to write and produce six weekly series of similarly high production values. In an effort to save the programs, Swenson and the school board notified parents of the imminent threat and asked them write to the school board and station KGW asking them to reverse their decision. The Board also distributed a survey to all elementary schools asking teachers to disclose how frequently they used the threatened programs. The results were impressive. For five of the six programs between 50 percent and 70 percent of the intended teachers tuned in. Satisfied of the demand, managers of KGW decided to continue writing and producing the in-school programs (Swenson, 1958). It is unclear how long they continued doing so.

Support Materials

While the Portland radio operation achieved distinction in many areas, it faltered in the important area of preparing and distributing printed support materials to the schools. Since the mid–1930s, the Radio Committee of the KBPS directors had mimeographed and distributed weekly KBPS program bulletins, which listed the programs for classroom use to be broadcast by KBPS and the commercial stations. The bulletins also listed the educational programs available from the network SOAs— NBC's *Music Appreciation Hour* and CBS's *American School of the Air*— and broadcast by the city's commercial stations.

However, what teachers needed most in order to integrate radio into their classrooms was a semester schedule and guide with program descriptions so they could make long range lesson plans. The commercial stations had distributed their own semester program announcements, but not until 1944 did Gilmore finally get a KBPS semester schedule into the hands of classroom teachers. It provided program titles, dates, broadcast times, and intended grade levels for the 26 programs to be broadcast by KBPS during the 1944–1945 school year, but for some reason distribution of the semester schedule was discontinued in 1946 or 1947.

Gilmore had recognized the deficiencies in the area of program support materials. In her 1945 report to the Superintendent of Portland Schools she called for the preparation of a teacher handbook for each series. The handbook should present, she said, a resume of each program in the series, suggestions for teacher preparation for and follow-up to the broadcast, vocabulary, and a list of supplementary readings (Swenson, 1958). Many years passed before the handbooks that Gilmore had called for were finally prepared and distributed.

The problem may have stemmed from the fact that in 1944, the newly formed Curriculum Council put the school's radio operation under the auspices of the subcommittee on Audio Visual Aids, later called Instructional Materials Department. That change took the responsibility for preparing and distributing radio supplemental materials away from the radio people and gave it to the Audio Visual people who may not have understood the importance of semester schedules and teacher guides (Swenson 1958).

Fortunately, in spring of 1947 Gilmore's replacement, Patricia Green Swenson, issued the first comprehensive KBPS Program Guide, which covered all programs broadcast over KBPS regardless of originator. For each program, it provided the originating station, series, title, time, day, suggested grade level and the recommended curricular area. Also she included for the first time the schedule and descriptions for the in-school programs broadcast by the Oregon School of the Air, station KOAC. Unfortunately, distribution of the Guide was discontinued again in 1948. In a letter to classroom teachers announcing the beginning of the 1949 radio broadcast year, Swenson mentioned that the Guide was not in production and that teachers should refer to the weekly bulletins to learn about the radio offerings (Swenson 1958). Unfortunately, lack of documentation makes it impossible to determine how frequently Swenson distributed Guides in subsequent years.

Not all of the many taped series that KBPS borrowed through the NAEB tape library included print support materials. To fill the gap, Green Swenson organized teacher committees to help prepare what they called "broadcast utilization materials," e.g. teacher guides. Teachers received these materials every week on a just-in-time basis.

By the 1953–1954 school year, the distribution of radio support materials had become more extensive, but confusing. To meet teacher requests for the titles, dates, and broadcast times of KBPS programs a year in advance, the Department of Instructional Materials distributed a KBPS Broadcast Guide. On its opening page, Green Swenson explained the confusing situation in which schedules and titles were provided for some series, but not others. The Guide included no descriptions or any other information about the programs. Green Swenson stated that the broadcast utilization materials were delivered weekly to the schools as part of a separate publication. It is unclear why such a confusing dual situation was necessary. The most probable answer, lack of staff.

By the mid–1960s, the school of the air operation seems to have gotten in synch with the Department of Instructional Materials. From that point on, at the beginning of each semester, the schools distributed a giant blue book, the KBPS Program Schedule. It included program series titles, broadcast times, and descriptions for all in-school series. It was a long time coming.

Philosophy and Methods

We can construct a general idea about what educational philosophy might have guided the development of KBPS programming by examining the development of the KBPS effort. Portland's school board originally set up KBPS as a laboratory where students at Benson Polytechnic could gain on-the-job training and experience running a real radio station. Later on, school administrators expanded that vision by offering radio-based instructional support to teachers throughout the city schools. More important, they continued to encourage active learning by extending to all Portland high school students the opportunity to plan, write, and perform radio programs. These actions stemmed from a vision of learning by doing, a vision that seemed influenced by Dewey's progressive thought. Dewey's Progressivism stressed active learning in real world contexts, though KBPS sources make no mention of him or progressivism.

After her appointment as station direction, Patricia Green Swenson offered a more instrumental perspective. She described radio as a "tool of learning, a teaching tool that no teacher should ignore" because students were living in the radio age. "Most children in school had never been without radio, they were accustomed to listening to it at home for information and enjoyment" (p. 106). Radio offered the teacher a great opportunity and challenge to use a tool of learning with which most young people were already familiar (Swenson, 1958).

Later in an article sent to teachers and school administrators, Swenson characterized radio as the "Fourth R" because to many it had become a significant factor in the total learning process. But she qualified that characterization saying radio lived up to that designation only when classroom teachers considered carefully how best to use it with their students. Factors that affected radio's effectiveness included determining whether radio instruction suited the learning topic and goals better than other media, the receptivity of a specific class to the anticipated programs, and finally how best to utilize the radio lessons. When all of these factors were folded into the learning situation, then radio can indeed be the Fourth R (Swenson, 1950, pp. 1–12).

Insight into how those who guided or ran Portland's in-school radio operation viewed education by radio can also be gained by studying what they did *not* say about radio. They made no grand statements about radio inaugurating world peace or a people's university or bringing the world into the classroom. They made no mention of master teachers or the voices of society's great leaders, artists, or scientists. Instead, they seem to see radio as affording students the opportunity to get actively involved in a variety of sophisticated learning activities that might not be available without radio. Indeed, thousands of Portland students did so.

Borrowing from KOAC

One of the mainstays in KBPS broadcast week were the 10 taped programs borrowed from Oregon's station, KOAC, managed by James Morris. Though KOAC also worked on a shoestring budget, the programs were professionally produced and as such represented a valuable addition to Swenson's schedule. However, the borrowing was not always a turn-key operation. Each program carried some baggage of special considerations and problems associated with its acquisition. Morris and Green Swenson were well acquainted and corresponded often on personal and business matters. Below are excerpts from their correspondence dealing with a problem Green Swenson faced in airing the KOAC astronomy series, *Starry Skies*. The exchanges show the difficulties that directors of the respective SOAs faced in getting programs of broadcast quality.

Patricia Green Swenson to James Morris, Sept. 1, 1949

Dear Jimmie: ... Mr. Rehmus, our Superintendent, called me into his office this morning to discuss Mr. Pruett and his *Starry Skies* with me ... Eugene Allen, a member of our school board is an amateur astronomer, and in the course of correspondence with Mr. Pruett learned that he [Pruett] was getting only 25 cents a week from both KBPS and KOAC for his radio scripts. Mr. Allen [believes] that Mr. Pruett is an astronomer of some note and importance ... [and should be getting more than 25 cents a week for his materials]

I told Mr. Rhemus we were considering using the *Starry Skies* programs (which you rewrite into 15 minute programs), but we could not pay the price that Mr. Pruett had asked. Mr. Rhemus feels that Pruett's material must be worth more than 25 cents and that the Portland Public Schools is willing to pay more.

— This is so long to put into a letter —

...but the board member has been very persistent. We must come to some decision on it. I told Mr. Rhemus that I hadn't heard the programs as you rewrote them so I was not able to set a price.... Could you please send five or six ... scripts of *Starry Skies* which you have expanded.

How noted is Mr. Pruett? I enjoy reading his material in the paper, [Pruett wrote an astronomy column for the local newspaper] but I don't think his five minute script's straight narration has much value for boys and girls as they are.

James Morris to Patricia Green Swenson, Sept. 14, 1949

Dear Pat: ... a word of explanation concerning the series, *The Starry Skies* which is furnished by Professor Pruett ... the material which he writes for newspapers is very inadequate for broadcast purposes and especially for our use on the Oregon School of the Air.... I contacted Professor Pruett a year and a half ago about the possibilities of planning an Astronomy series and bringing out a workbook or broadcast guide. Pruett gave me no concrete ideas of cost of such a project. The results was that we use on our *Starry Skies* a carbon copy of the material which he sends to the newspapers and that is used in the Sunday Oregonian.

The material is not rewritten, rather I talk from his material, ad-libbing my own elaboration, defining some of his technical terms in words that youngsters can understand, and taking from my own knowledge of astronomy as well as from his script. I have no complete script of any broadcast which I could send to you as an example. Professor Pruett seems very happy with this association.... His only payment from KOAC is for the added expense involved in making the carbon copies and the postage for mailing the scripts to us.

...Frankly, the present arrangement is only a stop-gap ... sooner or later we must face the need for a substantial expenditure in return for program material that teachers can have in advance and use intelligently in their educational programs.

The exchange demonstrates political and financial pressures that both SOA directors faced in getting programs on the air with their limited budgets and staff. Other SOAs, Wisconsin and Chicago, had paid script writers who could have easily written scripts out of Pruett's materials. Both could have paid Pruett an acceptable compensation.

Audience

Portland's school administrators occasionally conducted surveys to discover how many teachers used the KBPS programs and how often. No data on the findings of those studies exists except for the 1949 survey mentioned above. Based on those results, Swenson (1958) developed estimates of listenership for the six in-school programs produced by station KGW. Those results are presented in Table 64. They show that a substantial majority of Portland's elementary teachers used the six programs produced by the commercial stations, though it remains unclear how regularly. Interestingly, even though radio was thought to be a great medium for keeping students up to date on the news, *Current Events* was least used. The popularity of the *Great Moments* series probably stemmed in part from the fact that following World War II many state legislatures pressed the schools to teach state history, an early unfunded mandate. To comply, school boards often turned to radio where available because it offered a low cost solution.

TABLE 64. RESULTS, TEACHER LISTENING SURVEY, KBPS, 1949
(Swenson, 1958, pp. 182–183)

Programs	Total # of teachers and grade level surveyed	% of targeted population listening
Great Moments in Oregon History	90 eighth grade teachers	96.7% listen, most regularly
Our Magic World	72 second grade teachers	48.6%
	81 third grade teachers	70.4%
Science By-Ways	94 sixth grade teachers	48.9%
	71 seventh grade teachers	64.8%
	90 eighth grade teachers	52.2%

Pan America	94 sixth grade teachers	86.2%, (three fourths every week)
Let's Be Healthy	84 fourth grade teachers	81%
	78 fifth grade teachers	69.2%
Current Events	71 seventh grade teachers	39.4%
	90 eighth grade teachers	33.3 %

A few other indicators of KBPS audience and reputation also exist. For example Swenson, who served as the chair of the Radio Coordinator Committee and the program director for KBPS, claimed that "everyone of our [Portland's] 73 schools utilizes the services of KBPS in some aspect of their instructional programs" (Swenson, 1958, p. 128). If true, then Portland's teachers gave education by radio a ringing endorsement. Another indicator of the interest in and use of radio can be seen in the numbers of people who visited the KBPS station. Swenson (1958) made several claims, one that in 1948 approximately 400 children visited the KBPS studios each week. Another more precise claim was that in the 1949–1950 school year, 2,476 students and 333 teachers not counting staff visited the station. That adds up to roughly 5 percent of Portland's school population at that time.[30] Finally as a sign of KBPS's national reputation, it was invited to participate in one of I. Keith Tyler's radio research studies (Swenson, 1958, p. 49). Tyler headed up the federally funded Evaluation of Radio Broadcast research program at The Ohio State University.

On the negative side, Swenson (1958) mentioned several surveys conducted by the school board intended to learn how frequently teachers made use of the radio programs, but she provides no report on the results. This omission is curious. Perhaps the results were disappointing and, as a school board employee, she felt uncomfortable reporting bad news. Swenson made no report of any evaluation of the educational effectiveness of the radio programs. As for how KBPS impacted learning in the Portland schools, no data are available.

The 1960s

Despite the fact that contributions from the commercial stations had ceased by the early 1960s, KBPS continued to provide Portland schools with curricular enrichment and supplemental radio instruction. Working with a small staff, Swenson seems to have developed a consistent routine for delivering a full schedule of educational broadcasting. In addition, almost all the series were supported with print materials that included detailed program descriptions and schedules and in some cases teacher guides. Table 65 below provides a snap shot of the KBPS schedule for fall 1964 along with the intended grade level. Note the division between new and old programs.

TABLE 65. KBPS RADIO SERIES, FALL 1964
(KBPS Guide, 1964)

In-school Programs, New Series	Grade Level
History Highlights II	8–11
Introspect	7–8
Poetry Piper	6–8
King Arthur and his Knights	6–8
Some Merry Adventures of Robin Hood	6–8
Exploring Numbers	5–7

[30]Portland Public School enrollment was approximately 49,000 in 1945 (KBPS Bulletin, 1945).

Sense of the World	4–6
Portland Our Town	3
Linda Visits Afar	1–3
Playtime	K–3

In-school Programs, "Old Series"	Grade Level	In-school Programs "Old Series"	Grade Level
Art		**Oregon**	
Men of Art	6–12	*Exploring Scenic Oregon*	4–8
Journeys in Art	5–12	*Great Moments in Oregon*	
		History	8
		Northwest Adventure	4
Foreign Languages		**Science**	
Ecoutez!	7–10	*Alphabet of Science*	6–8
Gesundheit	5–8	*Exploring Science*	4–8
Speak Russian	5–8	*Making Friends with Science*	1–3
Speak Spanish	5–8	*Science By-ways*	5–8
Voici Mimi	2–6		
Re-voici Mimi	3–6		
Music		**Primary Stories**	
Come Listen Awhile	1–3	*Ever After*	2–4
Fun with Music III	1–3	*Just Why Stories*	K–3
It's Fun to Sing	K–3	*Our Magic World —*	1–3
Making Friends		*Mr. Buttons*	
with Music	6–8		
History and Social Studies		**Literature, Myth and Poetry**	
A Day to Remember	4–6	*Tales from the Troubadours*	5–8
Growing Up	1–3	*Tales from the Yet to Come*	6–8
How It Began	3–8	*Treasure Chest of Poetry*	4–6
Lives of Man	7–9	*World of Myths and Legends*	5–9
The Old World Today	7		
Pan America II	6		
The Story of Numbers	6–8		
Miscellaneous		**Miscellaneous**	
Meeting the Situation	6–8	*This Land of Ours*	5
Radio Almanac	8–12	*What's the Big Deal?*	4–8
Then and Now	7–10	*World of Wonders*	4–6
Think Your Answer	3–4		

The schedule shows that in the fall of 1964, KBPS broadcast 10 new and 40 "old" programs designed chiefly for grades K–9. Surprisingly, the schedule included six foreign language series; no other SOA at any level offered as many. More important, most series were supported by comprehensive printed materials consisting of program descriptions, broadcast schedules and for many series, full-blown teacher guides.

The question arises, how did Swenson working with an absurdly small staff composed of two full-time professionals and a few dozen high school students maintain such a formidable broadcast schedule? The answer is complex and simple at the same time. First, Swenson regularly solicited feedback from teachers. Sometime during the school year, she asked teachers to evaluate programs and request new topics to be covered. Based on the results, she planned the broadcast schedule for the following year. Then, taking full advantage of KBPS's affiliation with the National Association of Educational Broadcasters (NAEB), Swenson borrowed many outstanding program series from other educational radio stations, and from university, government, scientific, and cultural centers throughout the United States. Swenson continued her long time relationship with Oregon's state owned station by re-broadcasting series from the Oregon School of the Air (KOAC). Also, Swenson regularly encouraged Portland's teachers and students to plan and develop original series. Though the creators of most programs on the 1964 schedule cannot be identified, those with titles that included the words Oregon, Portland or Northwest were most likely home grown. Finally, KBPS and Swenson apparently had the full support of the Portland school board and administration. The Portland school's audio visual department prepared and distributed print support materials for nearly all in-school radio series (KBPS Guide, 1964). Despite working with bare bones staff and budget, throughout the 1960s, KBPS probably offered and supported as many quality in-school broadcasts as the big city SOAs in Chicago, Cleveland, and New York City.

Listening Text

While most local SOAs seemed to have hit their stride during the period from just after World War II to the end of the 1960s, Portland's SOA achieved its zenith much later. As of 1970, KBPS became a member of National Public Radio, giving it access to NPR's library of instructional programs, many of which were added to the KBPS broadcast schedule. During the 1970s, the Portland Public Schools integrated in-school broadcasting with school curricula more fully than had been the case in earlier decades. Moreover, the school system overall seemed more involved with educational radio and the KBPS staff grew larger. An overview of the Portland Public School's radio operation of the late 1970s can be obtained from a publication called the *KBPS Listening Text*, published throughout the 1970s and 1980s. *The Listening Text* for 1978—1979 contains descriptions of each instructional series, the broadcast schedule, appropriate subject areas and grade level designations. It also coordinates each program with appropriate learning skills and learning goals. Also included are teacher guides for most series. Overall, the *Listening Text* represented the most comprehensive printed radio support materials prepared by any local school board.

According to the *Listening Text* for 1978–1979, KBPS operations were directed by the Educational Media Department of the Portland Public Schools. Preparation of the *Text* involved a staff of six including Patricia Swenson who at that time carried the clunky title of Supervisor, Radio/Manager KBPS. The station's staff, in addition to Swenson, now included a production coordinator, chief engineer, production assistant, and a student intern who also served as a production assistant. While that group seems larger than in earlier years, it was still small compared to the roughly 25 full-timers who staffed New York's WNYE.[31]

REVISED VISION AND PEDAGOGY

The *Listening Text* section entitled "How to Use Instructional Radio" demonstrates that Swenson and the school administration had updated their conception of how to use educational radio in the classroom in several ways. In the early years, radio educators had advocated either a "one size fits many" approach or that one size could be tailored to a specific topic and grade level, but in either case, every student in a class listened to the same programs. The *Text* advocated a new approach, i.e., using programs not just for the whole class, but for small groups or individual learning as well. The classroom teacher decided how best to incorporate the series or individual programs into her lesson plans. Of course, the approach entailed new technology, namely listening stations where a small group or an individual could plug into a radio for private listening while the teacher worked with other members of the class. A few other SOAs mentioned using radio in this way, but the Portland system fully supported it.

The *Text* authors also asserted that just like reading skills, listening skills must be taught. "Edu-

[31]Not surprisingly many of the taped programs borrowed from NAEB were created by WNYE.

cation is increasingly utilizing electronic techniques. It isn't all the printed word anymore. The world is weighted toward the rapid transmission of vital information by picture and spoken work ... and the most often used [communication] skill is LISTENING" (KBPS Listening Text, 1978, p. 12).

By focusing on listening skills— rather than good listening habits— the PSA connected the old technology of radio with the then new ideas in education, namely the skills approach. Perhaps this focus enabled radio instruction to remain relevant to the city's elementary teachers.

CURRICULAR CORRELATIONS

Table 66 shows the program series offered for 1978 – 1979 by curricular area and intended grade level.

TABLE 66. KBPS RADIO SERIES, 1978–1979
(KBPS Listening Text, 1978)

Portland Public Schools	Recommended Grade Level				
Curriculum Areas and Series Title	K–3	4–6	5–8	7–8	9–12
ART					
*Arnie's Art Shop	X				
CAREER EDUCATION					
*Mystery Guest	X				
People Works			X	X	
*This Could Be You		X			
*Who's Behind It?	X				
CONSUMER EDUCATION					
*Watcha See Is Watcha Get			X	X	
*Wise Choices I Make	X				
If You've Got a Dime, You've Got a Choice		X	X		
HEALTH/PE					
*Catch Yellow Bus	X				
Healthy, Happy and Wise	X				
Healthy, Well-Fed and Wise	X				
*Movin' Free	X				
Getting to Know You		X	X		
LANGUAGE ARTS					
Better to Listen With	X				
Drama	X	X	X	X	X
Listening/4		X	X		
Mr. Saymore Says	X				
News Capsules	X	X	X	X	X
*Spell Down I – II	X	X	X	X	
*Spelling Bee I – II	X	X			
Spotlight	X	X	X	X	X
The Poem Maker		X	X		
The Spider's Web					
Turn On Your Ear	X	X	X	X	X
LAW RELATED					
Inquiry: The Justice Thing			X	X	
*Law Is ...		X	X		

Portland Public Schools	Recommended Grade Level				
Curriculum Areas and Series Title	K–3	4–6	5–8	7–8	9–12
MATHEMATICS					
*Make It Metric			X	X	
*Math Whizzes	X	X	X		
More or Less	X				
MULTI-CULTURAL					
Out of Many, One		X	X	X	
MUSIC					
*Catch a Sound	X				
Music and Me	X				
SCIENCE					
Exploring Science II	X	X			
Pollution/Energy		X	X	X	
SOCIAL SCIENCES					
Animal Focus	X	X	X		
Mail Bag			X		
*Who Cares?	X	X			

* Indicates series mostly likely developed within the Portland Schools

The chart covers 37 program series in eleven curricular subject areas. Using a Master Matrix, each series was further categorized according to the language arts skills they helped develop. For example, the main curricular thrust of *Arnie's Art Shop* was art of course, but it could also be used to build the communication skills of listening, reading, speaking, and writing. Remarkably, 15 series were developed by teachers or subject experts from within the Portland school system. Below are examples of the program descriptions and goal statements for representative series at various broad grade levels:

Primary, K–3, Arnie's Art Shop

Goals: Students will develop concepts and skills of art through a wide variety of media experiences.

Description: Listeners participate actively following Arnie's directions as they explore painting, stitchery, appliqué and collage, and print making.

Skills: Learning skills include problems solving/critical thinking, observation. Technical skills include material and tool use, drawing, painting, ceramics, textiles.

Intermediate Level, Listening/4

Goals: Students will examine their role as consumers and develop skills to extend their consumer competencies. Students will increase their vocabulary related to consumer education and their ability to listen critically for relevant information.

Description: The series emphasized five major listening skills: identifying details, identifying main ideas, making inferences, listening for sequences and summarizing. The format was deliberately unpredictable, and the content was planned to intrigue, surprise, and challenge. Worksheets were provided.

Upper Elementary Level, The Justice Thing

Goal: Students will identify a variety of law-related problems that may be encountered in real life situations.

Descriptions: Encourages respect and understanding for the laws and legal system. The purpose is to inform and to stimulate discussion, not to advise (KBPS Listening Text, 1978).

Following the section on series overviews, the *Text* provided teacher lesson guides for nearly every series. The whole *Listening Text* publication ran over 300 pages.

Final Years—Student Involvement

In a memo dated 1982, Swenson outlined the services that KBPS provided to the Portland schools. They included among other things:

• Career education in radio
• In-school programming in many subject areas prepared in cooperation with the curriculum department
• Musical and dramatic performance opportunities for students at all grade levels
• Participation in school dramas and city competition in spelling and math
• Assistance to school personnel in writing, producing and narrating radio programs
• Drama workshops (Swenson, 1982).

It is an impressive list for a station that boasted only 5 full-time staff. All but the first service, career education, related directly to KBPS' function as a school of the air. Throughout the 1980s, Swenson continued broadcasting a full schedule of in-school programs similar to that shown in Table 66, primarily by drawing heavily from a wide range of sources including NPR, American Public Radio, and Radio Netherlands, to name a few.[32] Throughout the final years, Portland's teachers and students continued to develop new programs and perform them.

The last four items on Swenson's list all related to student participation in radio, which during the final years became the focus for KBPS's service to the school—a testament, perhaps, to the Portland school administrator's refusal to abandon in-school broadcasting. Student involvement had always been a strong part of the KBPS identity, and as the availability of instructional radio programs on tape declined, KBPS filled the void by putting more students on the air. The 65th anniversary brochure of 1988 trumpets "many opportunities for creative student performances. Daily broadcasts include newscasts, storytelling, dramas, debates, panels and forums" (KBPS, 1988).

Remarkably in 1993, more than a decade after most other local SOAs had gone silent, KBPS distributed a bouncy brochure describing a surprising array of in-school broadcasts. The extent of that participation is spelled out clearly in the brochure *KBPS at a Glance, 1993–1994,* which highlights student participation and performance. Portland classroom teachers are invited to get their students involved in one of several student panel discussion programs in which an adult author or a subject expert led a discussion with a panel of students drawn from various schools. For a series on radio drama, billed as "A whole-language learning experience," students performed and recorded plays that were broadcast later over KBPS. Scripts at the appropriate reading level were written by KBPS staff or volunteer teachers. One scripted series covered Oregon history. The readings were broadcast as part of the long running series, *Old Tales and New,* in which students celebrated Oregon history by performing radio plays about the Oregon Trail (KBPS, 1993).

For the adventurous, the station regularly presented an "audio showcase for original student work," which could include plays, music, poetry, and short stories. All grades K–12 were

---

[32]In 1983, the Portland Schools launched KBPS FM, creating even more opportunities for in-school broadcasting. In the following year, the new facility broadcast a series targeted to high school students, and judging from several of the series titles, they must have thought FM appropriate for high brow programming. The titles included among others *Beethoven Lectures, Chautauqua Lectures, Radio Smithsonian, BBC Science Magazine, and City Club of Portland.* This list suggests the early days of instructional radio when SOA administrators thought prep school subject matter would draw listeners. No information is available on how many students listened in.

invited to participate. Such an "open mike" arrangement was almost guaranteed to produce a range of performances from exceptional to ghastly, but it demonstrated the station's willingness to experiment and to continue to run KBPS as a service for students (KBPS, 1993).

The KPBS schedule balanced student participation programs with regular broadcasts of old favorites such as the Holiday Special, *The Cinnamon Bear*. Billed as a Portland family tradition, the adventures of Paddy O'Cinnamon and his friends had been broadcast by KBPS annually since 1937.

Multi-cultural programming included broadcasts of ethnic folk tales and stories of different cultures and customs from around the world. The *Japanese Visitor* presented a Japanese student who shared cultural traditions with a Portland family. Other multicultural highlights included the drama series, *The Global Beat*. A computer malfunction sends three students off to explore world music. The documentary *Spirits of the Present* presented the legacy of Native Americans.

Kid Rhythm Radio filled the afternoon hours Monday through Friday with a series that offered teachers, parents and students "the best and most recent children's music and news." Each hour included music intermixed with brief reviews, interviews and news highlights by and for students, K through 5th grade.

Music made up a large part of the KBPS FM in-school broadcast day. Twice a week, *Music and You* offered a unique format consisting of students discussing with local performers the art of music making. Each program included a live, in-studio performance.

Competition in math and spelling made up two popular series. *Solvit* gave fourth, fifth and sixth graders the opportunity to apply their math skills and to solve word problems on the air. The goal was to promote skill in step-by-step problem solving methods. The competitions, one for each grade level, were aired for two hours several times each semester. All on-air participants received recognition as a Challenge Winner or a First Round Winner. KBPS made guides for *Solvit* available. *Spelldown* was open to students in grades 3 through 5. Students first took a written spelling test. Those who scored 80 percent or better qualified to participant in the on-air spelling competitions. All participants and their schools were recognized (KBPS, 1993).

Looking at the 1993–1994 KBPS brochure one can't help but be impressed with the vitality and creativity of Portland Public Schools broadcast effort. This was no derelict radio station approaching the end of a long and rough life. Rather KBPS AM and FM showed every intention of serving students with audio instruction and opportunities for direct learning involvement for years to come. Yet, the end was near.

Demise

The KBPS brochure for Spring 1995 showed signs that the station's long history of in-school broadcasting was nearing its end. The brochure is smaller than previous materials, and the name of long time director, Patricia Swenson, did not appear in the staff listing. Indeed, her name was last seen on the 1988, 65th Anniversary Program. A note from the Children's Radio Producer, Jackie Loucks, gave a sense of the precarious situation facing KBPS. She said that at the end of 1994, the Portland School district had eliminated the budget for radio operations. From that point on, the school board would retain the broadcast license but would no longer provide operating funds—though it would continue to provide in-kind services. KBPS was free to appeal to grants, "underwriting" and listener contributions for financial support (KBPS, 1995). In October 1994, as a way to raise money for operating KBPS, Benson Polytechnic made an agreement with Portland State University to share time on KBPS under the non-licensed call letters KPSU. That helped, but to stay alive during 1995, the station turned to that now familiar activity, the on-air fundraiser.

These changes meant that KBPS would have to pursue a different path. School children and their teachers could not be expected to donate the tens of thousands of dollars needed to support a radio station. Grants and underwriting would produce only supplemental funds for designated programs. In order to attract enough money from listeners to support operations, KBPS would have to broadcast programs that appealed to an adult audience. In-school programming did not fit into that picture.

One bright spot is that KBPS did not disappear or become another NPR station. In fact it has come full circle by reverting to its origins. It is once again dedicated to serving the students of the Benson Polytechnic School who are interested in careers in broadcast radio. The students write and produce programs in sports, local politics, and music for elementary schools.

Summary

While no entity in Portland ever called itself the "Portland School of the Air," radio station KBPS served that function for over 60 years.[33] Starting as a laboratory for training high school boys in radio broadcasting at Portland's Benson Polytechnic High School, the station's mission evolved gradually to providing instructional support to all of the city's schools. Throughout the years, Portland's teachers and high school students became involved at all phases of radio, script writing, production, broadcasting, and performing, a level of student involvement unmatched by any other SOA. Also notable was the high degree of cooperation KBPS achieved from several commercial stations. For the first decade of KBPS educational operation, NBC affiliate stations provided the schools with six in-school programs on a turn-key basis. But even after they stopped donating free air time to the schools, for another decade station KGW continued to write and produce six scripts a week for the schools. Finally, KBPS distinguished itself with programming that made 50,000 students aware of Portland's civic and cultural organizations. Several of these organizations developed instructional series for broadcast on KBPS.

A large part of the credit for KBPS's accomplishments must go to the women directors Kenyon, Gilman, and Swenson. Despite gross understaffing and limited funding, each woman expanded the station's vision and activities while remaining true to its original mission of being a laboratory for radio broadcasting.

During the final two decades KBPS in-school broadcasting received an extra infusion of funding and attention from school administrators. Programs became more closely integrated with school curricula and print support material more comprehensive and appealing. KBPS balanced its reliance on borrowed programs by emphasizing student involvement as creators and participants in educational radio, to an extent much greater than other SOAs. Even though KBPS now serves a limited audience, it continues to provide rich educational resources to the Portland schools.

WNYE School of the Air

New York City (NYC) is recognized for having the first school system in the country to experiment with broadcasting to the classroom. In June of 1923, just two and a half years after the landmark Westinghouse broadcast of the 1920 presidential election results, the NYC school board broadcast a program on American history intended for the DeWitt Clinton high school, probably one of the few schools in the city — or the country for that matter — equipped with a radio receiver. Since the broadcast came near semester's end, most likely it was a one-off event, and we know little more about it. However, the following year, 1924, the school board launched a

---

[33]Perhaps because the radio station of the University of Oregon, KOAC, used the title of the KOAC School of the Air and later the Oregon School of the Air, Portland's school administrators decided to avoid using the school of the air name to prevent any possible confusion.

more ambitious radio experiment. "Education by Radio" read the headline over a small article in the *New York Times* of February 10th. The article explained that the school authorities planned to broadcast "short educational talks or features each school day." The "entertainment" offered would include talks on educational topics, presentations by glee clubs, music lessons, songs, "recitations in English, history, civics, geography, arithmetic, nature study, science, spelling lessons" and special holiday programs. (Curiously, the article appeared at the end of the sports section.) These broadcasts were intended primarily to promote the schools to the general public (Atkinson, 1942c, pp. 12–13).

Later that semester, the *Times* reported on broadcasts aimed specifically at the classroom. The headline read, "Solve Problems by Radio: Pupils Here Get Questions Broadcast from Newark." Accountancy students at the Haaren High School, with adding machines ready, responded to accounting problems broadcast from what then seemed like distant Newark, New Jersey. At the end of the session, the broadcaster read the correct answers so students corrected their own tests. Also listening to the test were various school administrators located at the Board of Education building on Park Avenue. The Board issued an extensive report on the radio effort, but during the next decade, the NYC schools used radio infrequently.

Not until the mid 1930s did the NYC schools experiment again with radio for the classroom, but an experiment grew into one of the country's largest school of the air programs. The NYC broadcasting effort was unique because unlike other schools of the air that started before World War II, NYC's program never relied on commercial radio stations. From the beginning, NYC broadcast from its own radio facilities, WNYC and then WNYE. Furthermore, while it got off to a slow start, the New York system continued to expand and produce original programs, well into the 1980s. Because of their rich production values, the WNYE school of the air (WNYE-SA) programs received critical acclaim. Schools of the Air (SOAs) around the country frequently used taped versions of popular WNYE programs. New York's educational station remained true to its educational roots far longer than SOAs in other cities. Unfortunately, while New York built a big reputation for broadcasting to the schools, the documentation is scarce, so only part of the WNYE story can be told. The term "school of the air" was not widely used by NYC school administrators. In this work, the term WNYE-SA will be used.

Origins

In 1936, New York City offered the Board of Education an opportunity to initiate an experiment in education by radio using the city owned station, WNYC. The Board eagerly accepted the challenge and set aside $5,000 to fund a rigorous test of educational radio. It asked twenty schools to participate and keep careful record of the results of the radio instruction (Atkinson, 1942c). To launch the experiment, the school administration selected broadcast series that fit the schools' elementary curricula for specific grade levels. They also selected outstanding teachers to develop scripts and set a daily broadcast schedule. While the results of the tests are not available, the school board must have been satisfied, because following the test, support for education by radio increased steadily, though documentation on the experiment is sparse.

Starting in 1938, school administrators created three committees to advise and guide the radio work. They were the High Schools Radio Committee, the Junior High Schools Radio Committee and the Elementary Radio Committee. The following year, James Macandrew was appointed Radio Coordinator with full responsibility for radio operations, a position that Macandrew held for several decades. During that time, he became widely known as one of the nation's preeminent educational broadcasters working in radio and in television. By 1942, the radio staff working under Coordinator Macandrew consisted of a production manager, chief engineer, and a studio engineer. By 1944, the staff grew to nine, making it the country's the largest full-time staff devoted to radio for the classroom (Robertson, 1982). The radio school offered programs in a wide variety range of subjects including foreign languages, history, English, music, literature, and physics (Atkinson, 1942c).

Broadcasting

Broadcasting to the schools started with shared time on the city owned station, WNYC, but many city agencies used the station. Radio educators soon grew dissatisfied with that shared arrangement; they needed more air time and more control of their broadcasting schedule. To solve the problem, Macandrew and administrators of the Brooklyn Tech High School[34] persuaded the Board of Education to apply to the Federal Communications Commission (FCC) for a license to create a new broadcasting station to be operated by the schools. The FCC quickly approved a license to operate a short-wave station — the new bandwidth that the federal government advocated as the educational alternative to AM radio. Macandrew recalls, "in 1938, there probably weren't more than ten schools in the city of New York that owned radio sets" (Robertson, 1982, p. 4). While Macandrew may have exaggerated, it was true that very few of New York's 900 schools[35] possessed a short-wave receiving set. Consequently, the school programs continued to be broadcast over the city station, WNYC-AM, for several years more. Nevertheless, the new station was established, and Macandrew recalls they wanted a distinct educational identification. They considered the call letters WAOC for "all our children," but the radio people were overruled by a higher authority, and the station received the call letters, WNYE. "E" was for education. Macandrew explained:

> At that time Fiorello LaGuardia was mayor.... Now the mayor was ... a dynamic and impulsive human being ... and he was very much aware of the value of broadcasting ... Mayor LaGuardia said, "NY is New York, and we have NYC for the city, and P for the Police department and F for the fire department, and this is education, so that station there that the Board of Education put together, that's going to be WNYE." It was to no avail and a waste of breath to say that ... the letter "E" and the letter "C" (sound) fairly similar. And over and over we (WNYE) were to be confused with WNYC as the years went by. But that's the way it was, and that's the way it still is ... after 40 years[36] [Robertson, 1982, p. 7].

Shortwave never gained traction with the schools; the FM frequency was more attractive. In 1942, Edwin Armstrong, a Columbia college professor and the father of FM radio, donated some of his FM transmission equipment to WNYE and encouraged Macandrew to shift the station to FM. Based on Armstrong's recommendation, the Board of Education applied for and soon received a license to operate WNYE-FM (Robertson, 1982). That meant that the city's 900 plus schools had to be equipped with FM receivers, a job that was finally completed in 1950 (WNYE, 1951). Throughout the 1940s, however, the school board expanded its support for educational radio (Robertson, 1982).

The All-City High School Radio Workshop

During the first two decades, much of the radio program production, acting, and sound effects were performed by student members of the Board of Education (Radio) Workshops. Early on, radio educators realized that drama was the most successful format for classroom instruction. Drama of course required actors, but no money existed for hiring professionals or for releasing talented teach-

[34]At this time, Brooklyn Tech offered technical training designed to prepare students to become radio station engineers.

[35]MacAndrew estimated that by 1940, the NYC school system consisted of approximately 900 schools, about 90 of which were high schools, one million pupils, and between 60,000 and 70,000 teachers (Robertson, 1982).

[36]WNYC remained a city owned station until 1997 when it was transferred to a public-private foundation which operates it with a public radio format. WNYE became the official radio station of the city of New York.

ers. To fill the need, Macandrew and his staff turned to high school students. "We invited high schools to send candidates for what would become an all-city high school radio workshop ... we would hold auditions and a great many high schools sent students" (p. 8). The selected high school students were released early from their classes and received credit for a term of English. They also gained enormous practical experience in the skills of radio broadcasting. The Workshop became a kind of finishing school for young people seeking careers in fields of performance, "some very good names in American broadcasting and theater started in this little high school student workshop in Brooklyn, for instance, Barbara Streisand" (Robertson, 1982, p. 8). Later the workshop players were augmented by the WNYE Players, composed of gifted Workshop alumni (WNYE, 1954).

Programs

Documentation covering specific programs broadcast during the 1940s is scarce, but brochures exist for *Know Your City,* which during the early and mid–1940s served as a series on neighborhood history and diversity education. Its aim was to show that New York City is, "the largest and greatest city in the world today because of the contributions of all nations, races and creeds" (Know Your City, 1946). Jointly developed by the Board of Education and the City History Club, the series brought students from various schools into WNYE studies to participate in quiz format programs devoted to specific neighborhoods of New York. Students in school-based "Know Your City" clubs submitted questions and listened eagerly to the answers offered by a regular group of students in the studio. The program became enormously popular and captured a great deal of press attention.

Fortunately documentation from the decades of the 1950s and 1960s is available. The 1953–1954 schedule and program bulletin shown in Table 67 lists 12 programs broadcast multiple times during the week, starting in early October and continuing to the second week of May.

TABLE 67. WNYE PROGRAM SCHEDULE, 1953–1954
(WNYE 1954)

Program	Descriptions	Frequency
This Way to Story Land	Tales of people and places, animals and ideas, selected from the latest in children's literature.	M, T, W, Th, F
Tales from the Four Winds	Dramatized stories of legends and folk tales from around the world.	M, T, W, Th, F
* *Uncle Dan from Froggy Hollow Farm*	Presented children's experiences with animals, plants and insects. Designed to stimulate interest in the natural world.	M, T, W, Th, F
Science at Our Door	Highlighted different aspects of science; designed to arouse scientific curiosity.	M, T, W, Th, F
Sing Along	"Phil the folk singer" invited listeners to sing along with his guitar accompaniment.	M, T, W, Th, F
* *Making Friends with Music*	Music appreciation, intended for 5th and 6th grades. Informal presentations on good music.	M, T, W, Th, F
Language in Song	Designed for foreign language classes. Each program takes listeners on a foreign language trip in the language being studied.	Wednesday, 4 broadcasts
Americans to Remember	Dramatic presentation of the men and women who built America. Integrated with the Social Studies Curriculum.	M, T, W, Th, F

* The American Trail	Dramatic series that traced the growth of the United States.	Mondays, 4 times
Famous New Yorkers	Episodes in the careers of New Yorkers who contributed to the growth of the city.	Thursdays, 3 times
Safety Sam Returns	Through a series of adventures, Detective Sam highlighted safety awareness.	M, 2 times; Th and F.
Senorita Jones	Intended to promote better understanding between Spanish speaking and English speaking pupils.	M, T, W, Th

All programs were 15 minutes long and all aimed at the elementary grades. Counting all the repeat broadcasts, WNYE aired 50 broadcasts per week, a total of 12.5 hours during school hours. Most likely programs were aired once live, taped, and then the taped version broadcast as needed.

A comparison of the radio manuals for 1953–1954 and 1967–1968 reveals a surprising growth in operations. In the spring of 1968, during the hours 9:00 am to 3:30 pm, WNYE-SA aired 37 different program series compared with only 12 in 1953. Each program was aired several times during the week so the total number of weekly broadcasts reached 120. Table 68 shows the programs series organized by curricular areas.

TABLE 68. WNYE PROGRAM SCHEDULE, 1967–1968
(WNYE, 1967)

Curricular Area	Program Series and Descriptions*	Grade Level
Art	Men of Art	5–9
English as a	Senorita Jones	4–9
Second Language	Say It in English	4–6
Foreign Language	Songs of Other Lands	4–7
Guidance	What Would You Do?	1–3
Human Relations	Out of Many, One: A Nation of Minorities	4–12
	The Negro in America	4–12
Language Arts	Specially for You	K–2
	Tales from the Four Winds	1–3
	Stop, Look and Listen!	4–6
	Speak Up, Speak Out!	4–6
	The World of Myths and Legends	4–8
	American Folk Tales	4–8
	Meet Mr. Shakespeare	9–12
	Listen and Write	4–6
	Teen-Age Book Talk	7–12
Music	It's Fun to Sing	K–3
	Let's Make Music	4–6
	The Man and His Music	5–9
	Hall of Song: The Met	9–12
	Music We Like	7–12
	Toscanini Conducts	9–12
Safety	Safety Sam Returns	4–6
Science	A World of Wonder	K–2
	Pioneers of Science	5–9
	Science in Man's World	10–12
	March of Medicine	7–12

Social Science	*Where Does It Come From?*	1–3
	People and Places	3–5
	Friendly Helpers	K–2
	Man's Home: The Earth	5–9
	The Big City	5–9
	Americans to Remember	4–9
	Pacific Portraits	10–12
	Let's Look at the News	5–8
	What's in the News?	3–6
	Speak Your Mind	9–12

Table 68 shows the 37 program series organized into ten curriculum areas plus the grade level designations for each. Compared with the schedule from 1953, the 1968 schedule demonstrates a closer integration of radio with the school curricula. While the focus remained on programming for elementary grades, eight of the programs were intended for high school students. WNYE teacher guides for some series were distributed to the schools. Some of the more popular or innovative programs are described below.

Men of Art. (Art) The series introduced 15 notable artists whose work has enriched the world. Intended to lead listeners toward an interest in great artists, the series provided another example of how much educators of those days valued art in the elementary curriculum, a value that has since diminished substantially.

Senorita Jones. (English as a Second Language) Dramatic sketches in which the Senorita helps Pablo understand life in New York. The goal was to promote understanding between English and Spanish speaking pupils. This series became widely used by SOAs across the country.

Tales from the Four Winds. (Language Arts) A drama series that presented favorite tales and

Handling Sound Effects at WNYE (courtesy of New York Public School System).

legends from many lands, it was designed to stimulate primary children's imagination, develop literary taste, and foster a feeling of kinship with the children of other lands. Members of the WNYE All-City High School Radio Workshop presented the dramas.

The Man and His Music. (Music) This series introduced opera, operetta, and musical comedy to students in grades 5–9. Using narration, drama and music, paired programs dramatized the life of a composer one week and presented highlights from the composer's major works the next. Perhaps this topic would only work in New York City. Teacher manuals were available.

Out of Many, One: A Nation of Minorities. (Human Resources) The series explored the role and contributions of minority groups to American life through life-stories of prominent persons in each group.

A World of Wonder. (Science) This series supplemented the city's new science curriculum for grades K–2.

Pacific Portraits. (Social Sciences) Not all series originated at WNYE. Aired in response to "Mounting pressures in the Orient"— perhaps a reference to the Vietnam War — the series presented "varied aspects of the Pacific in terms of outstanding personalities, explorers, scientists, missionaries and colonial administrators who have contributed to its (the Pacific?) growth" (WNYE, 1967, p. 34). The description gives the impression of a propaganda piece. Created by the Wisconsin School of the Air, for mature high school students.

In addition to the in-school broadcasts, WNYE's High School of the Air offered special supplementary programs for home-bound students.

The WYNE staff continued to grow. In 1967–1968, still directed by Macandrew, the radio staff included 24 people, counting secretarial help, three professional script writers, and two announcers.

Support Materials

For many years, the WNYE distributed its Radio Manual throughout the city schools. A comprehensive annual program schedule and guide, the Manual provided an overview of the entire radio program, brief descriptions of each series, an illustrated schedule, and teacher guides for selected series. It also contained information on WNYE, a program evaluation form for teachers to complete, announcements of awards garnered during the previous year, a list of the WNYE radio staff, and the names of people who sat on the Radio Advisory Council. Significantly, the manual for 1953–1954 lists 12 programs. Each was broadcast weekly throughout the school year from October to the end of May. The 1967–1968 manual is much larger, listing nearly 40 programs. The larger manual indicates that unlike many other SOAs, the city school's radio effort had grown throughout the 1960s.

Philosophy and Methods

It is possible that NYC school administers, Macandrews or his staff did define an educational philosophy or ideas about methods, but little documentation of that exists. Even a close reading of the WNYE Manual statements reveals little. The editors offer only brief, cautiously worded suggestions regarding how to use the programs in class. For most series, suggestions are offered under headings such as: "Before the broadcast, why don't you..., During the broadcast, you will discover with us..., After the broadcast, you will have fun if you..." (WNYE, 1967). No rationals or bigger ideas are presented. What caused this lack? Possibly, Macandrew and others in the school administration wished to avoid giving the impression that the radio people knew more about instruction than did the classroom teachers, an impression that would cause many teachers to turn off their radios.

Program Development

The 1967–68 manual describes the process used to develop and produce new programs: "A single classroom program follows a long road. It begins frequently in the suggestions and recommendations sent by principals, supervisor, and teacher to their district superintendents, continues through the subject area directors and curriculum specialist and the deliberations of the Radio and Television Council, is prepared and produced by the staff of WNYE, is transmitted by the engineers over one of the twin transmitters" (WNYE, 1967, p. iii).

From this we can infer that in 1967 professionals developed the programming at WNYE, including scriptwriting. The role of teachers and students seemed much reduced mainly to suggesting program ideas, and to reach the station, it seems those ideas had to travel a bureaucratic maze. No mention is made of the All-City High School Radio Workshop.

The 1967–1968 Radio Manual provides one statement about the purpose of radio programs in the schools, and that statement opens a small crack in the door to the administration's philosophy of radio education. The purpose cited was, "to contribute to the achievement of that excellence in education for the children of New York City public schools to which we are all dedicated" (p. iii). An unfortunately vague statement, but, coming from the Acting Deputy Superintendent, it does tell us that as of 1967, radio still had a high enough profile that a top School administrator felt compelled to write something about it.

Audience and Evaluation

No data exist regarding the results of any teacher surveys that might have been conducted during the years from 1945 to 1970. However, Macandrew discusses teacher attitudes toward instructional television which might also have applied to radio in the classroom. He asserted the expression, "master teacher ... did an awful lot of damage" to teacher acceptance of instructional television (Robertson, 1982, p. 29). He explained that the elementary teachers, responsible for teaching five or six disciplines, recognized their limitations in specialized subject areas and consequently had no problem with allowing an electronic master teacher into their classrooms. High school teachers, however, were all trained in a given subject area and tended to think of themselves as master teachers in their area. They probably did not welcome the radio master teacher into their classrooms to teach their kids (Robertson, 1982, p. 29).

Another angle on the same issue was that the 1960s and 1970s saw the rise of teacher unions across the country. In that context, Macandrew argues, many teachers might have seen instructional television and its "master teachers" as an attempt by school boards to de-skill teaching and thereby justify lower teacher salaries. It is likely that some high school teachers perceived radio in much the same way.

The 1967–1968 manual included a questionnaire that asked teachers to identify the series they listened to and to respond to eleven Yes—No questions about those series. The questionnaire also asked teachers to comment on the programs and the teacher guides, and to offer suggestions for future programs. There were no questions about how frequently teachers used the programs or how many students listened in. Furthermore, the questionnaires were difficult to find in a 200 + page manual, and there appeared no statements about when the teacher responses would be tallied or what would be done with the results (WNYE, 1967). It seems safe to say that teacher feedback was a low priority, and that the results were for internal use only.

Demise

WNYC remained a city owned station until 1997 when it was transferred to a public-private foundation which operates it with a public radio format. WNYE became the official radio station of the city of New York.

Detroit

The Detroit public schools enjoyed a reputation for being early adopters of new technology into the schools so it is not surprising that they began experimenting with radio in the late 1920s. At first they had little interest in using radio for classroom instruction. Designed to promote the schools, those first radio programs consisted of little more than talks delivered by school administrators, an approach that failed utterly to interest listeners. Nevertheless, school administrators did not give up on the new medium. In 1931, they launched a new, listener friendly approach. A dramatized series, *Mrs. Peevey's Boarding House*, portrayed everyday life in a Detroit boarding house where the residents, curiously, regularly discussed the activities of the Detroit schools (Stewart, 1939). Like the previous effort, the new programs were designed to inform listeners about the schools and create positive public relations.

In 1934, school administrators expanded their view of radio to include programs intended, among other purposes, to support classroom instruction. The wider focus influenced programming directly for at least 5 years as demonstrated in the radio program schedule for 1937–1938, shown in Table 69.

TABLE 68. BROADCAST SCHEDULE, DETROIT PUBLIC SCHOOLS,
1937–1938 (STEWART, 1939; TYLER, 1967)

Program and Description	Audience	Day and Time	Station
History in the Making News events of the day are dramatized and discussed	Grades 7 — 12	Tuesday 11:15–11:30 A.M.	WJBK
The Schools Present Original radio scripts using high school musical talent	Grades 5–9	Tuesday 2:45–3:00 P.M.	WMBC
The School Spotlight An inter-disciplinary approach consisting of dramas that supplemented elementary grade instruction in nearly all subjects.	Grades 4–8	Thursday 2:45–3:00 P.M.	WWJ
The Contemporary Scene Planned and presented by Wayne University[37] faculty; covered a variety of topics, mostly world affairs	General Public	Wednesday 1:30–1:45 P.M.	WXYZ
Wayne University Students Variety shows put on by students of the Wayne University Broadcasting Guild	General Public	Friday 5:15–5:30 P.M.	WMBC

[37]Detroit's municipal college.

Public Education in Detroit School board originated programs that interpreted school policy to parents.	General Public	Friday 7:15–7:30 P.M.	CKLW
Public-School Talent Talent shows put on by local high schools	General Public	Saturday 9:45–10:00 A.M.	WJR
March of Youth Music and talk about subjects of interest to high school students.	General Public	Saturday 12:00–12:30 P.M.	WWJ

Table 69 shows that the Detroit school administrators used radio to serve several goals and audiences. They offered only three programs for classroom use, and those were designed for enrichment and aimed at a wide range of grades. The other five programs were intended for general audiences. Below are descriptions of the broadcasts intended for in-school listening:

History in the Making. The series used drama and commentary to present important contemporary issues. Dramatic sketches performed by actors from Detroit's municipal college, Wayne State University, portrayed contemporary situations in politics, international affairs, business, and the local community. A narrator provided background information and laid out the basic issues and challenges. Aimed at grades seven through twelve, the program was adapted to history or social studies classes. The hope was that after the broadcasts, students would continue with classroom discussion.

The Schools Present. Dramatic programs alternated with musical presentations from students at various Detroit schools. Students produced the programs. The main goals were to provide many students with experience in radio broadcasting and to offer supplemental music instruction.

School Spotlight. This series provided supplementary instruction for grades 4 through 8 in a range of subjects including literature, social studies, arithmetic, science, health, music, history, and biography. The goal was to help students integrate the lessons received from the study of different subjects (Stewart, 1939).

Broadcast

Table 69 shows that the Detroit schools broadcast its three in-school programs over three different commercial stations, an arrangement bound to cause problems. With different stations came frequent changes in broadcast times, which played havoc with listening schedules particularly in the junior and senior high schools. School administrators acknowledged that commercial commitments at the stations sometimes conflicted with the schools' need for consistent broadcast times throughout the school year. Even when stations did maintain announced schedules, multiple stations and broadcast times complicated planning for teachers and administrators. On the other hand, the stations typically offered the schools free air time, technical support, and rehearsal space (Stewart, 1939). No documentation exists to tell how well the relationship between the schools and the broadcasters worked, but in 1948, the Detroit Public Schools began broadcasting over its own FM station, WDTR. That story is recounted later in this segment.

ORGANIZATION AND STAFF

From 1934 to 1938, the responsibility for radio programs at the Detroit schools lay with the Advisory Committee on Visual and Auditory Education [sic]. Appointed by the superintendent of schools, the Committee set policy for relationships with commercial broadcast stations, program selection, script writing and review, and the use of pupils and teachers in the broadcasts. The Committee's view of radio's role in education can be seen in the objectives it set. The objectives were:

1. Interpret the schools to the community by means of radio
2. Supplement other forms of classroom instruction
3. Provide selected pupils with learning experiences in broadcasting
4. Develop in all pupils better taste and discrimination in radio listening (Stewart, 1939).

While the people in charge of radio defined their objectives precisely, they never did get around to giving the radio operation a distinct name. It seems that people just referred to it as the Radio Advisory Committee.

By 1938, the Board of Education moved to build up broadcasting for the classroom by funding a full-time radio staff and an initially part-time director. Mrs. Kathleen Lardie, who served as radio director until her retirement in 1963, headed a staff of 5 full-time people including a music specialist, a script writer, two people responsible for announcing, rehearsals, and production, and one clerical position. After several years, the director position became full-time. The radio staff worked out of a substantial broadcasting facility that included two studios equipped for rehearsal and recording. From that location, the staff developed program ideas, wrote and produced scripts, conducted auditions and rehearsals, and recorded programs (Stewart, 1939; Tyler, 1967).

NEW ADMINISTRATION

In 1938, a new school administration shifted responsibility for the radio effort to the Department of Visual and Radio Education located in the Division of Instruction at Detroit's municipal college, Wayne University. As a result, the radio staff became integrated with the Wayne University operation. One desirable outcome of the new administration was that the radio staff met with the commercial broadcasters to hammer out a broadcast schedule for the entire year. Also from that point on, Lardie and her staff prepared and distributed to the schools a broadcast schedule for each semester in advance, enabling teachers to incorporate radio into their semester lesson plans.

The new administration also set new goals that shifted the focus away from using radio as a promotional tool for the schools and toward classroom use (Atkinson, 1942c). The new goals included: (1) to supplement and enrich the regular instructional program, (2) to bring events and personalities into the classroom, and (3) to provide some instructional materials that are not readily available otherwise. Despite the new focus, with the exception of music, Lardie and school administrators did not integrate radio into the curricula of various subjects or align programs with specific grade levels.

The new administration did increase the number of programs intended for classroom use. Several new programs are described below:

The School Music Hour. This series supplemented the school's regular music curriculum. Each program of the series was one complete unit and could have been used for many different grade levels. Teachers were asked to use their own judgment about how to fit it in to their lessons.

Know Your Local Government. Designed for grades 6 through 12, this series introduced the purpose and activities of various departments of Detroit city and county government. Many broadcasts featured department heads, school officials, as well as the Mayor of Detroit.

The School Spotlight and History in the Making were continued as before (Atkinson, 1942c).

SUPPORT MATERIALS

Starting in 1939 the Department of Radio Education prepared and distributed weekly radio bulletins that listed all the Board of Education programs and other educational programs broadcast outside of school hours. The Department also prepared pamphlets to accompany the programs *The School Spotlight* and *History in the Making*, and had them posted on school bulletin boards throughout the city (Atkinson, 1942c). The pamphlets described upcoming programs in each series and offered suggestions for preparation and follow-up to the broadcasts.

Philosophy and Methods

In the early days, Detroit school administers used radio first as an instrument for public relations. They viewed radio's educational potential narrowly as a type of audio visual aid, similar to film. In this view, individual radio programs like individual films could be plugged into a single lesson as an optional enrichment or treat for the students (Tyler, 1967). By the early 1940s, however, Director Lardie had imposed a different view that recognized radio's broad instructional potential. In addition to enriching specific lessons, radio could also bring events and personalities into the classroom and provide some new instructional materials that might not otherwise be available (Atkinson, 1942c). Lardie's expanded view of radio may have encouraged school administrators to acquire an educational FM station to service Detroit schools. Nevertheless, throughout its history in the Detroit schools, radio programs were seldom designed to directly deliver elements of curricula for specific grades or to enable students to achieve specific educational objectives. Without this latter vision, for most teachers, radio remained an optional "nice to do" luxury rather than an integral part of the lesson plan.

In the area of instructional methods, Lardie and her staff broke no new ground. Their scripts used the established techniques, drama and story telling to supplement instruction in literature, history, and current affairs, but they expressed very narrow ideas about how radio should be used in the classroom. Teacher preparation and follow-up activities, they suggested, should be tailored to the program topic and needs of the class. That reasonable advice was seriously undercut by their insistence that during the broadcasts, in most cases, students should listen attentively and no more (Stewart, 1939). They urged classroom teachers to avoid having students draw, take notes, write on the board, discuss, or do any action during the broadcasts. Learning resulted from listening. This limited view of how to use radio in the classroom probably resulted in lower motivation on the part of students. It encouraged teachers to see radio as a source of information that could enrich the classroom lesson, but not as a tool for engaging students in active learning (Catalog, 1955).

WDTR-FM

In February of 1948, the Detroit schools began airing programs over its new FM station, WDTR. As with many other local SOAs, owning the station enabled a huge expansion of programming, 75 per week in 1948–1949 and over 100 per week by 1958. Lardie and her staff wrote and produced twenty-three of those programs. Tyler (1967) says that owning the station gave the Detroit schools the opportunity to integrate radio into the curricula and to design programs that pursued specific educational objectives. Regretfully, they did not do that. Instead, WDTR programming continued to reflect the idea that radio provided enrichment, something teachers might use to spice up a lesson, if time permitted.

Evaluation and Audience

By 1948, the Detroit schools had done little to evaluate the educational effectiveness of its radio broadcasts intended for classroom use or to survey the opinions of teachers or school administrators about the program (Stewart, 1939). Compared to most other local SOAs, Detroit's lack of evaluation activity seems glaring. That lack might have stemmed in part from their view of radio as just another type of audio visual aid. Had the school administrators viewed radio in the classroom as a great experiment in the application of technology to education, they most likely would have vigorously conducted evaluations and opinion surveys.

In 1966, Detroit school administration engaged I. Keith Tyler to survey the school's use of radio and TV and make recommendations for future action. Tyler, probably the country's preeminent authority in educational broadcasting[38] at that time (1967) issued an extensive report that included data about the size of WDTR's listening audience, at least for 1966–1967. He reported that regular WDTR listeners totaled 11,330 students or 7 percent of Detroit's 170,000 elementary school students and occasional listeners totaled 20,940, or 12 percent (Tyler, 1967, p. 29). Tyler expressed disappointment with these numbers, but he gave no indication about what level of listenership would have satisfied him. One possible explanation for the small audience size was that by 1967, the radio operation was already in serious decline, as explained further in the following segment. No data is available about the size of the student audience prior to 1967.

Demise

Tyler (1967) dates the beginning of radio's decline in Detroit around 1955, when the school administration turned their attention seriously to educational TV. In that year, the radio staff became part of the Department of Radio-TV Education, an office of 28 employees most of whom worked on television. As a sign of the times, one of the two radio studios was converted to television use. Certainly by the mid–1960s the radio operation had become a shadow of the former operation. In the early 1960s Lardie had retired and following that the radio staff trimmed. In 1965, only three original series were aired, in part because by then the entire radio staff had shrunk to just two people, a director and an engineer. Increasingly, radio became a "playback operation" broadcasting tapes borrowed from the library of the National Association of Educational Broadcasters (NAEB) and playing taped programs from the library of programs produced years earlier. Tyler also notes neglect on the receiving end. In the schools functioning receivers became more and more scarce as sets broke down or were stolen. Clearly school administers no longer gave priority to education by radio.

During the 1980s and 1990s, WDTR experimented with a variety of non-commercial radio formats including classical music and jazz, community service and news while retaining some programming for the classroom. The idea was to provide something for everyone in a potential audience that could consist of students, parents, extended family and teaching staff. But Carol Nolan, who engineered Chicago's WBEZ's transition from a school station to an independent NPR format, declared the missions to educate school children and to provide information incompatible. "It is difficult to imagine WDTR both attracting the general public and serving as an educational tool for Detroit's student body."

Through its history, however, WDTR retained its role as laboratory for high school students who wanted to learn the trade of radio broadcasting. A number of Detroit students got their start in radio broadcasting by serving as interns at the station. Among them is Casey Kasim. Finally, in 2005, the school board, pressed by financial deficits, agreed to lease management of the station to a commercial outfit that operates the station with a jazz and classical format. That move ended the station's 57 year history as an educational asset of the Detroit schools.

Summary

In Detroit, radio was seen initially as a multi-faceted communication tool for use in reaching a variety of goals, only one of which was supplementing classroom instruction in general ways. This defused view restricted the use of radio through the 1930s and resulted in only three series being offered for in-class use. Furthermore, radio never became an important contributor

---

[38]Tyler for many years headed the federally funded Evaluation of School Broadcasts project located at The Ohio State University.

It is Nature Study Time (courtesy of Detroit Public Schools).

to school's curricula. Rather it remained an enrichment tool to be used as needed by the classroom teacher. Nevertheless, Detroit continued in-school broadcasting for at least 35 years, carried forward mainly by the school administration's commitment to using audio/visual technology as enrichment to daily lessons and the fact that the school board owned a radio station. While the administration's view of radio's educational potential did expand somewhat during the early 1940s, the earlier view of radio as an audio/visual aid continued to dominate, restricting the exploration of radio's educational potential in the classrooms of Detroit.

In his 1967 report, I. Keith Tyler found that despite many positive factors the use of educational radio in Detroit had been seriously hampered by a lack of vision about the potential of radio. "... a clear-cut philosophy is lacking, there is a lack of genuine commitment, use of broadcasts is purely optional" (p. 206). Tyler goes on to say that while investing in production facilities would be laudable, educational broadcasting will never live up to its potential in Detroit, if the administrators lack commitment to making radio or TV instruments of direct instruction that lead to specific educational objectives.

Limited Data Local Schools of the Air

The availability of documentation for the remaining local SOAs covered in this study is limited. They are not included in the end of section summary.

Alameda City School of the Air

It's remarkable that a town of 35,000 people developed a nationally recognized local school of the air. Small budgets and limited staff would seem to make such a development difficult if not impossible. Nevertheless, the Alameda story demonstrates that when educators were motivated to incorporate radio in the schools and the climate of the times was supportive, even a small school system could accomplish big results. From 1933 to at least the mid–1940s, the Alameda City School of the Air (ACSA) served mostly rural schools in the east San Francisco Bay area and surrounding counties with daily radio instruction for classroom use. Furthermore, in 1945, the major scholars of the school of the air movement judged the ACSA to be one of the top local SOAs in the country (Woelfel and Tyler, 1945).

What motivated the Alameda school board to undertake education by radio? In the early 1930s the California State Commissioner of elementary education, Ms. Grace Stanley, launched a series of classroom broadcasts with the goal of enriching the curricula of the state's poor rural schools. Within a short time local school boards assumed the planning for these broadcasts. When the state ended its involvement in the programs a few years later, the various city public schools decided either to stop their radio work or continue on their own. Alameda was one of the latter. Working with local commercial stations, the Alameda school board developed a radio effort consisting of 6 weekly program series that attracted over 600 teachers in Alameda and many surrounding communities. Remarkably, almost all the people involved in the effort were volunteers.

Origins

In 1933, the Alameda City School of the Air (ACSA) broadcast just one program, *California History*. Strong demand for the topic had existed throughout the state's school system, but no textbooks or other resources were available. The ACSA filled the void, and it did so creatively. Lacking text books, the ACSA program developers sought out and uncovered original source material such as letters, deeds, and photos, and gathered first-hand stories from remaining pioneer Californians. From those found materials and interviews the developers fashioned original scripts. Initially they wrote 30 minute scripts aimed at junior and senior high students. Before long, elementary teachers with students as young as fourth grade tuned in the program. The ACSA responded by crafting scripts with more limited vocabulary appropriate for younger children (Atkinson, 1942c; Stewart, 1939).

The ACSA encouraged local involvement by announcing that it would broadcast a program about any locality that supplied historical material on a local town or important local figure. Students responded by submitting letters, essays, photos, and art work. "Teachers and pupils cooperated on these projects and a program related to each region was presented. Pupils interviewed local pioneers, visited local historical landmarks, studied old diaries and letters and engaged in research about their districts. The information (they compiled) was incorporated into radio scripts" (Willey and Young, 1948, p. 43).

The *California History* program clearly hit the mark both in terms of numbers of listeners and creative handling of material. Demand for the program continued strong even after a number of text books on California history became available. Furthermore, the director of the ACSA asserted that the California history series attracted many teachers outside of Alameda City and was chiefly responsible for making the ACSA a regional rather than a local broadcast.

Educational Programs

Despite the success of the *California History* series, the ACSA waited four years before launching additional programs. By 1937, the schedule included six weekly programs. Table 70 shows the schedule for 1937–38.

TABLE 70. PROGRAM SCHEDULE, ALAMEDA CITY SCHOOL
OF THE AIR, 1938–1939 (STEWART, 1939)

Program	Description
California History	The first program offered by the ACSA, it depicted the lives of important people in California history. Arranged in chronological order, the series also treated the settlement and growth of various regions in the state.
Myths and Legends	Dramatized myths and legends selected from a variety of places, times, and cultures, from Ancient Greece and Rome, to Norse, Teutonic, Chinese and Hindu.
United States History	For grades 7 through 12, this series supplemented and enriched the in-school course in U. S. History with dramatized highlights of key events.
Sonny's Magic Merry-Go-Round (Nature Study)	For K–6th grade, the Magic Merry-Go-Round carried Sonny to many places where he met different animals. The dramatized adventures wove nature-study facts into an imaginative story.
Great Moments from Literature	For junior and senior high students, the programs dramatize key scenes from books on the Alameda schools recommended reading list. It was hoped that dramatized scenes would entice students to read the entire work.
Nature's Secrets	This series presents to junior and senior high pupils stories of a college professor and his general-science class as they take field trips to places of scientific interest. The trips are interspersed with class discussion.

All programs but one aired at 1:30 P.M., a time selected by the schools. *Sonny's Magic Merry-Go-Round* was broadcast at 11:15, because teachers believed that children would listen best in the mornings.

The ACSA selected programs based on several criteria: (1) availability of subject experts within the system, (2) needs and requests expressed by teachers and school administrators, (3) adaptability of the subject to radio, (4) benefits to the pupils, and (5) the program's fit with the school curricula (Stewart, 1939). These criteria ensured that the programs meshed well with the needs and preferences of classroom teachers, local schools and communities, and the capabilities of the ACSA staff. School director Erle Kenney's stated recipe for success was "close harmony between the classroom teacher and the broadcaster" (Atkinson, 1942c, p. 77).

ACSA programming sought to offer programs not only for the Alameda schools, but for all the schools in the listening area that wanted to participate. Director Kenney invited teachers from all schools in the area to bring their classes to visit the ACSA radio studios and watch a broadcast. As many as 120 students at one time have packed the radio studio. By promoting this wide community, the ACSA became known and accepted in schools well beyond the city limits. That in turn kept the Alameda school administration enthusiastic about radio in education (Atkinson, 1942c).

Organization, Staff, Personalities

Given that the Alameda schools allocated no funds for radio staff or equipment, it is not surprising that the ACSA operation depended chiefly on volunteer efforts. The originator, driving force, and long time director of the school, Erle Kenney, had taken a leave of absence from his school job to devote full time to educational broadcasting.[39] Script writers, actors, producers and technicians for the various programs came in part from the Alameda Evening High School class in radio technique that Kenney supervised. In addition, talented volunteers such as former school teachers and retired actors also participated in the ACSA. Their mature voices suited well the history and literature dramas that required elder characters, such as Ben Franklin. Kenney and other school officials recognized, however, that a volunteer effort, no matter how effective, was unstable; to operate with stability, the ACSA required a reliable funding source (Stewart, 1939).

Broadcast

All ACSA programs were broadcast over station KLX, in Oakland, California. The station provided the schools with the same time slot, 1:30 P.M. five days per week, a benefit to classroom teachers because they could more easily work a regular listening time into their schedules. Furthermore, the station on several occasions declined advertisers who wanted the school's time slot. Kenney lauded KLX for its dedication to educational programming and boasted that from its beginning in 1933 through 1940, the ACSA had not missed one scheduled program due to the station's lack of cooperation. In addition to air time, the station also provided an announcer who opened and closed the school program session, rehearsal studio space, and access to some sound effects. Occasionally, the station accommodated classes of students who visited the studio. The ACSA submitted program scripts in advance so the announcer could prepare, but director Kenney asserted the scripts were never censored in any way. KLX provided its services on a sustaining basis; that is, at no cost to the schools (Stewart, 1939).

Kenney stressed that he and the ACSA staff worked hard to maintain a good relationship with the station owners. The ACSA never asked station staff to assist in the preparation or production of the programs, and Kenney claimed they furnished programs that were up to, or above, the general level of offerings on the station. Even in the early programs on California history, Kenney claims to have put on a program that would stand comparison with any program that was on the air at that time (Stewart, 1939). The truth of such claims can't be determined today, but they certainly show the determination of the ACSA director and school administrators to maintain a relationship that made radio instruction possible for the teachers and children of Alameda and its surroundings.

Despite all Kenney's efforts, the ACSA suffered the same fate as other SOAs that relied on commercial stations to broadcast their programs. In the fall of 1941, KLX switched the ACSA programs to a lower power station, KROW also in Oakland (Atkinson, 1942c). That same year the number of ACSA programs aired dropped from the previous year's six to three.

Philosophy and Methods

Director Kenney's statements about using radio in the classroom suggest a rigid teacher-centered view of education that saw students as passive learners. He summed up the classroom teacher's role in radio instruction with three words, "planning, listening, and correlating" (Atkinson, 1942c, p. 77). Planning consisted of reading the monthly program bulletin that gave information about upcoming programs, reviewed any available visual aids, and oriented students to the upcoming program. However, teachers were warned to avoid over preparing the class with extensive lecture or discussion. Too much preparation, they were told, would detract from the effectiveness of the broadcasts and from student interest.

[39]It is not clear whether Kenney's leave was paid. If so, that would represent a substantial subsidy for the radio operation.

Kenney asserted emphatically his beliefs about how students should behave during the broadcasts. He said: "We do everything we can to discourage teachers from requiring any pupil activity.... Any visual material to be consulted by pupils should be placed before the broadcast. During the program pupils should devote themselves to listening and 'living in' the broadcast. Teachers are urged to sit quietly during the program and set their pupils an example of attentive and interested listening. No teachers in Alameda point to maps, etc., or write on the board during a program, and we sincerely hope that no teachers elsewhere do, either" (Stewart, 1939, p. 201).

This quote shows that Kenney believed attentive listening to be the only effective method to be used during broadcasts. He even suggested correct listening posture. In the third step, "correlating," Kenney referred to the traditional types of lesson follow-up activities such as question and answer, discussion, short writing assignments, or even art work, if appropriate.

Conducting the steps precisely as directed was crucial to Kenney. If the classroom teacher disagreed with any of them, Kenney advised that the teacher avoid using the radio programs altogether because, he said, "they would not contribute to her classroom instruction" (Atkinson, 1942c, p. 77).

He also believed that the radio programs should be synchronized as much as possible with the school curricula both in terms of subject matter and the rate at which classroom teachers moved through the subject matter. According to Kenney, the ACSA routinely asked a sample of participating teachers to report where their classes would be in the subject each week during the school term. Based on that information, the ACSA then adjusted the broadcast schedule to follow the pace of the average classroom as it moved through the semester's lessons. Such action underscored Kenney' desire to serve the needs and preferences of the traditional classroom teacher.

Overall, Kenney's ideas about educational philosophy and methods show an inflexible teacher-centered view of pedagogy that probably was common in his day. He gave no trace of being influenced by Dewey's thought on active learning or by the progressive views on promoting a child centered classroom that were gaining popularity among educators of that period.

TEACHERS AND RADIO

Stewart (1939) asserted that Alameda City teachers were never required to use the radio programs, but that the degree of urging to do so varied according to the desires of each school's principal. Some principals provided in-school assistance in radio use while others let teachers make up their own minds about radio. The Alameda City Superintendent, according to Stewart, "believed that each teacher knows the needs of her class better than anyone else and in any case will use radio effectively only if she is convinced of its value" (p. 206). Stewart also asserts that there existed no organized resistance to radio among the city's teachers and no teacher ever complained about being asked to use radio in the classroom. Despite Stewart's assurances that Alameda teachers were free to refuse to use radio in the classroom, he makes clear his own negative views toward those who did. He said, "The teachers who do *not* use radio usually show a lack of initiative or a professional caution that approaches apathy" (206). This unsupported backhanded remark signals Kenney's frustration at those teachers who did not use radio.

Instead of requiring or urging teachers to use radio in the classroom, Kenney suggested that school administrators acquaint teachers with the benefits of radio in the classroom through a gradual process of education. He recommended that principals reward teacher enthusiasm for radio with quality receiving equipment. Kenney recognized that despite all his efforts, without the teacher's enthusiastic support, education by radio could not succeed, and he remained conflicted over what to do about teachers who ignored or rejected radio. One wonders why Kenney apparently conducted no research to determine why teachers chose or refused to use radio.

Audience and Evaluation

Erle Kenney considered the ACSA to be a regional operation that served schools throughout northern California. He asserted that the ACSA did not address programs only to Alameda schools, but gave equal attention to the needs of all schools that used the programs. "We make every feasible effort to secure listeners outside Alameda" (Stewart, 1939, p. 228). Kenney reported that the audience for ACSA programs included several hundred schools distributed over 32 California counties. He drew information on audience usage and location from responses to occasional mailed surveys and from the program bulletins mailing list. Kenney reported that in the city of Alameda, 605 teachers responded to a mail questionnaire that asked about radio equipment in the classroom. Given this sketchy data, it is difficult to make reliable estimates of the numbers that listened to ACSA programs (Stewart, 1939).

As for evaluation, Kenney referred to a simple learning test tool that was distributed to participating classroom teachers. The tool consisted of a one page test on a specific program that pupils were asked to complete a day or so after the broadcast. Question formats included fill-in the blank, multiple choice, and true and false. The completed tests were collected and scored by the classroom teacher who sent them to the ACSA. These results gave classroom teachers a measure of the radio program effectiveness and the broadcasters an idea about the level of difficulty for specific programs. Based on that feedback, radio teachers and producers could revise program content and their instructional approach. Kenney did not report results.

Demise

No data has been uncovered about the operation of the ACSA after World War II. However, Willey and Young refer to it in their book which was published in 1948 so it seems plausible that the ACSA broadcast programs at least until that date.

Summary

The ACSA got a jump start from the state initiated regional cooperative effort to provide rural schools with additional educational resources. By filling the need for programming on California history, the ACSA demonstrated for educators in surrounding areas that radio could meet basic educational objectives effectively and in an innovative way. The success of the ACSA owes much to the driving force of one person. Like Ben Darrow at the OSA, Erle Kenney combined talent and passion in the areas of education, and radio broadcasting with a persuasive personality. That combination built confidence and support for a new endeavor that seemed outside the comfort zone of many educators or local school boards. Probably because of the small size of the Alameda district, Kenney had to rely on volunteers from outside the schools to develop and produce programs.

Akron, Ohio

The Akron Board of Education School of the Air (ABESA) represented yet another successful variation on the use of radio in local schools. Like school boards in several other cities, the Akron board began experimenting with radio as a vehicle for public relations. Those first programs, written and presented by administrators and high school teachers, were predictably dull and soon ended. However, Akron educators continued their commitment to radio for the classroom, and by the end of the 1937—1938 school year, the ABESA had broadcast 180 programs, most of 6 weeks duration or less. Nonetheless, they represented quite an accomplishment for a mid-sized city of approximately 250,000. ABESA's extensive radio series in first aid instruction attracted national attention and recognition for its excellence.

Origins

In the fall of 1935, the ABESA launched its first radio course for classroom use, fifth grade geography and in the following spring, sixth grade geography. The following year the ABESA introduced science lessons and in the spring another science offering, *Things We Know*. The forward momentum continued the following year with the hiring of a full-time Director of Radio Education, Josephine French. Ms. French brought to ABESA a background in speech, acting, and radio work, which among other things enabled her to serve as the radio voice on many programs. She selected other adult voices as needed, based on their dramatic ability. Students selected from the schools performed dramatic scripts. French selected program directors and gave them responsibility for supervising and coordinating the various broadcast components such as music, announcements, sound effects, auditions, dialogue, rehearsals, and engineering. All except French served as unpaid volunteers (Stewart, 1939).

Ms. French oversaw a big expansion of program offerings. By the end of the 1937–1938 school year, the ABESA broadcast programs in 13 subject areas, including one series dedicated to remote broadcasts from school classrooms. Table 71 demonstrates the scope of radio activity offered to schools of Akron and surrounding communities.

TABLE 71. BROADCASTS, AKRON BoE SCHOOL OF THE AIR, 1937–1938 (STEWART, 1939)

Subject Area	Series
History	The U. S. Constitution
	The American Indians
	History Dramas
	News Flashes from History
	Current-History Exams (13 half hour quiz programs)
Science	A Preparation for Winter
	Weather
	Science Dramas
Geography	Cities of the U.S. Q and A
	Geography Dramas
Safety	Dramas
Literature	Dramas
Music	Lessons
	Opera
French Lessons	Seventh-Grade French Lesson
	Eighth-Grade French Lesson
Temperance Talks	Talks on the value of avoiding over indulgence in alcohol
Holidays	Thanksgiving, Christmas, Lincoln's Birthday, Washington's Birthday, Northwest Territory Celebration, Memorial Day
Remote-Control Broadcasts from the Classrooms	Central High School
	Bowen School (elementary)

All programs were 15 minutes long and broadcast in the mornings between 9:45 and 10:45 A.M. Most series ran for six weeks and were followed by another in the same subject area. Grade levels were not given, but it appears that many were aimed at the high schools. Some of the note-worthy program series are described below:

Program Descriptions

Sidelights on the Constitution. Some of the six programs in this series were based on origi-nal research conducted by Akron teachers who uncovered unusual information not found in the text books. They condensed their findings into six fifteen-minute presentations. Director French believed that the programs provided history teachers with unusual information and new points of view that aroused student interest, though she offered no support for that belief. A seventh broadcast consisted of an on-air quiz that served as a learning review. After each question, the radio teacher paused so students in the classrooms could write an answer. The broadcaster also provided correct answers.

Primary Story Hour. The 6 programs presented the best in children's literature for primary students. The writers' goal was to build a common background of stories for all Akron children. Some high schools used this program as a model for good story telling.

News for Youth. The series presented current events in language suitable for students in grades six to eight (Atkinson, 1942c). According to Atkinson, no weekly pattern emerged for the series in any one subject area. Teachers may have found this lack of regularity confusing.

Radio First Aid. Beginning in 1939, the ABESA offered American Red Cross first aid lessons aimed at seventh and eighth graders. The series soon attracted a wide and enthusiastic follow-ing not only in Akron but in surrounding towns and in Cleveland despite that city's well estab-lished program of in-school radio. Many adult listeners also tuned in. Topics included home safety, treating wounds with iodine and dressing, treating burns, blisters, poison ivy, and frost-bite. Other programs admonished students to keep medicines and household chemicals away from children or what to do for someone who breaks a bone. (Don't move them).

The appeal lay mostly in the dramatized situations that featured students at home or at play. In the first episode, while hanging curtains, Mom falls from a stool and injures herself. Her injury is made worst by bad first aid treatment. In the remainder of the program the narrator under-scored the need for knowledge of effective first aid. Programs on bandages gave good opportu-nity for follow-up activity in the classrooms and even demonstrations by the local boy scout troops. Subsequent programs covered injuries typical for the season, for example hunting acci-dents in fall and frostbite in winter.

For each lesson, certified first aid instructors prepared scripts and worksheets, 5,000 of which were distributed weekly to the schools. Students completed the worksheets immediately follow-ing the broadcasts. The instructors also wrote a final exam. By June of 1940, over 2,000 eighth grade students in Akron and many surrounding communities had passed the final exam and received their first aid certificates (Atkinson, 1942c). The first aid series put Akron's radio pro-gram on the map and attracted hundreds of complimentary letters from parents and students.

Director French estimated that each 15 minute broadcast required 30 hours of preparation, and a good part of that was devoted to writing and editing the script.

Volunteer teachers selected by French wrote the scripts. She looked for willing teachers who demonstrated writing skills rather than those with reputations for teaching prowess. She imposed three requirements: the script must be interesting, authentic, and sixteen minutes long. The writer determined the script's format, whether drama, interview, or talk. The entire cost of developing the broadcasts consisted of two salaries, French and a stenographer, and the cost of office supplies.

The Akron school board demonstrated their commitment to radio education by insisting that the broadcast take place at the same time every day and by encouraging junior and senior high schools to set aside a 15 minute period for radio listening. To make room for the 15 minute radio period, school principals had to shorten class periods slightly.

Support Materials

The Radio Director's office distributed two types of support materials, a program schedule for the upcoming semester and an announcement in the Superintendent's weekly bulletin. The announcement gave the title and description of the programs to be broadcast that week. Visual support materials such as slides and charts were used infrequently.

Philosophy and Methods

In Director French's view the ABESA operated as "an independent concern, doing its own work, in its own way" (Stewart, 1939, p. 159). She made no attempt to fit the programs into any course of study or school curricula. Most programs ran for 6 weeks, few for an entire semester. These sparse facts suggest that French followed no formal educational philosophy per se. Perhaps she believed learning to be a purely natural phenomenon that resulted automatically from any education activity that gained a learner's attention. Certainly she did not advocate radio as a supplement to the school curricula; nevertheless, the series *Radio First Aid* did constitute the entire curriculum for that topic. This inconsistency probably stemmed from the fact that the ABESA did not start with a clear idea about the role of radio instruction in the schools. To French, it seemed to be either enrichment to, or a diversion from, the regular classroom lessons.

French did have strong views on the proper methods for using radio in the classroom. She stated that listening was a powerful learning mode in itself, and teachers did best by getting out of the way of deep listening. Most ABESA programs involved drama of some kind, which French believed required little advance preparation. "A radio lesson can be ruined, as far as the pupils are concerned, if there is too much or even any preliminary work, just as a play or novel can be spoiled by too much advance information" (Stewart, 1939, p. 168). Listening, she had said, should be voluntary and pleasant, just as with popular entertainment. In fact she believed that the radio lessons should compete on the same level with entertainment radio. Students should do nothing during the broadcasts except listen and think. For follow-up, she advocated one to two minutes of absolute silence so "the child can think about the things he has just heard (p. 168). Teachers should be ready to answer questions—if they arose—and to conduct a conversational discussion, but only if the students are interested in doing so. French stated emphatically that teachers should require no forced follow-up to broadcasts of any kind. On the spectrum of methods for using radio in the classroom, French's views represented the extreme unstructured end. Perhaps French's ideas represented a precursor to Sesame Street.

Audience and Evaluation

For most ABESA programs, little data exist about audience size or evaluations that may have been conducted. An exception was the First Aid series. We know that ABESA distributed up to 5,000 lesson worksheets weekly to participating schools. Students were asked to complete the worksheets immediately following the broadcasts and those completed worksheets give some idea of the listening audience for that program. By June of 1940, over 2,000 eighth grade students in Akron and many surrounding communities had received certificates for having passed the final exam (Atkinson, 1942c). Those results represented irrefutable evidence of the effectiveness of education by radio.

Demise

No data uncovered.

Summary

It is unknown who or what provided the spark that ignited Akron's radio program for the schools in 1934, but four years later it broadcast an impressive array of nearly 24 programs for all grade levels, K–12. A large part of that success can be attributed to director Josephine French's strong leadership which attracted the volunteer talent necessary to make the low-budget local SOA operate effectively for at least 10 years. ABESA achieved a national reputation chiefly based on one program, *Radio First Aid.* Using an imaginative approach, Akron schools got over 2,000 senior high students qualified to receive first aid certificates. Ironically, it appears that *Radio First Aid* succeeded by contradicting most of French's ideas about how to use radio. The program covered the complete curriculum for the topic, including a required follow-up exam. Limited documentation prevents drawing conclusions about the overall success and longevity of the ABESA.

Summary: Local Schools of the Air[40]

Local school boards entered the field of radio broadcasting for the classroom somewhat reluctantly. After early experiments, New York and Chicago dropped educational radio for years. KBPS in Portland and Rochester started very slowly with one or two series. Detroit backed into programming for the classroom after discovering that radio did little to enhance the public image of the city schools. Only Cleveland entered the field with a planned approach and a record of continuous development. However, after some lack luster starts, local SOAs distinguished themselves in a variety of ways. Cleveland and Rochester gained national attention for delivering parts of the schools' science and math curriculum through radio. Local SOAs also highlighted the culture, economy and values of their respective communities to a depth not possible by the state and national entities. Chicago, Cleveland and Portland, for example, developed program series cooperatively with local museums, libraries, and other cultural organizations; in other cities, even local police and emergency services got involved with radio education.

Student participation was another area in which local SOAs distinguished themselves. About half of the local SOAs got students involved with many of the creative and technical aspects of educational broadcasting, and classroom teachers in several SOAs wrote scripts and served as on-air teachers. Grassroots operation helped ensure that radio broadcasting stayed in touch with the schools.

Despite their similarities, local SOAs developed in different ways, in part because of differences in school district size. Clearly, the large urban school boards such as Chicago and Cleveland could not only afford to own operate their own radio station, they also could pay the salaries for professional and technical staff.[41] Smaller districts such as Rochester and Portland had to rely more on cooperation from local commercial stations at least in the early years. By 1950 almost all commercial AM radio stations had withdrawn from broadcasting to the schools, and all local SOAs still operating owned and operated their own stations. Owning the radio station brought advantages to all local SOAs— it enabled school districts to develop a solid base for their operations and broadcast the entire school day—but it's surprising how well small districts' SOAs performed relying on volunteers to do much of the work.

Local SOAs experienced varying degrees of success in terms of audience, longevity, innovative educational production and educational impact. Table 72 summarizes operations, characteristics, and accomplishments of six local SOAs for which adequate documentation exists. Following that is a brief discussion of similarities and differences and some factors that may have accounted for differences.

---

[40]This summary covers the six local SOAs for which adequate documentation exists.

[41]The FM set aside of the mid–1940s enabled local school boards to own and operate their own radio stations.

The summary of findings shows that local SOAs enjoyed great longevity with five of the six operating between 45 and 60 years. That longevity is a testament to the confidence that educators had developed in the efficacy of radio in the schools. Key to the long life was to own and operate the radio station. School owned stations could set broadcast schedules that best suited the school curricula and re-broadcast popular programs as often as practical. Most local SOAs filled the school day with instructional programs and then added after school programs that combined education with entertainment.

Local SOAs varied substantially in their educational philosophy, goals and instructional methods. SOAs such as Cleveland and Rochester used radio to deliver curriculum, achieve learning objectives, and to train teachers. Others such as Detroit and Chicago saw radio primarily as a vehicle for lesson enrichment. Rochester emphasized the master teacher concept, while at the other end of the spectrum, Portland's KBPS saw radio instruction as a tool for getting students actively involved in learning and for advanced career preparation.

Within a few years of their inception, most local SOAs prepared print support material—primarily weekly bulletins that summarized the week's upcoming program—and distributed them to all schools in the system. The larger cities—Chicago, Cleveland, NYC, and Detroit—developed semester and annual radio manuals that listed broadcast times, described programs, and gave usage tips. Most local SOAs prepared teacher guides for some series. KBPS, for many years unable to prepare even a semester schedule, later on developed the *Listening Text,* the most comprehensive set of radio support materials prepared by any SOA. It included among other elements, broadcast schedules, program descriptions, skills and objectives matrix charts, and teacher guides.

Few local SOAs consistently collected audience data, or if they did, they failed to make the data public. Chicago and Rochester issued some audience data prior to 1950. Tyler's 1967 study for WDTR found that 7% of Detroit's elementary students listened regularly and 12% occasionally. Overall though the lack of audience data is perplexing, unless we consider that at the local level the entity that ran the SOA also funded it. In that environment, there existed no need to make audience numbers public. During their formative years from the 1930s to after World War II, most SOAs conducted teacher surveys and some evaluations. After 1950, few did.

More so than the network and state-based SOAs, local SOAs involved students in the technical and creative functions of educational radio. Portland's KBPS was staffed by student technicians, many of whom went on to careers in commercial radio. Portland's high school students wrote, produced, and performed radio lessons in many subject areas and won some national recognition. Elementary students in Chicago played roles in dramas for a variety of subject areas, while older students performed on discussion and quiz shows. New York's All City High School Radio Workshop became an elite training school for students pursuing performance careers in radio and television. That Workshop gave a start to several well known names in American broadcasting and theatre, including Barbara Streisand. Moreover, those student performances enhanced WNYE's reputation for quality radio productions.

Impact and Accomplishments

Local SOAs did not archive their records the way university based SOAs did so documentation on impact is quite lean. Nevertheless, we can infer some conclusions about the likely impact and accomplishments of local schools of the air. All SOAs enriched lessons and curricula with drama, story telling, current events, music, fine arts, and specialized expertise, but local SOAs focused their enrichment on local culture, history, personalities and institutions, thus expanding the learning environment from the confines of the classroom to the wider community. All local SOAs developed some programming cooperatively with local cultural institutions including libraries, historical societies, symphonies, museums, or local governmental entities such as

TABLE 72. SUMMARY OF FINDINGS: LOCAL SCHOOLS OF THE AIR

FINDINGS	CSA	CPSA	RSA	KBPS	WYNE	Detroit
Longevity	47 years - 1929–1976	45 years (approx) - 1931–1934; - 1938–1980(?)	16 years separate - 1932–1948; and 20 years as part of ESSA - 1948 –1968	62 years - 1933–1995	Approximately 45 years - 1936–1980s	50 years (approx.) - 1934–1980s(?)
Major Personalities	- Alice Keith, inspiration - Ida Black, experiment in math by radio - William Levenson, Supervisor of Radio, widely respected and published expert in educational radio	Harold Kent, director from 1938–1942. Kent became a leading figure in educational radio.	- George Eastman, benefactor - William Fey, manager, WHAM - Harry Carpenter, science supervisor	- Patricia Green Swenson, director of SOA activities and later director of station KBPS (1942 to 1988) - Mary Gilmore, director, 1941–47 - Hazel Kenyon, director, 1939–41 - The "Benson Boys"	James Macandrew, long-time director of WYNE	Kathleen Lardie, Director of Radio, 1938–1963
Broadcast Facility	- Commercial stations, 1929 to 1935 - WBOE short wave, 1936 – mid 1940s - WBOE FM, from the mid 1940s	- Commercial stations through 1942 - Gradual shift from commercial stations to WBEZ FM, 1943 to 1948	Three commercial AM stations: - WHAM (NBC) clear channel - WHEC (CBS) - WSAY	- KBPS AM, 1933–1995, run by students at Benson Polytechnic - Comm. stations, KEX/KGW, broadcast 1934 to 1943; KGW produced programs until mid-1950s	Three publicly owned stations -WNYC AM -WNYE, short wave -WNYE FM (Never used a commercial station)	- Six commercial stations, 1934–1948 - WDTR FM, 1948–1980s

Educational Philosophy	- Radio as a tool for direct teaching and achieving specific learning objectives - Teacher training through use of master teachers	- Radio supplemented the teachers. Teacher decided best use of radio in classroom. - Radio served as an "ornament' to the curriculum	- Master teachers and subject specialists bring high quality instruction to classrooms - Radio enabled classroom teachers to gain new skills	- Radio provides opportunities for on-the-job training - Radio was the "Fourth R," important to total learning - A tool for instruction that gave access to media savvy students	No data	Early years: – radio was an instructional aid for lesson enrichment After 1945: – radio exposed students to great minds and unique learning opportunities
School Goals	Use radio to distribute instructional expertise and correct curriculum throughout the system	- Enrichment for teacher selection - Supplement curricula in special topics such as safety	Use radio to distribute instructional expertise and correct curriculum throughout the system	Provide for: - In school and after school programming - Career training - Student participation Serve the wider community	No data	Early years: - radio used for PR After 1945: - Supplement and enrich instruction - Bring events and personalities to students - Provide instruction that was not available otherwise
Instruction Methods	- Direct teaching, master teacher took control of the classroom - Classroom teacher follows prescribed procedures - Students active during broadcast	- Teacher decides methods - Pre-broadcast should focus on motivating students - Students active during broadcast	- Direct teaching, master teacher took control of the classroom - Classroom teacher provides support for individual students	- Get students involved in the creative and technical aspects of ed. radio - After 1970, lessons used by individuals or small groups	– Briefly introduce the radio lesson – No suggested activity during broadcast – Following broadcast teacher discusses highlights and assigns activities	Learning resulted from passive listening During broadcast, avoid student activity such as drawing, note taking, or writing on board

TABLE 72 (*continued*)

FINDINGS	CSA	CPSA	RSA	KBPS	WYNE	Detroit
Support Materials	Extensive use of radio support materials including comprehensive teacher guides and visual aids delivered just in time for each lesson	- Weekly bulletins - Broadcast Handbook incl. schedule, stations, objectives, summary descriptions and learning activities - Tours and lectures at local cultural institutions	- Weekly bulletins - Specialist material to support special topics - Visual support materials	- Weekly bulletins - KBPS Program Guide - Broadcast utilization materials created to accompany taped programs - Listening Text (comprehensive guides)	- Weekly bulletins After 1950: - comprehensive radio manual published and distributed to all schools - separate teacher guides made available for some series	- Weekly bulletins listing all available educational broadcasts - Pamphlets prepared to accompany some series
Estimated Audience and %	Two-thirds of schools used radio lessons, according to Seerley Reid	- 1944: 97,000 - 1954: 400,000 claimed; probably reflected total enrollments, not individuals	- 53,000 listeners claimed, 1938, - No other data available	% of targeted teachers listening to specific programs ranged from 33.3% to 96.7%	No data	Tyler's 1967 study: - 7% of elementary students listen regularly - 12% listened occasionally
Evaluations and Surveys Conducted	Up to 1950, rigorous formative and summative evaluations: - teacher ratings - teacher made tests - commercial tests	- Weekly reports from listening groups - End of semester reports from teachers - School visits	- Survey of 168 teachers, 1939 - National study found that RSA science series increased knowledge of and interest in science - Formative evaluations	No data	No data	I. Keith Tyler surveyed Detroit school's use of radio and TV in order to develop recommendations for future development

Student Participation in Broadcasting	Little or no student participation	- Elem. students performed child roles after brief training and coaching - Students participated in panel discussion and quiz shows	Occasional participation in discussion and music programs	- Benson students operated KBPS - Portland HS students performed dramas and wrote scripts - In last decade several series used only students on-air	The All-City High School Radio Workshop trained HS students in professional performance. Many Workshop graduates went on to careers in broadcasting.	WDTD served as a laboratory for high school students to learn technical and on-air skills associated with radio broadcasting
Demise	- 1976, WBOE switched to NPR format - 1978, WBOE closed as a cost saving measure	- Transition to NPR format began in late 1970s - By 1990, in-school broadcasting had ceased - Radio never seen as integral to curricula	1948, WHAM AM shifted RSA broadcasts to WHAM FM, prompting RSA to form a state-based network	- 1994, Portland school board ceased funding KBPS - KBPS serves students of Benson Polytechnic as a training lab for careers in radio	No data	- Tyler said radio's decline began in 1955 when the school converted part of the radio operation to TV - Radio became a "play back" operation during 1960s - Teachers lost interest

the fire department. They developed programming that introduced students to local history, historical figures, and legends, and they brought the workings of local government into the classroom. Several local SOAs become training grounds for students who wanted to pursue careers in broadcasting. In some cases, local SOAs provided the main source of curriculum for special subjects such as local history, safety, and multicultural awareness. They also prepared school boards, administrators and teachers in thousands of school districts to rapidly accept new forms of educational technology, namely television and computers.

Most local SOAs achieved recognition for special accomplishment in one or two areas: KPBS for student participation in broadcasting; WNYE for high quality program productions; Cleveland, before 1950, for using radio to deliver curriculum; Rochester for teacher training through radio; and Chicago for developing several programs that crossed over to become popular on commercial stations. Despite this recognition, no single local SOA stood out the way the Wisconsin School of the Air did among the state-based SOAs, at least not according to the available documentation. Clearly, local SOAs made great use of radio as a community based educational resource. Unfortunately, available documentation does not allow us to determine whether local SOAs made the best possible use of radio's educational potential.

Section V

Opportunity Lost?

This section summarizes findings and draws conclusions about the development of radio based Schools of the Air in this country, the contributions that they made to education, and why some succeeded more than others. It also poses and tries to answer a fundamental question raised by this work, namely, in view of the many obvious benefits that some states and cities derived from radio instruction, why did many more fail to take advantage of this relatively low cost educational resource?

When broadcast radio burst on the American scene in the early 1920s, it excited the public imagination with fantastic possibilities. Businesspeople, politicians, social activists, religious and foundation leaders, and educators all saw great, though different, potentials emanating from the incredible new communication technology. Some said that radio would make possible a vast people's university, and many took up the challenge. By 1925, educators and engineers at dozens of colleges were broadcasting adult home-study courses, both noncredit and for credit. Soon, farsighted educators and social activists agitated for broadcasting to the nation's schools. In 1927 a movement arose to establish a national school of the air that could bring the world and a few talented teachers into the classrooms of America. Radio, it seemed, might cure many of the nation's educational deficiencies.

During the same period, as radio's huge commercial potential became clearer, a bitter conflict shaped up over the direction and control of the airwaves. The main battles occurred in Washington, D.C. at the Federal Radio Commission (FRC), which held power to assign broadcasting licenses, frequencies, power, and hours of operation. Working to bring order to the chaos of multiple stations broadcasting on the same wavelengths, the commission reassigned all broadcast licenses in the country. The FRC's new license assignments favored commercial stations with coveted evening hours, strong signals and, in some cases, clear channels. They restricted the college-based educational stations to low-power daytime operation, crippling adult home-study programs. Within a few years, many colleges shuttered or sold their radio operations.

The Payne Fund, led by Ben Darrow and Armstrong Perry, promoted a plan to create a national school of the air (NSoA) using foundation funding (from the Commonwealth Fund) and persuading the National Education Association (NEA) to operate or at least oversee the school. When the NEA rejected that idea, Darrow returned to Ohio to promote his ideas while Perry agitated at the federal level to extend government protection to the remaining college-based educational stations. Perry hoped that the college stations could form a network for a future NSoA. Interestingly, the Payne Fund supported both Darrow's and Perry's efforts. When the Wilbur Committee failed to make any provision to protect college stations, Perry and others refocused their efforts on getting the federal government to set aside 15% of all radio stations for public service including education.

TABLE 73. SUMMARY OF FINDINGS: SOA OPERATION—NATIONAL, STATE AND LOCAL LEVELS

FINDINGS	Network Sponsored SOAs	State-based SOAs	Local SOAs
Longevity	- NBC's MAH, 14 years, 1928 to 1942 - CBS's ASA, 15 years 1930 to 1945. Plus 3 years as an after-school program.	- Four of six continued broadcasting until the mid-1970s - TSA and ESSA ended in 1960 and 1968 respectively	- Most continued operating until the 1980s - Portland continued SOA broadcasts into the mid-1990s
Supporting Institutions	- Networks provided 100% of financial support - Education associations provided advisory and consulting services - Networks provided rich resources	- Land-grant universities provided limited access to free broadcast facility (except for TSA and ESSA) paid staff, volunteer expertise in education. Also some volunteer or low cost performers. - State legislatures and educational bureaucracies provided funding and legitimacy	- Local school boards: — set policy — provided supervision and funding — provided day-long use of broadcast facility — gave legitimacy — distributed bulletins to entire school system
Goals	- Improve public image - Demonstrate that the American system of privately owned radio could provide quality educational services - Live up to the terms of the Cooperation Agreement	- Serve the unmet educational needs of schools, particularly in rural areas - Bring the outside world and the voices of prominent people into the classroom - Offer educational resources that otherwise would be unavailable - Deliver special curricula	- Enrich classroom lessons - Supplement curricula - Use the latest technology to demonstrated the best pedagogy and deliver quality curricula - Provide opportunities for student training in broadcasting - Deliver special curricula, particularly with a local slant - Cooperate with local cultural and governmental entities
Educational Philosophy	- Essentialism for most of ASA's broadcast history - Affect over cognition (Damrosch) - Subject matter paramount - Radio enriches curricula - Bring great minds and exotic experiences to the classroom (ASA)	Wide variations: - Radio supplements curricula - Radio enriches curricula - Master teachers and great minds motivate students - Learner centered instruction situated in state culture and economy	Widest variations: - Radio supplements curricula - Radio enriches curricula and individual lessons - Radio as a tool for direct teaching and achieving specific learning objectives

		- Wisconsin Idea, e.g., radio enables the university to serve all citizens - Dewey's Progressivism	- Teacher training through use of master teachers - Radio is a field for on-the-job training
Instructional Methods	- Drama, dialog, story telling, panel discussion, mini-lectures - Teachers conduct pre- and post broadcast lecture, discussion and learning activities - Damrosch's 5-step pedagogy	- Drama, dialog, story telling, panel discussion, direct teaching, and mini-lectures - Wide variations, some emphasized active student engagement while others stressed passive listening - Active learning	- Drama, dialog, story telling, panel discussion, direct teaching and mini-lectures - Wide variations, some emphasized active student engagement while others stressed passive listening - Classroom teacher decides how best to use radio - Students participate in broadcasting
Community-Based Learning	Little or none	Several SOAs, most notably the WSA, developed strong programs of regional and state-wide community learning events	- WNYE, WDTR, WBEZ developed workshops in which selected students could participate - Student participation in studio performances - KBPS included students at all levels of broadcasting
Audience and Approx % of Student Enrollment in Listening Area	- Audiences reached approximately two million from late 1930s to demise - Between 7% and 8% of national enrollment for 1940, K–12 - Audiences well documented by university based researchers	- Audiences peaked in period from 1950 through 1965 - Percentage of potential total student audience that listened varied widely, from 10% for the OSA to 47% for the WSA	- Reliable audience data not widely available
Impact	- Enriched curricula - MAH supplemented music curricula and promoted European Classical music - ASA promoted tolerance toward different races, religions, and ethnicities - ASA introduced international cultures, music and literature - Both promoted acceptance of educational technology in the classroom	- Supplemented school curricula - Delivered specialized curricula such as conservation, state history, and multiculturalism - Enriched curricula - Promoted acceptance of educational technology in the classroom	- Supplemented school curricula - Delivered specialized curricula such as local history, personalities, and government - Cooperated with local cultural institutions to expand educational horizons - Promoted multiculturalism - Enriched curricula

TABLE 73 (*continued*)

FINDINGS	Network Sponsored SOAs	State-based SOAs	Local SOAs
Impact			- Provided career training in broadcasting - Promoted educational technology in the classroom
Demise	Business decision	- Consolidation of small schools undercut the need for state-based SOAs - Loss of interest by supporting institutions - Competition from alternative forms of educational technology, TV and computers	- Competition from alternative forms of educational technology, TV and computers - Reduced budgets due to demographic changes in most urban areas

The set-aside proposal stirred firm opposition from commercial broadcast interests led by the networks. CBS president and founder William S. Paley argued that the set-aside provision would destroy the American system of free-enterprise broadcasting, which he said served the public well and provided ample opportunities for education, if the educators would only take advantage of them. The networks shored up their arguments by launching their own limited schools of the air, thereby undercutting the argument for a federally supported NSoA. By 1934, the broadcasters had won the day; the set-aside issue was defeated. But the networks and the association of station owners did sign on to a cooperation policy in which they agreed to develop and broadcast the highest quality educational programs.[1]

In response to these setbacks, advocates of an NSoA pursued a dual policy. Some pressured the networks and commercial station owners to provide educational programming promised in the cooperation policy. Others advocated the development of schools of the air (SOAs) at the state and local levels. The dual policy seems to have produced concrete results. During the next ten years, the network SOAs, specifically the ASA, produced some remarkable programming, and SOAs sprang up in a half dozen states and cities. The resulting SOA movement — it couldn't be called a system — lacked any central goals, direction, funding, purpose, or performance standards. In other words it mirrored the fragmented educational system that operated throughout the U.S. Table 73 summarizes the finding of this work for each of the three levels at which SOAs operated.

Discussion of Findings

Longevity

The fact that two commercial organizations (NBC and CBS) operated nationwide schools of the air for well over a decade at no cost to participants is a remarkable and probably unique event in the history of American education. In the late 1920s the fledgling networks launched schools of the air (SOAs) because they made good business sense for a variety of reasons, but fifteen years later, things had changed; network broadcasters found that even 30 minutes of daily week-day air time was far too valuable to donate to the roughly two million school children who tuned in regularly[2] (Summers, 1958). By the mid–1940s both network national schools of the air, *Music Appreciation Hour* and the *American School of the Air*, ceased operating. Furthermore, the public's attitude toward radio had evolved substantially. Gone was the high-minded disapproval of a commercialized medium. In its place, there flourished a boundless fascination with broadcast entertainment. Perhaps the public came to see commercials as a kind of admission price for the right to the home entertainment that radio delivered. At any rate, when the networks discontinued their broadcasts to the schools, the public voiced few complaints. This outcome would not have surprised Armstrong Perry. In 1929 he had predicted that when commercial stations could sell all their daytime hours, they would end support of educational radio (McChesney, 1993). His concern appears to have been well founded.

Supporting Institutions

A more hospitable long-term environment for SOAs proved to be publicly funded state universities and local school districts. They provided SOAs with broadcast facilities, professional and technical expertise, and access to talented volunteer student performers for the numerous dramas,

[1]As described in Section I, the broadcasters agreed to cooperate with educators by making the airwaves available for educational programs and even developing some programs (Leach, 1983).

[2]For the year 1936–37, CBS and NBC offered a total of 141 unsponsored programs, called sustaining programs, for free or a small fee. By the 1946–47 broadcast year, the number had dropped to 94 and the total number of weekday sustaining programs had dropped even more dramatically (Summers, 1958).

TIMELINES: SCHOOLS OF THE AIR

Section 1, National Broadcast Networks:

• NBC's Music Appreciation Hour	1928–1942
• CBS's American School of the Air	1930–1945 (1948)

Section 2, State-Level SOAs:

• Ohio School of the Air	1928–1937; 1940–1960
• Wisconsin School of the Air	1931–mid 1970s
• Minnesota	1938–1979
• Texas School of the Air	1940–1960
• Oregon Schools of the Air (KOAC)	1933–mid 1970s
• Empire State FM School of the Air	1948–1968

Section 3, Local School Boards:

• Cleveland (WBOE)	1929–1976
• Chicago (WBEZ)	1938–1970?
• Rochester, New York (WHAM)	1933–1948
• Portland, Oregon (KBPS)	1933–1995
• New York City (WNYE)	1936–mid 1980s
• Detroit (WDTR)	1934–mid 1980s

quiz shows and discussion formats that made up most of broadcasting for the schools. No wonder that state-supported SOAs continued operating for up to three decades after the commercial networks had stopped broadcasting to the schools. Local SOAs operated even longer with several broadcasting until the mid–1980s, and Portland's KBPS continuing to the mid–1990s. Curiously, contemporary scholars of educational technology fail to mention the longevity of state and local SOAs.

Goals

Both NBC and CBS launched SOAs primarily to demonstrate their commitment to education. That commitment helped allay the public's fear of monopoly control and over-commercialization of radio. It also fended off attempts to have the government set aside stations for educational use. In addition, William Paley used the ASA to gain competitive advantage over NBC in both domestic and international markets. For the networks, gaining substantial acceptance from classroom teachers wasn't really necessary; they could accomplish their main goal of demonstrating commitment by creating the appearance of a serious educational effort. In that, they succeeded well.

Walter Damrosch, founder of the MAH, worked ceaselessly to spread the European classical music tradition throughout the United States. His programs never achieved the mass appeal of entertainment radio; nevertheless, many music educators and scholars acknowledged that his broadcasts to the schools succeeded in building appreciation for European classical music in the American heartland. ASA's director Alice Keith and its dean of faculty advisors William C. Bagley shared the goal of exposing students to society's great artists, thinkers, scientists, explorers, and political leaders. Later under the leadership of Sterling Fisher, that goal shifted to exposing students to the role that culture and the arts played in history and society of the U.S. and Latin America. Based on Fisher's work, CBS refashioned the ASA into the *School of Air of the Americas*, a vehicle for competing with NBC in the broadcast markets of South America.

Five of six state-based SOAs were supported chiefly by universities. Universities had jumped into broadcasting for the schools because as the centers of teacher education they felt a responsibility to make the new education technology available to schools in their states. Also, four of the six were broadcasting pioneers; they owned and operated radio stations and experimented with programming so they were ideally positioned to take up a leadership role in educational broadcasting once it became feasible.

All the state-based SOAs except the OSA focused on serving the basic, but unmet, educational needs of rural and small town schools, particularly in subjects such as music, art, science, history, current events, and story telling for young children. The directors and teachers at the WSA frequently articulated one main goal: to support the curricular needs of teachers in one-room and state-graded schools. Not only did they articulate that goal, their actions — conducting field visits and organizing community-based festivals, exhibits, demonstrations, and contests — showed their continued focus on fulfilling the educational needs of teachers. More so than in any other SOA, Wisconsin educators and teachers incorporated WSA programs into their teaching practices and relied on the broadcasts to build curriculum. Meanwhile Oregon and Minnesota devoted substantial effort to fostering a strong appreciation of their state's history, culture, and unique environments. However they never achieved the high degree of acceptance from the educational communities in their states that the WSA did in Wisconsin. At the other end of the spectrum, Ben Darrow in Ohio shared the goal articulated by the ASA: to bring the world's experts, leaders and artists into the classroom.

During the mid and late 1930s local schools embarked on educational radio for diverse motives. Some such as Cleveland were genuinely impressed with radio's educational potential and clearly planned to use radio as a primary source of instruction and teacher training. A polio epidemic motivated the Chicago Public Schools return to in-school broadcasting, and like educators in Detroit they thought radio would provide good public relations. Rochester entered because a local philanthropist and radio station manager made an offer that the school board could not refuse. Soon, however, the Rochester school board realized that radio could provide high quality science instruction for students stuck in elementary schools where adequate resources for science instruction were unavailable. In Portland, educators first shaped radio narrowly as a tool for career training in the technical and managerial aspects of broadcasting. Gradually, their vision expanded to using radio for in-school broadcasting and community service. New York City's Mayor's Office apparently sparked the use of radio for the schools by offering the Board of Education funding for an experiment and air-time on the city owned radio station, WNYC.

While the local SOAs seemed to have launched their in-school broadcasting efforts for a variety of reasons, the FCC's action in setting aside a part of the FM radio band for education gave a strong boost to in-school broadcasting at the local level. By 1948 all surviving local SOAs, except KBPS, operated their own FM radio stations, and the organizational structure that grew up to support the stations also contributed to the longevity of the local SOAs. Career training for jobs in radio provided several local SOAs, particularly KBPS in Portland and WTRD in Detroit, with a strong argument for the continued funding of school based radio.

Educational Philosophy

Interestingly the two network SOAs demonstrated divergent ideas about radio education. Damrosch, the gifted and dedicated teacher, offered his own sweat and blood so to speak as demonstration that radio education should strive to develop appreciation for the subject matter before building cognitive knowledge. Indeed he was often criticized for his emotional and fanciful descriptions of musical passages. For the first ten years of ASA's operation, William Bagley's Essentialism dominated with emphasis on subject matter mastery over affective learning. Both the MAH and the ASA brought into the classroom great minds, artists, and leaders. Damrosch himself was the great mind in music while the ASA filled their program hours with numerous and sometimes esoteric experts in various subjects. Neither Bagley nor Damrosch seemed much influenced by Dewey's progressive ideas, offering little in the way of learner centered curricula.

State-based SOAs reflected surprisingly diverse ideas about the use of radio in education. The master teacher concept dominated at the OSA and the ESSA. OSA's Ben Darrow believed that master teachers and exposure to great minds would motivate students to high achievement. He also believed that educational radio's strength lay in its ability to bring the real world into the classroom to counter the abstract world of books. Darrow experimented frequently with new approaches to programming, looking for ways to enhance what he called the "actuality" of the listening experience. Dewey's progressivism — with its emphasis on student centered curriculum, active learning, and community-based learning — seemed most influential at the WSA, TSA and to a lesser extend at the MSA and the ORSA. Programs such as the WSA's *Let's Draw, Let's Sing, Young Experimenters*, and *Rhythm and Games* involved students actively in learning during the broadcast. Others such as the TSA's *Open Your Eyes* and the MSA's *Sense of the World* encouraged extensive student engagement following the broadcasts.

The Wisconsin Idea — that the borders of the UW campus were the borders of the state — motivated WSA directors and teachers to shape the WSA into an institution that could address the educational needs of residents throughout Wisconsin. I. Keith Tyler (1967) underscored the importance of a having broad vision and overarching philosophy when he urged the Detroit school administrators to develop a written philosophy stating the role of radio in a school's instructional program (p. 79). We don't know if The Wisconsin Idea was actually written down somewhere, but it did spur WHA directors Engel and McCarty to build the state's FM network, which in turn enabled the WSA to become an integral part of the state's educational system.

Local SOAs seemed less inclined toward Dewey's Progressivism, perhaps indicating that his influence was strongest among university based educators. At any rate, local SOA administrators in Cleveland, Rochester, and to a lesser extent in Detroit believed radio would be a powerful tool for teacher training. Master teachers would model superior pedagogy and excellent content knowledge, which novices and less talented teachers could then imitate. Leaders of the CSA and RSA also believed strongly that radio instruction should be integrated thoroughly with curricula.

In Chicago Harold Kent had set the pattern for WBEZ programming on enriching the curricula and letting classroom teachers decide how best to incorporate radio lessons into their practice. By the 1950s however all local SOAs were focused chiefly on enrichment. Local SOAs in Portland, New York and Detroit used radio as a great tool for career training in various aspects of broadcasting: technical, program production, station management, or on-air performance. Others used students in various aspects of broadcasting but mostly out of necessity because they lacked funds to hire adequate staff.

Instructional Methods

Ben Darrow can take credit for pioneering at the OSA many of the instructional methods that became commonplace among the SOAs that followed him. Darrow strongly discouraged the college-lecture style of exposition that had plagued educational radio during the late 1920s (White, 1947). He advocated plain, direct talk, and his method for achieving such speech was to have the radio teacher imagine one child in the audience and talk directly to that child. He also used question-and-answer and dialogue, typically between the radio teacher and a student. Using these techniques, Darrow achieved exposition without lecture.

Darrow wasn't the first to use dramatization on the radio, but he did refine and expand its use. Mainly, he used professional and college-based drama troupes to create a sense of reality in a variety of OSA programs including history, literature, and social science. He also advocated using music and sound effects to stimulate the imagination (Darrow, 1932, 1940).

By the late 1930s there had emerged a consensus on the subject of instructional methods best suited for radio. All SOA administrators agreed that they wanted to avoid the deadly lecture hall sound and to take advantage of radio's attributes to make the broadcasts lively and appealing. In a study of the popular ASA program, *Tales from Far and Near,* Reid (1941c) found classroom teachers in agreement that broadcasts should be "dramatic rather than expository, emotionally stimulating rather than conversational" (p. 42). By 1940, SOA broadcasts at all three levels, with one exception, used the following instructional methods:

- Dramatization for literature, history, social science and even geography
- Story telling for younger students, mostly K–3
- Dialogue between the radio teacher and one or more students, used most for science and current events
- Multi-voice formats such as quiz show and panel discussion
- Music and sound effects to heighten emotional impact
- Voices of celebrities, renowned experts, and leaders (The idea was that lecture was acceptable from a celebrity or respected expert but not from the radio teacher.)
- Direct teaching that engaged students during the broadcast

The one consistent exception to the above list was Walter Damrosch. He had developed his teaching style in front of live audiences of New York schoolchildren, and those methods translated very well to his radio audiences. He grounded his instructional approach in an educationally sound five-step process composed of greeting, recall, preview, demonstration, and presentation. The recall segment tied each broadcast to the larger subject while the preview, demonstration, and presentation steps provided a simple but logical lesson structure. This approach won Damrosch the respect of music educators throughout the country (Martin, 1983). Damrosch stressed that to be successful his broadcasts needed the active cooperation of the classroom teacher who had to ensure that the students listened carefully to the broadcasts. Then, following the broadcasts, the teacher must lead a discussion of the music and guide students to read and do the activities suggested in the student notebook (Wiebe & O'Steen, 1942, p. 2). In order to give students on-air exposure, local SOAs made greater use of instructional formats such as quiz shows and panel discussions.

The ASA demonstrated little innovation in instructional methods, seemingly content to adapt the methods pioneered by Darrow at the OSA. The ASA teaching repertoire relied heavily on drama, storytelling, exposition, and dialogue, but little direct teaching. As the years passed, the ASA made greater use of drama, probably because the school could borrow from the CBS stable of talented radio writers, which included at one time or another Orson Welles, James Thurber, Dorothy Parker, and Norman Corwin,[3] among others (Lewis, 1992).

While the WSA frequently used exposition, drama, and storytelling, it also made greater use of direct teaching than the other SOAs. In long-running programs such as *Let's Draw, Let's Sing, Young Experimenters,* and *Rhythm and Games,* radio teachers took control of the classrooms during the broadcasts and engaged students in learning activities such as drawing, singing, performing experiments, and moving rhythmically.

Any discussion of instruction methods should confront the fact that teaching, whether live or mediated, is as much art as science. Methods alone could not explain Damrosch's appeal as an educator. Most observers attributed much of Damrosch's success as a teacher to his charm, passion, energy, and imaginative verbal imagery. While some music educators and critics of the time criticized his methods, most scholars now assert that whatever the demerits of finding heroic narratives in Beethoven's music, it undoubtedly appealed to youthful listeners and made more accessible the European music tradition.

---

[3]Though unfamiliar to all but a few media scholars today, from the late 1930s to the early 1950s Norman Corwin was known to many as the premier writer of quality radio programs. He possessed an appealing ability to weave political and social themes into dramas. For the 1944 election the Democratic Party got Corwin to write a nationwide get-out-the-vote program that supported Roosevelt's reelection (Barnouw, 1966; Lewis, 1992).

While Ben Darrow decried radio lectures, he readily acknowledged that the popularity of the OSA's geography series was due in large part to the fact that the radio teacher, Dr. McConnell, "was an unusually interesting lecturer" (Darrow, 1940 p. 28). Similarly, at the WSA, although *Afield with Ranger Mac* consisted of nothing but one man talking, it achieved great popularity that endured for many years. These anecdotal examples serve to demonstrate that the success of an educational endeavor cannot be attributed solely to instructional methods.

Evaluation

The Ohio based Evaluation of School Broadcasting project headed by I. Keith Tyler and Seerley Reid performed the most rigorous and reliable evaluation of the effectiveness of radio instruction versus traditional classroom learning. They found that radio instruction improved vocabulary acquisition, writing skills, and enhanced student interest and motivation for some subjects such as science. However, they also found that radio instruction did not produce more cognitive learning than did the traditional classroom. Subsequently, the value of such media comparison studies has been shown to be very low due to confounding variables. All of that, however, overlooks radio's most valuable contribution to education. It enables educators to deliver to the classroom learning resources that might otherwise not be available. For example Damrosch brought to thousands of classrooms a level of music instruction that simply could not be duplicated by local music teachers. Additionally, Wisconsin's *Young Experimenters* brought science instruction to rural classrooms where such curriculum had not existed.

The master teacher concept represented an interesting but unevaluated feature of SOA history. Did master teachers produce better instruction than the average classroom teacher, and how much did novice and poorly prepared teachers learn from the expert radio teacher? Regarding these intriguing questions little or no data exists.

Community-Based Learning

The WSA consistently promoted community-based extracurricular learning as adjuncts to its radio broadcasts. The regional and statewide music festivals associated with E. B. Gordon's *Adventures in Music Land* and *Let's Sing* became popular events throughout the state. *Let's Draw's* regional statewide art fairs and traveling exhibitions enabled tens of thousands of rural parents, teachers, and students to share the experience of admiring the artwork produced by children who had listened to the radio broadcasts. *Ranger Mac* got tens of thousands of Wisconsin students developing Conservation Corners in their classrooms and participating in school-sponsored reforestation projects. *Let's Write* held annual creative writing contests.

While no studies focused specifically on the community-based activities, the fact that tens of thousands participated annually allows us to infer that parents, educators, state officials, and teachers all believed that these WSA-related activities provided educational and social value to their children and communities.

Audience

In his study, *Teachers and Machines*, Cuban (1986) argues that educational radio, as with most educational technology in this country, had failed to attract widespread acceptance among America's teachers and educators. He and other scholars asserted that although the network-sponsored SOAs did reach several million listeners, the number was far fewer than that claimed by network executives. Studies based on the Ohio School of the Air found that less than 10 percent of the potential audience in Ohio listened regularly. Scholars projected data to the rest of the country and pronounced the SOA movement a brave try, but ultimately, a failure. That might be a fair judgment of the network SOAs, which attracted roughly 8 percent of the nation's school children, but as we have seen, the networks' educational efforts took second place to their corporate goals. Furthermore the judgment of failure based on audience size clearly does not apply to the other state-based SOAs whose penetration of audiences reached from 20 percent to as high as 47 percent for the Wisconsin School of the Air (WSA).

By any measure Cuban's assertion does *not* apply to the WSA; it did achieve a broad audience of student listeners and widespread teacher support. During the period 1954 through 1964, nearly 50 percent of the state's students, kindergarten through eighth grade, listened regularly to at least one WSA program, a level that far exceeded the hopes of many proponents of educational radio. Using the criteria of teacher acceptance, the WSA must be considered a rousing success.

Any discussion of audience size raises the question, How big need the audience be? For an educational endeavor to be considered a success, what proportion of the potential audience must participate? Woelfel and Tyler (1945) expressed ambiguity over this question. Referring to their study of the audience for the network SOAs, they said that the audience numbers were discouraging when compared to inflated network claims, but encouraging if one considering that listeners to network-sponsored programs represented the largest classrooms in the world.

Conclusions

More than just an effort to inject the latest educational technology into education, the school of the air movement reflects a desire to fundamentally reform — even transform — American education. The would-be reformers believed radio could bring the world's leaders, artists, and experts to even remote rural or deprived urban schools, overcome boring school routines, motivate students to higher achievement, make master teachers and quality curricula available to all, train new teachers, help develop a common national curricula that emphasized democracy and tolerance, and bring unity to the country's fragmented educational system — all in one big technological leap.

By documenting the Schools of the Air (SOA) story, this study fills part of a gap in our knowledge of the history of American educational media and also sheds new light on the school of the air movement. In the following section, we first develop conclusions about why the movement declined. That's crucial to our understanding. But it's also important to highlight the successes of the movement and in particular the questions raised by those successes.

Reasons for Demise

The movement started with the effort to create a national school of the air (NSoA). Promoted vigorously by Payne Fund representatives, Ben Darrow and Armstrong Perry, the movement foundered when, at critical junctures, the National Educational Association (NEA) and the federal government failed to provide support. Early on, the networks had offered free airtime (McChesney, 1993), but Armstrong Perry resisted giving commercial broadcasters complete control of the NSoA effort. He wanted educators at the NEA to develop the curriculum and run the school. When the NEA declined to take an active role in launching an NSoA, the funding source backed out,[4] and no others emerged. Why did the NEA table the most promising educational innovation to come along in decades? Their motives are unclear, though it seems that partly to blame was their general mistrust of innovation.

---

[4]The Commonwealth Fund had promised funding to launch the NSoA if the NEA would commit to planning and administering the effort.

Faced with that disappointment, Darrow returned to Ohio to found a state-based OSA, but Perry continued to agitate for an NSoA based on a network of publicly owned educational stations. Perry's efforts were frustrated twice by government rejection: first in 1930 when the Interior Department's Wilbur Commission failed to support the preservation of college stations and again in 1934 when the newly formed Federal Communications Commission failed to support the legislation calling for a 15 percent set-aside of radio channels for educational use (McChesney, 1993).

The refusal by the federal government to provide any solid support[5] stemmed in part from the structure of American education. At that time, the federal government played no significant role in education. No federal agency existed that could fund or administer a national school of the air, and any move to initiate such a role was opposed by many (Perry, 1929, p. 41). In addition, states jealously protected their educational prerogatives. In that environment, the concept of a federally supported nationwide education effort faced an uphill battle.

Furthermore, the radio broadcast system in the United States was largely owned by private individuals and corporations, and they exercised strong influence with federal regulators. In contrast to most other countries where governments had taken the lead in developing the broadcast system, in the U.S. private enterprise and free market concepts ruled. Consequently, private interests looked askance at public ownership of radio, even those stations controlled by colleges. Throughout the late 1920s and early 1930s, network executives and local station owners stood guard, ready to attack any real or imagined infringement on a purely market-based broadcasting system. Those efforts were illustrated by Harold McCarty's story of his battle to preserve UW's station, WHA, against attacks by the owners of several Wisconsin newspapers who wanted to privatize the college station (Lowe, 1972). Facing the triple barriers of inaction by professional educators, refusal by government agencies to support a public educational radio system, and powerful opposition from the owners of commercial radio, the movement to create a publicly supported national school of the air soon died out.

Nonetheless, schools of the air did flourish. In an environment of diverse media ownership, diverse SOAs emerged at three levels: national, state, and local. All achieved notable successes, had lasting impacts, but ultimately ceased operations. Following is a summary of the likely causes behind the decline of SOAs at the three levels and some lessons learned. The bulk of this section is devoted to analysis and conclusions about the successes of the school of the air movement based on the data presented, with particular focus on why more SOAs did not arise at the state and local level.

Causes for Demise

The documentation points to several probable causes for the demise of schools of the air.

- At the national level, changing market conditions, changes in social expectation for media, and the FCC's set aside of part of the FM radio band for education stations.
- At the state level, the school consolidation movement undercut key support for three of the most successful state-based SOAs, the WSA, MSA and ORSA. Consolidation movements eliminated many one-room and small schools that had relied most heavily on the state-based SOAs for curriculum support. Also larger schools meant more specialized teachers and less need for the supplements and enrichments offered by in-school radio. For the TSA and ESSA, over reliance on commercial radio for broadcast services spelled doom quickly. When the commercial stations withdrew their sustaining services, the TSA and ESSA had no where to turn for

---

[5]William Cooper, then commissioner of the Office of Education in the Department of the Interior, did express support for the idea of government supported educational radio, but his influence was no match for the powerful political forces that opposed that idea (McChesney, 1993; Saettler, 1990).

affordable broadcast services. Finally, competition from educational television also played some role in the demise of all state-based SOAs, but particularly in New York, Ohio, and Oregon.
- At the local level: Specific causes for demise are not clear. Possible candidates include the decline of American urban areas and resulting budget tightening, replacement of radio by educational TV, teacher resistance, and the rise of computers as a more sophisticated form of educational technology.

Lessons learned from the demise of the SOA movement might include:

- America's fragmented education system presents benefits and problems to innovation. Successful innovations often stagnate in the place of origin unable to hop from one state or district to another.
- The federal government still plays only a limited role in education, though clearly that is changing with passage of the No Child Left Behind laws.
- Once commercial interests get entrenched in a new medium, it is very difficult for government to extend any control.
- Educational researchers follow the interests and tone set by business, foundations and government funding. When those entities lost interest in radio and turned to educational television, educational researchers were compelled to follow.

Successes

This work is dedicated to uncovering the wide scope of educational activity and accomplishments achieved by the SOA movement. In no way unified or cohesive, the movement represented essentially separate operations at three levels: national, state and local. In that, it resembled the nation's fragmented educational system. Nevertheless the movement as a whole scored notable successes, the most important being the quality and characteristic of the educational resources deliver to students. Overall SOAs delivered:

- Live learning experiences. Unlike other forms of educational technology such as film, records and slide tapes, radio brought immediate experience to the classroom. Ben Darrow believed, "radio students get a sense of being in the presence of those who actually make history rather than those who merely write or talk about it" and that was, he thought, a powerful motivator for learning (Darrow, 1932). At all levels, SOAs enabled students to experience and learn from gifted teachers. Unfortunately, live broadcasting gradually diminished during the 1960s as more and more SOAs turned to taped programs. The trade-off was higher production values.
- Dramatized learning experiences that stimulated the imagination and motivation. Dramatization became the most commonly used pedagogy in radio, one that classroom teachers could not reproduce. It was acknowledged by nearly everyone as radio's single greatest strength.
- Active learning. Programs on drawing, music, and science got children actively involved in learning even during the broadcasts.
- Curricula enrichment. Radio was used most frequently to enrich school curricula or specific topics, even individual lessons.
- Curricula supplement. Particularly in rural schools, radio was used to fill "gaps" in curricula or to strengthen what would have been a weak offering. Subjects most often supplemented included music, art appreciation, science, storytelling, and current events.
- Career preparation. Through SOAs, thousands of students gained practical experience with the technical and creative aspects of broadcasting.

At the national level, the ASA invested its quality writing and production resources to create program series on folk music, history, geography, natural science and literature. It also succeeded to a small degree in emphasizing democracy as a fundamental goal for all Americans, a goal that fit well with Seerley Reid's vision for a national school of the air. Walter Damrosch brought not only high production values, but inspired teaching to music education.

At the state level, SOAs emphasized state and local culture, history, economy, population, and government. States that supported SOAs used them to deliver required curricula on state history and government. The state-based SOAs also supported state curricular goals, particularly in the areas of literature, social and natural science. Community gatherings of radio students in music and art became common in Wisconsin, Minnesota, and Oregon.

At the local level, student participation became a defining feature of education by radio. Students participated in script writing, broadcast production, and especially on-air performance. Local SOAs extended education to the wider community by developing cooperative programs with local museums, historical societies, and government entities. They also delivered programs on safety and local government.

The SOA movement is most often evaluated in terms of the size of the listening audience, and that issue will be covered extensively later in this section. However, few scholars of schools of the air seem aware of their longevity. The benefits listed above were delivered to several million students for over 60 years, starting in 1928 with NBC's *Music Appreciation Hour* and continuing until the mid–1990s when Portland's KBPS broadcast its last program for the schools.[6]

Why Did Not More Teachers Use Schools of the Air?

In 1945, after reviewing their findings on SOA audiences, radio researchers at the Evaluation of School Broadcast project at The Ohio State University had boiled down the status of radio in education to one simple question: "Why is it ... that teachers have not made [greater] use of radio?" (Woelfel & Reid, 1945, p. 3). They derived that question from the results of their audience survey studies conducted in Ohio in 1940–1941, in which they found that only 15 percent of Ohio's schools — not teachers, but schools — regularly listened to any SOA. They projected their findings to the rest of the country. The validity of those projections can be questioned on several counts. (1) The Ohio study took place just after the OSA's low point following the dismissal of Ben Darrow. The OSA audience was probably quite low at that point. (2) School data were essentially meaningless because enrollment varied widely from school to school. Rural one room schools, which at that time made up nearly 25 percent of Ohio's schools, typically enrolled fewer than 40 students while some big city high schools might have enrolled several thousand students. The meaningful data would have been numbers of teachers or students who used OSA programs. That was not provided. (3) The researchers ignored or were unaware of the WSA audience, which even in the early 1940s exceeded Ohio's audience[7] by a considerable amount. (I will discuss the exception of the WSA later in this chapter.) Also, many state and local SOAs hit their stride in terms of audience from the late 1940s through the 1960s. Despite these drawbacks, Woelfel and Reid's question can serve as a useful tool for analyzing other SOAs covered in this study.

American School of the Air

Why did the ASA with the full resources of the CBS network at its disposal fail to attract more than 5.5 percent of the nation's school children to its programs? Cuban (1986) argued that

---

[6]Portland's KBPS ceased broadcasting to the schools sometime between 1993 and 1995.

[7]By audience I mean the portion of the state's school enrollment, kindergarten through 12th grade, that listened regularly to the state's SOA.

the reason lay primarily with teacher rejection. While that appears true, we need to know more about why teachers chose not use the ASA programs. One likely reason was that throughout its history the ASA offered programming chiefly for high schools and junior high schools. Locked into rigid classroom schedules, many high school teachers could not tune in to the ASA broadcast times. For example, high school teachers who taught literature, history, or current events in the mornings or late afternoons could never make use of ASA's early afternoon programs. Had the programs been aired twice a day, morning and afternoon, listenership might have increased substantially, but of course the network would have had to forgo substantial ad revenue. That choice would have been unlikely, given that ASA was developed chiefly to support the public relations needs of a large corporation during its early growth period. Why didn't the ASA offer more programming for elementary grades when clearly such offerings would have attracted more teachers? Existing documentation offers no clues. The ASA did succeed in creating an effective national school of the air, but it was limited in effect because ASA management placed the needs of commercial broadcasting over those of teachers and students.

Music Appreciation Hour

While the ASA focused on the upper grades, the MAH offered programming suitable for students across the range from 4th through 12th grade. We might ask, then, why didn't it attract a larger audience than the 600,000 regular listeners that Reid (1941a) estimated for the series? This question puzzled the researchers, who were unsure whether to view Damrosch's radio audience as a disappointment or an encouraging success (Woelfel & Tyler, 1945). Given that the MAH broadcast only once a week and covered a single topic, European classical music, and then only a portion of that, we should conclude that MAH audience was quite large and that the MAH represented a great success.

The percentage of a state's students attracted by the state-based SOAs varied widely from roughly 10 percent for the OSA to nearly 50 percent for the WSA. This work has discussed several factors that attracted teachers to the state-based SOAs. One that correlates with high levels of teacher use of radio is station ownership. Those state-based SOAs that relied on donated air time tended to attract a smaller portion of state teachers than did SOAs that broadcast over state-owned stations. The WSA, MSA, and ORSA attracted larger audiences and operated longer than did the TSA and the ESSA. Another determining factor of teacher use related to whether an SOA's goals were curriculum enrichment or curriculum supplement. This topic is discussed more later in this section. Finally, audience data for local SOAs are too scarce to draw conclusions about why teachers did or did not use radio in the classroom.

All SOAs suffered from the movement's lack of cohesion. Regardless of level — national, state, or local — each SOA operated as a separate entity and none attracted much attention outside their home town or state. By the 1960s when the federal government was seriously considering providing support to non-commercial radio, the outlook for educational radio seemed weak and waning.

The following is from a NER report on the condition of educational radio 1966. "Overshadowed by commercial radio and then television it [educational radio] has suffered long neglect arising from disinterest among the educational administrators who control much of its fortunes. As a result, educational radio lacks cohesion as a medium; its purposes are varied and often confused, and it struggles for the beginnings of recognition as a potentially valuable national resource" (Holp, 1974, p. 42).

It's hard to tell from the quote what part of educational radio the author referred to.

The Wisconsin Exception

In light of the findings of this study, Woelfel and Reid's (1945) question about teachers not accepting radio should be revised to, "Why did so many teachers in Wisconsin make use of radio in their classrooms compared to teachers in other states?" This restatement is based on the finding that the WSA audience of regular listeners comprised at one point nearly 50 percent of the state's school population. One tool for answering the rephrased question can be found in the type of programming offered. For the purposes of this study, I distinguish between enrichment and supplemental programming.[8] I define *enrichment* as essentially ornamental to an ongoing course or curriculum, as Tyler noted, "...enrichment...tends to be considered...a kind of educational luxury" (Tyler, 1967). For example, a competent high school literature teacher who regularly taught a segment on Shakespeare might have decided to incorporate a dramatization of *Romeo and Juliet* using a film, record, or radio. The dramatization may have been highly effective at enhancing student appreciation and understanding, but it was not essential to the teacher's lesson or the school's curriculum. Students would have received competent instruction on Shakespeare regardless of the availability of the media enrichment.

I define the term *supplement* as a program that filled a curriculum gap that otherwise might have been filled poorly or not at all. For example, a small school may have no teachers experienced in specialized subjects such as drawing, music, science, or even geography. As a result, these specialized subjects might not be offered, or offered only inadequately. In these cases, radio instruction could be used to supplement (fill gaps in) the school's curricula. The classroom teacher's role would be to facilitate the radio instruction in the supplemented topic.

Given this distinction, we can look as some of the SOAs covered in this work in terms of whether they provided chiefly enrichment or supplemental programs. The ASA described its mission as providing educational enrichment to the schools (School and Society, 1930a). For example, in 1936–37 the ASA offered a music program for upper grades and high schools that presented music composed by famous people in Western history such as Henry VIII, Jean-Jacques Rousseau, and Martin Luther, to name a few (ASA, 1938). The history series for that year devoted programs to individual U.S. cities. Those programs provided enrichment opportunities but were hardly crucial to a curriculum of music education or American history. It is doubtful that either of these broad-scope courses could be adopted as a full semester's offering in music or American history (ASA, 1938).

The OSA also leaned heavily toward enrichment, though less so than the ASA. Darrow's vision was grandiose and global. In the early days of radio, he had talked effusively of radio blowing the roof off the classroom and moving the walls back to the circumference of the earth (Darrow, 1932). Those ideals, while visionary, were not geared to filling the basic educational needs of Ohio students in its small towns and rural schools. The OSA offered *Art Appreciation* by the Cleveland Museum of Art, as well as *Literature by Living Writers* and *Geography of Foreign Lands*, but there was no indication that these subjects were what teachers and students in Ohio's rural areas needed on a regular basis. Consequently, these courses were likely seen as ornamental, not fundamental to a school curricula.

At the local level WNYE's award winning *Tales from the Four Winds* offered dramatized legends and folk tales from around the world, and in most cases would be considered enrichment. Chicago's Harold Kent announced early on that radio would be used exclusively to enrich curricula of the city's schools.

---

[8]Use of the terms enrichment and supplemental differs from the way they were used in the literature issued by the SOAs covered in this study. Their use was inconsistent, often treating the two words as synonyms. For example, some ASA teacher manuals described their programs as supplementing the teacher's instruction and enriching the curriculum (ASA, 1938).

The MAH provided such in-depth treatment of one rather specialized topic, European classical music, that it could be seen as either enrichment to a general music course or as the main element in a school program that focused on classical music. For schools and teachers that already offered a general music appreciation course, Damrosch's broadcasts could serve as fine enrichment. For those who wanted to focus on European classical music but lacked the resources or personnel to do so locally, the MAH could fill that essential curriculum need.

At the other extreme, during its first two decades, the CSA (Cleveland) designed radio series for elementary grades to fulfill all the learning objectives set for subjects such as science, geography, and math. In other words, the radio not only supplemented the curricula, it delivered it (or most of it). The Rochester School of the Air took a similar approach with its renowned science program headed by master teacher Harry Carpenter. In truth, no SOA presented only enrichment or supplement. They all blended their approaches to some degree, and individual teachers used programs as they saw fit, but most SOAs did emphasize either enrichment or supplement.

The WSA stands out for having set curriculum supplement as one of its original goals. From its earliest days, the WSA offered a variety of programs that could be used to fill gaps in curricula, allowing small schools to offer instruction in topics desirable to the communities they served. WSA programs such as *Let's Draw, Afield with Ranger Mac, Let's Sing, Young Experimenters,* and *Rhythm and Games* did not fit Darrow's vision of bringing society's great minds and leaders into the classroom. Nor did they fit the ASA's stated goal of enriching and vitalizing classroom learning (ASA, 1938) or Cleveland's rigorous standards for radio directed lessons. They did, however, enable teachers to accomplish basic educational tasks such as developing their students' creativity in art and music, exploring the local environment, learning the elements of modern science, and engaging in rhythmic movement.

We can infer a relationship between an SOA's program type and penetration of its potential audience. The data suggest SOAs that sought to supplement curricula (fill gaps) attracted a greater portion of the available audience than did those that offered mainly enrichment. At its simplest, this distinction can be seen as the difference between "nice to do" and "need to do." The ASA produced some creative programs that excited many educators, but apparently, many teachers did not find those programs central to their instructional practice. The WSA seems to have discovered early on that teachers make greatest use of broadcast series that helped them expand their basic educational curriculum and that meshed well with the local community. That centeredness on teacher and community distinguished the WSA curriculum from the other SOAs. It largely explains why the WSA attracted so many of the state's elementary teachers and roughly half of the state's students as regular listeners. While the state's FM network made it possible for all Wisconsin teachers to tune in to the WSA, it was the school's programming and administrative focus that enticed so many to do so regularly.

Other Measures of Success

Evaluating SOAs solely on the basis of audience size and penetration overlooks the richness and complexity of the SOAs covered in this work. The data suggest that all succeeded in some ways, one being in terms of the founders' vision. The network SOAs, for example, fulfilled well the goals of their corporate founders and sponsors. Whatever their educational goals, the MAH and the ASA were elements of corporate public relations strategies, designed to help convince legislators, government agencies, and the public that commercial networks could be trusted to deliver on radio's educational promise, thereby making publicly supported educational broadcasting unnecessary. Just such an argument was made by CBS president William Paley before the Federal Communications Commission (FCC). In 1934, while the FCC deliberated on the 15 percent set-aside proposal, Paley argued that the nation's system of private broadcasting already provided educational programming for the schools and adults at home. The proposal to set aside radio channels, he claimed, would destroy a system that already worked well, a system that gave the public what it wanted in entertainment *and* education (Paley, 1934). Paley pointed to the ASA as a living illustration of his network's commitment to education.

On the surface it looked impressive. Directed by prestigious educators, the ASA delivered a traditional prep school curriculum that Paley claimed benefited upward of 8 million students. In opposition to Paley's concrete example, what could the advocates of government-sponsored radio offer? They could only describe abstract plans and visions. Because Congress and the FCC eventually sided with the commercial broadcasters, I conclude that the network SOAs contributed substantially to the goals of the corporate sponsors.

Considering educational goals, the MAH proved to be a modest success. True, Damrosch failed to make the average American a knowledgeable fan of Bach, Beethoven, Mozart, and Wagner. However, in terms of the educational goal of raising awareness and appreciation of European classical music among American schoolchildren, the MAH should be judged a success. Support for this judgment can be found in the opinions of knowledgeable observers of the MAH operation. During his radio career, Damrosch received the respect and genuine admiration of music teachers, scholars, students, and critics. They characterized the MAH as the most popular school radio program in the country, responsible for greatly increasing the use of radio in the classrooms (Atkinson, 1942b; Woelfel & Reid, 1945). Martin (1983) claimed it was the best use of either radio or television for an educational purpose, and Sanders (1990) said it served as a model for other music educators interested in education by radio. These accolades demonstrate that knowledgeable observers of that time had high regard for the MAH's educational impact and value. I infer from this wide support that the MAH did indeed succeed educationally, albeit in an educational niche.

Evaluating the OSA's successes and failures is problematic. On the one hand, the OSA can be seen as a personal triumph for Darrow. He established the country's first state-supported SOA and gained a position in the Ohio educational bureaucracy and the support of a powerful commercial broadcaster. He fulfilled his personal vision to bring the world into the classroom and expose students to great minds and leaders from all walks of life. Then he was fired and the OSA lost its state funding. The OSA did recover, but as a weaker entity, one that never gained the same level of attention and support from Ohio's educational establishment that Darrow had claimed.

Perhaps, in the end, the OSA was too much Darrow's personal enterprise. He did, after all, embody the spirit of a 19th-century entrepreneur more than that of an educator. With a limited background in education, grounded neither in theory nor practice, Darrow knew well how to promote his own visions, but he did not know how to integrate an educational experiment into Ohio's educational family.

For a while, the TSA succeeded in bringing advanced technology to the educational system of a conservative state. Its success grew out of a state-wide cooperative effort that included faculty and staff from four universities, the state's department of education, a half dozen commercial radio stations, and numerous civic organizations. All played a role in launching and operating an educational effort that was unique not just to Texas, but most likely to the entire country.

For over forty years, the MSA and the ORSA broadcast educational resources to isolated but politically powerful farm communities that recognized the value to their communities. The longevity of both SOAs demonstrated their success at meeting the perceived educational needs of rural schools.

All local SOAs could boast some signs of success, though the documentation is scare. A common success indicator for many of the local SOAs was that local school boards continued to support them, in some cases long after educational television had become well established. In fact there is little evidence that school boards abandoned radio in favor of television. Rather most seemed to have continued broadcasting radio and television programs simultaneously. Many locally produced program series won national recognition, for example: WNYE's *Tales from the Four Winds,* Chicago's *Battle of the Books,* Alameda's *Radio First Aid* series, and Portland's student written *Jeff Hi Latin Club*. At the time of this publication, KBPS continues to offer Portland students instruction and practical experience in broadcasting and educational radio.

Ultimately, educational endeavors should be evaluated in terms of the differences they make in the lives of students, teachers and schools. Our ability to determine such long-term effects is typically limited because of scarce documentation. However, documentation for the WSA is plentiful and rich. The following anecdote demonstrates how the WSA affected one student into adulthood.

The story is recalled by a woman who taught in a rural one-room Wisconsin school from 1953 to 1955 and used WSA programs regularly. She recalls:

> *Let's Sing,* the children kept that forever. Five years ago when we retired, we moved back to this area [where she taught]. So I see the adults now who were the children I taught. (My) next door neighbor is a woman I had in class when she was in 5th and 6th grade. Plus there are others up the road ... and one of the young men who's a singer. He said, "Oh, you taught me how to sing!" And of course I didn't, it was *Let's Sing*. He could even remember some of the songs; that would have been 45 years later. So it was lasting, definitely. Children love to sing [L. Mader, personal communication, November 19, 2003].

The story demonstrates a long-term learning influence on the students that continued years after the WSA ceased operation.

Questions and Lessons Learned

Questions

Historical work often raises as many questions as it answers. By documenting the stories of 14 SOAs, we raise the question of why, after the demise of network broadcasting for the schools, so few scholars of educational radio reported on SOAs that flourished at the state and local levels. Were their interests confined solely to national broadcasting? Like Seerley Reid (Woelfel and Tyler, 1945) did they believe that the national SOAs performed certain educational functions that state and local ones could not? Or perhaps their research subjects were determined by government and foundation grants, which at that time began to focus on educational television.

By establishing that the WSA became an important part of Wisconsin's educational family, this work raises the possibility that previous radio scholars have asked the wrong question. Instead of inquiring exclusively about why the SOA movement as a whole failed to attract more classroom teachers, a more fruitful approach might have been to ask why Wisconsin classroom teachers used radio so frequently? What educational needs did the WSA meet for them?

Another fruitful line of research might be to investigate why Wisconsin's successful model for a state sponsored school of the air prompted few imitators in neighboring states. Other than Minnesota, no other Midwestern state developed a school of the air. Moreover, why did only a handful of other states follow the Wisconsin example by creating a statewide FM educational radio network, and of those, why did only one build a state-based school of the air? After all, in 1948 FCC Chairman Wayne Coy said the Commission urged states to develop state-based educational radio networks. He said:

> The Commission favors the creation of State-wide networks as they seem to afford the greatest possibilities for the logical coverage of a State and the most efficient use of frequencies. Such

plans should be in conformance with the Commission's announced policy that such systems should afford 'fair treatment to public and private educational institutions, both urban and rural, at the primary, secondary, higher, and adult educational levels alike' [Dunham, 1948, p. v].

One possible reason why few other states did not build a statewide FM network is suggested by a bit of data regarding the Nebraska State Educational Television Commission. In the early 1970s, that commission expressed a desire to inaugurate a public radio system similar to Wisconsin's FM network. To convince the "powers that be," the Nebraska state legislature and governor, the commission administrators needed to demonstrate how radio could be used in the schools. For that reason, they requested tape copies of several WSA programs to use as examples of radio instruction for the schools (Nebraska Educational Television Commission, 1975). In an internal memo the director of Wisconsin's station WHA explained that the Nebraska commission had great plans and good dedication to public radio, but had "...encountered considerable adverse pressure from the many 'mom and pop' commercial radio owners in Nebraska who believe that Public Radio is both an unnecessary competitor and luxury for the people of their own state" (Borstein, 1975).

The quote highlights how farsighted WHA directors were in the mid–1940s, when they created Wisconsin's FM system years before the establishment of commercial FM stations. By the 1970s, it appears that even small commercial FM stations were strong enough to block the creation of a public radio network in Nebraska. This story raises another question, how often did this conflict between educators and owners of commercial FM stations play out in other states?

Still another area of inquiry that should be explored is the role played by foundations in steering the development of SOAs at all levels. The Payne Fund played an essential role in the birth of both the OSA and the WSA. What role did other foundations that were active in educational radio such as the Carnegie and Rockefeller foundations play in the development of SOAs at the federal, state, or local levels? Future research is needed to uncover the actions and motives of such key foundations.

Sattler (1990) has remarked that after 1945, educational researchers across the nation lost interest in educational radio. This is not surprising, because by that time NBC and CBS had discontinued broadcasting to the schools and the OSA was in a dormant phase. Most likely funding sources were turning their attention to educational television. What is puzzling, however, is why during the 1950s and 1960s so few educational researchers based in Wisconsin studied the WSA. Besides Kelly's (1990) study of *Let's Draw*, no Wisconsin based educational researchers focused on the WSA. Certainly others must have been aware of it. That neglect raises a larger question of who sets research priorities.

Lessons

One reason for writing an historical work is to develop alternative perspectives and evaluations of current educational issues. Certainly, the SOA narratives suggest a number of lessons that reflect on the contemporary educational scene in 2005. Most prominently, the WSA story provides at least one instance where educational technology played a significant and sustained role in one state's educational history. At the local level KBPS served a similar role in the Portland schools. What meaning do these accomplishments and the other SOA narratives hold for educators and scholars in 2007 who advocate that e-learning should play a key role in the schools? Probably the most obvious lesson that comes to mind is Cuban's (1986) assertion that teachers are important gatekeepers in determining whether and how technology will be used in the classroom. By concentrating on meeting teacher needs, the WSA succeeded in becoming part of the state's educational community. The same sort of concentration today increases the likelihood that e-learning and computer-based education will be adopted widely, not just by the technologically inclined. If widely accepted, e-learning could become a powerful educational resource for helping schools meet No Child Left Behind (NCLB) requirements or for supplementing those parts of the curriculum that have been reduced in order to make room for NCLB preparation.

One of the more intriguing ideas that emerges from the SOA narratives is to what extent could or should advocates of e-learning and distance education, K through 8, try to become embedded in state and local educational bureaucracies and communities? The WSA was an integral part of the University of Wisconsin, received quasi-formal recognition from Wisconsin's educational bureaucracy, became a mainstay of the state's radio network, developed strong ties to the state's powerful agricultural community, and conducted community-building programs that regularly attracted tens of thousands. In Portland, for 60 years KBPS served an important educational resource for city schools, students at KBPS, teachers and numerous civic organizations. Perhaps educational innovators today should attempt to become embedded in a manner similar to the WSA and KBPS.

Another lesson that emerges from the school of the air (SOA) narratives is that our country's educational structure — controlled by the states rather than the federal government — throws up barriers to nation-wide educational innovations. Advocates of the national school of the air not only stirred up hostility from commercial interests, they also challenged this country's tradition of states rights. Forming a national school of the air would have required the federal government to encroach into an area that had been states' domain since our nation's founding.

A corollary to the above point is that while state-based control of education encourages multiple innovations in various states, the results are often uneven, fragmented, and isolated. The OSA for example, struggled for survival and continuity, and the WSA's fine achievements were replicated to a lesser degree only in Minnesota and Oregon. Under our state-based systems, it appears that many fine educational ideas and programs fail to take off or fall by the wayside for reasons unrelated to educational effectiveness. The local SOAs documented here all seem to have started from scratch with little leveraging of the radio experience gained by state or other local school systems. Perhaps educational innovators need to focus on regional (multi-state) programs that would help ensure that one state's success gets transferred to others and that state-based educational innovators can learn from each other rather then trying to build continually from scratch.

The narratives of the network-sponsored SOAs demonstrate that when educational innovation relies on commercial organizations for support, that support is subject to abrupt termination. For marketing reasons, producers of new technology hardware and software are eager to see the schools adopt the latest technology and often invest heavily in the effort, but when market conditions change, commercial organizations may quickly withdraw their support. This was demonstrated when NBC and CBS, in response to a changing market environment, terminated their relatively successful SOAs within a few years of each other.

Another important issue raised by the SOA stories is who should control the technology that makes the Internet possible? Related to that is the question, will today's open-range Internet access remain unfenced? Or, as happened with broadcast radio, will powerful interests arise that restrict Internet access to only the most profitable options? The SOA narrative suggests that when educators play a primary role in directing the use of educational technology, it can become an integral part of America's educational family, benefiting teachers and students.

This history partially fills the gap in our knowledge of the school of the air movement. It documented 14 SOAs that operated at the national, state, and local levels. The data related to network-sponsored SOAs revealed a typically American narrative of conflict between profit and social obligation, between the goals of private media and the needs of public education. The network narratives include significant achievements but also significant opportunities missed. The study of Ben Darrow and the OSA illustrates the power of one man's vision and persistence but also the limitation of individual quests into the complex landscape of public education. The

ESSA and TSA demonstrated the power of decentralized grassroots efforts and widely cooperative efforts, but also their limitations. Finally, the WSA history reveals a puzzling situation where
an apparently long-term successful application of technology to public education failed to attract
the attention of scholars or stimulate interest among educators outside of Wisconsin. The non-
transfer of educational success stories remains one of the puzzling characteristics of American
education.

References

Apps, J. (1996). *One-room country schools, history and recollections from Wisconsin*. Amherst, MA: Amherst Press.

ASA (1930). *The American school of the air. Teachers manual and classroom guide, 1930–1931*. A. Keith and H. Johnson (Eds.).Chicago: Grigsby-Grunow Co.

_____ (1931). *American school of the air teacher's manual and classroom guide, 1931–1932*. A. Keith & H. Johnson (Eds.).New York City: Columbia Broadcasting System.

_____ (1936). *The American school of the air 1936–1937*. Teachers manual and classroom guide. H. Johnson (Ed.).New York: Columbia Broadcasting System.

_____ (1937). Gaspe peninsula, radio script. [Radio broadcast script, April 21, 1937]. New York: Columbia Broadcasting System.

_____ (1938). *The American school of the air: Teachers manual and classroom guide 1938–1939*. S. Fisher (Ed.).New York: Columbia Broadcasting System.

_____ (1941). *School of the air of the Americas, teachers manual 1941–1942*. S. Fisher (Ed.):Columbia Broadcasting System.

_____ (1943). *American school of the air*, teachers manual and classroom guide, 1943–44. L. Bryson (Ed.).New York: Columbia Broadcasting System.

_____ (1945). *CBS American school of the air, calendar manual for 1945–1946*. L. Bryson & L. Levine (Ed.) New York: Educational Division, Columbia Broadcasting System.

Atkinson, C. (1938). *Education by radio in American schools*. Dissertation. Nashville: George Peabody College for Teachers.

_____ (1942a). *Radio network contributions to education*. Boston: Meador Publishing.

_____ (1942b). *Radio program intended for classroom use*. Boston: Meador Publishing.

_____ (1942c). *Public school broadcasting to the classroom*. Boston: Meador Publishing.

_____ (1942d). *Broadcasting to the classroom by universities and colleges*. Boston: Meador Publishing.

Badger. (1953). *UW's school of the air. Badger Report, v. III*. March and April, 1953

Bagley, W. (1940a). The American school of the air. *Current History, 51*, 40–42.

_____ (1940b). Just what is the crux of the conflict between the progressives and the essentialists? *Educational Administration and Supervision, 26*, 508–511.

Bannerman, R. L. (1986). *Norman Corwin and radio: The golden years*: University of Alabama Press.

Barnouw, E. (1966). *A tower in Babel: A history of broadcasting in the United States* (Vol. I to 1933.). New York: Oxford University Press.

_____ (1968). *The golden web: A history of broadcasting in the United States* (Vol: II-1933 to 1953.). New York: Oxford University Press.

Barr, A. S., Ewbank, H., & McCormick, T. (1942). *Radio in the classroom: Report of the Wisconsin research project in school broadcasting*. Madison: University of Wisconsin Press.

Barts, J. (1945). Report of school visit. University of Wisconsin Archives, WSA 41/06/02–5 10/B/4 034 003, School Visits 1944–1950s

Bauer, N. (1975). Departmental correspondence, March 25, 1975. To Claire Kentzler. University of Wisconsin Archive, 41/06/02/02–5 10/B/3 032 018: WSA: Kentzler, Claire (corres.) 1970–76.

BBC, (1945) School broadcasting, I. Keith Tyler Papers (RG 40/62/1), British Broadcast Corporation: London County Council: 1931

Bird, W. W. (1939). *The educational aims and practices of the National Broadcasting Company and the Columbia Broadcasting System* (Unpublished Thesis). Seattle: University of Washington.

Bliven, B. (1927, February, 1927). The coming of the radio university. *Popular Radio, XI,* 127–130, 167–172.

Borstein, R. (1975). Memo, September 2. *To: Clair Kentzler.* University of Wisconsin Archive, 41/06/02/02–5 10/B/3 032 018: WSA: Kentzler, Claire (corres.) 1970–76.

Broadcast (1922). The people's university. *Radio Broadcast, May, 1922.*

Brown, J. S., Collins, A., & Duguid, B. (1989). Situated cognition and the culture of learning. *Educational Researcher, 18,* 32–42.

Carle, W., M. (1959). *An evaluation of the Ohio school of the air: June 1959.* Columbus, Ohio: Ohio State University Archives, Ohio School of the Air (RG 8/d-6/1).

Carpini, M. X. (1995). Radio's political past. In E. E. C. Pease (Ed.), *Radio the forgotten medium* (pp. 21–30). New Brunswick and London: Transaction Publishers.

Catalog, 1955. *Catalogue of radio scripts: first semester, 1955–1956.* Department of Radio TV Education, Division of Instruction. Detroit Public Schools

Caton, C., F. (1951). *Radio station WMAQ: A history of its independent years (1922–1931).* Northwestern University, Evanston.

Clauder, L. (Personal Communication). November 7, 2003.

Courier. (1929). *The courier: The Ohio school of the air program listing 1929–30:* The Ohio State University Archives, Ohio School of the Air (RG 8/d-6/1).

_____ (1931). *The courier: The Ohio school of the air 1931–1932* (Vol. III). Columbus, Ohio: Ohio State Department of Education. Available: The Ohio State University Archives, Ohio School of the Air (RG 8/d-6/1)

Crowley, Richard (1971). *Radio Station WHAM, Rochester, New York: its origins, development and programming practices, 1922–1941.* Master's Thesis, University of Maryland.

Cuban, L. (1986). *Teachers and machines: The classroom use of technology since 1920.* New York: Teachers College, Columbia University.

Damrosch, W. (1930). *My musical life.* New York: Charles Scribner's Sons.

Darrow, B. (1932). *Radio, the assistant teacher.* Columbus, Ohio: R. G. Adams and Co.

_____ (1940). *Radio trailblazing: A brief history of the Ohio school of the air.* Columbus, OH: College Book Company.

Douglas, G. (1987). *The early days of radio broadcasting.* Jefferson, NC: McFarland Publishers.

Douglas, S. J. (1999). *Listening in.* New York: Times Books.

Dunham, Franklin. (1948). *FM for education.* U. S. Office of Education. Washington, D. C.: U. S. Government Printing Office.

Engel, H. A. (1935a). Wisconsin state station completes new studio. *Education by Radio, 5* (12), 45–48.

_____ (1935b). Miscellaneous papers. University Archives. University of Wisconsin, Engel Papers.

Ensign, W. (1930). Personal communications, October 9, 1930 To: A. Keith. State Historical Society of Wisconsin, Alice Keith papers. Box 1, Folder: Correspondence 1907–Sept. 24, 1938.

ESSA (Empire State FM School of the Air) Annual Meeting, (1959). Minutes of Annual Meetings of the ESSA Board of Trustees, April 1, 1959. Syracuse University, Archives and Records Management. Box 5659, Folder: Empire State FM SOA. Syracuse, NY.

_____. Annual Meeting, (1960). Minutes of Annual Meetings of the ESSA Board of Trustees, April 12, 1960. Syracuse University, Archives and Records Management. Box 5659, Folder: Empire State FM SOA. Syracuse, NY.

_____ (1964). Minutes of Annual Meetings of the ESSA Board of Trustees, April 1, 1964. Syracuse University, Archives and Records Management. Box 5659, Folder: Empire State FM SOA. Syracuse, NY.

_____ (1965). Minutes of Annual Meetings of the ESSA Board of Trustees, March 31, 1965. Syracuse University, Archives and Records Management. Box 5659, Folder: Empire State FM SOA. Syracuse, NY.

_____. Cosgrove, (1967). Memorandum to Board of Trustees, July 15, 1967. Syracuse University, Archives and Records Management. Box 14618, Folder: Empire State FM SOA, 1964–1969. Syracuse, NY.

_____. ETV (nd). *A Report on the effects of educational television on the usage of school of the air programs.* Syracuse University, Archives and Records Management. Box 14618, Folder: Empire State FM SOA, 1964–1969. Syracuse, NY.

_____. News Bulletin X, (1959). Newsletter, *the Empire State FM School of the Air.* August 21. Syracuse University, Archives and Records Management. Box 17331, Folder: Empire State FM School of the Air, Speech and Drama. Syracuse, NY.

_____. News Bulletin (1966). Empire State FM School of the Air, Pre-Program Bulletin, Vol 18, No. 31. April 18, 1966. Syracuse University, Archives and Records Management. Box 14618, Folder: Empire State FM SOA, 1964–1969.

_____. Program Evaluation (1962). *Program Evaluation Report.* Syracuse University, Archives and Records Management. Box 5659, Folder: Evaluation Reports, 1960–1965. Syracuse, NY.

_____. Smith (1968). *The future of the Empire State FM School of the Air.* Syracuse University, Archives and Records Management. Box 14618, Folder: Empire State FM SOA, 1964–1969.

Field, Jerry. (1991). *A history of educational radio in*

Chicago with emphasis on WBEZ-FM: 1920–1960. Dissertation. Chicago: Loyola University

Foster, Eugene. (1955) Letter to Federal Communication Commission. In Truscott, 1958, *Empire State FM School of the Air: A historical account of the origin, growth and development.* Dissertation. University of Buffalo School of Education.

_____ (1952) in Truscott, 1958. *The Empire State FM School of the Air: A historical account of the origin, growth and development.* Dissertation. University of Buffalo School of Education.

Girling, Betty, T., (1947). *Report on Survey of the Minnesota School of the Air.* University of Minnesota.

_____ (1975). *Girling, Betty Thomas,* U. P. 45, Minnesota School of the Air: Box 10, Folder: Annual Reports—Teacher Evaluation. Minneapolis: University Archives, University of Minnesota

_____ (1978). *Girling, Betty Thomas,* U. P. 45, Minnesota School of the Air: Box 10, Folder: Annual Reports—Teacher Evaluation. Minneapolis: University Archives, University of Minnesota

Goodell, S. M. E. (1973). *Walter Damrosch and his contributions to music education.* Catholic University of America, Washington, D. C.

Harrison, Burt (1978). *James M. Morris: An interview conducted in Mr. Morris home.* Public Radio Oral History Project. Available at: National Public Broadcasting Archive, University of Maryland, College Park, Maryland.

Harrison, M. (1937). *Radio in the classroom: Objectives, principles and practice.* New York: Prentice-Hall, Inc.

Hill, A. N. C. (1997). *The Texas school of the air: An educational radio endeavor.* (Unpublished Thesis). University of Texas at Austin: Austin, Texas.

Hill, F. E. (1942). *Tune in for education.* New York: National Committee on Education by Radio.

Hill, J. R., & Raven, A. (2002). Online learning communities: If you build them, will they stay? *ITFORUM available on line at: http://it.coe.uga.edu/itforum/paper46/paper46.htm.*

Holp, Karen, P. (1974). *Format Public Radio: an alternative for educational radio.* Thesis, M.A. Akron: University of Akron.

Infoplease (2006) *United States— U. S. Statistics— Population by State.* Available online at: http://www.infoplease.com/ipa/A0004986.html. Accessed Feb. 20, 2006.

Johnson, R. (1972). Personal communication, December 11, *To Chancellor Durward Long.* University of Wisconsin Archive, WSA, 41/06/02/02–5 10/B/3 032 018: Kentzler, Claire (corres.) 1970–76.

KBPS (Portland School of the Air) Bulletin (1945). *The School Bulletin.* V. XXXII N. 4. Portland, Oregon, Feb. 15, 1945.

_____. Guide (1964). *Broadcast Guides, 1953–1964.* KBPS Records. Box 3, Folder 62. Available at: National Public Broadcasting Archives. University of Maryland.

_____. KBPS (1988). *KBPS 65, 1923–1988.* KBPS Records. Box 2, Folder 19, KBPS Brochures. Available at: National Public Broadcasting Archives. University of Maryland.

_____. KBPS, (1993). *KBPS at a glance.* KBPS Records. Box 2, Folder 19, KBPS Brochures. Available at: National Public Broadcasting Archives. University of Maryland.

_____. KBPS, (1995). *KBPS AM 1450.* KBPS Records, Box 2, Folder 19, KBPS Brochures. Available at: National Public Broadcasting Archives. University of Maryland.

_____. Listening Text (1978). *KBPS Listening Text 1978–1979.* KBPS Records. Box 2, Folder 61. Available at: National Public Broadcasting Archives. University of Maryland.

Keith, A. (1928). Promotional pamphlet, *radio in education.* State Historical Society of Wisconsin, Alice Keith papers. Box 3, Folder: Booklets and Pamphlets by Alice Keith, nd.

_____ (1932a). Letter, May 2, 1932. To: Carl Russell Fish. State Historical Society of Wisconsin, Carl Russel Fish papers. Box 9, Folder: Correspondence 1932.

_____ (1932b). Letter, May 25, 1932. To: Carol Russel Fish. State Historical Society of Wisconsin, Carl Russel Fish papers. Box 9, Folder: Correspondence, 1932.

_____ (1934). Education by radio. *Independent Woman,* January. 9, 30–31.

_____ (1936). Letter to William Bagley, August 14, 1936. State Historical Society of Wisconsin, Alice Keith papers. Box 1, Folder: Correspondence 1907–Sept. 24, 1938.

Kelly, M. F. (1990). *Art education by radio, a historical study of "Let's Draw."* Unpublished PhD dissertation, University of Wisconsin, Milwaukee, Milwaukee, Wisconsin.

Kentzler, C. (1969). Memo, April 1, To: Ron Borstein. University of Wisconsin Archive, 41/06/02/02–5 10/B/3 032 018: WSA: Kentzler, Claire (corres.) 1970–76.

_____ (1972a). Memo, April 12, To: Ron Borstein and Ralph Johnson. University of Wisconsin Archive, 41/06/02/02–5 10/B/3 032 018: WSA: Kentzler, Claire (corres.) 1970–76.

_____ (1972b). Memo, November 17, To: Ralph Johnson. University of Wisconsin Archive, 41/06/02/02–5 10/B/3 032 018: WSA: Kentzler, Claire (corres.) 1970–76.

_____ (1975). Memo, June 4, To: Ron Borstein. University of Wisconsin Archive, 41/06/02/02–5 10/B/3 032 018: WSA: Kentzler, Claire (corres.) 1970–76.

_____ (1969–76). Correspondence. WSA: UW Archive, 41/06/02/02–5 10/B/3 032 018

King, A. (1993). From sage on the stage to guide on the side. *College Teaching, Winter 1993, Vol 41(1),* p 30–36.

King, K. P. (2001). *Technology, science teaching, and literacy: A century of growth*. New York: Lower Academic Plenum Publishers.

Know Your City (1946) *Know Your City: Radio Broadcasts for elementary and junior high schools*. Board of Education and the City History Club of New York.

Lawson, C., M. (1942). *The development of radio education in the Chicago public schools*. Chicago: DePaul University.

Lazarfield, P. F. (1940). *Radio and the printed page*. New York: Duel, Sloan & Pearce, Inc.

Leach, E. F. (1983). Tuning out education: The cooperation doctrine in radio. *Current (available on line)* (January, February and March, 1983).

Levenson, W. B. (1945). *Teaching through radio*. New York: Farrar & Rinehart, Inc.

_____. & Stasheff, M. A. (1952). *Teaching through radio*. New York: Rinehart & Company, Inc.

Lewis, T. (1992). A godlike presence: The impact of radio on the 1920s and 1930s. *OAH Magazine of History, 6* (Spring 1992).

Lincoln, B. (1938, December 27, 1938). Teaching used as furtherance: Career woman. *Cleveland Plain Dealer*.

Linton, B. A. (1953). *A history of Chicago radio station programming 1921–1931, with emphasis on stations WMAQ and WGN*. Unpublished Thesis. Northwestern University, Evanston.

Long, D. (1973). Letter, February. 2nd, To: Ralph Johnson. University of Wisconsin Archive, WSA, 41/06/02/02–5 10/B/3 032 018: Kentzler, Claire (corres.) 1970–76.

Lowe, S. (1972). *Harold Engle and Harold McCarty: An interview conducted by Steven Lowe*. University Archives Oral History Project, University of Wisconsin, Engel Papers. Transcript. Madison, WI: University of Wisconsin.

MacLatchy (Ed.). (1935). *Education on the air (1935) fifth yearbook*. Chicago: University of Chicago.

Martin, G. (1983). *The Damrosch dynasty*. Boston: Houghton Mifflin Co.

McCarty. (1956). Memoranda and flyers. University of Wisconsin Archive. 41/06/02/02–5 10/B/3 032 022: WSA: Miscellaneous.

McCarty, H. (1941). *Ten year report,* University of Wisconsin Archives: WSA 41/06/02–5 10/b/3 032 0167. Madison: WHA radio.

_____ (1967). *Statewide classroom without walls: The Wisconsin school of the air*. Personal papers, typed. University of Wisconsin Archives, 41/06/02–5, 1949.

_____ (nd). Reminiscences of the founder and director. Unpublished personal papers. University of Wisconsin Archives, 41/06/02/02–5 10/B/3 032 022: WSA: Miscellaneous, various dates.

_____ In MacLatchy (Ed.), *Education on the air* (Vol. 1935). Chicago: University of Chicago.

McChesney, R. W. (Ed.). (1993). *Telecommunica-tions, mass media, and democracy: The battle for control of U.S. broadcasting, 1928–1935*. New York and Oxford: Oxford University Press.

McKelvey, Blake (1970) Radio and Television in the Life of Rochester. *Rochester History*. Vol. XXXII, July, 1970, No.3.

McKellar, A. (1964). Memo April 6, 1964. To staff. University of Wisconsin Archives: WSA 41/06/02–5 10/B/3 032 022: Miscellaneous, various dates.

Metz, Robert, (1975) *CBS: Reflections in a Blood Shot Eye*. Chicago: Playboy Press

Milbauer, R. S. (1949, June). The Wisconsin school of the air. *Amerika*. United States Department of State. University of Wisconsin Archives: 41/06/02–5 10/B/3 032 010 WSA: Articles re, 1947–56.

Milwaukee (1975). Letter (from Milwaukee public schools). To C. Kentzler. University of Wisconsin Archive, WSA, 41/06/02/02–5 10/B/3 032 018: WSA: Kentzler, Claire (corres.) 1970–76.

Morris, James (1946–1949). School of the Air Correspondence. *KOAC Records, 1923–1965*. Available at: Corvallis, Oregon, Oregon State University Library, Archive, RG-15.

_____ (1972). *The Remembered Years. a personal view of 50 years of broadcasting*. Corvallis, Oregon: Continuing Education Publications

MSA (Minnesota School of the Air) Annual Report (1948) *Survey of School Broadcasting* U. P. 45, Girling Betty Thomas, Box 10 Minnesota School of the Air: Folder: Annual Reports— Teacher Evaluation. Minneapolis: University Archives, University of Minnesota

_____. Annual Report (1960). *Biennial Report: 1960–62*. U. P. 45, Girling Betty Thomas, Box 10 Minnesota School of the Air: Folder: Annual Reports— Teacher Evaluation. Minneapolis: University Archives, University of Minnesota

_____. Annual Report (1971). *Biennial Report: 1970–71*. U. P. 45, Girling Betty Thomas, Box 10 Minnesota School of the Air: Folder: Annual Reports. Minneapolis: University Archives, University of Minnesota

_____. Bulletin (1938). *The 1937–1938 Bulletin: KUOM. The Minnesota School of the Air*. U. P. 45, Girling Betty Thomas, Box 12. Minneapolis: University Archives, University of Minnesota

_____. Bulletin (1943). *The 1943 -44 Bulletin: Program Schedule*. Bulletin of the University of Minnesota Extension Service. U. P. 45, Girling Betty Thomas, Box 12. Minneapolis: University Archives, University of Minnesota

_____. Bulletin (1950). *The 1949–50 Bulletin: KUOM. The Minnesota School of the Air*. U. P. 45, Girling Betty Thomas, Box 12. Minneapolis: University Archives, University of Minnesota

_____. Bulletin (1952). *The 1952–53 Bulletin: KUOM. The Minnesota School of the Air*. U. P. 45, Girling Betty Thomas, Box 12. Minneapolis: University Archives, University of Minnesota

_____. Bulletin (1960). *The 1959–1960 Bulletin: KUOM. The Minnesota School of the Air.* U. P. 45, Girling Betty Thomas, Box 12. Minneapolis: University Archives, University of Minnesota

_____. Bulletin (1966). *The 1965–66 Bulletin: KUOM. The Minnesota School of the Air.* U. P. 45, Girling Betty Thomas, Box 12. Minneapolis: University Archives, University of Minnesota

_____. Paulu, Burton (1978). U. P. 45, Girling Betty Thomas, Minnesota School of the Air: Box 10, Folder: Annual Reports— Teacher Evaluation, Memo, May 17, 1978. Minneapolis: University Archives, University of Minnesota

_____. Teacher's Manual (1958). *Teacher's manual for the centennial broadcasts of the Minnesota School of the Air 1957–1958.* Minneapolis: University Archives, University of Minnesota.

_____ (1979) *Teacher Manuals.* Minnesota School of the Air: Box 13–14, Multiple boxes of teacher manuals, 1976–1979. Minneapolis: University Archives, University of Minnesota

_____. Thompson, (1965). U. P. 45, Girling Betty Thomas, Minnesota School of the Air: Folder: Box 10, Annual Reports— Teacher Evaluation. Minneapolis: University Archives, University of Minnesota

NBC (1931). *Music appreciation hour, instructor's manual*, Ernest La Prade (Ed). New York: National Broadcasting Company.

_____ (1937). *Music appreciation hour, teacher manual.* New York: National Broadcasting Company.

Nebraska (1975). Letter from Nebraska educational television commission. To C. Kentzler, University of Wisconsin Archive, 41/06/02/02–5 10/B/3 032 018: WSA: Kentzler, Claire (corres.) 1970–76.

Null, J. W. (2003). *Disciplined progressive educator: The life and career of William Chandler Bagley.* New York: Peter Lang.

ORSA (Oregon School of the Air) Audience (1962). IV. Questionnaires and Listener Research, 1926 - 1962. *KOAC Records, 1923–1965.* reels 8–9. Available at: Corvallis, Oregon, Oregon State University Library, Archive, RG-15.

_____. Correspondence (1959). II. Dean Powers Files, 1932–1959, *KOAC Records, 1923–1965.* reels 3. Available at: Corvallis, Oregon, Oregon State University Library, Archive, RG-15.

_____. KOAC Records (1965) *KOAC Records, 1923–1965.* Oregon State University Archives, Corvallis, Oregon) (RG 15) Available online: http://osulibrary.oregonstate.edu/archives/archive/rg/rg015des.html.

_____. Oregon, (1968). *Educational Television and Radio in Oregon: A Report.* Oregon. Educational Coordinating Council. Salem, Oregon.

_____. Teacher Guides (1963). VI. Radio Program Series, 1926–1962, *KOAC Records, 1923–1965.* reels 10–18. Available at: Corvallis, Oregon, Oregon State University Library, Archive, RG-15.

Paley, W. S. (1934). *Radio as a cultural force*: Columbia Broadcasting System.

_____ (1979). *As it happened: A memoir.* Garden City, NY: Doubleday & Company, Inc.

Perry, A. (1929). *Radio in education: The Ohio school of the air and other experiments.* New York: The Payne Fund.

Potter, Florence (1942) *The development of a broadcasting program for 5A geography in the Cleveland Public Schools.* Thesis. Teachers College, University of Cincinnati.

Quinton, A. (1977). John Dewey's theory of knowledge. In R. S. Peters (Ed.), *John Dewey reconsidered.* London: Routledge and Kegan Paul.

Radio, Roots of Broadcasting. Available on-line at: http://www.tvhandbook.com/History/History_radio.htm as of 8/9/05

Ray, J. L. (1928). Letter, May 4, 1928. To Alice. Keith. State Historical Society of Wisconsin. Alice Keith papers. Box 1, Folder: Correspondence, 1907, 1938.

RCA (1928). *Teacher's manual for RCA educational hour.* E. L. Prade (Ed.).New York: Radio Corporation of America.

Reichelderfer, R. (1934). *Annual report Ohio school of the air 1933–34.* Columbus, Ohio: Ohio State University Archives, Ohio School of the Air (RG 8/d-6/1).

Reid, S. (1939). *Some effects of school broadcasts in literature. An evaluation of certain educational outcomes of radio literature programs used in seventh and eighth grade classes in Chicago public school.* Thesis. The Ohio State University.

_____ (1941a). *The classroom audience of network school broadcasts: Bulletin 34.* (Research report). Columbus, Ohio: Ohio State University.

_____ (1941b). *Network school broadcasts: Some conclusions and recommendation* (No. 35). Columbus: Bureau of Educational Research, Ohio State University.

_____ (1941c). *Tales from far and near: A critical appraisal of twenty-five school broadcasts. Bulletin #38.* Columbus, Evaluation of School Broadcasts, Ohio: Ohio State University.

_____ (1941d). *Radio and the Teaching of English: a study of the English 10A curriculum in Rochester, New York.* Bulletin #22. Columbus, Ohio: Evaluation of School Broadcasts, Ohio State University.

_____ (1942). *Radio in the schools of Ohio.* Washington D.C.: Federal Radio Education committee.

Report of Activities (1942). *Report of activities, First semester, 1942–1943.* Station WBOE, Cleveland: Cleveland Public Schools

Robertson, James (1982). *An interview with James Macandrew.* Available at: Mass Communication History Center of the State Historical Society of Wisconsin, Madison, Wisconsin

Rounder (2004). Alan Lomax collection: Time line: Rounder Records Company.

Saettler, P. (1990). *The evolution of American educational technology*. Englewood, Colorado: Libraries Unlimited, Inc.

Sahr, R. (2005, January 3, 2006). Inflation conversion factors for dollars 1665 to estimated 2013. Available at: http://oregonstate.edu/Dept/pol_sci/fac/sahr/sahr.htm.

Sanders, C. A. (1990). *A history of radio in music education in the United States*. Unpublished Dissertation, University of Cincinnati.

Schneiker, J. (1949). *History and development of the Wisconsin school of the air*. Unpublished Masters Thesis, University of Wisconsin at Madison, Madison.

School and Society (1930a). March 8. Expenditures for the public schools of Massachusetts. *School and Society, XXXI*, 793.

_____ (1930b). Education by radio. *School and Society, XXXII*, 284.

_____ (1937). January 16, 1937). American school of the air. *School and Society, 45*, 84–85.

_____ (1941). February, 15. The far-flung tentacles of the school of the air. *School and Society, 53*, 208.

Schwalbach, J. (1952). *Let's Draw 1952–53*. Teachers manual, University of Wisconsin Archives, 41/06/02–5 10/B/5 Box 37, 013 WSA

_____ (1948–1949). *Let's draw teacher's manual*. Jim Schwalbach (Ed). University of Wisconsin Archives, WSA Box 37 41/06/02–5 10/B/5 037 012: Teacher Manuals 1947–48).

Seels, B., Berry, L. H., Fullerton, K., & Horn, L. J. (1996). Research on the learning from television. In D. Jonassen (Ed.), *Handbook of research for educational communications and technology*. New York: Macmillian LIBRARY Reference USA.

Smith, S. B. (1990). *In all his glory: Life and times of William S. Paley*. New York: Touchstone Books, Simon and Schuster.

Stead, O. (1937). *A comparative study of schools of the air relative to function and organization*. Unpublished masters thesis, University of Wyoming, Laramie, Wyoming.

Stewart, Irvin (1939) *Local broadcasts to school*. Chicago: University of Chicago Press.

Stone, G. P. (1922). Radio has gripped Chicago. *Radio Broadcast*, 503–511.

Summers, H. (1958). *A thirty-year history of programs carried on national radio networks in the United States: 1926–1956*. New York: Arno Press and The New York Times.

Swenson, Patricia (1950). Some People Call it the 4th R. *The School Bulletin*. January, 1950, Portland: Portland Public Schools

_____ (1958). *Radio in the Public Schools of Portland, Oregon*. Dissertation. New York: New York University

_____ (1982). *Radio station KBPS*. KBPS Records. Box 1, Folder 93. Administrative files, operations, and staff information. Available at: National Public Broadcasting Archives. University of Maryland.

Taylor, M. W. (1974). *Ben Darrow and the Ohio school of the air*. Unpublished Ph.D. dissertation, Ohio State University, Columbus, Ohio.

Tracking the RRN, 2002. *Tracking the old Rural Radio Network*. Tower Site of the Week, January 16–23. Available online. Accessed 8/15/05 at: www.fybush.com/site-02116.html

"Teaching Appreciation" (1925). Teaching appreciation of music is her work. Cleveland Plain Dealer. July 29, 1925.

Tenerelli, Joseph, P., Jr. (1972). *Programming practices of noncommercial educational FM radio stations*. Masters Thesis. Western Illinois University.

Tribune (1938). Piracy on the air waves. *Chicago Tribune*. Wisconsin State Historical Society, Harold A. Engel Papers, 1922–1968, Box 3, folders 1 & 2

_____ (1939). Schools invade radio stations' business field. *Chicago Tribune*. Wisconsin State Historical Society, Harold A. Engel Papers, 1922–1968, Box 3, folders 1 & 2

Truscott, Natalie, A. (1958). *The Empire State FM School of the Air: A historical account of the origin, growth and development*. Dissertation. University of Buffalo School of Education.

TSA, (n/d). *Teachers' Manual and Classroom Guide*. State Department of Education: Texas.

_____, (1941). Reading Is Adventure. *Teachers' Manual and Classroom Guide*. State Department of Education: Texas.

_____, (1943). *Open Your Eyes*. Teachers' Manual and Classroom Guide. State Department of Education: Texas.

_____, (1944). *Reading Is Adventure*. Teachers' Manual and Classroom Guide. State Department of Education: Texas.

Tyler, I. K. (1939). Radio's function in education. *Educational Methods, XVIII* (No. 4), 147–154.

_____ (1946–1953). *Ohio school of the air, history: 1946–53*.Columbus, Ohio: Ohio State University Archive, I. Keith Tyler Papers (RG 40/62/8).

_____ (1967). *Instructional television and radio in the Detroit public schools: Survey and recommendations*. Columbus, Ohio: Special Survey Group.

Waller, J. (1923, February 17, 1923). *Radio Digest, IV*, 5.

_____ (1937). *Education by radio*. Paper presented at the 8th Institute of Education by Radio, May, 1937. Columbus, Ohio.

_____ (1946). *Radio, the fifth estate*. Cambridge, MA: The Riverside Press.

WBEZ (1978). *Radio Guide*. April, 1978. Vol. 6, Number 4. Chicago: Chicago Board of Education

WBOE (1938). *WBOE Radio Report of Activities: WBOE, 1938–1939*. Cleveland: Station WBOE, Cleveland Public Schools.

_____ (1939). Social Studies, 5A Radio History. *WBOE Teachers Guides, 1939–1942*. Cleveland: Station WBOE, Cleveland Public Schools.

_____ (1942). Radio Report of Activities: WBOE,

1942–1943. Cleveland: Station WBOE, Cleveland Public Schools.

WHA (1969a). *The first 50 years of University of Wisconsin broadcasting: WHA 1919 to 1969.* WHA radio, Madison: University of Wisconsin.

_____ (1969b). *WHA, radio pioneer.* (Xeroxed program). Madison: University of Wisconsin.

White, L. (1947). *The American radio: Report on the broadcasting industry in the United States.* Chicago: University of Chicago Press.

Wiebe, G. D., & O'Steen, A. (1942). *A study of Series A: Damrosch music appreciation hour.* Columbus: Bureau of Educational Research, Ohio State University

Willey, Roy & Young, Helen. (1948). *Radio in Elementary Education.* Boston: D. C,. Heath and Company.

Willis, F. (1932). Business letter, June 16. To: Carl Russell Fish. State Historical Society of Wisconsin, Carl Russell Fish papers. Box 9, Folder: Correspondence 1932.

_____ (1936). Business letter, August 21, 1936. To L. Windmuller. State Historical Society of Wisconsin, Alice Keith papers. Box 1, Folder: Correspondence 1907–Sept. 24, 1938.

Witherspoon, J., & Kovitz, R. (1989). *The history of public broadcasting* (2nd ed.). Washington: Corporation for Public Broadcasting.

WNYE, (1951). *WNYE Broadcasts for the Schools 1950–1951.* Board of Education of the City of New York.

_____ (1954). *1953–54 WNYE Manual.* Board of Education of the City of New York.

_____ (1967). *1967–1968 WNYE-FM Radio Manual.* Board of Education of the City of New York.

Woelfel, N., & Reid, S. (1945). Radio in American education. In N. Woefel & I. K. Tyler (Eds.), *Radio and the school* (pp. 1–21). Yonkers-on-the-Hudson, NY: World Book co.

Woelfel, N., & Tyler, I. K. (1945). *Radio and the school.* Yonkers-on-the-Hudson, NY: World Book co.

WSA (1932–1971). WSA enrollment data. University of Wisconsin Archive, WSA, 41/06/02–5 10/B/3 032 014 WSA: Enrollments 1932–71. Madison.

_____ (1935). WSA program schedule and description, 1935. University of Wisconsin Archive, WSA, 41/06/02/02–5 10/B/5 037 010: Teachers Manuals).

_____ (1944). *Report of school visits* (Hand written and typed report forms.). University of Wisconsin Archives, WSA 41/06/02–5 10/B/4 034 003, School Visits 1944–1950s.

_____ (1946 -1947). *Exploring science, teacher's manual,* 1946–1947. Lloyd Liedtke (Ed). University of Wisconsin Archive, WSA Box 37 41/06/02–5 10/B/5 037 011: Teacher Manuals).

_____ (1947–1948). *Exploring science, teacher's manual,* Lloyd Liedtke (Ed) University of Wisconsin Archive, WSA Box 37 41/06/02–5 10/B/5 037 011: Teacher Manuals).

_____ (1948). WSA schedule of radio program for elementary school. University of Wisconsin Archive, WSA, 41/06/02/02–5 10/B/5 037 012: Teachers Manuals).

_____ (1949). Report of school visits. Typed records. University of Wisconsin Archives, WSA 41/06/02–5 10/B/4 034 003, School Visits 1944–1950s.

_____ (1953). *Afield with Ranger Mac, teachers manual,* 1952–1953, Wakelin McNeel (Ed). University of Wisconsin Archives, WSA 41/06/02–5 10/B/5 037 012: Teacher Manuals, 1952–1953.

_____ (1958). WSA schedule of radio program for elementary school. University of Wisconsin Archive, WSA, 41/06/02/02–5 10/B/5 037 012: Teachers Manuals WSA.

_____ (1962–1963). *Young experimenters, teacher's manual.,* Lloyd Liedtke (Ed). University of Wisconsin Archives, WSA Box 37 41/06/02–5 10/B/5 037 015: Teacher Manuals 1962–63).

_____ (1967–1968). *Let's write, teacher's manual.* Mauree Applegate (Ed). University of Wisconsin Archives, WSA Box 38, 41/06/02–5 10/B/5 037 001: Teacher Manuals, 1967–68.

_____ (1969–1971), The Darker Brother. University of Wisconsin Archives, WSA 41/06/02–5 10/B/5 038 01: Teacher Manuals (1969 -71).

_____ (1970). WSA schedule of radio program for elementary school, 1970. University of Wisconsin Archive, WSA, 41/06/02/02–5 10/B/5 038 002: Teachers Manuals, 1970–71.

_____ (Various dates). Typed sheets, flyers, memos. University of Wisconsin Archives: WSA 41/06/02–5 10/B/3 032 022: Miscellaneous, various dates.

Index